COMMERCIAL LAWS
OF EAST ASIA

Recommended Stockists

Australia
LBC Information Services Ltd
Brisbane, Sydney, Melbourne, Perth

New Zealand
Brooker's
Auckland

Canada and USA
Carswell
Ottawa, Toronto, Calgary, Montreal,
Vancouver

Pakistan
Pakistan Law House
Karachi, Lahore

Hong Kong
Bloomsbury Books Ltd

Singapore & Malaysia
Thomson Information (S.E. Asia)

India
N.M. Tripathi (Private) Ltd
Bombay

South Korea
Information & Culture Korea
Seoul

Eastern Law House (Private) Ltd
Calcutta

M.P.P. House
Bangalore

Thailand
DK Book House Co. Ltd
Bangkok

Universal Book Traders
Delhi

Nibondh & Company Ltd
Bangkok

Aditya Books
Delhi

Pasit Limited Partnership
Bangkok

Japan
Kinokuniya Co. Ltd
Tokyo

UK/Europe
Sweet & Maxwell Ltd
London

Kokusai Shobo Ltd
Tokyo

Maruzen Co. Ltd
Tokyo

Yushodo Co. Ltd
Tokyo

COMMERCIAL LAWS
OF EAST ASIA

Edited by

Alan S. Gutterman, JD DBA

and

Robert Brown, JD MBA

HONG KONG • SINGAPORE
SWEET & MAXWELL ASIA
1997

Published in 1997 by
Sweet & Maxwell Asia
a division of
The Thomson Corporation (Hong Kong) Ltd
17/F Lyndhurst Tower, 1 Lyndhurst Terrace
Central, Hong Kong

Affiliated Companies

AUSTRALIA
LBC Information Services Ltd
44–50 Waterloo Road, North Ryde
NSW 2113

CANADA
Carswell
Corporate Plaza,
2075 Kennedy Road
Scarborough, Ontario M1T 3V4

NEW ZEALAND
Brooker's
PO Box 6343, Auckland

SINGAPORE / MALAYSIA
Thomson Information (S.E. Asia)
30 Prinsep Street, #05-02
LKN Prinsep House, Singapore 188647

UNITED KINGDOM/EUROPE
Sweet & Maxwell Ltd
100 Avenue Road, London NW3 3PF

Typeset by Best-set Typesetter Ltd.,
Hong Kong

Printed in China

Index compiled by Don Brech,
Records Management International Limited

A CIP catalogue record for this book is available from the British Library

ISBN 0 421 55040 6

Acknowledgments

The editors would like to acknowledge and thank each of the contributors for their excellent work in putting together the materials presented in this book. The editors appreciate how difficult it can be to balance the demands of the practice of law and the research and writing required to assist their colleagues in understanding the diverse commercial laws of the region. The editors would also like to thank Rory Manchee of Sweet & Maxwell for his support and enthusiasm for the project, and Kate Wyllie of Sweet & Maxwell for her tireless efforts in helping them bring this massive project together.

Aleksandr Solzhenitsyn had his Invisible Allies. These are ours.

Alan S. Gutterman
Robert Brown
January 1997

The Editors

Alan Gutterman

Alan S. Gutterman has had almost two decades of experience in counseling entrepreneurs, managers, investors and small and large business enterprises in the areas of general corporate and securities matters, venture capital, mergers and acquisitions, international law and transactions, strategic business alliances, technology transfers and intellectual property law.

For most of his professional career, Alan Gutterman has been affiliated with internationally recognized law firms and has served in a number of capacities within the American Bar Association sections of Business Law, International Law and Practice, and Science and Technology.

He has published numerous articles and several books, on a diverse range of topics, including international law, technology transfer and business financing. He has also been an adjunct professor and lecturer on corporate finance, venture capital, corporations law, Japanese business law and law and economic development at Hastings College of Law, Golden Gate University, University of San Francisco, University of Santa Clara and Boalt Hall School of Law (Berkeley).

He received his A.B., M.B.A. and J.D. from the University of California at Berkeley and a D.B.A. in international business from Golden Gate University. He is also currently pursuing a Ph.D. in Law and Economics at the University of Cambridge in England, where he is affiliated with the ESRC Centre for Business Research.

Robert Brown

For over 20 years, Robert Brown has been involved in international transaction, with particular emphasis on Asia and Europe. During that period he was senior in-house counsel for the US subsidiary of one of Japan's largest enterprises, Mitsui & Co. Inc. He has also been special counsel at Heller Ehrman White and McAuliffe, and was the partner who established the Tokyo office of Pillsbury Madison & Sutro. He was a principal in an investment bank assisting Asian clients raise debt and equity in the US, and is now general counsel of an emerging hi-tech company. He has also created and taught courses on international issues at Berkeley and the University of San Francisco.

While attending three years of law school, he also obtained a Masters degree in Community Development and a Master of Business Administration. In addition, he has a Masters degree in Japanese Studies from Sophia University (Jochi Daigaku) in Tokyo. He is currently pursuing a Ph.D. in law and economics at the University of Cambridge in England.

He has served as Chair of a number of ABA committees on Privatization and on Asia, and has been president of a number of Asian organizations.

The Contributors

Cambodia

Professor Dolores A. Donovan, who specializes in the legal systems of Cambodia and China, is the Director of the Asian Pacific Legal Studies Program at the University of San Francisco School of Law. She teaches Comparative Law, Asian Legal Systems, and International Human Rights. Professor Donovan has been involved in Asian legal studies and Asian law reform efforts for over 20 years, including work as an advisor to the Cambodian government on the 1993 Constitution of the Kingdom of Cambodia. She is Co-Director of USF's Cambodia Law and Democracy Program.

Professor Jeffrey S. Brand is the Director of the University of San Francisco's Cambodia Law and Democracy Program. He teaches Constitutional Law, Civil Procedure, Evidence, Remedies and International Human Rights. Professor Brand specializes in the training of judges and most recently has been the architect of government-sponsored training programs for the judiciary and prosecutors of Cambodia and Vietnam.

Hong Kong

David M. Lederman is a lawyer with Wang & Wang based in Taipei, Taiwan. Mr Lederman would like to express a special thanks to his wife Rachel for her support in writing this chapter.

Indonesia

Darrell R. Johnson is a lawyer with Soewito, Suhardiman, Eddymurthy & Kardono. A resident of Indonesia for over 19 years, Mr Johnson's expertise includes Indonesian finance, banking and capital markets law, foreign investment, oil and gas law, and corporate and commercial law. Mr Johnson is a 1966 honors graduate in political science of the University of Southern California and a 1969 J.D. graduate of the Stanford Law School, where he was a member of the Board of Editors of the Stanford Law Review. Mr Johnson is admitted to practice before the US Supreme Court and the Federal District Court (Central District) of California. Mr Johnson also manages the ELIPS Project on behalf of the Project's contractors and is a founding member of its Board of Advisors and has written and spoken frequently on Indonesian legal matters.

Malaysia

The chapter on Malaysian commercial law was jointly written by **Rabindra Nathan, Chuah Jern Ern, Gerard Tham, Nurul Nisa Fuad** and **Ong Gaik Ee**, all Advocates and Solicitors of the High Court of Malaya.

People's Republic of China

Preston M. Torbert and **Jia Zhao** are both partners of the international law firm of Baker & McKenzie, Chicago office. Preston Torbert received his J.D. degree from Harvard Law School and his Ph.D. in Chinese History from the University of Chicago. He advises clients on strategic planning for China, the legal, tax and practical aspects of trade, licensing and investment as well as the negotiation of contracts in China. Since 1979 he has participated primarily in the drafting and negotiating of equity and cooperative joint venture contracts on behalf of a broad range of clients.

Jia Zhao received her J.D. from Harvard Law School. Ms. Zhao was the first PRC national to become a member of the Bar in the United States and the first person to be admitted to the Bar in both China and the United States. Her work has involved advising clients about investment and trade in China and their legal, political and cultural aspects. She has been involved in the establishment of more than two dozen equity joint ventures, wholly foreign-owned entities and other investments in the manufacturing and service sectors.

Both authors wish to thank their colleagues for their assistance in preparing the chapter on PRC Commercial Law, with particular thanks to Xiong Yin and Xinzhong Yu, China Law specialists and Yuanxi Ma, Supervisor of Translation of Baker & McKenzie, Chicago office.

Philippines

Jacinto D. Jimenez is a lawyer with Romulo, Mabanta, Buenaventura, Sayoc and De Los Angeles, based in the Philippines. He teaches law at the Ateneo de Manila University and the University of Santo Tomas.

Singapore

Christopher J. Murphy is an international telecommunications legal specialist in Washington, D.C. He has recently received his second LL.M. degree from Georgetown University Law Center, Washington, D.C. He would like to acknowledge the kind assistance of Mya Saw Shin, Senior Legal Specialist, Eastern Law Division of the Law Library of the Library of Congress, U.S.A.

South Korea

Joseph S. Cha, LL.M. International Legal Studies, New York University, J.D., Whittier College, is an associate with Heller Ehrman White & McAuliffe in its Singapore office. He would like to thank Kim Hyung-Jin for his assistance in reviewing the chapter on the commercial laws of Korea, and Professor Song Sang-Hyun for introducing him to the study of Korean law.

Taiwan

Gregory Klatt, J.D. University of California at Berkeley (Boalt Hall), is currently an associate at the Los Angeles office of Jones, Day, Revis & Pogue. He would like to thank Paul-Andre Ruff and Michael Fedrick for their significant contributions to the chapter.

The Contributors

Thailand

Bentley J. Anderson is currently Associate General Counsel at Inter-Regional Financial Group, Inc. in Minneapolis, MN. He received his LL.M. degree, with distinction, from Georgetown University Law Center, and his J.D. from the University of Minnesota Law School. He has previously published articles on various aspects of foreign direct investment law and is co-author of a forthcoming book on international intellectual property rights.

Vietnam

Per Bergling, LL.M., has been affiliated with the Department of Legal Science at Umeå University in Sweden, and has participated in several missions to Vietnam to provide advice regarding the development and implementation of commercial laws in that country. He recently was a visiting scholar at Boalt Hall School of Law at the University of California in Berkeley, and lectured on various aspects of legal reform in Vietnam as part of a seminar on law and economic development at the University of San Francisco Law School.

Contents

Contents

A CAMBODIA

B HONG KONG

C Indonesia

Contents

D Malaysia

E People's Republic of China

F Philippines

G Singapore

Contents

H SOUTH KOREA

I TAIWAN

J THAILAND

K VIETNAM

Contents

Table of Cases

xix

Table of Cases

Table of Cases

Table of Legislation

Table of Legislation

Indonesia

Table of Legislation

Table of Legislation

Table of Legislation

Table of Legislation

Table of Legislation

Table of Legislation

Table of Legislation

Table of Legislation

EAST ASIAN MARKETS:
AN OVERVIEW

Introduction

In this book, we survey the commercial laws of many of the countries that   1.01
fall within the region often referred to as East Asia.[1] The region has undergone substantial economic, political and social changes since the end of
World War II, and a number of the countries in the region are now classified
among the so-called "big emerging markets" as they position themselves to
enter ever higher tiers of importance in world trading markets. In relation to
other parts of the world, recent and projected economic performance of
countries in the region is exceptional, even though growth has moderated
somewhat recently.[2] In this chapter, we will briefly describe the general
characteristics of the region, many of which will be referred to again in
greater detail in the chapters that follow.

Demographic and Economic Characteristics

The countries in our survey vary dramatically in their size and population.   1.02
More than 1.7 billion people, about 30 per cent of the total population of the
world, live in these countries.[3] Over 1.2 billion of those reside in the People's
Republic of China, which is the largest country in the world. At the other
extreme is Singapore, which has just under three million people, but has
achieved astounding economic success in recent years. Five of the countries
located in the region (*i.e.* China, Indonesia, Vietnam, the Philippines, and
Thailand) rank among the 20 most populous countries in the world. Population growth is projected to continue rapidly through the year 2020, when it
is anticipated that more than 2.1 billion people will live in these countries.[4]
The economic importance of the area is even more important when one
remembers the size of some its immediate neighbors, such as India (936
million people) and Japan (125 million people).

The demographic characteristics of the countries in the region vary substantially. For example, about 80 per cent of Vietnam's population resides in

1

rural areas, and 80 per cent of the population is under the age of 40. This geographic concentration explains why 65 per cent of Vietnam's population are current involved in agricultural and farming activities. The Philippines also has a very young population, with about 40 per cent of its residents between 15 and 40; however, in contrast to Vietnam, almost half of the population in Vietnam now live in urban areas.

The standard of living enjoyed by residents within the region varies substantially. For example, per capita gross national product (GNP) in both Hong Kong and Singapore was over $15,000, while the same figures for China and Indonesia were $470 and $670, respectively.[5] The average growth rate of per capita GNP from 1980 to 1992 in several of the countries exceeded that of Japan (3.6 per cent) for the same period. For example, average growth in Korea was 8.5 per cent, and impressive gains were also achieved in China (7.6 per cent), Taiwan (6.4 per cent), and Thailand (6.0 per cent). In contrast, Malaysia (3.2 per cent) and the Philippines (−1.0 per cent) had difficulties in keeping up with their neighbors over the period. When gross domestic product (GDP) is used as a measure of growth, the achievements of countries in the region are even more impressive, with several countries (China, Korea, Taiwan, and Thailand) achieving growth rates in excess of 8 per cent from 1980 to 1992.[6]

1.03   In most cases, economic activity in the region, measured as a percentage of GDP, was concentrated in the industrial and service sectors.[7] For example, industrial activities as a percentage of GDP ranged from 38 per cent to 45 per cent for each of Indonesia, Korea, Singapore, Taiwan, and Thailand, while the proportion attributable to services in those five countries was anywhere from 40 per cent (Indonesia) to 62 per cent (Singapore). Hong Kong (77 per cent) had the highest level of dependence on service activities among the countries surveyed, while China (38 per cent) had the lowest; however, the service industry in China grew at an average annual rate of 11 per cent from 1980 to 1992, a rate that was exceeded only by Taiwan (13.2 per cent) during that period. Agricultural activities remained quite important for China (27 per cent of GDP)[8], the Philippines (22 per cent), Indonesia (19 per cent), and Thailand (12 per cent), but generally amounted to less than 10 per cent of GDP in the other countries.[9]

With regard to the growth of exports from 1980 to 1992, the performance within the region has varied significantly.[10] Four of the countries (China (11.9 per cent), Korea (11.9 per cent), Malaysia (11.3 per cent), and Thailand (14.7 per cent)) were able to achieve average annual growth rates in excess of 10 per cent, while other countries (Hong Kong (5.0 per cent), Indonesia (5.6 per cent), and the Philippines (3.7 per cent)) achieved more modest rates of growth comparable to that of Japan (4.6 per cent) during the period. The composition of exported goods and services also differed between countries. For example, machinery and transportation equipment were important exports for Korea, Malaysia, and Singapore, while Indonesia exported significant amounts of fuel and minerals. In general, primary goods remain important to the export activities of China, Indonesia, Malaysia, and Thailand.

Forecasts of real economic growth and real export growth from 1994 through 1996 are also illustrative of the tremendous market opportunities in the region.[11] With regard to increases in real GDP/GNP for 1996, China and Thailand are expected to continue to register annual growth rates in excess of eight percent; however, significant growth is now also expected to take place in Indonesia (7.1 per cent), Malaysia (8.2 per cent), and in Vietnam (9.5 per cent).[12] As to export growth, a number of countries are expected to achieves gains far in excess of those anticipated for Japan (7.7 per cent) and the United States (9.0 per cent). For example, the following countries are projected to increase their exports by more than 17 per cent: China (17.5 per cent), Malaysia (20.0 per cent), the Philippines (18.0 per cent), and Vietnam (23.5 per cent).

Another striking characteristic of the region is the degree of economic integration which is being achieved therein.[13] For example, if one looks at the exports to, and imports from, the countries in the so-called Pacific Economic Cooperation Council (PECC), which includes not only countries in East Asia, but also other countries bordering on both sides of the Pacific (*e.g.* Australia, Canada, Japan, the United States, as well as countries in Latin America like Peru and Chile),[14] we find that 72.4 per cent of the exports from PECC countries in 1993 went to other PECC countries, and that 72.0 per cent of the imports received by PECC countries in 1993 were from other PECC countries.[15] While the United States and many of the Latin American countries within the PECC look to the PECC for no more than about 60 per cent of their exports, Asian members are very reliant on PECC trade, with 93.2 per cent of Taiwan's exports in 1993 going to PECC members.

Regional Organization and Integration

Countries in the region belong to the new World Trade Organization, which has replaced the General Agreement on Tariffs and Trade (GATT). The most important economic and political association in the region is the Association of Southeast Asian Nations (ASEAN). ASEAN was founded in 1967 by Indonesia, Malaysia, the Philippines, Singapore, and Thailand in order to increase the level of economic cooperation in various business sectors, including food production, industry and commerce, shipping and telecommunications.[16] Since that time, membership has been extended to Brunei and Vietnam, and Laos is currently an observer. ASEAN is headquartered in Djakarta, Indonesia, and its principal organs include the ASEAN Heads of Government; the ASEAN Ministerial Meeting, which is an annual meeting among the foreign ministers of the member states to set general policies; the Standing Committee; nine Permanent Committees, five of which deal with economic cooperation in the areas of financing and banking, food, agricul- 1.04

ture, and forestry, industry, minerals, and energy, trade and tourism, and transportation and communication; Ad Hoc Committees and Working Groups, and the ASEAN Secretariat.

ASEAN has spawned a variety of subsidiary agreements, including the ASEAN Free Trade Area (AFTA), a free trade zone formed in 1992 and made up of the members of ASEAN, and the ASEAN Preferential Trading Agreement, which is designed to ensure that the member states of ASEAN afford each other reciprocal trade treatment. AFTA is designed to reduce intraregional tariffs, and to offer foreign investors and manufacturers simplified access to business opportunities in the region. Originally, the agreement was to be phased in over 15 years, since countries like the Philippines and Indonesia had concerns about the competitiveness of their economies in relation to their fellow member states. However, the target date for final implementation of the AFTA has subsequently been moved up first to the year 2003, and now to the year 2000.

1.05   Another important association in the region is the Asia-Pacific Economic Cooperation group (APEC), which was founded in 1989 and which includes members on both sides of the Pacific.[17] Among other things, APEC is designed to be a forum in which the member states may discuss a broad range of economic issues. In addition, it is hoped APEC can promote increased multilateral cooperation among the market-oriented economies of the region. APEC members have shown an interest in studying methods that might be used to harmonize custom procedures and reduce various impediments to "market access" among members. Of note is the so-called Bogor Declaration of late 1994, where the members adopted a "declaration of common resolve" to pursue "free and open trade and investment" over the period extending to the year 2020. The Declaration contemplates that the region's developed nations would dismantle their trade barriers by 2010, and that the other member states would follow suit by 2020.

Another interesting association is the East Asian Economic Caucus (EAEC), which was formed as an alternative to what was to be referred to as the East Asian Economic Grouping (EAEG). The EAEG was to be an alternative economic bloc including the ASEAN members, Hong Kong, Myanmar, Korea, and possibly Japan and Vietnam, but not those nations with a predominantly non-Asian population.[18] It was originally contemplated that the EAEC would operate under the "umbrella" of the APEC, but would be directly coordinated by the ASEAN economic ministers. However, progress has been somewhat slow. For example, Japan has appeared to be hesitant to move forward, and has called for including Australia and New Zealand in the association in an effort to reduce some of the apprehensions expressed by the United States. Problems also exist as to how to reconcile the interests of China, Hong Kong, and Taiwan, each of which would be important participants in such an association.

1.06   The declining United States military presence in the region has lead to the creation of the ASEAN Regional Forum (ARF), which is to be a regional security forum designed, among other things, to facilitate the peaceful reso-lution of disputes and promote regional stability. Members of the ARF include the ASEAN members, Australia, Canada, China, the European Un-ion, Japan, Korea, Laos, New Zealand, Papua New Guinea, Russia, the United States, and Vietnam. The ARF has considered a variety of issues, including North Korea's nuclear posture, the escalating arms race in the region, and certain political and military actions taken by China; however, there has not yet been any formal agreement regarding conflict-resolution mechanisms that might be used throughout the region.

ASEAN, and the various other associations and forums referred to above, provide a framework for regional economic and political integration that will continue to grow in importance in the years to come. ASEAN is closely observing the efforts to develop regional cooperative efforts in the European Union and in North America, and has begun to focus on projects designed to harmonize laws and regulations relating to trade and business. For example, ASEAN is now considering the implementation of a regional patent, and similar initiatives can be expected in the near future. Membership is ASEAN is also expected to expand, with Cambodia, Laos, and Myanmar expected to join over the next few years.

Other Regional Characteristics and Trends

Ethnic Diversity

East Asia is a geographic and economic region of tremendous diversity, with a number of large and important ethnic groups. For example, while in Malay-sia the largest ethnic group is the *bumiputera*, the indigenous Malays, the country also has a significant number of Chinese and Indian inhabitants. In many cases, the various ethnic groups have become involved in different types of economic activity within the country, as has been the case where the native Malays focused primarily on farming while the immigrant Chinese and Indians concentrated on the development of the industrial and manufac-turing sectors. In some cases, this has led to internal discord, and govern-ments have been forced to undertake programs designed to redistribute capital, employment opportunities and managerial resources and opportuni-ties. There is also significant religious diversity in the region. For example, religious groups in Singapore include Buddhist (Chinese), Muslim (Malays), Christian, Hindu, Sikh, Taoist, and Confucianist. 1.07

Infrastructure Development

Countries are beginning to focus on developing and improving the infra-structure necessary for efficient economic growth. For example, Taiwan embarked upon a $300 billion program dedicated to improvement of its telecommunications, housing, roads, and system of mass transit, although the 1.08

scope of the program was reduced in light of budgetary constraints. Singapore prides itself on the scope and quality of its infrastructure, noting the extent of its paved highways and railroads, as well as it excellent airports and ports. In fact, Singapore objective of becoming the major airport hub of the region by the end of the current decade has facilitated the development of more than 50 local firms dedicated to aircraft component manufacturing, maintenance and aerospace activities.

Targets for Economic Development

1.09   A number of countries in the region have pursued economic development by focused concentration on specific industries and commercial areas. For example, in recent years, China has sought economic development and inbound foreign investment by attempting to enhance its resources in the areas of agriculture, industry, defense, and science and technology. Generally, this has led to the establishment of an administrative and legal framework that would support foreign investment activities, including laws and regulations relating to economic contracts, joint ventures, sales contracts, and intellectual property rights. In many cases, this has led to significant increases in export activities, much of which could be attributed to new foreign investment. Using China as an example once again, total exports rose from $26 billion in 1984 to just under $100 billion in 1993, and the percentage of exports attributable to foreign investment activities rose from almost nothing in 1984 to a little over 25 per cent by 1993.

The more developed countries in the area have been forced to turn their attention to high technology industries. One reason for this has been the fact that the wage rates in those countries have risen substantially, undermining the competitiveness of low-end manufacturers. In some cases, such as in Taiwan, firms have actually begun to move their manufacturing activities into areas where labor costs are much lower, such as mainland China. These countries now look to high technology industries to create new jobs for workers who have been displaced from the manufacturing sector. Countries have increased the level of national research and development spending and have implemented tax holidays and other measures to induce foreign high technology firms into the local economy. As a result, several countries have become major players in the computer and semiconductor industries, and it is anticipated that similar progress will eventually be made in other areas, such as medical equipment and biotechnology.

1.10   The desire of local governments to create employment opportunities has had other profound effects in the region. For example, in Malaysia, the transition from an economy based substantially on the export of primary commodities like tin and rubber to a industrialized areas has led to increased amounts of government intervention in the economy. The government has established wholly owned companies or joint ventures with local and foreign partners in various sectors of the economy, thereby undermining the laissez-faire tradition which had dominated in the past. While this strategy has often been useful in the formation and early development of new industries, eventually the government is forced, due to changing priorities and budgetary constraints, to turn direction of the industry over to the private sector. As a result, privatization has become one of the key policy issues in the region; however, it can be expected that governments will continue to play a much more active role in the economic aspects of countries in the region than is normally the case in the United States and Europe.

Another striking feature of economic development in the region is the direction of inbound and outbound trading. One important element is the degree to which countries rely on trade within the region, rather than on relationships with the United States and Europe. For example, Singapore's exports in 1994 were primarily computer equipment, rubber and rubber products, petroleum products, and telecommunications equipment, and its main trading partners included not only the United States (19 per cent), but also Malaysia (19 per cent), Hong Kong (9 per cent), Japan (7 per cent), and Thailand (6 per cent). Major imports, in the form of aircraft, petroleum, chemicals, and foodstuffs, came mainly from Japan (22 per cent), Malaysia (16 per cent), the United States (15 per cent), Saudi Arabia (4 per cent) and Taiwan (4 per cent).

Legal and Regulatory Development

The development of commercial laws throughout the region is impacted by   **1.11** the tremendous historical and social diversity among the various countries. For example, several countries, such as Hong Kong, Singapore and Malaysia, base a number of precedents on their experiences with the English common law. However, other countries, such as Indonesia, Vietnam and Cambodia, have been profoundly effected by long periods of civil law influence, and the commercial laws of the Philippines were, for a long time, based on the Spanish Code of Commerce. The situation is further complicated by the fact that portions of national laws are based on other bodies of law, such as Islamic law in the case of Malaysia. Finally, rules of commerce and trade in various communities often follow native laws, many of which are unwritten and unavailable to persons living outside of these communities.

There has been a substantial amount of activity in the region with respect to reform and revision of commercial laws and regulations. Most countries in the region have moved to make substantial modifications to the their laws and practices in the areas of economic contracts (*e.g.* sales of goods), foreign investment, business entities, and intellectual property laws. However, mere changes in the form and content of the laws have not always been sufficient. For example, while China has made a substantial number of changes in its economic laws over the last few years, concerns remain regarding the transparency of the new legal framework in China. Many of the new laws, while now widely published, have not yet been subjected to critical analysis, and judicial and administrative interpretations are also lacking. Foreign investors also remain concerned about the inaccessibility of local judicial systems, a problem which has led to development of international conventions and agreements relating to dispute resolution for commercial contracts. Finally, the substantial involvement of government agencies and representatives in economic activities is troublesome and unfamiliar to foreign investors, although it is unlikely that this will change substantially in the near future.

Notes

[1] This definition is somewhat imprecise. For example, in the *Asia 1995 Yearbook* published by the Far Eastern Economic Review, countries in the East Asian region included the People's Republic of China, Hong Kong, South Korea, Taiwan, and Japan. Japan has not been included in this survey, since our emphasis is on developing and emerging market countries. Other countries forming part of this survey, including Indonesia, Malaysia, the Philippines, Singapore, Thailand, and now Vietnam, are often categorized as so-called "ASEAN countries," by virtue of their membership in the Association of Southeast Asian Nations. We have also included Cambodia in this survey.

[2] See, *e.g. World Financial Markets* September/October 1995, published by Morgan Guaranty Trust Company, New York, September 1995. This report indicated that in 1994, real GDP growth in the OECD, United States, Japan, and Emerging Asia, was 3.1 per cent, 4.1 per cent, 0.5 per cent, and 8.4 per cent, respectively, and that projected growth for the same areas in 1996 was 2.6 per cent, 3.0 per cent, 1.5 per cent, and 7.5 per cent, respectively. China's actual and projected growth in those years was quite exceptional (*i.e.* 11.8 per cent in 1994 and 10.7 per cent forecast for 1996), that the report included rates for Emerging Asia excluding China (*i.e.* 7.1 per cent in 1994 and 6.3 per cent forecast for 1996). The report indicates that inflation has been picking up in the region, and that trade accounts are deteriorating rapidly. Countries included as part of "Emerging Asia" include China, Hong Kong, India, Indonesia, Korea, Malaysia, Philippines, Singapore, Taiwan, and Thailand.

[3] In contrast, approximately 292 and 509 million people live in North America and Europe, respectively. Source for all figures is United States Department of Commerce, Bureau of the Census.

[4] This increase of approximately 23.5 per cent should be compared to the projected population increases in the United States (23.1 per cent), Japan (0.3 per cent), and the United Kingdom (3.2 per cent) over the same period.

[5] Source: *Asia 1995 Yearbook*, (Far Eastern Economic Review, Review Publishing Co. Ltd, Hong Kong, 1995).

[6] In contrast, the average annual growth of GDP in Japan from 1980–92 was approximately 4.1 per cent.

[7] The source for all information in this paragraph is the *Asia 1995 Yearbook* (Far Eastern Economic Review, Review Publishing Co. Ltd, Hong Kong, 1995).

[8] The average annual growth rate of agricultural sector activities in China from 1980 to 1992 was 5.4 per cent, while industrial activities and service activities grew at the rates of 11.1 per cent and 11.0 per cent, respectively.

[9] Figures were not available for Malaysia, and Cambodia and Vietnam were not included in the survey. It can be expected that these countries had a relatively high level of dependence on the agricultural sector at that time.

[10] The source for all information in this paragraph is the *Asia 1995 Yearbook*, (Far Eastern Economic Review, Review Publishing Co. Ltd, Hong Kong, 1995).

[11] The source for all information in this paragraph is the *Pacific Economic Outlook 1995–96* (Pacific Economic Cooperation Council, San Francisco, 1995).

[12] Many of the countries in the region are expected to exceed the estimated 1996 growth rates of the United States (2.0 per cent) and Japan (2.8 per cent); however, the rate of growth in countries such as Hong Kong (5.8 per cent), Korea (6.7 per cent), Singapore (7.0 per cent) and Taiwan (6.9 per cent) often is comparable to, or less than, the rate of growth experienced in those countries over the last few years.

[13] The source for all information in this paragraph is the *Pacific Economic Outlook 1995–96* (Pacific Economic Cooperation Council, San Francisco, 1995).

[14] Members of the PECC include Australia, Brunei, Canada, Chile, China, Columbia, Hong Kong, Indonesia, Japan, Korea, Malaysia, Mexico, New Zealand, Peru, Philippines, Singapore, Taiwan, Thailand, United States, and Vietnam.

[15] In order to put this in further perspective, consider that 34.1 per cent of the exports from all over the world in 1993 went to PECC countries, and that 32.6 per cent of the imports received by countries all over the world in 1993 came from PECC countries. Both of these figures had actually exceeded 40 per cent in 1992, an indication of the importance of the PECC countries to world trade.

[16] The purpose of the association is

> ". . . to accelerate economic growth, social progress and cultural development in the region . . . to promote social collaboration and mutual assistance on matters of common interest in the economic, social, cultural, technical, scientific, and administrative fields . . . to collaborate more effectively for the greater utilization of ['the member states'] agriculture and industries, the expansion of their trade, including the study of problems of international commodity trade, the improvement of their transport and communication facilities and raising the living standards of their people."

[17] Members include Australia, Brunei, Canada, Chile, China, Hong Kong, Indonesia, Japan, Korea, Malaysia, Mexico, New Zealand, Papua New Guinea, Philippines, Singapore, Taiwan, Thailand, and the United States.

[18] Initial reaction to the formation of the EAEG was mixed, and the United States warned that such an association might weaken key established alliances, including those with the United States.

2

LAW AND ECONOMIC DEVELOPMENT

Introduction

A survey of the commercial laws of East Asia provides an opportunity to compare and contrast economic and legal systems which vary substantially in their content and maturity. It is particularly important to understand the relationship between commercial laws and economic development, since this facilitates an understanding of how a country's commercial laws may change and evolve over time. In this chapter, we briefly review some of the models of economic development which might be followed by the countries in the region, including the dynamic cooperative growth model which characterized the rapid post-war development of Japan and Korea. This background is important in understanding the industrial and economic policies which serve as the foundation for commercial laws and institutions in a country. We then go on to discuss the relationship between law and economic development, with a particular emphasis on the economic costs associated with incomplete or inefficient legal systems and institutions.

2.01

Models of Economic Development

Every nation seeks to enhance the welfare of its citizens through the pursuit of appropriate policies to achieve economic development and steady growth of output and income. However, the actual policies to be followed by any specific nation depend, in large part, on its historical and ideological background. Also, immediate economic goals and objectives are often established by analyzing the internal and external challenges facing the nation and, not unimportantly, by referring to the national consensus regarding the appropriate and legitimate role of the state and the legal framework in setting and implementing the policies to achieve those objectives.

2.02

In order for any nation to achieve economic progress, it must acquire technology, capital, and related resources which will allow it to create wealth for its citizens. Nations may choose from a variety of strategies for economic development. For example, advocates of so-called "free trade" policies will typically argue for "export-oriented" development strategies based on open domestic markets and pursuit of trade opportunity in areas where the developing nation might have a competitive advantage (*e.g.* cheap labor, natural resources, etc.). On the other hand, nations may select an "inward-oriented" strategy, which depends on development of domestic firms and industries under state protection from foreign competition. Finally, the recent economic successes of nations such as Japan and Korea suggest still another model for rapid economic growth.

Export-Oriented Development Strategies

2.03   An "export-oriented" development strategy is one in which the economic and trade practices of the developing nation do not discriminate between production for the domestic market and exports, or between purchases of domestic and foreign goods. This classical model of economic development assumes that the developing nation will adopt a free trade policy and that government involvement will be limited to providing across-the-board incentives and subsidies to exporting firms and to actions calculated to ensure that the exchange rate with major trading partners remains realistic. Domestic firms are expected to compete in international markets in industries that are usually relatively labor-intensive in the early years of development, thereby giving the developing nations a comparative advantage. Such competition facilitates the movement of domestic labor and capital to the most efficient firms. Little or no effort need be made toward unprofitable production in industries where goods could be more efficiently imported and financed from the revenues obtained from the nation's export activities.

Economists advocating classical free trade practices would discourage developing nations from "import substitution", a term which loosely refers to attempts to undertake domestic production of goods in an industry in which the nation does not have a comparative advantage. In such cases, imports of the goods would be heavily restricted to protect the domestic industry from competition, and firms often operate at substantial losses because of their inability to obtain needed technologies and other resources. In addition, the decision to divert resources away from export industries may create trade imbalances and ultimately lead to restrictive monetary and fiscal policies to address mounting levels of foreign indebtedness.

In its purest case, a successful "export-oriented" development strategy requires the creation and maintenance of a number of conditions: a strong government commitment toward export promotion and away from import substitution; a realistic exchange rate level and policies that assure exporters that adjustments will be made in accordance with differentials in inflation rates with major trading partners; no quantitative trade restrictions; access by exporters to international markets for raw materials and other factor inputs; a highly-developed infrastructure; liberalized policies with respect to capital, labor, and domestic product markets; competition between domestic and international firms both at home and abroad, causing a shift in the nation's resources to more efficient producers; and broad support for all export activities, rather than selective policies focusing on specific commodity areas.

Inward-Oriented Development Strategies

In contrast, a nation might choose to pursue various commercial, industrial,   2.04 and exchange rate policies which, taken collectively, have been identified as "inward-oriented". In those cases, policy makers utilize direct controls, such as import licensing and quantitative restrictions, rather than tariffs; hidden import duties, such as stamp taxes; advance deposit requirements; and a number of other quasi-tariff measures. In addition, inward-oriented regimes are generally characterized by high levels of protection for manufacturing, direct controls on imports and investments, overvalued exchange rates, and fiscal policies which provide production subsidies, credit subsidies, wage subsidies, and various tax holidays.

Many of the nations which practice "inward-oriented" policies are attempting to export primary commodities while simultaneously building domestic industries through import substitution policies. Arguments against export-oriented policies cite "export pessimism", the belief that the markets for primary and semi-finished exports are decreasing and that "infant industries" need to be protected. However, it is not clear that the market for primary commodities is declining at the rate cited by proponents of the "export pessimism" argument. Even in those cases where a valid reason exists for some form of government assistance to developing industries, it is believed that a policy of subsidies and incentives to the industrial sector is to be preferred to the costs of protecting an entire industry from import competition. Conversely, observers such as Peter Drucker have speculated that due to an apparent overabundance of raw materials in the world marketplace, it is no longer possible for developing nations to follow the "export-driven" growth model.

New Approaches to Economic Growth and Export-Oriented Development Strategies

The implicit differences between the classical definitions of "export-   2.05 oriented" and "inward-oriented" policies lie in the role which government plays within industry and trade. Usually, the government limits its involvement in export-driven growth to macroeconomic matters: providing the infrastructure for economic growth, promoting market efficiency, maintaining stable fiscal and monetary policies and, in some cases, stimulating the economy through special tax measures and government procurement policies. However, in recent years, several countries, notably Japan and Korea, have pursued exports as an appropriate national objective while rejecting the limited role of the state in favor of a series of microeconomic or industrial policies, each of which is supported by the history, culture, and national ideologies of the particular country.

The industrial policies of countries such as Japan and Korea cannot properly be characterized as either "export-oriented" or "inward-oriented," since they have freely borrowed from the practices of both models. They do share a common interest in rapid growth in the economy, which necessarily depends upon an ability to produce and sell more and more goods into the domestic and export markets. As such, global competitiveness becomes the overriding policy objective, leading to social practices, such as high savings and investment, which tend to improve productivity while deferring consumption. This national ideology drives the manner in which economic and commercial laws and regulations are drafted, interpreted, and enforced.

As we shall see, the economic conditions of the countries within East Asia are tremendously diverse, and each country will face its own unique series of hurdles as it strives for growth in the years to come. Nonetheless, the experiences of some of the more developed countries in recent years provide us with a sense of those elements that might be most important in the formulation of coherent national economic policies. Among those elements are the following:

Structure of Governmental Institutions

2.06 The ability of a nation to formulate and implement specific industrial policies greatly depends on the structure of its government institutions. Japan and other countries have adopted governmental and political structures which are characterized by the presence of a talented and elite bureaucracy with broad discretion regarding overall economic policy, an executive branch with only limited political opposition, a relatively weak legislative branch, a central economic planning function, and integrated regulation of fiscal, monetary, credit, and foreign investment policies through the finance and trade ministries.

One of the most striking elements of the structure of government institutions in many of these countries is that it has developed in a manner which is generally consistent with the traditional social hierarchies that have long existed within the country. For example, while most of the countries have a number of formal governmental and political institutions, they have, in many cases, remained largely underdeveloped in relation to their counterparts in the United States and Europe. Central planning authority remains largely vested in the ministries and in the bureaucratic infrastructures, and many of the industrial leaders in the private sector have served in the bureaucracy. As such, consensus regarding the nation's economic goals and objectives is often achieved outside of the political process.

Target Industries

Many emerging countries now regularly target those industries they believe 2.07
are essential to their national economic security. Having identified those
industries, a series of tariff and non-tariff barriers are established to "protect"
the domestic industries from foreign firms. Even more importantly, domestic
firms chosen to be active in target industries become the beneficiaries of a
wide variety of additional policy measures implemented to provide, without
substantial governmental subsidies, a number of competitors with the capital,
technology, and training necessary for rapid development of the capacity to
satisfy domestic demand and gain entry into the global marketplace.

Like the classical model of economic growth, the selection of target industries by each nation focuses overall industrial planning and dictates the use of
regulatory tools in the areas of trade, foreign investment, banking and credit,
and antitrust. However, what is striking is that these countries do not limit
their choices to "lower-end" goods, rather they often focus on goods and
industries where the technical requirements are quite complex, yet the market opportunities are greatest. Also, while some countries continue to use
state-owned enterprises as the vehicles for competition in the targeted industries, it is now becoming more common for the burdens of national economic
growth to be placed upon the shoulders of private firms, some of which
have been recently "privatized" or converted for their status as government
affiliates.

Strategic Planning and Administrative Guidance

The industrial policy of any nation consists of the microeconomic actions 2.08
taken by the government for the purpose of achieving a specific strategic
economic objective. For many years, the hallmark of industrial policy in
countries such as Japan and Korea has been the presence of a dedicated
bureaucratic elite, an apolitical group empowered to establish broad goals for
the economy and entrusted with a myriad of tools to encourage the appropriate actions at the firm and industry level. It is impossible to understand the
regulatory framework of many of the countries in the region without appre-
ciating the planning and administrative process and the deference shown by
politicians, banks, managers, employees, and consumers.

A number of the countries have established some form of central planning
agency which develops annual, medium, and long-term overall goals and
forecasts that guide and influence all of the major economic variables, including investment, savings, consumption, government spending, growth of the
money supply, aggregate output and supply, and imports and exports, as well
as the expected resource allocation within various sectors and industries.
Once established, these guidelines provide the framework for the administrative guidance supplied to private industry by the various ministries within
the government as well as for the interpretation of the regulations which are
applicable to economic activities. Moreover, announcements by the planning

agency identify target industry strategies, as Japan emphasized in building heavy and chemical industries and in improving the industrial structure during the 1960s and early 1970s.

2.09   Policymakers are often given broad discretion to change, without legislative approval, taxes, tariffs, interest rates, subsidies, controlled prices of selected goods, and other matters. In addition, rather than attempting to regulate the economy through a mass of detailed and universally applicable rules, bureaucrats can target certain industries for development through their control and leverage regarding the access of firms to credit and low-interest loans, imported raw materials, foreign investment, currency for foreign exchange purposes, and business licenses. Finally, central planners reward firms for outstanding performance and actively participate in the ultimate decisions regarding who will produce what, how much will be produced, and the fate of recalcitrant or inefficient firms within the nation.

While administrative guidance and an appropriate level of government intervention may be necessary to achieve industrial policy objectives, there are clearly several disadvantages to such practices. First, the broad discretion granted to various policymakers regarding rules and regulations undermines the goal of developing a consistent and transparent set of commercial laws and regulations which can serve as the foundation for long-term private transactions between domestic firms, and between domestic firms and foreign investors. Second, even though there has been a steady path of privatization throughout the region, the role that the state continues to play in its industry policy efforts may well lead to difficulties in the development and maturation of the nation's private firms, banks, local governments, and labor unions. For example, one can observe that the state's role in a country's banking and credit systems can clearly influence the development of its private financial institutions, and that too much control may make it difficult for those institutions to marshall the technical and capital resources to provide ongoing financial support to the country's firms in foreign markets.

Consultation

2.10   Consensus-building plays an important part in the implementation of industrial policies in many of the nations in the region. As such, each nation has developed a number of mechanisms for involving the various governmental ministries, industry groups, and others in formulating positions with respect to major economic policy matters. This type of consultation is often the focal point of industry structure, and is facilitated by the common educational and social experiences of the ministry personnel and industry leaders.

Capital Allocation

2.11   An important element of industrial policy is the government's ability to ensure that domestic firms obtain the capital which is necessary to fund the acquisition of new technologies and the rapid expansion of facilities and human resources. Capital allocation strategies can include direct subsidies, tax incentives, and low-interest loans provided by "semi-governmental" banks. However, the central government's most potent policy tool has often been its influence over the banking system, whereby commercial banks coordinate their lending efforts with those of the government, fostering cooperative relationships between firms and their banks, particularly since debt remains the preferred financing vehicle for many nations in the region.

Competition and Cooperation

One of the most tenacious debates in the United States regarding industrial policy concerns antitrust prohibitions on cooperative efforts among firms in the same industry. However, in Japan and other emerging countries in the region, competition and cooperation are key aspects of the industrial structure. While protection from foreign competition is often a fundamental concern for domestic firms, cooperative research and development projects regarding technology in target industries are encouraged and supported by the government as well as by the firms themselves, provided that each firm is left free to compete on its own terms with the resultant technology. Also, a wide variety of organizations, including ministerial councils, facilitate dissemination of competitive information throughout the domestic industry. **2.12**

Economic Development and the Role of the State

The growth and economic development strategies of modern Japan and other recently successful Asian economies can be readily distinguished from other models of economic development by the degree to which the state has intervened at the level of the firm or industry in order to achieve specific national economic objectives. Lodge has identified four areas where government can influence the effect of business (*e.g.* firms and industries) on the economic well-being of the general community: promotion of marketplace competition; regulation of competition; establishment of a partnership with business; and regulation of the grant and maintenance of the corporate or business license.[1] The second and fourth methods are consistent with the role of government under the classical model of economic growth; however, it is the first and third methods which have often proven to be effective in steering growth in the emerging economies of Asia, even in cases where the country may lack certain advantageous resources thought to be necessary for success in world markets. **2.13**

It can be expected that, in the future, governments in the region will follow economic development strategies that may have proven to be successful for their neighbors. The experience of Japan and Korea dictates that policymakers should pay attention to the needs of entrepreneurs and enterprises in the economy, as well as to the methods that might be used to enhance the level of dynamic competition in the marketplace. In some cases, this may require substantial interventions by the state of the type described above. However, while the state may take an active and visible role at some stage of economic development, ultimately the time will come a time for the state to step aside and allow the market to develop independently. In order for this type of transition to occur, however, the state must work to establish and maintain an environment within which market transactions can occur efficiently. One prerequisite to this environment is the establishment of a set of laws and legal institutions for the conduct of business and commerce.

Law and Economic Development

2.14   As developing countries begin to transform their economic systems away from government control over decisions relating to production and distribution to so-called "private ordering", where the private sector assumes responsibility for providing and delivering goods and services, the role of the government must change substantially. For example, the former primary role of the government in issuing licenses and permits, and in directly intervening in production, trade, and finance, is gradually subordinated to a new indirect management mode which emphasizes policies and regulations which provide the support necessary for the establishment and maintenance of efficient markets, including the legal framework that provides the basis for market contracts and transactions.

Economic transitions and reforms in developing countries generally include a number of changes in the legal, regulatory, and judicial environment in which business enterprises exist and commercial transactions take place. Specifically, there is a need to develop "rules of the game" for economic activity and provide procedures to ensure these activities are carried out efficiently and effectively. Developing countries can learn a good deal from studying how economic laws have evolved over time, as well as from the lessons to be gained from economic studies of the adverse effects of an inefficient legal system on economic growth and development.

Historical Development of Economic Laws

2.15   The relationship of law to economic development has been followed by a number of historians and economists. The rules that govern commercial activities today have their roots in the 11th and 12th centuries, which is when mercantile law, or *les mercatoria* as it was known, first began to develop. The growth of a separate commercial law was encouraged by the growth of cities and merchants residing there. Assisting their emerging trade were the Crusades and colonization efforts occurring at the time. This brought greater exposure to foreign cultures and goods, and a subsequent demand for such goods either as cheaper sources or as goods not otherwise available.

In order for this exchange of goods to occur, merchants needed order, particularly with respect to external trade with parties outside of the local market area. Before they were willing to undertake long distance trade, merchants needed to know what the rules were so they could calculate their risks and profits. Beyond order, there was also a need for justice. If one party broke its promises there had to be a system to grant the injured party its bargain. To regulate the increasing number of transactions, rules were developed concerning not only sales, but also the transportation, financing and insurance of goods being sold.

The merchant law which eventually developed had all the characteristics **2.16** of a legal system. It had objective standards, universal applicability (to those who were subject to its rules), established reciprocal rights, established rules for adjudication of disputes and allowed the parties to a dispute to participate, was an integrated system or rules applicable to the merchant society and how they did business, and allowed for growth and evolution of the rules. The characteristics of merchant law that evolved at that time have been summarized as follows:

1. "the sharp separation of the law of movables (chattels) from the law of immovables (land and fixtures attached to land);

2. recognition of rights in the good-faith purchaser of movables superior to those of the true owner;

3. replacement of the older requirement of delivery of goods in order to transfer ownership by the device of symbolic delivery, that is, transfer of ownership (and of risk of loss or damages) by transfer of transportation documents or other documents;

4. the creation of a right of possession of movables independent of ownership;

5. recognition of the validity of informal oral agreements for the purchase and sale of movables;

6. limitation of claims for breach of warranty, on the one hand, and development of the doctrine of implied warranties of fitness and of merchantability (*marchandise loyale et marchande*), on the other hand;

7. the introduction of an objective measure of damages for nondelivery of goods, based on the difference between the contract price and the market price, together with the introduction of fixed monetary penalties for breach of some types of contracts;

8. the development of commercial documents such as bills of exchange and promissory notes and their transformation into so-called abstract contracts, in which the document was not merely evidence of any underlying contract but itself embodied, or was, the contract and could be sued on independently;

9. the invention of the concept of negotiability of bills of exchange and promissory notes, whereby the good faith transferee was entitled to be paid by the drawer or maker even if the latter had certain defenses (such as the defense of fraud) against the original payee;

10. the invention of the mortgage of movables (chattel mortgage), the unpaid seller's lien, and other security interests in goods;
11. the development of a bankruptcy law which took into account the existence of a sophisticated system of commercial credit;
12. the development of the bill of lading and other transportation documents;
13. the expansion of the ancient Graeco-Roman sea loan and the invention of the bottomry loan, secured by a lien on the freight or by shares in the ship itself, as means of financing and insuring a merchant's overseas sales;
14. the replacement of the more individualistic Graeco-Roman concept of partnership (*societas*) by a more collectivistic concept in which there was joint ownership, the property was at the disposition of the partnership as a unit, and the rights and obligations of one partner survived the death of the other;
15. the development of the joint venture (*commenda*) as a kind of joint-stock company, with the liability of each investor limited to the amount of his investment;
16. the invention of trademarks and patents;
17. the floating of public loans secured by bonds and other securities, and
18. the development of deposit banking."[2]

To those of us accustomed to thinking of the Middle Ages as the Dark Age where little progress in civilization or culture occurred, it is a surprise to see how much progress in the field of commerce occurred that time. While many of the elements of culture that had already been known (such as art, sculpture, etc.) entered into a period of decline during this period, in an area much less developed by the Greeks and Romans, the people of the Middle Ages progressed much further than their cultural ancestors. In fact, much of what we now have in the commercial field was developed not by the Greeks or Romans but, as can be seen from the above list, during the Middle Ages.

Legal System Inefficiencies and Economic Development

2.17 While the elements of modern commercial and economic laws have been around for some period of time, they nonetheless remain quite new for many developing countries. While most developing countries are attempting to reform and modernize their economic laws, there is often a lack of understanding of need to make such reforms, and the adverse consequences which might flow from the failure to push forward with the development of a comprehensive system of commercial laws and institutions. Advocates of legal and regulatory reform in developing countries argue that it is necessary not only to increase equity in the society and raise productivity, but also to reduce various costs which adversely impact the rate of growth of economic activity in particular markets. Among the costs which are of greatest concern are transactional costs, costs of avoiding the formal legal system, and capital costs.

Transaction Costs

In order to understand what transaction costs are, let us go back to the origin of the phrase. In his 1960 article, "The Problem of Social Cost", Coase first used the phrase "the costs of market transactions". These became known as "transaction costs". According to Coase, what he had in mind was: **2.18**

> "In order to carry out a market transaction it is necessary to discover who it is that one wishes to deal with, to inform people that one wishes to deal and on what terms, to conduct negotiations leading up to a bargain, to draw up the contract, and to undertake the inspection needed to make sure that the terms of the contract are being observed. These operations are extremely costly, sufficiently costly at any rate to prevent many transactions that would be carried out in a world in which the pricing system worked without cost."[3]

Carl Dahlman categorized transaction costs as search and information costs, bargaining and decision costs, and policing and enforcement costs:

> "It is necessary to take the definition of transaction costs by Coase a little further. A natural classification of transactions costs consistent with his definition can be obtained from the different phases of the exchange process itself. In order for the exchange between two parties to be set up it is necessary that the two search each other out, which is costly in terms of time and resources. If the search is successful and the parties make contact they must inform each other of the exchange opportunity that may be present, and the conveying of such information will again require resources. If there are several economic agents on either side of the potential bargain to be struck, some costs of decision making will be incurred before the terms of trade can be decided on. Often such agreeable terms can only be determined after costly bargaining between the parties involved. After the trade has been decided on, there will be the costs of policing and monitoring the other party to see that his obligations are carried out as determined by the terms of the contract, and of enforcing the agreement reached."[4]

Transactional costs accrue throughout the process of negotiating a particular commercial transaction. For example, parties incur search and information costs as they begin to seek appropriate business partners and information regarding their resources and capabilities. Once the potential partner has been selected, parties are faced with bargaining and decision costs, including the direct costs associated with drafting all required legal documents for the transaction and, if necessary, forming new enterprises to participate in the   **2.19** transaction. Then, after the contract has been completed, the parties are faced with the costs of monitoring performance under the contract, including the possibility that adjustments will be required in cases where the transactions begin to stray from their initial objectives. Finally, there may be significant enforcement and award costs in the event that material disputes arise between the parties.

Transaction costs are a major impediment to efficiency, even in developed countries. North has estimated that almost one-half of the United States' national income is spent on transaction costs. Even more disheartening, this is a significant increase over a century ago.[5] Not surprisingly, transaction costs are an even greater impediment in emerging economies. Once again, it is North who found:

> "When we compare the cost of transacting in a Third World country with that in an advanced industrial economy, the costs per exchange in the former are much greater — sometimes no exchange occurs because costs are so high. The institutional structure in the Third World lacks the formal structure (and enforcement) that underpins efficient markets."[6]

Transactional costs can quickly become excessive, a problem which is exaserbated when the number and ideological diversity of the economic actors increases. As parties with widely divergent interests (*e.g.* entrepreneurs in developing countries and foreign investors from developed countries) being to engage in negotiations regarding economic contracts, it becomes impossible for them to rely on the use of informal agreement and enforcement mechanisms. Such parties need an objective framework within which to organize their transactions, or the transaction costs will be so high that the transactions will be so expensive that they will not be attempted.

Avoidance Costs

2.20 When transaction costs are excessive, access to the formal legal system is limited, or the risks of using the formal legal system remain too high due to inadequacies in the content and/or enforcement of laws and regulations, then parties may instead turn to strategies which avoid the formal legal system. For example, rather than applying for the licenses and permits which are nominally required as a condition of using the formal legal system, the parties may simply pursue the transaction without any formal legal approvals. While this may permit them to avoid some of the formal legal costs, it does expose them to another set of costs, including the need to pay protection money, bribe local officials, or downsize the scope of their activities in order to avoid detection. While activities conducted within this informal system may provide productivity gains, it is likely that those gains will be less than those that might have been achieved if the business had been conducted in the formal legal sector.

Capital Costs

An inadequate formal legal system can have an adverse impact on the cost of   **2.21**
capital and the availability of credit for financing new transactions. This is
due to the fact that the cost of capital is closely linked to the legal certainty
and predictability implicit in a country's formal legal system. Capital costs
reflect the relative security of a future claim with respect to a current transfer
of resources. For example, in a commercial loan transaction, the lender is
asked to transfer capital to the borrower in the present in exchange for a
future right to receive the capital back along with some additional compensation for the loss of use of the capital during the time that the loan was
outstanding. If the formal legal system does not include reliable enforcement
mechanisms which increase the lender's confidence regarding the return of
capital, then the cost of capital (*i.e.* the interest rate, collateral coverage) will
be much higher in order to compensate the lender for the increased risks
flowing from inadequacies in the legal system.

The problem is exacerbated in the case of developing countries, since
many of the borrowers are new enterprises with no established track records,
and many of the projects carry their own independent levels of business risk,
such as market and production uncertainties. These business risks necessarily
must be factored into the lender's decision-making process. When the higher
foreclosure and insolvency costs are added on to these inherent business
risks, the lender may either cease lending all together, reduce the pace of its
loans until market conditions become clearer, or restrict its lending activities
to projects in only a few selected sectors. In each case, the rate of growth and
development in the economy is adversely impacted. Moreover, if international lenders perceive that investment risks may be lower in one country as
opposed to another, perhaps because the formal legal systems in one country
are more advanced, then the flow of capital to the riskier country will be
reduced and then diverted to other countries, perhaps creating an inbalance
among countries in the same geographic region.

Economic Costs of Legal System Inefficiencies

Inefficient legal system costs critically affect development. The greater the   **2.22**
inefficiency and costs associated with doing business, the greater the handi-
cap to development. Where inefficiency is reduced and costs minimized,
development is more likely to take place. This does not guarantee that it will,
since there are too many other variables which must be taken into account.
We can only say that the more handicaps are removed, the more likely it is to
take place. The following passage from a recent issue of the *Wall Street
Journal* illustrates how important the legal system infrastructure can be to a
country's ability to attract foreign investment:

> "Recently, Vietnam's top planning ministry called in an international
> consulting firm to discuss why U.S. investment had been so far below its

expectations. Hanoi had hoped for a gold rush after the U.S. economic embargo ended a year and a half ago. Instead, there was an initial flurry of deals, followed by a cautious appraisal. Part of the consulting firm's answer was that most U.S. multinationals have big legal departments that prefer the comfort of established, stable law and tax systems. Vietnam has neither."[7]

The costs of an inefficient legal system have also been studied with respect to Peru by De Soto, who found that the costs of not having property rights for market participants included inefficient use of resources; reduced investment; a bias toward the use of multiple, small-scale operations rather than larger, more efficient, firms; limited use of property as collateral; and stagnation resulting from the lack of a system for transferring and organizing property rights. As to the costs associated with their inability to use a contract system, market participants ran up against an inability to use legal coercion to ensure compliance with agreements; unenforceable agreements; fewer long-term agreements; slower economic progress due to the need to develop personal relationships to replace contract-based relationships; increased time and costs associated with investigating and monitoring contractual relationships; restrictions on the scope of business relationships to kin and villagers, rather than the most qualified partners; greater use of violence for enforcement of agreements; an inability to separate control from ownership and an inability to offer limited liability as a means for inducing investment; and an inability to establish separate companies with separable liabilities.[8]

2.23   Inefficiencies in the legal system also had adverse effects on the public and the general economy in Peru. For example, the public was forced to deal with unregulated and uninsured informals. As for the economy as a whole, De Soto found:

1. Declining productivity as informals rely on smaller scale and more labor, since capital could be seized. Investment was also reduced for the same reason.
2. Inefficient tax system since as costs of formality increase more businesses remain informal thereby shifting more of tax burden to few formal businesses which in turn creates a vicious cycle.
3. Increased utility rates in a similar vicious cycle.
4. Limited technological progress since inventors are less likely to expend efforts on research unless they are certain of being able to reap benefits under well-established property rights in the invention.
5. Difficulty in formulating microeconomic policy since so much of the economy is run by unrecognized, unregulated, and difficult to quantify informals. This usually means that underemployment, employment and inflation are overestimated.[9]

Conclusions

Historical studies of Spain, France, the Netherlands or England during the **2.24** 18th and 19th centuries, America in the 19th and 20th, and Japan in the 20th, all appear to support the view of many economists that an inefficient legal system with uncertain property rights retards development. As North wrote, ". . . the institutional framework plays a major role in the performance of an economy . . . [it] is the critical key to the relative success of economies, both cross-sectionally as well as through time".[10] Inefficient legal system costs do much more than increase the costs of doing business. Where inefficiency exists, uncertainty prevails. This means profit maximization no longer controls decision-making and success is often determined not by skill but by luck. Obviously, an economy which is no longer built on profit maximization and skill is not resting on the best foundation. The following passage is enlightening:

> "Basically, what property rights, contracts, and extracontractual liability do is reduce uncertainty for people who want to invest their labor or capital in the development of existing resources. . . . In any country, uncertainty or legal instability reduces the volume of long-term investment and investment in plant and equipment. People save less and invest the little they do save in such socially unproductive goods as jewelry, gold, or luxury property. The flight of capital from countries . . . is only one more result of the desire to avoid uncertainty. . . . Thus, the actual value of an economic opportunity is not the value it would have it if could be realized without cost, but rather its estimated value, taking into account the cost of the red tap, the degree to which it can be protected against third party appropriation, and the ease with which it can be sold. The less costly the transaction and the more secure the right to enjoy the fruits of investment, the greater the real value of an economic activity. A law that is efficient in dealing with these elements will encourage people to identify and seize existing opportunities and will systematically increase the value of economic activity."[11]

The areas which should be covered in a comprehensive system of economic **2.25** laws and regulations are not difficult to identify, and have not changed much since the first set of mercantile laws were developed in the Middle Ages. However, although the value of such laws is readily accepted, their effectiveness in a given situation is more problematic, since it depends on a variety of factors such as the following:

1. the clarity of the laws and regulations and the availability of information regarding such laws and regulations;
2. the enforceability of legal contracts and instruments;
3. the general level of experience, education, and competence in economic, commercial, and legal matters;

4. the predictability and stability of laws, regulations, and enforcement mechanisms;
5. the moral and ethical behavior norms which exist in the community;
6. the perceptions in the community regarding the content and legitimacy of the prevailing legal system; and
7. the preference within the community for consensus or informal mediation over confrontation or formalistic litigation, or vice versa.

Notes

[1] See Lodge, *The American Disease* (1984).
[2] Berman, *Revolution*, 349–350.
[3] Coase, R.H., *The Firm, The Market, and the Law* (Chicago: The University of Chicago Press, 1988), p.114.
[4] Dahlman, *Externality*, 147–148. North also uses similar terminology in describing transaction costs:

> "The transfer of goods between economic units requires the provision of information about the opportunities for exchange or *search costs*, the negotiation of the terms of the exchange — *negotiation costs* — and determining procedures for enforcing the contract — *enforcement costs*. The costs of providing all the services involved are called here *transaction costs*."

North, *Rise*, 93.
[5] North wrote:

> "Wallis and North . . . measuring the size of transaction costs that go through the market (such as costs associated with banking, insurance, finance, wholesale, and retail trade; or, in terms of occupations, with lawyers, accountants, etc.) in the U.S. economy found that more than 45 percent of national income was devoted to transacting and, moreover, that his percentae had increased from approximately 25 percent a century earlier. Thus the resources of the economy consumed in transacting are of considerable magnitude and growing."

North, *Institutions*, 28.
[6] North, *Institutions*, 67.
[7] Greenberger, "Vietnam", W.S.J., A-11.
[8] De Soto, *Path*, 158–177.
[9] De Soto, *Path*, 158–177.
[10] North, *Institutions*, 69.
[11] De Soto, *Path*, 180, 181, 182–3.

LAWS AFFECTING BUSINESS AND COMMERCIAL ACTIVITIES

Introduction

As suggested in the previous chapter, the substantive requirements for a   **3.01**
comprehensive set of laws and regulations for business and commercial
activities have been well established. In the country-specific chapters which
follow later in this book, we survey the content of various economic and
business laws, including competition law, contract law, commercial law,
company law, capital markets and securities law, laws and regulations with
respect to arbitration and other dispute resolution methods, banking and
lending law, consumer protection law, health and safety laws, environmental
law, employment and labor law, foreign investment law, tax laws and accounting rules, and intellectual property law. In this chapter, we provide a
brief overview of these areas, focusing on the generic characteristics of the
laws and regulations in each area and the importance of such laws to reducing
inefficiencies in the legal system.

Commercial Laws

The increasing reliance in developing countries on market-based transactions   **3.02**
among independent contracting parties requires a system of commercial
laws. The importance of commercial laws for developing countries stems not
only from the need to formulate rules for transactions between domestic
parties, but also from the need for foreign investors to achieve some level of
comfort in their dealings with local firms in the course of licensing, distribution, production, and sales arrangements, as well as joint ventures. Among
the key legal and regulatory concerns in this area are the development of
general contract laws, laws relating to sales of goods, debtor-creditor laws,
and consumer protection laws. In addition, a number of countries regulate

commercial activities through regulations on sales agents and representatives, import controls, and product standards.

Contract Laws

3.03 Prior versions of contract law in developing countries focused primarily on the content of specific types of contracts (*e.g.* supply and installation contracts, loan contracts) and set out in detail the contractual terms of transactions involving state-owned enterprises. In many cases, the contract law really reflected the priorities of the state planning process in that contracts were used primarily as a means for setting out the economic targets established by the state and rights of the state in the event that the targets were not met. Early contract laws made little or no reference to market-based transactions, since they were largely not permitted.

As developing countries move toward market-based economies, contract laws are needed in order to allow economic transactions between parties without the need for administrative controls. Developing countries are now working to establish a commercial legal framework for economic contracts, including written agreements relating to production, exchange of goods, provision of services, and development and commercialization of technology. The structure of rights and obligations with respect to such contracts are no longer limited to meeting state-established targets or objectives. Instead, parties are allowed to determine the essential elements of economic contract, such as quantity, quality, and price, and can also establish their own terms relating to delivery, guarantees, and duration. Economic contract laws also include rules for dispute resolution, as well as provisions for mortgaging property, guarantees, and penalties, all of which are designed to ensure performance of the contracts.

3.04 Some countries, such as the PRC, have been using a two-tier system of contract laws which distinguish between contracts between domestic parties and contract between a domestic party and a foreign party. These foreign contract laws are generally limited to stating basic principles relating to formation of the contract, performance of obligations under the contract, and the consequences of a breach or violation of the contract. In many cases, special types of contracts (*e.g.* joint ventures, know-how licenses) must comport with other regulations which may have been adopted regarding such contracts. Dispute resolution procedures and choice of law provisions are typically covered in the foreign contract laws.

Foreign contract laws often refer to international practice for guidance in situations where no provision in the local law covers the particular issue. Typically, this means the parties may look to the rules set out in the United Nations Convention for the International Sale of Goods (CISG), and provisions in the foreign contract laws of many developing countries will often be borrowed from the CISG. Standard contracts continue to play a large part on contract negotiations between domestic and foreign parties in many developing countries, particularly since local parties still lack the experience and knowledge to assess some of the alternative provisions which might be suggested by foreign parties. However, this situation is changing in various areas, such as licensing agreements and joint venture contracts, as local entrepreneurs and government specialists gradually become more familiar with such transactions through increased contacts with foreign investors.

Sales of Goods Transactions

Many developing countries do not yet have comprehensive regulations covering such common commercial transactions as sales of goods and secured transactions. In many cases, sales of goods transactions are covered, if at all, in the country's general law relating to economic contracts, or in regulations relating to the purchase and sale of specific goods or services. Laws relating to domestic sales of goods tend to be more comprehensive than the laws relating to sales transactions involving foreign parties, and foreign sales contracts tend to be construed in accordance with international practice, which typically means the CISG.   **3.05**

Debtor-Creditor Laws

As an inducement for firms and investors to enter into commercial transactions, provision must be made to protect the rights of creditors who lend capital or other assets for use in a business enterprise. One of the priorities in this area is the establishment of laws which provide for the registration and enforcement of security interests, including mortgages on movable property and intangible property in a manner similar to mortgages on real property. Secured transactions laws permit banks and other creditors to finance equipment purchases by businesses by taking out a security interest on the equipment and protecting their legal and financial rights against other claimants (*e.g.* other creditors) without having to retain physical possession of the equipment. The registration system also includes a method for establishing priorities among various creditors, as well as a method for allowing prospective creditors to determine their priorities in relation to prior lenders.   **3.06**

In many developing countries, the laws and regulations relating to secured transactions are unclear and incomplete. For example, some laws either require physical possession of the asset in order for a mortgage thereon to be enforceable, or limit security interests to a narrow scope of assets, such as ships or airplanes. Moreover, even when security interests are available, the procedures may be quite time-consuming and expensive. As a result, banks and other lenders have little choice but to charge higher rates of interest or demand other collateral or guarantees that make it impossible for many businesses to acquire credit. Accordingly, economic development in these countries is hampered until there is a centralized register for all types of tangible and intangible assets, hopefully accompanied by a system which uses modern technology (*e.g.* computerized registers). Progress can also be fostered through refinement of the legal concepts of guarantees and pledges.

3.07   In addition to secured transactions laws, developing countries need procedures for restructuring or, if necessary, liquidating enterprises which experience financial or business difficulties. Developing countries are now beginning to adopt bankruptcy laws which provide for rectification and reform of enterprises which, with some protection from the immediate claims of creditors, be rehabilitated and continue to operate. In cases where liquidation is required, such laws provide a clear procedure for sale and distribution of the remaining assets of the enterprise, as well as priorities among secured creditors, workers, and unsecured creditors. Provision is often made for the resettlement of workers, and some laws actually set out some economic sanctions and criminal penalties for deriliction of duty that leads to bankruptcy. Bankruptcy laws which clearly set out the protections available to creditors can be invaluable as a means for increasing the willingness of financial institutions and others to provide financing for business activities.

At present, some countries, such as the PRC, limit the beneficial elements of its bankruptcy laws to state enterprises. In such cases, it can be expected that the relevant governmental agency will be heavily involved in the bankruptcy process, and might even intervene to stave off bankruptcy by providing funds to pay off the debts of creditors. Obviously, intervention of this type is not to be expected in the case of a troubled private company, and bankruptcy laws for private enterprises might have to be substantially modified. Those bankruptcy laws which do apply to private enterprises often do not contemplate such things as reorganization and rehabilitation, and the fate of any of the dislocated workers of a failed private enterprise is far more uncertain, given the lack of a social safety net in most of the developing countries.

Consumer Protection Laws

3.08   Competition and sales of goods laws are not adequate to protect consumers from unfair competitive practices, such as publication of false or misleading information regarding goods and services, or from defects in products which might cause harm to the user or his properties and assets. In order to achieve these safeguards, countries must begin to develop legal standards relating to consumer protection and product quality. Consumer protection laws address the quality and accuracy of information provided to consumers regarding products and services, as well as the quality of the products themselves. For example, laws may require that products not be sold if they present "unreasonable dangers" with respect to their use. Similarly, some products can only be sold if they have been produced, stored, and transported in accordance with specified safety and hygiene standards. Laws regarding warranties and product performance guarantees must also be addressed, including the responsibilities of the manufacturer and seller with respect to damages caused by defective goods.

Regulation of Local Sales Representatives

Foreign investors often attempt to engage local parties to act as their agents or representatives in a developing country as a first step in selling their goods into that country. Many countries have adopted laws as to agents and distributors which are designed to protect a specified class of these "intermediaries" in a manner similar to the way labor laws protect the rights of employees. Persons who fall within the designated group of intermediaries may themselves be subject to regulation, including requirements as to nationality, citizenship and registration. In some cases, the definition of "intermediary" is very broad and includes any person other than a salaried employee charged with one or more duties in relation to the promotion or distribution of a product. Certain countries use the concept of an intermediary in the context of actually prohibiting their use, and accordingly regulate any person who, directly or indirectly, participates in preparing, negotiating, concluding, or executing a sale of goods contract.   **3.09**

Sales agency and representative laws may regulate certain aspects of the arrangement. For example, many such laws cover remuneration of agents, and require that agents be compensated at a level commensurate with the custom or practice in the agent's territory and industry. Another area in which the sales agent or representative relation is heavily regulated is the termination of the representative's contract or agreement, particularly the amount of compensation that should be paid to the agent or the representative and distributors upon termination. As a general rule, local laws require that any termination compensation payable to a representative be based on "lost profits". Although countries calculate lost profits in a number of different ways, the following factors are usually considered: the average profits of the representative; the length of service; the amount usually earned by the representative in the length of time equal to the period of notice required by statute, and the length of the unexpired term of the contract.

Other regulations which might impact the rights of the parties in a sales agent or representative agreement in a given country include the following: **3.10**

1. In some countries, representatives who are natural persons will be given certain protection as if they were employees under local labor laws. In some cases, these representatives will be covered by rules which restrict termination of employees, require termination benefits or indemnities, and require that the principal contribute toward mandated employee benefits.
2. Some countries, particularly in the developing world, require that foreign sales representative agreements must be governed by local law.
3. Some laws and regulations place strict limitations on the ability of a manufacturer to impose restrictions, such as non-competition

agreements, on the activities of the local representative following termination.

Foreign Import Controls

3.11   The sale of goods into a foreign market may be subject to a variety of tariffs and import quotas. While developing countries often regulate the types and amount of goods which are imported into the country as part of the government's overall attempts to control the flow of currency and the skills of the local economy, tariffs and import quotas may also apply to sales which might be made into the larger, more developed, economies. For example, in Japan, formal import controls are regulated by that country's Foreign Exchange and Foreign Trade Control Law (FEFTCL), which applies to any type of "foreign investment", and the Import Trade Control Order.[1] Although most goods now automatically qualify for free export into Japan, certain goods still remain subject to import quotas and other special restrictions and approvals, such as the need to secure an "import license".[2]

Tariffs and import controls have often been criticized as having negative economic effects on the grounds that revenues to the state from the imposition of such costs are insufficient to offset the wasted resources associated with the efforts of firms to have the state implement regulations that protect the domestic industries. For example, opponents of tariffs and similar types of import controls argue that in the absence of such protection, firms would be forced to compete by more conventional methods, such as by implementing new technologies, anticipating market changes, or improving production processes. These activities are, in the eyes of these commentators, more likely to result in long-term improvements to the innovative capacity of the general economy than if such firms devoted their energies to acquiring a portion of the economic rents which the state makes available by its regulatory practices.

Product Standards

3.12   Another consideration in exporting products into a new territory is the possible application of formal certification standards in the foreign country which would require that products must be pre-cleared through government testing and approval before they can be offered for sale. Certain product testing standards which apply in the United States have previously been explained, and a number of other important export markets also have used some certification procedures from time to time. Once again, Japan is a good example. In contrast to the system in the United States, which requires only post-production analysis of performance (*i.e.* product liability regulations), many products in Japan must meet detailed specifications for their design. Moreover, even when a product receives governmental approval, it often faces "voluntary" standards imposed by trade associations, which, while neither legal nor compulsory, are generally required by wholesale and retail purchasers in Japan.

Dispute Resolution Techniques

Dispute resolution processes, as well as court systems, allow reforms in other areas, such as contract law, to proceed more smoothly by increasing the level of confidence that parties have that their contracts and agreements will be enforced. In addition, a well-functioning system for dispute resolution is necessary in order to assure that the rights of enterprises will be enforceable even when the state is no longer directly involved in the operation of the enterprises. **3.13**

Arbitration and other alternative dispute resolution procedures are often preferred as a means for settling disputes which might arise in the course of any economic transaction. For example, in the PRC and other parts of Asia, arbitration is clearly consistent with traditional preferences for settling disputes through "negotiation and mediation", and a number of countries have promulgated laws and regulations which dictate the rights of parties with respect to arbitration. In addition, countries have begun to develop a court system, and have promulgated laws and rules of civil procedure that provide not only for litigation of civil cases, but also for conciliation and the honoring of arbitration clauses which might be included in foreign economic trade, transport and maritime contracts. Also, in the contract law area, some countries have established systems of contract arbitration, with provisions for arbitration of special types of contracts (*e.g.* licenses and technology transfer contracts).

In the past, mediation in developing countries has often meant involvement by some administrative branch of the state, since state-owned enterprises were the primary economic actors in the economy. However, as private market transactions increase, the role of the state has also begun to change. For example, mediation in the PRC is often conducted by so-called "people's mediation committees", as well as by government departments, arbitration organs and courts. Also, special mediation centers are often established to deal exclusively with dispute resolution for international contracts, and separate arbitration laws and regulations are generally used for labor-related matters.

Dispute resolution is clearly an important issue for prospective foreign investors, and is generally reflected in the negotiations relating to choice of law provisions and enforcement of awards and judgments. As mentioned in the context of sales of goods transactions, choice of law issues with respect to economic contracts have been mitigated through the growing acceptance of international treaties like the CISG. Similarly, while there is still no broadly accepted international agreement that requires recognition of foreign judgments[3], the New York Convention on the Recognition and Enforcement of

Foreign Arbitral Awards of 1958 (New York Convention)[4] provides parties with the comfort that foreign arbitral awards rendered in any jurisdiction which is a party to the New York Convention will be honored in any other jurisdiction which is also a party to the New York Convention.

Related Commercial Law Issues

3.14 The need for sophisticated and transparent laws and legal principles for economic contracts extends beyond contracts for the sale of goods to include other areas which are necessary for enterprises in developing countries to expand the scope of their domestic business transactions and enter into a broader range of business transactions with foreign parties. For example, one of the fundamental elements of any sale of goods transaction is payment of the purchase price for the goods to the seller by the buyer. Any payment transaction in which the goods are shipped and delivered prior to payment raises issues of creditworthiness, particularly when there have been few or no prior dealings between the parties. Moreover, payments from a foreign buyer to a domestic seller in an international sale of goods transaction involve substantially more risk, due to differences in currency valuations, the great distances between the parties, language difficulties, and problems that the foreign party might have in attempting to enforce its rights to payment in local courts.

In order to induce domestic and foreign parties to enter sales of goods contracts, developing countries must develop their laws with respect to various financing methods, including laws relating to letters of credit, installment sales, wire transfers, factoring, and negotiable instruments and commercial paper. These devices, coupled with laws relating to secured transactions and guarantees, can significantly reduce the transaction costs to each of the parties in commercial transactions, and allow small- and medium-sized enterprises in developing countries to enter into the same sorts of transactions that heretofore may have only been available to large enterprises and state-owned firms. In addition, procedures must be developed for developing accepted forms of documentary title instruments, which would further facilitate sales of goods transactions.

Company Laws

3.15 While the success of any business arrangement generally turns on the compatability of the persons and resources involved in the particular project, the actual legal structure of the relationship usually involves various business organizations, each of which have distinct characteristics that impact the manner in which the transaction is structured and the business relationship itself is managed. For example, when the business arrangement takes the form of a joint venture, the parties may choose to form a new legal entity, separate and distinct from the existing activities of the joint venturers, within which the business activities of the joint venture will be conducted. On the other hand, while a licensing or distribution arrangement often does not call for formation of a new legal entity, each party needs to understand the legal environment within which the managers of the other party must operate, and the internal decision-making procedures mandated by law or regulation.

Company law, sometimes referred to as enterprise law, is necessary to define the legal entities (*i.e.* organizational forms) or enterprises which can be used to conduct commercial activities, as well as the rights and obligations of each enterprise and the governance process for the enterprises. In particular, a legal framework must be established with respect to formation, operation, and termination of enterprises, so that private investors have sufficient confidence regarding the rules which are applicable to local enterprises. For developing countries, some of the key issues in this area include defining and broadening the scope of enterprise autonomy and, in the case of state and collective enterprises, effecting the separation of ownership and management. The overall objective is to create a business and legal environment in which all enterprises, include those which may be owned and financed through the state, are able to function as independent actors in the domestic economy.

Company Law in Developing Countries

Some developing countries, particularly those who are attempting the trans- **3.16** formation from a state-managed economy to a private market economy, have been grappling with making state enterprises more autonomous and with developing new governance structures which permit such enterprises to be run as "profit-pursuing" businesses by independent managers. As part of this process, the state must also separate its responsibilities as a regulator from the rights of an owner, and attempt to concentrate its regulatory activities on strengthening regulation at the macroeconomic level, developing a market system, and providing social services to enterprises.

At the same time, developing countries must also lay the foundations for private enterprises, since these are generally perceived as the primary vehicles for development of a market-based economy. Developing countries are beginning to develop basic structures for governance of private enterprises. For example, laws and regulations have begun to recognize the separate legal powers and duties of members (*i.e.* shareholders), either in their individual capacities or acting through the shareholders' meeting, and the directors and managers of the enterprise. An enterprise may also have a board of management and inspectors, elected by the shareholders, and shareholders sometimes have the right to vote on distribution of profits and approval of annual business plans. The board of management is designed to protect the interests of the shareholders in relation to the company managers, and inspectors serve as auditors and inspect the firm's books and render reports to its shareholders.

Law Affecting Business and Commercial Activities

Although progress is being made in constructing a legal framework, developing countries continue to regulate and monitor the organization and operation of enterprises by registration requirements and minimum conditions for the recognition of formal legal status. For example, private businesses may be subject to government approval processes when the enterprise is established, and upon dissolution or whenever there is a change in operations. In addition, the government often retains the authority to limit the sectors that would be open to private businesses, and can influence the operations of enterprises through its ability to provide incentives (*e.g.* favorable consideration of land use, priority in borrowing capital, reduction or exemption of duties, import-export facilitation) for private businesses and companies which invested in certain specified fields. Apart from the fact that the government's role continues to go beyond that of pure administration, problems are caused by the fact that the grounds for governmental approval or disapproval of an application to start a new business are often not clearly specified in the law.

3.17   It would appear that the future effectiveness of company law reforms in developing countries depends upon a reduction in, if not elimination of, the government's role in approving the registration of new enterprises. Also, corporate governance standards could continue to be improved by establishing common rules and procedures for company directors and boards of management, such as by issuing model corporate bylaws that would offer a greater level of clarity and certainty in these areas. Laws will also need to be changed to clarify that members or shareholders own a proportionate shares of the legal entity, but not its assets, in order to reinforce the artificial corporate structure which permits limited liability.

Capital Markets and Securities Laws

3.18   Financial laws are necessary to provide access to capital through a market-driven system rather than through a centralized planning mechanism. Banking laws and regulations address the need in many developing countries for the availability of credit at reasonable cost, of deposit facilities for surplus cash and temporary investment, and of facilities which permit prompt clearance and settlement of payments. Securities laws are needed to facilitate the development of a market-oriented system for capital formation through the issuance of equity securities and debt instruments.

Developing countries are beginning to plant the foundations for a modern banking system, including a central bank and a system of commercial banks and other financial institutions that can begin to assume their respective functions of a central bank and the financial institutions in market economies. This means that the central bank will move away from the direction of providing credit through state-owned banks to merely supervising state-owned banks and other institutions, all of which would operate on an equal footing. Laws and regulations are also being developed that would serve as a basis for a transparent process relative to the establishment, operation, and dissolution of financial institutions. In addition, commercial banks would be held to various standards of accountability and performance, and would be required to implement measures to improve the quality of their credit management processes.

Securities laws and regulations are necessary to develop a market-driven system for enterprise financing, rather than having capital management defined as part of a state planning system. There are at least three important aspects of financial market regulations which are important in establishing a legal framework for enterprise financing: the definition of the rights associated with securities, the regulation of the securities markets, and the development of rules and procedures under which securities transactions can be conducted. These regulations are necessary in order to provide clear rules for investors, enterprises, and financial intermediaries in securities transactions.

The rights associated with securities are generally a function of the laws **3.19** relating to enterprises, and developing countries have taken to adopting various regulations relating to "shareholding companies", which are enterprises that permit and contemplate ownership by managers, employees, and others. There are generally various types of shareholding companies, with variations based on the number of incorporators and anticipated financing sources. In any event, the laws with respect to such companies spell out the basic rights relating to their equity securities, including provision for common and preferred shares, and limitations on ownership and transfer of the securities.

As developing countries begin to build their own domestic securities markets, it will be imperative that they develop laws and regulations for management of the markets and the parties involved in the financial transactions occurring therein (*e.g.* financial institutions, underwriters, dealers, appraisers, accountants, and lawyers). For examples, countries will move to develop securities laws which cover the regulatory structure for securities transactions; the registration or approval process for issuance of new securities; transactional rules (*e.g.* rights and duties of underwriters and brokers); settlement procedures; information requirements; dispute settlement procedures; legal prohibitions (*e.g.* self-dealing, insider trading, etc.); and investigative procedures and sanctions.

Foreign Investment Laws

Most countries have some sort of "investment law" or an "investment code" **3.20** which would apply to foreign investment in the country, including direct investment or a joint venture with one or more local partners. Foreign investment laws may regulate any type of foreign investment or may be limited to investments in a specified industry sector, such as tourism, agriculture, services or certain manufacturing areas. Foreign investment laws usually require review of the transaction by at least one, and sometimes more than one, governmental authority. In addition, investments by foreigners may be impacted by other local legislative acts, including laws and statutes regulating foreign exchange, unfair and restrictive business practices, and mergers and acquisitions. Regulation of foreign investment is not limited to the developed countries, since industrialized nations including Japan, Canada and the United States all have some legislation in this area.

General Areas of Foreign Investment Regulation

3.21 Foreign investment laws and regulations define the policy of the local government regarding foreign participation in the local economy. While there are a myriad of potential variations in the scope of regulation, foreign investment laws and codes, in almost every case, will cover the following areas: restrictions on foreign investment in specified industry sectors; limits on the percentage ownership by foreign investors in a project; incentives and guarantees, and controls and conditions.

Restrictions on Investment in Specified Industries

3.22 Many foreign investment laws restrict foreign investment in one or more specified areas. At a minimum, foreign investment will be precluded in certain sensitive areas on the basis of national security and defense considerations. As such, it is common to find many countries restricting investments by foreigners in the areas of armaments or telecommunications.[5] In order to provide guidance to potential investors, the government will generally publish guidelines, which usually are subject to periodic revision, which specify those areas within the local economy in which foreign capital will be permitted to operate. Often, the law will define such permitted areas in rather general terms similar to the following: "foreign capital shall be permitted to invest in industrialization, mining, energy, tourism, transportation, and other fields". In other cases, the government will attempt to highlight those areas in which foreign investment is specifically desired by formulating a separate set of investment laws and regulations which might apply to the chosen industry, such as an agricultural investment law, an industrial investment law, or a tourism investment law.

Restrictions on Percentage of Foreign Ownership

3.23 Some countries will limit the percentage of an enterprise that may be owned by a foreign investor, thereby creating the need to form a joint venture with local partners. Joint venture requirements serve a number of different purposes for the local economy, including: integration of the foreign partner and its assets and resources into the host country economy; creation of local management skills and transfer of technology; reduction in the risk of real or apparent foreign domination of the economy; access by the local interests to the foreign partner's international marketing network; responsiveness to government policies, and the opportunity to assume control over the entire project, either through nationalization or negotiated purchase. The exact nature of the joint venture requirement will vary with the situation. For example, some countries require that all foreign investments must be made in the form of a joint venture, and local laws may restrict aggregate foreign ownership to no more than 49 per cent of the equity interests in the project. In other cases, countries may adopt different standards with respect to the maximum permitted foreign investment percentage for various economic sectors.

Incentives and Guarantees for Foreign Investors

Many countries have used a wide range of incentives and guarantees to induce foreign investment. These include tax and fiscal incentives; customs duty exemptions; "free trade" zones, in which a joint venture project will be exempted from customs duties and taxes on the condition that it does not service the local market; guarantees that similar foreign investments will not be approved for a certain period of time; government loan guarantees and debt servicing; subsidized factors of production; guarantees against nationalization and expropriation; special dispute settlement procedures; and grants. **3.24**

Investment Controls and Conditions

In addition to providing incentives, investment codes and related laws often impose certain controls and conditions on any foreign investment projects. For example, foreign exchange and repatriation controls are frequently encountered, which may have the effect of limiting the availability of foreign exchange for debt servicing, repatriation of profits, payment of royalties or the purchase of spare parts. Some investment codes provide for multiple exchange rates and allow certain transactions to take place at a more favorable rate than others. Other types of controls include government price controls, controls on labor and employment, prescribed debt-equity ratios, restrictions on the type of contributions to be made by the foreign investor to the joint venture (*e.g.* hard currency and/or absorbable technology), ceilings on the reinvestment of profits or permissible rates of return, and local content requirements. **3.25**

Procedural Considerations

As noted above, proposed foreign investments, including joint venture, often need to be approved at their inception by one or more governmental agencies in the host country. While a number of countries have established a single, centralized agency for this purposes, developing countries often use inter-ministerial investment boards or commissions to coordinate foreign invest- **3.26**

Law Affecting Business and Commercial Activities

ment matters. Other structures involve simultaneous review by two or more agencies, such as the country's central bank, the ministry with responsibility for the particular industrial sector, and the agency charged with oversight of trade and business development.

Assuming that some sort of screening, authorization or notification process exists with respect to foreign investments, there are a number of variations on the actual procedures which might need to be followed. Among the possibilities are each of the following:

1. Prior approval may be unnecessary, but prior notification may be required.
2. Approval may be required but, in practice, it may be readily or even automatically given, unless the proposed investment falls within a restricted sector.
3. Approval may be required only when an application is made for local tax and other incentive benefits.
4. Investment may be permitted up to a certain amount without prior authorization.
5. Approval may not be necessary unless a certain percentage of shares (e.g. 50 per cent) in the local concern is to be acquired by the foreign investor.
6. Approval may not be required in certain industries.
7. Approval may be required from local, as well as national or federal authorities.
8. Approval may be required, or may be subject to a higher level of review, when the transaction is an acquisition of a local concern, rather than the establishment of a new entity, since the government may be concerned about the conversion of the business from national to foreign ownership.
9. Approval may be required not only for the initial investment but for reinvestment earnings.

3.27 Foreign investors will usually be called upon to provide, together with their local partners, a significant amount of data and information during the course of the application and review process. For example, in developing countries, it is common to find that all or most of the following information is needed:

1. An investment and financial plan showing the amount of investment in external and local currencies.
2. A production scheme indicating the annual volume and value of the production of the proposed joint venture.
3. A services scheme, indicating the creation of services and the volume and value of the services intended to be rendered by the joint venture.
4. An import and export plan indicating the anticipated volume of imports and exports emanating from the joint venture.

5. Local inputs indicating the anticipated volume of raw materials to be used.
6. An employment plan and forecast showing a program of training for local persons to acquire the requisite skills in the particular enterprise.
7. The industry to be established and the product to be produced.
8. The locality in which it is proposed to carry on such industry.
9. The anticipated completion date for the project or the date that the proposed joint venture is to commence operations.

In supplying the required information, an effort should be made to demon- **3.28**
strate the anticipated benefits and advantages to the local economy. For example, if possible, the application can be used to demonstrate proposed increases in local training and in the level of employment; the active involvement and training of local management personnel; the transfer of new technology to the local company and its personnel; import substitution; and the investment of new capital from overseas. In addition, developing countries are particularly interested in evidence that the joint venture will increase exports and improve the country's balance of trade.

The process of screening, review and approval for a new foreign investment often culminates in a formal agreement or other written instrument between the foreign investor and the appropriate governmental authorities in the host country which sets forth certain commitments of the investor and/ or conditions upon which the investment approval has been granted. For example, the government might require that the investment be made within a specified period of time. In other cases, the investor will be required to supply the government with periodic reports on the progress of the project and to submit to inspections of the plant and facilities of the new enterprise. Other types of commitments might include an agreement to submit disputes to local arbitration or to the jurisdiction of local courts, and agreements regarding the number of new jobs to be created in the course of the project and/or the amount of training which will be provided to local personnel.

Sanctions

The sanctions and penalties for failure to comply with foreign investment **3.29**
laws are as diverse as the underlying laws and regulations themselves. Country variations can be found, as well as differences which arise from the goal that the particular law or regulation is intended to serve. For example, a failure to register an infusion of foreign capital in a particular country may prevent the investor from repatriating any amounts from the country in the future. As noted above, if a technology transfer agreement is subject to investment regulations, non-compliance with any registration and review requirements may invalidate the entire agreement. Finally, in some countries, any violation of the foreign investment laws can result in fines and other penal sanctions against the companies involved, or against individual officers, directors, and other managerial personnel.

Competition Laws

3.30 Competition law is designed to promote fair and effective competition among autonomous enterprises and ensure that the interests of consumers are protected without the need for direct state management of the enterprises or competition. Among the specific objectives of competition laws in developing countries is the prevention of unfair competition in enterprise operations, particularly in market behavior; ensuring that enterprise mergers do not create barriers to entry into the market; regulation of monopolies, which in developing countries can include not only natural monopolies but also sectors which remain controlled by the state or its affiliates; and protection of consumers against cartel-like behavior of enterprises.

Many developing countries lack a comprehensive system of laws and regulations relating to competition, although they may have some general laws referring to the need for fair competition among enterprises and addressing concerns regarding behavior that is perceived as monopolistic. Developing countries interested in broadening the scope and sophistication of its competition laws will need to consider establishing a strong relationship between the agency with responsibility for enforcing such laws and the government's economic policy departments, particularly since a number of competition-related issues can be expected to arise in the context of mergers and combinations of enterprises. Also, reforms may be required in company laws, at least to the extent that the government continues to control new entrants through its authority with respect to registration of enterprises.

Antitrust or competition laws in developed countries typically deal with a variety of business collaborations involving two or more firms which might have a specified impact on competition in the relevant market. These laws not only cover mergers and joint ventures, but also other types of business collaborations (*e.g.* licensing or distribution agreements) that might result in some combination of the business assets and resources of actual or potential competitors in a manner which reduces competition. Competition may also be regulated or controlled by foreign investment laws, which focus upon the role that foreign firms and capital will have in the domestic economy of the regulating country, and by laws which are designed to vet specific forms of business collaborations (*e.g.* regulation of technology transfer agreements).

3.31 As to regulatory content, countries may adopt rules which impose outright restrictions on the use of certain contractual provisions (*e.g.* a rule that no patent owner may fix the prices to be charged by a licensee of the patent, or a restriction on the ability of a venturer in a joint venture to prohibit the other venturer from engaging in competitive activities). Rules of this type declare certain practices to be *per se* illegal, without reference to any surrounding circumstances which might mitigate the effect of the provision or justify its use. Alternatively, the applicable regulatory body may apply a "rule of reason" and assess a provision in an agreement in relation to things such as the intent of the provision, the market power of the parties, and the effect of the provision on the relevant market. In most situations, substantive law is a combination of *per se* rules and rule of reason analysis.

Procedural regulation of contractual arrangements generally takes one of three distinct forms, based on the timing and purpose of the review. Some countries, such as Canada, Germany, the United Kingdom, and the United States do not require pre-effective review of licensing and distribution agreements, and limit regulation to an after the fact analysis, generally in the context of potential or actual litigation proceedings, of anti-competitive effects. In contrast, the European Community (EC) and Japan have adopted policies which anticipate the review of commercial agreements in advance of effectiveness, and have promulgated detailed lists of acceptable and unacceptable provisions to serve as guidelines for drafters and regulators. A third method, generally used in the developing countries, is to condition the legality of agreements on review and approval by the government.

National practices regarding the regulation of joint ventures are somewhat **3.32** uniform, at least in those cases where the proposed collaboration involves participants of a specified size in relation to the effected market(s). For example, in the United States, joint ventures may be subject to review prior to the consummation of the transaction, although recent statutory changes have led to a more liberal attitude toward joint ventures which will be limited to research and development and production of the results of the joint research. The EC also reviews joint ventures and other collaborative arrangements in the same manner as it deals with commercial agreements. Finally, countries that extensively regulate direct foreign investment will generally be involved in reviewing any proposed joint venture between a local party and a foreign investor.

While competition law is certainly concerned with the regulation of competition among enterprises at the macroeconomic level, developing countries must also adopt laws and regulations which address unfair competitive practices which enterprise might engage in the course of day-to-day activities in the marketplace. Unfair competition laws address the general rules of trade in the market, and sanction such things as trademark infringement, fraudulent and improper sales practices (*e.g.* bribery or false advertising), misappropriation of trade secrets and confidential information, and unethical interference with the activities or reputation of competitors.

Intellectual Property and Technology Transfer Laws

The ability of any commercial enterprise to achieve its economic objectives, **3.33** in the form of a fair return to all of its stakeholders on their invested capital and other dedicated resources, is a function of a number of variables. For many years, "capital", in the form of machinery, land, buildings and other tangible assets, and "labor", in the form of human resources measured on both a quantitative and qualitative basis, were perceived to be the most important factors of production in the economic analysis of a given business enterprise. However, particularly in light of the literal "globalization" of business activity in the last quarter century, it is clear that a new set of assets, denominated as "knowledge" and "innovation", have now moved to the forefront of business strategy for both large and small enterprises around the world.

This new factor of production is often referred to as "technology" which has competitive significance. The use of this term connotes a set of tangible assets which can be used by their owner and, like any other type of asset, may be susceptible to obsolescence, misappropriation and duplication. However, the legal framework that has been constructed to contain, define and allocate ownership and control of these technological assets, in the form of so-called "intellectual property rights", provides an owner with far more that a set of property rights. Instead, technology rights provide a tool which permits the owner to forge and maintain an overall competitive advantage based, in part, on its ability to use, and prevent others from using, the valuable innovations and ideas which meet the requirements of law around the world.

3.34   The major forms of intellectual property rights which are recognized around the world and available to protect the valuable information, techniques and symbols developed and used by various business enterprises are patents, trade secrets, copyrights and trademarks. Each form of intellectual property right is designed to cover a different element of the creative process. Patents are used to protect new inventions, trade secrets recognize the value of proprietary business information, copyrights are used to protect books, records and other tangible forms of creative work from unauthorized copying and misappropriation, and trademarks protect the distinguishing words and symbols developed by firms to identify their goods and services in the eyes of consumers.

Each of the various forms of intellectual property right extend only to the border of the country in which the right has been granted. Thus, the holder of a United States patent can preclude others from using, making or selling the invention only in the United States because protection in foreign countries may not be derived from a United States patent grant. If a foreign country has an established patent law regime that covers the subject matter of the invention, the inventor may be able to apply for a patent in that country and thereby preclude others from unauthorized use or sale of the invention in that market. However, if the foreign country does not provide the appropriate patent protection, the inventor will be unable to prevent others in that country from using or selling the invention.

In the world today, intellectual property laws are far from uniform. This inconsistency reflects the fundamental schism that exists between developed and developing countries regarding the benefits and perceived dangers of property rights in technologies and related items. An inventor in a developed

Intellectual Property and Technology Transfer Laws

country will seek strong intellectual property protection to prevent those located in developing countries from "free-riding" on his work and to establish additional markets through which to recover the costs of development. On the other hand, governments in many poor and developing countries are reluctant to provide any strong degree of protection to foreign inventors and firms, since protection of this sort may work as a disincentive to local innovators to build their own research and marketing capabilities and, perhaps more importantly, allow foreign firms to exercise undue control over the availability and affordability of the protected items.

In spite of their fundamental discomfort with intellectual property rights, **3.35** developing countries have been forced to begin adopting some rudimentary form of intellectual property law. This movement has been driven by multilaterial negotiations on a variety of trade-related issues (*e.g.* the Uruguay Round of the GATT negotiations), in addition to well-publicized concerns of many developed countries regarding various inadequacies in the content and enforcement of intellectual property laws in the developing countries, including no preliminary or final injunctive relief, lack of seizure and impoundment relief, lack of exclusion of infringing imports, inadequate civil remedies (*i.e.* monetary damages), and inadequate fines or other criminal penalties.

The relationship of intellectual property protection to economic development has been studied in great detail. In one case, a researcher using multiple regression analysis claimed that the level of economic development is closely correlated with the existing level of intellectual property protection, and also concluded that many developing countries that failed to implement such protection systems experienced a correspondingly lower level of economic development, as well as a slower evolution in the size and complexity of their local markets. A survey of some of the arguments made supporting enhanced intellectual property protection includes the following:

1. An innovator's ability to obtain the monopoly rights inherent in the grant of an intellectual property right provides an incentive for higher levels of investment in innovative activities.
2. The availability of intellectual property protection for new products increases the flow of products into the developing country, thereby increasing the welfare of the population.
3. Enhanced intellectual property protection should increase the rate of inbound investment and technology transfer from foreign firms.
4. A strong intellectual property law regime improves the knowledge base concerning technical development due to increased imports, licensing activities, and patent application filings in the local market.
5. If enforcement regimes are improved, welfare gains are realized through a reduction of agency costs attributable to surveillance, verification, compliance, and enforcement.

Law Affecting Business and Commercial Activities

3.36 Little doubt exists that developing countries are quite anxious to reduce what they perceive as a critical technological gap between developed and developing countries.

However, many of these countries fear that patent protection for new products and technologies will merely enable large multinational corporations to secure global monopolies[6] and charge exorbitant prices for their goods.[7] Also, lacking the scientific and financial infrastructure necessary to create patent-induced innovations, developing countries are far more interested in technology transfer than in encouraging domestic innovation.[8] It is not surprising, therefore, that developing countries have little or no interest in creating a system that impedes their own ability to "appropriate" new technologies and products developed by foreign innovators.[9] Another fundamental problem is that many developing countries do not necessarily share the same cultural attitudes regarding the nature of private rights to own and use various types of tangible and intangible property. For example, in some countries, certain forms of intellectual property (*e.g.* pharmaceuticals) are viewed as public goods, and some cultures are genuinely hostile to any notion that knowledge is a private capital good, a premise that is fundamental to the intellectual property systems of the industrialized economies.

Developing country policies regarding recognition and enforcement of intellectual property rights must often be read in conjunction with laws and regulations with respect to inbound technology transfers (*e.g.* licensing agreements). Many nations have enacted specific legislation regulating the content of technology transfer agreements. These regulations are intended to serve a number of objectives, most of which are generally related to the overall economic development of the local country, although some statutes are also drafted in a manner which serves to protect the relative bargaining position of the transferee. For example, a survey of the various regulations regarding technology transfers which have been adopted in South America indicated the following principal objectives[10]:

1. Increasing the bargaining power of the local transferees, such as by prohibiting the use of package licensing and other similar practices.
2. Increasing the amount of information available to local parties with respect to possible sources of technology.
3. Controlling the nature of imported technology and improving the quality and local assimilation of any new technology which is to be transferred.
4. Protecting local innovation and technology.
5. Regulating remuneration for transferred technology in order to protect and improve the balance of payments position of the local economy, control foreign exchange operations, and prevent tax avoidance.
6. Limiting the protection of industrial property by restricting the

prohibitions which might be imposed upon disclosure and use of such information.

7. Promoting other local public policy goals, such as the use and training of local employees and protection of the environment.

As a general rule, technology transfer regulations operate by requiring the international technology agreement be submitted to, and approved by, a national administrative authority in order for the agreement to be enforceable. Governmental bodies charged with reviewing technology transfer agreements often refer to statutory lists of objectionable business practices which must be excised from any agreement as a condition of approval. Among the most common areas of concern are royalty rates and other forms of remuneration, the scope and content of controls the technology provider seeks to impose on the local transferee, the nature of any implied representations and warranties regarding the quality and performance of the transferred technology, the term of the agreement, governing law, and dispute resolution procedures.

3.37

A number of countries have structured their technology transfer laws to encourage and promote imports of technology for use in specified industrial areas. For example, a country may provide that the general technology transfer rules will be modified in relation to certain technologies, such as by providing for expedited reviews, liberalizing restrictions on the level of foreign investment participation, creating incentives for local manufacturing, permitting components needed for use in local manufacturing to be imported at concessional rates, and authorizing development subsidies, tax credits and tariff protections. Industry promotion may be accomplished by announcing areas in which incentives and concessions will be available or by the use of "lists" which identify the type of regulations and restrictions on foreign investment in industries specified thereon.[11]

Labor, Health and Environmental Laws

Employment and Labor Laws

Employment and labor laws are necessary for economic development to create a labor contract system, and a system for providing workers' rights and benefits which are not permanently linked to a particular employer. Labor and employment laws in developing countries cover such things as regulation of worker dismissals, recruitment, and unemployment insurance, as well as regulations establishing the respective rights and obligations of the parties to a labor contract. These laws and regulations play an important role in enhancing the level of worker confidence in the labor system, and in promoting the labor mobility which is often required for developing economies to rapidly shift its human resources to sectors which are best suited for the further development and growth.

3.38

Law Affecting Business and Commercial Activities

Many developing economies have experienced extended periods of labor unrest, which often adversely impacted the productivity of numerous enterprises, if not entire industries. While the response of the state was sometimes combative, most developing countries have begun to lay the foundation for a comprehensive set of laws and regulations relating the terms and enforceability of labor contracts (*e.g.* description of duties, compensation, benefits, term, termination, and liabilities for breach), trade unions, health and safety regulations in the workplace, labor disputes and mediations, and pension and disability benefits. In some cases, special regulations have been promulgated for various industries considered to be of strategic importance.

Health, Safety and Environmental Laws

3.39 Most developing countries have recognized the need for strong and enforceable laws and regulations relating to health and safety, both generally and in the workplace in particular, as well as the need to address the potential impact of commercial activities on the local environment. Health and safety laws cover a variety of matters, including safety conditions in the factories and other workplaces, infectious diseases, health and sanitary conditions in public places, food hygiene, and safety conditions in specific industries (*e.g.* maritime transport, public utilities, etc.). These laws impose specific obligations on employers and other business operators.

Environmental protection is a growing area of concern for many developing countries, not only as part of their investment approval process, but also as a means for preserving natural resources which may be necessary for sustainable development. Developing countries are struggling to develop various laws and regulations. For example, Vietnam has been working to develop regulations governing and establishing an environmental impact assessment regime. In addition, countries are attemping to address urban environmental problems, such as water quality and noise, industrial discharges, and toxic gas and ambient air standards. Environmental protection standards for forests and marine areas are also under consideration. It can be anticipated that governments will be issuing numerous regulations addressing environmental concerns in specified industrial sectors.

Tax Laws and Accounting Rules

3.40 Enhanced commercial activity in developing economies requires substantial changes in governmental systems relating to imposition and collection of income and related taxes. There remains substantial diversity among countries with regard to the manner in which economic activities are taxed, with countries often using a combination of income, consumption, and "value-added" taxes. A number of emerging economies do not impose any tax on capital gains, and separate taxation schemes are often implemented for strategic industries as a means for inducing new investment by domestic and foreign entities. Tax reporting requirements also mandates development of accounting standards; however, accounting practice in a number of developing countries remains fairly unsophisticated and loosely regulated.

Related Laws and Legal Institutions

1. Development of private property rights, including rights of individuals and artificial legal business enterprises to own and control real and personal property. Implementation of a private property rights systems also calls for transfer of control from the state to the private sector (*i.e.* privatization).   **3.41**
2. Land law reforms, including procedures for unfettered transfers of title, land leases, and regulation of land usage (*e.g.* zoning).
3. Development of law-making and law-implementing institutions, such as ministries of justice and local regulatory boards and agencies.
4. Development of a judicial system, including a system of courts and prosecutorial officers. Consideration might be given to establishing separate courts which would deal exclusively with economic and commercial contract matters.
5. Training for lawyers, judges, instructors, and others involved in the law-making and enforcement process.

Notes

[1] Imports are further regulated by the nation's Customs Duty Law, Customs Tariff Law, and Customs Duty Temporary Measures Law, as well as certain excise and commodity taxes.
[2] Import licenses from the Japanese Ministry of International Trade and Industry (MITI) are required for the import of products falling into four broad areas: (i) certain articles listed with GATT for the protection of national security, public health, and morals (the "negative list"); (ii) imports from certain countries; (iii) imports designated as "restricted" by MITI; and (iv) imports involving unusual settlement terms. Imports of items on the negative list are allocated by quotas and MITI periodically publishes an "Import Notice" listing all the items that are subject to quota restrictions and require its prior approval.
[3] As a general matter, recognition of foreign judgments turns on principles of comity, which is a matter of national law.
[4] The New York Convention was adopted on June 10, 1958. See 330 U.N.T.S. 38).
[5] Other commonly prohibited sectors for foreign investment include postal services, utilities, broadcasting, transportation, newspapers, banking, and insurance. Many countries also restrict or prohibit the ownership of land by foreigners.
[6] *See* Dembo, Dias & Morehouse, "Technology to Aid the Poor: Constraints to Access Resulting from the Privatization — The Case of Biotechnology," in *The International Context of Rural Poverty in the Third World* 103, 124–25 (1986).

Additionally, Gao Lulin, Director General of the Chinese Patent Office, argued that international consideration should be given to the economic development of less developed countries and stated that developed nations have a greater interest in protecting their own patent rights than in the economic growth of less fortunate countries. "Asia-Pacific Countries Agree to Cooperate on Patent Issues", 4 World Intell. Prop. Rep. (BNA) 53 (Mar. 1990).

[7] Economists from developed countries argue that the fear of high prices arising from patent protection is based on a mistaken view of the competitive marketplace. They assert that while patents allow innovators to capture gains from their innovation, ordinarily the gains take the form of "foothold" access to well-populated, competitive markets which permit sellers to do no more than charge competitive prices and earn competitive returns, including the returns on innovation. There are, to be sure, cases where an innovation represents so drastic a departure from the status quo that an entirely new market is created and prices and profits are high.

[8] Robert P. Merges, "Battle of Lateralisms: Intellectual Property and Trade", 8 B.U. Int'l L.J 239, 244 n.9 (1990) (citing *Science and Technology: Lessons for Development Policy* 353 (R. Evenson & G. Ranis eds., 1990)) (adopting current international intellectual property conventions might be globally optimal for developing countries, but not in the best interests of individual developing countries, since the best regime for them is one that facilitates the transfer of technology).

[9] Arguments for the non-implementation of patent systems often refer to the longstanding practice of tariff protection, a practice permitted under the GATT and used to stimulate "infant industries" by protecting them from foreign import competition.

[10] See G. Cabanellas, *Antitrust and Direct Regulation of International Transfer of Technology Transactions*, 30–47 (1984).

[11] For example, South Korea originally used a "positive list system" which enumerated those industries in which foreign investment was permitted. See *Foreign Capital Inducement Law*, April 12, 1973. Subsequently, as the economy matured, South Korea changed to a "negative list system" under which all industries other than those on the "negative list" would be open to foreign investment. See *Foreign Capital Inducement Law*, effective July 1, 1984.

LEGAL ASPECTS OF COMMON BUSINESS ACTIVITIES AND TRANSACTIONS

Introduction

As we have seen, the countries of East Asia have become important and thriving locations for commercial activities. Domestic enterprises have been created and expanded, and are now engaging in a wide range of business relationships, all of which have called for development of a coherent set of commercial laws and regulations. In addition, the volume of cross-border business arrangements involving domestic and foreign firms has also increased. As a result, entrepreneurs and regulators in each of these countries have had to increase their familiarity with the key economic and business issues which generally arise in the course of negotiating the terms of these arrangements. In this chapter, we provide a brief overview of some of the common methods used to conduct business in the emerging markets of East Asia, including the impact that laws and regulations generally will have on such arrangements.[1]

4.01

Sale of Goods Transactions

The most frequent form of cross-border business arrangement is the simple sale of goods transaction, pursuant to which one party sells specified goods to the other party under the terms of a sale and purchase contract. In general, the standard terms of any such contract would cover most of the following matters.

4.02

General Terms of Sale and Purchase Contracts

Acceptance — The agreement should set out the basis for acceptance of the terms of the order by the seller. As a general rule, the seller will be unwilling

4.03

to accept orders which do not incorporate the terms and conditions of the seller's standard form of purchase order.

Change Orders — The agreement should cover the rights of the parties in the event that the buyer wishes to make any changes in the product specifications, volume of products, time and place of delivery or method of transportation. If the buyer is allowed to make any changes, some equitable adjustment should be made to the purchase price to take into account any increase or decrease in the cost of the products resulting from such change. In order to mitigate the effect of any changes, the buyer may insist that the seller not purchase any materials, or make material commitments, or production arrangements, in excess of the amount, or prior to the time necessary to meet buyer's original delivery schedule.

Cancellation — In the event that the buyer cancels the order, the seller will be entitled to receive some compensation in relation to the amount of work done in connection with the order. For example, the cancellation charge might be set as a percentage of the order price reflecting the percentage of the work performed prior to the notice of termination, provided that if cancellation occurs too close to the delivery date, the buyer will be obligated for the entire amount of the purchase price.

Pricing — Pricing is generally based upon prices that are published by the seller from time to time. The seller may be willing to provide discounts from published prices for orders that exceed a certain dollar amount and, in some cases, buyers will negotiate for the "most favored customer" clauses that guarantee that they will receive the lowest price charged by the seller to similar customers.

4.04   *Terms of Payment* — The agreement will provide for payment within a specified period of time following the date that the products are shipped or delivered to the buyer. The payment period determines the amount of "credit" which the seller is willing to provide to the buyer. Most agreements provide for a "service charge" equal to a specified percentage of the purchase price in the event that the buyer is late in making payments. The seller will retain a purchase money security interest in the products until payment is made.

Shipping Terms and Risk of Loss — The agreement should specify the shipping dates for the products and the time that the risk of loss is to pass to the buyer. Shipping instructions must be set out in the agreement, including the manner of shipment.

Nonconforming or Defective Shipments — The buyer will have the right to inspect the products received from the seller and may reject any nonconforming or defective goods. The seller will be obligated to replace or repair any nonconforming or defective goods and the buyer will be entitled to reimbursement for the expense of returning such goods to the seller. The buyer must complete the inspection within a reasonable period of time after delivery of the goods.

Warranties — The seller will provide standard warranties with respect to the products and will agree to repair or replace any goods which do not conform with the warranty for a specified period of time following sale. However, the seller will disclaim any other express or implied warranties, including any warranties of merchantability or fitness for a particular purpose. Also, the seller will insist that it not be liable for any incidental or consequential damages.

Indemnification — Although the seller will seek to limit liabilities to the buyer to the scope of the warranty provision, there may be situations where the buyer may require the seller to indemnify it against certain claims arising out of the buyer's purchase and use of the products, including intellectual property infringement claims made by third parties, the failure of the goods to comply with specified performance characteristics, and defects in the design of the products.

Force Majeure and Excuse — As a general rule, the parties will agree that the seller's performance will be excused by the occurrence of specified events, such as fire, explosion, flood, riot, labor dispute, shortage, accident, act of God, regulation, law, or other event or circumstance beyond seller's reasonable control which prevents or delays seller's performance. **4.05**

Default — Should the seller fail to deliver the purchased products in a timely fashion, or deliver substantial amounts of non-conforming or defective goods, the buyer will have the right to terminate the agreement for cause. In such cases, the parties may provide for some sort of liquidated damages.

Choice of Law — The parties should include a choice of law provision which determines how the terms of the agreement will be interpreted and the legal rights of the parties apportioned. In the United States, for example, this requires the selection of that version of the Uniform Commercial Code that has been adopted by the state chosen by the parties. As to international sale agreements, the parties must not only select the governing law, but must decide upon the application of various international treaty provisions, such as the United Nations Convention on the International Sale of Goods (CISG).[2]

United Nations Convention on the International Sale of Goods

An international sales contracts, albeit relatively straight-forward, can nonetheless raise a number of potential legal and regulatory issues. For example, the parties must always consider the effect of export (*e.g.* export controls) **4.06** and import controls on the transaction, including duties and tariffs which might be imposed with respect to the goods. Defects in the goods will generally trigger products liability issues. However, it is usually the content and interpretation of the sale contract itself which is most important to the parties. Many developing countries are attempting to develop their own internal law with respect to sales contracts, and the influence of the CISG can be seen as legal and business practice evolves in this area.

The CISG sets out rules governing the formation of international sales contracts, and determines the rights and obligations of each party to an international sales contract. An international sales contract is broadly defined in Article 1(1) of the CISG, which provides that the CISG "applies to contracts of sale of goods between parties whose place of business are in different states". It is important to note that application of the CISG turns on the place of business of the parties, and that the nationality of the parties is irrelevant. Obviously, a party may have more than one place of business; however, for purposes of determining whether the CISG applies to a given transaction, the relevant place of business is that with the most appropriate relation to the contract and its performance. The CISG may also apply where the rules of private international law dictate that the law of a Contracting State (*i.e.* a state that has ratified or acceded to the CISG) is applicable.

While the CISG was intended to provide a general set of universally acceptable rules which can be applied to most sales contracts between parties from different Contracting States, it is clear that the drafters intended to allow the parties to have a significant amount of freedom to substitute their own terms for those otherwise mandated under the CISG. Article 6 of the CISG explicitly endorses the principle of freedom of contract: "The parties may exclude the application of this Convention or, subject to Article 12, derogate or vary the effect of any of its provisions".

4.07   Under the CISG, the seller must deliver the goods, hand over any documents relating to the goods, and transfer the property in the goods. In the absence of any nominated place of delivery, the seller is required under Article 31 of the CISG to deliver the goods to the first carrier for transmission to the buyer in the case of any contract which involves the carriage of goods.

In the case of other contracts, the seller will satisfy the requirements as to delivery by merely placing the goods at the disposal of the buyer, which can even be at the seller's place of business. If there is no fixed date or period of time regarding delivery set out in the contract, the seller may deliver within a reasonable time following execution of the contract.

The CISG does not concern itself with transfer of property in, or possession of, goods. These subjects have been left to private international law. However, there are provisions relating to the passage of risk from seller to buyer. As a general rule, the CISG provides that risk passes when the goods are taken by the buyer. However, Article 67 of the CISG provides that in the case of contracts of sale involving the carriage of goods, where the seller is not bound to hand them over at a particular place, the risk will pass to the buyer when goods are handed over to the first carrier, although risk will not pass under this first carrier rule until the goods are clearly identified by markings on the goods, by shipping documents, or by a notice given to the buyer. If the seller is bound to hand the goods over to a carrier at a particular place, risk does not pass until the carrier is actually in receipt of the goods at that place. Article 62 of the CISG contains different rules which apply to passage of risk with respect to goods sold in transit.

Article 35 of the CISG requires the seller to deliver goods which are of the quality, quantity and description, and in the manner of containment or packaging required by the contract. This is one of the most important provisions of the CISG, particularly since Article 35(2) of the CISG states that goods will not be deemed to conform to the contract unless they satisfy the following required implied warranties: **4.08**

1. Fitness for the purpose for which goods of the same description would ordinarily be used.
2. Fitness for any particular purpose expressly or impliedly made known to the seller at the time of the conclusion of the contract (except where it is clear that the buyer did not rely on the seller's skill and judgment).
3. Possession of the qualities which the seller held out to the buyer as a sample or model.
4. Containment in a manner usual for such goods or in a manner adequate to preserve and protect such goods.

Under Article 39 of the CISG, the buyer must give notice to the seller of any lack of conformity of the delivered goods within a reasonable time after the time at which the defect was discovered or ought to have been discovered; however, in no event should the notice period extend beyond two years from the date upon which the goods were actually handed over to the buyer. Obviously, this period can be extended by contractual terms of guarantee, and the parties are also free to include a specific notice period in the sale contract itself, which can be set by reference either to the date that the buyer discovered or ought to have discovered the non-conformity, or the date on which the goods were actually handed over to the buyer. **4.09**

The CISG provides the buyer with four broad options in the event of seller's breach of the sales contract:

1. The buyer may compel performance by the seller (*i.e.* specific performance).
2. The buyer may reject the goods and rescind the contract; however, this remedy is only available in cases involving a "fundamental breach" of the contract.
3. The buyer may accept the goods, in spite of the nonconformity, and then claim damages.
4. The buyer may seek a reduction in the price for the non-conforming goods.

4.10 Where damages are claimed, these can be calculated in accordance with Articles 74–76 of the CISG. Damages are defined as the sum equal to the loss, which can include any loss of profits flowing directly from the breach of the contract. However, the total amount of damages are restricted to the loss which the seller in breach either foresaw or ought to have foreseen as the possible consequences of the breach at the time that contract was concluded. Article 77 of the CISG imposes a duty on the non-breaching party to mitigate his damages, and the party in breach is entitled to have a reduction in the damages payable in the event of any failure to mitigate. While the CISG contains no specific provisions relating to the use of liquidated damages clauses, the parties are free to include them in the sale contract and their validity will then be governed by the relevant applicable national law.

The major obligations of the buyer are to pay the price and take delivery of the goods in accordance with the contract terms and/or the provisions of the CISG. In the absence of an express or implied term as to purchase price, the default provisions of Article 55 of the CISG, which are referred to above, will apply. If the sales contract does not govern the place of payment, which they often will do in order to guard against currency risks, the CISG requires the buyer to pay at the seller's place of business or at the place at which the goods and documents will be handed over. Where the time of payment is not specified, the buyer will become obliged to pay once a seller places the goods or documents at the disposal of the buyer. Except in the case of a contract for a documentary sale, however, the buyer will have the right to examine the goods prior to payment of the purchase price. With regard to delivery, the buyer must do what is required under the contract in order to enable the seller to make delivery, and must in fact take the goods as required.

4.11 In the event of any failure by the buyer to comply with her duties under the sales contract, the CISG provides the buyer with three primary remedies:

1. The seller may compel performance by the buyer (*i.e.* specific performance).
2. The seller may rescind the contract; however, this remedy is only available in cases involving a "fundamental breach" of the contract.
3. The seller may claim damages.

A good deal of the rules considered above in relation to buyer's remedies also apply directly to the seller. In addition, under Article 62 of the CISG, the seller can compel the buyer to accept the goods in order to render him liable for the purchase price. The seller will almost certainly be able to avoid the contract upon a failure by the buyer to pay the purchase price, as non-payment clearly constitutes a fundamental breach of the sales contract. As for damages, the seller will be able to pursue them in the same manner as the buyer might proceed against the seller.

Licensing Arrangements

One of the most basic elements of many of the forms of business relation- **4.12** ships discussed below is the "license", which facilitates the transfer of valuable legal rights and technology from one party to the other party in order to further the overall purposes of the relationship. A licensing arrangement is created when one party, the "licensor", which owns, or otherwise controls the right to specify the uses of, a valuable legal right, grants to the other party, the "licensee", the right or license to utilize the legal rights for the purposes specified in the contract between the parties.[3] In consideration for the grant of the license, the licensee agrees to compensate the licensor, perhaps by the payment of a flat fee or by payment of an amount determined by reference to amounts received by the licensee from the use of the licensed rights. However, in some cases, the compensation may be "in-kind," such as when the licensee agrees to deliver finished goods to the licensor for resale.

A license is not an outright assignment of the legal rights from the licensor to the licensee, since the licensor will retain actual ownership of the licensed subject matter. When the term of the license expires, the licensed rights will revert back to the licensor and the licensee will generally not be able to use any of the elements of the licensed subject matter which may still be eligible for legal protection. As such, a license actually amounts to a form of rental arrangement with respect to the subject matter and the amount of compensation requested by the licensor is often computed with the intent of arriving at a fair rate of return in relation to amounts expended by the licensor in developing the licensed technology. For its part, a licensee compares the rental costs of the license to the burden of independently developing legal and viable alternatives to the licensed subject matter.[4]

While a license is appropriate when the licensee simply wishes to exploit **4.13** its own technology without being "blocked" by the rights of the licensor, it is common to see a license used as a fundamental tool in the other forms of international business transactions. For example, in order for a party to manufacture and distribute the products developed by another party, it must generally be granted a license to make and sell the products. In such cases, the agreement between the parties includes the basic technology license and an agreement covering the terms upon which the products will ultimately be sold to consumers. Also, a joint venturer may contribute technology to a joint venture through a licensing arrangement.

Licensing agreements can be characterized by the subject matter of the license, such as a patent or trademark license, or by the permitted functional uses of the licensed subject matter, such as a manufacturing or distribution license. While, as a practical matter, the license agreement will cover each type of intellectual property right which may be required in order for the licensee to perform the specified functional activity (*e.g.* manufacturing or distribution), there may be situations where, due to local law or otherwise, it may be necessary for the parties to enter into a series of separate license agreements covering each element of the overall technology package.

Regulation of Licensing Agreements

4.14   Licensing agreements obviously raise intellectual property law issues, since the intellectual property rights are the main subject matter of the agreement, and it is generally agreed that the volume of inbound licensing activity is partly a function of the legal rights available to the licensor with respect to the protection of the licensed technology in the country in which the license is operative. Licensing agreements may also be subject to regulation under export control laws of the licensor's country and the technology transfer laws of the licensee's country. In addition, as market activity increases, license agreements will generally become subject to any antitrust/competition laws that might be applicable to either of the parties, particularly in situations where it is perceived that the intellectual property rights covered by the license provide a substantial competitive advantage and/or the terms of the license itself may adversely impact the ability of one or both of the parties to compete in the marketplace.

Key Terms of Licensing Agreements

Definition and Use of the Licensed Technology

4.15   Obviously, the clause granting the licensee the various legal rights to exploit the technology embodied in the licensed subject matter is one of the most important terms of the license. As such, it is important for the parties to clearly understand all of the legal rights possessed by the licensor which may be relevant to the proposed transaction, as well as the intended use of each of these rights by the licensee. This information allows the "granting clause" of the license to be drafted in a manner which precisely enumerates the rights which are to be given to the licensee and the permitted uses of the technology.

    The key issues which need to be considered in formulating a granting clause are the definition of the actual legal rights that are to be the subject of the license, the permitted uses of such rights, whether or not the licensee is to have the exclusive right to practice and use the legal rights granted in the license for the purposes specified and whether the licensee itself will have the right to grant further licenses (*i.e.* sublicenses) of the licensed rights to third parties. The answers to each of the aforementioned issues will determine the scope and utility of the license grant, as well as the amount of consideration which a licensee might well be asked to pay for the use of the license.

Warranties and Guarantees

4.16   In some countries, like the United States, the grant of a license does not include any implied warranties regarding the subject matter, such as a guarantee that the technology has commercial utility or that patents or copyrights included in the subject matter don't infringe upon the rights of third parties. However, in other countries, a license actually imposes a number of affirmative rights and obligations on each of the parties, including the rights of the licensee to use any inventions which may be covered by the license and the duty of the licensor to facilitate the lawful use of the licensed subject matter by the licensee. For example, in Germany a patent license carries an implied warranty that production using the patented invention is technically possible and that all of the representations set forth in the license agreement with respect to the functionality of the invention are true and correct.

In most cases, the parties to a license agreement will not rely upon any implied warranties regarding the licensed subject matter. Instead, the license agreement will generally contain a number of representations and warranties from the licensor with regard to the legal status and utility of any of the inventions and technical information being transferred to the licensee. A common representation requested by licensees is an affirmative statement that the licensed subject matter does not infringe upon the rights of any third party and has been lawfully developed or acquired by the licensor. However, the licensee will usually attempt to secure broader representations which would cover the performance characteristics of the licensed subject matter. In turn, the licensor will seek to limit or disclaim any express or implied warranties regarding the licensed subject matter.

Rights and Obligations of the Parties

The license agreement will usually contain a number of very specific rights and obligations of the parties which must be meant over the term of the relationship. A few of these obligations, such as the duties which relate to the protection of the licensed subject matter, are shared by both parties. The obligations of the licensor, aside from those emanating from the representations and warranties, generally run to continuing technical assistance to the licensee and honoring any contractual rights of the licensee with respect to exclusivity. As to the licensee, it may have a number of responsibilities, the most important of which will relate to the duty to actively exploit the licensed rights and refrain from engaging in competing activities. Of course, the licensee will also have the separate contractual obligation to pay the consideration set out in the license agreement.

4.17

The technical assistance and training to be provided by the licensor is an important part of ensuring that the technology will be effectively transferred to, and used by, the licensee. For example, the information contained in a patent will generally not be sufficient to allow the licensee to begin production and manufacturing and trade secrets, by their nature, will require "hands-on" training in addition to the information included as part of any documents which may be provided to the licensee. Accordingly, unless the licensee has the requisite technical skills and experience in the use of the licensed subject matter of the license, the parties should anticipate that the licensing relationship should include some ongoing technical assistance and training from the licensor to the licensee. In fact, this type of assistance is of crucial importance for technology transfers into developing countries' economies, since the licensee often does not have the technical experience necessary for efficient exploitation of the licensed technology.

Compensation for Use of Licensed Rights

4.18　In most cases, the license will call for payment of some form of compensation by the licensee to the licensor for the use of the licensed subject matter. The form of compensation, be it cash or "in-kind", as well as the amount and timing of the payments will be determined by negotiation between the parties and each side will seek to satisfy their own financial and accounting objectives with respect to cash flow management, cost recovery and minimization of tax obligations. While industry standards are helpful in arriving at an appropriate "value" for the license, each transaction will be unique and the compensation package will ultimately depend on the needs of, and alternatives available to, the parties.

　　Cash payments are the most common type of compensation paid under a licensing arrangement. Cash payment can be classified in one of two ways: "royalties", which are measured by reference to the actual use of the licensed technology by the licensor; and "lump sum" or other periodic forms of payments, which may be made in addition to, or in lieu of, royalties and which are typically unrelated to the licensee's use of the licensed technology. The two types of cash payments are not mutually exclusive and, in many cases, the agreement calls for some lump sum payment at the time of execution, which covers the licensor's initial costs of negotiating the agreement and transferring the technology; additional minimum periodic royalty payments to ensure that the licensee is serious about using the technology; and "performance-based" royalties which are tied to the licensee's actual use of the technology over the term of the license.

　　The level of compensation in the license agreement is a common concern of regulators administering technology transfer laws in developing countries, and it has been quite common for such laws to restrict the royalty rate charged by the licensor and/or place a cap on the total amount of royalties which the licensee might be obligated to pay over the license term. In addition, royalty payments may well be subject to restrictions under local currency controls and, as a practical matter, the licensor may find that remittances in local currency may have little value due to difficulties in exchanging local currency for marketable currencies (*e.g.* dollars, yen, etc.).

Term and Termination of the License Agreement

4.19　Although the parties are typically most concerned about establishing the guidelines necessary to insure the success of the relationship, great care must be taken with respect to determining the circumstances, if any, which might lead to termination of the licensing agreement. First of all, the parties should determine the natural duration of the licensing arrangement, absent an event which might lead to an early termination. The agreement should then specify the events which might lead to early termination, the consequences associated with *any* termination of the agreement, the effect of termination upon the then-existing rights of the parties, any post-termination covenants or restrictions with respect to the licensed rights and, if appropriate, any additional remedies and liabilities relating to termination.

Evaluating Potential Licensing Partners

Licensing partners can be used to assist the licensor in conducting further research and development work, production and manufacturing of products which embody the licensed technology and the distribution of products which may have previously been manufactured by the licensor or another licensee or manufactured by the distributor-licensee. While the search for a licensing partner in a developing economy may be made more difficult due to problems in acquiring necessary information regarding the skills and activities of potential licensees, licensors nonetheless will analyze some of the same factors which they use in assessing a prospective licensee in their home country, like the following:

4.20

Technical and Functional Experience — The potential licensee should be able to demonstrate experience in specific technical area and in the particular function or functions which are at the essence of the particular relationship. For example, if the relationship is being established for the distribution of products, the licensee/distributor should be able to provide proven skills in marketing similar or complimentary products in the target market(s).

Formal Strategic Plan — The potential licensee should be able to provide a formal strategic plan setting out in detail the steps that will be taken to fully exploit the licensed technology. The plan should include firm estimates of the licensee's proposed expenditures and the anticipated revenues and income, which estimates might be incorporated into the license agreement in the form of covenants.

Management Skills and Support — The potential licensee should have one or more senior managers with the skill and experience to ensure that the licensee is able to execute its strategic plans. Such persons should be able to serve as in-house "champions" for the business relationship in the face of competing opportunities.

Financial Resources — The potential licensee should be able to provide sufficient capital to fund the formal strategic plan, as well as to finance additional work which might be required on the licensed technology.

Distribution Arrangements

4.21 Developing countries are generally perceived as being attractive potential markets for products manufactured by and for firms in the developed world, and these foreign sellers may well seek out partners in the developing countries to assist them in the sale and distribution of their products in these markets. The arrangement in such situations may take the form of a sales agency or representative agreement, under which a local party attempts to locate purchasers for the products, the products are sold directly to purchasers by the manufacturer, and the agent or representative receives a commission or fee based on sales which it is able to arrange. Alternatively, the parties may enter into a distribution arrangement, which would involve a sale of goods by the manufacturing entity to the distributing entity for resale by the distributor, combined with a license covering all the patents, trade secrets and trademarks required in order for the distributor to market and service the products. This arrangement will allow the manufacture to take advantage of the sales network of the distributor. In turn, the distributor gains access to new products without incurring the costs of internal development.

The contractual terms for a distribution arrangement includes many of the aspects of a direct sales agreement. For example, it will generally cover the description of the goods and services, the manner in which the subject goods are to be priced and delivered and allied requirements with respect to shipping and insurance; the form and timing of payment and related credit arrangements and any warranties and limitations which might be imposed on the respective liabilities of the parties to the agreement. However, the usual terms covering the sale of goods will be supplemented by additional provisions regulating how the distributor is to pursue the manufacturer's principal objective of penetrating a market in which direct sales efforts are either inappropriate or economically infeasible.

Regulation of Distribution Agreements

4.22 Distribution agreements must obviously take into account relevant contract laws, particularly laws relating to the sale of goods. In addition, many countries have special laws regulating the activities of sales agents and distributors, as well as the terms of sales agency and distribution arrangements. Also, a number of developing countries regulate distribution arrangements under the antitrust/competition laws in much the same way as they regulate licensing agreements. Regulators in these countries are particularly concerned about the competitive effects of exclusive distribution arrangements.

Key Terms of Distribution Agreements

Goods Covered by Distribution Arrangement

4.23 The distribution agreement should enumerate all of the products which are to be made available to the distributor for resale, terms upon which spare parts and supplies relating to the main products are to be stocked by the distributor, the treatment of enhancements and improvements to the main products which might be developed by the manufacturer during the term of the agreement and, in some cases, the agreement between the parties regarding extension of the arrangement to cover new products which might be developed by the manufacturer in the future.

Scope of Appointment

As with licensing agreements, distribution agreements raise various issues **4.24** regarding the scope of the appointment. It will be necessary for the parties to define and geographic, market or customer limitations which will be imposed upon the activities of the distributor. In addition, the agreement should always set out the expectations of the parties regarding the distributor's use of subdistributors and dealers to assist in the sale and marketing of the products in the specified market. Finally, whether or not the appointment is to be exclusive is a crucial question which must be resolved by the parties.

Pricing and Payment Terms

Generally, a distribution arrangement involves a sale of products by the **4.25** manufacturer to the distributor, along with an agreement by the distributor to pay for the products within a specified number of days following delivery of the products. As such, the parties enter into a credit arrangement under which the manufacturer, in effect, extends credit to the distributor on the terms provided in the agreement. The distribution agreement must describe the manner in which the products will be priced for sale to the distributor and the terms of payment following delivery of the products.

Ordering and Shipping Procedures

Ordering and shipping procedures are key elements of the planning process **4.26** in the distribution relationship, particularly in the case of new products where the manufacturer will be gradually "ramping-up" its production capabilities to meet the demand that may be generated through the activities of its distributors. The distribution agreement should establish guidelines for placement of orders, allocating the burden of any scarcity of products among the manufacturer's distribution partners and the procedures for shipping the purchased products.

Resale Pricing

As noted above, the distributor's net income from the relationship is derived **4.27** from the "spread" between the price at which the distributor is able to resell the products to its customers and the total costs, including the price of purchasing the products from the manufacturer, incurred by the distributor with respect to acquiring, storing and marketing the products. Since the manufacturer's profit is not directly related to the resale price charged by the distributor, given that the parties will agree on a fixed transfer price, there will usually be no limitations placed upon the right of the distributor to determine the prices or terms at which the products may be resold; however, the suggested retail price prescribed by the manufacturer may have a significant impact upon the price which the distributor may be able to reasonably charge to consumers.

One area of particular concern to the distributor results from the fact that the manufacturer may need to vary the amount of the suggested retail price from time to time during the term of the distribution agreement as costs and competitive factors change and the financial objectives of the manufacturer with respect to the product evolve. Any change in the suggested retail price will have a significant economic impact on a distributor, particularly if the manufacturer reduces the suggested retail price at a time when the distributor still holds a significant amount of inventory that was purchased at higher prices. In some cases, distributors may demand some form of protection against the adverse effects of price decreases and in almost all cases the manufacturer must provide the distributor with prior notice of any price changes.

Product Warranties

4.28 Distributors will, on behalf of themselves and their end users, request a variety of warranties and guarantees from the manufacturer regarding various aspects of the products which are to be the subject of the distribution agreement. For example, in almost all cases, the manufacturer will be required to provide some warranties with respect to the design and functionality of the products, although the scope of the warranties will generally be quite restricted and the remedies of the distributor and end user limited to repair of the defective products provided that a claim is made during the specified "warranty period". In other cases, the manufacturer may be asked to provide representations and warranties regarding the integrity of the legal rights that may underlie the specified product, such as a statement that the products do not infringe the intellectual property rights of any third parties.

Duties of the Distributor

4.29 While the manufacturer is certainly interested in making a profit on sales made to the distributor, it will also want to be sure that the distributor is able to successfully penetrate the specified market, thereby assuring the manufacturer of enhanced sales over the term of the arrangement. Accordingly, the parties will include various covenants and agreements by the distributor to ensure that it uses it best efforts to develop the full sales potential of the products within the territory. Among the items that are typically included are the following:

1. The distributor will agree to promote the products, identifying them by their correct names as products of the manufacturer. The distributor will also agree to maintain a qualified sales force and distribution organization, although it may be necessary for the manufacturer to supply appropriate training with respect to the uses and functions of the products.

2. The distributor will maintain a staff of trained technicians and a stock of spare parts and technical literature adequate to provide technical support and service to its customers. Once again, it may be necessary for the manufacturer to provide training in the appropriate service techniques, particularly when concerns exist regarding the overall quality and reputation of the product offerings.

3. The distributor will establish and maintain a place or places of business in areas throughout the territory adequate to provide good customer support and marketing coverage.

4. The distributor will agree not to sell or distribute products which are competitive with the products that are produced by the manufacturer.

5. The distributor will be obligated to maintain an inventory of products sufficient to satisfy customer orders on a timely basis; however, the obligations of the distributor in this regard must be made subject to any other agreement covering the allocation of limited products supplies among other distributors.

6. The distributor should provide the manufacturer with periodic reports regarding product sales, competitive goods and prices and additional information relating to the markets in which the distributor's activities are being conducted.

7. The distributor will be obligated to conduct its business in a manner that will reflect favorably on the manufacturer and will agree not to engage in any deceptive, misleading, illegal or unethical business practices. It is important to understand the importance of local regulations and customs regarding the sale and distribution of goods, particularly if they differ materially from those that might exist in the home market of the manufacturer.

8. Warranty obligations with respect to the products should be clarified, as should the allocation of the costs and responsibilities associated with any warranty repairs. The distributor should agree to promptly inform the manufacturer of any complaints regarding the products.

Distributor Review

One of the fundamental goals and objectives of any form of distribution arrangement is to generate revenues from sales of products and, in turn, to build and maintain market share. While in some cases the obligation of a distributor under the agreement will be limited to the use of its "best efforts", 4.30

it is generally most desirable for the manufacturer to impose various standards under which the performance of the distributor will be measured. However, the ability of the manufacturer to effectively monitor the performance of the distributor will depend upon a number of factors, including the relative size and experience of the parties and the consequences attached to any failure by the distributor to meet the expectations of the manufacturer. Performance criteria can take a number of different forms, such as sales quotas, minimum inventory purchases, levels of staffing, shelf or floor space requirements, number and geographic coverage of dealer appointments, warehouse locations and the amount of expenditures on promotional activities. Whatever the form of criteria, it is important to provide ongoing incentives for the distributor and to take into account anticipated changes in market conditions and in the various strategic objectives of each of the parties. One method for ensuring that a distributor will diligently attempt to meet any performance measures is to condition any ongoing right of exclusivity on the achievement of the objectives. If the distributor does not attain the goals set forth in the agreement, the manufacturer may have the right to engage other distributors and, in some cases, to terminate the entire relationship.

In addition to any objective performance measures, the agreement may include a number of other procedures calculated to build and reinforce communication between the parties regarding the conduct of the relationship. For example, it generally makes sense to provide for periodic financial and marketing reports, on-site inspections of distributor facilities, training sessions and other meetings or telephonic conferences between representatives of each of the parties. Ongoing contact of this sort will give the manufacturer a good sense of the distributor's commitment to the relationship and the feasibility of expanding the scope of the arrangement into other areas.

Term and Termination

4.31 Although each of the parties may certainly contemplate that the distribution arrangement will continue for a long period of time, it is necessary to give careful consideration to the term of the arrangement, any conditions with respect to renewal of the arrangement and, most importantly, the circumstances under which it will be possible for one or both of the parties to terminate the arrangement prior the end of any specified term. Also, the agreement should describe the effect of any termination of the agreement, as well as any procedures that may be established to regulate the resolution of disputes among the parties with respect to their respective rights following any termination of the agreement.

Termination of the distribution agreement may expose the terminating party to potential claims with respect to damages that might be suffered by the other party due to termination of the relationship. While both parties will attempt to limit their exposure with respect to such claims by including disclaimers of any liability for damages or restitution arising out any decision to terminate the agreement, such provisions may not be effective under the laws of various nations. Also termination generally does not effect the rights of the parties to receive payments that may be owed as a result of activities which occurred prior to the date of termination.

A number of countries now have laws which provide various protections for local agents and distributors upon termination of an international distribution relationship. For example, it may be possible for the terminated distributor to obtain compensation for the value of the goodwill which may have been developed with respect to the manufacturer's products, for the loss of expected profits during the remaining term of the agreement, for the value of capital investments which the distributor may have made in the course of marketing the products and, in some cases, for the cost of employee severance benefits paid to those employees which the distributor needs to lay off as a result of the termination of the distribution agreement. The manufacturer can avoid liability if the termination is "justified"; however, most laws contain a very narrow definition of "just cause", limiting it to criminal acts and gross incompetence.

Manufacturing Arrangements

Another common and important type of business transaction involves the manufacture of specified goods. Firms in developed countries may realize greater efficiencies in production by utilizing low-cost manufacturers overseas to make their products. The firm may achieve these cost savings by granting a license to the manufacturer to make the products and agreeing to repurchase the products at a fixed price, perhaps at some multiple of the manufacturer's actual cost. The license almost always must include some agreement as to technical assistance, since the manufacturer must be trained in a manner which guarantees that its products are similar in quality to those that would otherwise be produced by the licensor. | 4.32

Manufacturers in developing countries stand to gain a good deal from a balanced manufacturing arrangement. First, and most importantly, the arrangement provides employment for the local workforce and enhances the technical skills of the firms in the developing country, even if the scope of their use of the basic technology is limited to the products covered by the agreement. Second, revenues from the arrangement can be used by the local firm to expand its current operations and purchase new equipment. Third, if appropriate, manufacturers can begin to serve as local distributors for the products covered by the agreement, or work with the foreign party on developing complimentary products that are best suited to the needs of the local market. Finally, the relationship with the foreign party may enhance the credibility and reputation of the local firm and allow it to gain access to further resources (*e.g.* new financing).

Regulation of Manufacturing Agreements

4.33 Manufacturing agreements involve issues of contract and commercial law, since the underlying relationship is based on terms and conditions regarding manufacturing specifications, deliveries, and other matters which are set out by agreement. The purchase of the finished products by the foreign party will typically be governed by terms similar to those usually set out in a sale of goods agreement. If the foreign party provides the manufacture with technology, the arrangement may be subject to the same conditions governing any other licensing agreement (*e.g.* technology transfer regulations). Finally, manufacturing and production projects often raise concerns with regard to the environmental impact of the manufacturing process.

Key Terms of Manufacturing Agreements

Definition of Licensed Products

4.34 As with licensing or distribution arrangements, careful consideration must be given to defining the products that are to be the subject of the agreement. The process begins by defining the type of product, such as a $5\frac{1}{4}''$ half-height winchester technology based disk drive, and then describing how any new or improved versions of the basic product are going to be included in the arrangement. For example, the parties may define products to include any version of the basic product which goes into commercial production within a specified time period following the date of the agreement. In other cases, the parties may include newer models to the extent that they continue to fall within a specified range of performance characteristics.

Technology Licenses and Technical Assistance

4.35 In order for the manufacturer to commence and continue manufacturing the products, the agreement must provide for a license of the foreign party's patents and other intellectual property rights to the manufacturer for the purposes described in the agreement, as well as for the actual transfer of technical information, such as trade secrets, which is need to build and manufacture the products. In addition, the foreign party should agree to provide some training to the manufacturer's personnel regarding the use of the technical information and the parties will attempt to work together to minimize the costs of raw materials and other inputs into the manufacturing process.

Foreign Party's Obligation to Purchase Products

4.36 The parties should specify the number of products to be purchased by the foreign party, the price to be charged for the products, and the manner of payment. As noted above, the price will usually be set at a level which provides the manufacturer with a specified profit over its manufacturing costs. Payment for products purchased under the agreement will usually be in stages. For example, the foreign party may agree to pay a portion (*e.g.* 50 per cent) of the total price of the amount of products ordered for a particular month or other period at the time that the order is given to the manufacturer, which is generally 60 to 90 days prior to the delivery date. The balance will be due within a specified number of days (*e.g.* 30, 45 or 60) following delivery. The parties should agree on an order forecast to permit proper planning by the manufacturer. Forecasted orders should be laid out in monthly increments, although the foreign party will generally have the right to delay or accelerate shipments within specified limitations.

Joint Venture Arrangements

One of the most common forms of organizational strategic business relationship is the "joint venture". The joint venture utilizes a separate business entity to conduct the specified business activities. The use of a separate entity allows the parties to limit the liabilities associated with the relationship and, in fact, the structure may be required in order for the parties to avail themselves of incentives and concessions offered under any local foreign investment programs when the joint venture is used as a means for selling and distributing products and services into a foreign market.
4.37

Joint ventures can be classified by the various functions which may be performed by the enterprise. For example, a joint venture may be formed to conduct research and development work on new products or technical application, to manufacture or produce various products, to market and distribute products and services in a specified geographic area or to perform some combination of the aforementioned functions. The function of the joint venture will be linked to the overall objectives of the parties and will dictate to a large extent the substantive terms of the joint venture arrangement.

Motivations for Joint Venture Relationships

A joint venture carries with it a number of advantages and disadvantages. On the one hand, a joint venture can provide a party with access to resources and skills which are unavailable to it at any reasonable cost. However, on the other hand, use of a joint venture can be quite risky given the reliance that must be placed upon the ability and willingness of the other party to perform its obligations during the term of the arrangement. In considering whether or not to enter into a joint venture, notice should be taken of some of the following motivations which might drive a party toward such a relationship:
4.38

1. The party may not have sufficient financial resources to take on a particular project by itself and may seek a partner to assist in sharing the financial burden and other risks of the project. Projects which require a substantial amount of investment in development work and

product testing may be good candidates for the joint venture structure. In some cases, a partner may even be willing to provide most, if not all, of the funding in exchange for gaining access to the intangible assets of the party.

2. The party may want to gain access to the technical resources and skills of another party. A joint venture which brings together managers and scientists from each party will facilitate the rapid exchange of information regarding existing and new technologies.

3. The party may seek a joint venture with a local party in a new foreign market as a means of accelerating the pace of market penetration. The local party should be able to provide the requisite knowledge of local tastes and customs and providing for equity involvement by the local partner will ensure that it will provide the best services to the joint venture. A joint venture may also be required in order to satisfy host country rules which require local participation.

4. The party may use a joint venture to decrease the costs associated with the manufacture of its products while retaining some control over the quality of the process and the technology used in the course of completing the manufacturing activities.

5. A party may choose a joint venture structure, rather than a network of contractual relationships, in order to ensure that it is in a position to directly manage the specific functional process, be it research work, manufacturing or distribution. Also, a joint venture may be appropriate when the party believes that it will need to provide personnel to facilitate rapid transfer of trade secrets and other information for use in the collaborative venture.

Regulation of Joint Venture Relationships

4.39 The formation and operation of a joint venture generally raises a number of legal and regulatory issues, including the following:

1. Antitrust and competition laws are always an area of concern whenever a joint venture is to be formed, since the consolidation of resources from two or more parties which might otherwise compete with other will always, by its very nature, raise questions about the effect of the joint venture on competitive conditions in the marketplace. The parties may need to make filings with antitrust regulators in one or more countries setting out various information about their current activities and the proposed business of the joint venture.

2. With regard to international joint ventures, there may be a need to obtain approval from local regulators of an investment by a foreign party. The regulators may also review the amount and form of the contribution which is to be made by the foreign party, particularly if local currency, rather than hard currency, is to be used or the foreign party is making an "in-kind" contribution.

3. If a foreign party is to obtain a license to use any of the technology developed by the joint venture, a review might be made of the royalties which are to be paid by the foreign party to ensure that they allow the local party to receive a reasonable return through its interest in the joint venture.

4. In countries where hard currency is scarce, regulators may closely scrutinize any arrangement which permit a foreign party to repatriate joint venture profits in hard currency or receive payments from the venture for components or technology in hard currency.

5. Many countries offer various incentives to induce foreign parties to invest in joint ventures with local partners. If the joint venture wishes to qualify for a tax holiday, low-cost government loans or other types of benefits, application may need to be made at the time the joint venture is formed.

Another threshold legal issue is selecting the form of business entity which will house the joint venture's activities. While it is difficult to generalize, a number of developing countries are working to create business enterprises that have characteristics that are familiar to potential investors in the developed world. These entities can be distinguished by reference to the following factors: **4.40**

1. The amount of the potential liabilities of the owners of the entity.
2. The degree of participation in the management of the entity which is available for the owners.
3. The transferability of ownership interests in the entity.
4. The amount of information regarding the entity and its owners which must be available to regulators and to the general public.
5. Limitations on the aggregate number of owners (*e.g.* shareholders) of the entity.

One possible form of business enterprise is a so-called "public company", which is popular in civil law countries. While an ownership interest in these entities is denominated by shares, the share interests need not be "publicly traded". Instead, the use of the term "public" refers to that fact that such entities are required to publish accounts annually and must also have public auditors. Local laws often require that a public company be used if the foreign shareholder is a publicly traded company in its own country. Examples of such companies include the following: **4.41**

— *Aktiengesellschaft* or A.G. (Germany), literally, a "stock company";
— *Societe Anonyme* (France, Switzerland, Belgium), *Societa Anonima* (Italy) or Sociedad Anonima (Spain, Mexico, Latin America, generally) or S.A. literally, "anonymous company";
— *Naamlooze Vennootschaap* or N.V. (Netherlands, Netherlands Antilles), literally, "anonymous (nameless) company";
— *Kabushiki Kaisha* or K.K. (Japan) a public company; and

— PLC (UK), a publicly traded entity, typically on the London Stock Exchange.

A "private" limited liability, or "stock company", is an entity which permits the owners to enjoy limited liability. Such entities, akin to corporations in the United States, are based on recognition of an artificial legal person separate and distinct from its owners. This concept is fairly new for many developing countries, and recognition of such entities has proceeded slowly, often delayed until complimentary laws and regulations for the protection of creditors (*e.g.* bankruptcy laws and mortgage and secured transactions laws) have been developed. Private limited liability or stock companies are widely recognized in a number of countries. For example, Germany's Gesellschaft mit beschrankte Haftung or G.m.b.H., permits limitation of the equity holders' liability to the amount of their capital contributions. Equity interests are not represented by stock certificates or other security instruments and may be transferred by notarial deed. Interests may be freely transferred or made subject to transfer restrictions. The law requires that the entity have a "managing director", but it is possible to provide that the director can act only pursuant to instructions from the equity holder(s).[5]

Finally, many countries recognize partnership-type entities, most of which are pass-through entities for tax purposes. These entities are sometimes similar to general partnerships in the United States, with unlimited liability for each participant, or to limited partnerships, with limited liability for at least some of the participants. In some cases, notably in Japan, the entities are treated as separate legal bodies for tax purposes, resulting in undesired tax consequences.

Key Terms of Joint Venture Arrangements

4.42   While the interdependence created by the use of a joint venture makes it difficult to generalize regarding the key issues in forming and operating a joint venture, it is usually the case that the parties will need to expend a good deal of time and effort on discussing the following areas: the functional and financial objectives of the joint venture, the contributions which each of the parties are to make to the joint venture, the capital structure of the joint venture corporation, management and control, operating the joint venture, restrictions on transfers of ownership, pre-termination withdrawals of either of the original venturers, and the term and termination of the joint venture.

Defining the Objectives of the Joint Venture

4.43   At the outset of every proposed joint venture, it is necessary for the parties to arrive at some understanding of the basic objectives of the proposed enterprise. This includes an identification of the nature and scope of the proposed activities of the joint venture and a description of the expectations of each of the parties as to the ultimate financial and technical performance of the joint venture. The process of defining the basic objectives of the joint venture is usually facilitated by the preparation of a summary of the key business terms of the transaction, as well as a formal business plan.

In defining the objectives of the joint venture, it is necessary for the parties to take into account the scope of the joint venture business, the size of the joint venture, the way in which the parties will allocate management responsibility for the day-to-day operations of the joint venture, the decision-making process for major decisions regarding the venture, the terms of any ancillary agreements between the joint venture and either of the parties and the term of the joint venture and any events that might lead to an early termination of the business relationship.

Contributions to the Joint Venture

The planning and negotiation process prior to the actual formation of the joint venture should include an analysis of the financial, technical and functional requirements of the venture throughout the proposed term of its existence. Although this type of analysis should initially be conducted without regard to the specific capabilities of the parties in each of these areas, it will ultimately be necessary for the parties to focus upon each of the specific contributions which are to be made by the parties. **4.44**

Since the venturers are something more than passive investors in the joint venture, the range of possible contributions will be much broader than is normally the case. For example, not only will the venturers contribute cash and cash equivalents to finance the operations of the joint venture, they may also provide the venture with services, tangible property (*e.g.* equipment or facilities), intangible property rights, and specific functional expertise in such diverse areas as research and development, manufacturing and distribution. In addition, the venturers may be able to contribute their experience and contacts in dealing with local regulators and in obtaining supplies of scarce raw materials.

Capital Structure

Whatever form the initial capital contribution might take, a joint venture actually commences operations upon the sale and issuance of ownership interests to the parties. The parties become the owners of the enterprise with such rights as may be created under the laws of the jurisdiction where the enterprise is organized, as well as any contractual agreements between the venturers. The ownership interests to be issued to the parties carry a number of rights with respect to management and control of the enterprise as well as the manner in which the holder can expect to receive a return with respect to its invested capital. **4.45**

Legal Aspects of Common Business Activities and Transactions

Management and Control

4.46 Devising an appropriate structure for the management and control of the venture is one of the most important matters to be negotiated between the parties. Assuming that the choice is made to utilize the corporate form of business entity, the parties must consider various issues relating to the election of the board of directors, the selection of the officers and key managers, the respective voting rights of each of the parties on matters deemed to be material to the existence and operation of the enterprise and the specific duties of the board of directors, the officers and any committees created by the parties to manage one or more of the business functions of the enterprise. Also, while hopefully the parties will not reach a situation where they are unable to agree on a certain matter, the parties should agree upon a procedure for the orderly resolution of disputes.

Generally, each of the parties will have the right to designate one or more representatives to act as members of the board of directors or officers of the corporation. In addition, either as a matter of law or by contractual agreement, each of the parties will have various voting rights on matters of importance to the corporation. Also, it is not unusual for the corporation to contract with one or both of the parties for the conduct of one or more specific functions or services, including such things as basic research and development, manufacturing and distribution. As a result of these contractual arrangements, the party effectively assumes control over a material aspect of the operations of the venture, even though nominal authority remains in the board of directors and in the officer or manager selected to oversee the specific function or service.

The parties need to strike an appropriate balance between permitting the officers and managers of the joint venture to make appropriate decisions regarding the operation of the enterprise and reserving the right, as the owners of the venture, to review and approve certain matters. The matters which are subject to the "shared control" of the owners, thereby requiring approval of both joint venture partners, should be limited to those items that are material to the performance of the venture, since making numerous actions subject to a unanimous vote will diminish, or even eliminate, the ability of the venture to quickly respond to appropriate business opportunities and changes in competitive and other environmental conditions.

4.47 While there are seemingly endless possibilities for the listing of items which might require the unanimous consent of the shareholders, or a supermajority vote of the board of directors, the following matters are typically considered:

1. Capital expenditures or indebtedness in excess of a specified dollar amount at any one time, other than as provided in the annual operating budget.
2. Sale of assets the value of which exceeds a specified dollar amount at any one time or the aggregate value of which exceeds a specified dollar amount within any six month period.

3. Creation of material liens, mortgages, encumbrances or other charges of any kind on any asset of the venture or guarantees of payment by or of performance of the obligations of any third party.

4. Approval of the annual operating budget and annual capital expenditure budget of the joint venture, as well as any amendments thereto.

5. Any commitment of the joint venture which either creates a liability in excess of a specified dollar amount or which obligates the joint venture to perform under any arrangement, contract or agreement which is not within the ordinary course of its business.

6. Any amendment to the articles of incorporation or bylaws of the joint venture corporation.

7. Any issuance of additional shares of the joint venture corporation, declaration of dividends or reinvestment of earnings at a time when the corporation is otherwise permitted by law to pay dividends.

8. Any agreement or material transaction between the joint venture and either (1) a shareholder or any affiliate of a shareholder or (2) a director or executive officer of the joint venture.

9. Adoption of or change in any major policy of the joint venture relating to operations, manufacture, sale of products, or changes in product lines.

10. A dissolution, liquidation, merger, consolidation, other business combination or sale of substantially all the assets of the joint venture.

Operating the Joint Venture

Although a good deal of the emphasis during the period of negotiating the **4.48** terms of the joint venture is placed on issues relating to capitalization and management, it is important for the parties to remember that the venture company will become an independent operating entity with a life of its own. As such, the joint venture documents should cover the key points relating to operation of the venture, including the responsibilities for the functional activities of the company (*e.g.* research and development, manufacturing and/or distribution); operational matters, such as legal compliance, insurance, staffing and other similar issues; accounting and financial reporting matters; and the allocation and distribution of joint venture income.

Restrictions on Transfers of Ownership

As a general rule, the parties will generally agree to a strict prohibition on any **4.49** sale or transfer of the shares for a specified period of time, usually corresponding to the initial term of the venture. Precluded transfers will include not only an outright sale of the shares, but also any pledge or other encumbrance of the shares, although in some cases a party will be permitted to transfer the shares to a successor corporation or a wholly-owned subsidiary of the party. Waiver of the restriction on transfer would require the consent of the other party.

After the restriction period has ended, the parties will usually agree to a "right of first offer" or a "right of first refusal". The right of first offer obligates the party wishing to find a purchaser for its shares to first offer them to the other shareholder on the terms at which the potential seller would like to complete the transaction. If the other shareholder is unwilling to purchase the shares on those terms, the seller would them have a specified period of time to find a purchaser on terms no less favorable to the seller than those originally offered to the other shareholder. The right of first refusal is slightly different, since the selling shareholder must first have an offer to purchase the shares from a third party at the time the transaction is proposed to the other shareholder.

Pre-Termination Withdrawals of a Joint Venture Partner

4.50 There may be a variety of situations in which one of the joint venturers will be allowed, or required, to withdraw from the venture prior to the date upon which the parties originally contemplated that the relationship would terminate. For example, a fundamental change with respect to one of the parties, such as a change in ownership of the party, may cause a sufficient amount of uneasiness for the other, or "non-changing" party, to trigger a right in the hands of the non-changing party to purchase the shares of the other party. Another situation where withdrawal may be appropriate is when a party which is not actively involved in the management of the venture is dissatisfied with the level of performance which the venture has achieved in the hands of the other party and seeks to have its interest purchased by the party that is in control of the venture.

Withdrawal of one of the parties and continuation of the business by the other party is obviously an alternative to simply dissolving and liquidating the entity. In some cases, continuing the business without both of the original parties is simply not a viable alternative, particularly when the withdrawing party takes with it certain resources, technical or otherwise, which are of fundamental importance to the success of the venture. However, since dissolution and liquidation often diminish the value of the interests of both parties, some effort will generally be made to establish equitable procedures for liquidating the interests of the parties without terminating the business itself.

Duration and Termination of the Joint Venture

4.51 The joint venture documents must include provisions which specify the duration of the enterprise, the events which may lead to the termination and dissolution of the joint venture and the manner in which the assets and resources of the entity will be redistributed to the parties upon liquidation. The duration, or "term", of the joint venture will depend upon the specific goals and objectives of the parties and the amount of time which will be needed in order to achieve the required investment return. Termination and dissolution may occur either at the end of the fixed term or upon the occurrence of specified events prior to the termination date otherwise specified in the venture documents. The process of liquidation is generally governed by applicable law, although the parties do have some freedom to specify how the remaining assets of the joint venture will be allocated between them after the claims of creditors have been satisfied.

Evaluating Potential Joint Venture Partners

There are few subjects that have been more extensively analyzed then the 4.52 selection of potential joint venture partners. Clearly, a joint venture presents special problems since, by its very nature, a joint venture requires partial integration of the skills, attitudes, bias and experiences of the organizations of each of the partners, as well as many of the persons within them. Accordingly, it should come as little surprise that the focal points of evaluating potential joint venture partners include not only functional characteristics, but also take into account the likelihood of compatibility between the partners. Among those factors which should be considered are the following:

Compatibility — The potential partner should be compatible with the firm in a number of areas, such as the level of commitment to the joint venture, the size and structure of the organization and the underlying national and corporate cultures. Under the best of circumstances, the parties will have had some sort of prior relationship with one another.

Functional Skills and Resources — The functional skills and resources of the potential partner must compliment those of the firm. For example, in an international joint venture formed in order to take advantage of the local partner's ability to rapidly access the market, the firm should be more concerned about the skills of the prospective partner in the distribution area than about the partner's ability to assist in developing any new products.

Managerial Resources — The potential partner should have the managerial resources required to provide all needed assistance to the joint venture, particularly in those areas in which the partner is to have primary functional responsibility.

Facilities and Support — Although the joint venture is often operated as a wholly separate entity, it is sometimes useful to have a partner that is willing and able to provide facilities and administrative support for a portion of the joint venture's activities.

Governmental and Regulatory Acumen — There are cases, such as in international joint ventures and in ventures which involve products which are subject to government testing and approval, when the skill and experience of a prospective partner in dealing with the government can be extremely important. For example, in a number of foreign countries, the government exercise actual or de facto authority over local distribution.

Financial Resources — The potential partner must have sufficient financial resources to support the joint venture, as well as any functional activities that it will be called upon to undertake for the joint venture.

Reputation — A joint venture is perhaps the most "visible" form of business relationship. If possible, an effort should be made to find a partner with a solid reputation in the market, as well as in the functional skills and resources that the partner is being asked to provide to the joint venture.

Formation of New Entities and Acquisitions

4.53   A foreign party may enter a new market by forming a new business entity and attempting to establish a new business. This strategy can be extremely risky unless the firm has substantial familiarity with the market and is able to recruit qualified local personnel to assist in the venture. A foreign party may also sometimes decide to enter a new foreign market by purchasing a significant equity interest in an existing local entity or by purchasing the entity outright. Obviously, this type of strategy can involve a significant amount of cash and other resources and the success thereof may ultimately depend on the foreign firm's ability to retain key local employees and continue to capitalize on the reputation and local contacts which the local firm has developed prior to the acquisition.

Formation of a new business entity, or acquisition of an existing entity, will each generally require approvals under the applicable foreign investment regulations of the host country. In some cases, foreign investors will be subject to restrictions regarding their percentage ownership of local businesses, and may not be allowed to invest in certain industries or make an acquisition for amounts over a specified valuation. Transactions of this type also can raise complex tax and accounting issues. Finally, acquisitions must be completed in a manner consistent with local requirements relating to labor contracts and other types of employee benefits.

Notes

[1] One common form of business arrangement, a research and development agreement or project, is not discussed herein because most developing countries still lack the economic and scientific infrastructure required to make them attractive candidates for research funding from foreign investors. It can be expected, however, that this situation will change in the years to come, and that foreign investors may well have great interest in funding research activities by local firms to develop new products customized to local requirements and tastes.

[2] The United Nations Convention on the International Sale of Goods, which was prepared by the United Nations Commission on International Trade Law, is an attempt to provide a "neutral" body of sales law which can be applied to sales

transactions between parties whose "places of business" are in different countries. A number of countries, including the United States, have ratified the Convention and the Convention may apply to international sales contracts involving parties from the United States unless the parties specifically agree *not* to have the Convention apply or vary the Convention's provisions in the sales agreement.

[3] As used herein, the term "valuable legal right" includes not only intellectual property rights, such as the authority to lawfully practice a patented invention without fear of being sued for infringement, but also the right to use technology, knowledge, trade secrets and technical data, all of which are considered to be a form of property held and controlled by the owner thereof.

[4] A potential licensee may attempt to develop substitutes for a patented product which do not infringe upon the claims set out in the patent which might be the subject of a license or, as to trade secrets, may undertake to independently develop the process, knowledge or other information through inspection of the licensor's products or reverse engineering.

[5] Other examples include *Societe à Responsabilité Limitée* (France, Switzerland, Belgium); *Sociedad de Responsibilidad Limitada* (Mexico, Latin America, Spain); Yugen Kaisha (Japan); and the Limited Company (United Kingdom).

CAMBODIA

Professor Dolores A. Donovan and Professor Jeffrey S. Brand

I. Summary of Business and Political Conditions

Basic Demographic, Political and Economic Information

Cambodia is committed to developing a free market economy and to encour- **A.01**
aging foreign investment. Cambodia's Constitution states that Cambodia
"shall adopt a market economy system" and recent law reform efforts, including reforms in legal education,[1-2] are geared toward the integration of
Cambodia into ASEAN and the world economy.

The Kingdom of Cambodia is a constitutional monarchy with a population of 9.3 million persons, 12–15 per cent of whom are concentrated in
urban areas.[3] Buddhism is the state religion. The economic life of the nation
is centered in the capital, Phnom Penh, which has a population between 1 and
1.5 million. Although large-scale plans for development of tourism facilities
in Siem Reap, near Angkor Wat, have been approved by the government, the
provinces are, on the whole, devoid of significant commercial activity. The
only possible exceptions to this rule are Cambodia's port city, Sihanoukville,
also known as Kompong Som, and the provincial capital of Battambang.
Sihanoukville is the point of entry for most goods imported from abroad.

The language of Cambodia is Khmer. English is in the process of replacing
French as Cambodia's second language. Until 1975, instruction in the French
language was mandatory in all secondary schools and French is still spoken
by most educated persons over the age of 40. However, English is increasingly popular, especially among the younger generation.[4]

The Cambodian economy, with substantial assistance from international **A.02**
donors, is on the mend. The current government, elected in the U.N.-
sponsored elections of 1993, is making every effort to rebuild the economy,
destroyed by the Khmer Rouge reign of terror in the period 1975–1979 and

by the subsequent twelve years of civil war. The table below[5] chronicles the
results of the government's efforts.

Basic Indicators	1991	1992	1993	1994
GNP per capita (US$)	203	204	210	214
GNP (Cambodian Riels bn.)	280.3	302.8	319.5	335.5
Real GNP growth (%)	7.6	7.0	5.7	5.0
Inflation (%)	197	75	114	25
Exports (US$ mn.)	67.3	51.3	37.7	60.9
Imports (US$ mn.)	99.8	137.5	225.5	263.2
Current Account (US$ mn.)	−27.7	−49.6	−136.9	−211.5

The Royal Cambodian Government is focused on repairing Cambodia's
infrastructure. As a result of higher infrastructure spending and lower revenues, the budget deficit expanded in 1993 and 1994 to 5.7 per cent and 6.8
per cent of the Gross National Product, respectively. Revenues are steadily
increasing, but it is unlikely that the government will achieve its goal of a
balanced budget in the near future. Major areas of expenditure are public
works (19 per cent) and defence (18 per cent); major sources of revenue are
tax revenue (46 per cent) and foreign aid (31 per cent).[6] The spending on
defence is necessitated by the fact that the Khmer Rouge still hold about 15
per cent of Cambodia's territory, mostly in the jungle along the Thai-
Cambodian border.

The Kingdom of Cambodia's constitutional monarch is King Norodom
Sihanouk, who was restored to the throne by the Constitution of 1993,
written in the wake of the U.N.-supervised elections of May, 1993. The
elections, conducted according to a system of proportional representation,
produced a three-way split between the three major parties, each of which
claims to espouse the ideology of liberal democracy. The two leading
parties, FUNCINPEC (the French acronym used by the party headed by
Prince Norodom Ranariddh) and CPP (Cambodian People's Party), formed
a government loosely modeled on the parliamentary systems of France and
England.

A.03   The unicameral legislature is called the National Assembly and is composed of 120 Members of Parliament (MPs). In a parliamentary system, the
members of the executive branch of government are usually chosen from the
ranks of the members of parliament, rather than being appointed from outside the legislature. Cambodia has adhered to the parliamentary model in this
respect. However, Cambodia has deviated from the norm in that, instead of
the usual Prime Minister and his or her Cabinet, there are two Co-Prime
Ministers. This result was dictated by the inability of the two leading parties

to reach a compromise. The two Co-Prime Minsters are Prince Norodom Ranariddh for FUNCINPEC and Hun Sen for the CPP.

The inability to compromise extended to the naming of Ministers: most Ministries are headed by a Minister from one party seconded by an assistant minister, titled Secretary of State, from the other party. Two key Ministries, Interior and Defence, even have Co-Ministers. Although this dualist system of government is, at first glance, startling, it is best understood as the outcome of a recently-concluded civil war, during the twenty years of which the members of FUNCINPEC and CPP confronted each other across the barrels of guns rather than bargaining tables. Old habits die hard.

Legal History

The civil war that had battered Cambodia for more than 20 years, having its origins in the Vietnam War fought by the U.S. Government, came to an end on October 23, 1991, when the warring factions signed a peace treaty, known as the Paris Agreements, brokered by the five permanent members of the U.N. Security Council. In the Paris Agreements, the four factions, the dominant three of which had, in the past, espoused communism or socialism, committed themselves to the key features of liberal democracy, including a multiparty system, an independent judiciary, and a market economy. The Agreements provided for the U.N.-supervised elections of 1993, in which the factions were to field candidates to elect a National Assembly that would write a new constitution for Cambodia.[7]   A.04

The Constitution of 1993, the final product of the U.N. intervention, is the seventh constitution adopted by Cambodia since its independence from France. Cambodia had no constitution prior to 1947, for it had been ruled by a long line of god-kings dating at least as far back as the 9th Century, when the temples of Angkor Wat were built. However, in the 17th, 18th and 19th centuries the power of the Cambodian kings waned and Cambodia fell under the influence of Thailand, Vietnam and, in 1863, the French. The French established a protectorate that was to endure until World War II.

After the death of King Monivong in 1941, 18-year-old Prince Norodom Sihanouk was placed on the throne by the French governor-general of Japanese-occupied Indochina, on the mistaken assumption that Sihanouk would acquiesce in continued colonial rule. In 1945, when the Japanese imprisoned French personnel in Indochina, King Sihanouk seized the opportunity to declare Cambodia an independent state. Seven months later, however, the French regained control, leaving Sihanouk on the throne, promising a constituent assembly, and permitting the formation of political parties. The constitution of 1947 followed in fairly short order.

In 1954 the Geneva Conference was convened to bring a formal conclusion to the Indochinese War, in which Vietnam had won its independence   A.05

Cambodia

from France. A "side-show" at the Geneva Conference was the question of whether Sihanouk's government, established by and under the protection of France, or the Cambodian resistance government, composed of the victorious Viet Minh and members of the Cambodian Communist Party, was the legitimate government of Cambodia. The Conference determined that the Sihanouk government was the legitimate government of Cambodia. Shortly thereafter, in 1955, King Sihanouk abdicated the throne in favor of his father in order to enter politics full-time, re-taking the title "Prince" Sihanouk. King Suramarit, Sihanouk's father, died in 1960, leaving the throne vacant. It remained vacant until 1970, when Lieutenant Gen. Lon Nol abolished the monarchy.

In 1970, Lon Nol, supported by the United States, seized power from Sihanouk in a military coup. Lon Nol declared the monarchy abolished and himself the premier of the new Khmer Republic.

In 1975 the Lon Nol government was overthrown by the Khmer Rouge, who established the People's Republic of Democratic Kampuchea. The Khmer Rouge are the Cambodian faction, led by members of the Cambodian Communist Party, who controlled Cambodia, or Kampuchea, as they called it, during the years 1975–1979. Espousing the political tenets of radical Marxism-Leninism-Maoism, they sought to remove all vestiges of modern Western civilization from Cambodia in order to create an agrarian Communist utopia. In the process of purging Cambodia of all Western influence, the Khmer Rouge killed or caused the deaths by starvation of an estimated one to two million Cambodians, or at least 15 per cent of the total Cambodian population.

The prime targets of the Khmer Rouge were the intellectual elite who, through the process of education, had been exposed to the influence of Western thought. Lawyers, legislators, prosecutors and judges, because of their identification with the processes of governance, were the focal point of the slaughter. With the death of the persons who operated the legal system came the collapse and eradication of the apparatus of the law. Law books were destroyed and the buildings that had housed the courts and the faculty of law put to other uses. Estimates of the number of legal professionals remaining in Cambodia at the end of the massacres range from six to ten. Cambodia's legal system was completely destroyed by the Khmer Rouge.[8]

A.06 Cambodia actually had two legal systems: the formal court system inherited from the French and its own ancient informal conciliation-based dispute resolution system. The Khmer Rouge destroyed both of them. The French, whose mid-nineteenth century arrival in Cambodia is of recent vintage relative to the existence of a Cambodian civilization flourishing in the 9th Century A.D., had attempted to combine the Khmer conciliation system with the French judicial system. The executions of lawyers, legislators and judges by the Khmer Rouge brought about the collapse of the French system; the destruction of the fabric of Cambodian society eradicated the traditional system.

In 1979 Vietnam invaded Cambodia, causing the Khmer Rouge to flee to the Thai border. Vietnam installed a client regime composed of Khmer Rouge defectors. This government began to rebuild a formal court system. Because it, like most communist regimes, devalued law, it was slow to rebuild the legal system generally and to restore legal education in particular. The few laws that were enacted and courts that were created bore the imprint of Soviet concepts of socialist legality.

In 1989 Vietnam began its withdrawal from Cambodia, leaving behind a regime that became known as the State of Cambodia (SOC), with Hun Sen as Prime Minister. Under the SOC regime the government began to create a functioning legislative and judicial system, but the on-going civil war and lack of money prevented significant progress. Nonetheless, decrees were issued and laws were enacted, many of which remain in effect today. Indeed, some of the major pieces of legislation in the commercial law area date back to the SOC regime. The most important of these are Decree 38, governing contract law, and the SOC Labor Law of 1992.

The current government has supplemented the legislative structure it inherited from the SOC regime with additional key pieces of legislation. The Foreign Investment Act of 1994[9] ranks first among them. Other welcome additions to Cambodia's legislative portfolio have been the Financial Law of 1995, setting up a tax system, and the Law of the Supreme Council of the Judiciary. Several other important pieces of legislation, such as a company law (a law governing forms of doing business), an arbitration and commercial court law, a law governing the performance of commercial contracts, and an intellectual property law are now in draft form. The enactment of the draft legislation will complete Cambodia's legislative and judicial structure for regulation of commercial activities. However, pending enactment of these draft laws, the combination of the SOC laws and decrees and the laws enacted by the National Assembly provide the necessary, though minimal, framework for doing business in Cambodia.

Business Opportunities for Foreign Investors in Cambodia

The Cambodian government is eager for foreign investment and is in the process of creating the legal infrastructure required to ensure investor confidence. Several recent commercial laws, including a Foreign Investment law containing many incentives to foreign investment, have been passed, and more are in draft form. The dispute resolution system is being restructured and its personnel re-trained and upgraded, also with an eye to assuring foreign businessmen that their investments will be protected.

A.07

The challenge facing the government lies as much in the realms of politics and economics as in the legal arena. As all the world knows, the Cambodian government and economy were all but destroyed in the 1970s by the Khmer

Cambodia

Rouge's attempt to create an agrarian communist utopia within the boundaries of Cambodia. From one to two million human lives were lost through murder or starvation during the Khmer Rouge regime. Even after the fall of the Khmer Rouge government in 1979, a vicious civil war continued for another twelve years. Not until late 1991 did the warring Khmer factions agree to lay down their arms and embark upon the reconstruction of their country.

Pursuant to the peace treaty signed by the parties to the civil war, United Nations peacekeepers, accompanied by platoons of civil servants, occupied Cambodia in 1992 with the purpose of setting the country on the path to reconstruction. In 1993 U.N.- supervised elections were held to elect a government that would establish a functioning liberal democracy backed by a viable market economy. The U.N. process was, on the whole, successful. A representative government was selected by the Cambodian people in elections that were free and fair. That government will remain in office until 1997, when new elections are scheduled.

On the economic front, the challenge facing the Cambodian government is massive. The state of Cambodia was teetering on the edge of bankruptcy at the time of the U.N. take-over and is still subsisting largely on loans from international donors.[10] The World Bank and the Asian Development Bank are among the major contributors to the Cambodian treasury, as are the countries of Japan, France, Australia and the United States. The on-going low-level war with the Khmer Rouge remains a significant drain on the government's meager finances.

A.08   Agriculture comprises 50 per cent of Cambodia's gross domestic product and accounts for 80–85 per cent of its labor. Exports consist largely of rubber and timber. Tires are the only significant domestically manufactured product. Illegal exports of lumber and gemstones are said to be substantial.[11] Until 1991 Cambodia relied on the Soviet Union for import of capital goods, machinery and oil. Until 1993 the private sector in Cambodia was virtually non-existent. The arrival of the United Nations artificially stimulated the growth of a private sector, which continues to function, in reduced form, even now that the U.N. has gone.[12]

The Cambodian economy has the potential for growth.[13] Agricultural exports to the rapidly industrializing nations in Southeast Asia could become substantial once the landmines are cleared from the fields. Several foreign companies are drilling for oil and natural gas. The potential for growth in tourism is enormous. The infrastructure for tourism, including hotels and restaurants, developed largely because of the surge of growth in the service sector engendered by the United Nations' 18-month tenure. Plans for restoration of Angkor Wat and the many other magnificent and beautiful historical and religious sites of Cambodia are underway. Cambodia's coastal areas are marked by scenic beaches. The majority of these prospective tourist sites are in areas securely held by the Phnom Penh government. The prospect for a boom in tourism is good.[14]

Business Opportunities for Foreign Investors in Cambodia

The growth of the private sector is critical to both political and economic development in Cambodia. The government has taken steps to ensure that the necessary growth occurs. In 1993, the first year in which Cambodia had a private sector worthy of the name, the Ministry of Commerce had registered more than 500 trading companies. Also in 1993 the port of Sihanoukville (Kompong Som) was opened to international shipping and licensing regulations were removed from most commodities for trading by registered companies. These measures, combined with low customs duties, have given Cambodia a foothold as a transit point for regional trade.[15]

In Phnom Penh, as in Sihanoukville, the Cambodian private sector is lively   A.09
and growing. Activity in Phnom Penh focuses on the service sector: the city is filled with hotels, restaurants, photocopying establishments and computer stores. Most foreign investment is targeted on Phnom Penh and Sihanoukville. These urban centers account for only 15–20 per cent of the Cambodian population. In the long term, the task for the government is not only to attract foreign investment and its accompanying private sector activity, but to expand it to the provinces, where the vast majority of the Cambodian people live.

The government has realized a modest degree of success in attracting foreign investment. By mid-1995, Cambodia's Council for the Development of Cambodia (CDC), the Government's "One Stop Service" investment agency, had approved foreign direct investment projects valued at more than US$ 2 billion. These investments were approved pursuant to Cambodia's 1994 Foreign Investment Law, which, in an effort to redress Cambodia's trade deficit by attracting export-oriented manufacturing and light industry, features such attractions as full import duty exemptions for export-oriented projects, free repatriation of profits, tax holidays of up to eight years, and a nine per cent corporate income tax.

On the political front, the Royal Cambodian Government has defied all predictions of disaster by preserving a fragile coalition between two ruling parties, presided over by a constitutional monarch, King Norodom Sihanouk. The 1993 elections produced a three-way split between a royalist liberal democratic party, known by its French acronym of FUNCINPEC, which received roughly 45 per cent of the vote, the newly-reformed and newly democratic former socialist party known as the CPP (Cambodian People's Party), which received 38 per cent of the vote, and the Buddhist Liberal Democratic party (BLDP), which received approximately 10 per cent of the vote. The Khmer Rouge, which had been one of the original parties to the peace talks, refused to take part in the U.N.-supervised elections and returned to its stronghold in the jungle along the Thai-Cambodian border.[16]

FUNCINPEC, as the party of cosmopolitan expatriates, acquired the portfolios of ministries such as Foreign Affairs and Finance that dealt with the world outside of Cambodia's territorial boundaries. The CPP retained control of ministries concerned with the internal administration of the country. During the intervening two and a half years, the balance of power has slowly shifted towards the CPP.

A.10   By late 1995 the balance of power had shifted so significantly in favor of the CPP that FUNCINPEC, originally expected to take the lead in implementing liberal democratic reforms, began to align itself with the CPP on almost all major issues. A concurrent development has been the silencing and, in some cases, the expulsion from the National assembly, of the few remaining critics of the Government. The resulting absence of a loyal opposition has led to a noticeable increase in the authoritarianism of the Executive Branch of the Government.

A question in the minds of many observers of the Cambodian political scene is whether the CPP is confident enough in the degree of power it presently wields to let matters rest until the scheduled 1997 elections, or whether the CPP will attempt to consolidate its power by a coup d'etat prior to the elections. Because the CPP controls the armed forces, such a coup could be almost bloodless. What such a coup would do to investor confidence and whether the Cambodian Government's loans from large international investors would be withdrawn are open questions.

Certainly the CPP understands the need for a stable political and economic environment to assure foreign businessmen that their investments in Cambodia will be protected. Authoritarian regimes have, in other countries, generated conditions conducive to economic growth and development. The question is whether the CPP, acting alone, would be capable of achieving these results.

Cambodia and the International Economic Community

A.11   To understand the current status of Cambodian commercial law, one must also be aware of Cambodia's developing relationship with the world-wide economic community and how that relationship might affect Cambodia's economy. That, in turn, requires an examination of Cambodia's relationship with its ASEAN neighbors (Indonesia, Malaysia, Singapore, the Philippines, Thailand, Brunei and most recently Vietnam), Cambodia's relationship with international economic institutions including the World Bank, the Asian Development Bank (ADB) and the International Monetary Fund (IMF), and Cambodia's relationship to one of the remaining so-called super-powers, the United States.

Cambodia and ASEAN

A.12   It has been nearly 30 years since Cambodia was first asked to become a member of ASEAN. That first invitation, however, was rejected by then-Prince Norodom Sihanouk whose foreign policy was moving Cambodia closer to both China and Vietnam. Lon Nol's ascendancy in 1970 might have provided Cambodia with an opportunity to join ASEAN, but political instability prevented any such move. Of course, Cambodia's tortured political history from 1975 to 1989, including the nightmarish rule of Pol Pot and the Vietnamese occupation after his downfall, precluded any thought of ASEAN membership.

The UN-sponsored elections in 1993, however, changed Cambodia's political structure and brightened prospects for entry into the ASEAN community. In fact, in July 1994 Foreign Minister Norodom Sirivudh went to Singapore for talks concerning membership in ASEAN. Thereafter, in January 1995, Cambodia's new Foreign Minister, Ung Huot, on behalf of the Cambodian government, agreed to be bound by the Treaty of Amity and Cooperation which is a predicate to membership in ASEAN.[17]

Cambodia took its first concrete step toward full membership in ASEAN by attaining observer status in August, 1995. Observer status in ASEAN amounts to an opportunity for Cambodia to prepare itself for full membership without being burdened by substantial costs incurred by full ASEAN members. Prince Ranariddh recently commented on the significance of observer status, noting that "we have a stake, a desire and an interest in ASEAN. It is in the observership that we must learn the rules and the nature of the game."[18] There is as yet no timetable for Cambodia's full membership in ASEAN, a status that will demand from the government substantial financial and diplomatic resources as well as further industrial development.

There is no question that ASEAN status would greatly change both the perception and economic reality of Cambodia's economic development. First, as noted, admission to ASEAN would in and of itself signal a significant growth in Cambodia's economy. It would also require Cambodia to open its markets to products produced by other ASEAN nations and to lower its tariffs by 2003 as a member of the ASEAN Free Trade Area (AFTA).

Cambodia's Membership in ASEAN and its Effect on Relations with the United States

Cambodian membership in ASEAN may also have a substantial beneficial effect on its economic relationship with the United States. As a first order of priority, ASEAN membership is likely to accelerate Cambodia's receipt of Most Favored Nation (MFN) status from the United States. MFN status prohibits the duty charged on the goods of the MFN from being any higher than duties charged on goods from other nations. Moreover, if the United States subsequently enters into a tariff agreement with another country for lower rates, the MFN automatically enjoys the benefit of that agreement with the third country.[19]

For many of the same political reasons that have opperated to prevent Cambodian entry into ASEAN, the United States has heretofore refused to accord MFN status to Cambodia. The factors most commonly cited by both ASEAN and the United States as grounds for refusing to deal with Cambodia have been the Communist ideology of its government and its lack of a market economy. Of course, the U.N.-sponsored elections and Cambodia's new constitution and political structure have changed all that. There is now growing support in the United States for granting MFN status to Cambodia. Still, political resistance to such status remains.[20] Cambodia's admission to ASEAN would be the equivalent of a bill of political and economic good health from some of the most vibrant and rapidly-growing economies in the world.

Even more valuable than MFN membership, and also more likely once Cambodia has achieved ASEAN status, would be the receipt of Generalized System of Preferences (GSP) status from the United States. The United States, through its GSP program, allows certain developing countries the privilege of exporting goods to the United States while paying reduced tariffs or no tariffs at all. This status has historically been conferred by the United States only on developing countries which it views as friends and allies. These reduced tariffs apply not just to goods manufactured wholly in the qualifying developing country, but also to goods not manufactured wholly in the qualifying country, so long as 35 per cent or more of the value of those goods is attributable to components from or the cost of processing in the qualifying country. This 35 per cent "rule of origin" under the United States GSP program is of inestimable value to a developing country like Cambodia which produces few manufactured goods of its own but rather functions as an assembly point for manufactured goods whose major components are manufactured elsewhere.

A.14 It is at this point that the benefits of prospective Cambodian membership in ASEAN become inextricably intertwined with the benefits of prospective receipt of GSP status from the United States. Without membership in ASEAN, Cambodia would find it difficult to receive the full benefits of a grant of GSP status from the United States. Because Cambodia manufactures few if any of the components of the export goods it assembles and then ships to the United States, it is not likely that even 35 per cent of the appraised value of these goods at the time of their arrival in the United States can be attributed to Cambodia. However, under GSP regulations, contributions made by any member of a regional trading organization such as ASEAN are counted toward the required 35 per cent total for an import from a particular member of the trading organization.[21] Thus, if the value of a component from Singapore is 25 per cent of the appraised value at the time of arrival in the United States, and the value of the processing or assembling in Cambodia is 10 per cent, the goods in question, when exported from Cambodia to the United States, would qualify for preferential tariff treatment under the GSP program.

When all is said and done and the complications of trade calculations are stripped away, the bottom line benefit for Cambodia of membership in

ASEAN combined with GSP status from the United States may be enormous. Estimates are that the current duties of 50 per cent and more charged by the United States on Cambodian goods would drop to as low as 2–4 per cent and, in some cases, to nothing.[22]

Cambodia and Other World Banking Institutions

The fate of Cambodian economic development must also be viewed in light   A.15
of its relationship to regional and world banking institutions that have invested substantially in Cambodia and will help shape its destiny. While a short chapter on Cambodia is not the place to detail Cambodia's complex relations with world banking institutions, a brief note on Cambodia's relationships to the International Monetary Fund (IMF), the World Bank, and the Asian Development Bank (ADB) is instructive.

The IMF

The IMF assists member states experiencing balance of payments difficulties.   A.16
The IMF was established after World War II to help stabilize monetary exchange policies of countries throughout the world. Presently, virtually every country in the world, including Cambodia, belongs to the IMF. The IMF looks at a country's monetary policy, its exchange rate, and its budget policy to insure a coherent economic strategy. For Cambodia, this has translated into loans totalling nearly $130 million.

Thus, the IMF will continue to monitor closely Cambodian monetary and economic reforms and adjust its support accordingly. IMF policies might dramatically affect how other economic institutions support Cambodia. As Joshua Charap, an American economist and resident representative of the IMF in Cambodia, noted: "The World Bank usually does not go ahead in the absence of a Fund program. A lot of donors look to see that the Fund (IMF) says the government policies are appropriate."[23]

The World Bank

The World Bank's legal programs in Cambodia are of very recent origin.   A.17
They are targeted on the legislative process, specifically on legislation in the commercial and economic areas. A major program of assistance to secondary education in Cambodia is also in the offing.

The Asian Development Bank

The ADB has loaned Cambodia $120 million and has another $150 million in   A.18
loans committed for 1996 and 1997. Over the long term, $2 billion in ADB aid is projected for Cambodia. That aid, however, is not guaranteed and will be influenced heavily by events in Cambodia. Thus, it was recently reported that ADB was concerned by the apparent lack of vitality of the Cambodian economy and the fact that it was "only being propped up by massive infu-

sions of foreign aid". The ADB has also been concerned with "lack of programs to create jobs, continuing violence, overlap in various aid projects and the increase in purported human rights violations".

Nonetheless, the ADB seems intent on continuing its assistance to Cambodia. As Linda Tsao Yang, the U.S. Ambassador to ADB noted:

> "(Overall) I think we're pretty impressed with the government's basic economic policies, its fiscal policies, its monetary policy and its controls. This country is in a really difficult position, even among developing countries. The real challenge is whether it's going to be able to mobilize the revenues necessary to cover its tightened down expenditure."[24]

II. Laws and Institutions Affecting Business and Commercial Activities

Commitment to a Free Market Economy

A.19 Cambodia's commitment to a free market economy accessible to foreign investors is reflected in recent ministerial decisions. In March of 1996 the Council of Ministers formally decided to align Cambodia's laws in the business and commercial areas with those of other ASEAN nations. Knowledgeable insiders report that the ministers explicitly recognized that their decision would require revision of almost all of the Ministry of Commerce's French-influenced legal drafts to ensure that the future statutes, discussed below, would be compatible with those of Cambodia's major trading partners in the Anglo-American legal tradition, such as Malaysia and Singapore.

Recent legislative pronouncements have struck the same theme. For example, the Financial Law for 1995 provides a mechanism for the government to privatize public assets and establishes a Commission for the Privatization of Public Enterprises.[25] Most critically, the brevity, tone and simplicity of Cambodia's Law on the Investment of the Kingdom of Cambodia (hereinafter the Investment Law) reflect a desire on the part of the Royal Cambodian Government (RCG) to foster confidence among foreign investors.

The Foreign Investment Law

A.20 First and foremost, the Investment Law seeks to streamline investment procedures by creating the Council for the Development of Cambodia (CDC) as the "sole and one-stop service organization responsible for the rehabilitation, development and the oversight of investment activities".[26] Moreover, a 45 day deadline is imposed on the RCG to respond to requests for approval of foreign investment,[27] and failure to meet the deadline may result in criminal sanctions imposed against government officials.[28] The CDC and the investment bureaucracy generally will be discussed in Section B of this chapter.

Investor Guarantees and Incentives

In addition, the Investment Law is laden with investor guarantees and incentives aimed at encouraging the flow of capital into the country. With respect to the former, the Investment Law guarantees that all investors will be treated in a "non-discriminatory manner"[29], that the RCG "shall not undertake a nationalization policy which adversely affects private properties"[30], that price controls will not be imposed[31], and that foreign currencies will be available for purchase within Cambodia and useable to pay obligations incurred in connection with any investment.[32]   **A.21**

With respect to the former, the Investment Law identifies preferred areas of investment including, technology, job creation, exports, tourism, agriculture, energy, physical infra-structure, and the environment, and provides incentives for investments in these areas as well as for investment in "other such important fields."[33] Incentives for investment in these areas include: a 9 per cent cap on corporate tax rates for natural resources exploration; corporate tax holidays of up to 8 years; non-taxation on the distribution of "dividends and profits" resulting from the investment; and, a 100 per cent import duty exemption on materials used for investment in certain areas (primarily export-oriented projects, tourism-related projects, and projects designated by the CDC as Special Promotion Zone investments).[34] In addition, foreign investors are granted a 100 per cent exemption from export taxes. Finally, liberal policies are detailed permitting foreign nationals to work in Cambodia.[35]

Limits on Investors

Despite the apparent simplicity and incentive-based nature of the Investment Law, investors in Cambodia should not fail to recognize limitations on foreign investment and the bureaucracy that has grown up around the operation of the CDC. Key limitations within the Investment Law include: **A.22**

1. Investment incentives are not assignable or transferrable.[36]
2. 51 per cent of the ownership of land necessary for investment must be vested in Cambodian citizens or legal entities deemed to be citizens of Cambodia. Foreign investors, however, may lease land for up to 70 years and, if permitted by law, may, in rare cases, own land or personal property in Cambodia.[37]
3. Employment of foreign nationals is limited to certain management

personnel, industry experts, and family members.[38] In addition, there must be a showing that the expertise of a foreign national does not otherwise exist in Cambodia, and that training to develop such expertise is being offered to Cambodian employees. Further, an employer hiring foreign nationals must demonstrate that Cambodian staff is being promoted to "senior position . . . over time".[39]

4. Rights and benefits granted the investor by the CDC may be withdrawn if the investor "violates or fails to comply with the conditions stipulated by the Council (CDC)".[40]

The Investment Bureaucracy

A.23   As noted, the simplicity of the Cambodian Investment Law may be deceiving. In fact, a commercial lawyer practicing in Phnom Penh noted that the "absence of the 'fineprint' of a sub-decree, which would enable potential investors to understand the criteria applied by the Cambodia Investment Board (the body within the CDC that oversees private sector development) in reviewing an investment application and thus structure their applications to secure maximum benefits was a point of serious criticism."[41] In response, the government recently issued a sub-decree detailing the structure of the CDC and the duties of each of its departments.

The Commercial Registry Law

A.24   Another building block of the Cambodian legal structure for regulation of commerce is the Commercial Registry Law,[42] enacted in mid-1995 as a companion to the Chamber of Commerce Law (discussed below, in the section detailing Cambodia's Business Assistance Programs). The purpose of the Registry law is to obtain and make available to the government and the public the information that the government needs to regulate entities doing business within its borders and that the public needs in order to do business with these entities.[43]

Virtually all persons doing business in Cambodia, ranging from the largest corporations ("moral" persons) to individuals selling goods in markets ("physical" persons), are required to register with the Ministry of Commerce fifteen days prior to the opening of their business.[44] It is anticipated that the function of maintaining the commercial registry will eventually be transferred to the control of a new institution, to be called the Commercial Court, which is still in the planning stages.[45]

Persons doing business are required to submit declarations containing certain specified information to the Registry. The information in question is that typically required to be available to the government and the public in industrialized democracies. Thus, a commercial enterprise must provide to the Registry its name and address, the names of its directors and shareholders, the capital contributions of shareholders and the names of authorized signatories.[46] This information is to be published by the Clerk of the Registry in an official journal.[47] Also required is additional information such as patents and trademarks held by the business in question, judgments for and against the business entity, including judgments of bankruptcy, mortgages on its real property and liens on its assets.[48] Once a properly-completed declaration has been submitted, the Registry's clerk will issue to the commercial enterprise in question a certificate with a registration number.

Merchants or directors of companies who fail to file within the prescribed time limit, or who file incomplete declarations, shall be fined 50,000 to 500,000 riels.[49] Merchants or directors of companies who file incomplete declarations "in bad faith" shall be imprisoned from one to five years and fined one to 10 million riels.[50]

The Commercial Registration law also sets certain standards for doing business in Cambodia. These standards, such as keeping accounting records, are those that would be complied with in any event by any respectable commercial enterprise.[51]

Draft Commercial Code

The Laws of the Commercial Registry and the Chambers of Commerce   A.25
constitute Books One and Six, respectively, of the future Cambodian Commercial Code and are the only portions of that Code that have, as yet, been enacted. The subject matter of Books Two through Five is as follows: Book Two — the Law on Business Organizations; Book Three — the Law on Commercial Contracts; Book Four — the Law on Appointment of a Receiver and Liquidation of Assets; Book Five — Law on Settlement of Legal Disputes and Commercial Jurisdiction. The draft of Book Five contains the framework for a system of commercial arbitration in Cambodia, reviewed in the discussion of dispute resolution immediately following this inventory of Cambodian commercial law.[52]

Drafts of Books Two through Five of the Commercial Code had been prepared by French advisors to the Ministry of Commerce and at least one of them, the draft Law on Business Organizations, had begun its progress through the complex Cambodian legislative process. However, the decision of the Council of Ministers in March of 1996 to review all pending commercial legislation for compatibility with the laws of Cambodia's trading partners in the Anglo-American legal tradition has slowed the drafting and law-making process.

The heart of the draft Commercial Code is, of course, the law on Commercial Contracts. At the time of the Council of Ministers' decision, more than two years had been spent on the drafting of a Commercial Contracts Law that virtually replicated the corresponding provisions of the French Commercial Code. That draft is now under review for conformity with the commercial contract laws of other ASEAN nations. The same is true of the draft of Book Four — the Law on Appointment of Receiver and Liquidation of Debts.

The outcome of this battle of the drafts remains to be seen. However, the odds at the moment appear to be heavily weighted in favor of the eventual predominance of Anglo-American, not French, legal concepts in the fields of business and commercial law.

Draft Law on Business Organizations

A.26 Passage of a draft Law on Business Organizations, often referred to as The Company Law, had been expected early in 1996. However, that draft Law had been heavily in the French tradition. The Council of Ministers' March, 1996 decision to review all of the drafts in the business and commercial areas for conformity with the laws of other ASEAN nations caused withdrawal of the French draft. An American advisor to the Ministry of Commerce has completed a new draft Company Law.[53]

The merits of this clash between French and Anglo-American models for a Company Law are difficult to determine. What can at present be said is that certain French organizational forms of doing business are arguably not conducive to the internal growth of a company, to good relations between owners and management, or to effective decision-making. The recent travails of Airbus are a case in point. From this perspective, it appears that a company law in the Anglo-American tradition would be more conducive to the growth of business in Cambodia.

Cambodian Contract Law

A.27 Pending enactment of Book Three of the Commercial Code, contract law in Cambodia is governed by *Decree #38 D Referring to Contract and Other Liabilities* (Decree 38), adopted in 1988. Because the National Assembly has not enacted any laws governing contracts since the formation of the Royal Government in 1993, Decree 38 remains in effect and governs Cambodian contract law.[54] The language of Decree 38 is similar to some of the contract law provisions found in the French Civil Code, but it also has unique aspects. Because of its importance, Decree 38 is discussed here at some length.

Consistent with other contract laws around the world, Decree 38 defines a contract as an agreement, freely entered into by two or more people or legal entities, which affects their rights and obligations.[55] In addition, a contract, under Cambodian law, is treated as a private "law", applying only to the parties.[56] Decree 38 also defines the elements necessary for a valid, enforceable contract and outlines what remedies, if any, are available when a party fails to fulfill its obligation under the contract. Decree 38 also provides specific provisions for certain types of contracts, including contracts for the sale of goods, the loan of money, employment, and transport of goods or passengers.

Parties to a Cambodian Contract

Under Article 1 of Decree 38, a party to a contract may be either a natural person or a legal entity.[57] Decree 38 does not define these two terms, but under general contract law, a "natural person" is a human being (*i.e.* a real person) and a "legal entity" can be any one of the various forms of business organization such as a partnership, a corporation, or a limited liability company.

A.28

Under Article 1, if the party is a legal entity, then the contract can be entered into by a representative of that entity.[58] Article 1 does not indicate whether an authorized representative or agent of a natural person also can enter into a contract on behalf of the natural person. It is quite possible that authority to do so is implicit or that it was omitted inadvertently from Article 1. Nevertheless, until the National Assembly passes legislation revising or superseding Decree 38, or a functioning Cambodian judiciary determines that representatives of natural persons can sign contracts on behalf of natural persons, this uncertainty will remain. Accordingly, anyone entering into a contract under Cambodian law with a natural person should insist that the natural person, rather than his or her representative, sign the contract.

Formation of a Contract Under Cambodian Law

Under Cambodian law, a valid contract is simply a contract which is legally enforceable by the parties through Cambodia's legal system.[59] If a contract is *not* valid, the court will not use its power to enforce it.

A.29

The five elements necessary to form a valid, enforceable contract under Cambodian contract law are as follows: agreement, consideration,[60] capacity, legality, and formality. These elements of Cambodian contract law are analogous to the general contract law provisions found in both the civil law and common law traditions. Each element will be briefly reviewed below.

Under Decree 38, a contract which does not satisfy the five elements of a valid contract is either "void" or "voidable". A void contract is without any legal effect and cannot be enforced through the legal system. A voidable contract is a contract that, depending on the circumstances, one or both of the parties may choose to cancel or void.[61]

The Agreement

Article 1 of Decree 38 defines a contract "as a freewill agreement between two or more persons". Thus, an agreement is an explicit requirement of a

A.30

valid contract under Cambodian law. Under Articles 3 & 6, the agreement also must be "real". In other words, the agreement must contain a valid offer and acceptance, including any essential terms of the contract.

For example, Article 3 of Decree 38 specifically provides that to be valid, a contract must have "a subject matter that is certain". Article 17 of Decree 38 also provides that, for the sale of goods, "every contract dealing with items used in commercial trade shall clearly and separately describe the items according to their quality and quantity". Thus, an agreement which lacks these essential terms may be invalid. In certain circumstances, however, the court can supply or construe certain terms of a contract. For example, under Article 23, the court can interpret "unclear terms" of a contract "according to common practice or custom of the place where the contract has been made" as long as the custom or practice does not conflict with a specific provision of Decree 38.

Article 23 of Decree 38 also provides that any "ambiguity" in the contract will be interpreted in favor of the party who owes the obligation under the contract. Article 23 calls for construing any ambiguity in a contract in favor of the "debtor". To understand who is a debtor, it is necessary to look at Article 30 which states that "each party to a contract is a *debtor* regarding the obligations to be executed [under the terms of the contract]".

Finally, the agreement must be voluntary and must *not* be the result of mistake, duress, or fraud.[62] If no valid agreement is formed, the contract is voidable.[63]

Consideration

A.31 Traditionally, *common law* jurisdictions required that all contracts must have consideration to be valid and enforceable. In the United States, the modern approach is to define consideration as a "detriment to the promisee that is bargained for by the promisor". Under the *civil law* tradition, a contract, in certain circumstances, may be enforced without consideration. Under Cambodian law, it is unclear whether consideration is a requirement for a valid, enforceable contract. Consideration is not explicitly listed as a required element in Decree 38. Under Article 12 of Decree 38, however, inadequate consideration is grounds for rescinding a contract.

Under general contract law principles, *consideration* is generally defined as (1) the bargained-for exchange (2) of something of legal value. Consideration may be exchanged in the form of money, goods, services, or other property. Consideration, however, need not necessarily be something of economic value to be legally sufficient, valid consideration.

Capacity

A.32 Under Cambodian law, all parties to a contract must have the *capacity* to enter into a contract. Minors (persons under the age of 18), the mentally ill, and those otherwise legally restrained from administering their business affairs are generally held *not* to have the capacity to enter into a contract.[64] Minors, however, may enter into a valid contract with the consent of their legal guardian or into a contract for a basic necessity of life, even without the consent of a guardian.[65] Contracts in which a party lacks capacity are enforceable only by the party lacking capacity.[66] If one party lacks capacity, then the contract is voidable by the party who lacks capacity or his or her legal guardian.[67]

Legality

Under Cambodian law, *legality* means that the purpose of the contract must be legal and must not be against public policy. Specifically, Article 5 of Decree 38 provides that a contract will be invalid if it "is illegal, not consistent with public order or good custom . . . [or] not consistent with social interests or principles of social ethics". Moreover, Article 3 provides that a valid contract must be "lawful and consistent with public order and good custom". Under Cambodian law, if the contract is illegal or contrary to public policy, it is void.[68]

A.33

Formality

Under Article 4 of Decree 38, a valid contract must be in the form required by law. For example, Article 4 requires that any contract "regarding money or item(s) worth more than five thousand riels must be in writing". Other contracts, such as a contract for an interest-bearing loan[69] or a contract of suretyship,[70] also must be in writing. Under Cambodian law, all contracts which are *not* in the form required by law are void.[71]

A.34

In sum, the elements of a valid contract under Cambodian law are, in general, quite similar to the contract law principles of many legal traditions.

Breach of Contract

If one party fails to perform his or her obligation under the contract, the other party may file a civil lawsuit asking the court to enforce the contract through the judicial system. As noted, currently in Cambodia, there is a proposal to set up a Commercial Court to hear and decide these types of lawsuits. In addition, Cambodia has a long history of non-judicial dispute resolution or conciliation. Historically, Khmer culture has embraced a system of conflict resolution based on personal, family, social, and religious values and customs.

A.35

In Cambodia, the judicial system is just now reemerging from the chaos and tragedy of the past 20 years. As the Cambodian courts re-establish themselves, they will resume their role as the enforcement mechanism for resolving contractual disputes. At present, however, the court system is woefully under-trained, under-staffed, and under-financed, severely limiting the judicial system's ability to process, resolve, and enforce judgments relating to contractual disputes.

Finally, under Article 25 of Decree 38, a lawsuit must be filed within five years from the date of performance or the date the contract was formed or it will be time barred. If the defendant is certified by the local authorities as absent from his or her residence, the time period is tolled.[72] The statute of limitations can be asserted by the defendant and, if not, then the "[c]ourt shall do it instead".[73]

In a contract case, it appears that a Cambodian judge typically would require the breaching party to pay monetary damages. The court will award an amount of money sufficient to put the non-breaching party in the same position that he or she would have been in had the contract been fulfilled. Although not specifically mentioned in Decree 38, monetary damages generally will include any reasonably foreseeable damages resulting from the breach. Under Article 24 of Decree 38, a party is required to "satisfy his obligations under the contract by payment from personal and real properties available now and in the future".

Paying Taxes in Cambodia

A.36 As might be expected, Cambodia's developing economy has brought with it a variety of tax laws and mechanisms for their enforcement. Since the tax structure remains a work-in-progress, rates and procedures are subject to change and it is critical that practitioners and business persons check carefully with local counsel to determine applicable taxes. Nonetheless, a general tax structure is now is place and, as of December 1995, can be summarized as follows.

The current tax structure is largely defined by the Financial Laws of 1994 and 1995. These laws, however, must be read in conjunction with international treaties to which Cambodia is a party and other laws passed by Cambodia's National Assembly, most notably the Investment Law detailed above, to determine exemptions that might apply to a particular transaction.

Income or Wage Tax

A.37 Chapter III of the Financial Law for 1995 mandates promulgation of an income tax to increase budget revenue.[74] The tax is levied monthly on all income, whether it be paid in cash or any other form, for services provided in Cambodia. The tax must be paid on benefits as well as wages. Moreover, income received for work in both the public and private sectors is subject to the income tax.

Persons or entities subject to the tax include residents of Cambodia (regardless of whether they are working in Cambodia or abroad), and non-residents of Cambodia providing services in Cambodia. Employers are required to deduct the tax directly from the employees' wages and to pay them directly to the state treasury.[75]

Exemptions from the income tax include:

1. repayment of certain loans spent on vocational training by employees under the order of and for the benefit of employers;
2. severance payments to employees required by the Labor Code;
3. travel allowance payments (not including payments made by employers for overseas expenses for the benefit of the employee)[76];
4. work supplies or equipment received from the employer;
5. those exemptions provided for by international treaty or convention or by acts of the National Assembly. For example, pursuant to the Investment Law, the corporate tax rate is limited to 9 per cent and corporations may be exempted altogether from tax payments for up to eight years.

Finally, tax credits are available if income is also taxed in a foreign country.[77–78]

Income tax rates set forth in the 1995 Financial Law are as follows:

Income	Rate
$300–$400	5%
$401–$4,000	10%
$4,001–$8,000	15%
$8,001 and above	20%

Enterprise Profit Tax

Cambodia now imposes a monthly tax on businesses based on profits, interest, and capital gains. The so-called Enterprise Profits Tax applies to incorporated businesses, manufactuerers, and commercial enterprises with an annual turnover of 200,000,000 riel (approximately US$ 77,000). The tax also applies to service business with an annual turnover of 100,000,000 riel. Moreover, the tax is applicable to importers, exporters, businesses covered under the Investment Law, and hotels and restaurants.[79] The amount of the tax is determined by a formula taking into account profit margins and turnover. Refunds are not given in the case of a loss, but the loss may be carried forward for three years.[80]   **A.38**

It is critical that those doing business in Cambodia check carefully with the Ministry of Commerce for rates applicable to a particular business. Generally, however, corporations tend to be taxed at a flat rate of 20 per cent whereas individual businesses are taxed at progressive rates ranging from 10–30 per cent.[81]

Tax on Undeveloped Land

The 1995 Financial Law also provides for landowners to pay a 2 per cent tax on land without construction and land that has construction but is "left over"   **A.39** (presumably non-productive). The rate is 2 per cent of the fair market value of land. The 1995 Financial Law establishes a committee to identify such land, to value the land and to help resolve disputes concerning the tax.[82] In addition, a 4 per cent tax is payable on the sale of property (see Registration Tax below). Finally, a 10 per cent tax on the lease of real property based on the rental value of the lease is payable by the lessor/owner.[83]

Sales Tax (Business Turnover Tax (BTT))

A.40   A Sales Tax or Business Turnover Tax (BTT) is imposed as follows: 1 per cent of the gross income of the business, excepting service businesses which are taxed at 2 per cent of gross income and hotels, hotel-related services, massage parlors, bars, entertainment establishments, restaurants and the like, that are taxed at 10 per cent of gross income.[84]

Registration Tax

A.41   The sale of land or other "immobile assets" as well as the sale of trucks, vans, cars, motor bikes, motor boats and other seafaring vessels triggers a so-called Property Transfer Tax. The rate of the tax is 4 per cent of the fair market value of the item for land, buildings, cars, trucks, and vans and 2 per cent for motorcycles. Generally, the purchaser is responsible for the payment of the Property Transfer Tax unless the parties agree otherwise. Exemptions exist for sales ordered by the government and sales by public utilities and other charitible organizatinos. In addition, a tax in an amount set by statute must be paid on the registration of various legal documents.[85]

Business License Fee (Patent Tax)

A.42   This Business License Fee tax is levid on most buinesses and those rendering professional services. The tax is based on the estimated or actual turnover during the previous calendar year. The tax for new businesses is based on an estimate by the taxing authority. Note that farmers are not subject to the tax. The rate of the tax depends upon the business or industry being taxed. For example, Class 1 businesses (manufacutring and handicrafts) are taxed at the rate of 0.5 per cent; Class 2 businesses (fisheries, construction, transport, small services, restaurants and trade) are taxed at the rate of 0.8 per cent and Class 3 businesses (primarily service businesses) are taxed at the rate of 1.0 per cent.[86]

Importing Goods into Cambodia

A.43   As noted, the Investment Law exempts payment of certain import duties to encourage the flow of foreign capital and goods into Cambodia. Nonetheless, Cambodia requires payments of various import and export duties on most items. With respect to the former, a tariff is placed on all imports pursuant to the Harmonized System of Classification effective September 16, 1993. Rates are *ad valorem* and, as noted in the *Cambodian Investment Handbook* published by the Ministry of Commerce, "are levied on a cost-insurance-freight (c.i.f) basis".[87] However, certain items accounting for nearly 80 per cent of Cambodia's imports are taxed at a fixed rate set by the government. These include cigarettes, beer, petroleum products, motor cycles, soft drinks, televisions, video cassette recorders and radio cassette players.[88] Overall, there are basically four import duty rates: 7 per cent for essential consumer goods; 15 per cent for machinery and equipment; 35 per cent for non-essential consumer goods; and, 50 per cent for luxury consumer goods, cigarettes and alcolholic beverages.

In addition, export duties on levied on various items. For example, a 10 per cent rate is applied to many animals and wook products. A 50 per cent rate is appllicable to certain cut flowers, perfumes and chemicals.[89] The duty is an *ad valorem* tax on the f.o.b. value of the item.

Cambodia recently has taken measures to scrutinize more carefully the nature, quality and quantity of goods imported into the country. The result likely will be that certain foreign exporters will pay more in the way of tariff and import taxes, but the heightened scrutiny may also increase the quality of imports and foster fair competition among foreign investors.[90]

Specifically, Cambodia has hired the Swiss company, Societe Generale de Surveillance (SGS), to conduct pre-shipment inspections on goods at their site of origin. SGS currently conducts similar operations for other ASEAN countries. Announcing the program, the RCG issued "Regulations on the Implementation of Pre-Shipment Inspection Services", dated September 8, 1995 and Declaration No 321, dated October 8, 1995. SGS inspection will verify the quality, quantity and value of the goods. Based on SGS findings, the relevant Cambodian ministry will assess levies and taxes. Goods valued at less than US $5,000 are exempted from pre-shipment expenses as are certain goods listed in directives from the Ministry of Commerce, including some gem stones, certain publications, livestock, personal effects and humanitarian aid.[91]

Labor and Employment Law

A new Labor Code may soon be enacted by the RCG. Pending such legisla- **A.44** tion, however, the State of Cambodia's Labor Law for 1992 (hereinafter SOC Labor Law) remains in effect today. The SOC Labor Code is a clear response to the forced labor that led to massive starvation during the time of Pol Pot and represents an effort by the Cambodian government to protect the rights of both employers and workers. Since the Labor Code aims to define the relations between employers and a wide range of workers including indus-trial workers, artisans, service employees, agricultural workers and transportation workers, it is likely applicable to most employees of foreign investors in Cambodia.[92]

The Code is a long detailed document which defines various kinds of employees within Cambodia, the nature of labor contracts, working conditions for men, women, children and agricultural employees, conditions upon which foreign labor may be brought into the country[93], health and safety regulations for laborers, laborers' right to organize, mechanisms for resolving labor disputes,[94] and penalties that may be imposed on employers. Only the Code's salient features can be outlined here.

1. Forced, non-voluntary labor is absolutely prohibited.[95]
2. All business enterprises must register with the Ministry of Labor and Social Action, detailing the nature of the enterprise, its physical plant, the nature of its work and the nature of the work force.[96]
3. Employers with labor forces of 10 or more employees are also required to file with the Ministry of Labor and Social Action "internal rules" which set forth in detail the conditions under which the laborers work, including their wages and benefits.[97]
4. All laborers, except seasonal agricultural workers, are required to possess a "labor book" identifying jobs held and wages received. The labor book is issued by the labor inspector of the province or region along with a laborer identity card.[98]
5. Contracts between employers and employees may be oral or written. Employment contracts for a specified time, however, must be in writing. The lawful length of an employment contract takes into account such factors as the amount of time an employee will be separated from his or her family.[99]
6. The Labor Code sets forth grounds for termination of employment contracts and specifies periods of advance notice required to terminate a contract (generally, the longer an employee has worked, the more notice is required.)[100]
7. Chapter Six of the Labor Law details minimal working conditions. For example, "labor-charges (wages) must be adequate to assure every laborer a standard of living consistent with human dignity". Any agreement, oral or written, violating that standard is void. Other specific articles of Chapter 6 detail minimum pay for piece work, and require that an employer make rates of pay and other working conditions known to its work force. Finally, the Labor Code requires payment of wages directly to the employee, specifies the time of payment (at least twice monthly), and prescribes procedures for the employee to bring a civil action to recover his or her wages. (There is a one year statute of limitations for complaints by employees with respect to wage payments.[101])
8. Debts of employers to employees take precedence over other debts in bankruptcy proceedings.[102]

9. Generally, work days for laborers are not to exceed eight hours, work weeks for laborers are not to exceed 48 hours, overtime is to be paid, and, in some instances, permission to extend the work week must be sought from the Ministry of Labor. A holiday at least 24 hours long is required every six days and Sundays are mandated as a day of rest. Paid vacations are also mandated.[103]

10. Special provisions define working conditions for women and children, generally requiring that a company employing women and children under 18 "should care for their dignity".[104] The Ministry of Labor and Social Action is required to detail a list of dangerous occupations from which women and children are barred from employment. Children under the age of 18 are not permitted to apprentice, but may work in a family setting under the "supervision of father, mother or guardian". 90 days paid pregnancy leave is required for women.[105]

11. General sanitation and safety measures require that businesses be maintained in a manner that protects the worker's health. Monitoring and enforcement procedures are set forth in the Code.[106]

12. Employers are required to provide health benefits for their employees and their families. The size of the enterprise, however, determines the types of benefits that are available to workers.[107]

13. Employers are responsible for all accidents occurring at work, apparently regardless of fault. Medicines, nursing care, and death benefits are all required to be paid by the employer.[108]

14. Organized representation of workers is envisioned through "personnel delegations" whose numbers, membership structure, voting rights and the like are all to be determined by the Minister of Labor and Social Action. The duties of the delegations include informing employers of worker complaints, informing the labor inspector regarding health, safety and other regulatory violations, proposing remedial measures in cases of health and safety problems, and offering advice with respect to the internal rules of business enterprises.[109] In addition, the code allows for "associations of occupations", consisting of laborers and employers engaged in the same work, whose purpose is to protect the particular occupation and its workers' interests.[110]

Intellectual Property

At the present time, Cambodia has no intellectual property law as such. **A.45** However, drafts exist of a Marks Protection Act, a Patent and Design Act, and a Copyright Act. Under the Marks Protection Act, properly registered trademarks are protected in Cambodia for a period of ten years from the filing date of the application for registration and may be renewed for an additional ten years so long as application fees are paid and there is no change made to the mark.[111] Not all marks, however, may be registered. Specifically precluded are marks which are in the public domain, marks which suggest the characteristics of the goods or service to which they relate, marks which are likely to mislead the public, or marks which are "contrary to morality or public order, customs or law".[112] The owner of a validly registered mark has the exclusive right to use the mark to distinguish the owner's goods or service.[113]

The draft Patent and Design Act, also known as the Inventions, Designs and Models Protection Act (hereinafter Patent and Design Act), mirrors the structure of the Marks Protection Act. The draft Patent and Design Act protects new or novel inventions which involve an "inventive step" and which are "industrially applicable". Generally, a "new" invention is one which could not have been anticipated by "prior art" which is defined to include "everything disclosed to the public by publication in tangible form or by oral disclosure".[114] Discoveries, scientific theories, mathematical methods, methods for doing business and methods for human or animal medical treatment are not patentable, nor are inventions "contrary to public order or morality" or biological methods for breeding plants or animals.[115] In addition, designs and models which are "new" as defined above may also be protected by registering the new design or model with the Ministry of Industry.[116]

Once a valid patent is obtained, the owner has the right to prohibit the marketing, importing or using for any purpose, any product within the scope of the patent. Patent protection, however, extends only to the commercial and not to the private use of the otherwise infringing product.[117] Civil remedies, including damages and injunctive relief, may be obtained in civil court for violation of a patent. The statute of limitations for such an action is two years. Foreigners have the same rights as Cambodian citizens under the draft Patent and Design Act.[118] However, foreigners involved in administrative or judicial proceedings under the Act must appoint a representative domiciled or maintaining a place of business in Cambodia to represent his or her interests.[119]

Finally, the draft copyright law is formally titled Law on Copyright and Related Rights (hereinafter Copyright Law). Under the Copyright Law, the author of a work enjoys, by the sole virtue of his or her creation, an exclusive incorporeal property right in the work. A work is deemed created by the mere fact of its realization, even if uncompleted, by its author. Public disclosure is thus not required in order for the copyright to come into being. All creations of the mind are covered by the draft Cambodian copyright law. The list of covered works of the mind includes:

— books, brochures and other literary writings, both artistic and scientific
— lectures, speeches, sermons

— plays and musicals
— choreography, pantomimes
— musical compositions, with or without words
— films and other works consisting of a series of animated images
— designs, paintings, architectural plans, engravings, lithographs
— graphic and typographic works
— photographs
— applied arts
— illustrations, maps, blueprints
— computer programs

Also protected, by virtue of the protection afforded the pre-existing works, are derivative works such as anthologies.

The author of a work, who is the holder of the copyright, has the exclusive **A.46** right to decide if, when, how and under what name his or her work will be divulged. The work is divulged, or made public, when it is made accessible, for the first time, by the author or with his or her consent, to a large number of persons who do not constitute a circle of closely-linked persons such as relatives or friends. Further, the author has the exclusive right to decide if, when and in what manner his or her work will be exploited. In particular, the author of a computer program and the producer of an audiovisual work have the exclusive right to rent the original or copies of their work.

The draft Cambodian copyright law does contain penalties for infringement of copyright which, if enforced, would constitute a significant deterrent. The penal sanctions for knowingly, with the intent to profit, infringing upon the copyright of another consist of a fine of ten million riels and imprisonment for a maximum of five years. Civil remedies are also envisioned: the draft law confers on the courts the power to enjoin suspected infringers from distribution and sale of the goods in dispute upon a showing of good cause to believe that irreparable harm will occur. Violation of such a court order is punishable by a maximum fine of 10 million riels. In addition, administrative remedies are provided through the customs service.

Environmental Law

Cambodia's forests and waterways are in great need of legal protection, both **A.47** in the domestic arena and internationally. Wholesale logging, both legal and illegal, threatens to destroy Cambodia's rain forest.[120] China, Laos and Thailand plan to build dams along the upper reaches of the Mekong River, threatening the destruction of the ecology built around the lower stretches of the river in Cambodia and Vietnam.[121]

Protection of the forests is addressed in the draft Law on Environmental Protection, which requires the government to assess the impact on the environment caused by the development, use and management of each natural resource.[122] Such environmental impact plans would be required for projects involving use of development of specific listed resource, including biodiversity, fishery, forestry, marine and coastal resources, water, minerals, and energy resources.[123] The draft law proposes the preparation of a National Action Plan to set national priorities and strategies for the conservation, management and use of natural resources, "to ensure sustainable development".[124] Under the draft law, the Ministry of the Environment would be empowered to prescribe enforcement mechanisms and sanctions, to include fines, payable to an "Environment Fund" to finance environmental quality enhancement and resource conservation projects.

On the international front, Cambodia, Laos, Thailand and Vietnam signed, in April of 1995, the Agreement on Cooperation for the Sustainable Development of the Mekong River Basin. Administration of the Agreement will be performed by the Mekong Commission, a regional organization first formed in 1957. The Agreement is promising in that it formalizes for the first time in almost forty years the principle of cooperation between nations who have long been hostile to one another. On the other hand, the Agreement allows diversion of water from the Mekong by the upstream nations without the consent of the downstream nations, except during the dry season. Extensive diversions by Thailand and Laos are to be expected in light of these two nations' plans for building several power plants along the Mekong. The diversions could prove extremely harmful to Cambodia's Tonle Sap lake, its fisheries, and the people and agriculture who rely on it.[125]

Draft Securities and Banking Law

A.48 Despite the very small number of commercial companies in Cambodia, a Hong Kong consulting firm has been retained by the Cambodian government to assist in the drafting of a securities law. Once that law has been enacted, Cambodia expects to set up a Securities and Exchange Commission and open the doors of a small stock exchange, hopefully in 1997. A banking law is being drafted on a parallel track. New accounting standards are also in the offing.[126]

Arbitration and Other Forms of Dispute Resolution in Cambodia

Past and Present

A.49 Alternative dispute resolution is now in vogue in the West, but for centuries, in many Asian countries, including Cambodia, traditional dispute resolution has depended on mediation and consensus rather than adversarial proceedings. Thus, it is somewhat ironic that Cambodia's system of alternative dispute resolution for resolving commercial disputes is as undeveloped as it currently is.

This is not to say that alternative means of resolving disputes play no role in Cambodia. In fact, at least one, and often two mediations (called reconciliations), precede the filing of claim in Cambodia's trial courts — the Provincial and Civil Courts — where most commercial claims are heard. Moreover, at the Court of Appeals level, where claims are heard *de novo* by a panel of three judges, a mandatory effort at reconciliation precedes the contested hearing.

Nonetheless, the first priority in reconstructing the legal system destroyed by the Khmer Rouge holocaust and years of civil war has been the rebuilding of the formal court system. Judge training, construction of calendaring systems, and other such routine but fundamental matters have taken precedence over the creation of an alternative dispute resolution system for use in the commercial arena. Within the framework of reconstruction of the formal legal system, the education of judges and court personnel in business and commercial law has been assigned a high priority. It is well understood by the Minister of Justice that integration of Cambodia into ASEAN and the world economy will not be possible without trained legal personnel capable of resolving complex commercial issues.

Despite the Ministry of Justice's focus on the formal court system, Cambodia's new legislation does at times draws on its tradition of alternative dispute resolution to resolve disputes in particular areas. Similarly, Ministries often make use of informal dispute resolution techniques.[127] In addition, Cambodia's slow but sure integration into the international economic community has resulted in its being a party to international treaties and conventions which include arbitration as a form of dispute resolution. The following examples illustrate these points: **A.50**

1. Cambodia's Investment Law[128] reflects its tradition of seeking resolution in an informal, conciliatory arena rather than in a court of law. Thus, Article 20 of the Investment Law requires that in the event of dispute it "shall be settled amicably as far as possible through consultation between the parties".[129] In the event the parties cannot reach agreement, the matter may not be brought to a court of law until an effort has been made to conciliate the matter before the CDC which has the authority to either render an opinion *or* to refer the matter to the Cambodian courts.[130] Once in the courts, as noted, additional efforts at reconciliation would be required. Of course, to the extent that international rules are applicable to resolve a dispute, those rules would apply.[131]

2. Similarly, an exhaustion of administrative remedies requirement exists to resolve tax disputes arising under the Financial Law of 1995.[132] Thus, taxpayers have two months from the date of the tax notice to file a written complaint with the tax authorities.[133] If no decision is forth-

coming from the taxation division within two months, the complainant may file an action in civil court. If an adverse decision is rendered, the complainant has two months from the date of the decision to file a civil action.[134]

3. In addition, labor disputes, whether they be between an employer and an individual employee or between an employer and an association of employees, must first be submitted for resolution through reconciliation and/or before the labor inspector in the province or region. Only after such efforts have been made, may an action be filed in civil court.[135]

4. The Draft Marks Protection Act[136] allows for the filing of a civil action to protect a trade mark or to enjoin an unfair labor practice, but also provides that the "institution of civil proceedings shall not prevent the use of arbitration".[137]

5. In the international arena, Cambodia is a signatory to the Convention on the Recognition and Enforcement of Foreign Arbitral Awards (The "New York" Convention) which requires Cambodia to enforce arbitration awards rendered in signatory states and to agree to arbitrate a matter if a party to the dispute is a citizen of a State that is also a party to the Convention.[138]

Draft Arbitration and Commercial Court Law

A.51   In fact, a law on arbitration and commercial jurisdiction is in draft form. The long-awaited Commercial Code[139] contains in Book Five of the draft the articles that will implement the dispute resolution provisions of the Foreign Investment Law and other laws governing commercial activity in the Kingdom of Cambodia.

The draft of Book Five creates two new forums for settlement of commercial disputes: an arbitration tribunal and a commercial court. The arbitration tribunal will have jurisdiction over disputes arising under contracts containing written clauses expressly providing for arbitration; the commercial court will exercise jurisdiction over disputes that arise under contracts not containing arbitration clauses and disputes arising from transactions relevant to business and commerce within the boundaries of Cambodia.

As presently envisioned, the Arbitration Tribunal will operate according to the rules that contracting parties agree upon among themselves according to international legal conventions and Cambodian law. The contract clause providing for arbitration must have been part of the contract as originally drafted and must be expressly set forth in the contract itself or in a document to which the contract refers. If a contract containing an arbitration clause becomes the subject of litigation, the parties may still, at any time, enter into an agreement to submit the substance of their dispute to arbitration. The judge of the court in which the litigation is taking place may not abrogate such an arbitration clause.

Arbitration and Other Forms of Dispute Resolution

The draft provides that the establishment of an Arbitration Tribunal pursuant to a written arbitration clause automatically deprives other jurisdictions of competency to hear the commercial dispute in question. However, disputes over points of law may be submitted to a court designated in the arbitration agreement entered into by the parties or, by default, to the Commercial Court. The President of the designated court or of the Commercial Court is designated as the judge for such interlocutory matters and his or her decisions are not subject to interlocutory appeal.

The drafters contemplate an Arbitration Tribunal composed of one or more arbitrators, as agreed by the parties. The Ministry of Justice will publish a list of official arbitrators. However, freedom of contract requires that the parties be permitted to select arbitrators not on the list. The arbitration must be completed within six months of its commencement. The parties may be represented by counsel throughout the proceedings. The arbitrators shall adjudicate like judges; they must apply the law. If they are authorized to adjudicate like arbiters ("amical compositeur"), they may render decisions in equity.

The troublesome question of the force and effect of arbitral decisions is dealt with in the draft in a straightforward manner. The decisions of the arbitration tribunal have the authority of *res judicata* relative to the issues settled. They are subject to appeal in the normal fashion. However, the arbitration awards are not enforceable until they have been certified as valid and enforcement ordered by the president of the Commercial Court. An enforcement order is not subject to appeal. However, should the president of the commercial court refuse to order enforcement of an arbitration award, that refusal may be appealed.

The jurisdiction of the Commercial Court is carefully defined so as not to interfere with that of the Arbitral Tribunal. The draft legislation envisions a Commercial Court that shall have jurisdiction over all commercial disputes involving claims exceeding 10 million riels and as to which the Arbitration Tribunal is not competent. Its jurisdiction shall include all disputes between natural persons and legal persons relevant to commerce within the Kingdom of Cambodia. Appeals shall be to a special chamber of the Court of Appeal.

Recent conversations with government officials indicate that the composition of the Commercial Court is a matter of some debate. One view, held by the Ministry of Justice, is that the judges of the Commercial Court should be experienced adjudicators with training in the law; the other school of thought is that some or all of the Commercial Court judges need not be law-trained and hence may be drawn from other relevant ministries or even the private sector. The draft currently provides that the Commercial Court shall be composed of a president and six judges, three of whom shall be from the ranks of the judiciary and three elected by the Chamber of Commerce. The electoral list for Chamber of Commerce elections to judgeships on the Commercial Court shall be from a list made up by a Commission presided over by the Ministry of Commerce and composed of representatives of the

A.52

Ministries of Economy and Finance, Industry, Transportation, Agriculture, and Interior.

Parties to a proceeding before the Commercial Court may request whatever measures they deem necessary to protect their interests. Apparently, this includes interlocutory remedies such as injunctions.

The procedure and rules of evidence proposed for the Commercial Court are a matter of some interest. The draft suggests that proof by oral testimony shall always be admissible in the Commercial Court. The means of gathering evidence shall be three-fold: (1) by hearings (l'enquete) such as take place in ordinary civil cases; (2) by expert opinion, delivered according to the rules set forth in the (as yet not enacted) Code of Civil Procedure; (3) by referral to a referee, akin to the Special Masters in U.S. federal courts, who shall have the task of conciliating the parties and, in the case of failure to conciliate, filing a report clarifying the matters at issue with the Clerk of the Commercial Court.

Pending passage of the draft Law on Commercial Contracts, commercial disputes will be generally resolved the way other civil disputes are resolved in Cambodia. That is, very informal efforts at mediation, conducted by untrained personnel, are followed by a rather summary civil trial that has remarkably little form and few rules to guide it. The government is aware of the deficiencies of its court system and serious efforts are now being made to re-educate and, where necessary, replace current personnel.

Law of the Supreme Council of the Magistracy

A.53   The December, 1994, passage of the law of the Supreme Council of the Magistery should allow for the beginnings of true independence for Cambodia's judiciary. The Law, which provides for a large, though not total, measure of self-governance for the judiciary, through the Supreme Council of the Magistery, is, hopefully, the first step towards separation of Cambodia's judiciary from the executive branch of government which has heretofore dominated it.

III. General Considerations in Negotiating Business Transactions in Cambodia

Cultural Factors

A.54   Good personal relationships are, in Cambodia, the foundation of successful business relationships. Prospective foreign investors usually have no relationship at all with their Cambodian counterparts, let alone a good personal one. Thus, it behooves the prospective investor to make the initial contacts with or through a Khmer or Khmer-American personally acquainted with the Cambodians involved. Once the relationship is established, it should be nurtured with care. Small gifts are appropriate and even expected.

Two factors are critical to maintaining good personal relationships within Cambodian society. The first is a cuturally appropriate demeanour and the second is an understanding of the hierarchies around which Khmer society is built. Khmer culture, even more than most Asian cultures, rewards calm and courteous behavior. Polite requests, accompanied by a smile, get far better results than loudly-voiced demands. To lose one's temper, to shout, to pound a table, are the height of bad manners and viewed as signs of inferior breeding and education. The emphasis on an a smiling and unruffled demeanor is carried to such an extreme that a Khmer will often interpret the absence of such a demeanor as an indication that something is amiss. The intensity and abruptness that characterize many successful American businesspersons is likely to prove counterproductive in Cambodia.

Khmer society is hierarchical, organized on the principle of patronage. Each hierarchy has a patron at the top. Persons at the bottom of a hierarchy render service to the man at the top and he, the patron, rewards this service by protecting and promoting the welfare of those at the bottom.

The common denominators of these hierarchies are kinship and politics. It is common in Cambodia to find many members of the same family working in a particular ministry, NGO or business. Such an arrangement is viewed as natural and practical. Nepotism is not a Khmer concept.

The counterpoint to the theme of kinship is the theme of political factionalism. Just as some hierarchies are organized around the theme of kinship, others, often overlapping, are organized around political factionalism. Ministries, and even sometimes departments within ministries, are viewed as the domain of one or the other of the two leading political parties, or of a particular faction within a party. Thus, when doing business in Cambodia it is helpful to ascertain the party affiliation of the government official at the top of the particular ministry hierarchy or departmental hierarchy with which you are doing business. Once in possession of that knowledge you can begin to build a network of complementary relationships capable of bridging factional disputes. Even more helpful would be knowledge of the (usually complex) kinship relationships involved, but these networks are not easily accessed by foreigners.

Cambodia is a very small country. The members of its elite generally know or know of each other. More often than not they are connected through attendance at the same school, service in the same military unit, or membership in the same extended family. It is to the advantage of a foreign investor to be aware of and sensitive to these inter-relationships.

Local Counsel

A.55   Prospective investors would do well to consult with local counsel prior to attempting business negotiations in Cambodia. Pending the enactment of the draft legislation discussed above, much of the commercial activity in Cambodia is governed by sub-decrees not readily obtainable by persons outside the goverment. In the absence of a sub-decree, the verbal representations of the official responsible for a particular transaction tend to function as the law of the case. The proliferation of sub-decrees and the personal fiefdoms created and presided over by certain officials combine to render the advice of local counsel indispensable. Local counsel may be able to provide, and translate, the applicable sub-decree or, in the absence of a sub-decree, obtain favorable verbal representations from the government official handling the business venture in issue.

Unfortunately, the number of lawyers in Cambodia is very small. As stated above, most were killed by the Khmer Rouge. A local bar association, composed almost entirely of returning expatriates, was formed in mid-1995. Its total membership is 38. Very few of these 38 lawyers have the training and background necessary to advise on and facilitate major international business transactions.

An Institute of Business and Law, focusing on the training of commercial lawyers, may open its doors within the next two years.[140] The Institute's Faculty of Law would teach Cambodian law in a comparative context, familiarizing its students with the commercial law of both the common law and civil law traditions.

Until the graduates of the Institute appear, or until the local bar broadens its understanding of commercial law, foreign investors should supplement the advice of their Cambodian local counsel by consultations with foreign lawyers having offices in Phnom Penh or Bangkok. Three or four American law firms have opened offices in Phnom Penh, and several major international law firms maintain branch offices in Bangkok.

The role of foreign lawyers within the Cambodian legal system is in the process of clarification. A Bar Statute was passed this year[141] and implementing regulations are still being written. As is the case in many Asian nations, foreign lawyers will not be allowed to appear in court. Only Khmer lawyers may do so.[142] Foreign lawyers who are admitted to the Bar in their country of origin may "practice the legal profession" in conjunction with a Khmer lawyer.[143] However, foreign lawyers may not "represent" clients.[144] This pattern of restrictions on foreign lawyers is common throughout Asia as a form of protection of the local bar. Not so common are the provisions of the Law on the Bar stating that foreign lawyers will be licensed to practice their profession in Cambodia only when their country of origin provides the same possibility to Cambodian lawyers.[145] This reciprocity provision has caused temporary difficulties for American lawyers in Phnom Penh. Meanwhile, most of the foreign law firms having offices in Phnom Penh have associated local Khmer lawyers as partners or contract employees, and are continuing to practice the legal profession pending resolution of the reciprocity problem.

Business Assistance Programs

The Cambodian Development Council (CDC)

The creation of the CDC was mandated by the Foreign Investment Act of 1994. The CDC meets monthly. The make-up of the CDC reflects the effort generally of the RCG to maintain the political balance necessary to sustain the fragile coalition government that rules Cambodia. The First and Second Prime Ministers co-chair the CDC. Other members of the CDC include the senior minister in charge of Rehabilitation and Development (CDC vice-chairman), the senior minister in charge of Culture, Arts, Land Management and Urbanization, and the Ministers of Public Works and Transport, Foreign Affairs, Economy and Finance and Planning. Rounding out the membership of the CDC are its Secretary-Generals and the Secretary-Generals of the Cambodian Rehabilitation and Development Board (discussed below) and the Cambodian Investment Board (also discussed below). The Co-Chairs, Vice Chairman, and three Secretary Generals comprise the executive committee of the CDC which meets twice monthly and is in charge of its general affairs.   **A.56**

The CDC itself is itself divided into three bodies: (1) the General Secretariat which oversees the work of the CDC and has divisions for Legal and Dispute Resolution, Finance and Administration, Personnel Management and Strategic Planning; (2) the Cambodian Rehabilitation and Development Board (CRCB) which oversees public sector investments and works closely with donor countries, international organizations and NGOs; and, (3) the Cambodian Investment Board (CIB) which oversees private investments.

One-Step Investment Shopping in Cambodia?

In theory, the CDC has high level representation from all Ministries necessary to make "one-stop" investing a reality. Thus, representatives of the Ministry of Foreign Affairs and International Cooperation, the Ministry of Economy and Finance, the Ministry of Planning, and representatives of the Cabinet from the Council of Ministers are all represented on the CRDB. Similarly, representatives from the Ministry of Economy and Finance, the Ministry of Commerce, the Ministry of Planning and representatives from the Cabinet of the Council of Ministers are all represented on the CIB. Moreover, the CRDB and the CIB may request additional representation from additional Ministries as needed.   **A.57**

One-stop investment shopping in Cambodia, however, may presently be more of a goal than a reality. Part of the explanation is structural. Ultimately, the CDC is responsible to the Council of Ministers for the approval of certain investments, including investments in excess of $50 million dollars, investments affecting politically sensitive issues, investments affecting natural resource development, and investments which might have a negative impact on the environment. In addition, Cambodia has always been a country where personal contacts are critical. A Phnom Penh practitioner recently reported that "at present, contact with the individual ministries (by the investor) remains an important part of establishing and operating investment and development projects in Cambodia".[146]

The Chamber of Commerce

A.58 Cambodia's recently established Chamber of Commerce may prove to be a critical agency to assist foreign investors. At a minimum, foreign investors must be familiar with the Chamber and the projected role it will play in Cambodia's economic development.

Pursuant to an Act of the National Assembly passed in May 1995, a Chamber of Commerce is to be established in each province and operate under the auspices of the Ministry of Commerce.[147] Each Chamber's membership is broad-based and includes elected officials (president and one or more vice presidents) as well as management *and* employee representatives from commerce, industry, agriculture and craft enterprises.[148]

The *Phnom Penh Post* reported that business people in Phnom Penh hoped that the Chamber "would smooth out problems between the government and business people and advise prospective foreign investors (by putting) them in contact with local companies and give information on government licensing regulations". It was also reported that the Chambers were intended to help "streamline licensing procedure" and help to "reduce corruption".[149]

Certainly, the statutory authority of the Chamber is consistent with these broad objectives. Thus, each Chamber is designated a "public institution" and charged with establishing relationships with economic sources within and without the country, improving economic efficiency, researching economic and commercial issues, acting as an intermediary between government and business, and acting as an arbiter for business disputes. Moreover, each Chamber is required to provide opinions on draft business regulations, proposed economic legislation, fee and tax schedules, and the utility and feasibility of public works projects. In fact, the Chamber may, upon the request of private or state donors, manage both public and privately-owned commercial, industrial, agricultural and craft institutions, including warehouses, public retail spaces, department stores, galleries and museums, professional business and industrial training schools, public markets and tourist complexes.[150]

Given this broad mandate, the Chambers are likely to play a key role in facilitating foreign investment within Cambodia. In fact, a negative response on the part of a Chamber to a proposed private or public investment will have a substantial effect on whether the project is ultimately approved or disapproved by the RCG. Given the power that the Chamber could wield, it is not surprising that competition for Chamber posts has been brisk.[151]

Practical Considerations in Negotiating Business Transactions in Cambodia

Infrastructure

Newcomers to Cambodia will be taken aback by the decayed or non-existent   **A.59** state of Cambodia's infrastructure, especially in the provinces. Even in the city of Phnom Penh, electrical black-outs are common and roads are filled with potholes and, during the rainy season, flooded. The state telephone system is almost non-functional; cellular telephones are a must if reliable local, let alone international, communication is desired. What this means is that completion dates for construction, delivery dates for goods, and even the provision of basic services in the service sector are all highly unreliable. Flexibility in scheduling and a large contingency fund in the project budget are prerequisites to doing business in Cambodia.

Personal Contacts

Doing business in Cambodia is likewise impossible without personal con-   **A.60** tacts within the state bureaucracy. As previously noted, business relation- ships, once established, must be nurtured with care. Gift-giving in the business context is common and, indeed, proper throughout Asia.

In Cambodia, problems can arise when foreign investors and their Cam- bodian contacts have differing views as to what sort of gift is appropriate. Civil servants, even at quite high levels in the bureaucracy, make only US$20 or $30 per month. It is not possible to support a family in Phnom Penh on that amount of money. Because of the very small salaries paid most govern- ment employees, generosity is appreciated and even expected. On the other hand, bribery of a government official is a crime under the Cambodian criminal law (though such a prosecution has never yet been brought). The line between gift-giving and bribery is a fine one that every foreigner doing business in Cambodia will have to walk.

Conclusion

Perhaps the biggest problem confronting those doing business in Cambodia   **A.61** is the difficulty in obtaining accurate information regarding applicable laws and regulations. As noted throughout this chapter, many laws are in draft form and decrees and circulars are constantly being issued by various Ministries. Those doing business in Cambodia are urged to check carefully with Ministries to determine precisely what regulations might be applicable to a particular business transaction. The recent publication of *Business and Investment Handbook*, published by the Ministry of Commerce and cited here, marks a significant effort by the Cambodian government to add certainty to the risky business of doing business in Cambodia. It is easily obtainable from the Ministry and even at local newstands. Moreover, those doing business in Cambodia are urged to contact the growing number of foreign law firms now working in Cambodia. The lawyers in these firms are likely to have developed the necessary personal contacts to insure that information is accurate and that proper procedures are being followed.

A.62 The absence of reliable and sophisticated dispute resolution mechanisms in Cambodia should be an investor's major source of concern. Viewed from this perspective, one yardstick for investment in Cambodia is the level of risk an investor is willing to tolerate. Under the present state of affairs, it is unlikely that a foreign investor would be able to recover in Cambodia for a breach of contract where the breaching party is the Royal Cambodian Government or someone closely connected to the Government. If inability to recover for breach outweighs the potential benefits of doing business in Cambodia prior to any breach, the prospective investor may prefer to invest in a more stable and rule-of-law oriented society than Cambodia. On the other hand, Cambodia could be a very attractive investment prospect for a businessman or woman who is not risk-adverse. The Cambodian economy is likely to expand dramatically in the next year or two and the potential for profits to be reaped by knowledgeable investors is high.

Notes

[1-2] Cambodia has supported the establishment of a new law faculty and curriculum intended to teach basic business law concepts to insure Cambodia's ability to transact business throughout the world. This effort at legal education reform is being assisted by the University of San Francisco School of Law.

[3] *Kingdom of Cambodia: Legal Services Country Profile*, Australian International Legal Cooperation Program, Attorney-General's Department, Australia, March, 1995. These are 1993 figures. At its current growth rate of 3.3 per cent, the Cambodian population should have passed the 10 million mark by mid-1996.

[4] On several recent occasions, university students have demonstrated against the mandatory instruction in the French language which is a condition of French foreign aid to technical institutes of higher education. The demonstrating students demanded that they be given the opportunity to study English.

[5] This table is based on one set forth at p.8 of *Kingdom of Cambodia: Country Legal Services Profile*, above at n.3, which in turn is based upon *Country Economic Brief*, February, 1995, Department of Foreign Assistance and Trade, Australia, and *Country Report: Indochina*, 3d Quarter, 1994. The GNP is given in 1989 constant prices; inflation rate is based on consumer prices (period averages); the export figures exclude re-exports; the import figures exclude re-exports; the current

account figures exclude official transfers. In interpreting the table it should be noted that hundreds of free-spending U.N. employees, journalists and entrepreneurs injected huge amounts of foreign currency into the Cambodian economy during the period February 1992 to June 1993 attendant upon the U.N. occupation of Cambodia leading up to the elections of May, 1993. The economy did not return to normal until late in 1993.

6   *Ibid.* at p.10.

7   In 1992 the Khmer Rouge refused to participate further in the electoral process, preferring instead to withdraw to their jungle strongholds. From there, they continue to wage war against the Cambodian government.

8   Donovan, D., "The Cambodian Legal System: An Overview", in Brown, F. Ed., *Rebuilding Cambodia: Human Resources, Human Rights, and Law* (c.1993).

9   Law of Investment of the Kingdom of Cambodia, enacted August 4, 1994.

10 The 1995 budget of US $410 millions was 44 per cent funded by international donors. Hayes, Michael, "Narcotics Trafficking Debate takes Center Stage", *Phnom Penh Post* November 17–30, 1995, pp.1,4.

11 The Khmer Rouge are widely believed to support their troops by the illegal sale of lumber and gemstones to the Thais.

12 Shawcross, William, *Cambodia's New Deal* (Carnegie Endowment for International Peace 1994) p.76.

13 According to the World Bank, Cambodia must achieve the following four benchmarks if economic recovery is to take place: 1) to maintain real growth rates of 78 per cent per annum; 2) to reduce inflation to 5 per cent; 3) to reduce the account deficit to 9 per cent of the gross domestic product; 4) to increase international reserves. Shawcross, p.77.

14 See generally, Shawcross, pp.77–78. On the down side are the facts that more than half the population is under the age of 15 and that the population is growing at the rapid rate of 2.8 per cent per annum. The average Cambodian dies before the age of 50. Op cit.

15 Shawcross, pp.76–77.

16 The Khmer Rouge continue to hold approximately 15 per cent of Cambodia's territory in the rain forest along the border with Thailand. However, the Phnom Penh government's hold on its 85 per cent of Cambodian territory is secure enough to have engendered the confidence of many recent foreign investors.

17 For a full discussion of the history of Cambodia's path to ASEAN membership *see* Granger, Matthew, "History of Slow Boat to ASEAN", *Phnom Penh Post*, Vol.4, no.15, July 28–August 10, 1995 p.16.

18 As quoted in Granger, Matthew, "First Step to ASEAN 'Family'", *Phnom Penh Post*, Vol.4, no.15, July 28–August 10, 1995, p.1.

19 For an excellent summary of MFN status *see*, Popkin, Michael, "The Rule of Law", *Phnom Penh Post*, Vol.4, no.11, June 2–15, 1995, p.13.

20 *Ibid.*

21 *See* Doran, David "Rule of Law: ASEAN and U.S. Trade Law", *Phnom Penh Post*, Vol.4, no.16, August 11–24, 1995, p.6 for a detailed example of the operation of the 35 per cent requirement.

22 *Ibid.*

23 "New IMF 'Res Rep' Opens the Books", *Phnom Penh Post*, Vol.4, no.18, September 8–21, 1995, p.14.

24 As quoted in Postlewaite, Susan, "ADB Board Worried About Tattered Economy", *Phnom Penh Post*, Vol.4, no.19, September 22–October 5, 1995, p.13.

25 *See* Financial Law for 1995, Chapter IV, Arts. 81 and 82.

26 Investment Law, Chap. 2, Art. 3.

27 Investment Law, Chap. 3, Art. 7.

28 *Ibid.*

Cambodia

[29] Investment Law, Chap. 4, Art. 8.

[30] Investment Law, Chap. 4, Art. 9.

[31] Investment Law, Chap. 4, Art. 10.

[32] Investment Law, Chap. 4, Art. 11.

[33] The list is clearly non-exclusive and is likely to be construed broadly by the CDC.

[34] These projects are developed by the CDC in a "development priority list" which is available to investors. Chap. 5, Art. 14(4)b. Additional projects qualify for import duty exemptions and certain restrictions apply. See generally Chap. 5, Art. 14(4). The CDC has already announced that Special Promotion Industrial Zones are being developed in Phnom Penh and in Sihanoukville, Cambodia's main deep water port. According to the CDC, investment in these zones will qualify investors for additional incentives. See "Why Would Anyone Want to Invest in Cambodia?", published by the Council for the Development of Cambodia.

[35] Chap. 5, Art. 14(5) and (6).

[36] Investment Law, Chap. 5, Art. 15.

[37] Investment Law, Chap. 6, Art. 16.

[38] Chap. 5, Art. 14(6).

[39] Investment Law, Chap. 6, Art. 18. The State of Cambodia Labor Law of 1992, which is still applicable, also details restrictions regarding the employment of foreign labor including the requirements that foreign laborers: have a "Labor Card" issued by the Ministry of Labor and Social Action; have entered Cambodia lawfully and have the right to reside in Cambodia; have a valid passport; be of good reputation and behavior; be physically qualified for the position and have no communicable diseases. 1992 SOC Labor Code, Arts. 258 *et seq.*

[40] Investment Law, Chap. 9, Art. 25.

[41] Kennedy Michael I., "How Cambodia Measures Up For Investors: One Year On", *Phnom Penh Post*, October 20-November 2, p.14.

[42] The official title of the Commercial Registry Law is "the Law concerning Commercial Rules and the Registry of Commerce".

[43] *See* Doran, David, "The Rule of Law", *Phnom Penh Post*, May 5–18, 1995.

[44] Arts. 1–2, 14, 17, Law of Commercial Registration. The exceptions include artists, family members exchanging goods or services among themselves, a spouse selling goods produced by his or her merchant spouse, salespersons employed by a merchant, and minors. Arts. 3–6, Law of Commercial Registration Law.

[45] *See* Arts. 54, 57, Law of Commercial Registration.

[46] Arts. 14–15, 17–18, Law of Commercial Registration.

[47] Art. 38, Law of Commercial Registration.

[48] *Ibid.*

[49] Art. 40, Law of Commercial Registration. The exchange rate is 2300 riels to $1.00 U.S.

[50] Art. 43, Law of Commercial Registration.

[51] *See, e.g.* Arts. 47–53, Law of Commercial Registration.

[52] The provisions of Book Five relating to arbitration and the proposed commercial court are discussed in the text below in the section entitled "Draft Arbitration and Commercial Court Law".

[53] For informative discussions of the French-influenced notions regarding forms for doing business in Cambodia, see the *Mekong Law Report: Cambodia*, May 31, 1995, published by the law firm of Dirksen, Flipse, Doran & Le, Phnom Penh, Kingdom of Cambodia; *see also* Popkin, Michael, "The Rule of Law: The Company Law", *Phnom Penh Post*, July 14–27, 1995.

[54] Laws, like Decree 38, which predate the Khmer Constitution remain in effect pursuant to Art. 139 of the Constitution. *See* Khmer Constitution, Chap. XIV, Art. 139 ("[l]aws and standard documents in Cambodia that safeguard properties,

rights, freedom and legal private properties and in conformity with national interests, shall continue to be effective until altered or abrogated by new texts, except those provisions that are contrary to the spirit of this Constitution").

55 *See* Decree 38, Art. 1 (defining a contract as "a freewill agreement between two or more persons to create, change, or terminate one or more obligations, relevant to them").

56 *See* Decree 38, Art. 22 (providing that a "contract is regarded as law as between the parties ... [and] binds only the parties to the contract").

57 *See* Decree 38, Art. 1 (defining a "person" in a contract as either "a natural person or a legal entity").

58 *See* Decree 38, Art. 1 (providing that "[a] legal entity can enter into a contract through his/her own representative").

59 *See* Decree 38, Art. 1 (defining a contract "as a freewill agreement between two or more persons to create, change, or terminate one or more obligations, relevant to them").

60 Under Cambodian law, consideration is not explicitly required for a valid contract. Nevertheless, it appears to be an implicit requirement, as is discussed below.

61 The procedures for canceling a voidable contract are outlined in Art. 19 of Decree 38 as follows: the party entitled to void the contract must (1) notify the other party that he or she intends to void the contract and (2) file a claim in court within 12 months of notice. If the contract is canceled or "voided", Art. 21 of Decree 38 provides that "the situation prior to entering into contract shall be restored". Under Art. 20, however, if after filing suit, the party "agrees to carry out his/her obligations or agrees, in writing, to withdraw the action", the right to void the contract under "Article 19 shall cease". These are the same procedures whether the "contract is voidable because of incapacity, mistake, duress, or fraud".

62 *See* Decree 38, Art. 3, 6–10.

63 *See* Decree 38, Art. 6 ("[t]he following shall be deemed voidable: every contract not resulting from a real ... agreement").

64 *See* Decree 38, Arts. 14 & 15. Art. 14 provides that any one over the age of 18 can enter into a contract except "detainees". The word "detainee" apparently also has been translated as "interdicted" persons. *See Cambodia Law Notes*, Asia Foundation (using this definition combined with glossary of terms annexed to *SOC Decree #lOOD referring to Land Law*; defining an "interdicted" person as "a person of low awareness and intelligence, or a person ... [legally] restrained from administer[ing] his own property").

65 *See* Decree 38, Art. 15.

66 Decree 38, Arts. 6 &, 16, 19. Art. 6 provides that "every contract made with a party lacking capacity ... shall be deemed voidable". Arts. 16 and 19 provide that the "aggrieved" party (*i.e.* the party lacking capacity) can sue to cancel the contract within certain time limits, but that the other party cannot "get out of his/her obligations on the grounds of incapacity of the other party".

67 *See* Decree 38, Arts. 6 & 16.

68 *See* Decree 38, Art. 5.

69 *See* Decree 38, Art. 57.

70 *See* Decree 38, Art. 112.

71 *See* Decree 38, Art. 4 ("[e]very contract not consistent with the formalities fixed by law shall be deemed void"). In the United States, the rule is that contracts which violate the Statute of Frauds are voidable, not void. The Khmer language does not appear to have precise equivalents to the terms "void" and "voidable". It is possible that the intent of the Cambodian drafters was to render contracts not consistent with the formalities fixed by law voidable rather than void.

[72] *See* Decree 38, Art. 26.
[73] *See* Decree 38, Art. 27.
[74] Financial Law for 1995, Chap. III, I, Art. 9.
[75] Financial Law 1995, Arts. 10, 11, and 19.
[76] Financial Law 1995, Art. 15.1
[77-78] *See* Financial Law 1995, Article 16. *See also: Mekong Law Report*, Cambodia, prepared by the Phnom Penh-based law firm of Dirksen, Flipse & Le.
[79] *See, Business and Investment Handbook* at 311, n.83, above.
[80] *Ibid.*
[81] *Ibid.*
[82] Financial Law 1995, Arts. 26–36.
[83] *See Mekong Report*, cited n.78 above.
[84] *See* 1995 *Financial Law*, Arts. 37–38 and *Mekong Law Report*.
[85] *See* 1995 *Financial Law*, Art. 40.
[86] *See, Cambodia: The Remergence of New Opportunities, Business & Investment Handbook*, published by the Cambodian Ministry of Commerce (1996).
[87] n.83, above, at 317.
[88] *Ibid.*
[89] *Ibid.*
[90] *See* "Cambodia Hires World's Largest Import Auditors", *Phnom Penh Post*, Vol.4, no.18, September 8–21, 1995, p.15
[91] The regulations and their implications are analyzed in Doran David & Dararith, Kim Yeat, "The Rule of Law", *Phnom Penh Post*, Vol.4, No.22, November 3–16, 1995, p.14.
[92] SOC Labor Law, Chapter One, Section 1, Art. 1. The various types of employees are defined in Chapter One Arts. 2–11.
[93] Discussed more fully above.
[94] Discussed more fully below.
[95] SOC Labor Law, Art. 12. Those in military service, incarcerated, or otherwise under the control of the government are excepted.
[96] SOC Labor Law, Arts. 14–17.
[97] SOC Labor Law, Arts. 19—23.
[98] SOC Labor Law, Arts. 24–30.
[99] SOC Labor Law, Arts. 62–67.
[100] *See* generally Arts. 69–91 for additional issues relating to the entering into and termination of employment contracts.
[101] SOC Labor Code, Arts. 101–116.
[102] SOC Labor Code, Art. 120.
[103] SOC Labor Code, Arts. 133 *et. seq.*
[104] Labor Code, Art. 168.
[105] *See generally* Arts. 168 *et. seq.*
[106] SOC Labor Code, Arts. 224 *et. seq.*
[107] SOC Labor Code, Arts. 231 *et. seq.*
[108] SOC Labor Code, Arts. 242 *et. seq.*
[109] SOC Labor Code, Arts. 263 *et. seq.*
[110] SOC Labor Code, Arts. 271 *et. seq.*
[111] Draft Marks Protection Act, Section 9(1) and (2).
[112] Draft Marks Protection Act, Section 2(1)(a–e).
[113] Draft Marks Protection Act, Section 12(1).
[114] Draft Patent and Design Act, Sections 1–2.
[115] This does not include products used in the treatment of animals or humans, only the methods of treatment. Design and Patent Act, Section 1(3)(c). Regarding patents contrary to public morality, *see* Section 4(b).
[116] Draft Design and Patent Act, Part 2, Section 34. The statutory scheme for such

designs and models is nearly identical to that for patents. The reader is referred to the draft statute for particulars.

[117] Draft Patent and Design Act, Sections 13–14.

[118] Section 70(2).

[119] Section 57.

[120] The Khmer Rouge are widely believed to have sold logging concessions to Thai companies, giving these companies access to substantial portions of the Cambodian forest under Khmer Rouge control along the Thai-Cambodian border. For its part, the Phnom Penh government has sold the logging rights to vast tracts of Cambodian forest, in some cases equivalent in size to entire provinces, to Malaysian and Indonesia companies. Even the logging rights to rubber trees on rubber plantations have been sold. These depredations of Cambodia's forests are so wide-spread as to have moved King Sihanouk to a public protest. *See, e.g.* Channo, Mang, "Samling Says Green Study in Progress", *Phnom Penh Post*, August 25-September 7, 1995, p.14; Fitzgerald, Tricia, "Samling: Half Our Trees Are Gone", *Ibid.*; Jeldres, Julio, "Logging Samling Style: Malaysian Record Raises Royal Concern for Cambodia", *Phnom Penh Post*, August 25-September 7, 1995, p.15; Postlewaite, Susan, " 'Anarchy' in Cambodia's Rubber Plantations", *Phnom Penh Post*, October 20–November 2, 1995, p.12.

[121] *See, e.g.* Nette, Andrew, "Damming the Mekong, Damning the Consequences", *Phnom Penh Post*, October 20–November 2, 1995, p.17; Nette, Andrew and Wallengren, Maja, "The Mekong Region's Politics of Power", *Ibid.*, p.16.

[122] Art. 9, draft Law of Environmental Protection.

[123] Art. 16, *ibid.*

[124] Art. 11(b), *ibid.*

[125] Nette, Andrew, "Damming the Mekong, Damning the Consequences".

[126] Postlewaite, Susan, "Stock Exchange on the Way — But Who'll Be on It?" *Phnom Penh Post*, November 17–30, 1995, p.11.

[127] For example, within the Ministry of Commerce, an informal system of dispute resolution exists to resolve issues relating to weights, measures and quality control.

[128] The Investment Law is discussed more fully in section II above.

[129] Investment Law, Chap. 8, Art. 20.

[130] *Ibid.*

[131] *Ibid.*

[132] The Financial Law of 1995 is discussed more fully in section II above.

[133] Financial Law of 1995, Art. 76. A taxpayer may only complain that unlawful tax procedures have been followed or dispute the amount of the tax levied.

[134] Financial Law of 1995, Art. 76.

[135] The State of Cambodia (SOC) 1992 Labor Law remains in effect. The dispute resolution provisions are found in Chapter 12, Sections 1 and 2. For a fuller discussion of the SOC Labor Law, see section II above.

[136] Described more fully in section II above.

[137] Draft Marks Protection Act, Section 45.

[138] Convention on the Recognition and Enforcement of Foreign Arbitral Awards, Article II, Codified at 9 U.S.C. 201 *et seq.*

[139] Readers are cautioned that the version of the Commercial Code finally enacted may differ in major and minor ways from the drafts discussed here. The enacted law should be carefully examined in order to determine the points of difference that will inevitably arise.

[140] Such an Institute would likely be funded by USAID. The concept is currently being developed under the tutelage of the University of San Francisco School of Law (USF). USF has a broad mandate to develop legal education in Cambodia for law students (undergraduates following the French model), persons in the public

and private sector, and for the fledgling Cambodian Bar Association. USF has a full staff in Phnom Penh and several professors, including the authors of this chapter, working on the project here in the United States.

[141] The Law on the Bar, enacted June 15, 1995.

[142] Art. 5, *Ibid.*

[143] *Ibid.*

[144] *Ibid.*

[145] Art. 6, *Ibid.*

[146] *See* Doran, David, "Rule of Law: The Council for the Development of Cambodia", *Phnom Penh Post*, August 25–September 7, 1995. Mr. Doran is a partner in the firm of Dirksen, Flipse, Doran and Le and, along with Michael Popkin, frequently writes excellent analyses of specific Cambodian financial laws. The same article also details the structure of the CDC.

[147] Law on the Chambers of Commerce, Chap. 1, Art. 1.

[148] Law on the Chamber of Commerce, Chap. 1, Art. 5.

[149] *See* Cheng, Heng Sok, "Biz Chamber Candidates Gear Up for Vote", *Phnom Penh Post*, August 25-September 7, 1995, p.12.

[150] Law on the Chamber of Commerce, Chap. 1, Arts. 9, 10, and 11.

[151] *Ibid.*

HONG KONG

David M. Lederman

I. Summary of Business and Political Conditions

Basic Demographic, Political and Economic Information

Demographics

Hong Kong is a British colony composed of Hong Kong Island, the Kowloon peninsula and the New Territories. Its population of 5.865 million people (1993) makes it one of the most densely populated areas of the world.[1] It has a total land mass of about 412 miles (1,067 square km).[2] The population is roughly 98 per cent ethnic Chinese and about 2 per cent other minorities.[3] The predominant religions are Taoism, Buddhism and Christianity.[4] The port of Hong Kong is one of largest container ports in the world.[5]

B.01

Language

There are three dominant languages spoken in Hong Kong: Cantonese, Mandarin and English. Presently English predominates the legal profession. In the past the "official language" of Hong Kong was English. However, that changed in 1974 with the Official Languages Ordinance.[6] All new statutes are written in both English and Chinese, in preparation for Hong Kong's future reclamation by China in 1997, however English is still the dominant language used in the higher courts. The July 5, 1995 amendment to the Official Languages Ordinance removed one of the last English language restrictions.[6a] Today both Chinese and English are the "Official" languages and are given equal weight. This may continue after the Chinese resume sovereignty over Hong Kong. According to Article 9 of the Basic Law (Hong Kong's constitution come 1997) English "may be used as an official language". Mandarin

B.02

Hong Kong

is the "official language" of the People's Republic of China. It therefore is becoming more widely spoken in Hong Kong. However, most Hong Kong Chinese speak Cantonese as their native language.

Although there are many dialects spoken in China the written language is essentially universal. One of the major changes brought about by the Communist government was the simplification of the Chinese writing system, naturally referred to as "simplified characters" (*jian ti zi*). This simplification of the language was supposed to make the written language more accessible to the common people. Both Hong Kong and Taiwan continue to use the traditional characters often referred to as "complex characters" (*fan ti zi*). The key difference between the two systems is the number of brush strokes required for each character.

Economic Information

B.03   The local currency is the Hong Kong dollar (HK$). The Hong Kong Monetary Authority (HKMA) has tried to keep the Hong Kong Dollar (HK$) pegged to the US dollar (US$) at 7.8 HK$ to 1 US$ since 1985.[7]

Throughout most of the 1990s, unemployment remained at around 2 per cent,[8] however, recent statistics have shown a modest rise to around 3.2 per cent.[9] Real Economic growth is at 5.5 per cent.[10] At the end of 1994 Hong Kong's foreign exchange reserves stood at a healthy US$ 49.2 billion (which was up US$ 7.2 billion from the prior year).[11] Inflation is around 9 per cent.[12] Rent in Hong Kong is one of the highest in the world at $137 per square foot.[13]

The economies of Hong Kong and southern China have become highly integrated. For those interested in doing business in China, Hong Kong should be carefully examined for use as a headquarters for operations in China. Hong Kong is China's largest trading partner accounting for two-thirds of its direct foreign investment (1991).[14] However, at least some of these investors are of foreign origin using Hong Kong firms with expertise in setting up business ventures in China. As Hong Kong has a very limited supply of natural resources it imports most of its resources.[15] The largest source of imports for Hong Kong is the Peoples Republic of China (PRC).[16] China is Hong Kong's third-largest source of direct foreign investment.[17]

The present government of Hong Kong has taken a very minimalist policy towards business regulation, and taxes are relatively low.[18] In general there are no legal impediments to foreign trade or investment. Foreign firms are on the whole treated the same as domestic ones.

Rule of Law

B.04   As opposed to other East Asian nations Hong Kong has a strong common law tradition based on the English system. The common law was imposed on

Hong Kong in 1844.[19] This provided a source of stability upon which business flourished. Hong Kong adopted many of the UK's laws dealing with business and corporations. As such, Hong Kong's legal system is well equipped to handle most commercial disputes that may arise. However, as Hong Kong prepares to revert to China the rule of law and the integrity of Hong Kong's legal system become questionable.

The Basic Law, which is to be Hong Kong's constitution, will leave the capitalist system untouched for 50 years, and further provides that the laws previously in force shall be maintained.[20]

Synopsis of Hong Kong's Political System

History

Article 3 of the Treaty of Nanking signed in 1842 China ceded Hong Kong Island to England in perpetuity.[21] This was the first of what was later to become known as "the unequal treaties", resulting for the most part from Chinese resistance to the British Opium trade. In 1860 part of the Kowloon peninsula was ceded to Great Britain and became part of Hong Kong under the Convention of Peking,[22] as a continuation of Sino-Anglo hostilities over the Opium trade. Finally, the area known as the New Territories was given to Great Britain as a part of the second Convention of Peking in 1898 on a 99 year lease.[23] It is this lease which is due to expire on July 1, 1997. Britain realized that due to the integration of the Hong Kong territory the maintenance of Hong Kong Island and Kowloon without the New Territories would be impossible after the expiration of the lease. On July 1, 1997 China will reclaim all of Hong Kong, laying to rest a century and a half of British colonial rule.

China has, since the founding of the PRC, held consistently to the position that the entire territory of Hong Kong is an inalienable part of China.[24] It is China's view that the treaties were the result of oppression, hence the reference to "unequal treaties", and are therefore not valid.[25]

Hong Kong's Governance

The following is a brief description of the most important governing bodies of Hong Kong. Hong Kong's constitution is currently composed of the *Letters Patent* and the *Royal instructions*.[26] Both documents taken together delineate the powers of Hong Kong's governing bodies. Hong Kong's constitution differs from the American Constitution in that the *Letters Patent* and the *Royal instructions* are not the supreme law of the land, and can be amended by an act of Parliament.[27] This state of affairs will last as long as Britain is sovereign over Hong Kong. That sovereignty is due to end at midnight on June 30, 1997. At that time the Basic Law will come into effect.[28]

B.05

B.06

Hong Kong

The Basic Law was enacted by the National People's Congress of the PRC on June 4, 1990. It is Chinese law that embodies the principles agreed upon between the UK and the PRC in the Joint Declaration.[29] It is the centerpiece of Deng Xiao-ping's philosophical experiment of using "One country–two Systems" to unify China.

As of July 1, 1997 Hong Kong will be called the Hong Kong Special Administrative Region (HKSAR). Under the Basic Law as agreed to in the Joint Declaration the "capitalist system and way of life shall remain unchanged for 50 years". Further, under Article 12 of the Basic Law the HKSAR is to be locally administered and will "enjoy a high degree of autonomy".[30]

Although the way of life will remain unchanged for 50 years, the government will change. The following discussion of Hong Kong's government will discuss each body of government as it stands today, and the changes to be made pursuant to Chinese sovereignty and the Basic Law.

The Governor

B.07 The office of the Governor is created by the *Letters Patent*. He is the chief executive authority of Hong Kong representing the UK. The Governor can be dismissed any time and is accountable to the Prime Minister. In practice the normal tenure for a Governor is five years.[31] The Governor appoints counsels, public officers, and Judges. Additionally he presides over the Legislative and Executive Councils.[32] His basic job is to govern. He is empowered to make law with the advice and consent of the Legislative Council (LegCo).[33]

Key Basic Law Differences[34]

B.08 On July 1, 1997 the position of Governor will cease to exist and will be replaced by that of the Chief Executive. The Chief Executive will be accountable to the Central People's Government.

The Key differences are that the Chief Executive:

1. Will be selected by "election or through consultation held locally and be appointed by the Central People's Government". The Chinese Government's stated goal in the Basic Law is to ultimately allow the Chief Executive to be elected based on universal suffrage through a type of electorial college system.[35] If implemented this would give the people of the HKSAR far more of a say over who is elected Chief Executive than they did over the appointment of the Governor.
2. The term of appointment will be for a period of 5 years.[36]
3. The Chief Executive can veto a bill from the Legislature by sending it back. LegCo can then override the veto by a majority of two-thirds of *all* the members.[37] If LegCo get the two-thirds majority the Chief Executive would then have the option either to sign the bill into law or, after consulting ExCo, *dissolve the legislature.*[38]

This power effectively gives the Chief Executive the final say over any bill. However, if the new legislature passes the same bill a second time the Chief Executive would be obliged to resign.[39]

The Executive Council (ExCo)

ExCo is similar to the United States' cabinet. It has no independent legislative or administrative powers. Its primary function is to advise the Governor. It is composed of official members and unofficial members.

B.09

The four official members are as follows: the Commander of the British Forces, the Chief Secretary, the Attorney General, and the Financial Secretary. The remaining 10 unofficial members composing the majority of ExCo are prominent citizens appointed by the Governor.[40]

The Governor is required in most instances to consult ExCo prior to making decisions unless exigency requires immediate action. However the final decision is his. If he rejects ExCo's recommendations members may require that the grounds of the rejected opinion be recorded in the minutes, and he must report to the UK and explain why he acted in opposition to ExCo.[41] Exco also has an administrative appeals function from decisions of civil service department heads.

Key Basic Law Differences

No significant difference. Article 65 states simply: "The previous system of establishing advisory bodies by the executive authorities shall be maintained."

The Legislative Council (LegCo)

LegCo is the Legislative branch. It approves bills and advises on the enactment of Ordinances. This branch is currently in the greatest state of flux. In the past it was composed of 10 official members: the Chief Secretary, the Financial Secretary, the Attorney General and seven other civil service officers. In addition to the 10 official members there were 22 appointed members.[42] In 1987, 12 were elected by an electorial college and the remaining 12 were elected by functional constituencies.[43] The functional constituencies are professional organizations and labor unions.

B.10

In 1991 the UK allowed for direct elections of 18 LegCo members. Indirect elections via professional organizations accounted for another 21 members, for the first time putting the Governor's appointees in a minority.[44]

On September 17, 1995 for the first time LegCo was fully elected.[45] Twenty seats were elected by universal suffrage, 10 by local councilors, and the remaining 30 by the functional constituencies.[46] The term of this newly elected legislature was intended to last until 1999, two years after the transference of sovereignty to the PRC.[47] They were to be elected in conformity with the *Decision of the National People's Congress on the method for the Formation of the First Government and the First Legislative Council of the*

Hong Kong

Hong Kong Special Administrative Region.[48] The decision stated that those so elected in conformity with the Basic Law and who pledge allegiance to HKSAR shall be the first (transition) Legislative Council for first two years of the HKSAR. However, this continuum is in doubt.

Key Basic Law Differences

The Chinese Government has said that it will dissolve the legislature at midnight June 30, 1997 and replace it with its own provisional legislature.[49]

The Judiciary

B.11 Until July 1, 1997 the highest Court of Appeal for Hong Kong is the British Privy Council (located in London). Hong Kong has a Supreme Court (comprised of a Chief Justice and Justices of the Court of Appeals and the High Court), and lower District Courts and magistrates. Supreme Court Judges are appointed by the Governor in consultation with the Judicial Services Commission.[50] While decisions of the Privy Council are directly binding on Hong Kong Courts, decisions of other British courts are also given deferential persuasive respect.

Key Basic Law Differences

The judicial system as it previously existed shall be maintained except for those changes necessary to create the Court of Final Appeal to replace the prior system of appeals to the Privy Council.[51] The common law system is supposed to be maintained after the transition.

Article 82 of the Basic Law states that the Court of Final Appeal will have the power of final adjudication in HKSAR. Article 85 goes on to state that the courts of the HKSAR shall "exercise judicial powers independently, free from interference." However, the power to interpret the Basic Law is vested in the Standing Committee of the National People's Congress.[52] One aspect of the power to interpret the Basic Law is the power to define its scope.

According to the Basic Law Article 19 the HKSAR has no power over acts of state "**such as** defense and foreign affairs".[53] A somewhat tortured interpretation of this may include breaches of contract by PRC state run enterprises. This could represent a serious curtailment of the power of Hong Kong's judiciary to settle commercial disputes with PRC traders. One would hope that the NPC exercises restraint in its power to interpret the Basic Law. However, the foreign investor should be aware of the potential impact this may have on the future of dispute resolution in the soon to be ex-colony.

Hong Kong's Regulatory Environment

B.12 The Hong Kong government has generally adopted a policy of nonintervention in the private sector. Presently there are few barriers to foreign investment. The government of Hong Kong has traditionally been committed to free trade, allowing private enterprises to shape economic growth.[54] Therefore business regulations are minimal. However, all business must be registered, whatever the form, under the Business Registration Ordinance.[55] Foreign firms are treated equally with domestic firms except that all companies incorporated outside of Hong Kong that establish a place of business in Hong Kong must register in accordance with the Companies Ordinance part IX.[56]

To register a foreign firm will need to supply the Registrar of Companies with the following information:

1. a certified copy of the firm's bylaws (or documents serving the same purpose, *i.e.* constitution);
2. list of the directors (including enumerated detailed personal information);
3. name of secretary;
4. name and address of at least one person who is authorized to accept service of process on behalf of the corporation, as well as a memorandum of appointment for the designated person under the corporation's seal;
5. address of principle place of business in Hong Kong, as well as place of incorporation;
6. certified copy of the firms Articles of Incorporation, and
7. a certified copy of the corporations most recent accounts (exception provided for Hong Kong Private company or comparative entity such as the United States' statutory close corporation).

Jurisdiction of the Courts[57]

District Courts

The District Courts can hear contract and tort cases where the amount in controversy exceeds $5,000 and is less than $60,000. Cases less than $5,000 need to be brought before the Small Claims Tribunal. There is no right to a jury at this level.   B.13

The High Court of Justice

The High Court of Justice hears civil cases in excess of $60,000. While most cases are heard by the judge sitting without a jury, a party may request one and deposit with the Registrar sufficient funds to cover the costs.

The Court of Appeal

The Court of Appeal hears appeals from *inter alia* the District Court and the High Court of Justice. Until July 1, 1997 this is the highest appellate court in Hong Kong.

Hong Kong

Post-1997: The Final Court of Appeals

Presently appeals from the Court of Appeal goes to the Judicial Committee of the Privy Council in London. After the People's Republic of China resumes sovereignty over Hong Kong appeal will go the Final Court of Appeals. In theory this will be the court of the highest appellate jurisdiction replacing the Privy Council. However, on questions concerning the interpretation of the Basic law (Hong Kong's post-transfer constitution) the final arbiter is the National People's congress.[58]

Regional Trade Forums

B.14   Hong Kong as a British colony lacks full diplomatic powers, therefore its participation in international treaties is by way of extension through the UK. However, the Governor has been given the authority to enter into and implement international and regional trade agreements and organizations.[59] As such, Hong Kong is a member of GATT/WTO, the Asian Development Bank, Interpol and the United Nations.[60] Through the UK, Hong Kong is a member of the Berne Convention, Universal Copyright Convention, the Paris Convention, Patent Cooperation Treaty 1970.[61]

Under the Basic Law it is assumed that this state of affairs will be unchanged. Article 151 states that HKSAR "may ... maintain and develop relations and conclude and implement agreements with foreign states and regions and relevant international organizations in the appropriate fields, including the economic, trade, financial ... fields".[62]

II. Laws and Institutions Affecting Business and Commercial Activities

Competition Law

B.15   Hong Kong has no formal barriers to foreign firms entering the market place. According to one author the guiding principle of the Hong Kong economy is positive non-intervention or laissez-faire.[63] As such there is very little by way of formal anti-competition laws similar to the United States Sherman Act. The one key area of anti-competition law in Hong Kong is intellectual property. That subject is discussed separately under its own heading. There are no anti-trust laws, however, there are still a few areas where there is a government monopoly or foreign investment is restricted.[64]

This section will discuss the major areas of competition law: the common law torts of passing off, conspiracy, and restraints on competition in the employment context. These areas are the product of English common law as modified (if at all) by the courts of Hong Kong.

Passing Off

The elements of the tort passing off are discussed briefly in the section on intellectual property. It is a tort that occurs when a seller of goods misrepresents those goods to the public in such a manner that it misleads the public into thinking the goods are actually those of another.[65] For example, an infringer may sell a counterfeit product by altering the name of the famous name brand. For instance, a pair of sunglasses bearing the name Ray Bons written in the same script as the name brand Ray Bans would be actionable under the tort passing off.

Conspiracy

The common law elements of conspiracy require the following:

1. two or more persons;
2. joined together;
3. with the intent to cause economic injury to another, and
4. damages.

In a civil conspiracy suit, if the defendant was acting to protect his own legitimate interests that was a defense.[66]

Restrictive Covenants

A restrictive covenant in the employment context is a promise or undertaking whereby an employee agrees not to engage in certain activities which may harm the employer's business.[67] To be effective a restrictive covenant needs to be reasonable and not contra public policy.[68]
According to Anne Carver, there are four main types of restrictive covenants. They are covenants:

1. Not to disclose or use confidential information, trade secrets or confidential technology belonging to the employer's business.
2. Not to solicit other employees to leave the employer within a specified period after leaving the employment.
3. Not to solicit customers of the employer within a specified period after leaving employment.
4. Not to compete with the employer's business for a specified period after leaving the employment.[69]

The courts in determining whether they will enforce any of the above restrictions will rely on a variety of factors. The contract must be reasonably tailored to meet the parties' needs.[70] To be reasonable a restraint of trade must be:

> "(a) reasonable in point of time; (b) reasonable as to the geographic area of its operation; and (c) reasonable as to the restraint it imposes on the employee in respect of the type of work in which the employee is forbidden to engage."[71]

The courts will not endeavor to reform contracts that violate the above rules. The offending clause will simply be excised from the agreement.[72] However, the common law courts may construe the clause to conform to the intent of the parties if it is reasonable to do so.[73]

Contract Law

B.16   The law governing contracts in Hong Kong is the common law rules of England subject to modifications by statutes and minor deviations through Hong Kong's own case law. As with other common law nations, Hong Kong has adopted a separate ordinance to address the sale of goods. The biggest modifications to the common law are for the sale of goods (discussed under the section on Commercial Law), the Control of Exemption Clauses Ordinance,[74] and the Misrepresentation Ordinance[75] (both discussed under Consumer Protection).

The law of contracts is rich and well known to most common law attorneys. This section seeks to highlight some of the fundamental aspects of contract law which are not addressed in the Sale of Goods Ordinance. The reader should note that this is merely introductory in nature.

The law of contracts can be easiest broken down into the following elements: offer, acceptance, consideration, and defenses. Each area will be discussed briefly. The reader will note that the author occasionally resorts to the United States, Restatement of Contracts 2d. This is simply for convenience and clarity. In those instances the Restatements are the most lucid statements of the law.

Offer

An offer is according to the Restatement of Contracts, 2d, a "manifestation of willingness to enter into a bargain, so made as to justify another person in understanding that his assent to that bargain is invited and will conclude it."[76] To determine if the parties manifested an intention to enter into a bargain, the courts will "look to the intention of the parties, as evidenced by their behavior".[77]

Certain actions are presumed not to be offers. These include: invitations to offer such as in the auction context,[78] and advertisements.[79] However, at least with respect to advertisements, if the offeror manifests a willingness to be presently bound, so that all the offeror needs to do is give his assent, that is an offer. The essence of whether or not an offer was made is a question of fact.

Only the person to whom the offer is addressed may accept the offer forming a binding contract. The offer can be to one person or many people however, if made to many it may appear more like an invitation for an offer, especially if the communication lacks specificity.[80]

The offer will terminate in any one of the following ways: acceptance, rejection, revocation, and lapse. Acceptance (discussed below) terminates the offer by maturing it into a full contract. On the other hand a rejected offer cannot be accepted afterwards unless the offeror renews the offer. Third, until the offer is accepted the offeror can unilaterally revoke the offer. However, when the offeree has paid consideration (discussed below) to keep the offer open for a period of time, the offeror cannot revoke the offer until that period of time has elapsed. That type of offer is called an option. An option is itself a binding contract.

Finally an offer can end by the mere passage of time. That amount of time could be an expiration date stated by the offeror or, if none it would be the mere passage of reasonable amount of time. What is reasonable depends on the circumstances of the offer.

Acceptance

Acceptance is made by the offeree expressing a present willingness to be bound by the terms of the offer. There are two basic ways an offer can be accepted. The first is by the offeree making a reciprocal promise, called the bilateral contract. The second is by performance, or the unilateral contract. The most common form of business contracts is the bilateral contract.[81] The method which the offeree must use to accept the offer must be the form in which the offeree designated. The offeror can demand acceptance in any manner he chooses.[82] When no manner of acceptance is designated the proper manner will be whatever is reasonable under the circumstances.[83]

B.17

Consideration

According to one author, "every legal system distinguishes between promises that it chooses to enforce and promises that it will not enforce. One who seeks to enforce a promise in a common law jurisdiction must affirmatively establish a basis for finding the promise enforceable . . . Consideration is the primary basis for promise enforcement in the common law system".[84]

Consideration is what distinguishes enforceable promises from gratuitous promises, or gifts. Simply defined it is bargained for legal detriment.[85] Courts will not look to test the sufficiency of the consideration, that is the for the parties to decide.[86] The detriment can take the form of merely promising to do something or forebearing from doing something which the offeree was legally allowed to do.

What would normally be considered an unenforceable promise can be made enforceable by giving some nominal consideration in exchange.[87] However, the lack of consideration will rarely, if ever, be an issue in an arms length business agreement.

Conclusion

There are far too many defenses to contract formation to discuss in detail in this introductory essay on contracts. However, in general, each defense is an attack on one of the three elements of a contract. For example, the defense of duress is an attack on acceptance. The party arguing duress will try to persuade the judge that the acceptance of the offer was not of his own volition, *i.e.* he was not willing to assent to the offer.

Commercial Law

The Sale Of Goods

B.18 The Sale of Goods Ordinance (SOGO) is substantially the same as the English Act of 1893.[88] SOGO applies only to the sale of goods. Goods are defined as "all chattels personal other than things in action and money".[89] SOGO is not as comprehensive as the United States' Uniform Commercial Code (UCC). SOGO does not address some of the basic common law rules such as offer and acceptance (which are discussed under the section on contracts). Therefore the common law rules apply. Further common law defenses such as undue influence, mistake and misrepresentation also apply.[90] What follows is a basic guide to SOGO.

Formation

SOGO applies to both the present sale of goods and agreements to sell goods in the future. A contract may be formed either in writing or orally. Unlike the UCC, there is no statute of frauds provision in SOGO.[91]

While at common law the element of consideration merely requires legal detriment or bargain for exchange, SOGO is more restrictive. In order for a sale of goods to be governed by SOGO the consideration paid must be money. Therefore it does not apply to barter contracts.

SOGO section 15 distinguishes between sale by sample and sale by description. If the sale is by both, the description of the goods predominates. If the goods conform to the sample, but not the description the seller is in breach.

Price

Price can be fixed either explicitly in a contract or by course of dealing between the parties. If no price is stated, the price is a reasonable price based on the facts and circumstances of each particular case.[92]

If the price is left to be fixed by a third party and the third party cannot or does not make the valuation, the agreement is void.[93] However, the buyer must pay a reasonable price for that portion of which was already delivered. If the third party is prevented from making the valuation due to the fault of either party, the party not at fault may bring an action against the wrongdoer.

Warranties

Warranties which apply to the sale of goods include implied warranties. (SOGO sections 14–17 lists the implied warranties.)

As in the UCC there is an implied warranty of merchantability (quality), unless the defect is made known to the buyer, or the buyer had the opportunity to examine the goods and the defect was one which would have been revealed by a reasonable examination.[94]

Where the buyer makes known to the seller the particular purpose for which the goods are purchased there is an implied warranty that the goods will be reasonably suitable for that purpose. Further, the seller implicitly warrants that he has the right to sell the goods or at the time of the agreement to sell, will have that right.

Further warranties will be discussed in the section on consumer protection.

Risk of Loss

Unless the parties otherwise agree, the risk of loss remains with the seller **B.19** until the goods are transferred to the buyer.[95] However when there is a delay in delivery through the fault of either party to the contract, the party who caused the delay will bear the risk of loss to the extent of their fault. Note by its terms SOGO draws a distinction between the time when property passes, shifting the risk of loss to the buyer, and "delivery" of the goods, which does not determine the passing of the risk of loss.

The distinction between the two concepts delivery and passing of property is determined by discerning the intent of the parties. SOGO section 20 lists five rules of construction to aid discovering that intent.

SOGO distinguishes between two basic classifications of goods which have an effect on who bears the risk of loss. Goods can be either specific or unascertained. Specific goods are goods which are identified and agreed upon at the time of the contract. Unascertained goods are goods not yet selected at the time of the formation of the contract. According to SOGO section 9 when there is an agreement to sell specific goods and the goods, through no fault of the seller or buyer, are destroyed the agreement is "avoided". If the goods perished before the making of the contract without the seller's knowledge the contract is void.[96] However, when the goods are unascertained the contract cannot be avoided by the destruction of the goods.

When the parties agree that the seller will deliver the goods to a place and time other than when and where they were sold, the buyer will bear the risk of "deterioration in the goods necessarily incident to the course of transit", unless the parties agree to the contrary.[97]

Hong Kong

Title

SOGO adheres to the concept that a seller cannot pass better title than he has. One selling a good to which he has no title may be in breach of the warranty that he has good title to sell (SOGO section 14). However, a bona fide purchaser (BFP) in the ordinary course of business in a shop or market does acquire good title.[98] Further when the seller has voidable title, the buyer gets good title provided he is a BFP, irrespective of the place of sale.[99]

Performance

Performance of the contract is governed by Part III of SOGO. It contains a series of gap filler provisions many of which are similar to the UCC. Section 30 states that, unless otherwise agreed, delivery of the goods and payment of the price are conditions concurrent. If nothing is said as to the place of delivery then the place of delivery is the seller's place of business. If he has none, then the place of delivery is his residence. Further, the buyer has a reasonable time to inspect the goods before acceptance. If the buyer unreasonably delays inspecting the goods he will be deemed to have accepted the goods.[100] As such, much like under the UCC, after the time to inspect has passed the buyer will no longer be able to reject the nonconforming goods. A buyer also accepts nonconforming goods by an act inconsistent with the seller's ownership rights in the goods.[101]

If when the contract was made the goods were in some other place and both parties knew this to be so, then that is the place of delivery. If nothing is said as to time then the time for delivery is a reasonable time.

The general rule as to delivery of nonconforming quantities of the goods is that the buyer has the right to accept the nonconforming portion and reject the rest or reject the whole and sue for breach of contract.[102] Unless agreed the buyer cannot be forced by the seller to accept delivery in installments where no such provision was contracted for. However, whatever the buyer accepts he must pay for at the contract rate.

The seller and the buyer will have the traditional common law remedies for breach of contract. Theses remedies include both legal damages and equitable remedies such as specific performance.

International Contracts

Although China is a signatory of the United Nations Convention on Contracts for the International Sale of Goods (CISG) neither the UK nor Hong Kong are. As such the CISG does not apply by operation of law as it does in other nations. Therefore SOGO will apply to the international sale of goods, unless the contract selected another forum's law to control the transaction.

However, the Basic Law provides that the laws previously in force in

Hong Kong will be maintained, subject to amendment by the Hong Kong legislature. This raises the question as to whether the CISG could be applied to Hong Kong by a favorable vote of the legislature, or perhaps come 1997 the CISG will apply by virtue of the PRC's membership in that convention.

Secured Transactions

As not all purchasers of property have the available cash to make the desired purchases, the law developed the concept of secured transactions. Hong Kong has developed several methods by which a seller can retain some interest in the goods sold until the time the buyer makes full payment. This section will briefly examine the following types of secured transactions: credit sales, liens, mortgages, pledges and hire-purchase agreements. Note that unlike the UCC Article 9, there is no statutory system for registering all security interest.[103] The following discussion only addresses secured transactions as they related to transactions in goods.

B.20

Liens

In a lien the seller retains a property interest in the goods. The Sale of Goods Ordinance Part IV addresses the rights of the seller against the goods. Under SOGO the seller has a lien interest in the goods as long as the goods remain in the seller's possession. As soon as the goods are transferred to the buyer the security interest in the goods dissipates. Where there is part delivery the seller may still exercise his right to retain the remainder, unless the circumstances show that the seller, by partial delivery waived his right to the lien.[104] A vendor's lien is a lien that aries out of the agreement from which the debt arose. An example of this kind of lien is when one takes one's automobile to be serviced. The service station will have a lien on the car for the work done. Liens can also be created by agreement or court order.[105] However, where the intent of the parties was to have a credit sale, the seller will have no basis for a lien. His only recourse would be to sue for breach of contract.

Mortgages

A mortgage is essentially the bifurcation of possession and title to the goods. The mortgagor (borrower) will have the right to possession, while the mortgagee (creditor) will have the right to seize the goods if the mortgagor does not pay (because the mortgagor has title).[106] Mortgages need not be in writing. However, when the mortgage is in writing and refers to goods it is called a bill of sale. Bills of sale must be registered under the Bill of Sale Ordinance within seven days of its execution.[107] If not registered in accordance with the Ordinance, the bill of sale is void. As such the goods cannot be foreclosed upon. When a mortgage affects the personal property of a company it must be registered under the Companies Ordinance to have effect.[108]

Hong Kong

Pledges

In the instance of pledges the property itself is the security. Unlike other forms of security, the debtor actually hands over the property itself to the creditor. The creditor (pledgee) keeps the property until the debt is fully paid.[109]

Hire-Purchase Agreements

The hire-purchase agreement is much like a lease agreement with an option to purchase. In the hire purchase agreement the price paid towards the lease would apply to satisfaction of the purchase price. If the lessee defaults as payment becomes due the owner may then resume possession. Unlike in the UK, this type of agreement is not controlled by statute. Its origin is in the common law.

In order for the seller/owner to protect himself from the sale of the chattel to a BFP it is necessary to register the agreement to give the world constructive notice.[110]

Companies Law

B.21 The law of companies as well as other business entities are largely the result of the evolution of the common law. Most of the principles are the same as those shared by other common law nations. The ordinances addressing this area are essentially codification of the preexisting common law rules. There are no special laws promulgated to address joint ventures. Each of the business forms discussed in the following sections can be used as a vehicle for a joint venture. The most common form for a joint venture is the limited liability company.[111] This section will describe the vehicles available to the foreign investor to conduct business in Hong Kong.

Whatever the business entity, it will be necessary for it to register under the Business Registration Ordinance.[112] This will require that the business register with the Commissioner of the Inland Revenue Department in accordance with the forms attached to the Ordinance. The business registration certificate is valid for one year and must be renewed annually. The Commissioner must be notified within one month of any changes with respect to the application.[113]

Unincorporated Business

Sole Trader

B.22 By its very name the sole trader is unavailable as a vehicle for joint ventures. However, it is important to discuss it this volume on commercial laws because it is an option for foreign individuals considering doing business in Hong Kong. The sole trader is not a product of any statute, however, if created it must comply with Business Registration Ordinance,[114] and if it employs others it must comply with the relevant employment statutes. As the sole trader is not covered by any liability sheltering statutes he is subject to unlimited personal liability. In addition, the sole trader does not pay a salaries tax on his earnings. His profits are subject to the profits tax (see tax section).

Contractual Joint Venture

This is merely a contractual arrangement between two or more entities whereby they agree to cooperate on a certain business venture. This arrangement is more tenuous than a partnership and does not create a separate business entity. Their obligations and responsibilities towards each other must be carefully detailed in the joint venture contract (see practical considerations). This form of venture is less than a partnership. The parties must be careful not to fall within the definition of a partnership (see below). To do so will subject the partnership to a joint tax assessment (see tax below).

Partnership

One potential vehicle for foreign investors to do business in Hong Kong is through a partnership. There are two basic types of partnerships. The first is the unlimited liability partnership,[115] the other is the limited liability partnership.[116] Both types will be discussed in brief. The main focus in the following discussion of partnership law is its applicability to foreign business for joint venture.

Unlike a company, a partnership is not an independent legal entity. It is simply the "relation which subsists between persons carrying on a business in common with a view of profit".[117] It is a product of contract and can be formed either in writing or orally. In accordance with the Business Registration Ordinance the partnership must be registered with the Commissioner of the Inland Revenue Department.[118]

In neither of the above mentioned types of partnership can the number of partners exceed 20. The partners with respect to the business venture own each other a high fiduciary duty. They must seek to avoid conflicts of interest in which they must choose between their own self interest and that of the partnership. The rights and duties of the partners to the partnership is normally governed by contract. If however, the partners mutual obligations are not stipulated then the Partnership Ordinance and the Limited Partnership Ordinance delineate the partners respective rights and duties.

Limited Partnership

The limited partnership limits the liability of some partners (the limited partners) to the amount of capital contribution. A limited partnership is composed of two types of partners. The first is the general partner. The general partner is fully liable for the debts of the partnership without limitation, while the limited partner is only liable for up to his paid in capital. The limited partner has no authority to manage the partnership and cannot bind the partnership. A corporation can be a limited partner, however it will still be taxed at the corporate rate (*see* Tax Law).

According to section 4 of the Limited Partnerships Ordinance[119] limited partnerships must be registered with the Registrar of Companies. If the partnership is not registered then it will be deemed to be a general partnership by default and all of the partners will be subject to unlimited liability.

To register, the limited partnership must pay a fee to the Registrar of Companies and deliver to them a memorandum signed by the partners containing the following information:

1. the firm name;
2. the general nature of the business;
3. the full name of each partner;
4. the duration for which the partners entered the partnership (if it is so limited) and the date of its commencement;
5. a statement that the partnership is limited and description of every limited partner as such, and
6. the amount of contributed capital by each of the limited partners and method of payment (*i.e.* cash, property).

Unlimited Partnership

In an unlimited partnership all of the partners can generally participate in the management of the partnership. Each partner has potentially unlimited liability for the partnerships debt and is jointly and severally liable for the partnership's torts.

Company Law

B.23 In general the key distinction between a company and a partnership or sole trader is that the company is seen as an independent legal entity with the power to sue and be sued. There are two broad types of companies available in Hong Kong. The first is the unlimited liability company. The unlimited liability company is rarely used because it provides its shareholders the same unlimited potential for liability as a partnership. Its advantages over the partnership are that it is not limited to 20 members and has a potentially unlimited life.[120] Under the Hong Kong Company Ordinance any business, with the exception of a few professional organizations, that has over 20 persons joined together with a profit making motive must be incorporated.[121] The second type of company is the limited liability company. As opposed to the unlimited liability company the limited liability company means that the extent of a shareholder's liability is the amount of paid in capital (share price).

To register as a limited liability company the firm must pay a filing fee with the Registrar of Companies and file, *inter alia*, the following documents:[122]

1. a memorandum of association stating:
   (a) the company's name (ending with the word limited);
   (b) that the registered office of the company will be in Hong Kong;
   (c) an "Objects clause";
   (d) a limited liability or a guarantee clause and
   (e) authorized share capital;
2. articles of association, and
3. a declaration by a solicitor or director engaged in the formation of the company that the company has complied with all of the requirements of the Company Ordinance.

The memorandum of association contains the information most useful to outsiders such as creditors and other business relations. In Hong Kong for all companies formed after August 31, 1984 the company law has provided for a list of implied powers that are delineated in Schedule 7 of the Company Ordinance. In addition, the objects clause should contain all of the powers and purposes for which the company was formed. An activity that is performed outside the Objects clause is illegal as *ultra vires*. An *ultra vires* contract is void and cannot be enforced. However, the third party trying to enforce the contract may be able to enforce the contract if it can prove that it was entered into in good faith and without notice that the purpose was unauthorized.[123]

A limited liability company can be either limited by shares or by guarantee. A company limited by shares is the most common form of corporation. The members' only exposure in this type of company is its share price. If the company is limited by shares the memorandum of association must state the total number of authorized shares and its par value. A company need not issue all of its authorized shares, however it cannot exceed that number. A guarantee company is one in which the member's liability extends only as far as his specified guarantee. That amount must be stated in the memorandum of association.

As discussed above any business association which has 20 or more members and is not in an exempted class must incorporate. A business which is required to incorporate and does not is void. Contracts made by the business will be considered unenforceable by the business.

Fraudulent Corporations

Forming a corporation offers the advantage of limited liability. In some instances an individual may be tempted to abuse the corporate form by using it to perpetrate some type of fraud. As a response in some instances the courts may be willing to disregard the corporate form and impose unlimited liability on the shareholders.[124] Further when there is only one shareholder and no

B.24

new shareholders added for a six month period that single shareholder will be personally liable for the company's debts.[125]

Private v. Public Companies

B.25 The Company Ordinance draws a distinction between private and public companies. The distinction between the two is similar to the distinction between the C corporation and the S corporation under the United States tax laws. The chief benefit of the private company is that it is not required to file a copy of its annual accounts with the Registrar of Companies. This saves the private company the expense of an annual audit as well as avoiding public disclosure of its accounts.

A private company is defined by the following restrictions. If a company does not have such restrictions in its articles of association it is by default a public company subject to the Company Ordinance disclosure requirements. A private company:

1. must restrict its members' rights to transfer shares (the method of restriction is not specified in the ordinance);
2. cannot have more than 50 shareholders (with the exception of employees and ex-employees who became members while employed), and
3. cannot invite the public to subscribe for shares.[126]

A large subcategory of the public company is the "listed company". That is a company that is listed on the Stock Exchange of Hong Kong, Ltd. The securities industry is supervised by the Securities and Futures Commission (SFC). Listing on the stock exchange requires that a prospectus be filed and approves with the stock exchange, SFC and the Registrar of Companies. This is an expensive process that normally requires several months and the assistance of both legal and financial advisors.[127]

The Overseas Company

B.26 Part XI of the Companies Ordinance requires that all companies incorporated outside of Hong Kong that establish a "place of business" inside of Hong Kong register in compliance with that part of the Companies Ordinance.[128] Section 341 exempts from the definition of a "place of business" "a place not used by the company to transact any business which creates legal obligations". It would appear that given this exemption, representative or liaison offices are excluded from the requirement of registering under Part XI, if they do not partake in contractual or business transactions. However, the scope of the above mentioned exclusion provision is unclear. A representative office will need to enter binding obligations to rent office space and equipment. A strict reading of section 341 would seem to include this type of transaction thus requiring even a representative office to register under this part. If a business is considering opening a representative office they should consult local counsel for the most recent interpretation of section 341.

An overseas company becomes registered in Hong Kong by filing the following documents with the Registrar of Companies and paying the required fee:

1. a certified copy of the firm's bylaws (or documents serving the same purpose, *i.e.* constitution);
2. list of the directors (including enumerated detailed personal information);
3. name of secretary;
4. name and address of at least one person who is authorized to accept service of process on behalf of the corporation, as well as a memorandum of appointment for the designated person under the corporation's seal;
5. address of principle place of business in Hong Kong, as well as place of incorporation;
6. certified copy of the firms Articles of Incorporation, and
7. a certified copy of the corporation's most recent accounts (exception provided for Hong Kong Private company or comparative entity such as the American statutory close corporation).

Further Companies registered under Part XI under the Companies Ordinance are under an ongoing obligation to update changes to the personnel on the board of directors, corporate address, charter, memorandum or articles of incorporation, etc.[129] Section 336 requires the foreign company to file a tax return and balance sheet, etc. annually.

If the company is being liquidated in its home country it is required to give notice to the Registrar within seven days.[130]

Capital Markets and Securities Laws

This section is a brief introduction into the securities laws and institutions of Hong Kong. This section first examines the institutions of the Hong Kong Stock Exchange (HKSE) and the Securities and Futures Commission (SFC) and is followed by a brief discussion of the Securities Ordinance, which is the primary legislation dealing with the securities industry, the statutory scheme for the protection of investors and the basic listing requirements. **B.27**

Hong Kong Stock Exchange (HKSE)

The HKSE, known also by it statutory designation as the Unified Exchange, was created in 1986.[131] The legislation that created the HKSE at the same time wound up the then existing exchanges:[132] the Far East Exchange limited, the Hong Kong Stock Exchange Limited, the Kam Ngan Stock Exchange Limited and the Kowloon Stock Exchange limited.[133] **B.28**

To be a member of the stock exchange one must be a shareholder in the Exchange Company.[134] Only members of the Stock Exchange are permitted to trade on the floor of the HKSE.[135] Trading must be conducted in Hong Kong Dollars (HK$), however, since the HK$ is freely convertible there is no problem exchanging currencies.[136] Further since the HK$ is pegged to the US$ if you are trading from US$ there is little to fear from currency fluctuations.

The language of the statute is in the negative—"no individual shall be eligible to be a member of the Exchange unless he is":

1. a dealer registered under Part VI of the Securities Ordinance (which states among other things basic requirements for registration as well as grounds for refusing to grant registration);[137]
2. of good moral character, and
3. born or is a long term resident of Hong Kong (however, if the individual is "in the opinion of the Commission, . . . a person of good reputation [sic] in dealing in securities" this provision can be waived).[138]

Corporations have similar rules under the Stock Exchanges Unification Ordinance. The Corporation must:

1. be a registered dealer under the securities act;
2. be incorporated in Hong Kong;
3. have as its only business "that of dealing in securities and those activities which are normally ancillary to a stockbroking business", and
4. be "of good financial standing and integrity".[139]

In addition to the above statutory requirements the Rules of the Stock Exchange impose additional requirements relating mostly to capitalization, disclosure, trust accounts, and other trading activities.[140] The aforementioned rules are subject to the statutory rules that will be discussed below.

The main stock index in Hong Kong is the Hang Seng Stock Index, which is modeled on the Dow Jones Industrial Average.[141]

Securities and Futures Commission (SFC)

B.29 The main regulatory body for the securities and futures industry is the SFC.[142] The SFC is a corporate body with the power to sue and be sued.[143] The SFC has the following obligations under the Securities and Futures Ordinance:

1. to advise the Financial Secretary on all matters relating to securities, futures contracts and property investment arrangements;[144]
2. to be responsible for ensuring that the provisions of the securities and futures related Ordinances are complied with[145] (a list of most of these Ordinances are listed as part of the definition of "the relevant Ordinances" of section 2 of the Ordinance);[146]
3. to report to the financial Secretary the occurrence of any dealings it suspects to be insider trading (to be discussed below);[147]

4. to be responsible for supervising and monitoring the activities of the Exchange Companies and clearing houses;[148]
5. to take all reasonable steps to safeguard the interests of persons dealing in securities or trading in futures contracts or entering into property investment arrangements;[149]
6. to promote and encourage proper conduct amongst members of the Exchange Companies and clearing houses, and other registered persons;[150]
7. to suppress illegal, dishonorable and improper practices in dealing in securities, trading in futures contracts, entering into property investment arrangements, and the provisions of investment advice or other services relating to securities, futures contracts and property investment arrangements;[151]
8. to promote and maintain the integrity of registered persons and encourage the promulgation by registered persons of balanced and informed advice to their clients and to the public generally;[152]
9. to consider and suggest reforms of the law relating to securities, futures contracts and property investment arrangements;[153]
10. to encourage the development of securities and futures markets in Hong Kong and the increased use of such markets by investors in Hong Kong and elsewhere,[154] and
11. to promote and develop self regulation by market bodies in the securities and futures industries.[155]

In addition to the above enumerated obligations the SFC has other powers and duties designated to it under the other securities regulations. All of the above obligations can be delegated by the Commission to any if the directors of the Commission, a committee or any employee of the commission.[156] The Commission must also publish an annual report of its activities for the Financial Secretary and Legco.[157]

Where an application for registration is refused or the SFC takes some type of disciplinary action against a trader (such as revoking or suspending registrations) the Ordinance provides for an appellate process.[158]

Securities Ordinance

Registration of Dealers

According to the Securities Ordinance section 48, all dealers in securities must be registered under the Ordinance.[159] A corporation cannot deal in securities unless one of the directors actively participates or is directly supervising the business of dealing in securities and that director is registered under the Ordinance.[160] Any person who knowingly violates the registration requirement will be subject to criminal fines.[161] There are exceptions to the registration requirement for certain investment advisors.[162]

Dealing in securities is defined under section 2(1) of the Ordinance as

B.30

making or offering to make an agreement or inducing or attempting to induce another into making an offer into an agreement:

1. to acquire, dispose of, subscribe or for underwriting securities, and
2. with the purpose or pretend purpose to secure a profit for any of the parties to from they yield of securities or by reference to the fluctuations in the value of the securities.[163]

To register an individual must show the following:

1. that he has at least three years experience in dealing in securities in Hong Kong or a SFC recognized stock market or passed the SFC approved examination;[164]
2. that he can meet the capitalization requirements.[165]

A corporation must make a similar showing except that it must be registered under the Companies Ordinance as either a Hong Kong or overseas firm.[166] In addition to the above requirements in the Securities Ordinance there is the additional requirement under the Securities and Futures Commission Ordinance that the Commissioner must refuse to register a person who is not "a fit and proper person to be registered".[167] The basic requirements that the commission is supposed to examine is that the person has a stable financial status, the proper education or other qualifications to perform, and that he has the character and integrity to deal in securities.[168]

Trading in Securities

The Securities Ordinance requires that with certain exceptions an offer to buy or sell securities must be in writing or be put in writing within 24 hours of the oral communication.[169] Unless the Commissioner previously consented otherwise the offer must be written in both English and Chinese. The offer must include among other things the following disclosures:

1. the name and address of the offeror and if any person is making the offer on behalf of the offeror, the name and address of that person;[170]
2. description of the securities sufficient to identify them;[171]
3. specific terms of the offer;[172]
4. where a dividend has been declared, is recommended, or anticipated before the transfer of securities the offer must state whether or not the securities will be transferred with the dividend,[173] and
5. whether or not the offeror will pay any stamp duty that the person will become liable as a result of the transaction.[174]

Protecting Investors

B.31 Another aspect of the Securities Ordinance is its consumer protection sections. Section 73 prohibits dealers from entering into a contract for the sale of securities by contacting people at their homes or business unless he does so at the persons invitation and includes the disclosures discussed above.[175]

However, excepted from this protection are investors who already hold securities in that corporation,[176] a person the dealer has made transactions for three times over the last three years,[177] or persons such as institutional investors, solicitors or professional accountants, etc.[178]

Where a contract is entered into in violation of section 73 the purchaser may rescind within 28 days, subject to the rights of any bona fide purchaser for value (BFP).[179] Subject to certain time restrictions upon request from a client, the dealer must provide him with a copy of the contract note relating to the dealing and a copy of his account with the dealer.[180]

Section 74 of the Ordinance generally prohibits persons (dealer or not) from "calling from place to place" soliciting people to enter into agreements to sell securities.[181] If he so solicits more than twice within two weeks it will create a rebuttable presumption that he has been "calling from place to place".[182] A conviction of "calling from place to place" subjects the defendant to fines and imprisonment.[183]

The Protection of Investors Ordinance in general makes it illegal for a dealer to fraudulently, or by reckless misrepresentation induce a person to enter into a contract for the sale of securities.[184] Such acts are punishable by fines and imprisonment.[185]

Insider trading is also prohibited. If found by the Insider Dealing Tribunal to have committed insider dealing the guilty insider can be barred from being a director, liquidator, receiver or manager of the property of a listed company for up to five years.[186] The insider may also be liable to pay a fine of any profit or treble the amount gained or loss avoided by any person as a result of the insider dealing.[187] However, no transaction will be avoided solely because it was conducted by an insider.[188]

Listing Rules in Brief

The listing rules are issued and administered by the HKSE.[189] A company **B.32** seeking to be listed on the HKSE must issue a prospectus under the Companies Ordinance,[190] and meet among others the following requirements:

1. meet the minimum capitalization requirements (presently at HK$100 million);
2. have made at least HK$20 million in profits for the most recent fiscal year, and more than HK$30 million for the prior two years;[191]
3. have at least HK$50 million worth of securities held by the public.[192]

In addition the company must meet the disclosure requirements including:

1. identifying directors and senior management;
2. disclosing the director's and senior management's compensation;
3. pension plans and costs;
4. major customers and suppliers.[193]

When a listing is granted, the company must enter into a listing agreement with the HKSE.[194] That agreement is the principle source of a listed company's continuing disclosure obligations.[195] That obligation includes continuing disclosure and audit requirements.[196]

Arbitration and Other ADR Techniques

B.33　There are four principle forms of alternative dispute resolution in Hong Kong:[197] negotiation, mediation, conciliation and arbitration. The first three are relatively informal and require merely a brief description. The fourth, arbitration, is fairly well developed and will be addressed in more detail.

Negotiation is the most informal method of dispute resolution. It involves no neutral third party. It is often used before and concurrently with the other methods. Mediation is a process involving a neutral third party. However, the third party does not have the power to make a decision. He or she can merely make suggestions and try to clarify the parties' positions. Conciliation is essentially the same as mediation except that the neutral third party plays a more active role in seeking to encourage the parties to come to an agreement.[198]

Arbitration

B.34　The Hong Kong International Arbitration Center (HKIAC) is the main organization which administers commercial arbitration in Hong Kong. There are two kinds of commercial arbitration in Hong Kong: Domestic and International. Arbitrations in Hong Kong are governed by the Arbitration Ordinance.[199] The Ordinance contains the following six schedules: Protocol on the Arbitration Clauses 1923, the Geneva convention on the Execution of Foreign Arbitral Awards 1927, the New York Convention on the Recognition and Enforcement of Foreign Arbitral Awards (1958), a schedule dealing with judge-arbitrators, and the Uncitral Model Law (Model law). The Ordinance laws out the legal framework for arbitrations in Hong Kong while the HKIAC lays out its rules of procedure.

As in other common law nations the decision to resort to arbitration is normally the result of an arbitration clause in a contract. If the parties to a contract do not agree at the formation stage of the contract to arbitration they will need to agree mutually to forgo litigation and resort to arbitration at the time of the dispute. Absent a contract term neither party can unilaterally impose an obligation to arbitrate. The determination as to whether or not there is a valid contract is not arbitration. If the contract is determined to be invalid the arbitration clause in the contract is also invalid and therefore no obligation to arbitrate will exist.

Hong Kong is a member of the New York Convention on the Recognition and Enforcement of Foreign Arbitral Awards.[200] This convention binds contracting parties to recognize arbitration awards granted in other member

States. China is also a member of this agreement, and as such, after the transition the convention should still apply.

Model Law and Arbitration Ordinance Compared

Under the Model Law an arbitration is international if any of the following apply:

1. the parties at the time of the formation of the contract have their place of business in different States; or
2. the agreed jurisdiction for arbitration is outside the State where the parties have their place of business; or
3. a substantial part of the performance of the contract is to be performed outside the State in which the parties have their principle place of business or the place with which the subject matter of the dispute is most closely connected, or
4. the parties agree that any dispute will be "international".[201]

International arbitrations are governed by the Model Law while domestic arbitrations are governed under the Arbitration Ordinance essential as it existed before the adoption of the Model Law.[202]

Under Article 7 of the Model Law an "arbitration agreement" is an agreement by the parties to submit to arbitration all or certain disputes which may have arisen or which may arise between them in respect of a defined legal relationship whether contractual or not. An arbitration agreement may be in the form of an arbitration clause in a contract or in the form if a separate agreement.

Under Hong Kong law there is no requirement that an arbitration clause designate Hong Kong as the situs of the arbitration nor if the arbitration is in Hong Kong must Hong Kong's substantive laws control. However, if the forum choice is Hong Kong the substantive and procedural rules cannot contravene public policy.[203]

Under the Arbitration Ordinance, in domestic disputes, the parties have a right to appeal issues of law.[204] However, under the Model Law there is no such right. This type of finality of findings makes the Model Law more attractive to those who want to seek a relatively quick determination of the parties rights and obligations.

Under the Arbitration Ordinance an arbitrator can be removed on the request of one of the parties on the grounds that the arbitrator is biased or there is a potential ground for bias.[205] This request to remove the arbitrator applies even if the aggrieved party knew of the arbitrator bias before the appoint of the arbitrator was made. If there has been misconduct on the part of an arbitrator the aggrieved party can petition the court to remove the arbitrator and set aside the improperly procured award.

In contrast the Model Law limits the parties right to remove the arbitrator for bias only for reasons that the party was unaware of at the time of the appointment of the arbitrator. Further the arbitrator has an obligation to disclose any bias he may have before his appointment.

If the arbitration agreement does not specify the number of arbitrators the Arbitration Ordinance specifies that one arbitrator will be the default.[206] This is in contrast to the Model Law which specifies three as the default number.[207]

Conciliation

B.35 A special feature of the Hong Kong Arbitration Ordinance is the emphasis given to conciliation.[208] Under the Ordinance the parties may appoint a conciliator and have that same person serve as an arbitrator if the conciliation process fails. If the parties so designate in the agreement the parties will not be able to object to the appointment of that conciliator as an arbitrator. Settlements derived through conciliation are deemed under section 2A(4), and are treated as arbitration awards for the purpose of enforcement.[209]

Banking and Lending Law

B.36 As of September 1995 Hong Kong has approximately 500 foreign banks. It is the fourth largest banking center in the world and is the fifth largest foreign exchange center.[210]

Hong Kong has no central bank. The powers normally given to a central bank are divided among several institutions. Its currency is issued by three commercial banks: Hong Kong Bank, Standard Chartered Bank, and the Bank of China. The currency issued by those banks are backed by US dollars.[211]

Most of what would be a central bank's regulatory powers have been granted to the Hong Kong Monetary Authority (HKMA). The HKMA controls the Exchange Fund.[212] The Exchange Fund tries to influence monetary policy as well as the overall cash supply.[213] In the past the Exchange Fund has been used as a lender of last resort to support failing banks. According to section 3 of the Exchange Fund Ordinance the "financial secretary may with a view to maintaining Hong Kong as an international financial centre, use the fund as the thinks fit to maintain the stability and integrity of the monetary and financial systems of Hong Kong". The overriding policy objective of the HKMA is to maintain the linked exchange rate of US$ 1 to HK$ 7.8.[214]

The Hong Kong Banking system is regulated through the Banking Ordinance. The mission of the Banking Ordinance is expressed in its long title as "to provide a measure of protection for depositors and to promote the general stability of the banking system . . ." All applications for bank licenses goes through the HKMA. The Banking Ordinance governs the following three types of institutions: licensed banks, restricted license banks and deposit-taking companies. The discretionary authority to grant licenses for banks and restricted banks rests with the Governor in Council and the

Financial Secretary. While the HKMA has discretionary power to grant licenses to deposit-taking companies.[215]

The Three Types of Banks

Licensed banks are essentially the full service banks. They can accept deposits of unlimited size or duration and operate savings and checking accounts. All licensed banks are required to be members of the Hong Kong Association of Banks (HKAB). The HKAB sets the minimum and maximum interest rates that the Banks can charge. Unlike the other two types of banks the licensed banks can use the word "bank" in their name and advertisements without restriction.[216] A licensed bank's minimum capitalization requirement is HK\$150 million.[217]   **B.37**

Restricted banks can engage in merchant banking and the capital markets. These banks can (with a few exceptions) only take deposits of a minimum of HK\$500,000.[218] Restricted banks can also use the word "bank" in their name and advertisements, however, the use must be qualified with adjectives that indicate the banks restricted nature. Restricted banks are not limited by HKAB's interest caps. Restricted banks have a minimum capital requirement of HK\$500,000.[219]

The third type of bank, called a deposit-taking company, cannot use the word "bank" in its name or advertisements. Deposit taking companies can accept minimum deposits of HK\$ 100,000. Their minimum capital requirement is HK\$100,000.[220]

The Governor in Council has broad discretion in the granting of licenses. If a license is denied he need not give an explanation. He may also attach conditions.[221]

Foreign Banks in Hong Kong need at least \$16 billion in assets, but a license may still be granted where the bank is of "unquestionable standing" and the granting of the license would be in the interest of Hong Kong.[222] However, new foreign banks opening in Hong Kong are restricted to a single office,[223] with one back office in a separate building. The back office can handle transaction processing, strategic planning, correspondence, etc.[224] Automatic Teller Machines (ATMs) are not considered branches for the purposes of the one office restriction. The result has been a proliferation of ATMs in Hong Kong.[225] Under certain conditions the Governor in Council may revoke a bank's license. However if he does he needs to give an explanation.

All licensed banks must be incorporated. A share holder seeking to acquire more than a 10 per cent voting share in the bank must seek approval from HKMA.[226] Banks must maintain an 8 per cent minimum capital adequacy ratio in accordance with the Basle Agreement.[227]

Relationship Between the Bank and Its Customers

Unless excluded by contract, the common law implies certain terms to the banker-customer relationship. The following implied duties are imposed   **B.38** upon the bank. The Bank has the duty to accept money and payments on behalf of the customer. Secondly, provided there are sufficient funds available in a customer's account, the bank has a duty to pay out in compliance with the customer's instructions. Thirdly the Banker must give reasonable notice before termination of a customer's account unless the customer is incapacitated. Finally the bank owes the customer a duty of confidentiality as to the customer's affairs.[228]

The banking consumer should be aware the terms of the relationship are a product of contract, as banks tend to want to limit their liability as best they can. Recently banks in Hong Kong have sought to limit their liability by using "conclusive evidence clauses".[229] These clauses have been sent to customers in the form of "additional terms and conditions" addendums. They state that the customer agrees that statement of account between the bank and the customer is conclusive evidence of the account balance and that if there is an objection it is waived unless the customer notifies the bank within a specified amount of time.

The above mentioned clauses may be proved invalid as adhesion contracts or as violative of the Control of Exemption Clauses Ordinance (CAP 71) which requires a general requirement of reasonableness in contract terms.

Lending

B.39 In general the law of lending is similar to that of other common law jurisdiction. However, Hong Kong does not have a universal system of registration for all securities.[230] In Hong Kong almost anything of value can operate as a security for the purpose of a loan. As discussed above banks under the Banking Ordinance can make loans. Those not authorized under the Banking Ordinance can loan money, however, they must be registered and comply with the Money Lender's Ordinance.[231] Money lenders are restricted from charging interest rates in excess of 60 per cent per annum.[232]

Loans are contractual in nature. As such the common law defenses of lack of consideration, undue influence, etc., apply. The law of lending in Hong Kong is similar to that in most common law jurisdictions.

Consumer Protection Law

B.40 Consumer protection in Hong Kong is not as developed as in many other modern countries. Consumers can find protection stemming from both statutory and common law sources. The main statutory sources of protection are the Control of Exemptions Clauses Ordinance,[233] the Misrepresentation Ordinance[234] and the Sale of Goods Ordinance.[235]

Control of Exemption Clauses Ordinance

B.41 Exemption clauses stem from the common law notion that parties to a contract are free to agree to any terms they wish.[236] The nineteenth century common law philosophy was *caveat emptor* (buyer beware).[237] Since then the common law has evolved to include requirements for adequate notice and penalties for misrepresentation.[238] To combat the common laws evolution away from *caveat emptor*, sellers started incorporating exclusion clauses into their contracts. Those clauses provided that the parties agreed that in the case of a certain contingency the other party would have only limited or no liability. The problem with this was that the parties were often not in equal bargaining positions. The Control of Exemption Clauses Ordinance was promulgated to assist the weaker party from the potentially unfair and harsh result of the common law.

Under the Control of Exemption Clauses Ordinance parties cannot by contract exclude or restrict potential liability for death or personal injury resulting from one party's negligence.[239] Other restrictions on a party's liability for negligence are void unless reasonable.[240] Whether a term is reasonable depends on the facts and circumstances known to the parties at the time of the formation of the contract.[241] This is further qualified by the Ordinance's caveat that just because a person agrees or is aware of the limitation of liability for negligence does not of itself indicate that he voluntarily accepted any risks.[242]

Liability cannot be excluded or restricted for goods damaged in the course of private use or consumption due to negligence on the part of the manufacturer or distributor if the goods are ordinarily supplied for private use or consumption.[243] The Ordinance does not apply to liability arising under international supply contracts or where the law is that of Hong Kong only by virtue of a choice of law selection.[244]

Common Law Protections

At common law there are several rules of construction that prevent exclusion **B.42** clauses from being effective. The first courts could simply resolve any ambiguities in the contract against the party that drafted it.[245] The courts could selectively strike out terms of a contract that contradicted one another, or were against public policy. However, with the enactment of the Control of Exemption Clauses Ordinance, there is no need for the courts to be so creative.[246]

Misrepresentation Ordinance

According to Chui and Roebuck in their mini treatise *Hong Kong Contracts* **B.43** a misrepresentation is:

> "an untrue statement of fact, made by one contracting party to the other, which statement was intended to, and did, induce the other party to enter into the contract."[247]

Under the Misrepresentation Ordinance, even if the misrepresentation has become a part of the contract or the contract has been performed, the aggrieved party would still be entitled to rescind the contract without alleging fraud.[248]

At common law, damages were only available for fraudulent misrepresentations. This changed under the misrepresentation Ordinance.[249] The Ordinance provides for both damages and recision even if the misrepresentation was not intentional.[250]

The Control of Exemption Clauses Ordinance proffers further protection against misrepresentation. It prevents the parties from excluding or limiting their liability for misrepresentation unless the terms were fair and reasonable under the Control of Exemption Clauses Ordinance standard.[251]

Consumer Protection Under SOGO

I .44   Sections 14 to 17 of SOGO are considered the "consumer sections".[252] They are implied in every contract for the sale of goods to a consumer.

Under section 14 the seller of goods implicitly promises that he has the right to sell the goods or, in an agreement to sell at some time in the future, will at the time the property is to pass to the buyer have that right.[253] Section 14 also provides for an implied warranty that there are no known undisclosed encumbrances on the property.[254] Under the Control of Exemption Clauses Ordinance section 11(a) this warranty cannot be excluded or restricted by contract.[255]

Under SOGO, section 15 where there is a sale by description there is an impled condition that the goods will correspond to that condition.[256] The Control of Exemption Clauses Ordinance, section 11(2) states the seller's liability for breach of the conformity requirement cannot be excluded or restricted by the terms of the contract.[257] This section of the Control of Exemption Clauses Ordinance applies to sections 16 and 17 of SOGO as well (discussed below).

SOGO section 16 states that there is no implied warranty of fitness for use or quality unless the goods are sold in the ordinary course of business. If the goods are sold in the ordinary course of business there is an implied condition that the goods are of a merchantable quality, unless the defect was brought to the buyers attention and he still purchased it, or the buyer examined the goods and should have discovered the defect.[258] In addition where the buyer makes known the purpose for which the goods are purchased, and it is reasonable to rely on the seller's skill or judgement there is an implied promise that the goods will conform to that purpose.

Where the sale is by sample section 17 applies. Section 17 implies that the bulk will be of the same quality as that of the sample.[259] It further provides a condition that the goods be free from defects rendering them unmerchantable, if upon a reasonable examination of the sample the defects would not have been readily apparent.[260]

Health, Safety and Environmental Law

The first part of this section briefly describes Hong Kong's health and safety **B.45** laws as they relate to employment. It will cover two primary statutes: the Factories and Industrial Undertakings Ordinance, which deals with the inspection, investigation of accidents and enforcement of safety standards for industrial work places[261] and the Employee's Compensation Ordinance. The second part of this section will examine Hong Kong's environmental regulations focusing on the four areas of principle legislation: the Air Pollution Control Ordinance;[262] Noise Control Ordinance;[263] Water Pollution Ordinance;[264] Waste Disposal Ordinance.[265]

Health and Safety

Section seven of the Factories and Industrial Undertakings Ordinance em- **B.46** powers the Commissioner of Labour to make detailed rules to regulate for health and safety in industrial work sites. Breaches of these rules are criminal offenses.[266]

Owners of "industrial undertakings", such as factories and construction sites are required by the regulations to report all incidents which resulted in serious injury or death to a factory inspector within 24 hours. Deaths must also be reported to the police.[267] In addition the proprietor must report any non-injury "dangerous occurrences, such as explosions, structural collapses, etc." within 24 hours.[268]

Under the ordinance proprietors have a general duty to provide a reasonably safe and healthy working environment by way of equipment maintenance; safety instruction and training, etc.[269] A breach of this duty subjects the owner to criminal penalties,[270] and civil suit.[271]

Officers are empowered under the Ordinance to enter and inspect any premises subject to the Ordinance, ask questions and take statements based on a reasonable suspicion of a violation of the ordinance. Like US whistle-blower statutes it is illegal to discriminate against an employee who provides the inspector with information. The statute further requires that the inspector keeps the complainant's identity confidential.[272]

The Employee's Compensation Ordinance provides compensation to employees injured on the job, regardless of whose fault caused the injury (excluding intentionally self inflicted injuries). This right to compensation is in addition to any common law damages an employee may have against his employer. However, any award of damages will be reduced by the amount paid or payable under the ordinance.[273] All employees are covered by this scheme.[274]

In order to be covered the injury must result in more than a three days' absence from work or result in some degree of permanent incapacity. Applicants for compensation must be made within 24 months to either the District

Court·or the Employer. Compensation for the employee is paid for by the employer.[275]

In addition to the Employees' Compensation Ordinance is the Pneumoconiosis Ordinance.[276] This Ordinance created a statutory Pneumoconiosis Compensation Fund out of which to pay compensation for employees (or owners) who suffer from a work-related Pneumoconiosis disease. There is an exception to having to prove the injury was work related for employees with asbestosis or silicosis. To be eligible under this statute the employee needs to have been a resident of Hong Kong for at least five years.[277]

In addition to the above mentioned statutory schemes, at common law employers owe their employees a duty of care. Breach of this duty subjects the employer to civil liability.[278]

Environmental Law

B.47   Hong Kong (in Mandarin *Xiang Gang*) means fragrant harbor. When Hong Kong was first ceded to the British it was, as Lord Palmerston noted, "a barren island with hardly a house upon it".[279] Over the last hundred years Hong Kong has grown exponentially in economic terms, surpassing its colonists' per capita income.[280] One of the casualties of Hong Kong's prosperity is its environment. Hong Kong is said to have a "First World Economy, but a Third World Environment".[281] This section will examine Hong Kong's environmental regulatory agency and the four major ordinances affecting environmental regulation.

Hong Kong's environmental regulatory structure is fragmented, however, the Environmental Protection Department (EPD) is the primary agency obligated to monitor and enforce the environmental regime.[282] The EPD seeks to regulate by having the polluters bear the costs of their pollution.[283] The Air Pollution Control Ordinance[284] gives the Governor in Council after consultation with Environmental Pollution Advisory Committee (EPAC) authority to declare parts of Hong Kong to be Air Control Zones (ACZs), and to set air control objectives for each area.[285] The Ordinance also provides for a licensing system for any premises using a "specialized process" (manufacturing process targeted for pollution control).[286] Owners of such premises are required to "use the best practicable means for preventing the emission of noxious of offensive emissions from such premises, and for preventing the discharge, whether directly or indirectly, of such emissions into the atmosphere, and for rendering such emissions where discharged harmless and inoffensive".[287]

Under the Ordinance the air pollution control authority (the authority) has wide discretion to investigate polluters. With the exception of residences the authority can make warrantless searches of suspected violators.[288] Violations are punishable by fines, imprisonment, and injunctions.[289]

The Noise Control Ordinance[290] deals with a large variety of noise problems. The most important of which is construction noise. Section 6 of the

Ordinance prohibits the use of machines and construction equipment during the night time hours, subjecting violators to potentially large fines.[291]

The Water Pollution Control Ordinance,[292] like the Air Pollution Control Ordinance provides for the Governor in Council to create Water Control Zones (WCZ).[293] Discharges into the WCZs are governed by a licensing system.[294] Further it is illegal to discharge noxious or poisonous substances into the water, even if no WCZ has been created.[295]

The Waste Disposal Ordinance[296] covers both industrial and animal waste treatment and disposal. The Ordinance provides the authority for the collection of waste[297] as well as providing a licensing scheme for those who seek to use land to dispose of waste or to collect waste.[298] Collection or disposal of waste without a license subjects the culprit to fines.[299]

Employment and Labor Law

This section is divided into three parts. The first part deals with the protections and duties of Hong Kong's labor force. The second part will discuss methods of terminating the employment contract and the final section addresses Hong Kong's labor unions.   **B.48**

Protections and Duties

Hong Kong has no statutory minimum wage with the exception of that for   **B.49**
foreign domestic workers,[300] nor any prohibition on discriminatory employment practices.[301] There are no restrictions on the number of hours adult men can work. According to the Employment of Children Regulations it is illegal to employ a child under the age of 13 years old.[302] Children between the ages of 13 and 15 can be employed part time and are subject to a variety of other limitations to ensure that they complete a basic level of education.[303]

Women and young persons under the age of 16 years are in general limited to working a 48 hour week. Women can work an additional two hours of overtime per day subject to other restrictions. Further, both women and young persons are subject to time of day restriction.[304]

Hong Kong has an Employees' Compensation Assistance Ordinance which provides for either lump sum or periodic payments to employees injured in work-related accidents.[305] The employer is primarily liable for the payments.[306] Unlike the American Workman's compensation scheme, an injured employee who receives compensation under the ordinance may still seek common law damages against the employer, subject to an offset for the amount of money already received.[307]

LegCo recently approved enabling legislation to establish the Mandatory Provident Fund (MPF), as a mandatory retirement plan. Legislation for the MPF is expected to be in place by mid to late 1996. The plan will require employees to contribute 5 per cent of their wages, matched by an equal contribution from employers.[308]

Hong Kong

The Employment Ordinance is the basic statute providing protection and benefits to employees.[309] The Ordinance designates the minimal rights protecting employees. These rights can be expanded by contract, however, they cannot be reduced below the Ordinance minimum standards.[310]

The Employment Ordinance provides for Maternity leave for women. If a women takes this leave she is entitled to return to her job and treated as if there was no break in service.[311] She also may be eligible for two-thirds of her salary for the duration of her leave.[312] The Ordinance also grants a minimum benefit in terms of rest days (at least one day a week),[313] sickness allowance,[314] holiday pay (paid time for Chinese holidays),[315] and annual leave (seven to 12 days depending on length of service).[316] In addition to the benefits required under the Ordinance, many employers also provide subsidized meals or food allowances, attendance bonuses, free medical insurance, and a Chinese New Year bonus equivalent to at least one month's salary.[317]

Sickness days are a statutory benefit. They accrue at a rate of two days per month for the first year of employment, and then at a rate of four per month, thereafter. Sickness days can be accumulated up to 120 days.[318] The rate of pay for each sickness day is two-thirds of the employee's normal rate of pay.[319] To be eligible for this benefit the employee must take at least four consecutive days off.[320] The employer will not be liable to pay for sickness days unless the employee furnishes him with a medical certificate.[321]

Under the Employment Ordinance the manner in which one's employment terminates affects the amount due at severance.[322] The Ordinance recognizes the following methods of termination: termination by notice[323] termination by payment in lieu of notice,[324] and termination for cause, without notice.[325]

In the absence of agreement, employment contracts are considered month to month contracts.[326] A termination by notice can be effected by either party giving notice of his intention to terminate the contract. This notice can be either oral or written.[327] For a month to month contract, unless otherwise agreed, the period of notice is one month, however in the case of a prior agreement the notice can be no less than seven days.[328] If an employer terminates the contract by notice the employee will be entitled to any outstanding wages, any other sums accrued but not paid, pro rata amount of year end payment and annual leave payments, as well as applicable severance or long term payments.[329] Where the employee terminates (excluding retirement) he will be entitled to outstanding wages, accrued entitlement not paid, as well as a pro rata annual leave payment.[330]

Where notice is not given it is referred to as termination by payment in lieu of notice. This requires the party desiring to terminate the opportunity to terminate the relationship by paying the other a sum equal to the amount of wages which would have accrued to the employee during the period of notice required above.[331] This applies to both the employer and employee.[332] The benefits to which the employee is entitled upon termination are the same as discussed with regards to termination by notice.[333]

An employer may terminate an employment contract for cause.[334] If so terminated the employee is still entitled to benefits already accrued. An employee has a corresponding right to resign without notice if under section 10, "an employer's conduct was such that it undermined the very basis of the contractual relationship".[335] If the employee resigns under section 10, in addition to amounts due as discussed under termination by notice the employee will be entitled to common law damages.[336]

Trade Unions

In Hong Kong people have the right to join and form unions. After the transition in 1997 this right will continue. Article 27 of the Basic law states that "Hong Kong residents shall have ... the right and freedom to form and join trade unions, and to strike".[337] **B.50**

All trade unions must be registered under the Trade Unions Ordinance within a month of their establishment.[338] To register all trade unions need at least seven members.[339] Registration requires the unions to incorporate. As a result the unions are given the status of a legal person and can hold property, enter contracts, sue and be sued.[340] However, trade unions do have some protection from civil suit for certain actions undertaken in "contemplation of a trade dispute ..."[341] There are at least 532 registered unions with a total of approximately 543,800 members out of a labor force of 2.6 million.[342] Under the Employment Ordinance employers are subject to a fine if they impose a condition that the employee will not engage in union activities as a condition for employment.[343]

Other than the limitation from liability for certain actions undertaken in "contemplation of a trade dispute ...",[344] there is no unequivocal right to strike. However, work stoppages are permitted.[345] Regardless, Hong Kong has one of the lowest number of work stoppages in the world.[346] Like work stoppages, there are only a small number of collective bargaining agreements in Hong Kong.[347] Most agreements between workers and management occur informally on the shop floor.[348]

Under the Basic Law the PRC has granted freedoms far beyond that of the current law with regard to strikes. The Basic Law guarantees "the right and freedom to join trade unions and to strike".[349]

Labor disputes can be resolved under the Labour Relations Ordinance.[350] The Ordinance provides for the resolution of disputes through conciliation and arbitration.[351] Another forum for resolving trade disputes is the Labour Tribunal.[352] The Labour Tribunal's jurisdiction is limited to claims for money arising out of breaches of employment contracts and questions of rights under the Employment Ordinance.[353]

Foreign Investment Law

Unlike the other nations discussed in this volume on Asia's commercial laws this section is necessarily short. On the whole it can be said that Hong Kong **B.51** treats foreign businesses no differently than domestic ones. Hong Kong does not distinguish or discriminate against foreign owned companies.[354] However, there are some restrictions as to the amount foreign investors can own in licensed television broadcasters.[355] Hong Kong has no specific foreign investment legislation.

In 1994 Hong Kong was named the "world's best city for business" in a survey conducted by *Fortune* magazine of executives.[356] As of January 15, 1994 Hong Kong was the regional headquarters of 624 foreign firms.[357] Hong Kong is noted for its efficient and relatively non-corrupt civil service, hard-working work force, modern infrastructure and commitment to free trade.[358]

Unlike China (see section on China) Hong Kong has no restrictions on the movement of capital and the repatriation of profits.[359] This tradition of the free movement of capital should not change after the transition to Chinese sovereignty in 1997. The Basic Law promises: "The socialist system and policies shall not be practiced in the Hong Kong Special Administrative Region, and the previous capitalist system and way of life shall remain unchanged for 50 years".[360]

Hong Kong does not discriminate in favor of foreign business and does not normally offer preferential tax treatment to incoming businesses. The government traditionally tries to foster free trade with limited governmental interference.[361]

One of Hong Kong's attractions to foreign visitors is its favorable tax system. The tax system does not discriminate against foreign companies. Foreign businesses in Hong Kong will be liable in Hong Kong for its profits tax only on income derived in Hong Kong.[362] There is no distinction in the taxes paid between residents and non-residents. Hong Kong's tax system is based on the territorality approach. That is its taxes are only paid on income earned in Hong Kong or derived from Hong Kong.[363]

Hong Kong, unlike the United States, does not have a comprehensive tax on income. Hong Kong has three main types of taxes: profits, salaries and property tax.[364] There is no tax on capital gains or interest from dividends.[365]

Technology Transfer

B.52 Hong Kong is considered a free trade port.[366] However, with regard to certain areas, such as technology, there are certain restrictions to either raise revenue or as the result of an International agreement or obligation.[367] Hong Kong has had access to strategic goods that are barred by the Co-Ordinating Committee for Multilateral Export Controls (COCOM) to other countries. In return for access to these strategic goods Hong Kong had to implement an enforcement regime that mirrored COCOM countries.[368]

Theoretically after 1997 Hong Kong will continue to receive goods that are restricted from sale to China. Paragraph 6 of the Joint Declaration signed between the PRC and Great Britain the two countries agreed that Hong

Kong would "retain the status of a free port and a separate customs area".[369] This was in substance reiterated in the Basic law.[370]

However, it must be remembered that the PRC will be Hong Kong's sovereign. It is difficult to believe that the PRC will allow foreign countries to dictate what can and cannot be imported into the mainland from Hong Kong.

One ramification of the PRC not abiding by COCOM terms could be that Hong Kong would loose its special status as a recipient of advance dual use technologies. Section 201 of the United States–Hong Kong Policy Act of 1992 states that:

> "Notwithstanding any change in the exercise of sovereignty over Hong Kong, the laws of the United States shall continue to apply with respect to Hong Kong, on and after July 1, 1997, in the same manner as the laws of the United States were applied with respect to Hong Kong before such a date . . ."[371]

However, section 202 goes on to state that "if Hong Kong is not sufficiently autonomous to justify" such treatment the President will have the authority to issue an executive order suspending such law with respect to Hong Kong.[372] If restricted goods were exported to China in violation of its trade restrictions, the President may exercise his discretion and suspend Hong Kong's preferential treatment.

Tax Law

This section first discusses the role of accountants under the Companies Ordinance, followed by a brief discussion of Hong Kong's tax system. This will include a brief introduction to tax accounting rules and then the three principle forms of taxation: the profits tax, salaries tax and finally the property tax. **B.53**

All companies incorporated under the Companies Ordinance[373] are required to appoint an independent auditor to examine the company's accounts and report its findings to the members (shareholders).[374] Section 29 of the Professional Accountants Ordinance[375] states that only registered professional accountants can serve as a company's independent auditor.

The Hong Kong Society of Accountants (HKSA) was incorporated under the Professional Accountants' Ordinance to register and formulate standards for the accounting profession.[376] The members of a company are required to appoint an auditor each year for a one year term at the annual general meeting.[377]

The auditor is required to be independent of the directors. His function is to examine the company's various accounts and gives his opinion as to whether they are a fair, accurate and reasonable statement of the company's affairs.[378] This information is to be provided annually at the general shareholder's meeting.[379] The Hong Kong's accounting standards and guidelines are based on those of the United Kingdom.[380] In Hong Kong the shareholders do not have the power to inspect the company's books.[381] Therefore the annual audit is their main method to evaluate the directors management over the company.[382]

Tax

B.54 The fiscal year ends on March 31st.[383] The tax year ending in 1996 will be referred to as the 1995/96 tax year. As referred to above there are three principle kinds of tax: profits tax, salaries tax and property tax. There is no separate tax system for corporation or partnerships alone.[384] The Profits tax applies to all business entities.[385] There is no double taxation for corporations, in the form of one tax at the corporation level and one at the individual's income level, as neither dividends nor capital gains are taxed.[386]

The most common accounting method is the accrual method. However, the cash method when it is applied consistently and does not distort profits is acceptable.[387] The Inland Revenue Ordinance (IRO) is the main body of law setting forth the tax system. It is administered by the Inland Revenue Department (IRD).[388]

Profits Tax

B.55 Individuals, corporations and other associations of individuals are liable to pay taxes on profits from a trade, profession or business in Hong Kong.[389] Simply put, businesses in Hong Kong pay taxes on profits earned in Hong Kong. Residency does not matter. The only requirement is that source of the profits be Hong Kong.

Although there is no corporate tax, individuals and corporations are treated a little different in that corporations pay a slightly higher tax rate than individuals. In the 1993–94 tax year the tax was at 17.5 per cent for corporations and 15 per cent for other business forms.[390] Partnerships that are beneficially owned by corporations are taxed at the 17.5 per cent rate while non corporate partners are taxed at the 15 per cent rate.[391]

Three conditions must be met in order for a legal person to be liable to pay a profits tax:

1. The entity must carry on a trade, business or profession in Hong Kong;
2. The profits must come from that trade, business or profession; and
3. The profits must arise in or be derived from Hong Kong.[392]

Whether a foreign corporation is conducting business "in Hong Kong" is a question of fact.[393] This issue will be largely resolved by the scope of the foreign corporation's activities in Hong Kong. If it has an agent with the authority to enter into contracts on behalf of the principle it will most likely be considered in Hong Kong for tax purposes.[394]

The key to liability under the profits tax is that source of profits be Hong Kong. This is a complex question which has lead to a mass of litigation. According to Departmental Interpretation & Practice Notes (DIPN) No. 21 4(b):

> "The broad guiding principle is that one looks to see what the tax payer has done to earn the profits in question and where he has done it. In other words, the proper approach is to ascertain what were the operations which produced the relevant profits and where those operations took place."

However, although the DIPN is the Inland Revenue Department's (IRD's) interpretation of the law it is similar to the United States' Internal Revenue Department's Treasury Regulations in that they are what the Departments will base their assessments of tax on, however they are not legally binding and can be challenged in future tax litigation.[395]

A few simple examples of what the IRD considers to be profits from a Hong Kong source are as follows: goods manufactured in Hong Kong, goods sold in Hong Kong, and profits from rental property located in Hong Kong.[396]

The general rule for the deducibility of business expenditures is that a deduction will be granted for all expenses which are incurred in the production of profits under the profits tax.[397] The following are a few examples of deductible expenses: foreign income taxes actually paid;[398] bad debts; intellectual property registration and scientific research (usually).[399]

Losses are determined in the same way as profits.[400] Losses can be carried forward indefinitely for future years. However, the rules are different depending on whether the entity is either an individual, partner or corporation.

When an individual incurs a loss in a taxable year it can be used in the same taxable year to offset other sources of income. However, if the individual seeks to carry over the loss for future years it can only be used against profits made in the same trade, profession or business in which the loss was incurred.[401] This same rule applies to individual members of partnerships with 20 or fewer members.[402]

As to corporations and partnerships of more than 20 members, the losses incurred are set off against any taxable profits in the same year and can be carried forward indefinitely to be used to offset any profits in future years.[403]

In addition there are some special rules for partnerships. They are assessed taxes as a single entity, and may choose which partners share the profits and which the losses pretty much as they like.[404]

Salaries Tax

In general the salary tax is a tax on employment income "arising in or derived from Hong Kong".[405] Therefore as with the Profits tax it is crucial to determine where the source of employment is to determine tax liability. That location is determined by examining the following three factors:

B.56

Hong Kong

1. the place where the contract was negotiated, concluded and enforced;
2. the location of the employer; and
3. where compensation is paid.[406]

While the above factors are important and will normally be determinative, the IRD will "in appropriate cases" look beyond those factors.[407]

The effect of this is that if it is determined that the employment is located in Hong Kong all income from that employment regardless of where the employee renders service is subject to Hong Kong's salaries tax.[408] However, even if the source is outside Hong Kong the employee will still be liable for income earned from services rendered in Hong Kong. The main exception to this rule is the 60 day rule. If the employee spends 60 or fewer days in Hong Kong he will be exempted from paying tax for the services he performed in Hong Kong. If on the other hand he visits Hong Kong for 61 days or more he will be liable for the amount of his salary attributable to the service performed in Hong Kong. This applies even if most of the time the employee is in Hong Kong on vacation.[409]

Furthermore, Hong Kong employees who travel abroad and are required to pay taxes on income earned in another jurisdiction will not have to pay Hong Kong tax on the earnings for which they have already paid tax to the other jurisdiction.[410]

Hong Kong's fringe benefit exclusion is worth mentioning briefly. In general a benefit received in a form other than money is not calculated as a part of salary for the salaries tax unless the benefit is either capable of being converted into money or is the discharge of the employee's debt.[411]

Property Tax

B.57   In general the property tax is a tax paid by the "owners" of land or buildings on the net assessable value of such property in Hong Kong.[412] The term owners in the IRO does not mean title holder. With few exceptions all land in Hong Kong is owned by the British government and is leased for periods of time to leases under what are called Crown leases.[413] The term owner for tax purposes is defined in section 2 of the IRO. It includes but is not limited to the Crown lease, life tenants, adverse possessors, mortgagors.[414]

The net assessable value of the property is essentially the consideration paid as rent or in lieu of rent less deductions. The two standard deductions are rates paid by the owner[415] and 20 per cent for repairs and outgoings.[416] The basic rate in the 1993/94 tax year was 15 per cent.[417]

Anti-Avoidance

B.58   The general anti-avoidance provisions are sections 61 and 61A of the IRO. These provisions allow the assessor to ignore transactions that were designed solely or mainly for tax avoidance or reduction reasons.[418] However, at least according to one author there is a large loop hole. That is "it cannot be applied so as to tax income that arises outside Hong Kong, even if the income arises outside of Hong Kong as a direct result of a transaction designed solely to avoid Hong Kong taxation. This is because each of the three taxes charged under the Inland Revenue Ordinance — profits tax, salaries tax and property tax — applies only to income arising in Hong Kong".[419] This is based on a DIPN which states that "the ultimate assessment made must be within the scope of the Inland Revenue Ordinance".[420]

Objections and Appeals

Taxpayers who wish to dispute an assessment must first file a timely objection with the Commissioner of the Inland Revenue Department.[421] If the objection is valid, the assessor on behalf of the Commissioner will try to resolve the matter with the tax payer through negotiation. However, if no agreement is reached the Commissioner can make a unilateral determination.[422] If the person disagrees with the Commissioner's determination he may appeal that decision within a limited time to the Board of Review. The Board of Review is comprised of individuals appointed by the Governor and is independent of the IRD. Under certain circumstances a grievant can appeal to the High Court or the Court of Appeals.[423]

B.59

Intellectual Property

Hong Kong's intellectual property regime reflects that of the United Kingdom. Hong Kong's laws either borrow from the UK or are directly controlled by the UK as in the case of patents. This section will examine briefly Hong Kong's general framework for protecting intellectual property. The following areas will be covered: copyrights, patents, trade marks, passing off and, *Anton Piller* Orders. As much of Hong Kong's intellectual property laws are dependent on England's laws, either by adopting Britain's statute by order (as with copyrights), or by requiring that certain acts be taken in Britain before the right will be enforced in Hong Kong (as with Patents) it is likely that these areas will change rapidly as the government sifts through what statutes it needs to "localize" before 1997.

B.60

Copyrights

The copyright law of Hong Kong is the United Kingdom Copyright Act of 1956 which was extended to Hong Kong subject to a few modifications that took place between 1972 and 1990.[424] The Copyright Act of 1956 breaks the subject matter of copyrights into two sections. The first deals with "Original Works", while the second addresses copyrights in "Sound recordings, Cinematograph Films, Broadcasts, etc".[425]

Part I and II of the 1956 Act requires that the work seeking protection be "original". That is that the work must "have originated from the

B.61

author . . . and have involved the author's skill and labour".[426] This applies to literary, dramatic, musical[427] or artistic[428] works under Part I and sound recordings, cinematograph films, television and sound broadcasts and, published editions under Part II. This list was extended in 1985 to include computer software under the UK Copyright Amendment Act of 1985.[429] The Act applies whether the work is published or unpublished as long as the author is "qualified".[430] A qualified person is either a subject or resident of a country to which the act is extended or a company incorporated in a country to which the act is extended.[431]

The countries covered by the act are those who have a right to protection via conventions. The principle convention by which Hong Kong extends protection is the Berne Convention. This treatment was recently expanded through the conclusion of the Uruguay GATT round which resulted in the Agreement on Trade-Related Aspects of Intellectual Property Rights (TRIPS).[432] Under TRIPS Art. 3 GATT member nations can treat member nations no less favorably than it accords its own nationals, with the exception of some stated exclusions delineated in the international conventions that deal with intellectual property.[433] TRIPS applies to most areas of intellectual property including, patents and trade marks.[434]

The protection offered copyrighted materials is in general the life of the author plus 50 years, with a few exceptions.[435]

Patents

B.62   At this time Hong Kong does not grant its own patents. However, Hong Kong does provide for the registration of patents granted in the United Kingdom.[436] Under the Registration of Patents Ordinance any person who owns a UK patent or a European patent designating the United Kingdom may apply to have the patent registered in Hong Kong.[437] To register, the grantee of a patent needs to apply within five years from the date the patent was granted.

By registering the patent, it is treated under Registration of Patents Ordinance, s.6 "as though the patent had been granted in the United Kingdom with an extension to Hong Kong".[438] However, the rights granted under the Ordinance "shall continue in force as long as the patent remains in force in the United Kingdom".[439]

Patents granted under the 1977 Patents Act are protected for 20 years from the date of filing the application.[440]

Trade Marks Ordinance

B.63   In Hong Kong a trade mark is a mark used or proposed to be used in relation to goods or services to indicate a connection between the goods or services and the person who provides them.[441] In order to reap the protection of the Trade Marks Ordinance a trade mark must be registered. The register is divided into two parts: A and B.

Registration in Part A requires that the trade mark contains at least one of the following:

1. the name of a company, individual, or firm, represented in a special or particular manner;
2. the signature (in other than Chinese characters) of the applicant or a predecessor in the business;
3. an invented word or words;
4. word or words not descriptive of the goods or services for which the mark is used and a geographical name or surname, or
5. any other distinctive mark. Underlying all of the above is the requirement that the mark be distinctive.[442]

Trade marks may also be registered under Part B, even if they do not meet the distinctiveness requirement, if they are capable of being distinguished as the property of the owner as distinguished from other goods or services which are not.[443]

Trade marks will be rejected if they are identical or similar to the mark of another already registered.[444] A mark will also be rejected if it is deceptive, or contrary to law or morality.[445]

A civil suit lies for violation of Part A if the plaintiff shows that the defendant uses a mark identical with or nearly resembling the plaintiff's registered mark.[446] A violation under Part B will fail if the defendant establishes that the use complained of is not likely to deceive or cause confusion.[447]

Trade marks registered in Hong Kong are valid for seven years and are renewable for 14 year periods.[448]

Trade Marks at Common Law (Passing Off)

In addition to the protection offered by the Trade Marks Ordinance, Hong Kong has an additional common law cause of action called passing off. The plaintiff in a passing off action must prove: (a) he has a good trade reputation or good will; (b) the defendant used a deceptively similar trade mark; (c) actual confusion or deception resulted from such use, and (d) damages have occurred or are likely to occur.[449]

Anton Piller Orders

An *Anton Piller*[450] order is an *ex parte* injunction.[451] The *Anton Piller* **B.64** order gives the plaintiff's solicitor the opportunity to petition the court to (a) require the inspection of a premises for counterfeits (b) require the defendant to disclose information, and (c) require the production of documents.[452]

Anton Piller orders were fairly common, however they have recently become harder to obtain.[453] These orders are not restricted to intellectual property and are often used to prevent the destruction of evidence.[454]

III. General Considerations in Negotiating Business Transactions in Hong Kong

Cultural Factors and Business Negotiations

B.65 Much of what is discussed here are values and attitudes shared with what has come to be called "Greater China". Greater China includes the Chinese mainland (the PRC) as well as Hong Kong, Macau and Taiwan. One aspect of culture that distinguishes Hong Kong from both the mainland and Taiwan is that the population of Hong Kong is far more accustomed to seeing and interacting with westerners.

In Hong Kong, the Chinese will tend to ignore westerners as well as other Chinese as they go on about their business. According to one author "when Chinese in Hong Kong deal with strangers, they are often rude or uncaring. Such behavior is a psychological necessity in a city as densely populated as Hong Kong . . ."[455]

Chinese society is strongly influenced by Confucianism. Confucianism is essentially the ethical teachings of Confucius, a Chinese philosopher/teacher who lived between 551–479 B.C.[456] Today we can see a slow shifting back to Confucianism as some people in modern society strive for the virtues of the Confucius gentleman: integrity, righteousness, loyalty, reciprocity and humanity.[457]

In its most basic modern form Confucianism refers to the way people treat each other in relation to their social or familial status. To the Western businessman in Hong Kong this means that he needs to be conscious of people's position in the corporate structure. Attention should also be paid to the respective ages of the people they are dealing with.

One manifestation of the importance of relationships is the concept of *guanxi*. *Guanxi* simply translated means relationship or connections. It is perhaps easiest to think of *guanxi* as the cultivation of good will. Good will is important to a successful business venture in any western nation, however, it is crucial to success in Hong Kong.

The western businessman should attempt to cultivate a long term relationship with his Chinese partner. This relationship should be based on mutual trust and respect. This type of relationship takes time and effort to develop. It will not just happen over night.

It is important in developing these relationships to exchange favors with each other. Sometimes the request for favors can come at inopportune times or they may involve something that the western attorney or businessman considers unethical. It is not crucial for the western businessman to "go native". The Westerner needs to be clear as to the form of the relationships and make it clear as to what he can and cannot do. However, this must be done tactfully.

Cultural Factors and Business Negotiations

The concept of *mienzi* or face is important in Hong Kong as in all of Greater China. Face is simply the way people perceive each other. It is a mark of status and dignity.[458] Westerners think that the Chinese are very polite. They are, and that politeness should be reciprocated. This goes also towards building *guanxi*. It is a good practice to compliment workers, associates or friends when they have done a good job. It's important for good relations in western nations and is crucial in Hong Kong. It is common for people upon meeting for the first time in Hong Kong to exchange business cards. It is polite to give and receive business cards using two hands. This is a sign of respect.

Sometimes it is hard for westerners to remember and pronounce Chinese names, this also applies to Chinese people remembering western names. Although this is less of a problem in Hong Kong where English is spoken quite widely it is still a good idea to have business cards printed up with English on one side and Chinese on the other. Chinese names have the surname before the given name. For example, in the name Liu Mei-yu, Liu is the surname, Mei-yu is the given name. Given names are usually two characters, however most surnames are monosyllabic. Among Hong Kong people it is also common to use an English given name followed by their surname, for example James Peng.

Another facet of Chinese culture in Hong Kong that the Westerner should prepare for is that in their spare time the Chinese like to have lively entertainment with their friends. The term for this is *renao*. *Renao* is distinguished by a high level of noise. Hong Kong Chinese, like their compatriots in Taiwan, like to go out to karaoke clubs. In these clubs the host would normally rent a private room for his guests. In the room is a large screen monitor to display music videos. The patrons select which songs they would like to hear. While the music is being played the screen will display a video with some scenes and the words to the songs. The guests will then take turns singing their favorite songs. The karaoke club will also supply food and drinks for an additional charge.

Hong Kong, as a British colony, cannot help but be influenced by the West. Since 1842 when China ceded Hong Kong to the British in the first of the unequal treaties, Hong Kong has been subject to British rule and British culture. As a result some Western values and manners have managed to slip into the culture. One example of this is the wearing of shoes in the house. Upon entering a home in the Chinese mainland or Taiwan it is customary to take off one's shoes, and either wear slippers that are provided by the host or if the floor is carpeted walk in wearing only socks. This tradition seems to have faltered in Hong Kong.

The Westerner should keep in mind that Hong Kong has not evolved independently from the mainland. In 1990 37 per cent of Hong Kong's residents were born in mainland China. Throughout Hong Kong's colonial history during times of social upheaval in the mainland there has been an increase in immigration from the mainland.

Role and Competence of Local Counsel

B.67   Attorneys in Hong Kong, like those in England, are divided into barristers and solicitors.[459] Barristers can only be retained through a solicitor.[460] They prepare pleadings and make court appearances. In addition they give advice normally through written opinions. Barristers work as solo practitioners in "chambers", which are single person offices. They cannot form partnerships, however they may associate with other barristers to share rent and general overhead costs.[461]

Solicitors, unlike barristers can form partnerships. They perform much of what would be considered the basic legal work. They prepare agreements, write wills and act as general consultants.[462]

As Hong Kong is a common law jurisdiction, the courts and legal counsel play a significant role in the development of the common law on a daily basis. The law Society of Hong Kong, much like the American Bar Association (ABA), acts as a lobbying group and proposes legislation.[463]

As Hong Kong is an international business and trade center, there are many foreign law firms set up to handle international transactions. With respect to domestic law, many attorneys are from other common law jurisdictions, mostly educated in Europe or other Commonwealth nations. In addition the University of Hong Kong has its own law school training many of today's lawyers.

The Law Society of Hong Kong is the ethical watchdog for the solicitors. The Society has the power to discipline a solicitor by: striking his name from the roll of solicitors (disbarment); suspension; fines; or censure.[464] Barristers are not policed by the law society. Their regulatory body are the courts themselves.[465]

As is the practice in the United States, solicitors owe the client a high fiduciary duty, on an obligation to avoid conflicts of interest. Clients do not have direct access to the barristers. The solicitor is in essence the middle man and must relay instructions from the client to the barrister.[466]

Government Resources and Business Assistance Programs

B.68   Unlike some other Asian nations Hong Kong has no system of economic planning.[467] The government is committed to the *laissez faire* approach to business. Its approach is that of minimal interference with the free market.[468] The Hong Kong Economic and Trade Offices located throughout the world are very helpful in providing information on Hong Kong.

The one area of business where Hong Kong appears to offer some type of assistance is in advanced technologies. For example, Hong Kong established the Industrial Estates Corporation to help provide factory sites to industries to help some firms shift from labor intensive processing to more technologically advanced production.[469]

In addition the government funds research and development projects in manufacturing technology, and is contemplating establishing a science park.[470] The government is also involved in quite a number of large infra-structure projects, such as, the construction of the new airport on Lantau island, a fourth tunnel between Hong Kong island and Kowloon.[471] These projects seem well timed to bolster confidence in the colony in the wake of its impending transfer to Communist rule.

Another method for the government to control and target areas for development is by attaching conditions to the crown leases. In Hong Kong the British government owns all of the land. The government leases the land and has a reversionary interest.[472] As a part of the lease the government can attach covenants or limitations on the use of the land. This can function as a tool for urban planning as well as for industrial targeting.

According to the Basic Law this state of affairs will continue. According to Article 7 of the Basic Law provides:

> "The land and natural resources within the Hong Kong Special Administrative Region shall be State property. The Government [sic] of the Hong Kong Special Administrative Region shall be responsible foe their management, use and development and for their lease or grant to individuals, legal persons or organizations for use or development . . ."[473]

As a result the Government of Hong Kong will be able to continue to be able to use the crown leases as a tool for urban planning and industry targeting, after the transition.

Sale of Goods Transactions

Many provisions of the Sale of Goods Ordinance are prefaced with the clause **B.69** "Unless a different intention appears from the terms of the contract . . ."[474] Therefore if the parties to a contract intend to use different terms to govern their contract they should so clearly state.

If the time of delivery is important such that one of the parties would want or need to be able to declare a breach of contract and sue for damages or avoid the contract if the delivery is late, the parties must include a clause in the contract that says "time is of the essence", or something to that effect.[475] It is prudent to use the language "time is of the essence" because that is the language used in the statute. The presumption under SOGO is that time is not of the essence (see SOGO, sec. 12). Therefore, unless otherwise stated, the courts will allow the parties a reasonable time for delivery.[476] The determination as to what is a reasonable time will be a question for the trier of fact to decide.

Further, when considering the time element of a contract the parties should be aware that if nothing is said as to time, the time for payment will be the time of delivery.[477] If nothing is stated in the contract the seller will have a reasonable time to deliver. This may mean that the buyer will have to wait, but when the seller does deliver the buyer must pay at that time.

According to SOGO section 22 the risk of loss passes at the same time as the property passes. The term "property" in SOGO is similar to the term "title" (*i.e.* ownership interest) and for the determination of risk of loss should be so considered. Under section 20 there are five rules that determine when property passes. The five rules are as follows:

1. in an unconditional contract for the sale of specific goods in a deliverable state, the property in the goods passes to the buyer when the contract is made, and it is immaterial whether the time of payment or delivery, or both, be postponed.[478]

2. in a contract for the sale of specific goods, if the seller is bound to do something to the goods to put them in a deliverable state (*e.g.* customize) then the property does not pass until the thing is done and the buyer so notified.

3. in a contract for the sale of specific goods in which the seller is obliged weigh, measure, test, or do some other act or thing to the goods, or for the goods, in order to ascertain the price, the property passes when that act or thing is done.

4. when the goods are delivered on approval or "on sale or return" (*i.e.* when the buyer is acting as a bailee) the property passes when:
    (a) the buyer signifies approval or does an act inconsistent with the seller's ownership interest (like selling the goods), or
    (b) he retains the goods without notice for a period stipulated by the parties or if none stipulate then for a reasonable time.

5. in a sale of goods to take place in the future property passes when goods, meeting the description in the contract, are appropriated for the contract and the buyer is so notified.

The key is that both rule 20 and 22 mentioned above are prefaced with the exclusionary language of "unless a different intention appears". In order for the parties to be protected it is best that they state clearly in the contract when the risk of loss passes and at what point property passes.

If the parties intend to have an installment contract, that too should be states in the terms of the contract. If not stated there is a presumption that the deliver was meant to be in a single shipment, in which case the buyer will not be bound to accept delivery installments as part of a continuing sale.[479]

Under SOGO the parties can choose elect, by using a choice of law clause in the contract, not to apply SOGO. In that case the parties must elect the law of another jurisdiction.[480] However, when the contract is a domestic one and the choice of law is another jurisdiction, the implied warranties in sections 14–17 will still apply (see Consumer Protection section).[481] However, where the contract is for the international sale of goods those warranties can be waived through a choice of law clause and a clear statement that sections 14–17 do not apply.[482]

Joint Ventures

B.70 Unlike mainland China, Hong Kong has no joint venture law, nor any requirement that foreign ventures have local partners. There is no prohibition against 100 per cent foreign ownership of business. In Hong Kong foreign firms are treated the same as local firms (with the exception of banks). The key consideration in deciding whether to enter a joint venture is solely the business objective of each party. To form joint ventures for whatever purpose the parties must look to the existing business entities existing in Hong Kong, such as the corporation or partnership. If the parties seek a joint venture of a more limited nature they could simply enter into a joint agreement, *i.e.* contractual joint venture.

There are many reasons why a firm entering the Hong Kong market will seek to go in as a joint venture, rather than alone. For one, the Western firm may be unfamiliar with local needs or customs. They may want a firm familiar with the local laws and regulations, although this is less important than in the mainland because the laws of Hong Kong are transparent. Another key reason to take on a joint venture partner in Hong Kong is to spread the risks, perhaps because of the uncertainties associated with Chinese sovereignty in 1997.

In most circumstances there will be no difference in the tax treatment of the joint venture regardless of whether they choose a corporation or a partnership as a business entity. Under the Inland Revenue Ordinance if the partners are corporations they are taxed at the corporate rates.[483] Since there are no special tax benefits to using a partnership as opposed to the corporate form, and the corporate form offers limited liability that is the most common business form for joint ventures in Hong Kong.[484]

In Hong Kong there are two principle documentary vehicles available for the equity joint venture as a limited liability company to delineate the parties rights and duties. They are the shareholder's agreement and the articles of association.[485]

The Companies Ordinance requires that the articles of association be filed with the Registrar of Companies.[486] As such that document is a public record. The articles are considered to be an agreement between the members of the corporation and the corporation itself.[487] A violation of the articles is not a breach of contract but would be invalid as *ultra vires* (not within the corporation's authority).[488]

The shareholders' agreement is a private agreement between the shareholders in which they define each other's rights and obligations.[489] A breach of the shareholder's agreement unlike the articles of incorporation does not invalidate the act but merely exposes the breaching party to civil damages under a contracts theory (including a possible injunction).[490]

Technology License Arrangements

Hong Kong has a host of methods by which investors or joint venture **B.71** partners can protect their technology in Hong Kong. Some of these methods are discussed in more detail above in the section on Intellectual Property.

One method to protect a firm's technology is to give up only partial control of the new technology transferred to the joint venture partner, *i.e.*

supply the essential features as finished projects. This limits the ability of the Hong Kong partner to exploit the new technology in ways that infringe on the partners intellectual property rights without having to go through burdensome litigation. This could be performed through a franchise.

As to licensing arrangements the parties are free to delineate what ever reasonable terms they want in a contract. There is no technology transfer requirement or burdensome regulations dictating how much technology needs to be transferred to Hong Kong over a period of time.

As discussed in the section on Intellectual Property patents must be registered in the United Kingdom to be registered in Hong Kong. Copyrights and trademarks can be directly registered in Hong Kong. The foreign holder of the original property right can lease or transfer the right to use that design in Hong Kong in return for payments or royalties.

Production and Manufacturing Arrangements

B.72 As mentioned above there is little difficulty for a foreign corporation to simply set up shop in Hong Kong. There is no discrimination against overseas investors. The major problem with setting up a production or manufacturing plant in Hong Kong is the price. As Hong Kong is experiencing a labour shortage, competition for labor is stiff. Hong Kong's wages surpassed that of the United Kingdom in 1992.[491] Hong Kong's land is limited and therefore expensive. As a result Hong Kong factories employ around three million people on the Chinese mainland in Guangdong.[492] That is slightly more than half the entirety of Hong Kong's population.

Hong Kong is uniquely situated to serve as the base and starting point for investment and manufacturing in the mainland China. Trade links between the mainland and Hong Kong are strong. The PRC is Hong Kong's largest investor, and Hong Kong represents two-thirds of all direct foreign investment in the mainland.[493] As a result of its location and degree to which the two economies have become integrated through trade, Hong Kong has a host of experienced consultants to assist in establishing ventures in China.

Distribution Arrangements

B.73 As discussed above there are no prohibitions restricting foreign businesses from setting up their own distributions systems. If the foreign business decides not to attempt to distribute alone they can go through pre-existing distributors or form a joint venture with a local partner. Also as discussed above the joint venture can take one of many forms. For a distribution system a contractual arrangement might prove them most useful.

The foreign firm may set up a franchise arrangement where the local distributor sells under the foreign name and purchases its goods from the foreign seller. In the alternative the foreign producer may permit the local firm to produce the goods under a royalty agreement. The foreign seller can use one dedicated distributor or many distributors competing for sales.

Employment Agreements

In general the Employment Ordinance applies to all domestic employees **B.74** irrespective of their earnings or profession engaged under an employment contract, with a few exceptions.[494] The contract need not be in writing, however if it is in writing a copy must be provided to the employee.[495]

Under the Ordinance the employer is required to inform the employee of the basic terms and conditions of employment.[496] These basic terms include wages, wage period, notice requirements to terminate employment, and what the end of year payment, if any will be based. As a matter of practice this should be clearly stated in the employment contract. In addition, any time there is a change in the conditions of employment the employee is required to be notified in "an intelligible manner," and upon the employee's request those changes too need to be stated in writing.[497]

The Ordinance also states that unless otherwise stated the wage period will be deemed to be a month.[498] Wages are defined as "all renumeration, earnings, allowances, tips, etc. with the exclusion of certain fringe benefits. Those benefits include:

1. accommodation, education, food, fuel medical care or water provided by the employer;
2. any contribution paid by the employer on his own account to any pension fund or provident fund;
3. any travelling allowance;
4. any gratuity payable on completion or termination of a contract of employment or;
5. any annual bonus which is of a gratuitous nature or which is payable only at the discretion of the employer.[499]

The employee should note that this definition of wages applies to the Employment Ordinance only, not to the Salaries tax (see section on tax).

Another area which is addressed in the Employment Ordinance is the subject of rest days. The Ordinance requires that the employee be give at least one day of rest out of seven.[500] Those rest days are in addition to the statutory holidays.[501] However, this requirement is the statutory minimum and can be increased and specified by the terms of an employment contract.

Under the Employment Ordinance, when the employer wants to dismiss a person with notice, if there is no agreement as to the length of notice that needs to be given, then the term will be deemed to be one month. As such, if the employer contemplates needing to terminate his employees on short notice he should consider a contract clause so stating. However, the statute does require a minimum of seven days notice be given.

As in most nations it is not necessary that there be a formal written agreement that goes into the full details of the employment. Many factors which are the subject of an employment contract such as wage, and notice of termination (which is discussed under the section on Employment and

Labor) are restricted by the Employment Ordinance. However, if the employee is given benefits in excess of the statutory minimums it would be prudent to reduce those terms, as well as the employer's expectations of the employee, to writing.

Loan Agreements

B.75 Loan agreements are contracts between the banks and the borrower. The banks will seek to maximize their chances of repayment while minimizing the risks of non-repayment. Loans made by banks, to say a corporation, will probably require that the corporation grant a right of recourse against property owned by the corporation as security against the debt.[502] If not the bank may require a guarantee from a person or corporation willing to be liable for the debt if the original debtor could not or does not repay the loan.

Regardless of whether the security for the debt is property or another's guarantee, the agreement itself is a binding contract.

Notes

[1] The World Bank, *The World Bank Atlas 1995* (1994), pp.8.
[2] Walden Publishing Ltd., *Country Reports: Hong Kong* (1995), available in LEXIS, World Library, Profile File.
[3] U.S. Central Intelligence Agency, *The World Factbook* (1994), available in LEXIS, Nexis Library, Profiles file.
[4] *Walden report* see n.2.
[5] Brian Hunter (ed.), *The Statesman's Year-Book: Statistical And Historical Annual Of The States Of The World For The Year 1994–1995* (1994), pp.679.
[6] Tomasz Ujejski, "The Future of the English Language in Hong Kong Law", in *The Future of the Law in Hong Kong*, 164, 173 (Raymond Wacks, ed., 1989).
[6a] C.K. Kwong (Hong Kong) in APAA News (Asian Patent Attorney Association), no.23, May 1996, p.103.
[7] Hong Kong Monetary Authority, *Global Investor* (1994), Vol.12, no.4; pp.11.
[8] Walden Reports, see n.2.
[9] "Asia's labour pains", *The Economist*, August 26th-September 1st 1995, at 51.
[10] "Prices & Trends: Hong Kong", *The Far Eastern Economic Review*, July 27, 1995, at. 84.
[11] "Emerging-Market Indicators", *The Economist*, August 5th–11th 1995, at 98.
[12] *Ibid.*
[13] *Ibid.*
[14] Timothy Conti, "China and Hong Kong Trade" in *Trade and Investment Law in Hong Kong* (Smart and Halkyard ed. 1993), p.368.
[15] U.S. Central Intelligence Agency, *The World Factbook* (1994), available in LEXIS, Nexis Library, Profiles file.
[16] Brian Hunter (ed.), *The Statesman's Year-Book: Statistical And Historical Annual Of The States Of The World For The Year 1994–1995* (1994), p.678.
[17] Ferris, "The Economy", in *Trade and Investment Law in Hong Kong* (Smart and Halkyard ed. 1993), p.36.
[18] *Ibid.*, p.26.

[19] Berry Fong-Chung Hsu, *The Common Law System in Chinese Context* (1992), p.11.

[20] "The Basic Law of the Hong Kong Special Administrative Region of the People's Republic of China, Article 8", in *Hong Kong's Transition to 1997: Background, Problems and Prospects* (Hungdah Chui, 1993), 43.

[21] Jonathan D. Spence, *The Search for Modern China* (1990), p.159.

[22] Hsu *op. cit.*, p.9.

[23] Thomas Boasberg, "One Country, One-and-a-Half Systems: The Hong Kong Basic Law and Its Breach of the Sino-British Joint Declaration" (1992) 10 *Wiscon. Int'l Law Journal* 285.

[24] *Ibid.*, p.288.

[25] Dennis Duncanson, "Hong Kong as a Crown Colony" in *Hong Kong: A Chinese and International Concern* (Domes and Shaw, ed. 1988), p.10.

[26] Laws of Hong Kong (1984 revised ed.) Vol.23 Appendix I, cited to in Peter Wesley-Smith, *An Introduction to the Hong Kong Legal System* (1987), p.24.

[27] *Ibid.*, p.24.

[28] *Ibid.*, p.167.

[29] Joint Declaration of the Government of the United Kingdom if Great Britain and Northern Ireland ad the Government of the People's Republic of China on the Question of Hong Kong [December 19, 1984] as reprinted in *The Hong Kong Basic Law: Blueprint for "Stability and Prosperity" under Chinese Sovereignty?*, (Chang and Clark ed., 1991), p.259.

[30] Basic Law, Art. 5.

[31] Wesley-Smith, *op. cit.*, p.27.

[32] Anne Carver, *Hong Kong Business Law* (1991), p.8.

[33] Wesley-Smith, *op. cit.*, p.42.

[34] Chapter IV of the Basic Law deals with the Political Structure. Arts. 43–58 deal with the Chief Executive.

[35] Basic Law, Art. 45.

[36] Basic Law, Annex I: "Method for the Selection of the Chief Executive of the Hong Kong Special Administrative Region."

[37] Basic Law, Art. 49.

[38] Basic Law, Art. 50.

[39] Basic Law, Art. 52.

[40] Wesley-Smith, *op. cit.*, p.29.

[41] Peter Wesley-Smith in, *Law In Hong Kong: An Introduction* (Penlington, 2d., 1986), p.29.

[42] *Ibid.*, p.30.

[43] Wesley-Smith, *op. cit.*, p.89.

[44] Diane Stormont, "Far East, Hong Kong: End of an Era for Hong Kong's LegCo", *Reuter News Service*, July 29, 1995, LEXIS, World Library.

[45] "Mother and Father do not know best", *The Economist*, September 23rd–29th, 1995, p.29.

[46] "Hong Kong: The real thing", *The Economist*, September 16rd–22th, 1995, p.40.

[47] The Basic Law of the Hong Kong Special Administrative Region of the People Republic of China [April 4, 1990], *Decision of the National People's Congress on the Method for the Formation of the First Government and the First Legislative Council of the Hong Kong Special Administrative Region*, as reprinted in The Hong Kong Basic Law: Blueprint for "Stability and Prosperity" under Chinese Sovereignty? (Chan and Clark ed., 1991), p.206.

[48] Adopted as an appendix to the basic law on April 4, 1990.

[49] "Hong Kong: First Fully Elected HK LegCo to Start Nomination", *Reuter News Service-Far East*, July 30, 1995. Lexis, World Library. See also Yash Ghai, "Back to basics: the provisional legislature and the Basic Law" (1995) 25 HKLJ 2.

Hong Kong

[50] See *Supreme Court Ordinances by Letters and Patent.*
[51] Basic Law, Art. 81.
[52] Basic Law, Art. 158.
[53] Basic Law, Art. 19.
[54] Price Waterhouse, *Doing Business in Hong Kong*, (1992), p.27.
[55] *Ibid.*, p.44.
[56] Laws of Hong Kong, (CAP) 32, s.332 et seq.
[57] Penlington, *op. cit.,* 43–55.
[58] Basic Law, Art. 158.
[59] Robert W.H. Wang & Co., Martindale-Hubbell, *Hong Kong Law Digest*, (1994).
[60] Walden Country Reports, *op. cit.* Membership in International Agreements (1995).
[61] Robert W.H. Wang & Co., *op. cit.*, p.HK-9.
[62] Basic Law, Art. 151.
[63] Frankie Fook-lun Leung, "Hong Kong", in *Competition Laws of the Pacific Rim Countries* (1991), p.HK-1.
[64] *Ibid.*, at HK1–12.
[65] *Ibid.*, p.258.
[66] *Ibid.*, pp.259–260.
[67] Carver, *op. cit.*, p.295.
[68] Kevin Williams, *An Introduction to Hong Kong Employment law* (1990), p.67.
[69] Carver, *op. cit.*, p.295.
[70] Williams, *op. cit.*, p.67.
[71] *Susan Bushanan v. Janesville Ltd.*, (1981) H.K.L.R. 700 as cited in Frankie Fook-Lun Leung, *op. cit.*, pp.HK1–7.
[72] Williams, *op. cit.*, p.70.
[73] *Ibid.*
[74] Control of Exemption Clauses Ordinance, (CAP 71), Laws of Hong Kong (Authority of the Attorney General of Hong Kong, Government Printer).
[75] Misrepresentation Ordinance, (CAP 284), Laws of Hong Kong.
[76] Restatement of Contracts 2d. *as cited* in *Contracts in a Nutshell* (Schaber and Rohwer, 1990), p.9.
[77] Carver, *op. cit.,* 89.
[78] Sale Of Goods Ordinance (SOGO), (CAP 26), s.60.
[79] Carver, *op. cit.,* 91.
[80] Chui and Roebuck, *Hong Kong Contracts* (1989), p.24.
[81] Carver, *op. cit.*, p.95.
[82] Chui and Roebuck, *op. cit.*, p.27.
[83] *Ibid.*
[84] Schaber and Rohwer, *op. cit.*, p.75.
[85] *Ibid.*
[86] Chui and Roebuck, *op. cit.,* 33.
[87] *Ibid.*
[88] Leung and Ho, "The Commercial Laws of Hong Kong" in *Digest Of Commercial Laws of the World* (1992), p.3.
[89] SOGO, sec. 2(1) "goods".
[90] Judith Sihombing, *Goods: Sales and Securities* (1989), p.29.
[91] Sale of Goods Ordinance (SOGO), (CAP 26), s.5 in *The Laws of Hong Kong.*
[92] SOGO, *op. cit.*, s.10.
[93] SOGO, s.11(1).
[94] SOGO, s.14(1)(b).
[95] *Ibid.*, s.22.
[96] *Ibid.*, s.8.
[97] SOGO, s.35.

[98] *Ibid.*, ss.24–25.
[99] SOGO, s.25.
[100] *Ibid.*, sec. s.36.
[101] SOGO, s.16(2).
[102] SOGO, s.32(1–2).
[103] Lee Aitken, "Secured Lending" in *Trade and Investment Law in Hong Kong*, (Smart and Halkyard ed., 1993), p.244.
[104] SOGO, *op. cit.*, p.44.
[105] Betty Ho, *Security for Credit: Law and Practice in Hong Kong* (1992), p.498.
[106] Penlington, *op. cit.*, p.277.
[107] Bill of Sale Ordinance (CAP 20) in the *Laws of Hong Kong.*
[108] Sihombing, *op. cit.*, p.143.
[109] Ho, *op. cit.*, p.163.
[110] Penlington, *op. cit.*, p.279.
[111] Philip Smart, "Business Associations" in *Trade and investment law in Hong Kong* (Smart and Halkyard ed. 1993), p.59.
[112] Business Registration Ordinance (CAP 310), s.5 in *Laws of Hong Kong.*
[113] *Ibid.*, s.8.
[114] *Ibid.*
[115] Partnership Ordinance (CAP 38) in the *Laws of Hong Kong.*
[116] Limited Partnership Ordinance (CAP 37) in the *Laws of Hong Kong.*
[117] Partnership Ordinance, *op. cit.*, s.3(1).
[118] Clement Shum, *Business Associations* (1989), p.30.
[119] Limited Partnership Ordinance (CAP 37).
[120] Pauline Wallace, *Company Law in Hong Kong*, (2nd ed. 1990), p.5.
[121] Companies Ordinance (CAP 32), s.345.
[122] *Ibid.*, s.5.
[123] Wallace, *op. cit.*, p.65.
[124] *Ibid.*, p.18.
[125] Companies Ordinance, *op. cit.*, s.31.
[126] *Ibid.*, s.29(1).
[127] Price Waterhouse, *op. cit.*, p.46.
[128] Companies Ordinance, *op. cit.*, s.332.
[129] *Ibid.*, s.335.
[130] *Ibid.*, s.337A.
[131] Stock Exchanges Unification Ordinance, s.27(3), Laws of Hong Kong CAP 361 as reprinted in Robert C. Rosen, *International Securities Regulations, Hong Kong, Booklet 2: Documents: Laws and Regulations.* 211, 221 (1992).
[132] *Ibid.*, Part IV.
[133] *Ibid.*, s.2(1).
[134] *Ibid.*, s.27(4).
[135] *Ibid.*, s.11.
[136] Edward G. Hinkelman, et al. (ed.), *Hong Kong Business, The Portable Encyclopedia For Doing Business With Hong Kong* (1994), p.209.
[137] Securities Ordinance (CAP 333), *op. cit.*, Part VI, s.47 *et seq.*
[138] Stock Exchange Unification Ordinance, (CAP 361), *op. cit.*, s.12.
[139] *Ibid.*, s.13(a–d).
[140] Larry LK Kwok, "Regulation of the Securities Industry" in *Trade and Investment Law in Hong Kong* (Smart and Halkyard 1993), p.283, 290 *et seq.*
[141] Price Waterhouse, *op. cit.*, p.210.
[142] Kwok, *op. cit.*, p.286.
[143] Securities and Futures Commission Ordinance (CAP 24), s.3(2) in the *Laws of Hong Kong.*
[144] *Ibid.*, s.4(1)(a).

[145] *Ibid.*, s.4(1)(b).   [146] *Ibid.*
[147] *Ibid.*, s.4(1)(c).   [148] *Ibid.*, s.4(1)(d).
[149] *Ibid.*, s.4(1)(e).   [150] *Ibid.*, s.4(1)(f).
[151] *Ibid.*, s.4(1)(g).   [152] *Ibid.*, s.4(1)(h).
[153] *Ibid.*, s.4(1)(i).   [154] *Ibid.*, s.4(1)(j).
[155] *Ibid.*, s.4(1)(k).   [156] *Ibid.*, s.9.
[157] *Ibid.*, s.12.
[158] *Ibid.*, Part III, s.18 *et seq.*
[159] Securities Ordinance (CAP 333), s.48(1) in the *Laws of Hong Kong.*
[160] *Ibid.*, s.48(1A).   [161] *Ibid.*, s.48(2).
[162] *Ibid.*, s.47(1)   [163] *Ibid.*, s.2(1)
[164] *Ibid.*, s.65A(1–2)   [165] *Ibid.*, s.65B.
[166] *Ibid.*, s.65A(3).
[167] Securities and Futures Commission Ordinance, *op. cit.*, s.23(1).
[168] *Ibid.*, s.23(2–3).   [169] *Ibid.*, s.72(1)(a).
[170] *Ibid.*, s.72(1)(b)(i).   [171] *Ibid.*, s.72(1)(b)(ii).
[172] *Ibid.*, s.72(1)(b)(iii).   [173] *Ibid.*, s.72(1)(b)(iv).
[174] *Ibid.*, s.72(1)(b)(v).   [175] *Ibid.*, s.73(1)(a–b).
[176] *Ibid.*, s.73(3)(b)(i).   [177] *Ibid.*, s.73(3)(b)(ii).
[178] *Ibid.*, s.73(3)(b)(iii).   [179] *Ibid.*, s.73(4).
[180] *Ibid.*, s.77(1).   [181] *Ibid.*, s.74(1).
[182] *Ibid.*, s.74(5).   [183] *Ibid.*, s.74(4).
[184] Protection of Investors Ordinance (CAP 335), s.3 in the *Laws of Hong Kong.*
[185] *Ibid.*
[186] *Securities (Insider Dealing) Ordinance 1990*, s.23(a) in John A. Luff and Helen Lee, "Hong Kong" in International Securities Regulation (Rosen, ed. 1992).
[187] *Ibid.*, s.23(1)(b–c).
[188] *Ibid.*, at s.14.
[189] Kwok, *op. cit.*, p.312.
[190] Wallace, *op. cit.*, p.108.
[191] Denton Hall, "The Exchange aims for quality", in *Asia Law*, March 1995, p.25.
[192] *Ibid.*, p.25.
[193] *Ibid.*, p.26.
[194] Kwok, *op. cit.*, p.315.
[195] Denton Hall, *op. cit.*, p.27.
[196] Price Waterhouse, *op. cit.*, p.211.
[197] J.A. McInnis, "Alternative Dispute Resolution", in *The Future of the Law in Hong Kong* (Wacks, ed., 1989), p.392.
[198] "Hong Kong's Role as a Regional Dispute Resolution Centre", *Reuter Textline, Euromoney Supplement*, July 16, 1991, Lexis, Nexis, World Library.
[199] Arbitration Ordinance (CAP 341) in *Laws of Hong Kong.*
[200] Martindale–Hubbell, Selected International Conventions (1994), p.IC-11.
[201] McInnis, *op. cit.*, p.504.
[202] *Ibid.*, p.505.
[203] *Ibid.*, p.513.
[204] Arbitration Ordinance CAP 341, *op. cit.*, s.23(2).
[205] *Ibid.*, s.25.
[206] Arbitration Ordinance, s.8.
[207] Model Law, Art. 10(2).
[208] *Ibid.*, s.2A.
[209] *Ibid.*, s.2A(4).
[210] Figures as stated by Barrie Wiggham, the Hong Kong Commissioner for Economic and Trade affairs, USA at a luncheon before the California Chamber of Commerce, in Sacramento, CA on September 28, 1995.

[211] Global Investor, *Hong Kong Monetary Authority*, Vol.12, no.4, p.11.

[212] *Ibid.*

[213] Derek Roebuck, et al., *Law Relating to Banking in Hong Kong* (1994), p.311.

[214] Global Investor, *op. cit.*, p.11.

[215] *Asia Law*, 30 May 1995, p.34.

[216] Hinkelman (ed.), *op. cit.*, p.202.

[217] Hong Kong Government Printers office, *Hong Kong, 1995* (1995), p.81 (herein "Hong Kong, 1995").

[218] Hinkelman (ed.), *op. cit.*, p.203.

[219] *Hong Kong, 1995, op. cit.*, p.81.

[220] Hinkelman (ed.), *op. cit.*, p.82.

[221] *Ibid.*, p.82.

[222] *Ibid.*, p.284.

[223] Price Waterhouse, *op. cit.*, p.56.

[224] *Hong Kong, 1995*, p.81.

[225] Hinkelman (ed.), *op. cit.*, p.203.

[226] Roebuck, et. al., *op. cit.*, p.285.

[227] *Ibid.*, p.287.

[228] Carver, *op. cit.*, p.350.

[229] S. Nossal, *The New Bank Terms and the Control of Exemptions Clauses Ordinance*, 23 HKLJ 422, 425 (1993).

[230] Aitken, *op. cit.*, p.244.

[231] Money Lender's Ordinance (CAP 163) in the *Laws of Hong Kong*.

[232] *Hong Kong, 1995, op. cit.*, p.96.

[233] Control Of Exemption Clauses Ordinance (CAP 71) in *Laws of Hong Kong*.

[234] Misrepresentation Ordinance (CAP 284) in *Laws of Hong Kong*.

[235] Sale of Goods Ordinance (CAP 284) in *Laws of Hong Kong*.

[236] Chui and Roebuck, *op. cit.*, p.121.

[237] Carver. *op. cit.*, p.147.

[238] *Ibid.*

[239] Control of Exemption Clauses Ordinance, *op. cit.*, s.7(1).

[240] *Ibid.*, s.7(2).

[241] Carver, *op. cit.*, p.152.

[242] *Ibid.*, s.7(3).

[243] *Ibid.*, s.10(1).

[244] Control of Exemption Clauses Ordinance, *op. cit.*, ss.16–17.

[245] Carver, *op. cit.*, p.157.

[246] Carver, *op. cit.*, p.158.

[247] Chui and Roebuck, *op. cit.*, p.66.

[248] Misrepresentation Ordinance, *op. cit.*, s.2.

[249] Chui and Roebuck, *op. cit.*, p.72.

[250] *Ibid.*, s.3.

[251] Control of Exemption Clauses Ordinance, Schedule 3, Amendment to Misrepresentation Ordinance, s.4.

[252] Carver, *op. cit.*, p.189.

[253] SOGO, s.14(a).

[254] *Ibid.*, s.14(b).

[255] Control of Exemption Clauses Ordinance, *op. cit.*, s.11(a).

[256] SOGO, *op. cit.*, s.15(1).

[257] Control of Exemption Clauses Ordinance, *op. cit.*, s.11(2).

[258] SOGO s.16(2).

[259] SOGO s.17(2)(a).

[260] SOGO s.17(2)(c).

[261] Williams, *op. cit.*, p.109.

[262] Air Pollution Control Ordinance (CAP 311) in *Laws of Hong Kong*.

[263] Noise Control Ordinance (CAP 400) in *Laws of Hong Kong*.

[264] Water Pollution Ordinance (CAP 358) in *Laws of Hong Kong*.

[265] Waste Disposal Ordinance (CAP 354) in *Laws of Hong Kong*.

[266] Williams, *op. cit.*, p.110.

[267] *Ibid.*, p.111.

[268] *Ibid.*, p.112.

[269] *Ibid.*, p.112.

[270] *Ibid.*, pp.112–113.

[271] Williams, *op. cit.*, p.116.

[272] *Ibid.*, p.114.

[273] Employees Compensation Ordinance (CAP 282), s.26, in *Laws of Hong Kong*.

[274] *Ibid.*, p.124.

[275] Williams, *op. cit.*, p.125.

[276] Pneumoconiosis Ordinance (CAP 360) in *Laws of Hong Kong*.

[277] *Ibid.*, s.4.

[278] *Ibid.*, pp.117–118.

[279] Hugh D.R. Baker, "Hong Kong: A View From Both Sides", *Asian Affairs: Journal of the Royal Society for Asian Affairs*, Vol.XXVI Part I, Feb. 1995, p.10.

[280] Richard J. Ferris, Jr., "Aspiration and Reality in Taiwan, Hong Kong, South Korea, and Singapore: An Introduction to the Environmental Regulatory Systems of Asia's Four New Dragons", 4 Duke J. *Comp. & Int'l L.* (1993) 125, 143.

[281] Roda Mushkat, "Environmental Problems and Policy Response In Hong Kong: An Evaluation From an International Legal Perspective", *Asian Yearbook of International Law*, Vol.2, 113–126 (Ko Swan Sik et al. eds., 1994), note 19 (quoting M. Appleyard, "Time to Tackle Pollution. HK's Third World Environment", *SCMP* 26 March 1989).

[282] Jill Cottrell, "Environmental Protection", in *Trade and Investment Law in Hong Kong* (Smart and Halkyard, ed. 1993), pp.211, 216.

[283] *Ibid.*, p.219.

[284] Air Pollution Control Ordinance (CAP 311) in *Laws of Hong Kong*.

[285] *Ibid.*, s.6.

[286] *Ibid.*, s.2.

[287] *Ibid.*, s.12(1).

[288] *Ibid.*, s.28(2).

[289] *Ibid.*, s.30.

[290] Noise Control Ordinance (CAP 400) in *Laws of Hong Kong*.

[291] *Ibid.*, s.6(3).

[292] Water Pollution Control Ordinance (CAP 358) in *Laws of Hong Kong*.

[293] *Ibid.*, s.4.

[294] *Ibid.*, s.19 et seq.

[295] Ferris, *op. cit.*, p.155.

[296] Waste Disposal Ordinance (CAP 354) in *Laws of Hong Kong*.

[297] *Ibid.*, s.9 et seq.

[298] *Ibid.*, s.21 et seq.

[299] *Ibid.*, s.23.

[300] *Hong Kong Human Rights Practices, 1994* (US Department of State 1995), Lexis, Nexis, World Library.

[301] Michael J. Downey, "Employment Law", in *Trade and Investment in Hong Kong* (Smart and Halkyard, ed. 1993), p.190.

[302] Employment of Children Regulations (CAP 57), s.4. in *Laws of Hong Kong*.

[303] *Ibid.*, ss.4–8.

[304] Women and Young Persons Regulations (CAP 57), s.8 in *Laws of Hong Kong*.

[305] Downey, *op. cit.*, p.196.

306 Kevin Williams, *Hong Kong Employment Law* (1990), p.125.

307 Downey, *op. cit.*, p.198.

308 "Mandatory Provident Fund for Hong Kong workers; passage ends 30 year debate", *East Asian Executive Reports*, July 15, 1995, p.6.

309 Employment Ordinance (CAP 57) in *Laws of Hong Kong*.

310 Downey, *op. cit.*, p.193.

311 Employment Ordinance, *op. cit.*, Part III, s.12.

312 *Ibid.*, s.14.

313 Employment Ordinance, s.17.

314 *Ibid.*, s.33.

315 *Ibid.*, s.39.

316 *Ibid.*, s.41, *et seq.*

317 Price Waterhouse, *op. cit.*, 87.

318 Employment Ordinance, s.33.

319 *Ibid.*, s.35.

320 *Ibid.*, s.33(3).

321 *Ibid.*, s.35(5)(a).

322 Employment Ordinance Part II, s.5 *et seq.*

323 *Ibid.*, s.6.

324 *Ibid.*, s.7.

325 *Ibid.*, ss.9, 10.

326 *Ibid.*, s.5(1).

327 *Ibid.*, s.6.

328 *Ibid.*

329 Downey, *op. cit.*, p.203.

330 *Ibid.*, p.203.

331 Employment Ordinance, *op. cit.*, s.7(1).

332 *Ibid.*, s.7(3).

333 Downey, *op. cit.*, p.204.

334 *Ibid.*, s.9.

335 Downey, *op. cit.*, pp.201–202.

336 *Ibid.*, p.202.

337 Basic Law, Art. 27.

338 Trade Unions Ordinance (CAP 332), s.5 in *Laws of Hong Kong*.

339 *Ibid.*, s.5(3).

340 Ng Sek-hong, "Employment and Human Rights in Hong Kong: Some recent developments", 24 *HKLJ* 108, 129 (1994).

341 Trade Unions Ordinance (CAP 332), s.42.

342 US Dept. of State, *Hong Kong Human Rights Practices, 1994* (1995), Lexis, Nexis, World Library.

343 Employment Ordinance, s.21C.

344 *Ibid.*, s.42.

345 Hong Kong Human Rights Practices, *op. cit.*

346 Ng Sek-hong, *op. cit.*, p.133.

347 *Ibid.*, p.135.

348 *Ibid.*

349 Basic Law, Art. 27.

350 Labour Relations Ordinance (CAP 55), Laws of Hong Kong.

351 Downey, *op. cit.*, p.206.

352 Labour Tribunal Ordinance (CAP 25), Laws of Hong Kong.

353 *Ibid.*, s.7.

354 Price Waterhouse, *op. cit.*, p.42.

355 *Ibid.*, p.43.

356 "Death of Hong Kong", *Fortune* 118, 119, June 26, 1995.

Hong Kong

[357] Sally Gelston, "Hong Kong Popular Choice for Asian HQs", *East Asian Executive reports*, Vol.16, no.1, p.6.

[358] Ferheen Mahomed, "A Foreign Investor's Guide to the Environmental Legal Regime of Hong Kong", 28 *San Diego L. Rev.* 787, 789 (1991).

[359] *Ibid.*, at 42.

[360] Basic Law, Art. 5.

[361] Andrew Halkyard, "Using Hong Kong for Regional Headquarters Operations", in *Trade and Investment Law in Hong Kong*, (Smart and Halkyard, eds. 1993) pp.353, 362.

[362] Price Waterhouse *op. cit.*, p.112.

[363] "Synopsis of Taxes Administered by the Inland Revenue Department of Hong Kong" (23rd Edition), as Appendix A to Andrew Halkyard, "Structuring Operations for Multinational Corporations Carrying on Business in Hong Kong" in *Trade and Investment Law in Hong Kong* 126, 153 (Smart and Andrew, eds., 1993).

[364] Andrew Halkyard, "Structuring Operations for Multinational Corporations Carrying on Business in Hong Kong", in *Trade and Investment Law in Hong Kong*, 126, 129 (Smart, Halkyard, eds., 1993).

[365] *Ibid.*

[366] Peter F. Rhodes, "Import and Export Regulation", *in Trade and Investment Law in Hong Kong*, pp.413, 416 (Smart, Halkyard, eds., 1993).

[367] *Ibid.*

[368] *Ibid.*, at 429.

[369] "Joint Declaration of the Government of the United Kingdom of Great Britain and Northern Ireland and the Government of the People's Republic of China on the Question of Hong Kong", reprinted in *Hong Kong's Transition to 1997: Background, Problems And Prospects* 25, 26 (Hungdah Chui) 1993.

[370] Basic Law Arts. 115–116.

[371] 22 USC 5721.

[372] 22 USC 5722.

[373] Companies Ordinance (CAP 32), Laws of Hong Kong.

[374] Wallace, *op. cit.*, pp.199–202.

[375] Professional Accountants Ordinance (CAP 335), Laws of Hong Kong.

[376] Wallace *op. cit.*, p.200, and Price Waterhouse, *op. cit.*, pp.96–97.

[377] Companies Ordinance, s.131.

[378] Wallace, *op. cit.*, p.202.

[379] Wallace, *op. cit.*, p.245.

[380] Price Waterhouse, *op. cit.*, p.98.

[381] *Ibid.*, p.246.

[382] *Ibid.*, p.245.

[383] David Flux, David G. Smith, *Hong Kong Taxation: Law and Practice 1993–94 ed.*, (1993), p.6.

[384] Price Waterhouse, *op. cit.*, p.127.

[385] *Ibid.*

[386] *Ibid.*, p.126.

[387] *Ibid.*, p.128.

[388] Flux and Smith, *op. cit.*, p.18.

[389] *Ibid.*, p.117.

[390] *Ibid.*

[391] *Ibid.*, p.119.

[392] "Departmental Interpretation & Practice Notes No. 21, Locality Of Profits in Hong Kong" as reprinted in Flux and Smith, *op. cit.*, pp.599, 600.

[393] Flux and Smith, *op. cit.*, p.120.

[394] *Ibid.*, p.120.

[395] *Ibid.*, p.152.
[396] "Departmental Interpretation & Practice Notes No. 21, Locality Of Profits in Hong Kong", *op. cit.*, ss.7–11, pp.601–602.
[397] Flux and Smith, *op. cit.*, p.170.
[398] *Ibid.*, pp.174–175.
[399] *Ibid.*, pp.177–179.
[400] *Ibid.*, p.189.
[401] *Ibid.*, p.189.
[402] *Ibid.*, p.189.
[403] *Ibid.*, p.189.
[404] *Ibid.*, p.118.
[405] Inland Revenue Ordinance (CAP 112), s.8(1) in *Laws of Hong Kong*.
[406] Flux and Smith, *op. cit.*, p.40.
[407] "Department Interpretation & Practice Notes (DIPN), No. 10 the charge to salaries tax", reprinted in Flux and Smith, *op. cit.*, as appendix 10 at 491, 493.
[408] Andrew Halkyard, "Structuring Operations for Multinational Corporations carrying on Business in Hong Kong", *op. cit.*, at 145.
[409] Flux and Smith, *op. cit.*, pp.42–43.
[410] Flux and Smith, *op. cit.*, p.44.
[411] "DIPN No. 16, Taxation of fringe benefits", Appendix 16 in Flux and Smith, *op. cit.*, pp.555, 557.
[412] "Synopsis of Taxes Administered by the Inland Revenue Department of Hong Kong" (23rd ed.) Appendix A, in Halkyard, "Structuring Operations for Multinational Corporations Carrying on Business in Hong Kong", *op. cit.*, pp.153, 159.
[413] Flux and Smith, *op. cit.*, p.29.
[414] *Ibid.*
[415] "Synopsis of Taxes Administered by the Inland Revenue Department of Hong Kong" (23rd ed.), *op. cit.*, p.160.
[416] Flux and Smith, *op. cit.*, 7.
[417] *Ibid.*, p.23.
[418] Jefferson P. Vanderwolk, "Can Tax Avoidance be Stopped? Limitations on the Scope of sections 61 and 61A of the Inland Revenue Ordinance", 23 HLKJ 207 (1993).
[419] *Ibid.*, pp.209–210.
[420] DIPN no.15, Part C, s.29(a), reprinted in Flux and Smith, *op. cit.*, p.545.
[421] Flux and Smith, *op. cit.*, 17.
[422] Flux and Smith, *op. cit.*, pp.363–364.
[423] Flux and Smith, *op. cit.*, pp.365–370.
[424] Eva Lau, "Protection for Intellectual Property", in *Trade and Investment Law in Hong Kong* (Smart and Halkyard, eds. 1993), p.93.
[425] "Copyright Act of 1956", reprinted as Appendix 3 in *Law of Intellectual and Industrial Property in Hong Kong* (Michael D. Pendleton, 1984), p.402.
[426] K.H. Pun, "Copyright Protection For Computer Software: Does Hong Kong Meet International Standards?", 24 HKLJ 56, 65 (1994).
[427] Copyright Act of 1956, *op. cit.*, s.2.
[428] *Ibid.*, s.3.
[429] Lau, *op. cit.*, p.96.
[430] Copyright Act of 1956, *op. cit.*, s.2(1), 3(2).
[431] *Ibid.*, s.1(5)(a) and (b).
[432] John H. Jackson, et al., 1995 Documents Supplement to Legal Problems of International Economic Relations 3d. (1995), p.335.
[433] *Ibid.*, Art. 3.
[434] *Ibid.*, at 335.
[435] John A. Connors, *Protecting Intellectual Property in Asia-Pacific* (1984) p.20.

Hong Kong

[436] Alan J. Jacobs, Elizabeth Hanellin ed. *Patents Throughout the World*, 4d. (1995), H-9.

[437] Registration of Patents Ordinance (CAP 42), s.3 in *Laws of Hong Kong*.

[438] *Ibid.*, s.6.

[439] *Ibid.*, s.7.

[440] Connors, *op. cit.*, p.22.

[441] Trademarks Ordinance (CAP 43) in *Laws of Hong Kong*.

[442] *Ibid.*, s.9.

[443] *Ibid.*, s.10.

[444] *Ibid.*, s.20.

[445] *Ibid.*, s.12.

[446] *Ibid.*, s.27(1).

[447] *Ibid.*, s.28.

[448] "Hong Kong Investment Climate Statement", *National Trade Data Bank*, Nov. 13, 1992, Lexis, Nexis, World Library.

[449] Lau, *op. cit.*, p.106.

[450] "Anton Piller K G v. Manufacturing Processors Ltd", (1976) Chap. 55. cited in Pendleton, *op. cit.*, p.306.

[451] Pendleton *op. cit.*, p.306.

[452] Pendleton, *op. cit.*, p.308.

[453] Michael Wilkinson, "Recent Developments affecting Anton Piller Orders", 23 HKLJ 79 (1994).

[454] *Ibid.*, p.307.

[455] Hinkelman, *et al.*, *op. cit.*, p.129.

[456] Frederick W. Mote, *Intellectual Foundations of China*, 2d., p.32.

[457] The four virtues are discussed in Fairbank, Reischauer, Craig, *East Asia: Tradition and Transformation*, (1978), p.46.

[458] Berry Fong-Chung Hsu, *The Common Law System In Chinese Context: Hong Kong in Transition* (1992), p.25.

[459] Peter Wesley-Smith, *An Introduction into the Hong Kong Legal System* (1987), p.91.

[460] Carver, *op. cit.*, p.49.

[461] Wesley-Smith, *op. cit.*, p.92.

[462] *Ibid.*, p.91.

[463] Alison E.W. Conner, "Regulation of Foreign Lawyers in Hong Kong", 22 HKLJ 132 (1992).

[464] Legal Practitioner's Ordinance (CAP 159), s.10(2)(a–d) in *Laws of Hong Kong*.

[465] *Ibid.*, s.31.

[466] Carver, *op. cit.*, p.52.

[467] Price Waterhouse, *op. cit.*, p.27.

[468] *Ibid.*, at 28.

[469] Walden Country Reports, Hong Kong, *op. cit.*

[470] Governor Christopher Patten's Annual Policy Address, delivered on October 11, 1995. Excerpts from the address were provided to the author courtesy of the Hong Kong Economic & Trade Office, San Francisco.

[471] Hinkelman, *op. cit.*, p.19.

[472] Albert H Y Chen, "The Basic Law and the Protection of Property Rights", 23 HKLJ 31, 40 (1993).

[473] Basic Law, Art. 7.

[474] See SOGO, ss.12, 20, 22, 30, 31(5), 33, 34(2–3), 36(2), 38.

[475] SOGO, *op. cit.*, s.12.

[476] Sihombing, *op. cit.*, p.77.

[477] SOGO, s.30.

[478] SOGO, s.20, rule 1.

479 SOGO, s.33.
480 SOGO, s.57A.
481 *Ibid.*
482 SOGO, s.62(5).
483 Price Waterhouse, *op. cit.*, p.160.
484 Tim Dobson, "Equity Joint Ventures", in *Trade and Investment Law in Hong Kong* (Smart and Halkyard, eds. 1993) p.63.
485 *Ibid.*
486 Companies Ordinance (CAP 32), s.15 *et seq.*
487 *Ibid.*, s.23.
488 Dobson, *op. cit.*, pp.63–64.
489 *Ibid.*
490 *Ibid.*, pp.64–65.
491 Hinkelman, et al., *op. cit.*, p.170.
492 Barrie Wiggham notes, *op. cit.*
493 Conti, *op. cit.*, p.368.
494 Employment Ordinance (CAP 57), s.4.
495 *Ibid.*, s.2.
496 Employment Ordinance, s.44.
497 *Ibid.*, s.45.
498 *Ibid.*, s.22.
499 *Ibid.*, s.2 "wages".
500 *Ibid.*, s.17.
501 *Ibid.*
502 Derek Roebuck (ed.), *Law Relating to Banking in Hong Kong* (2d., 1994), p.178.

INDONESIA

Darrell R. Johnson

I. Summary of Business and Political Conditions

Basic Demographic, Political and Economic Information

With over 13,000 islands occupied by more than 190 million people, spread   C.01
out over 3,000,000 square miles of ocean, Indonesia is the fourth largest
country in the world and the most prominent archipelagical country in the
world. Indonesia has five main islands that total 90 per cent of its land area
and contain over 93 per cent of its population. These are Java, Kalimantan,
Sumatra, Irian Jaya and Sulawesi. Indonesia's territory is similar in length to
the United States, stretching over 3,200 miles from the tip of Sumatra in the
west to eastern Irian Jaya. The country has over 300 distinct ethnic and
language groups, united by a national language called Bahasa Indonesia, or
Indonesian.

There is freedom of religion in Indonesia. Approximately 90 per cent of
the population professes the Islamic faith while the remainder are mainly
Christians, Buddhist and Hindu.

Indonesia's economic growth during the last 25 years has been dramatic.
Its average annual growth rate has been about 7 per cent during this period.
In 1967, Indonesia's per capita income was less than half that of Bangladesh.
Today its per capita income exceeds US$1,000 per annum, which places
Indonesia in the top rank of developing countries. During the late 1960s
and 1970s, Indonesia's economic growth rate was based primarily on oil
and gas. With depressed oil prices in the early 1980s, the Indonesian Government reoriented its economic planning to encourage the growth of non-oil
and gas exports and to make the private sector more competitive internationally. This policy has continued until the present time. Non-oil and gas
exports have risen dramatically and the country's dependence on oil and

gas revenues has been reduced. Whereas oil and gas revenues contributed about 75 per cent of export earnings in the 1970s, non-oil and gas revenues today contribute about that portion, with approximately a quarter of export earnings realized from the sale of oil and gas.

The country has a free foreign exchange system, by which the Government has allowed the Indonesian Rupiah to depreciate at a rate of approximately 4 to 5 per cent per annum.

General Summary of the Political and Governmental System in Indonesia

C.02   Indonesia adheres to what is commonly referred to as the "1945 Constitution", which provides for executive, legislative and judicial branches in a republican form of government. There are two houses of the legislative branch, the People's Consultative Assembly (the MPR) and People's House of Representatives (the DPR). The MPR is the highest body of the state. Its function is primarily to elect the President and the Vice President and to establish what is known as the GBHN, or the Outlines of State Policy. These functions are exercised every five years. The MPR is comprised of 500 members of the DPR and another 500 members representing various regional and working groups. One-third of the members of the MPR are appointed by the President. In addition to these bodies, the Government of Indonesia issues various types of promulgations that have the force of law. These are government regulations, presidential decrees, ministerial decrees, director general decrees and departmental circular letters.

The DPR has 500 members, 400 of which are elected, with the remainder appointed from the military. The DPR performs the legislative functions for the Government and, together with the President, enacts laws.

The next DPR election is in 1997, and will be followed by a Presidential election in 1998.

Indonesia has 27 provinces. Each province is headed by a governor who is elected by a local parliament which is subject to presidential approval. The provinces are sub-divided into municipalities and regencies. There are 50 to 60 municipalities and about 250 regencies in the country.

Historical Development of the Legal and Judicial System in Indonesia and the Role of Law in Economic Development

C.03   For nearly 400 years, Indonesia was subject to various degrees of control and occupation by The Netherlands. The greatest impact of Dutch colonialism was felt in Java. One of the Dutch legacies was the Dutch Civil and Commercial Codes. Dating from 1847, these Codes form the legal basis of commercial and corporate law in Indonesia today. It should be noted that the Indonesian Commercial and Civil Codes have not been officially translated into Indonesian, though two widely accepted Indonesian versions exist.

At independence, the Indonesian Government made a decision to incorporate all of the prior Dutch law into its legal system, except if specifically rejected. Accordingly, these Codes still have the force of law. In addition, codes that were specifically rejected, such as certain procedural codes governing judicial matters, may still be followed as a matter of guidance, even though they were specifically repealed at the time of, or shortly following, independence.

While the Dutch codes have been amended on numerous occasions, these amendments were not incorporated into the Indonesian Codes. As a result, the fundamental principles of Indonesian corporate and commercial law are based upon Codes that have been generally overtaken by business developments during the last 150 years.

To the extent that interpretations of Code sections are made by the judiciary and scholars, references are often made, to the extent possible, to Dutch jurisprudence (*i.e.* court decisions and scholarly comment) and to the more modern codes that exist in Holland. Indonesian courts are not required to make such references, which are entirely discretionary.

In addition to the Dutch influence on the legal system, the Indonesian   C.04
Government has adopted numerous laws and other promulgations since independence. Many of these economic laws and regulations date from 1967 and were accompanied by a change of government at that time. For the international investment community, the most significant law during this period was the Foreign Investment Law. This Law and its implementing regulations have gone through a number of changes since the Law was adopted in 1967. In addition, with the Government's deregulatory policy dating from the mid-1980s, numerous laws, government regulations and decrees have been adopted to stimulate the private sector. These were issued on a sector–by–sector basis, with perhaps the most important being issued by the Department of Finance, the Department of Industry and the Department of Trade.

The judicial system is comprised of three levels: District Courts, High Courts and the Supreme Court. The District Courts function as trial courts. Their procedures are based upon the civil law system, and there is no jury system. Appeals may be taken to the High Court and thereafter to the Supreme Court. The Supreme Court consists of a number of judges and decisions are made by a three-judge panel. Decisions are not reported in Indonesia and in any case do not have the *stare decisis* effect that is familiar to common law systems.

In addition to the Civil Code, there are Islamic courts that deal with domestic matters such as divorce and inheritance for persons of the Islamic faith, administrative courts, which hear disputes concerning charges against

Government departments and agencies, and a tax court that hears taxpayer appeals from decisions of the Indonesian tax authorities.

The Indonesian Government is aware that its commercial laws are not well-suited to a dynamic and growing economy. The Department of Justice's Law and Development Center is a permanent body whose function is to promote law and development and specifically new legislation to modernize Indonesia's legal structures. In addition, the Government has created the Economic Law and Improved Procurement Systems Project (the ELIPS Project), which is the largest single-country law and development effort in the world. In addition to substantive law reform, the ELIPS Project is focused on changes in law school curricula and legal information systems.

Legal and Judicial Structure for the Regulation of Commercial Activities in Indonesia

C.05   The legal structure for Indonesian commercial activities will differ depending upon whether domestic or foreign investment is involved. With regard to domestic investment, commercial activities may be undertaken by corporations, sole proprietorships, and partnerships. In some cases, Government regulations require the use of legal entities. Indonesia has adopted, as of March 7, 1996, a new Company Law to replace earlier provisions of the Indonesian Commercial Code dealing with company formation and operation. This Law is meant simultaneously to provide shareholders with flexibility in governing their affairs and also to protect minority shareholders and creditors.

If domestic investors seek facilities such as duty holidays and reductions on the import of capital equipment, they will fall under the jurisdiction of the Capital Investment Coordinating Board (BKPM) and the Domestic Investment Law of 1968.

Foreign investors that invest in manufacturing and some service activities also fall under the jurisdiction of BKPM but are subject to the Foreign Investment Law of 1967. Details concerning this Law and its procedures are described below. In addition, significant investment activities are regulated by the Department of Finance, in the areas of banking, finance (such as capital leasing and capital market activities) and insurance. Oil and gas investment is made by foreign oil companies under a production sharing contract regime with P.N. Pertamina, the state oil company, under the supervision of the Directorate of Oil and Gas of the Department of Mines and Energy. Indonesia was a member of GATT and is a member of the World Trade Organization. It is also a founding member of the Association of South East Asian Nations (ASEAN) and a founding member of APEC, the Asia Pacific Economic Cooperation.

II. Laws and Institutions Affecting Business and Commercial Activities

Competition Law

Indonesia does not have a comprehensive competition law at the present time. There is only one provision of Indonesian law that specifically addresses this topic, though in a general way. Article 382 of the Indonesian Criminal Code stipulates that unfair competition is considered a criminal act:

C.06

> "Whomsoever commits an act of fraud to mislead persons or a particular person, with the intent of establishing or increasing the proceeds of his own or another's trade or business, shall be punished, because of unfair competition, with a maximum imprisonment of 1 year and 4 months or a maximum fine Rp. 13,500, if the foregoing could cause a loss to his own or the other person's competitors."[1]

Various provisions of the Indonesian Civil Code are relevant to unfair competition. Article 1365 is a general tort provision and imposes civil responsibility for wrongful acts:

> "Every illegal act causing damage to another person shall oblige the person who caused the damage to pay compensation."

This provision is used in Indonesian litigation to support damage claims based on a wide variety of facts. It is possible that a criminal act under Section 382 of the Indonesian Criminal Code can be used as the basis of civil liability under Section 1365 of the Indonesian Civil Code. In addition, Sections 1320, 1335, 1337 and 1338 of the Indonesian Civil Code provide generally or are generally construed to provide that illegal agreements are considered null and void:

(i) Article 1320: "An agreement requires four conditions as follows:
   1. Consent of the persons involved;
   2. The capability to enter upon an agreement;
   3. A certain subject;
   4. A lawful purpose."
(ii) Article 1335: "An agreement made without any cause, or arising from a false or illegitimate cause, shall be invalid."
(iii) Article 1337: "A cause will be illegal if prohibited by law, or if contrary to good ethics or public order."
(iv) Article 1338: "All agreements which have been constituted legally shall be law to those having undertaken them. Such agreements cannot be revoked other than by bilateral consent, or on grounds

that are declared sufficient by law. These agreements shall be carried out in a bonafide manner."

If an agreement is illegal under Section 382 of the Criminal Code, these sections can be used to avoid the agreement for civil law purposes.

C.07 The Indonesian Government is considering a Competition Law or Fair Trade Practices Law, to be drafted in the future, with the aim of making the commercial legal framework more conducive to the development of a market driven economy in Indonesia.

Contract Law[2]

C.08 Modern commercial contracts in Indonesia are governed by the Indonesian Civil Code, Book III of which deals with contract law, or what is referred to in the Code as the law of obligations.

Article 1320 of the Indonesian Civil Code requires four basic conditions to be fulfilled to form a binding contract: (i) mutual consent; (ii) capacity; (iii) a certain subject matter; and (iv) a lawful purpose.

The requirement of mutual consent means that both parties must have entered into the contract as an exercise of their free will. Accordingly, they must not have entered into the contract by reason of mistake, fraud or duress.

To satisfy the capacity requirement, the parties must also be legally competent to enter into the contract. Among the types of persons who lack legal capacity are minors (defined by Article 330 of the Indonesian Civil Code as a person under 21 unless he or she is married) and prisoners, pursuant to Article 433 of the Indonesian Civil Code. Article 108, which provides that married women lack legal capacity, has been ruled invalid in a 1963 letter issued by the Indonesian Supreme Court.[3]

The requirement that there be a certain subject matter means that the contract must have a definite object or purpose, which means, simply, that the contract must set out the respective rights and obligations of the parties. The Indonesian Civil Code distinguishes between movable (Articles 509 through 513 of the Civil Code) and immovable property (Articles 506–508 of the Civil Code), but as a general matter, any service, right, goods or other thing is a legitimate object of a contract.

The fourth requirement, that of lawful purpose, means that the purpose of the contract must not violate Indonesian public order or policy. In such cases, the contract will not have been formed.

C.09 An important feature of Indonesian contract law is that the common law concept of consideration is not required for a valid contract to be created.[4]

Article 1338(1) of the Indonesian Commercial Code provides that once a contract has been formed, it cannot be revoked except by mutual agreement or for reasons of law. It appears that some contracts, such as pre-nuptial agreements, cannot be terminated even by mutual agreement.[5]

Article 1315 provides that as a general matter, only the parties to a contract are bound by it. Some third party beneficiary contracts, such as life insurance contracts, may be made.[6] Contracts made for the benefit of a third party may require positive action by the beneficiary to obtain the benefits of the contract.

If a contract has been legally formed, the parties are bound by its express terms. Pursuant to Article 1339 of the Indonesian Commercial Code, they are also bound by terms which, according to the type of agreement, are required by reasonableness, custom or nature. In addition, the parties to a contract are required by Article 1338(3) to perform it in good faith.

If a party defaults on the performance of a contractual obligation, the other party may sue for specific performance or for damages, including costs and interest.[7]

Article 1266, and possibly Article 1267 as well, require judicial confirmation of contract termination. To avoid this necessity, parties to a contract governed by Indonesian law generally waive these Articles, to the extent such judicial approval is required.

Commercial Law

The Commercial Law of Indonesia is based on the 1847 Dutch Civil and   C.10
Commercial Codes, which were incorporated into Indonesian law at the time of independence. Given the scope of these Codes, a summary would not be practical here; rather a sense of the topics covered in these Codes will be conveyed.

The Indonesian Civil Code consists of four books. Book One deals with persons and governs such matters as marriage, divorce, children, guardianship and related rights and obligations. Book Two concerns movable property (chattels and goods), the rights and obligations of ownership, labor, succession, inheritance, debt preferences, pledges and mortgages. Book Three addresses the broad area of obligations, the law of contracts, purchases and sales of assets, leases, partnerships and corporate bodies, loans and deposits, guarantees, interest, and settlements. Book Four concerns the law of evidence and the limitation of actions.

The Indonesian Commercial Code contains specific provisions on commercial matters; therefore matters that are generally addressed in the Civil Code may be covered by the special provisions on the same subject in the Commercial Code. Matters that are subject to the Commercial Code regulations are, among others, brokerage, partnerships, commercial paper (such as notes, bills and checks), insurance and shipping. In addition, Indonesia's Bankruptcy Ordinance, although a separate code, is considered part of the commercial law.

Indonesia

Company Law

C.11 On March 7, 1996, by Law No. 1 of 1995 Regarding the Limited Liability Company ("the Company Law") (March 6, 1995) was adopted. The Company Law superseded the previous company law found in Articles 36 through 56 of Wetboek van Koophandel (Staatblad 1847:23) (*i.e.* the Indonesian Commercial Code). The Company Law changes the former law in many areas. Implementing regulations for the new Company Law have not been issued as of the date of writing, but standard forms of articles of association have been issued by the Department of Justice.

The process for formation of a limited liability company under the Company Law is set forth in Chapter II, Articles 7 through 23. A company is established when its Deed of Establishment, which is executed in the Indonesian language and in notarial deed form, is approved by the Minister of Justice. The Deed of Establishment contains the Articles of Association. Once the Deed of Establishment is approved, the shareholders of the company are no longer personally liable for the acts of the company except in limited circumstances. The members of the Board of Directors, in contrast, continue to be personally liable for acts undertaken in the name of the company until the company's articles of association have been filed with the Department of Industry and Trade and published in the State Gazette.

C.12 The Company Law sets out various matters which must be included in the Articles of Association: the purposes, objectives and business activities of the company, the composition of the Boards of Directors and Commissioners, the procedures for holding General Meetings of the Shareholders, the number and classification of shares and the procedure for profit utilization and dividend distribution.

Amendments — Certain amendments to the Articles of Association require Department of Justice approval. All other amendments to the Articles of Association merely need to be reported to the Department of Justice. All amendments must be subsequently registered with the Department of Industry and Trade pursuant to Law No. 3 of 1982.

Capitalization — The Company Law requires a minimum authorized capital of Rp.20,000,000 (twenty million rupiah). On incorporation, at least 25 per cent of the authorized share capital must be issued, at least 50 per cent of which must be paid-in when the articles are signed, and the balance of which must be paid up at the time the Department of Justice approves the company's articles.

Classes of Shares — There may be one or more classes of shares, including classes with limited voting rights and dividend or liquidation preferences. Pre-emptive rights may be granted to existing shareholders, but the Company Law provides that if a shareholder does not exercise its pre-emptive rights, the shares must first be offered to the company's employees prior to any other persons.

Management and Control — The highest authority in the company is the Shareholders, who act through a General Meeting of Shareholders (the "GMS"). Majority requirements exist for both quorum and voting in regards to most corporate actions, but the GMS and other corporate bodies must first attempt to reach decisions on the basis of consensus. Super quorum and voting requirements exist for mergers, consolidations, acquisitions, amendments to the articles, a sale or other transfer of all or substantially all of the company's assets and dissolution of the company.

Directors are elected by the GMS and have responsibility for the management of the company. In this capacity the Directors owe their allegiance to the company and not to the shareholders. This duty of management includes the day to day affairs of the company, planning for the future, and undertaking new activities for the company. The Directors are bound by the duties of good faith and diligence and are subject to discharge by the GMS. The Company Law states that a company must have a Board of Commissioners, which is a change from the previous law, although most companies had such Boards. The Board of Commissioners' role is both to give advice to the Directors and to supervise the manner in which the Directors discharge their management responsibilities. The Commissioners are appointed by the GMS, and like the Directors, owe their duty to the company. In their supervisory role, the Commissioners are granted the power to obtain information from the Directors which they deem necessary. They also have the right to enter and inspect company property and to employ experts to assist in inspection or supervision. As well, the Board of Commissioners are vested with the power to suspend any Director who has violated the articles of association, committed a harmful act towards the company or failed to fulfill his duties to the company.

Minority Shareholder Rights — Minority Shareholders are afforded special rights under the Company Law. Every shareholder has the right to request the company to repurchase its shares at a reasonable price in the event of certain corporate actions that cause the shareholder a loss. These corporate actions include amendments to the Articles of Association, sales, pledges or exchanges of a large portion of the company's assets, and mergers, consolidations or acquisitions. Holders of 10 per cent of the shares have the right to sue Directors and Commissioners, investigate the company, request a court investigation and/or a dissolution, and call a GMS.

Mergers, Consolidations and Acquisitions — The Company Law expressly recognizes mergers, consolidations and acquisitions, which is one of the areas of improvement over the previous law which was silent on these issues. One of the key provisions is that any merger, consolidation or acquisition must also be in the interest of the target company, its employees and minority shareholders and must not be against the public interest. Any merger, consolidation or acquisition must be done with due consideration for fair competition. The Company Law is ambiguous as to whether all acquisitions are covered.

Dissolutions — Under the Company Law, a company may be dissolved in three ways: (i) a shareholder resolution (which requires a super majority vote and quorum requirement); (ii) the expiration of a duration stipulated in the Articles of Association; and (iii) a decision by a court. There are certain circumstances where a court can order dissolution of a company and appoint a liquidator. During liquidation, creditors are given protection by establishing the manner and procedure for conducting the liquidation of the company.

Indonesia has also adopted a new Capital Markets Law. See the discussion below. It should be noted that for public companies, in the event of a conflict between the Company Law and the Capital Markets Law, the Capital Markets Law shall prevail.

Capital Markets and Securities Laws

C.13   On November 10, 1995, the Capital Markets Law, Law No. 8 of 1995 (November 10, 1995) (the "Capital Markets Law") was signed by the President of the Republic of Indonesia into law after the House of Representatives passed the Capital Markets Bill. The Capital Markets Law took effect on January 1, 1996. Following the adoption of the Capital Markets Law, the Government issued 93 regulations and decrees to implement the new Law.

The Capital Markets Law replaced Law No. 15, enacted in 1952, and its implementing regulations. Previously, the regulatory framework for Indonesia's capital markets law was based upon a series of regulations promulgated to implement Law No.15 of 1952.

The purpose of the Capital Markets Law is to keep pace with a rapidly expanding public securities market. As part of its deregulatory reform efforts in the 1980s, the Government activated the Indonesian securities markets, which have grown, with two exchanges, from about 25 publicly-listed companies to more than 200. As a general matter, the Capital Markets Law is designed to give greater legal weight to the regulations and decrees which comprise the present regulatory framework of the capital markets, to provide protection to investors, to require greater disclosure from issuers, to increase the enforcement powers of the Capital Markets Supervisory Board ("Bapepam"), to increase the penalties for violations, to ensure tighter legal enforcement of the capital markets, to permit the establishment of open-end mutual funds and to ensure that the Capital Markets Law complements Indonesia's new Company Law.

The Capital Markets Law defines securities as valuable paper such as debt acknowledgment letters, commercial paper, shares, bonds, debt receipts, participation units of collective investment contracts, term contracts, and any derivatives of securities.

Capital Markets and Securities Laws

Capital markets in Indonesia are under the regulatory control of the Department of Finance which stipulates the general policies governing capital markets. Daily supervision is performed by Bapepam, which is directly responsible to the Department of Finance.

Bapepam has administrative authority over the capital markets, which includes such activities as the granting of business licenses, the issuance of guidelines and conditions for public offerings, the issuance of capital market policies, such as the determination of what instruments constitute securities, inspection authority, such as the right to audit and inspect public companies and issuers and investigatory authority for violations of the Capital Markets Law.

Disclosure Requirements

Investor protection is the main concern of the Government, and the Capital Markets Law emphasizes disclosure as one of the foundations to achieve this goal. The Capital Markets Law, among other things, further clarifies and expands disclosure requirements by requiring a greater emphasis on disclosure of important and relevant nonfinancial information. Under the new Law, a prospectus must disclose the following: (i) information concerning the public offering; (ii) the proposed use of the funds received from the public offering; (iii) discussion and analysis by management; (iv) a disclosure of business risks; (v) a legal opinion; (vi) information on how to place an order to buy the securities; and (vii) information on the articles of association.

C.14

Bapepam is granted discretionary power to require special disclosure with respect to pre-emptive rights, conflicts of interest, tender offers, consolidations, mergers and acquisitions. In addition, the new Law extends disclosure obligations to lawyers, notaries, appraisers and accountants, who are liable for losses suffered by investors if they provide incorrect or misleading statements of material facts or if they omit material facts in the registration statement.

The disclosure requirements of the new Law apply to the registration statement prior to public offering, to the public offering and as long as the issuer's securities are listed on the stock exchanges.

The disclosure framework recognizes the importance of fiduciary relationships and the need to uphold fiduciary duties. Disclosure requirements are an important check against "insider trading" and other related activities that can harm the unsuspecting investor.

Foreign Ownership of Shares

Foreigners are still limited in the percentage of stock they can own in a publicly listed company. Pursuant to Minister of Finance Decree 1055, foreigners may not own more than 49 per cent of a company's listed shares.

Indonesia

Investment Funds

A key change in the Capital Markets Law deals with investment funds. Previously, the capital markets regulations only recognized closed-end investment funds. Now, the Capital Markets Law also recognizes open-end investment funds.

Trading Systems

In addition to regulatory changes, the Indonesian Capital Markets have made significant improvements in updating their trading systems. The Jakarta Stock Exchange now uses electronic "scriptless trading" as part of its automated trading system so that it is not necessary for share certificates to actually change hands after the conclusion of a trade. This system helps eliminates the risk of loss, theft or damage to the certificates and should mean increased efficiency and reduction in paperwork.

Arbitration and Other ADR Techniques

C.15   Arbitration in Indonesia is provided for in the Burgelijke Reglement op de Rechtsvordering, or the Regulation on Civil Procedure, (State Gazette No. 52 of 1847 jo. No. 63 of 1849), sometimes referred to as the "RV". The RV requires an arbitration proceeding to be based on an agreement containing an arbitration clause or on a separate arbitration agreement.

Most disputes are arbitrable under the RV, but certain disputes may not be resolved by arbitration such as donations, legacies, divorce or separations, disputes concerning the status of any person and any other disputes which do not allow a compromise. The RV provides any adult person can act as an arbitrator. Attorneys are not excluded.

The parties to an arbitration may waive the right of appeal with an express statement that judicial recourse is waived. The Indonesian Supreme Court recognized the validity of such a waiver in its decision in *P.T. Multi Plaza Properties v. Yahya Widjaja* No. 1 Banding/Wasit/1981 (July 10, 1984), and in *Ahiu Forestry Company Limited v. Sutomo of P.T. Balapan Jaya* Reg No. 2924 K/Sip/1981 (February 22, 1982).

Institutional Arbitration

C.16   Parties are generally free to contract as to where and under what rules an arbitration may be conducted.

Indonesia has had a national arbitration centre since 1977. This is the Badan Arbitrase Nasional Indonesia, or the Indonesian National Board of Arbitration, commonly referred to as BANI.

BANI was established with the purpose of providing an equitable, fair and prompt means of settlement of commercial disputes arising in the fields of trade, industry and finance at the national as well as the international level. Its services, however, are not limited to dispute settlement. BANI also provides binding opinions regarding questions arising from contracts, such as the interpretation of ambiguous provisions and the formulation of new provisions. Once BANI has given its opinion, the parties are bound by that opinion, and a refusal to abide by it is considered a breach of contract.

The Board of BANI is comprised of a Chairman, a Vice Chairman, a number of members and associate members and a Secretariat. The Chairman, Vice Chairman and the Arbitrators are appointed by the Indonesian Chamber of Commerce (Kadin Indonesia) on the proposal of the BANI Board. They are lawyers and technical experts in particular fields of industry.

Although BANI is closely related to the Indonesian Chamber of Commerce and Industry, it is completely independent and free from the intervention of any other body or authority.

BANI's Rules and Arbitral Procedures are based partly on the Uncitral Arbitration Rules. BANI's Rules, which came into force on December 3, 1977, were revised in 1980.

BANI regulates the costs of arbitration which consists of registration and administration fees and the arbitrator's fee, which the parties to the dispute are required to pay before the arbitration procedure can commence.

Another arbitration institution was established under the name of Yayasan Badan Arbitrase Muamalat Islam Indonesia (BAMUI — the Indonesian Islamic Muamalat Board of Arbitration) on October 21, 1993. While BAMUI was established by the Islamic Council, its purpose is to deal with commercial disputes and to offer an alternative to BANI. It evidences a growing commitment in Indonesia to alternative dispute resolution mechanisms.

Recognition and Enforcement of Arbitral Awards

Article 637 of the RV provides that binding arbitral awards shall be enforced   **C.17** by the courts.

BANI's Rules allow a grace period within which the losing party is required to comply with the award. The chairman of BANI may request the chairman of the competent district court to enforce an award if, after the lapse of such a grace period, the losing party does not voluntarily comply with the award.

Until March 1, 1990, when the Supreme Court issued Regulation No. 1 (the "Regulation"), foreign arbitral awards were not enforceable in Indonesia, notwithstanding that Indonesia is a party to the U.N. Convention on the Recognition and Enforcement of Foreign Arbitral Awards of 1958 (the "New York Convention"). In ratifying the New York Convention, Indonesia made two reservations: that Indonesia will apply the New York Convention to the recognition and enforcement of awards made in the territory of another contracting state, only if such other contracting state enforces arbitration awards issued in Indonesia (the "Reciprocity Reservation"), and that Indonesia will apply the convention only to differences arising out of legal relationships which are considered as commercial under Indonesian law (the "Commercial Reservation"). Other than the foregoing, Indonesia can only refuse to enforce foreign arbitral awards in Indonesia if they are contradictory to public order or policy.

Foreign arbitral awards can be enforced in Indonesia by filing an application for exequatur with the District Court of Central Jakarta. The exequatur will be given by the Chairman or the Vice Chairman of the Supreme Court or by the Chairman of the Written Civil Law Department, which in this case is authorized by the Chairman of the Supreme Court or Vice Chairman of the Supreme Court.

It is to be noted that Indonesia is also a party to the Convention on the Settlement of Investment Disputes between States and Nationals of Other States on June 29, 1968, pursuant to Presidential Decree 32 of 1968. In the event that a foreign investor in a foreign investment law company has an investment dispute with the Government, the dispute may be referred to ICSID pursuant to this Convention.

ELIPS Project and a New Draft of an Arbitration Law

C.18   The ELIPS Project has prepared an academic draft Arbitration Law, which is being reviewed by the Indonesian Government.

Banking and Lending Law

The Banking Law

C.19   On March 25, 1992, the Government promulgated Law No. 2 on Banking (the "Banking Law"), the purpose of which is to improve the banking system and structure in Indonesia from that previously regulated by Law No. 14 of 1967.

Under the Banking Law, a bank is defined as a business unit to mobilize funds from the public, in the form of deposits, and to channel such funds to the public to raise general living standards. There are two kinds of banks:

(i)   a Commercial Bank ("Bank Umum") is a bank that provides payment services. A Commercial Bank can be owned by the central Government, by a regional Government, by a Cooperative or by private limited liability company.

(ii)   a Smallholder Credit Bank ("Bank Perkreditan Rakyat") is a bank that receives only time deposits, savings and/or other deposits of similar types. A Smallholder Credit Bank can be owned by a regional Government, a Cooperative, a private limited liability company or any other company stipulated by Government regulation.

Banks have two functions: collecting funds from the public and distributing funds to the public.

Any bank that collects funds is obligated to obtain an operating permit as a Commercial Bank or as a Smallholder Credit Bank from the Minister of Finance (unless the activity of collecting funds is otherwise regulated), after consultation with Bank Indonesia, Indonesia's central bank.

The distribution of funds is done at the bank's own risk. The bank is obligated to consider sound credit principles, such as the evaluation of the borrower's ability to repay the loan as scheduled, and its character, capital, security and business prospects.

Bank Indonesia requires a lending bank to ask a credit applicant to submit a copy of its tax registration number and, for a corporation, to submit a copy of its financial statements to the Indonesian tax authorities as an attachment to its Annual Income Tax Return ("SPT Tahunan PPh").[8] This must be for the most recent tax year, stamped as received by the relevant tax office. An individual credit applicant is also obligated to submit a copy of his annual income tax return, stamped as received by the relevant tax office.

Maximum Legal Lending Limits

Because a bank distributes public funds, a bank is obligated to reduce its risk **C.20** by adhering to Maximum Legal Lending Limits ("Batas Maximum Pemberian Kredit") prescribed by Bank Indonesia. The purpose of the Maximum Legal Lending Limits is to ensure that banks do not lend money to affiliates in excess of certain amounts. The Maximum Legal Lending Limits apply to the following:

(i)   the grant of credit facilities;
(ii) the grant of guarantee facilities;
(iii) the purchase of commercial paper; and
(iv) other similar credits such as factoring facilities granted by a bank to a borrower or group of borrowers.

The Maximum Legal Lending Limits are regulated by Bank Indonesia Board of Directors Decree No. 26/21/KEP/DIR Regarding Maximum Legal Lending Limits (May 29, 1993) ("BI Decree No. 26"). BI Decree No. 26 provides the following rules in this regard:

(i)   the Maximum Legal Lending Limit for a borrower or a group of borrowers not associated with the bank is 20 per cent of the bank's capital; and
(ii) the Maximum Legal Lending Limit for parties who are associated with the bank, for one or more loans, is a maximum of 10 per cent of the bank's capital.

"A group of borrowers", as stipulated by BI Decree No. 26, means a group of borrowers who are associated with one another in terms of ownership, management, and/or financial relationship. Pursuant to Bank Indonesia Board of Directors Circular Letter No. 28/63/KEP/DIR Regarding the Maximum Legal Lending Limits for Listed Companies in the Stock Exchange,[9] a company is categorized as a member of a group of borrower companies if it constitutes one of two or more companies having linkage in ownership, management or financial relationship which fulfills any of the following criteria:

   (i)   35 per cent or more of the ownership of each company is controlled by a company or an individual or jointly by a family;

  (ii)   one of the companies controls 35 per cent or more of the ownership rights of the other company;

 (iii)   a member of the board of directors, board of commissioners or other officials having executive functions in one of the companies is an executive official in the other company;

 (iv)   two or more of the companies are linked in ownership and/or management which fulfill none of the criteria stipulated in points (i), (ii) and (iii) above, but there is a financial relationship which results in business control by one of them.

A company within a group of borrower companies, as defined by the above criteria, or a company as a party associated with the bank, but which has its shares traded at a stock exchange totaling over 30 per cent of its paid-in capital, shall be treated as an independent company. As such, the Maximum Legal Lending Limit for such a company is 20 per cent of the bank's capital. Such exception will not be applicable if, in the future, the total shares of the company traded at the stock exchange become less than 30 per cent of its paid-in capital.

Offshore Loans

C.21   Indonesian borrowers can obtain loans from offshore banks. Such loans may be governed by foreign law. Indonesian courts will enforce loan agreements governed by foreign law as long as enforcement does not offend Indonesian public order or policy and the transaction has sufficient contact with the foreign jurisdiction under Indonesia's conflicts of law principles.

    Offshore loans must be reported to Bank Indonesia and the Offshore Loan Control Team by borrowers. In some cases, such as offshore loans to foreign investment law companies, loans must be approved by Bank Indonesia. If the foreign investment law company has a state-owned company as one of its shareholders and if the state-owned company owns more than 51 per cent of the company or if the loan is more than US$ 20 million, the loan must be approved by both the Department of Finance and by the Offshore Commercial Loan Team.

    Furthermore, if the offshore loan repayment is linked to a state-owned company in any way, the loan must be approved by the Offshore Commercial Loan Team. Examples of such linkage are a private power company that sells its power to the state-owned electricity company, PLN, and a petrochemical company that obtains its feedstock from Pertamina, the state-owned oil company.

The foregoing rules are contained in various decrees: Presidential Decree No. 59 of 1972 Regarding Receiving Foreign Credits (October 12, 1972), Minister of Finance Decree No. 261 of 1973 Regarding Executive Provisions on Receiving Foreign Credits (May 3, 1973) and Presidential Decree No. 39 of 1991 Regarding The Coordination of Management of Offshore Commercial Loans (September 4, 1991).

Secured Transactions

The statutory law governing secured transactions in Indonesia is not comprehensive, although most Indonesian commercial lending is done on a secured basis. In general, security rights are classified into two main categories: those conferred by law and those conferred by agreement.   **C.22**

Security Rights Conferred by Law

Article 1131 of the Indonesian Civil Code states that all assets of a debtor, movable as well as immovable, constitute security for its debts. All the debtor's creditors thus have *pari passu* pro rata rights to a debtor's assets, unless a preference has been created by law or has been given contractually to certain creditors. Preferences at law are governed by the Indonesian Civil Code and are granted to certain types of creditors. Article 1139 allows unsecured creditors preferences with respect to specific assets in certain cases: **C.23**

(i)   claims relating to leases of real property regarding the property concerned;

(ii)   claims of an unpaid seller of movable goods for the sales price of goods relating to such goods;[10]

(iii)   claims for costs incurred in connection with the storage or conservation of goods relating to such goods (*e.g.* the claims of an unpaid warehouseman or conservator);

(iv)   claims of workmen for work performed upon movable goods relating to such goods;

(v)   claims of an innkeeper in possession of goods belonging to the debtor left in the custody of the innkeeper;

(vi)   claims with respect to freight costs and expenses relating to the goods carried;

(vii)   claims of workmen for work performed in connection with the construction and repair of immovable property, including property

owned by the debtor, if the claims are not older than 3 years and the bankrupt debtor still owns the property; and
(viii) certain claims of public prosecutors.

It should be noted that tax liens have priority over all other claims except foreclosure costs, costs of salvage and preservation, and certain other claims pursuant to Articles 80 and 81 of the Indonesian Commercial Code, which are not relevant here. This preference is stipulated by Article 21(3) of Law No. 6 of 1983 on the General Provision and Procedure of Taxes, as amended by Article 21(3) of Law No. 9 of 1994.

Security Rights Created by Private Agreement

C.24 Article 1134 of the Civil Code provides that a secured creditor's claims based on pledges and mortgages have priority over all unsecured claims "except where otherwise provided by law". Pledges and mortgages are the only devices recognized by statutory law for creating security interests, respectively, over movable and immovable property. The priority of secured creditors is "otherwise" superseded by statute only with respect to the ranking of foreclosure costs and tax liens. These expenses are to be paid out of the proceeds of the sale of assets prior to payment to secured creditors. The fiduciary transfer security device is not provided for under Indonesian statutory law and is not, therefore, specifically referred to in the priorities listed in Article 1134. The fiduciary transfer has come into use, in effect, without a specific statutory basis. It has grown out of the commercial necessity for a financing device more flexible than the pledge, which requires physical transfer of the secured assets to the creditor. Claims arising out of a fiduciary transfer appear to have been accorded the same priority as specifically provided by statute for the pledge and mortgage.

Types of Security Documents

C.25 Security rights to movable property are established through a pledge, a fiduciary transfer or a fiduciary assignment, while security rights to immovable property can only be established through a hypothec, or mortgage.

Mortgages — A mortgage is a security right ("Hak Tanggungan") over immovable property. The term "immovable property" is associated with land. It should be noted that under the Indonesian Mortgage Law[11] only land covered by a Right of Ownership, a Right to Build, a Right to Use and a Right to Exploit can be mortgaged. A mortgage creates a preference in favor of a particular party and is valid notwithstanding any subsequent transfer of the property. An earlier registered mortgage has preference over a mortgage registered later. Land mortgages must be executed before a land official.

In accordance with Articles 314 and 315(b) of the Indonesian Commercial Code, some of the mortgage provisions that were formerly applicable to land are, insofar as the nature of the encumbered property permits, applicable to ships. The ships concerned must be greater than 20 cubic meters gross volume and must be registered in the Ship's Register/Main Register for Registration and Recordation of Transfer of Title to Vessels.

In addition, according to Article 12 of Law No. 15/1992 Regarding Aviation (May 25, 1992), aircraft and helicopters that are registered in Indonesia may also be hypothecated.

Pledges — A pledge is a statutorily recognized security device for movable property, whether tangible (such as machines or vehicles) or intangible (such as accounts receivable, shares or patent rights). Furthermore, a pledge is a possessory security, which means that it is created and perfected by obtaining possession of the property concerned. With tangible property, the property must be in the physical possession of the pledgee or at least must no longer be under the physical possession or control of the pledgor. Intangible property is more difficult to deal with in this connection. Usually there is some written evidence of the ownership of the property concerned, such as a deposit receipt or share certificates. In any case, possession should be taken by the pledgee of any document that gives the owner-pledgor control over the intangible rights concerned.

Article 1154 of the Indonesian Civil Code provides that it is not lawful to agree in the pledge agreement that the pledgee will become the owner of the pledged goods in the event of default by the debtor. Any agreement to that effect is null and void. This is commonly interpreted to mean that foreclosure and sale must be conducted through the auction office.

Article 1159 of the Indonesian Civil Code provides that a pledgee is entitled to keep the pledged property in its possession until the pledgor pays the full amount of its debt plus any interest and costs outstanding (including the cost of maintaining the pledged property in a safe condition).

Fiduciary Transfers — The fiduciary transfer is a peculiar Indonesian creation which creates security rights in movable property and intangible goods. The fiduciary transfer can also apply to intangibles, such as accounts receivables, bank accounts and contingent payments, such as insurance proceeds. A fiduciary transfer constitutes a theoretical transfer of ownership, and not merely a "lien", such as is created by a mortgage, although the transfer is expressly stated to be for security purposes only. **C.26**

Assignments of Receivables — Indonesian law recognizes the right of a party to assign receivables due under a contract, including insurance policies. As noted above, this is sometimes done by way of a fiduciary transfer. Indonesian law is significantly less clear on the ability of a borrower to make collateral assignments for security purposes of other contract rights. As a general matter, most practitioners would probably counsel that such an assignment, by which contract rights purport to be separated from obligations, may not be made.

Guarantees — Guarantees are not security in the sense of creating a preferred right of the secured party in specific collateral. Rather, they provide an additional party to pursue in the event of the debtor's default.

The Indonesian Civil Code requires prior exhaustion of remedies against the principal debtor before enforcing a guarantee. However, such provisions are not mandatory and are always waived in properly drafted Indonesia guarantees, which results in guarantees that are theoretically enforceable directly upon demand. Provisions in the guarantee to the effect that the obligations of the guarantor thereunder will not be affected by any extension of time or other forbearance given to the principal debtor are valid and enforceable. Guarantees of offshore debt must be reported to Bank Indonesia and the Department of Finance.

Until recently, state-owned banks were prohibited from granting guarantees in favour of non-residents of Indonesia. Pursuant to Presidential Decree No. 15 dated March 18, 1991 and two promulgations of Bank Indonesia issued on the same date (Bank Indonesia Board of Directors Decree 23/88/KEP/DIR Regarding the Issuance of Bank Guarantees (March 18, 1991) and Bank Indonesia Circular Letter No. SE/7/UKU Regarding the Issuance of Bank Guarantees (March 18, 1991)), all Indonesian foreign exchange banks, state and private, are now permitted to guarantee offshore credits to either state-owned or private borrowers in Indonesia. The value of guarantees which may be outstanding at any one time by an Indonesian bank and all its branches onshore as well as overseas is limited to 20 per cent of the bank's capital.

There are no prescribed formalities required in connection with the execution of guarantees. They can be either in private or notarial deed form.

Health, Safety and Environment Law

Health and Safety

C.27   Law No. 1 of 1970 Regarding Safety (January 12, 1970) ("Law No. 1") regulates safety in all workplaces whether on land, underground, on the water, underwater or in the air. The purpose of Law No. 1 is to guarantee a safe workplace for all workers and to protect them while they work. The Law also requires mandatory health examinations for all employees at the employer's expense. Examinations are required prior to employment and periodically thereafter.

The Department of Manpower is responsible for the implementation and enforcement of Law No. 1. Many of the specific safety standards and requirements are contained in other laws and regulations. Safety inspectors and experts from the Department of Manpower directly supervise employers' compliance with the laws. Employers are required to report accidents occurring in the workplace and workers are required to provide accurate information upon request to the Government's safety inspectors and experts.

Employers are required to post notices and to place safety and health posters in the workplace. Employers must also provide obligatory personal protective equipment. All persons entering a workplace must obey safety instructions.

Persons who violate Law No. 1 are subject to criminal sanctions of up to three months imprisonment or a fine of up to Rp. 100,000 (approximately US$43 at present exchange rates).

Environmental Law

General

The basic law governing the environment in Indonesia is Law No. 4 of 1982   **C.28** Regarding the Basic Provisions on Environmental Management (March 11, 1982) ("Law No. 4"). Consistent with the Constitution, Law No. 4 states that the natural resources belong to the State and are to be maximized for the benefit of the people. In addition to Law No. 4, various Government Regulations and Decrees have been adopted on specific environmental matters for specific sectors. For example, in the industrial sector, these are:

(i)   Government Regulation No. 20 of 1990 Regarding Water Pollution Control (June 5, 1990) ("GR 20");

(ii)   Government Regulation No. 51 of 1993 Regarding Environmental Impact Analysis ("Analisis Mengenai Dampak Lingkungan" or "AMDAL") (October 23, 1993) ("GR 51");

(iii)   Minister of Industry Decree No. 250/M/SK/10/1994 Regarding the Technical Guidance of Environmental Impact Preparation on the Industrial Sector (October 20, 1994) ("Decree 250");

(iv)   Minister of Industry Decree No. 148/M/SK/1995 Regarding the Stipulation of Industrial Types and Commodities, the Production Processes of which do not Damage or Endanger the Environment and do not use Natural Resources Excessively (July 11, 1995) ("Decree 148");

(v)   State Minister of Environmental Affairs Decree No. KEP-11/MENLH/3/1994 Regarding the Kinds or Activities which are Obligated to have an Environmental Impact Analysis (March 19, 1994) ("Decree 11"); and

(vi)   State Minister of Environmental Affairs Decree No. KEP-51/MENLH/10/1995 Regarding the Liquid Waste Quality Standards for Industrial Activities (October 23, 1995) ("Decree 51").

Law No. 4 provides that every person is obligated to maintain the environment and to prevent, as well as to remedy, the destruction and pollution thereof. Every person who conducts business activities is required to maintain a harmonious and balanced environment to support continuous development, and such obligation must be stipulated in every license issued by the Government. All licenses and permits issued to businesses and undertakings are thus required to restate the obligation to maintain a harmonious and balanced environment.

C.29   Management of the environment on the national level is implemented by the Office of the State Minister of Environment Affairs and the Environmental Impact Management Agency ("Badan Pengendalian Dampak Lingkungan" or "BAPEDAL"). Each Governmental Department also has environment management responsibilities within its sector.

The implementing regulation of Law No. 4 is GR 51. It further clarifies that every activity which impacts the environment should have an AMDAL, an Environmental Management Plan ("Rencana Pengelolaan Lingkungan" or "RKL") and an Environmental Monitoring Plan ("Rencana Pemantauan Lingkungan" or "RPL"). The AMDAL, RKL and RPL should be submitted to, and will be approved by, the department responsible for the business activities of the company concerned. The approval is valid for three years. When the AMDAL, RKL and RPL are no longer valid, a new application must be filed.

Industrial Business Activities Obligations

C.30   As noted above, the Department of Industry and Trade ("DOIT") and the Office of the State Minister of Environmental Affairs have adopted several decrees which refer to environmental matters, specifically Decree 250, Decree 148, Decree 11 and Decree 51.

The following is a summary of environmental rules for industrial business activities:

   (i)   All industrial business activities included in Attachment I of Decree 11 should prepare an AMDAL. Decree 11 does not specify further the standard report which should be conducted by these kinds of business activities.

   (ii)   All industrial business activities included in Attachment 1 of Decree 250 should prepare an AMDAL which consists of an Environmental Impact Analysis ("Analisa Dampak Lingkungan" or "ANDAL"), RKL and RPL. The AMDAL, RKL and RPL are environmental study activities used to prepare the environmental report necessary to obtain approval from the DOIT. The AMDAL standard report outline is determined by the DOIT. The DOIT, through its Head of the Industry and Trade Research and Development Agency ("Badan Penelitian dan Pengembangan Industri dan Perdagangan" or "BPPIP"), must issue a Recommendation Letter for the approved AMDAL. This Recommendation Letter is valid for five years and must be copied to BAPEDAL, the Governor or Head of the relevant

Region, and other Government agencies considered necessary pursuant to prevailing laws and regulations.

(iii) All industrial business activities included in Attachment II of Decree 250 should prepare an Environmental Management Effort Report ("Upaya Pengelolaan Lingkungan" or "UKL") and an Environmental Monitoring Effort Report ("Upaya Pemantauan Lingkungan" or "UPL"). The UKL and UPL are the statements from the owner regarding its intention to preserve the environment. The UKL and UPL report must be submitted to the DOIT for approval. The UKL and UPL standard report form is determined by the DOIT. The DOIT through its AMDAL Division Director must issue an approval letter for the UKL and UPL. This approval letter is valid for three years.

(iv) As stipulated in Article 9, Paragraph 1 of Decree 250, all industrial business activities which have an important impact on the environment and are located in an industrial estate, bonded zone or industrial complex which have been supported by an AMDAL, are not required to prepare an additional AMDAL, but still have to prepare an RKL and RPL, which references the industrial estate's bonded zone's or industrial complex's standard RKL and RPL.

To obtain approval, the AMDAL, UKL and UPL Reports must be presented to the AMDAL Commission, the members of which consist of several environmental experts from the DOIT, the Governor or Head of the Region concerned, BAPEDAL and other related Government agencies.

(v) All industrial business activities included in the Attachment of Decree 148 must prepare the Statement of Environmental Management ("Surat Pernyataan Pengelolaan Lingkungan" or "SPPL") to be submitted to the DOIT. The standard form of the SPPL is determined by the DOIT.

Reporting Requirements

Decree 250 and Decree 148 are silent as to the reporting requirements for C.31 AMDAL, UKL and UPL. The reporting requirements are stipulated in the standard reports which are determined by the DOIT. The AMDAL, UKL and UPL reports should be provided every six months to the DOIT. After five years for the AMDAL, and three years for the UKL and UPL, the AMDAL, UKL and UPL approvals should be renewed by filing new application forms to the DOIT.

In addition to the existing activities, if a company plans to establish new activities which will impact the environment, even though the AMDAL, UKL and UPL approvals are still valid, the company must submit new AMDAL, UKL and UPL applications for the approval of the new activities.

Indonesia

Inspection Authority

The promulgations discussed above contain no provisions requiring the DOIT to control the environmental activities of industrial companies. From experience, DOIT will only conduct an environmental control inspection if the local community reports that there is environmental pollution.

Sanctions

C.32 Polluters of the environment must pay damages to their victims. They are also subject to severe criminal sanctions under Law No. 4 and other environmental laws. Intentional destruction or pollution of the environment is a criminal offense and is punishable by up to ten years imprisonment and a fine of up to Rp. 100,000,000 (approximately US$43,000 at current exchange rates). Negligent destruction or pollution of the environment is subject to one year imprisonment and a fine of up to Rp. 1,000,000 (approximately US$430, at current exchange rates).

Employment and Labor Laws

Introduction

C.33 Indonesia has adopted comprehensive labor laws that are embodied in numerous laws, regulations and decrees.

As a general matter, Indonesian labor laws protect workers' rights, such as the right of association and right to organize and bargain collectively, the freedom to choose and change employment at will, the establishment of minimum wages, hours of employment and occupational safety and health, annual leave, termination of employment, severance benefits and the like.

The Department of Manpower is the agency responsible for implementation and enforcement.

Labour Unions

C.34 The establishment of labor unions in Indonesia is based on several major laws and regulations, namely, the 1945 Indonesian Constitution, Article 28 of which secures the right of Indonesian citizens to organize, Law Number 18 of 1956 Regarding the Ratification of the International Labour Organization Convention No. 98 of 1949 Regarding the Application of the Principles of the Right to Organize and to Bargain Collectively (September 17, 1956), Law Number 14 of 1969 Regarding the Basic Principles of Employment (November 19, 1969), and Minister of Manpower Decree Number KEP-1109/MEN/1986 Regarding Guidelines on the Establishment, Supervision, and Development of a Labour Union in a Company (October 30, 1986).

The All Indonesia Workers Association ("SPSI") is the only registered and recognized labor union in Indonesia at the present time. A company that has a minimum of 25 persons is required to allow its employees to establish a branch of the SPSI. The basic principle of the SPSI is "Pancasila Industrial Relations", the purpose of which is to establish and maintain harmonious relations among employers, employees and the Government.

The main goal in the establishment of the SPSI is to protect the interests of its members with regard to such matters as wages, working hours, overtime, allowances, termination, and other matters. In addition, the SPSI has, as a goal, to increase productivity and the creation of industrial peace among its members.

Employee Terminations

One of the most sensitive issues of the Indonesian labor law concerns termi- **C.35** nation of employment. Under Indonesian law, a unilateral termination of employment is not permitted. Except where an employee resigns voluntarily (which may occur as a result of a negotiated settlement), any employment termination requires the approval of the Regional Labour Committee or the Central Labour Committee (called the 'P4P") for the Settlement of Labour Disputes (called the "P4D"). The Labour Committee is an administrative court established under Law No. 22 of 1957 (April 8, 1957) for the settlement of employment disputes.

Certain acts permit immediate dismissal of an employee, subject to approval of the P4D under Minister of Manpower Regulation No. 03 of 1996 (February 14, 1996) ("Reg. 03"):

(i) swindling, theft or embezzlement from the employer, the employer's colleagues, or other employees;

(ii) false information or testimony or falsification of documents which cause loss to the company or the State;

(iii) drunkenness, the use of narcotics or illegal or sedative drugs at work;

(iv) commission of an indecent act or gambling in the workplace;

(v) commission of a criminal act, such as assault, extortion, fraud and drug dealing, inside or outside the area of the company;

(vi) personal injury of another, the threat of physical or mental injury, gross insults to the company's management or any employee or co-worker, including their families, in any manner;

(vii) the inducement of the company's management or other employees to commit an unlawful act, an act contrary to morality or the company's work rules;

(viii) intentional or grossly negligent damage to the company's property, or allowing damage to occur to the company's property;

(ix) allowing the employer or another employee to be in a dangerous situation, intentionally or in a grossly negligent manner.

(x)   the disclosure of confidential information or secrets of the company or the internal secrets of the company's management, except for the interests of the State;

(xi)   the commission of wrongful acts for which the employee was previously warned; and

(xii)   other actions provided under an employment agreement or the company's work rules.

C.36   In termination situations, Law No. 12 of 1964 Regarding Termination of Employment in Private Undertakings (September 23, 1964) and Reg. 03 require the employer to first negotiate the employee's resignation. If an employee will not agree to resign, the employer must then seek the conciliation services of the Department of Manpower. If conciliation fails, either of the disputing parties may apply to the Regional Labour Committee to settle the dispute. The P4D may first issue a non-binding recommendation on the issue. If the recommendation is not accepted, the P4D is entitled to hold a hearing and issue a binding decision.

The decision of the P4P may be appealed by either party to the Central Labour Committee except where the P4D's decision concerns a specific local matter. The P4D consists of five representatives from labor unions, five representatives from employer groups, and five representatives from government agencies. The P4P is also comprised of an equal number of representatives from labor, management and government agencies. A decision of the P4P is binding and enforceable through the courts if the Minister of Manpower does not postpone or vacate the decision within 14 days. The Minister of Manpower is authorized to vacate or postpone a decision of the P4P only where he considers it necessary to maintain public order and to protect the interests of the state.

Experience suggests that the P4P generally approves an employer's intent to discharge where reasonable grounds are given. Except in cases of criminal conduct or other serious misbehavior, the P4P's consent to terminate is always based on the payment of a stated severance allowance to the employee involved. The fact that an employer cannot unilaterally terminate an employee's contract and that the P4P's consent to termination is almost always premised on the payment of some severance allowance, encourages a negotiated termination, *i.e.* a mutual settlement between the parties prior to seeking P4P consent. Severance pay is payable in all termination cases, including termination for cause, except in cases involving moral turpitude or serious criminal conduct.

Negotiated, consensual terminations are often based on payments in excess of the statutory minimum because, as a practical matter, the P4P tends to award a minimum of two to three times the minimum severance pay required by law, where an employee has refused settlement and has forced the employer to apply to the P4P for consent to terminate. As a practical matter, then, negotiated settlements tend to result in payments of about this amount.

Foreign Investment Law

Introduction

There are two generally different regimes by which foreign investors may C.37
make equity investments in Indonesian companies: establishment of an Indonesian limited liability company under the Foreign Investment Law and
establishment of certain types of Indonesian limited liability financial companies under regulations issued by the Department of Finance. For all types
of manufacturing companies and most types of service companies, the Foreign Investment Law is the method of foreign investment in Indonesia.

Equity Investments in Indonesia under the Foreign Investment Law

As noted, most foreign investments are made pursuant to Indonesia's For- C.38
eign Investment Law, Law No. 1 1967 (January 10, 1967), as amended by
Law No. 11, 1970 (August 7, 1970) (collectively referred to as the "FIL").
The FIL has been supplemented by numerous Government regulations —
the most recent and significant of which was issued in June 1994 and is
known as the "June Package". The June Package continues the Government's
policy to further deregulate foreign investment.

The first issue a foreign investor must address is whether the Indonesian
Government will permit an investment in a desired line of business. As a
general rule, all business sectors are open for foreign investment unless
specifically prohibited. For this purpose, the Government publishes a Negative Investment List, known by its Indonesian initials as the "DNI". The
DNI specifies the business areas in which foreign investment is prohibited,
restricted or conditioned. A business area is open for foreign investment if
it is not listed in the DNI, subject to any specific controls issued by a
Government Department that may have jurisdiction over the activity
concerned.

Any type of foreign investment approved under the FIL must take the
form of an Indonesian limited liability company, known as a "Perseroan
Terbatas", or "PT". When this company is established and licensed under
the FIL, it is often known as a "PMA" company (the Indonesian acronym
for foreign capital investment) or a "joint venture company". A foreign
investor now may be a limited liability company or a foreign individual.
The Indonesian investor can be a limited liability company (wholly-owned
by Indonesian nationals), an Indonesian individual, or an Indonesian
cooperative.

In order to initiate a foreign investment under the FIL, it is necessary to
file a Model I Investment Application with the Indonesian Capital Investment Coordinating Board ("BKPM").

After an evaluation of the Model I Application, BKPM submits the application to the President of the Republic of Indonesia for approval. Assuming the application is approved, BKPM then notifies the applicants. The Notification of Presidential Approval is known as an "SPPP" and is in effect a temporary business license that permits the investors to go forward with their investment.

After the SPPP is issued, BKPM also issues additional permits and licenses. This process occurs concurrently while the Department of Justice reviews and approves the Articles of Association. Those permits and approvals include the following:

(a) master list approval, allowing the PT exemptions or reductions from import duties, value added tax, sales tax on luxury goods, on the importation of listed capital goods, spare parts and related raw materials;

(b) a limited import license ("APIT"), permitting the import of goods approved under the masterlist;

(c) a manpower utilization plan ("RPTKA") allocating expatriate employment and work permits ("IKTA") allowing expatriates to work in Indonesia; and

(d) a permanent operating license ("IUT"). The IUT is issued when the PT is certified ready for the commencement of commercial production.

C.39 The foreign investment license granted by BKPM is for a period of 30 years from the date of commencement of commercial production. This term may be extended at the discretion of the Government. As the FIL is only now approaching its 30-year anniversary, the Government has not yet extended foreign investment licenses, but the Indonesian investment community does not foresee any issue in this connection.

Under the June Package, a foreign investor may now form a PMA company with 100 per cent foreign equity with no minimum capital investment requirements. However, some divestment of an unspecified percentage must take place within 15 years. The amount of divestment was not clearly stated in the June Package but it is commonly believed that this amount is not greater than 5 per cent. Although a foreign investor may own up to 100 per cent in a PMA company, certain critical sectors of the economy are open only to PMA companies possessing at least 5 per cent Indonesian equity, with no further divestment requirement.

A PMA company already engaged in commercial production may purchase shares in a domestic investment law ("PMDN") company or a company which is neither a PMA nor a PMDN company. Under the Decree of the State Minister for Mobilization of Investment Funds/Chairman of the Capital Investment Coordinating Board, No. 21/SK/1996 Regarding Procedures for Application of Capital Investment Granted in the Frameworks of Domestic Capital Investment and Foreign Capital Investment (July 15, 1996)

(Decree "21") if the acquired company is a PMDN, its status need not change because of the acquisition. If, however, the acquired company is not a PMDN company, it must change its status to a PMDN company. In either case, the acquired company may not engage in activities listed on the DNI. Thus, for example, a PMA company at the present time may not acquire a trading company or, if it does, the acquired company must change its business purpose.

A PMA company may also establish subsidiaries. If the PMA company and a foreign national or entity own the shares of a subsidiary, the subsidiary will be a PMA company; if, however, the PMA company joins with an Indonesian national or entity (including another PMA company) to form a subsidiary, the subsidiary will be a PMDN company. However, the PMDN company may not engage in activities listed on the DNI.

A foreign legal entity (*i.e.* one not established in Indonesia) may purchase shares (i) in a PMA company, (ii) in a PMDN company or (iii) in a company which is neither a PMA company nor a PMDN company. The acquisition can be done by direct investment or through the Indonesian capital markets, but in the case of direct investment, the acquisition, in the case of a PMDN or a company which is neither a PMDN nor a PMA company, must meet at least one of the following four criteria: (a) the acquired company's project must be in the construction stage; (b) the new shareholder is a lender which is converting its debt to equity; (c) the acquisition is made to improve the acquired company's product marketing; or (d) the acquisition is made to improve the acquired company's exports or to obtain the benefits of new technology. These rules are contained in Decree 21. We note that an additional criterion was set forth in the June Package. This criterion, which appears to remain in effect, allows the acquisition if the acquired company is in financial distress. In the case of (ii) and (iii) above, the acquired company's business activities must be open for foreign investment and the acquired company's status must be changed to be a PMA company.

Investments Not Covered under the FIL

Certain types of investments fall outside the jurisdiction of the FIL and the BKPM. Most notably these include investments in the finance area and the oil industry. The Department of Finance regulates foreign investment in the formation and operation of certain types of finance companies. These include joint venture banks, finance companies, securities companies and insurance companies.

C.40

The oil industry is unique in that foreign oil companies must execute production sharing contracts for oil and gas exploration and production in Indonesia with Pertamina, the Indonesian national oil company. As a result of the contract, the foreign oil company then is permitted to open and operate a branch office in Indonesia.

Tax Laws and Accounting Rules

Tax Laws

C.41 The Government first restructured the Indonesian tax system in 1984 by replacing the previous system of taxation with a new income tax law, a value added tax law, a sales tax on luxury goods and general tax provisions dealing principally with tax administration and procedure. The new laws constituted a comprehensive revision of the Indonesian tax system. The old personal and corporation income taxes were replaced by a new income tax. The Value Added Tax ("VAT") was introduced in place of the old sales tax that had existed since 1951 (although a Sales Tax on Luxury Goods remains in effect). In addition, a new Property Tax on Land and Buildings was later introduced replacing old laws dealing with taxes in that area. The purpose of all these new tax measures was to enhance tax revenues for capital formation, to finance development and to promote equity in income and wealth distribution in Indonesia.

Effective January 1, 1995, the Government of Indonesia adopted new tax laws that amended the previous tax laws. These were the General Tax Provisions and Procedures, Law No. 9 of 1994 (November 9, 1994), the Income Tax Law, Law No. 10 of 1994 (November 9, 1994), the Value Added Tax and Sales Tax on Luxury Goods Law, Law No. 11 of 1994 (November 9, 1994) and the Land and Building Tax Law, Law No. 12 of 1994 (November 9, 1994).

Indonesian taxes are imposed at both the national and regional levels. The three basic categories are state taxes, regional taxes and customs and excise taxes. The Indonesian tax laws and their official elucidations are supplemented by Government Regulations, Presidential Decrees, and Minister of Finance Decrees. They are also supported by various circulars, rulings and letters issued by the tax authorities. These provide interpretation of the laws in the application to emerging and specialized issues, not fully addressed in the laws themselves.

Indonesian income tax law differs depending whether the taxpayer is a resident taxpayer or non-resident taxpayer. Resident taxpayers are in theory taxed on their worldwide income, whether or not remitted to Indonesia, although the Indonesian tax authorities have not enforced this provision in practice. There is a three-tier rate structure for all resident taxpayers at the same progressive rates, with a range from 10 to 30 per cent. Tax administration is by self-assessment.

Non-resident taxpayers are subject to withholding taxes on Indonesian companies subject to bilateral tax treaties. Indonesia has an extensive number of such treaties.

In general, VAT is imposed on the following:

(i)   the delivery of taxable goods within the Indonesian customs area;
(ii) the import of taxable goods;

(iii)   the delivery of taxable services within the Indonesian customs area;

(iv)   the use of intangible taxable goods and/or taxable services from outside the customs area within the customs area; and

(v)   the export of taxable goods.

The VAT rate is generally 10 per cent with the exception of exports where the rate is nil.

Each domestic entity or individual providing taxable goods or services must register separately for VAT. The Government has appointed certain entities as "VAT collectors". VAT collectors do not pay VAT to their suppliers but instead pay such VAT directly to the State Treasury. **C.42**

Input VAT (the tax payable on the purchase of taxable goods or services) can be credited against output VAT (the tax invoiced to customers on the delivery of taxable goods or services) in the same tax period. If in a tax period output VAT exceeds input VAT, the excess is payable to the State Treasury. However, if input VAT exceeds output VAT, either a request for reimbursement of the excess can be made, or this amount can be carried forward and offset or credited against future output VAT. Output VAT charged to VAT collectors is paid by the collector directly to the State Treasury. Such output VAT is outside the normal VAT input/output mechanism.

The Sales Tax on Luxury Goods is essentially an excise tax, imposed on the consumption of luxury taxable goods within the customs area, and is collected either at the time of sale by the manufacturer or at the time of import. The rates range from 10 to 50 per cent (the rate on the export of luxury goods is zero).

The Land and Building Tax is payable annually on land, buildings and permanent structures. The effective rates are nominal, typically no more than 0.1 per cent, on the value of property. Exemptions include land and buildings used for religious worship, social affairs, health, national education and culture, graveyards and archeological relics, protected forests, nature reserves, tourist forests, national parks, pastures under village control, and other state lands, diplomatic offices and consulates (on a reciprocal basis) and specified international organizations.

Accounting Rules

There is an Indonesian Association of Accountants known as the "Ikatan Akuntan Indonesia", or "IAI", to which all Indonesian accountants must belong. The IAI issued Indonesian accountancy standards in 1984 and since then have also issued a number of statements or accounting practices that cover a number of different areas ranging from how to account for equity to matters such as depreciation, leases and pension benefits. In practice, it may be necessary for foreign businesses in Indonesia to draw on accounting practices and policies in their home countries, as Indonesian accounting standards may not be as thorough or as detailed as those in more developed countries. **C.43**

Intellectual Property Law

C.44 Indonesia recognizes three types of intellectual property rights: patents, trademarks and service marks, and copyrights.

Patents

C.45 The Patent Law, Law No. 6 of 1989 Regarding Patents (November 1, 1989), became effective August 1, 1991. A "patent" is defined as "a special right granted by the state to an inventor for the results of his invention in the field of technology to personally use his invention or to authorize another person to implement it". There are three pre-requisites for a patent right to be granted to an inventor: (i) the invention must be new; (ii) it must contain an inventive step; and (iii) it must be industrially applicable.

There are two kinds of patents. The first is a simple patent, which is valid for five years from the date of the issuance of the Certificate of Simple Patent. A simple patent cannot be extended. The second type of patent is a regular patent, which is valid for 14 years commencing from the date of receipt of a completed patent application. This type of patent can be extended once for a further two years.

Under the Patent Law, the patent holder is entitled to license the right to use the patented creation to another party based on a license agreement. In addition, patent rights may be transferred by way of inheritance, will, grant, agreement or any other manner pursuant to law. All transfers of patent rights must be registered in the Patent Office and must be recorded in the General Register of Patents. There are no implementing regulations specifying how the transfer agreements should be registered with the Patent Office and recorded at the General Register of Patents but it appears that the transfer agreements themselves must be filed. There is no requirement that license agreements be registered with the Patent Office.

Trademarks

C.46 The Trademark Law, Law No. 19 of 1992, (July 23, 1992), became effective April 1, 1993. The Trademark Law introduced a registration system, pursuant to which trademark and service mark protection is afforded only to those marks which have been registered with the Trademark Office. Unless so registered, protection will not be given. Once the mark is registered, it gives the right to the owner to use, or grant permission to another to use, the mark for a period of ten years. This right may be extended for another ten years. Marks are registered by classes of goods or services, with only one class per registered mark. Therefore, an application must be filed for each class for which protection is sought.

An application for registration of a mark may be rejected, if it is similar to a registered mark of another person for similar goods or services belonging to a class. An application for registration will also be rejected (i) if it is offensive to morality and public order; (ii) if it has no distinguishing features; (iii) if it has become public property; (iv) or if it is related to goods or services for which a registration application is pending.

A mark will also not be registered if it resembles the name of a well-known person or if it resembles the mark of another person which is already protected by copyright law. These provisions are intended to protect famous or well-known marks that are registered in other jurisdictions but have not yet been registered in Indonesia.

Under the Trademark Law, the mark owner can license other parties to use his trademark. The licensee can, if permitted under the licensing agreement, further sublicense his rights. The licensing itself should be based on an agreement and should apply to each class of mark. The licensing period may not exceed the period of protection of the registered mark itself. All licensing agreements must be reported to the Trademark Office, recorded in the General Register of Marks and announced in the Trademark Official Gazette. Implementing regulations on the requirements and procedures to record a licensing agreement have not been issued.

Copyrights

The Copyright Law, Law No. 6 of 1982 (April 12, 1982), as amended by Law No. 7 of 1987 (September 7, 1987), provides copyright protection in Indonesia. A "copyright" is defined as the right of a creator of the creation to publish or reproduce his creation as well as to grant a license to others to use it subject to legal restrictions.   **C.47**

The major change made by the 1987 amendment was to expand the sanctions imposed on copyright violators and to expand the definition of copyright to expressly include computer programs.

Indonesia is not a party to either the Berne Convention or the Universal Copyright Convention. However, Indonesia entered into bilateral treaties regarding copyright protection with the United States on March 22, 1989 and with the European Community on May 27, 1988, in the latter case specifically related to sound recordings.

Under the Copyright Law, the creation of a work automatically receives protection and registration is not required to obtain the copyright. However, without registration, it would be difficult to prove the date the work was created. Registration of a work provides evidentiary proof of such date in the event of a copyright dispute.

There are three categories of term protection under the Copyright Law:

(i) copyright on creations covering books (including pamphlets and other written works), dances (choreography), art works, batiks, songs and architectural works. These works enjoy copyright protection for the lifetime of the creator plus 50 years. In case a copyright holder is a company, the copyright protection is valid for 50 years as of the date of first publication;

(ii) copyright on creations covering cultural performances for the public, speeches, lectures, maps, cinematographic works, musical recordings and translations. These works enjoy copyright protection for a period of 50 years from the date of first publication; and

(iii) copyright on creations covering photographic works, computer programs, adaptations, and compilations. These works enjoy copyright protection for a period of 25 years from the date of first publication.

Under the Copyright Law, a copyright can be transferred either by way of inheritance, will, grant, escheat to the state or by agreement. The transfer of a copyright may be made only in writing. The transfer must be recorded in the General Register of Creations and announced by the Department of Justice in the Supplement to the State Gazette of the Republic of Indonesia. The assignment document must be reported to the Directorate of Patents and Copyrights.

Other Intellectual Property

C.48   In addition to the above, Indonesia may provide protection for the design of industrial products pursuant to Law No. 5 of 1984 on Industry (June 29, 1984) ("Law on Industry"). Article 17 of the Law on Industry appears to prohibit the imitation of industrial product designs which have already been created and registered. However, there are no implementing regulations for this provision of law and it is not clear how one would register industrial product designs at this time.

III. General Considerations in Negotiating Business Transactions in Indonesia

Cultural Factors

The Importance of Relationships

C.49   As with many countries in Asia, the importance of relationships in business affairs cannot be underestimated. Indonesians tend to view an agreement as representing their basic understanding with the other party, a document that reflects an agreement that is subject to change as circumstances vary. At the same time, Indonesians appreciate the importance of written agreements, particularly to parties from the United States and Europe. With Indonesia's significant economic development over the last 20 years, Indonesian business groups have become sophisticated and experienced in conducting international business transactions and understand the importance and sanctity of written agreements. With this increased experience level, and a gradual strengthening of the legal system, differences between Indonesian and Western businessmen with regard to the importance of written agreements have somewhat diminished. Nonetheless, Indonesians will continue to emphasize the business relationship and will not necessarily fall back on the specific terms of an agreement previously reached when problems develop. There is also a practical reason for this: in most cases, the agreements will be in English and generally neither the Indonesian principals nor their attorneys will be as skilled in drafting English language documents as their foreign counterparts from the West. In short, the agreement reached may favor the other party and the Indonesian's negotiating position may be better served by focusing attention away from the agreement and onto the relationship.

Consensus Decision Making

Indonesia has a consensus philosophy that permeates its culture. In all organizations, decisions must be agreed upon at various levels, often from the bottom up, so that the head of an organization has the support of his subordinates before proceeding with an important transaction. This can tend to produce delays in decision-making and implementation. On the positive side, however, the process encourages the entire organization to officially commit its support to decisions, once made. **C.50**

Management Resources

Management resources in many Indonesian companies are thin, so that the burdens on senior management are intense. Businessmen therefore need to ensure that senior management of their Indonesian counterparts focus on and understand the transaction at hand. This avoids misunderstandings later, both prior to document execution and in implementation. Personal meetings to finalize agreements and transactions are essential; long distance negotiations by facsimile transmissions and letters rarely succeed. **C.51**

Role of Local Counsel

Foreign businessmen and their foreign lawyers often retain local counsel to assist them in negotiations and document drafting, whereas their local counterparts tend not to use counsel prior to the documentation stage. This practice tends to complicate and delay the finalization of documents and implementation of projects. If the Indonesian party does not have counsel, **C.52** the foreign party must take care that it does not over reach and cause one-sided documents to be prepared that will then be put aside once local counsel is retained by the other party, while, at the same time, avoiding harm to its own interests in an effort to avoid such one-sided documentation. As a general matter, it would be advisable to encourage the Indonesian counter-part to involve local counsel at an early stage. There are a number of law firms in Indonesia that can provide competent counsel on sophisticated business problems, notwithstanding that Indonesia continues to have the lowest number of lawyers, per capita, of any country in the world. While most law firms are familiar with Indonesian tax law, it is generally necessary to retain a tax advisor as well. The large accounting houses, as well as specialized tax advisors, have day to day working relationships with the Indonesian tax authorities which allows them an understanding of tax practice and implementation.

Government Resources and Business Assistance Programs

C.53 One of the hallmarks of the Indonesian Government is the accessibility of Government officials to the private sector. It is possible for appointments to be made with Directors and Directors General of Government Departments. Ministers are also available. Each Indonesian Government Department has an information section that can provide information to the businessman on various current issues and government programs. An important source of information for the foreign businessman is the Indonesian Capital Invest-ment Coordinating Board, which provides information to promote both domestic and foreign investments in Indonesia and is a useful source of information. Business organizations such as the American Chamber of Com-merce are also useful resources.

Practical Considerations

Language

C.54 English is used widely in commercial circles in Indonesia when foreigners are involved. It is common for agreements to be written in the English language, and also for negotiations to be conducted in that language.

Corporate Authorization

Indonesian law does not have a doctrine of apparent authority and it is important that authorization be determined precisely in order to ensure that a binding contract has been entered into. In order to achieve such comfort, it is necessary to obtain copies of the articles of association and all amendments of the company concerned, and the minutes of the last meeting of shareholders at which directors and commissioners were elected. Only if this is done will it be possible to determine whether the person purporting to exercise authority on behalf of a company is in fact empowered to do so. Review of the articles of association and the minutes will allow one to determine if that person occupies the position in the company with the authority to enter into the transaction and to determine whether any internal corporate approvals are required and have been obtained. Unfortunately, the principal source of the information is the company itself. It is accordingly also necessary for representations and warranties to be made in the agreement that all relevant corporate documents have been provided and corporate authorizations and approvals obtained. It is possible to verify this information through the company's registration at the Department of Industry and Trade. All companies are required to register their articles, amendments, the names of their directors and commissioners and other pertinent information. There is now good compliance with this requirement in Jakarta and most other urban centers.

Joint Ventures

With regard to joint ventures entered into between foreign and local entities to form an Indonesian company, it is important that the joint venture agreement be executed, or otherwise agreed as to major issues, before a foreign investment application is filed with BKPM. This ensures that the private business points between the parties have been agreed before the Government approval process is engaged.

Written Agreements

Written, detailed agreements are important in order for the parties to clearly and definitively document their understandings. Since oral agreements are enforceable in Indonesia, contractual parties should provide that any amendments must be made in writing. It is important to draft specific and definitive agreements because modern commercial transactions are undertaken in a context of a developing legal system. Indonesia's commercial law is based upon the 1847 Dutch Civil Code, which has not been amended in Indonesia (except as to land matters) since adoption. Many modern commercial transactions are not properly supported by this legal system. While the Indonesian Government has embarked upon the largest single-country law and development effort in the world, substantial time and effort will be required to achieve the necessary modernization in its legal system. Indonesian law recognizes the principle that a written contract represents the law between the parties as to that matter, unless the contract violates public order or policy. Accordingly, most standard provisions of an agreement lawful in other countries should be enforceable in Indonesia. Specifically detailed provisions help ensure the parties understand the agreement if a subsequent dispute or other issue of interpretation should arise and this helps close off areas of dispute and contention. The agreement should allow the dispute resolution body, be it an arbitrator or a judge, to clearly understand the transaction and enforce the agreement according to the parties' intent. The second reason why a written agreement is important is because of the developing judicial system in Indonesia. It is generally recognized that there are inefficiencies and weaknesses in the Indonesian judicial system and most parties to a contract will opt for arbitration in lieu of judicial dispute resolution. However, in the final analysis, the judicial system will be engaged, even if it is only to enforce an arbitration award. Every effort should thus be made to prepare an agreement that avoids ambiguity that would result in an interpretation contrary to the parties' intent.

Notes

* The author wishes to thank the partners and associates of Soewito, Suhardiman, Eddymurthy and Kardono for their support and assistance in preparing this chapter, with particular thanks to Dyah Soewito, Retty Suhardiman, Ira Eddymurthy, Yani Kardono, Susandarini Zein, M. Arif Widjaksono, Rusmaini Lenggogeni, Utiek R. Abdurachman, Saraswati Sastrosatomo, Rati Farini Srihadi, Deni Rijadi and R. Widuri. Appreciation is also due to J.R. Turman and Chanda Miller.

[1] This and the other translations of Indonesian text are unofficial translations.

[2] This section is taken from *Business Law, Contracts and Business Associations*, Padjadjaran University, Faculty of Law, Bandung, 1984. Only civil law principles are discussed here, but adat law, or customary law, is extremely important at the village level in Indonesia. These unwritten rules differ among ethnic groups but share some common principles. Generally, adat law does not impact on commercial issues involving foreigners, but could be important in some matters, such as land acquisition or water rights. For a good discussion of adat law, see S. Gautama, Indonesian Business Law, pages 68–74 (1995), Survey of Indonesian Economic Law, Padjadjaran University Faculty of Law, Business Law: Contract and Business Associations (1973) (herein "Survey"), pages 1–7, and S. Pompe (ed.), Indonesian Law 1949–89, pages 351–384 (1992).

[3] *See,* Gautama, page 79.

[4] *See,* Indonesian Commercial Code Articles 1313 to 1314.

[5] *See,* Indonesian Civil Code. Articles 149 and 1338, and Survey, page 9.

[6] *See,* Article 1317 of the Indonesian Civil Code.

[7] See Indonesian Commercial Code, Articles 1266 and 1243 through 1252.

[8] See Bank Indonesia Circular Letter No. 27/3/UKU (January 25, 1995), (as further implemented by Bank Indonesia Board of Directors Decree No. 27/121/KEP/DIR (January 25, 1995) Regarding the Submission of the Tax Registration Number ("NPWP") and the Financial Balance Sheet in Credit Applications ("Decree No. 27").

[9] (September 6, 1995) ("BI Circular Letter No. 28").

[10] In a sale of goods transaction subject to Indonesian law, a wholly or partially unpaid seller can reclaim the goods within 60 days from delivery of the goods to the buyer, if the latter still possesses the goods. For the first 60 days following

delivery, there is, in effect, only a conditional transfer of title to a non-paying buyer. This rule could be construed to mean that a security interest cannot be taken by way of a fiduciary transfer of title in such goods until the 60-day period expires, if payment for the goods has not been made.

[11] Law No. 4/1996, April 9, 1996 and Government Regulation 40/96, June 17, 1996.

MALAYSIA

Rabindra Nathan, Chuah Jern Ern, Gerard Tham,
Nurul Nisa Fuad and Ong Gaik Ee

I. Summary of Business and Political Conditions

Basic Demographic, Political and Economic Information

Situated in the centre of Southeast Asia, Malaysia covers a total land area of   D.01
approximately 331,000 square kilometers and is made up of two distinct
regions, namely, Peninsular Malaysia which covers an area of 132,000 square
kilometers and Sabah and Sarawak, with a total area of 199,000 square
kilometers. These two regions are separated by about 650 kilometers of the
South China Sea.

British colonial rule was largely responsible for shaping Peninsular
Malaysia whereas Sabah and Sarawak on the island of Borneo, were originally part of Brunei and the Sulu sultanates. Both states were privately
acquired prior to being ceded to the British Government. Having been
exposed to two separate histories, these two regions developed variations in
their legal and social structures. The present policy is however one of progressive removal of these differences. The commercial laws of both regions
are uniform.

System of Law

By virtue of its diverse cultural heritage, Malaysia has three parallel legal   D.02
systems, namely a common law system, an Islamic Law system and in Sabah
and Sarawak, a native law system.

Malaysia

Common Law

The common law system was imported from England and India, and adapted to suit local conditions. Where commercial laws are concerned, little modification was effected.

The judicial reliance on English common law has continued even after three decades of independence. The Civil Law Act 1956 (revised 1972) sought to consolidate the application of English Law as it stood on April 7, 1956 for West Malaysia, December 1, 1951 for Sabah and December 12, 1949 for Sarawak. The different dates reflect the original reception of English law in the component states. However, English land law was specifically excluded from application as Malaysian land law is one that is based upon registration, otherwise known as the Torrens title or systems of titles and interests registration.

Islamic Law

Islam predates the arrival of the European colonists and the introduction of the common law system. Colonial courts in the Straits Settlement and the Malay states however, only accorded it limited recognition and as such it is limited to the areas of marriage, divorce, maintenance, adoption, gifts, religious charities trusts and a range of minor religious offenses. The same limited jurisdiction is now entrenched in Malaysia's present Federal Constitution.

Native Law System

The native laws of Sabah and Sarawak are largely unwritten and consist of rules ordering the native communities of those states. While the range of native laws may satisfy rural village communities, its ability to meet urban commercial communities is limited. Thus the trend is to ignore native laws in favour of similar laws in the common law system.

Court Hierarchy

D.03 Each of the three systems of law had its own hierarchy of courts. With the coming into force of the Courts of Judicature (Amendment) Act, 1994, the previous three-tiered common law court structure (consisting of subordinate courts, two High Courts, and at the apex, the Supreme Court) has been replaced by a four-tiered system consisting of subordinate courts, two High Courts, the Court of Appeal, and at the apex, the Federal Court.

The two High Courts, one in Malaya and in the Borneo States, form the core of the common law judicial system. In addition to their unlimited civil and criminal jurisdictions, they also possess appellate and supervisory jurisdiction and further sit as the watchdogs of the Constitutions.

As a result of these recent amendments, there is now a new tier, namely the Court of Appeal. In respect of criminal appeals, it has jurisdiction to hear and determine any appeal against decisions made by the High Court; and in the exercise of its appellate jurisdiction in respect of matters decided by the Sessions Court, to hear appeals from the Public Prosecutor and to hear appeals from the Magistrate's Court on questions of law. In respect of civil appeals, it has jurisdiction to hear and determine appeals from any judgment or order of any High Court whether made in the exercise of its original jurisdiction or of its appellate jurisdiction, but in respect only of matters involving amounts of RM250,000 and above.

The final court of appeal is the Federal Court which has original and appellate jurisdiction. Appeals to the Privy Council have been abolished.

The Syariah or Islamic Courts are established by the states. State enactments regulate both the administrative content and provisions on Islamic law in that state. Coordinated legislative reform at state level has introduced a common structure of Islamic Courts in all states. The three levels of Islamic courts are the Syariah Subordinate Court, the Syariah High Court and the Syariah Appeal Court.

The Native laws in Sabah and Sarawak are administered in a special system of courts. In Sarawak, these are in the following ascending order, *i.e.* the Headman's Court, the Native Officer's Court, the District Officer's Court, the Native Officer's Court, the Resident's Native Court and the Native Court of Appeal. In Sabah, they consist of the Native Court, the District Officer's Court and the Native Court of Appeal.

Political and Economic Development

Governmental Structure

Malaysia has adopted the Westminster system of governance. Hence, although the Head of the State is the *Yang di-Pertuan Agong* (the King), the executive authority is in practical terms vested with the Prime Minister and his cabinet. **D.04**

Under the Federal Constitution, the judiciary is independent from the executive and the legislature.

The power to make delegated legislation may be conferred either on the Minister, or on the *Yang di-Pertuan Agong*, or partly on a statutory body, or on a designated official. The Minister is thus entitled to exercise powers of regulation-making in consultation with a designated authority, or at other times may allow the statutory body to make regulations with his consent.

State Monopolies

State monopolies exist over land ownership, water supply, extraction of minerals, timber and are subject to the granting of licences. Petroleum falls within the ambit of the Federal Government and by virtue of the Petroleum Development Act 1974, the entire ownership, rights and powers of exploring, exploiting, and obtaining petroleum whether onshore or offshore belongs exclusively to *Petroleum Nasional Berhad* (Petronas).

Economic Development and Outlook

D.05   The British colonial rule shaped the Malaysian economy into one that is trade related, although it was geared predominantly to support the British colonial empire. As a result of this, for many years, Malaysia was dependent primarily on its export of primary commodities.

Although the production of rubber and tin provided the country with a satisfactory rate of economic progress, overdependence on these two primary commodities subjected the country to much instability resulting from fluctuating international demands and prices. The realization that these industries were unable to generate sufficient employment opportunities also caused much concern. These factors had the effect of propelling the Malaysian Government to forge ahead to pursue economic diversification and industrialization as a major development strategy.

The result was twofold. Firstly there was a conscious effort to promote industrialization and secondly, by virtue of the fact that such development was spearheaded by the Government, it also resulted in a shift from the relatively *laissez-faire* type economy that was inherited from the British colonial rule to one based on direct state intervention premised upon the concept of trusteeship. The country thus witnessed much direct governmental participation through either wholly-owned industries or joint ventures with local or foreign partners in various sectors of the economy.

The Industrial Master Plan (IMP) (1986–1995) and the Investment Promotion Act 1986 were developed and implemented to encourage foreign investments. The IMP also highlighted Malaysia's need to undertake an increasingly more outward-looking industrialisation by encouraging export led growth. The results were positive. Real GDP growth reached a peak of 9.8 per cent in 1990, exports grew by 30 per cent per annum and the manufacturing sector grew by more than 20 per cent between 1986 to 1990. As a basis of comparison, the agriculture sector which had contributed about 45.7 per cent of the total GDP, decreased to some 20.3 per cent in 1985 and was only 17 per cent of the GDP in 1991. In contrast the manufacturing sector which accounted for only 8 per cent of the GDP in 1957 increased to 19.1 per cent in 1985 and is currently the single largest contributor to GDP at some 29 per cent.

Lessons learnt from the recession in the mid-eighties further propelled the Government to inject more dynamism into the Malaysian economy by moving towards a more flexible administrative guidance system, with the private sector encouraged to play a more positive role in the management of the economy.

Earlier studies herald privatization as a success story. For instance Jones and Fadil (1992), established in their study on the effect of partial divestiture on efficiency that, in the case of Kelang Container Terminal, there was a 55 per cent efficiency gain upon privatization and in the case of the national airline, MAS, there was a 22 per cent increase in efficiency. Privatization has also undoubtedly deepened Malaysia's stock market. The August 16, 1992 issue of *Malaysia Business* and the November 1992 issue of *Investors Digest* reveals that the public listing on the Kuala Lumpur Stock Exchange (KLSE) of 13 entities privatized by June 1992 had raised total market capitalization by RM201.09 billion, hence accounting for 28 per cent of total market capitalization, making KLSE the largest stock market in Southeast Asia and the fourth largest in Asia.

Apart from the economic advancement of Malaysia as a whole, much of the Malaysian economic agenda over the past decade had been influenced by what is known as the New Economic Policy (NEP) that spanned 1970 to 1990. This was the very framework that spawned the First Outline Perspective Plan (OPP1) which covered the period of 1971 to 1991. These development plans were introduced by the Government with the intention of promoting growth with equity and fostering national unity. In a nutshell, the NEP took a two pronged approach, namely:

1. to reduce and eradicate poverty by raising income levels, and increasing employment opportunities, irrespective of race, and
2. to accelerate the process of restructuring Malaysian society to correct the economic imbalances then existing, and to eradicate and eliminate the identification of race with economic functions.

The NEP served its most important function by fostering a climate of social stability, so allowing the Government to concentrate on the business of developing the nation into what it is today.

Starting from where the NEP left off is the Second Outline Perspective   D.06 Plan (OPP2), covering the period of 1991–2000 and embodying the New Development Policy (NDP). Its objective, simply, is to establish a more united and just society. Building upon the groundwork establish by the NEP, the NDP encompasses the following criteria:

1. striking an optimum balance between goals of economic growth and equity;
2. ensuring a balanced development of the major sectors of the economy so as to increase their mutual complementaries to optimize growth;
3. reducing and ultimately eliminating the social and economic inequalities and imbalances in the country to promote a fair and more equitable sharing of the benefits of economic growth by all Malaysians;
4. promoting and strengthening national integration by reducing the wide disparities in economic development between states and between the urban and rural areas in the country;
5. developing a progressive society in which all citizens enjoy greater material welfare, while simultaneously being imbued with positive social and spiritual values, and an increased sense of national pride;

6. promoting human resource development including creating a productive and disciplined labor force and developing the necessary skills to meet the challenges in industrial development through a culture of merit and excellence without jeopardizing the restructuring objectives;

7. making science and technology an integral component of socio-economic planning and development, which entails building competence in strategic and knowledge-based technologies, and promoting a science and technology culture in the process of building a modern industrial economy; and

8. ensuring that in the pursuit of economic development, adequate attention will be given to the protection of the environment and ecology so as to maintain the long-term sustainability of the country's development.

With the Prime Minister's vision of a developed Malaysia by the year 2020 firmly in progress, there is no doubt that the economic future of the nation promises to be an exciting one.

II. Laws and Institutions Affecting Business and Commercial Activities

Competition Law

D.07   At the time of writing, the Ministry of Domestic Trade and Consumer Affairs is in the midst of drafting the proposed Competition Act. This Act seeks to ensure fair competition for participants in economic activities.

The competition policy aims to regulate "workable competition" by helping to set a level playing field for companies operating in various industries. It focuses on problems associated with the concentration of markets, mergers and takeovers, and market manipulation. From the perspective of foreign investors, this Act is seen as an investment catalyst as established participants in the market place no longer have the competitive edge.

Prior to this proposal, the protection of consumers' interests had been covered by a variety of legislation. The provisions in the legislation responded to the need to prevent anti-competitive measures and the abuse of market power.

For instance, Section 28 of the Contracts Act 1950 provides that every agreement by which anyone is restrained from exercising a lawful profession, trade or business of any kind, is to that extent void. The exceptions to this general rule are:

1. One who sells the goodwill of a business may agree with the buyer to refrain carrying on a similar business, within specified local limits, so long as the buyer, or any person deriving title to the goodwill from him carries on a like business provided that such limits appear to the court reasonable regard being had to the nature of the business.
2. Partners may upon, or in anticipation of, a dissolution of the partnership, agree that some of all of them will not carry on a business similar to that of the partnership within such local limits as are referred to in exception 1.
3. Partners may agree that some one or all of them will not carry on any business, other than that of the partnership during the continuance of the partnership.

The policy reasons for this are clear. They prevent the party with the bargaining power from protecting his position by warding off future competition. This prevents the creation of monopolistic markets which is socially undesirable.

Malaysia's Intellectual Property laws also provide certain safeguards for the simple reason that intellectual property rights create temporary monopolies in the copyright work, patented product, registered design, and trademark. The owner of the intellectual property right is able to influence the market price and is able to control the output of the product, and hence is able to make an abnormal profit. Society bears the cost of the monopoly as there is a transfer of wealth from consumers to producers. One of the ways in which the intellectual property laws limit monopolistic tendencies is through the compulsory licensing provisions under the Patents Act 1983. For instance, Section 49 of the Patents Act 1983 provides that at any time after the expiration of three years from the grant of a patent, any person may apply to the Registrar for a compulsory licence if it appears at the time when such application is filed

1. that there is no production of the patented product or application of the patented process without any legitimate reason; and
2. that there is no product produced under the patent for sale in any domestic market, or there are some but they are sold at unreasonably high prices or do not meet the public demand without any legitimate reason.

Through the compulsory licensing mechanism, the owner of a patent is prevented from abusing his market advantage. In the case of extreme monopolistic power, for example selling the products at unreasonably high prices, the Patents Board may grant a third party the right to exploit the patent. The owner of the patent is forced to limit the operation of his exclusive right to maintain competition. (Legal position as at September 1995.)

Contract Law

D.08 The legislation in Malaysia governing contracts is the Contracts Act 1950 (Revised 1974). However, the Contracts Act only partially codifies the common law of contract and common law principles are still relied upon in interpreting and filling gaps in the Act by virtue of the reception of English law under the Civil Law Act 1956. Where the Contracts Act makes certain provisions which differ from English law, the provisions of the Contracts Act must prevail.[1]

Elements of a Contract

The following are the essentials of a contract:

1. offer
2. acceptance of the offer
3. intention to create legal relations
4. consideration
5. certainty
6. capacity

The Contracts Act provides as a general rule, that an agreement without consideration is void.[2] There are several exceptions under the Act:

1. an agreement made on account of natural love and affection between parties standing in near relation;[3]
2. an agreement to compensate for a past voluntary act;[4]
3. an agreement to compensate a person who did an act which the promisor was legally compellable to do;
4. an agreement to pay a statute-barred debt.

Under Malaysian law, consideration need not be adequate.[5] Consideration may be executory, executed or past.[6] The phrase "has done or abstained from doing" in s. 2(d) of the Contracts Act appears to cover past consideration.[7] Under the Contracts Act, consideration need not move from the person who receives a promise, *i.e.* a party to an agreement can enforce the promise even if he has given no consideration so long as somebody has done so.[8]

In Malaysia, the general rule that payment of a smaller sum is not satisfaction of an obligation to pay a larger sum does not apply. The Contracts Act provides that the promisee may dispense with or remit performance of promise.[9] In both situations, the discharge is effective.

The parties entering into a contract must have legal capacity to do so.[10] In Malaysia, the age of majority is eighteen years (Age of Majority Act 1971). Thus, the general rule in Malaysia is that the contracts made by minors are void. The exceptions to this rule are as follows:

1. contracts for necessities;
2. contracts of scholarship; and
3. contracts of insurance.

Formalities

The general rule is that a contract can be made informally. However, the need
for certain formalities in contracts depends on legislation dealing with special
contracts.[11] In the Contracts Act itself, there are two instances of agreements
requiring written form: **D.09**

1. agreements made on account of natural love and affection between
   near relations, and
2. agreements to pay a statute-barred debt.

Voidable Contracts

When consent to an agreement is caused by coercion, fraud or misrepresentation, the agreement is a contract voidable at the option of the party whose
consent was so caused.[12] Section 21 of the Contracts Act provides that where
both parties to an agreement are under a mistake as to a matter of fact
essential to the agreement, the contract is void. It would seem that if the
mistake is made by one party the agreement is valid. **D.10**

Void and Illegal Contracts

Some agreements are void as well as unlawful. The consideration or object of
an agreement is unlawful if: **D.11**

1. it is forbidden by a law;
2. it is of such a nature that it would defeat any law;
3. it is fraudulent;
4. it involves or implies injury to the person or property of another; or
5. the court regards it as immoral or opposed to public policy.[13]

The following agreements are also declared void by the Contracts Act:

1. an agreement made without consideration unless it is in writing and
   registered, or is a promise to pay a debt barred by limitation law;[14]
2. an agreement in restraint of marriage;[15]
3. an agreement in restraint of trade except for an agreement not to carry
   on business of which goodwill is sold or an agreement made prior to
   a dissolution of a partnership or an agreement made during the continuance of a partnership;[16]
4. an agreement in restraint of legal proceedings except for a contract
   agreeing to refer to disputes to arbitration or a contract relating to
   scholarships;[17]

5. an agreement, the meaning of which is not certain, or capable of being made certain;[18] or
6. an agreement by way of wager.[19]

The general rule under the Contracts Act is that the courts will not enforce an illegal contract: *ex turpi causa non oritur actio*. However, the Contracts Act also provides that when an agreement is discovered to be void, or when a contract becomes void, the person who has received any advantage under the agreement or contract is bound to restore it, or to make compensation for it to the person from whom he received it.[20]

Contracts in restraint of trade or legal proceedings are void to the extent of the restraint only. In other words, it is possible to sever that part which is invalid and to enforce the rest of the agreement provided it does not substantially alter the nature of the agreement.

Discharge of Contracts

D.12   A contract may be discharged by any of the following ways:

1. by performance;
2. by consent or agreement of the parties;
3. by impossibility; or
4. by breach.

Frustration of contract is a complete defence. The law on frustration is contained in the Civil Law Act 1956 which adopted the provisions of the United Kingdom Law Reform (Frustrated Contracts) Act 1945. When a contract has become impossible to perform or has been otherwise frustrated, there are provisions for adjustment of the rights and liabilities of the parties to the frustrated contract.

Remedies

In general, the whole range of legal and equitable remedies are available, although they are sourced in legislation such as the Contracts Act 1950 and the Specific Relief Act 1950. The principle remedies in contract are damages, specific performance, injunction and rescission. The rules of assessment of damages, although codified, are based on the English common law rules. Section 75 of the Contracts Act provides for penalties to be struck down if they are not a reasonable pre-estimate of damages. However, under the Contracts (Amendment) Act 1976, where a government scholarship agreement has been breached, the scholar has to pay the full sum stipulated in the agreement whether or not actual damage or loss has been caused by such breach and no consideration will be given for the period of service already performed under the contract.

Use of Standardised Contracts

Standard form contracts are permitted and are extensively used commercially. Legislatively prescribed standard form contracts apply in certain transactions such as hire purchase and the private purchase of homes from housing developers.

Requirements for Government Contracts

Some special rules apply to government contracts. The Government Contracts Act 1949 (Revised 1973) provides for the making of contracts on behalf of the federal and state governments. All such contracts must be in writing and signed by the Minister, if the contract is a federal government contract; or by the Chief Minister, if it is a state government contract or by any of their authorised officers. Such public officers cannot be sued upon any contract they have made unless they pledge their credit or unless they contract otherwise than as agents of the federal or state governments.

Commercial Law

Commercial law regulates the rights and obligations of persons engaged in   D.13
commercial transactions. The subject matter is varied and includes contracts, agency, partnership, negotiable instruments, sale of goods and insurance. Commercial law is based on the common law of England. For the purposes of this article, the general overview of the laws of agency, partnership, negotiable instruments, sale of goods and insurance will be discussed.

Agency Law

The law of agency is governed by Part X of the Contracts Act 1950 (Revised 1974). A contract of agency may arise as follows:

1. by express appointment by the principal;
2. by implied appointment by the principal;[21]
3. by ratification by the principal;[22]
4. by necessity *i.e.* by operation of law;[23] or
5. by the doctrine of estoppel or "holding out".

Consideration is not necessary to create an agency.[24]

In the absence of a contract of agency, the rights and duties of the principal and agent are laid down in the Contracts Act.[25]

Unlike the common law, when a principal is not identified even though he is disclosed and an agent is personally liable, the third party dealing with him may sue either the agent or the principal or both of them when he discovers the identity of the principal.[26] The liability in such a situation is joint and several. However, if the third party chooses to sue one only he may be estopped from suing the other party if he has allowed the party to believe that only the one he sued will be liable.

A contract of agency may be terminated by the act of the parties or by the operation of law.[27]

The Law of Partnership

D.14 The law of partnership is governed by the Partnership Act 1961 (Revised 1974).

The Partnership Act specifically excludes co-operative societies and registered statutory and chartered companies.[28] In West Malaysia, the partnership business must be registered under the Registration of Business Act 1956; in Sarawak under the Sarawak Cap. 64 (Business Names); and in Sabah, under the Trades Licensing Ordinance No. 16, 1948.

In the absence of a partnership agreement, the Partnership Act lays down certain situations which are not prima facie partnership.[29] They are co-ownership of property, sharing of gross returns and sharing of profits.

In the absence of agreement, the Act also lays down the rights and duties of partners.[30] The principle of "utmost good faith" between partners is implicit in every partnership agreement in that every partner must render true accounts, account for private profits and not compete with the firm.[31]

When a partner retires from the firm, he remains liable for the partnership debts incurred before his retirement. The retired partner is also liable to persons who had done previous dealings with the firm unless he had given notice thereof in the relevant Gazette[32] (either, the Federal, Sabah or Sarawak Gazette, depending on the principal place of business of the firm).

A partnership may be terminated or dissolved by agreement, by operation of law, by death or bankruptcy, by charging on shares, by supervening illegality or by court order.[33]

Sale of Goods

D.15 The law that is applicable in Peninsula Malaysia other than Penang and Malacca is the Sale of Goods (Malay States) Ordinance 1957. The position in Penang, Malacca, Sabah and Sarawak is governed by Section 5 of the Civil Law Act 1956. In general, courts in Penang, Malacca, Sabah and Sarawak have applied the English Sale of Goods Act 1893 in cases before them. The Sale of Goods Ordinance is modelled, with some modifications, after the English Act. Thus, the differences between the law in Peninsula Malaysia and that in Penang, Malacca, Sabah and Sarawak, are slight.

A contract for the sale of goods is basically the same as any other contract so that the general rules of contract are also applicable. However, the Sale of Goods Ordinance lays down special rules and some of these rules supersede that of the law of contract.

The Sale of Goods Ordinance implies a few terms in all contracts for sale of goods, although the contracting parties may exclude or modify them, such as:

1. implied undertaking as to title;[34]
2. sale of goods by description;[35]
3. implied terms as to quality or fitness;[36]
4. sale by sample.[37]

Hire-Purchase

The law relating to hire-purchase is governed by the Hire Purchase Act 1967 **D.16** (Revised 1978). This Act applies only to hire-purchase agreements relating to the following goods specified in the First Schedule of the Act:

1. all consumer goods, and
2. motor vehicles; namely invalid carriages, motor cycles, motor cars including taxi cabs and hire cars, goods vehicles (where the maximum permissible laden weight does not exceed 2,540 kg) and buses including stage buses.

Hire-purchase agreements on other goods are governed by common law.

Part III of the Hire Purchase Act deals with conditions and warranties in every hire-purchase agreement. These provisions are similar to the conditions and warranties implied in a contract for the sale of goods under the Sale of Goods Ordinance 1957.

Under the Hire Purchase Act, the hirer has the following statutory rights:

1. to be supplied documents and information;[38]
2. to require the owner to appropriate payments made in hire-purchase agreements;[39]
3. to apply to the Magistrate's Court for an order approving the removal of the goods to another place;[40]
4. to assign his rights, title and interest under the hire-purchase agreement;[41]
5. to have his right, title and interest passed on by operation of law;[42]
6. to complete the purchase of the goods earlier than the due date;[43] and
7. to terminate the hiring.[44]

At common law, when a hirer has committed a breach of his contractual obligations under the hire-purchase agreement, the owner is entitled to recover possession of the goods let on hire. However, the Hire Purchase Act imposes restrictions on the power of the owner to recover possession of goods as a means of protecting the interests of the hirer. When a hirer defaults, the following procedure has to be taken:

Malaysia

1. the owner must serve on the hirer a written notice of his intention to retake possession;[45]
2. after the repossession the owner must not sell or dispose of the goods for 14 days;[46]
3. the hirer's rights and immunities when goods are repossessed;[47] and
4. the hirer can regain possession of the goods in certain circumstances.[48]

Insurance

D.17 The law governing insurance companies is contained in the Insurance Act 1996 which repeals the Act of 1963 (The Insurance Act 1996 will be in force only in the first quarter of 1997). Under Section 5 of the Civil Law Act 1956 English insurance law is applicable in this country in the absence of local legislation. The Insurance Act classifies the insurance business as follows:

1. Life business *i.e.* all insurance business concerned with life policies, including any type of insurance business carried on incidental only to the life insurer's business and
2. General business *i.e.* all insurance business which is not life business.

If a person has no insurable interest, the policy is void.[49] There are exceptions:[50]

(a) a person's spouse, a person's child or ward being under the age of majority at the time the insurance is effected;
(b) his employee; or
(c) anyone on whom that person is at that time wholly or partly dependant. (NB. This section does not affect life policies issued before January 24, 1963)

Failure to disclose material information gives the other party the right to treat the contract as void. The exceptions to this general rule are that at common law a person is expected to disclose facts which he actually knows or reasonably ought to know[51] and under the Insurance Act, a policy is not voided by reason only of a misstatement of the age of the life insured.[52]

In order to curb the harshness of the general rule, the Insurance Act specifically provides that the proposal form must prominently display a warning that if a proposer does not fully and faithfully give the facts as he knows them or ought to know them, he may receive nothing from the policy.[53]

Other statutory exceptions under the Insurance Act relating to the duty of disclosure imposed on the insured would include matters that:

(a) diminish the risk to the insurer; or
(b) are of common knowledge; or
(c) the insurer knows or in the ordinary course of his business ought to know; or

(d) in respect of which the insurer has waived any requirement for disclosure.

Negotiable Instruments

The law of negotiable instruments in Malaysia is governed by the Bills of Exchange Act 1949. The present law is largely based on English law (Bills of Exchange Act 1882). The characteristics of negotiability are: **D.18**

1. the instrument and the rights contained in it which are transferred by mere delivery, or where it is payable to order, by indorsement plus delivery;
2. the holder who is in possession of the instrument can sue in his own name;
3. the debtor need not be given notice of this transfer; and
4. the transferee who has received it in good faith and for value gets a superior title and is therefore unaffected by previous defects.

Negotiable instruments include bills of exchange, promissory notes, bankers' draft, bank notes, treasury bills, share warrants, dividend warrants, debentures and travellers' cheques.

A person is not liable on a bill unless he has signed[54] it as a drawer, acceptor or indorser and delivered it.[55] As a general rule, when a bill has been dishonored by non-acceptance or non-payment, notice of dishonor must be given by the holder to the drawer and indorser[56] otherwise, they will be discharged from liability.[57] Section 49 of the Bills Of Exchange Act lays down the rules governing notice of dishonor.

Remedies Under Commercial Law

In general, the whole range of legal and equitable remedies are available and these are sourced in legislation such as the Contracts Act 1950 and the Specific Relief Act 1950. (Legal position as at September 1995.) **D.19**

Company Law

The law of companies in Malaysia are codified in the Companies Act 1965 (the Act). The Act only deals with the registration and administration of companies and does not concern itself with the regulation of investment or business, whether local or foreign. There are no foreign investment law per se in Malaysia although foreign investors should be aware of the existence of the New Development Policy (NDP). The objectives of the NDP build upon the now defunct New Economic Policy (NEP) and are essentially: (i) to reduce and eradicate poverty by raising income levels and increasing employment opportunities; and (ii) to accelerate the process of restructuring Malaysian **D.20**

society so as to correct the economic imbalance and to eliminate the identification of race with economic functions.

The Foreign Investment Committee of the Prime Minister's Department
has issued a non-statutory document entitled *Guidelines for the Acquisition
of Assets, Mergers and Take-overs* (the FIC Guidelines) to regulate the
acquisition of assets or interests, mergers and take-overs of companies and
businesses to ensure a greater distribution of wealth in line with the objectives of the NDP.

Forms of Commercial Organizations

D.21 There are two main forms of commercial organizations in Malaysia:

1. the limited company, which may be private or public, incorporated
   under the Act, and
2. the partnership, which is regulated by the Partnership Act 1961 (Revised 1974).

A company may be limited by share, by guarantee, by both shares and
guarantee, or be unlimited. No company may however be formed as, or
become, a company limited by guarantee with a share capital.

Private Companies

A company limited by shares may be incorporated as a company if its
memorandum or articles:

1. restricts the right to transfer its shares;
2. limits to not more than 50 the number of its members (joint shareholders are counted as one person and excluding employees (past or
   present) of the company or its subsidiary who are shareholders);
3. prohibits it to invite the public to subscribe for any shares in or
   debentures of the company; and
4. prohibits it from inviting the public to deposit money with it for fixed
   periods or payable at call, whether interest-bearing or not.

Foreign Companies

A foreign company which has a place of business or carries on business
within Malaysia is required to be registered under the Act, otherwise the
foreign company would be committing an offence. (A registered foreign
company is also known as a branch office to the Ministry of International
Trade and Industry (MITI)).

The Registrar of Companies has in the past been reluctant to so register
foreign companies as it is contrary to the Malaysian government's policy of
regulating the form and structure of foreign investment in accordance with

the New Economic Plan and the National Development Plan. The usual form of such regulation has been the imposition of equity restructuring conditions in respect of Malaysian companies which have foreign shareholders. Furthermore, the registration of foreign companies has usually been effected only with the approval of MITI and then only upon these companies having been awarded a contract by the Malaysian government or its agencies.

Under Malaysian law, a foreign company may establish a business presence in Malaysia in the following ways:

1. by acquiring control of a company incorporated under the Act, or incorporating such a company and carrying on business through such a company, or
2. by registering itself under the Act as a foreign company and thereby establishing a branch office in Malaysia.

Registration and Incorporation

A company is incorporated and registered by the lodgement of the memo- **D.22**
randum and articles of association of the proposed company with the Registrar of Companies together with other documents required to be lodged by or under the Act and the payment of the appropriate fees. The registration fee for a company having a share capital ranges from RM1,000.00 where its nominal share capital does not exceed RM100.00 to RM70,000.00 for a company whose nominal share capital exceeds RM100,000,000.00.

In addition to the lodgement of documents and the payment of the requisite registration fees, a registered foreign company is also required to appoint a local agent.

Establishment of Subsidiaries

The Act defines a subsidiary as a corporation which board of directors are controlled by another (parent) corporation or which has more than half of its voting power controlled by the parent corporation or which has more than half its issued share capital (other than preference shares) held by the parent corporation. Other than the above, there are no separate rules for the establishment of a subsidiary company. Subsidiary status, as such, is acquired only as a result of shareholding in or control by another company.

Board of Directors and Directors' Shareholdings

Every company must have at least two directors who must each have his principal or only place of residence within Malaysia. Directors are only required to hold qualifying shares to the extent provided in the Articles of the company. Where directors are required to hold such shares, the Act merely requires such directors to obtain their qualification within a period of two months or other shorter period fixed by the Articles.

Malaysia

Shareholders, Share Capital and Issued Capital

D.23 There must be a minimum of two shareholders in a company, each of whom must hold at least one share with a minimum nominal of RM1.00. The only exception to this is a company which is the wholly-owned subsidiary of another. There are no specific legislation limiting shareholdings by non-residents, but note the FIC Guidelines above. Shares may be paid for in cash or in the form of other valuable consideration. Where non-cash consideration is given for shares, there is no requirement for independent valuation. There are no restriction for the disposal of shares.

Companies are not required to issue all their authorized capital. There are no minimum paid-up capital requirements under the Act although minimum paid-up capital requirements may apply under legislation dealing with banking, insurance companies, etc.

Time Required to Set up Companies

Companies may be formed within a period of three to four months under the Act as long as there are no delays resulting from the selection of names.

Accounts

Under the Act, every company, through its directors and managers, is under an obligation to keep such accounting and other records as will sufficiently explain the transactions and financial position of the company. A company's records must enable the preparation of a true and fair profit and loss account and balance sheet and any documents required to be attached thereto. Such records must be kept in such form and manner as to enable them to be conveniently and properly audited.

Annual Return

Every company having a share capital is required to make an annual return in prescribed of information specified in the Eighth Schedule to the Act, including a copy of the last audited balance sheet and profit and loss account of the company.

Liquidation

A company may be voluntarily (Voluntary Winding Up) or compulsorily (Winding Up by the Court) wound up.

Voluntary winding up — A company is voluntarily wound up:

(a) on the expiry of the period fixed for the duration of the company by the Memorandum or Articles or on the occurrence of an event fixed by the Memorandum or Articles to be one which dissolves the company, and by a resolution of the company requiring the company to be voluntarily wound up; or

(b) by special resolution of the company.

A members' voluntary winding up is a voluntary winding up in which, within a period of five weeks immediately preceding the passing of the resolution for voluntary winding up, the directors make a written declaration to the effect that the company will be able to pay its debts in full within a period not exceeding 12 months after the commencement of winding up. A creditors' voluntary winding up is one in which such a declaration of solvency is not made. Shareholders in general meeting appoint and supervise the liquidator in a members' voluntary winding up while in a creditors' voluntary winding up the creditors do so.

Winding up by the court — A company may be wound up by court order (whether or not it is being wound up voluntarily) if:

(a) the company has resolved by special resolution resolved that it be wound up by the Court;

(b) default is made by the company in lodging the statutory report or in holding the statutory meeting;

(c) the company does not commence business within a year from its incorporation or suspends its business for a whole year;

(d) the number of members is reduced in the case of a company (other than a company the whole of the issued shares in which are held by a holding company) below two;

(e) the company is unable to pay its debts;

(f) the directors have acted in the affairs of the company in their own interests rather than the interests of the members as a whole, or in any other manner whatsoever which appears to be unfair or unjust to other members;

(g) an inspector appointed as reported that the company is insolvent and should be wound up or that it should be wound up in the interests of the public, the shareholders or the creditors;

(h) any time fixed for the duration of the company by the memorandum or articles expires or any event occurs on the occurrence of which the memorandum or articles provide that the company is to be dissolved;

(i) the court is of opinion that it is just and equitable that the company be wound up;

(j) the company has held a licence under the Banking Act 1973 or the Islamic Banking Act 1985, and that licence has been revoked or has expired and has not been renewed; or

(k) the company has carried on banking business in Malaysia in contravention of section 3, 5, or 6 of the Banking Act 1973.

(Legal position as at September 1995.)

Capital Markets and Securities Laws

D.24 "Capital Markets" in Malaysia refers to the market in longer-term financial assets, comprising all public and private debt instruments with securities exceeding one year, and corporate stocks and shares, for which there is no fixed maturity period. The market comprises the issue of Government securities, Government Investment Deposits, Cagamas bonds, securities on the stock market and Negotiable Certificates of Deposit.

The securities industry in Malaysia are essentially regulated by the following enactments:

1. Securities Commission Act 1993, which was recently amended by the Securities Commission (Amendment) Act 1995;
2. Securities Industry Act 1983, which was recently amended by the Securities Industry (Amendment) Act 1996;
3. Securities Industry (Central Depositary) Act 1991, which was recently amended by the Securities Industry (Central Depositories) (Amendment) Act 1996;
4. Futures Industry Act 1993 (recently amended by the Futures Industry (Amendment) Act 1995; and
5. Companies Act 1965.

Prior to March 1, 1993 there were nine regulatory bodies responsible for the supervision and management of the securites industry. They were the:

1. The Capital Issues Committee (CIC);
2. Registrar of Companies (ROC);
3. Foreign Investment Committee (FIC);
4. Panel on Takeover and Mergers (TOP);
5. The Kuala Lumpur Stock Exchange (KLSE);
6. Ministry of International Trade & Industry (MITI);
7. Central bank of Malaysia (CBM);
8. Ministry of Finance (MOF); and
9. Implementation and Coordination Unit of the Prime Minister's Department (ICU).

Under this system of regulation, applications by public companies were required to be made in a fragmented fashion to all the various authorities above. This often led to a duplication of functions, delays and excessive red-tape.

The Securities Commission (SC) was thus established by the Securities Industry (Amendment) Act 1993 to eradicate the unnecessary duplication of functions that prevailed in the previous fragmented systems of approvals. It is thus designed to not only create a more efficient system of regulation but also to enhance supervision and surveillance of the security industry. The SC also plays an important part in the long term planning and development of the securities industry. Upon its commencement of operation, in March 2, 1993, all powers of the CIC and the TOP were transferred to the SC.

Securities Commission

Structure

Members of the SC are appointed by the Minister of Finance and consist of an Executive Chairman, four members representing the Government of Malaysia and four other persons.[58] The first and current Executive Chairman is Dr. Mohammed Munir Abdul Majid.

D.25

Functions

The statutory duties of the SC include advising the Minister of Finance on all matters relating to the securities, and futures contract industries, the regulation of issues of shares and the designating of futures contracts, the regulating of take overs and mergers of companies and generally monitoring and supervising all securities and futures exchanges, clearing houses and the CDS.[59]

Securities Industry Act 1983 (SIA)

Overview

The present legislation which replaces the earlier Securities Industry Act 1973 came into force on July 8, 1983. It is aimed primarily at mobilizing capital more effectively to ensure the growth of an orderly capital market.

D.26

The SIA is modelled largely on the Australian Securities Industry Act 1980 with the difference being that whilst the Australian Act promotes self regulation, the Malaysian SIA not only facilitates the appointment of a government representative to act on the stock exchange committee[60] but goes so far as to ensure that the Minister of Finance is responsible for the securities industry.

With the promulgation of the Securities Commission in 1993 (as discussed above) the overall administration and enforcement of securities industry that formerly laid with the Registrar of Companies is now the responsibility of the Security Commission.

In short, the SIA regulates the stock exchange, stock brokers, persons dealing in securities apart from spelling out certain offenses relating to trading in securities and for other connected purposes.

The Stock Exchange

Under the SIA, the stock exchange may only be set up upon the Minister of Finance being satisfied as to there being a body corporate comprising at least 10 members carrying on the business of dealing in securities independently of

D.27

and in competition with one another, the rules of the body contains satisfactory provisions with regard to the admission of only persons of good character and high business integrity as members, lists comprehensive rules that pertains to the expulsion, suspension or disciplining of members, conditions under which securities may be listed, conditions governing dealings in securities by members, the class or classes of securities that may be dealt with by members and the general conduct of the stock exchange with due regard to the interests of the public.[61]

Section 8(3), SIA 1983, empowers the Minister to appoint any person to sit on the committee of the stock exchange to represent the interest of the public.

Licenses

Dealer, dealer's representatives, investment advisers and investment adviser's representative are required to be appropriately licensed under the SIA, before they can carry on business or holding themselves as categorized. Two further categories of licenses were added with the coming into force of the Securities Industry (Amendment) Act 1996. They are the Fund Manager's License and the Fund Manager's Representative's License. Prior to the recent amendments in 1996, the function of issuing licenses rested with the Licensing Officer, a public officer appointed by the Minister of Finance (under the now defunct s.15A. This function now lies with the commission). The tenure of licenses granted is for one year only. Applications are to be made in a prescribed form and accompanied by the appropriate fee and in the case of an application to renew, is shall be made not later than 30 days before the expiry of the license.

Records

Part V of the SIA provides for the keeping of records in the form of a Register of Securities in the form prescribed by the SIA (Form 14). Persons so required to keep records are dealers, dealer's representatives, investment advisers, investment representatives, fund manager, fund manager's representatives, financial journalist or any authorised depository agent appointed under Section 13 of the Securities Industry (Central Depositories) Act 1991.

The Security Commission or the Registrar of Companies may require the production of such register for inspection and failure to produce such register tantamount to the commitment of an offence. (s.33)

Accounts and Audit

D.28   Part VII of the SIA relates to the keeping of accounts by dealers, fund managers and their audit. The auditor's report is required to be lodged with the Companies Registrar within three months of the end of the financial year.

(s.49) The Auditor is also required by the SIA to report any suspected misnomers to the relevant authorities.

Payments made to dealers that are not paid over to the client by the next business day are required to be paid into a trust account (s.44) and monies paid into such accounts may only be withdrawn subject to stringent conditions. (s.45)

Compensation

Part VII of the SIA provides that all members of the stock exchange are required to contribute towards the stock exchange's compensation fund. The monies under this fund are used for purposes specified under s.64 to s.72 of the SIA and are designed essentially to protect the investing public against any defalsification committed by members of a stock exchange or their employees.

Other Protection

Part IX contains a whole array of provisions which protects against short-selling, wash sales, matched sales, market rigging, false or misleading statement, use of manipulative and deceptive devices for trading and insider's trading.

Enforcement & Investigation

The SC is empowered to appoint Investigating Officers to carry out investigations under the Securities Commission Act 1993. These Investigating Officers are endowed with extensive powers permitting them to even make forced entries if needed (s.36, 37 SCA).

Recent Developments

Formation of the Central Depository System (CDS)

The Securities Industry (Central Depositories) Act 1991 introduced the   **D.29**
Kuala Lumpur Stock Exchange ("KLSE") to a scriptless trading system with the aim of increasing the efficiency of KLSE's trading system and to further tightened KLSE's control over trading in the local bourse by eliminating trading of Malaysian shares outside the country, namely, Singapore. It is thus expected that in time to come, the CLOB international OTC market (Central Limit Order Buying) operating in Singapore will die a natural death.

Structure

The Central Depository is essentially a company limited by shares and incorporated under the Companies Act 1965. It is known as the Malaysian Central Depository Sdn Bhd (MCDS).

Malaysia

The KLSE is a shareholder of the MCDS and is empowered to require any security listed or proposed to be listed for quotation on its official list to be deposited with the MCDS. Such security is thereafter known as a prescribed security (s.14).

An advisory committee may be appointed by the Minister of Finance in respect of the MCDS which consists of the following members:

1. a Chairman;
2. a Deputy Chairman; and
3. a representative each from:
   (a) the SC;
   (b) the MITI;
   (c) the CBM;
   (d) the KLSE; and
   (e) the MCDS
4. not less than six but not more than eight other members who have had experience of and have shown capacity in, matters relating to the capital marker, finance or investment (s.6).

The advisory committee shall be responsible for advising the MCDS on matters relating to services provided by it, make recommendations or proposals to the Minister of Finance to improve the efficiency of the MCDS and to perform such other duties as prescribed by the minister of Finance.

Formation of a Futures Industry

D.30 In another effort to further develop Malaysia, in particularly, Kuala Lumpur, as a key financial centre, the Futures Industry Act 1993 came into force on March 1, 1993 and recently amended on November 25, 1995. The Act had been designed to regulate trading in options and financial futures with particular emphasis on the protection of investors.

The much awaited Malaysian Monetary Exchange (MME) and the Kuala Lumpur Options and Financial Futures Exchange (KLOFFE) has just recently commenced trading.

In fact MME is currently trading the three-month Kuala Lumpur Interbank Offer Rate. KLOFFE is currently trading the KLSE index.

It is hoped that these developments will produce a cost-effective hedging system to ensure an efficient transfer and distribution of financial risks in the economy. As a matter of fact, the central bank is supportive of these developments and is currently undertaking studies to further foster more conducive conditions to promote and enhance the financial futures markets.

Others

Lately the Securities Commission had been looking to introduce Securities Borrowing and Lending ("SBL") and shortselling. To this effect they are currently reviewing the existing security legislation. (Disclaimer: Legal position as at June 1996.)

Arbitration and Other ADR Techniques

Commercial arbitration in Malaysia is governed by the Arbitration Act 1952 **D.31** (Act 93) which is modelled on its English 1950 counterpart. In order to be subject to the Act, the arbitration agreement (defined by section 2 of the 1952 Act) must be in writing whether as a separate agreement or as a clause in the principal contract (the latter treated as an agreement in its own right). Therefore an oral arbitration agreement will be governed by common law.

By virtue of section 33, the 1952 Act is retrospective and therefore applies to all arbitration agreements entered into before it was enforced. Notwithstanding any statutory provision to the contrary, the said Act does not apply to any arbitration held under the Convention on the Settlement of Investment Disputes Between States and Nationals of Other States 1965, the UNCITRAL Arbitration Rules 1976 and the Rules of the Regional Centre for Arbitration at Kuala Lumpur: see section 34(1).

Parties to an arbitration agreement are not prevented from seeking remedy in court. However, section 6 provides that a party may apply to the High Court for a stay of any civil action provided that he has not taken a step in the proceedings and undertakes that he is ready and willing to do all things necessary for the proper conduct of the arbitration. The section 6 test is propounded in the case of *D&C Finance Bhd v. Overseas Assurance Corpn Ltd* [1989] 3 MLJ 240 following the English case of *Heyman v. Darwins Limited* [1942] 1 ALL ER 337. There must be an agreement existing between the parties and it contains arbitration provisions. Further, there must be sufficient reason why the matter should not be referred to arbitration. The courts have a discretion whether or not to grant a stay and may draw upon its inherent jurisdiction to do so (*Stolt Loyalty and Maya* case [1985] 1 CLJ 290).

Nevertheless, clauses which oust the jurisdiction of the courts are bad in law and not enforceable (*Perbadanan Kemajuan Negeri Perak v. Asean Security Paper Mill Sdn Bhd* [1991] 3 CLJ 2400). Section 22 expressly empowers the court to compel an arbitrator to submit a point of law for determination and this cannot be contracted out of (*Czarnikow v. Roth, Schmidt & Co* [1922] 2 KB 478).

On the other hand, a *Scott v. Avery* clause which provides for arbitration as a precondition to a court action is not void for it is not intended to oust the court's jurisdiction.

General principles on competency for referrals basically follow the English position. Infants and bankrupts (*Re Milnes and Robertson* (1854) 15 CB 451) may submit to arbitration and a company's right depends upon its nature of business and regulations which govern it. On the other hand, business partners would require express authority before they can do so (*Stead v. Salt* (1825) 3 Bing 101).

The construction of arbitration agreements are a matter of interpretation. Caselaw has established that contracts depend on express terms and parties' rights are governed by the terms therein (*Heng Cheng Swee v. Bangkok Bank Ltd* [1976] 1 MLJ 2670). The terms may be altered or amended by the mutual consent of the parties but not the arbitrator.

Arbitration under the Kuala Lumpur Centre for Arbitration

D.32   Disputes may be settled under the Malaysian Arbitration Act 1952, the Rules of Conciliation and Arbitration of the International Chamber of Commerce (ICC) in Paris or under the Rules of the United Nations Commission of International Trade Law (UNCITRAL) 1976.

Although the ICC is an established body, countries in this region are reluctant to submit to its jurisdiction due to the resulting exorbitant costs and inordinate delay.

On December 15, 1976, the United Nations General Assembly by its resolution No. XXXI 98 adopted the UNCITRAL Arbitration Rules. Acceptance of the said Rules by the United Nations Commission on International Trade and Law in 1976, immediately precipitated the Asian-African Legal Consultative Committee (AALCC) to recommend its member Governments to likewise accept and adopt them.

On April 1, 1978 following that recommendation, the Malaysian Government established the Regional Centre for Arbitration (the Regional Centre); a non-profit making institution now situated at Jalan Conlay in Kuala Lumpur. The Regional Centre renders assistance in the conduct of *ad hoc* arbitrations for the settlement of trade and commerce disputes including those held under the UNCITRAL Rules, assistance in the enforcement of arbitral awards and holding arbitration proceedings under its own auspices. The Regional Centre functions under the supervision of the AALCC and is headed by a Director. Its principal function is to provide fair, expeditious and inexpensive procedures so that arbitration institutions outside the region is no longer necessary.

The Regional Centre has adopted its own set of rules for Arbitration which closely follows the UNCITRAL Rules in some respects (the KLRC Arbitration Rules). Under these Rules, the Centre is the appointing authority unless the parties have agreed otherwise. When the Regional centre was set up, the Malaysian legislature amended the Arbitration Act 1952 to provide in section 34(1) that the provisions of the Arbitration Act 1952 would not apply to awards of the Regional Centre save as otherwise provided, thereby excluding such awards from the general registration and enforcement provisions of the Arbitration Act 1952, as well as from the supervisory jurisdiction of the High Court under that Act.

However, section 34(2) of the Arbitration Act 1952 provides that if an award is made under New York Convention on the Recognition and Enforcement of Foreign Arbitral Awards, 1958 or the Convention on the Settlement of Investment Disputes between States and Nationals of other States, 1965 (ICSID), then enforcement would take place in accordance with those Conventions. Malaysia has since incorporated the New York Convention into its domestic law through the Convention on the Recognition and Enforcement of Foreign Arbitral Awards Act 1985, and enforcement of awards falling within the ambit of the New York Convention is through the provisions of the Convention on the Recognition and Enforcement of Foreign Arbitral Awards Act 1985. Enforcement of awards falling within the ambit of the New York Convention is through the provisions of the Convention on the Recognition and Enforcement of Foreign Arbitral Awards Act 1985.

Investment disputes however can be resolved by conciliation or by arbitration under the Convention on the Settlement of Investment Disputes between States and Nationals of other States 1965 (ICSID) to which Malaysia become a party in 1966. Proceedings under the ICSID may be held in Washington, the Permanent Court of Arbitration or any other venue approved by the Commission or Tribunal after consultation with the Secretary General of ICSID. After 1979 however, these proceedings may be held at the KL Regional Centre.

Rules for Arbitration of Kuala Lumpur Regional Arbitration Centre

Arbitration under the auspices of the Regional Centre can be availed by **D.33** parties who have agreed in writing that the dispute be referred to the said centre. However, for purposes of enforcement, for reasons which will be explained shortly, it is preferable that the dispute is of an international character, *i.e.* the parties are resident or belong to two different jurisdictions or the dispute involves international commercial interests. The suggestion that the dispute possess an international character is to ensure that award comes within the New York Convention, and thus can be enforced under the Convention on the Recognition and Enforcement of Foreign Arbitral Awards Act 1985. There is some doubt as to whether an award made pursuant to an arbitration that lacks the attributes of a New York Convention award can be enforced, in view of the language of section 34(1) and (2) of the Arbitration Act 1952.

Requests must be in written form indicating that the parties have entered into an agreement under which they have agreed to refer disputes and differences for settlement by arbitration under the auspices of the Regional Centre (Rule 1 and 2 of the KLRC Arbitration Rules). This may be by virtue of a separate agreement or incorporation into the principal contract.

Unlike other institutional arbitrations, the KLRC Arbitration Rules allow for flexibility in the conduct of the proceedings and leaves a wide discretion to the parties to decide on the choice of arbitrators, place of arbitration and the applicability of the procedural rules.

The choice of arbitrators is left to the parties to be appointed in accordance with the UNCITRAL Rules but in the event of failure to appoint a sole arbitrator or the presiding arbitrator in the case of a three member tribunal, the appointment shall be made by a "appointing authority" chosen by the Parties.

Should the parties appoint the Centre as the appointing authority or if none is appointed, the sole or presiding arbitrator shall be appointed by the Centre out of the international panel maintained by the Centre in accordance with Rule 3 of the KLRC Arbitration Rules (pursuant to Articles 6 and 7 of the UNCITRAL Rules).

The names on the international panel have been included based on the recommendation of the appropriate authorities in the respective governments and consist of eminent Jurists, Judges and Diplomats drawn from Asian-African countries and those having close economic ties in the region.

The arbitration may be held in KL or any other place chosen by the parties. Facilities such as sittings of the tribunal, secretarial assistance and interpretation are provided for by the Director (Rule 4 of the KLRC Arbitration Rules). A complete set of records will have to provided by the parties to the arbitrator who in turn shall furnish them to the Director (Rule 5 of the KLRC Arbitration Rules). The centre will thereafter assist in the enforcement of any awards rendered in accordance with Rule 6 of the KLRC Arbitration Rules.

In accordance with Rule 7 and 8 of the KLRC Arbitration Rules and Article 38 and 41 of the UNCITRAL Rules, costs of arbitration including arbitrator fees and expenses reasonably incurred by the Regional Centre and administrative charges shall be borne by the parties in accordance with the award. There are no fixed schedule for fees or charges. The former depend on the complexity of each case, the nature of the dispute, length of hearings and eminence and standing of arbitrators which are fixed after consultation with the arbitrators and parties involved.

Ad hoc arbitrations may also use technical facilities and assistance available at the Regional Centre and charges will be fixed taking into account the expenses incurred by the Centre and its non-profit making character.

Arrangements have been made with other institutions such as the World Bank's International Centre for Settlement of Investment Disputes under which arbitration proceedings under its auspices may be held at the Centre.

Other ADR Methods

D.34 Parties to a contract may nevertheless mutually agree to submit initially to a domestic or internal arbitration forum to settle any disputes or differences arising between them. The conduct of such proceedings will depend on the terms of the contract itself and mediation is normally carried out by parties appointed and agreed to by the parties. There are no mediation institutions as such.

A leading case upholding a domestic arbitration/forum agreement is *Thiagarajah Pooinpatarsan v. Shanmugam Paramsothy* [1990] 2 CLJ 312. In this case, V.-C. George J. held that Statute has cast a prima facie duty on the courts to act upon such agreements.

Certain types of disputes such as International Loan Agreement disputes are invariably settled in accordance with the lending institution's rules while syndicated loan disputes rely on procedures agreed to between the parties.

There are no restrictions for seeking such remedies however, there are often safeguarding provisions whereby the parties may still refer to a proper arbitration institution in the event of failure to reach a compromise or solution. (Legal position as at September 1995.)

Banking and Lending Law

The Banking system in Malaysia is comprised essentially of monetary and non-monetary institutions. Whereas the former consists of institutions whose principal liabilities involve money, namely the Central Bank as the issuing source and the commercial banks as the institutions operating current accounts, the latter consists of institutions such as merchant banks, and finance companies, whose liabilities are accepted to be near money. There are also non-financial intermediaries that are supervised by various government departments and agencies. At the apex of the banking system in Malaysia is Bank Negara, the Central Bank of Malaysia.   **D.35**

Role of the Central Bank of Malaysia (Bank Negara)

Primary Role

Section 4, Central Bank of Malaysia Ordinance 1950 defines the role of Bank Negara as: **D.36**

1. To issue currency and keep reserves safeguarding the value of the currency;
2. To act as a banker and financial adviser/agent to the Government;
3. To promote monetary stability and a sound financial structure; and
4. To influence the credit situation to the advantage of the country.

Subsidiary Role

Bank Negara acts as the medium upon which licensing of financial institutions are effected. For instance, licenses for the licensed institutions, scheduled businesses and representatives are issued by the Minister of Finance only upon the recommendation of Bank Negara. Similarly, all Islamic banks   **D.37** under the Islamic Banking Act 1983 and all insurance companies, under the Insurance Act 1963 and the Takaful Act 1983, are required to obtain a licence from the Minister of Finance upon the recommendation of Bank Negara.

Bank Negara also acts as the supervisory authority of all the other financial institutions that make up the banking system. Since August 1, 1960, the Governor of Bank Negara also acted as the Controller of Foreign Exchange and through an amendment to the Central Bank of Malaysia Ordinance in 1989, the Central Bank was made directly responsible for all exchange matter and ceased to act merely as an agent for the Government. With effect from May 1, 1988, the Governor of Bank Negara also acts as the Director General of Insurance and the Director General of Takaful (the country's Islamic insurance).

Regulatory Regime

D.38 The banking industry is governed by the following legal and regulatory regime:

1. Central Bank of Malaysia Ordinance, 1958;
2. Islamic Banking Act 1983;
3. Banking and Financial Institutions Act 1989 (BAFIA);
4. Essential (Protection of Depositors) Regulations, 1986 enacted under Emergency (Essential Powers) Act 1979;
5. Insurance Act 1963;
6. Takaful Act 1984;
7. Exchange Control Act 1953; and
8. Offshore Banking Act 1990 (and related legislations such as the Offshore Companies Act 1990, the Offshore Insurance Act 1990, Labuan Trust Companies Act 1990, Labuan Business Activity Act 1990 and the Income tax (Amendment) Act 1990.

The main legislation is the BAFIA, which came into force in 1989 replacing the previous Banking Act 1973 and Finance Companies Act 1969. BAFIA represents a consolidated effort to review previous inadequacies in the banking legislations. Under this Act, the Central Bank is empowered to supervise and regulate all institutions involved in deposit-taking, and any form of provision of finance. Institutions licensed and supervised by the act are divided into the following categories:

1. Licensed Institutions, which cover:
   — merchant banks, commercial banks, finance companies, discount houses, money brokers and foreign exchange brokers;
2. Scheduled Institutions and Representatives Offices which cover:
   (a) building credit business (such as development finance institutions, building societies, housing credit institutions);
   (b) credit token business (such as issuers of charge or credit cards, travellers cheques and operators of cash dispensing machines);

(c) development finance business;

(d) factoring business;

(e) leasing business.

3. Non-Scheduled Institutions which cover:

— all other institutions and statutory bodies not included above which engaged in the business of providing finance.

Despite the extensive regulatory regime currently in existence, much guidance and reference is still made to the English common law principles. Section 5(1) of Malaysia's Civil Law Act 1956 reads as follows:

> "In all questions or issues which arise or which have to be decided in the States of West Malaysia other than Malacca and Penang with respect to the law of partnerships, corporations, **banks and banking**, principals and agents, carriers by air, land and sea, marine insurance, average, life and fire insurance, and with respect to mercantile law generally, **the law to be administered shall be the same as would be administered in England in the like case at the date of the coming into force of this Act,** if such question or issue had arisen or had to be decided in England, unless in any case other provision is or shall be made by any written law."

The Civil Law Act came into force in West Malaysia on April 7, 1956 and was extended to the States of Sabah and Sarawak on April 4, 1972. Suffice to say, much of the law on banker-customer relationship, the banker's duty of care, the banker's duty to make inquiries the bank's duty of secrecy and the legal implications entrenched in the myriad of financial services offered by banks to their customers derive essentially from the prevailing common law in England as at 1956. However by virtue of Malaysia's colonial heritage, Malaysian courts of law do continue to draw references and guidance from the common law. (Legal position as at September 1995.)

Consumer Rights in Malaysia

Malaysia does not currently have in place specific enactments pertaining to the protection of consumers' rights. There are however, piecemeal provisions in particular legislations which indirectly addresses consumers' rights and grants limited protection to consumers in specific situations or transactions. There is however a Consumer Protection Bill that is in the process of being drafted by the relevant authorities which, when implemented, ought to go some way towards ensuring the protection of consumers.   **D.39**

Legislations on the Protection of Consumers' Rights

The barrage of existing legislation on consumer protection comprises the following: **D.40**

Malaysia

1. Price Control Act 1946 (revised 1973);
2. Sale of Food and Drugs Ordinance 1952;
3. Housing Developers Act (Control and Licensing Act) 1966;
4. Hire Purchase Act 1967;
5. Weights and Measures Act 1972;
6. Standards and Industrial Research Institute of Malaysia (Incorporation) Act 1975;
7. Trade Descriptions Act 1972; and
8. Contracts Act 1950.

Product Safety and Information Standards

D.41 The Standards and Industrial Research Institute of Malaysia (Incorporation) Act 1975 (SIRIM) established a Council with the main objective of promoting public and industrial welfare, health and safety. The Council is thus active in the formulation of standards for consumer goods.

Goods that are manufactured in Malaysia fall within two categories, namely mandatory products for which a prescribed safety standard needs at all times to be fulfilled and the non-mandatory products for which safety standards are merely prescribed. The scheduled of mandatory goods, consists mainly of electrical goods, crash helmets and safety belts.

Electrical goods that are imported need to be accompanied by a certificate of approval issued by the Director General of the Department of Electrical Inspectorate Malaysia certifying that such goods conform to the Malaysian or British standard. Such requirements are also imposed upon imported seatbelts.

Exclusion of Warranties

D.42 The Hire Purchase Act 1967 and the Sale of Goods Ordinance 1957, provides limited protection to consumers in this area. Section 7 of the Hire Purchase Act 1967 for instance stipulates that every hire purchase agreement shall have:

1. an implied warranty that the hirer shall have and enjoy quiet possession of the goods;
2. an implied condition on the part of the owner that he shall have the right to sell the goods at the time when the property is to pass; and
3. an implied warranty that the goods shall be free from any charge or encumbrance in favour of any third party at the time when the property is to pass.

The section also expressly stipulates an implied condition that the goods are of merchantable quality unless the hirer has examined the goods or a sample thereof for defects and that such examination ought to have revealed defects.

The Sale of Goods Act 1957 provides that in a contract of sale, unless the circumstances of the contract are such so as to reveal a different intention, there is:

1. an implied condition that the seller has the right to sell or will have a right to sell at the time the property is to pass;
2. an implied warranty that the buyer will enjoy quiet possession of the goods; and
3. an implied warranty that the goods shall be free from any charge or encumbrance not declared or known to the buyer before or at the time of the contract.

Regulations on Restraint of Trade

S.28 of the Contracts Act 1950, renders all covenants seeking to restrain   **D.43**
trade, void even if the covenants in question are reasonable. The Malaysian courts has also taken the approach of invoking the doctrine of public policy as embodied in s.24 when they are of the opinion that a covenant is too harsh or onerous.

Various regulations and codes apply to mergers and takeovers so as to safeguard shareholders interests. The formulation of these regulations and codes are prescribed by s.179 of the Companies Act 1965. In mergers, the authorization of the Securities Commission (SC) and the Foreign Investment Committee (FIC) (where applicable) are also required to be obtained in advance.

Malaysian law on these issues are territorial in nature and do not apply to contracts made or performed outside the country unless the contract expressly provides that the laws of Malaysia shall apply. Apart from the above restrictions, there are no controls or regulations existing over contracts relating to exclusive dealings, monopolization, franchising and resale price maintenance.

Review of Unfair Contracts

S.14 of the Contracts Act 1950 endows the courts with the power to review   **D.44**
contracts to ascertain whether there are elements of coercion, undue influence, fraud, misrepresentation or mistake if it were alleged by one of the contracting parties. It is however a moot point as to whether the courts are willing to go so far as to review contracts which are alleged to be unfair or unconscionable. Practice has however shown that Malaysian courts often turn to the English common law for guidance when confronted with a gap in Malaysian law. The principles of the law of equity may thus have some limited application in certain cases.

Laws Governing Advertising and Promotion of Products

The Malaysian Code of Advertising Practice is fundamental to the system of control by which Malaysian advertising is regulated. The Code is voluntary in nature and is maintained by the Advertising Standards Authority of Malaysia.

The Authority comprises representatives from the Advertisers' Association, the Association of Accredited Advertising Agents, the Malaysian Newspaper Publishers Association and the Federation of Malaysia Consumers Association (FOMCA).

The Authority maintains close contact with the central and local government apart from the consumer organizations. It also deals with complaints received and sanctions advertisers that flout the Code by withholding advertising space or time from such advertisers.

In addition to this general control there are also specific controls exerted by specific statutes. For instance, the Trade Description Act 1972 (TDA) prohibits traders from applying a false trade description to any goods or supplies or offers to supply. The TDA also prohibits the importation of goods bearing a false indication of origin. Other legislations are the Food Act 1983 and its regulations which define certain restrictions on the advertisement of infant food products and the Sale of Drugs Act 1952 which delimits the manner in which the sale or advertising of drugs may be carried out.

Organisations Overseeing Consumers' Rights and Protection

D.45 The National Consumer Advisory Council for Consumer Protection, is a statutory body created by an Act of Parliament in 1975 for this specific purpose. The Council comprises members of various Government departments, consumer organizations, chambers of commerce, women's and trade representatives and others. The Council advises a multitude of ministries (where applicable) on consumer protection. For instance the Ministry of Trade and Industry's own Consumer Affairs Division is constantly in liaison with the Council. Various other ministries are also involved in the enforcement of legislation relating to their functions, for example, the Ministry of Health is responsible for the Sales of Foods and Drugs Acts, the Ministry of Housing and Local Government for the Housing Developers Act. These ministries often consult the Council for its views.

In addition to Government linked organisations, Malaysia has a relatively well established Consumers' Association. The first consumers' association in Malaysia was founded in January 1965 in Kuala Lumpur. There is now an association on a voluntary basis in almost every one of the States of the Federation. All the consumers' associations in the country are united under the Federation of Malaysia Consumer Association (FOMCA).

As well as the Consumers' Association, the following facilities also exist to protect consumers' rights:

1. Complaints Bureaux have been set up in all states to enable consumers to make any complaint regarding infringement of their rights.

2. Legal Advisory Clinics staffed by volunteer lawyers, exist to give free advice to consumers on their rights.

3. Consumer Education, set up to increase consumers' understanding through mass media and consumer club activities.

Health, Safety and Environmental Law

Health, Safety and the Environment in Malaysia are placed under the control of the Ministry of Health and the Ministry of Science, Technology and Environment.

D.46

The objective of the Ministry of Health is to raise the health status of Malaysians by providing promotive, preventive, curative and rehabilitative health services. Under the Fifth Malaysian Plan, the Ministry in line with the New Economic Policy is paying particular attention to facilitating the attainment and maintenance by the individual of a standard of health which will enable him to lead a socially and economically productive lifestyle.

The Public Health Programme covers the following activities:

1. personal health;
2. environmental health and food quality control;
3. prevention and control of communicable diseases; and
4. other services.

It is the policy of the Government generally and the Ministry of Health in particular to improve the health delivery system and also to rectify the imbalance in the distribution between the states and between the urban and rural areas of each state. Under the Fifth Malaysian Plan (1986–90) a total of 1,934 projects have been approved and funded for implementation. The development allocation under the Plan stands at RM737.97 million.

The objectives of the Department of the Environment under the Ministry of Science, Technology and Environment, are to enhance and improve the quality of environment, in order to achieve a better quality of life as well as to balance the goals of socio-economic development and environmental control and to promote the efficient and sustainable utilization of natural resources.

The Department of Environment (DEO) has adopted the following strategies:

1. control and prevention of pollution;
2. comprehensive development planning and integrated project planning;
3. environmental education and information; and
4. cooperation and involvement in activities at international and regional levels.

The main legislation is the Environmental Quality Act 1974 (Amendment) 1985 (EQA) and under it various sets of regulations have been formulated to carry out its underlined objectives.

Malaysia

Among the Regulations enforced under the Environmental Quality Act are as follows:

1. Environmental Quality (Clean Air) Regulations 1978;
2. Environmental Quality (Prescribed Premises) (Raw Natural Rubber) Regulations 1978;
3. Environmental Quality (Scheduled Wastes) Regulations 1989;
4. Environmental Quality (Prescribed Premises) (Scheduled Wastes Treatment and Disposal Facilities Order) 1989;
5. Environmental Quality (Prescribed Premises) (Crude Palm-Oil) Regulations 1977;
6. Environmental Quality (Licensing) Regulations 1977;
7. Environmental Quality (Prescribed Activities); (Environmental Impact Assessment) Order 1987;
8. Environmental Quality (Motor Vehicle Noise) Regulations 1987;
9. Environmental Quality (Sewage and Industrial Effluent) Regulations 1979;
10. Environmental Public Health (Public Cleansing) Regulations 1970; and
11. Environmental Public Health (Food Establishments) Regulations 1973.

Enforcement

Air Pollution Control

D.47   Air pollution is one of the environmental problems of great concern to Malaysia. In 1990 the Department of Environment with the cooperation of the Traffic Police conducted inspection of black smoke emission on 32,207 motor vehicles. A total of 6,292 drivers were summoned under the Motor Vehicles (Control of Smoke and Gas Emission) Rules 1977.

Water Pollution Control

To date, efforts on water pollution control are focused on the control of effluent discharges through the Environmental Quality (Sewage and Industrial Effluent) Regulations 1979. In 1990, a total of 88 formal samplings of industrial effluent were conducted during enforcement visits to the industries.

Noise Pollution Control

In 1990, 24 enforcement campaigns on noise emission from motorcycles were conducted throughout Peninsular Malaysia. From the campaigns about 391 motorcycles were tested and 211 were summoned for not complying with the standard stipulated under the Environmental Quality (Motor Vehicle Noise) Regulations 1987.

General

Out of 931 factories inspected under the Environmental Quality Act 1974 in 1990, a total of 19 factories were prosecuted, 416 were compounded and 540 were given warnings/directives for violating various Regulations.

Environmental Quality Act 1974

S.34A of the EQA also makes provision for an Environmental Impact As-   **D.48** sessment (EIA) to be carried out and submitted to the DEO for review, prior to the approval of projects or activities that may have a significant environmental impact. These activities are classified as "prescribed activities". Contravention of this provision would attract a fine not exceeding RM10,000 or an imprisonment up to two years or both. The offender is also liable to a further fine of RM1,000 for everyday that the offence is continued after he has been served with a notice from the Director-General of the Department of Environment requiring him to comply with the act. A statutory duty is thus placed upon the industrial sector to observe basic requirements for pollution control in the country.

The Environmental Quality (Prescribed Activities) (Environmental Impact Assessment) Order 1987 that was enacted pursuant to s.34A, classified 19 areas as "prescribed activities". The prescribed activities cover the following areas:

1. Agricultural;
2. Airport;
3. Drainage and irrigation;
4. Land reclamation;
5. Fisheries;
6. Forestry;
7. Housing;
8. Industry;
9. Infrastructure;
10. Ports;
11. Mining;
12. Petroleum;
13. Power generation and transmission;
14. Quarries;
15. Railways;
16. Transportation;
17. Resort and recreational development;
18. Waste treatment and disposal; and
19. Water supply.

In 1990 a total of 113 EIA reports were reviewed by the Department of Environment where 47 reports were approved and 15 rejected.

Another Act which concerns the environment and public health is the Environmental Public Health Act 1987.

In 1994 an Occupational, Safety and Health Act was enacted in order to make further provisions for securing the safety, health and welfare of persons at work. It is also meant to protect others against risks to safety or health in connection with the activities of persons at work. The Act also leads to the establishment of the National Council for Occupational Safety and Health and for matters connected therewith.

Under the Factories and Machinery Act 1967, several regulations were enacted concerning the safety of the workers such as the following:

1. Factories & Machinery (Safety, Health and Welfare) Regulations 1970;
2. Factories and Machinery (Building Operation and works on Engineering Construction (Safety)) Regulations 1986; and
3. Factories and Machinery (Fencing of Machinery & Safety) Regulations 1983.

Foreign Investment Law

D.49 On the whole, foreign investment is welcomed by the Malaysian government. The NEP, superseded by the NDP, aims at restructuring the ownership and control of companies and businesses in Malaysia to achieve a more balanced participation by Malaysian in the economic activities in the country.

The Malaysian Government imposes different restrictions on foreign ownership of business and companies depending whether manufacturing activities are undertaken by the businesses or companies.

A manufacturing licence is required from MITI if a company or business carries on manufacturing activities. Otherwise, or additionally, it might also have to comply with the FIC Guidelines.

In the following situations, a joint venture will require both the approval of MITI and the FIC:

1. shares in manufacturing companies are acquired in consideration of a transfer of shares;
2. a licensed manufacturing company acquires a non-manufacturing company by a transfer of shares;
3. companies (not being licensed manufacturing companies) which either carry out manufacturing activities or whose subsidiary is a licensed manufacturing company acquires a non-manufacturing company by a transfer of shares;
4. there is an acquisition of a manufacturing company exempted from licensing requirements under the Industrial Coordination Act 1975 (the ICA).

Regulation by MITI

The ICA requires any person undertaking a manufacturing activity to obtain **D.50** a licence from MITI in respect of the premises on which such activity is carried out. Manufacturers with fewer than 75 employees and less than RM2.5 million in shareholders' funds are exempted.

The issue of licences by MITI are invariably accompanied by conditions which imposes foreign ownership restrictions and requires further MITI approval prior to the transfer of any foreign-held shares. Foreign parties may typically hold between 30 and 70 per cent of shares, exceptionally up to 100 per cent. Royalty rates to be paid by a manufacturing joint venture to the technology providing foreign joint venture party also requires MITI approval. Royalty rates range from 1 per cent to 5 per cent of net sales and the presumed duration for sufficient full absorption of technology of five years if preferred in any technological assistance agreements.

Control of Foreign Investors

The Foreign Investment Committee in the Prime Minister's Department is **D.51** responsible for the implementation of the FIC Guidelines. The Guidelines are non-statutory, having been made to give effect to the NEP, as superceded by the NDP, which represents the national policy of the country.

The functions of the FIC are:

1. to formulate policy guidelines on foreign investment in all sectors of the economy to ensure the fulfilment of the objectives of the NDP set up by the government;
2. to monitor the progress and help resolve problems relating to foreign private investment and to recommend suitable investment policies;
3. to supervise and advise Ministries and government agencies concerned on all matters concerning foreign investment;
4. to coordinate and regulate the acquisition of assets or interests or mergers and take-overs of companies and businesses in Malaysia; and
5. to monitor, assess and evaluate the form, extent and conduct of foreign investment in the country and to maintain comprehensive information on foreign investment.

The FIC Guidelines apply specifically to the following situations for which the approval of the FIC is required:

1. any proposed acquisition by foreign interests of any substantial fixed assets in Malaysia;
2. any proposed acquisition of assets or any interests, mergers and take-overs of companies and businesses in Malaysia by any means, which will result in ownership or control passing to foreign interests;
3. any proposed acquisition of 15 per cent or more of the voting power by any one foreign interest or associated group, or by foreign interests

in the aggregate of 30 per cent or more of the voting power of a Malaysian company and business;

4. control of Malaysian companies and businesses through any form of joint-venture agreement, management agreement and technical assistance agreement and other arrangement;

5. any merger or take-over of any company or business in Malaysia whether by Malaysian or foreign interests; and

6. any other proposed acquisition of assets or interests exceeding in value RM5 million whether by Malaysian or foreign interests.

The Guidelines do not apply to projects specifically approved by the government such as acquisitions by Ministries and government departments.

The permitted equity proportion to be held by foreign interests varies depending on factors such as whether the industry type is one encouraged under Malaysian economic policy and the proportion of products to be exported.

For the promotion of the hotel and tourism industry, 100 per cent ownership is allowed for five years after which the company is required to restructure with at least 49 per cent ownership held by Malaysians, including 30 per cent being reserved for *bumiputeras*. (Legal position as at September 1995.)

Tax Law

D.52 At the time of going to press, the next Malaysian Parliamentary Budget Session was expected to bring significant changes in legislation governing Malaysian taxation, particularly with regard to Labuan as an offshore financial center.

For this reason, it was decided by the publishers and contributors that this area of Malaysian law should not be discussed in this chapter.

Intellectual Property Law in Malaysia

D.53 Intellectual property law is the branch of law that attempts to safeguard the rights of creators and other originators of intellectual product.

In recent years, there has been an increase in awareness and activity in the area of intellectual property law in Malaysia. In Malaysia, protection of patents, trade marks and copyrights are governed by statutes whereas registered designs are governed by the laws of United Kingdom. On the other hand, confidential information and trade secrets are protected under common law.

Patents

Patent law is a law designed to confer a monopoly on the creator of a   **D.54**
novel invention. In Malaysia, protection of patent rights is accorded through
registration under the Patents Act 1983 (hereinafter referred to as the 1983
Act).

Conditions of Patentability

Under the 1983 Act, invention is defined as an idea of an inventor which
permits in practice the solution to a specific problem in the field of technology. An invention is patentable if it is new, involves an inventive step and is
industrially applicable and may relate to a product or a process. An invention
is said to be new if it is not anticipated by prior art. The requirement for
an "inventive step" is designed to keep out pedestrian improvements or
obvious extensions to known products or process and an invention is considered as involving an inventive step if it would not have been obvious to a
skilled person in the art having regard to the prior act. An invention is
considered as industrially applicable if it can be made or used in any kind of
industry. However, the Act expressly excludes, the following inventions
notwithstanding that they may come within the meaning of invention of the
Act.

(a) discoveries, scientific theories and mathematical methods;
(b) plant or animal varieties or essentially biological processes for the
production of plants or animals, other than man-made living microorganisms, micro-biological processes and the products of such
micro-organism processes;
(c) schemes, rules or methods for doing business, performing purely
mental acts or playing games;
(d) methods for the treatment of human or animal body by surgery or
therapy, and diagnostic methods practised on the human or animal
body:
Provided that this paragraph shall not apply to products used in
any such methods.

Registration Procedure, Grant of and Duration of Patent

Registration is essential to patent protection under the 1983 Act. An application for patent registration is made to the Registrar and the said application
must comply with and contain the information as laid down in the Patents
Regulation 1986.

If the Registrar is satisfied with an application as having complied with all
the conditions of patentability and formalities, he shall forthwith grant the
patent by issuing a certificate to the patent owner.

The duration of the patent is 15 years and is subject to payment of annual
renewal fees.

Malaysia

The Rights of Patent Owner and Infringements

The patent owner shall have the exclusive rights to exploit, assign or transmit, and conclude license contracts in respect to the patent.

Exploitation of a patented invention is the doing of any of the following acts:

1. when the patent is granted for a product, the making, importing, offering for sale, selling, or using: or stocking the product for sale or offer to sell, selling or using;
2. when the patent is granted for a process, using the process: or doing any of the acts referred to in paragraph (a) in respect of a product obtained directly by means of the patented process.

The patent owner may licence another person to do any or all of the acts referred to above.

Performance of any acts referred to above, without consent from the owner and subject to other provisions of the 1983 Act, is an infringement of the rights of the owner. The patent owner has a right to institute High Court proceedings against any person who has infringed or is infringing the patent, and also against any person who has performed acts which make it likely that an infringement will occur. The remedies available to the patent owner are injunctions to prevent further infringement and an award of damages. However, proceedings against infringement may not be instituted after five years from the infringing act.

Utility Innovations

Malaysia has a two-tier system in that the law also provides for a petty patent or a utility model system of protection which is called "utility innovation" system. The purpose of having such a system is to enable those inventions which would otherwise fail to qualify for a full patent, to get a lesser degree of protection. Therefore, a lower level of inventive step is required, *i.e.* "any innovation which creates a new product or process, or any new improvements of a known product or process, which can be made or used in any kind of industry, and includes an invention" would qualify for a utility innovation certificate of grant.

A utility innovation certificate has an initial term of five years which is extendible by two consecutive terms of five years each if the proprietor is able to satisfy the Registrar that the innovation is still in industrial or commercial use in Malaysia.

Copyrights

D.55   Copyright law in Malaysia is governed by the Copyright Act 1987 as amended by the Copyright (Amendment) Act 1990. The Act provides that no copyright shall subsist otherwise than by virtue of the Act. Please note that amendments have been made to the Act via the Copyright Amendment Act A952 of 1996 but these amendments have not yet come into force.

The Scope and the Duration of Protection

Copyright may subsist in the following works:

1. literary works;
2. musical works;
3. artistic works;
4. films;
5. sound recordings; and broadcasts.

Works coming within any of the above categories are eligible for copyright protection but they must satisfy the requirement of originality, that is sufficient effort must has been expended to make the expression of the work original in character. A work which is "copied" from another work is not original, but a work which is based on the same idea can be original as long as the expression of the work is different. Since copyright law protects the expression of ideas and not the ideas itself, there is an added requirement that the work should have been written down, recorded or otherwise reduced to material form. However, once the work eligible for copyright is reduced in its material form, the copyright in it automatically vests on the originator of the work, unlike in the case of a patent where no right subsists on the owner until a formal grant of patent.

Malaysia, being a member of the Berne Convention for the Protection of Literary and Artistic Works 1986, has a very wide scope of copyright protection that goes beyond the national borders.

The general rule is that copyright will subsist during the life of the author and fifty years after his/her death. However, works which have not been published before the death of the author remains to be protected under copyright and the fifty years will only start to run from its first publication.

The Rights of Copyright Owner and Infringements

Copyright is the exclusive right to control in Malaysia the following in respect of the whole work or a substantial part thereof, either in its original or derivative form:

1. the reproduction in any material form;
2. the communication to the public;
3. the broadcasting;
4. the communication by cable; and
5. the distribution to the public.

However, the right to control does not include the right to control the doing of the above acts by way of fair dealing for purposes of non-profit research, private study, criticism, review or the reporting of current events, provided there is sufficient acknowledgement.

Infringement of copyright is actionable in the civil courts at the suit of the owner of the copyright. Reliefs available include damages, injunctions which include Anton Pillar Orders, an account of profits and other similar reliefs. In the case of exclusive licence, the exclusive licensee shall enjoy the same rights of action and be entitled to the same remedies as the owner.

On the other hand, statutory enforcement of copyright is undertaken by the Enforcement division of the Ministry of Domestic Trade and Consumer Affairs and the Police. Certain prescribed criminal offenses together with penalty are specified for the doing of certain acts in relation to works that are still protected under copyright when the act is committed.

Trade Marks

D.56 Trade Marks law in Malaysia is governed by the Trade Marks Act 1976 as recently amended by the Trade Marks (Amendment) Act 1994 (which is not yet in force).

A trade mark is a mark (which must be one of the following: a device, brand, heading label, ticket, name, signature, word, letter, numeral or any combination thereof) that is used to indicate the origin of the goods and therefore enables the customers to link the goods with the manufacturer, origin or source of the goods and consequently link with his/her own personal expectations as to the quality of those goods.

The purpose of regulating the use of trade marks is to prevent unfair exploitations of the already-established goodwill and reputation associated with a particular trade mark and to prevent confusion and deception.

Registration and the Duration of Trade Marks

Registration under the Act is essential in order to obtain protection in relation to one's trade mark. The requirements for registration are as follows:

1. it must be a "mark" within the definition of the Act;
2. there must be a connection with the course of trade between the proprietor and the goods;
3. there is a use in relation to the goods;
4. the mark indicates the trade origins of the goods;
5. the mark must acquire some distinctiveness.

However, registration of a trade mark is not permissible if:

1. its use is likely to deceive or cause confusion to the public or would be contrary to law; and
2. it contains or comprises any scandalous or offensive matter or would otherwise not be entitled to protection by any court of law.

A successful application will entitle the applicant of the particular trade mark to be entered in the Register as proprietor of the said trade mark. The duration of trade mark protection originally is seven years and is renewable for subsequent periods of 14 years. However, under the Amendment Act, the duration of protection is now 10 years and is renewable for subsequent periods of 10 years.

The Rights of a Trade Mark Proprietor and Infringement

The registered proprietor of trade mark has the exclusive right to use the trade mark in relation to goods and services registered subject to any conditions, amendments, modifications or limitations in the Register.

A registered trade mark is able to be assigned and transmitted with or without goodwill of the business concerned in the goods bearing the registered trade mark. In addition, the registered proprietor has the right to give permission for any person to become a registered user of a registered trade mark owned by the registered proprietor but it is for the Registrar to determine the duration of the registered use.

A registered trade mark is infringed by any person, not being the registered proprietor or registered user by way of permitted use, who uses an identical or closely resembling mark which is likely to deceive or cause confusion in the course of trade in relation to goods bearing the registered trade mark. Such an infringement entitles the registered proprietor to institute a civil action in the High Court and remedies available to him include injunctions, damages and costs. Criminal prosecution is carried out by the Enforcement Division of the Ministry of Domestic Trade and Consumer Affairs under the Trade Description Act 1972 for alleged false trade description through the wrong use of a trade mark. A Trade Description Order may be obtained from the High Court under the Act to assert such trade mark rights.

Service Marks and Unregistered Trade Marks

The Trade Marks (Amendment) Act 1994 enables the registration of service marks as well. The registration for such service makes is more or less similar to that of trade marks. The Amendment Act is due to be proclaimed into force by late 1996.

Unregistered trade marks, on the other hands, are protected under the common law of passing off and there is no pre-condition of registration for a valid cause of action in passing off. However, case law has laid down five characteristics that must be present for a valid cause of action, which are:

1. a misrepresentation,
2. made by a trader in the course of trade,
3. to prospective customers of his or ultimate consumers of goods or services supplied by him,
4. which is calculated to injure the business or goodwill of another trader (in the sense that this is a reasonably foreseeable consequence) and

5. which causes actual damage to a business or goodwill of the trader by whom the action is brought or (in a *qua timet* action) will probably do so.

The protection under the law of passing off is wider than the statutory protection for registered trade mark in that it covers not only trade marks but also distinguished features such as get-up, packing and any other conduct tending to associate the plaintiff's business with that of the defendant.

Industrial Designs

D.57   Malaysia has recently gazetted an Act that will regulate industrial designs, namely the Industrial Design Act 1996. However, this Act has not yet come into force and at present, Malaysia is still depending on the laws of the United Kingdom for the protection of industrial designs in Malaysia.

To obtain protection in Malaysia, a design must be registered under the laws of the United Kingdom. Once it is registered under the United Kingdom Registered Designs Act 1949, the registered proprietor of a design shall enjoy in Malaysia all the like privileges and rights as if the Certificate of Registration issued in United Kingdom had extended its operation in Malaysia.

Design is defined as any feature of any shape, configuration, pattern or ornament applied to an article by any industrial process or means, being features which in the finished article appeal to and are judged by the eye. Such design is only registrable if it is new in the patent sense; that is, it is must be original and novel and must not be the same as any design which before the date of application has been registered or published.

In the case of infringement, the registered proprietor has the right to institute High Court proceedings for injunction, damages and costs. Damages are not available if the defendant can prove that he was unaware of the infringement and had no means of making himself aware at the date of infringement that the design has been registered, although an injunction can still be applied for. In view of this, it is advisable that the registered proprietor should publish in Malaysian newspapers about the fact of registration of the designs in the United Kingdom.

Confidential Information and Trade Secrets

D.58   There is no legislative provision for protecting confidential information and trade secrets. As a result, this area of law is still governed by the common law under breach of confidence.

Any information that is derived through a position of confidence can be classified as confidential information and the breach of confidence law attempts to prevent any person in such a position of confidence to reveal the confidential information. Trade secrets are but part of confidential information and can be defined as confidential information of a commercial character.

Case law has laid down certain requirements for an action on breach of confidence to succeed, namely:

1. the information must have the necessary quality of confidence about it; in this connection,
   (a) the information must be information the release of which the owner believes will be injurious to him or of advantage to his rivals/others,
   (b) the owner must believe that the information is confidential,
   (c) the owner's belief under (a) or (b) must be reasonable;
2. the information must have been imparted in circumstances importing an obligation of confidence;
3. there must be an unauthorised use of that information to the detriment of the party communicating it.

A successful action in breach of confidence will entitle the plaintiff to equitable remedies.

Notes

1. *Song Bok Yoong v. Ho Kim Poui* [1968] 1 MLJ 56.
2. s.26 of the Contracts Act 1950 (Revised 1974).
3. *Tan Soh Sim, Chan Law Keong v. Tan Saw Keow* (1951) 17 MLJ 21.
4. *J.M. Wotherspoon & Co v. Henry Agency House* (1962) MLJ 86.
5. *Phang Swee Kim v. Beh I Hock* (1964) MLJ 383.
6. s.2(d) of the Contracts Act 1950.
7. *Kepong Prospecting Ltd and S.K. Jagatheesan v. A.E. Schmidt* (1968) 1 MLJ 170.
8. s.2(d) of the Contracts Act 1950.
9. *Ibid.* s.64.
10. s.11 of the Contracts Act 1950.
11. *Ibid.* s.10(2).
12. *Ibid.* s.19.
13. *Ibid.* s.24.
14. *Ibid.* s.26.
15. *Ibid.* s.27.
16. *Ibid.* s.28.
17. *Ibid.* s.29.
18. *Ibid.* s.30.
19. *Ibid.* s.31.
20. *Ibid.* s.66.
21. *Ibid.* s.140.
22. *Ibid.* s.149.
23. *Ibid.* s.142.
24. *Ibid.* s.138.
25. Contracts Act 1950, ss.164–178.
26. *Ibid.* s.8.

[27] *Ibid.* ss.154–163.
[28] Partnership Act 1961 (Revised 1974), s.3.
[29] *Ibid.* s.4.
[30] *Ibid.* s.26.
[31] *Ibid.* ss.30–32.
[32] *Ibid.* s.38. *Re Siew Inn Steamship Co.* [1934] MLJ 180.
[33] *Ibid.* ss.34–37.
[34] Sale of Goods (Malay States) Ordinance 1957, s.14
[35] *Ibid.* s.15.
[36] *Ibid.* s.16.
[37] *Ibid.* s.17.
[38] Hire Purchase Act 1967 (Revised 1978), s.9.
[39] *Ibid.* s.10.
[40] *Ibid.* s.11.
[41] *Ibid.* s.12.
[42] *Ibid.* s.13.
[43] *Ibid.* s.14.
[44] *Ibid.* s.15.
[45] *Ibid.* s.16.
[46] *Ibid.* s.17.
[47] *Ibid.* s.18.
[48] *Ibid.* s.19.
[49] Insurance Act 1996, s.152(1).
[50] *Ibid.* s.152(2).
[51] *Kathirvelu v. Pacific @ Orient Insurance Co. Sdn. Bhd.* [1990] 3 MLJ 312.
[52] Insurance Act 1996, s.147(1).
[53] *Ibid.* s.149(4).
[54] Bills Of Exchange Act 1949, s.23.
[55] *Ibid.* s.21(1).
[56] *Ibid.* s.48.
[57] *Ismail v. Abdul Aziz* [1955] 3 M.C. 52.
[58] s.4, Securities Industry Act 1983.
[59] s.15, SIA 1983.
[60] s.8, SIA 1983.
[61] s.8, SIA, 1983.

PEOPLE'S REPUBLIC OF CHINA

Preston M. Torbert and Jia Zhao

I. Summary of Business and Political Conditions

Basic Demographic, Political and Economic Information

The spectacular changes in China's economy in the last 15 years are reflected   E.01
in the challenges and achievements in the development of China's commercial law. China's policy of opening to the outside and transforming its domestic economy have required fundamental changes in China's commercial law. Essentially, these changes reflect the two major areas of focus of reform in China: China's foreign economic relations and its domestic economic structure.

As China began its current reform process in 1978, it had a socialist planned economy modeled on that of the Soviet Union. Although China's economy was much less centralized and planned than the Soviet economy, in comparison with Western market economies it was still characterized by a high degree of planning, state ownership and limited foreign trade with non-socialist economies. The challenge for China initially was how to reform this system to increase productivity and participate in the world economy.

While the process of reform is not yet complete, it can certainly be said that so far China has achieved a high degree of success. China's policy has been to implement reform both in its domestic business law and its foreign-related business law at the same time. This has resulted in the evolution of two separate legal and tax systems that have co-existed over the last 15 years. In the domestic economy, China encouraged the development of individual entrepreneurship and cooperative enterprises, as well as small scale private enterprises, and implemented price reforms that abolished state-set prices for many commodities. In the foreign sector, China allowed joint ventures, and

279

then wholly foreign owned enterprises, first in manufacturing, then in a broader range of activities including the service industries. Since China's domestic economy was still dominated by state-owned enterprises, the corporate, contract and tax legislation applicable to these enterprises was not appropriate for foreign invested enterprises. Therefore, China established two separate legal systems for domestic and foreign investment entities. The creation of these two different systems, while unusual, has worked well. The new legislation over the last 15 years has allowed China to effectively implement reform in both of these sectors.

A major challenge for the further development of China's commercial law and business environment, is the merger of these two systems. As China's economy moves closer to a market economy — "socialist market economy" — it appears that the legal framework for the domestic sector will become more similar to that for the foreign invested sector. Specifically, as noted below, China has recently introduced a new company law that provides for corporate structures similar to those for existing foreign invested enterprises and to those in the Western market economies. China has also introduced a variety of new taxes, including a value added tax similar to that in many European countries. China's contract law for transactions between domestic enterprises was also recently revised to adjust to the greater role that the market, rather than the plan, plays in the domestic economy. While additional steps still need to be taken, particularly in the area of tax legislation, China appears to be moving relatively quickly towards the unification of the legal bases for these two separate economic systems. Unification of these two legal regimes is a necessary prerequisite to the development of an integrated market economy.

Potential foreign investors should understand the tremendous changes China has undergone and is undergoing, but they should not overlook aspects of China's past that continue to affect the current business and legal environment. Specifically, in considering the prospects and evaluating the risks of doing business in China, foreign investors should take into account the following factors:

E.02   First, as noted above, China is changing from a socialist to a market economy. Over the last 15 years, China has moved from a "socialist planned economy", to a "socialist commodity economy", to a "socialist market economy". But this transition is not yet complete and many attitudes and institutions reflecting the planned economy still survive. Furthermore, China's "socialist" market economy is not a "capitalist" market economy. Although the cooperative and private sectors are growing rapidly, state-owned enterprises still play the largest role in the economy and are the most likely contracting partners for foreign companies doing business in China.

Secondly, although China has opened its economy to foreign trade and investment since 1979, significant restrictions remain. Foreign investment in the form of joint ventures or wholly foreign-owned enterprises was originally seen as an exception to a socialist economy characterized by widespread state ownership. Foreign investment is still seen as exceptional and is restricted to certain areas of the economy. While China is still continuing to open further to foreign investment, it is doing so at its own pace. The first question for any foreign company considering doing business in China is whether all its proposed activities are permitted by current Chinese law and policy.

Thirdly, as China moves ahead with its opening to the outside and its reform of the domestic economy and the related unification of the two separate economic systems, one of its greatest challenges will be the need for greater transparency. China's reform of its foreign economic relations has been very successful in no small part due to the greater transparency that it has provided to foreign investors over the last 15 years. Over this period, China's foreign related legislation has become considerably clearer and more detailed. This has allowed foreign investors to understand the legal basis for their investments in joint ventures and wholly owned foreign enterprises in China, and to evaluate more effectively the risks involved in investing in China. This has also permitted foreign parties to discern clearly the rights that they and their enterprises enjoy in China. China has significantly reduced the amount of "internal" (*i.e.* secret) legislation applicable to foreign economic relations, both trade and investment. Nevertheless, foreign investors are still concerned that, in certain cases, unpublished rules or policy may determine important aspects of their own activities or those of their foreign invested enterprises in China. China can reassure them by ensuring that unwritten law or policy do not take precedence over published law.

Fourthly, China faces a challenge in enforcing its new legislation. The effort to reform the economy and commercial legal system and to move closer to international practice in many areas of the law will not succeed if the numerous new laws and regulations remain mere scraps of paper. The foreign investment China needs for its further modernization will not come if foreign investors cannot rest assured that the contracts they sign will be enforced in accordance with objective procedures. Contract cancellations, such as these involving Japanese and German companies for the Baoshan steel complex in the 1980s and those involving U.S. securities firms for trading in derivatives in 1994, indicate that the sanctity of contract is not always respected in China. Unsuccessful efforts to enforce foreign arbitration awards (under the 1958 New York Convention on the Enforcement of Foreign Arbitral Awards) and the widespread violation of intellectual property rights that resulted in a recent special agreement to enforce such rights between the United States and China have raised serious doubts in the minds of potential foreign investors about the effectiveness of the new legislation which China has enacted since 1978. China can help to reassure them by effectively implementing and enforcing its legislation.

As China has undergone the transformation from a "socialist planned economy" to a "socialist market economy" and opened previously restricted areas to foreign investment, opportunities for doing business have increased considerably. It seems likely that this trend will continue in the future as E.03

China's policy and legal framework for doing business move closer to general international norms.

The opportunities, however, are commensurate with the risks. China has indeed made tremendous progress in the last 15 years in establishing a legislative basis for foreign investment and a legal system to uphold the rule of law. But the past weighs heavily on China's progress. Although the pace of China's development has been extremely rapid, much remains to be done before China's legal environment approximates that of many developed or some developing countries. Traditional attitudes and a lack of resources mean that it is easier to promulgate new laws than to vigorously enforce them.

Accordingly, while foreign companies will find many attractive opportunities in what is arguably the world's largest market, they will want to pay particular attention to protecting their interests to the maximum through careful planning based on a full appreciation and understanding of the rapidly changing legal environment for doing business there. It is hoped that this volume will assist in this effort.

II. Laws and Institutions Affecting Business and Commercial Activities

Competition Law

E.04   As China makes the transition from a planned economy to a market economy, more and more economic entities are gaining independence and freedom to participate in market competition. This competition does not necessarily mean fair competition. Counterfeiting of trademarks and goods, false publicity, infringements of patents, unauthorized use of unpatented technology and trade secrets, local blockades, and other unfair competitive practices are common. Thus, preventing unfair competition was the first step the Chinese legislative authorities took to establish a competition law framework in China. The second step in China's competition legislation, the anti-trust law, is still in the drafting stage.

Since 1980, China has adopted a number of regulations concerning competition, such as the 1980 Provisional Regulations on Development and Protection of Socialist Competition, the 1987 Regulations on Administration of Advertising, certain provisions in the Economic Contract Law, Patent Law, Trademark Law, Consumer Right Protection Law, etc. Some local authorities also made their local rules, such as in Wuhan Municipality, Shanghai Municipality and Jiangxi Province. In 1993, a National Statute, Law of the People's Republic of China Against Unfair Competition (the "Unfair

Competition Law" or the "Law"), was promulgated and became effective on December 1, 1993. It is the most important of China's competition legislation.

Scope of Application

The purpose of the Unfair Competition Law is to ensure the sound develop- E.05
ment of the socialist market economy, to encourage and safeguard fair competition, to prevent unfair competition practices, and to protect the lawful rights and interests of business operators and consumers. The term "unfair competition" is defined by the Law as the "practices of business operators that violate the provisions of this law by injuring the lawful rights and interests of other business operators and disrupting the social and economic order". All business operators are required to observe the basic market trading principles of voluntariness, equality, fairness, honesty and trustworthiness and to abide by generally accepted business ethics. "Business operators" that are subject to the Law are defined as legal persons, other economic organizations, and individuals engaged in product operations or in providing services for profit. These include foreign invested enterprises in China. One question that arises is whether, in certain circumstances, government agencies should also be considered as subject to the Law. They are not legal persons or economic organizations under the General Principles of Civil Code, and the definition in the Law of "business operators" does not specifically include government agencies. It seems likely therefore that government agencies are not generally covered by the Law.

Nevertheless, the Unfair Competition Law does contain some provisions restricting certain behavior of government agencies. Article 7, for example, provides that governments and their subordinate departments may not abuse their administrative powers by restricting other parties from purchasing the products of their designated business operators, by restricting the fair business activities of other business operators, or by restricting the entry of commodities from elsewhere into the local market or outflow of local commodities to other markets. It can be argued that government agencies may engage in unfair competition acts under the Unfair Competition Law because any restrictive acts taken by government agencies can affect fair competition. Further, the Unfair Competition Law, in the absence of other anti-trust legislation, could be considered a necessary measure to prevent government abuse and excessive intervention in market competition activities. Currently, the provisions in the Unfair Competition Law are not sufficient for this purpose because in China political power is still tightly linked to economic power.

Unfair Competition Practices

The unfair competition practices prohibited under the Law include trade- E.06
mark and name infringement, improper sales practices, trade secret infringe-

ment, public utilities monopoly, and other improper practices. Trademark and name infringement is possibly the most common unfair competition practice in China now, which includes "passing off" one's trademark as the registered trademark of another party; unauthorized use of the name, packaging, or trade dress unique to well-known products or use of a name, packaging or trade dress similar to that of well-known products; unauthorized use of the enterprise name or personal name of another party; counterfeiting of or unauthorized use of identification marks, marks indicating good quality products and other quality marks on products, falsification of place of origin or making false statements on product quality that mislead people. Consistent with Chinese Trademark Law, the Unfair Competition Law provides no protection for unregistered trademarks. The Law does not state to what degree a product can be considered as a "well-known" product nor does it mention the protection of the unregistered name, packaging and trade dress of a product not well-known.

Improper sales practices include various acts such as bribery, false publicity, below-cost sales, and certain prize sales. Granting or accepting secret off-the-book rebates will be treated as having given or accepted bribes. In the sale or purchase of products, business operators are allowed to grant aboveboard discounts to the other party, to pay commissions to middlemen, or to receive discounts and commissions, but they must book the same strictly according to the facts. Business operators shall not make false statements through advertising or by other means regarding the quality, composition, capabilities, uses, producers, validity period, and place of origin of products. They are also prohibited from selling products below cost for the purpose of forcing out competitors except for:

1. sales of fresh or live products;
2. disposal of products whose period of validity will soon expire or other overstocked products;
3. seasonal price reductions, or
4. sale of products at reduced price to settle debts, to shift to another product line or to close business.

Business operators may not tie the sale of a product to the sale of other products or attach other unreasonable conditions against the purchaser's wishes. Also, they may not conduct any prize sale which involves:

1. lying about the prize or deliberately letting internal personnel win the prize or resorting to other deceptive means;
2. resorting to the use of prizes to promote sales of expensive goods of poor quality, or
3. giving a highest prize exceeding RMB 5,000 when using the draw-prize method in prize sales.

E.07   Before promulgation of the Law, protection of trade secrets was one of the issues foreign investors were most concerned with. The term "trade secrets" is defined in the Law as technical information and business information which is of practical value, is unknown to the public, can bring economic benefits to the owner of the trade secrets, and for which the owner has adopted measures to maintain its confidentiality. A business operator will be deemed to have infringed trade secrets if it: (a) has obtained the trade secrets by theft, enticement by promises of gain, duress or other improper methods; (b) divulges, uses or allows others to use the trade secrets obtained by the above methods, or (c) divulges, uses or allows others to use the trade secrets in its possession, where such is in breach of an agreement or contrary to a confidentiality requirement. A third party will also be deemed to have infringed the trade secrets for obtaining, using or disclosing the trade secrets of others if it knows or should know of the above illegal conduct.

The only provision in the Unfair Competition Law that restricts monopoly is Article 6, which provides that public utilities, enterprises or other business operators that occupy a monopoly position under law may not restrict other parties from purchasing the products of their designated business operators in order to force out fair competition of other business operators. The Law also prohibits business operators from fabricating and spreading false information to injure the reputations of competitors or their products, and from any conspiracy in the submission or invitation of tenders.

Liability and Enforcement

Violation of the Unfair Competition Law results in three types of liabilities: **E.08** civil, administrative, and criminal liabilities. Business operators who have caused the injured business operators to suffer loss should pay damages. If the loss is difficult to calculate, the amount of damages will be the profits derived from the infringement by the infringing business operator during the infringement. The infringing business operator will also bear the reasonable costs paid by the injured party in investigation of the infringement. Administrative sanctions, which are imposed on every unfair competition practice, include fines of various amounts, orders to cease illegal acts, confiscation of illegal income and revocation of business license. Business operators who have committed serious violations in infringing registered trademarks, bribery, and selling counterfeit or substandard products will be criminally prosecuted.

The Unfair Competition Law can be enforced through two channels: the judicial system and the administrative system. It is worth noting that besides the formal judicial system, the administration for industry and commerce plays an important role in the fight against unfair competition. The county level offices of this administration have the authority to supervise, inspect and investigate the business conduct by business operators and to issue and enforce administrative sanctions.

People's Republic of China

Contract Law

E.09   Currently, China's contract legislation contains a two-tier system in dealing with domestic and foreign-related contractual transactions in accordance with the Economic Contract Law of the People's Republic of China ("Economic Contract Law") and the Foreign-Related Economic Contract Law ("Foreign Contract Law"). While the Economic Contract Law which was originally promulgated in 1981 formed the basis for the general provisions on contract law in domestic transactions, the Foreign Contract Law which became effective on July 1, 1985 is the major legislation that interests foreign parties doing business with Chinese entities. It should be noted, however, that a unified contract law is being drafted by the National People's Congress of the People's Republic of China, which, by replacing the Economic Contract Law and the Foreign Contract Law, would apply to both domestic and foreign-related contractual transactions in the near future.

The Foreign Contract Law

E.10   The Foreign Contract Law covers almost all types of contract between foreign firms and Chinese entities. This breadth of scope has two implications. First, the Foreign Contract Law is an extremely important piece of legislation that foreign parties should take into consideration in conducting almost any type of business activity in China. Second, the Foreign Contract Law of necessity sets forth general principles only. More specific rules are stipulated in legislation relating to particular types of contract, such as the Provisional Regulations on the Control of Technology Import Contracts.

    The Foreign Contract Law applies to economic contracts between enterprises or other economic organizations of the PRC and foreign enterprises, other economic organizations, or individuals, but not to international transport contracts. These contracts should be concluded in accordance with the principles of equality and mutual benefit and agreement through consultation, and should observe the laws of the PRC and not violate public policy. Parties to a contract may choose the applicable law to handle disputes as to the meaning of the contract, but where they have not done so, the law of the country with the closest connection with the contract will be applied. However, PRC law must be applied to certain contracts such as joint venture contracts. In the absence of PRC law, international practice may be applied.

    Under the Foreign Contract Law, a contract is made when the parties have reached agreement on the terms in a written form and have signed it, but if the approval of the contract by Chinese authorities is required, the contract is effective only upon approval. Contracts that violate the laws of the PRC or public policy and contracts concluded through deception or coercion are invalid.

    Parties to a contract should perform their contractual obligations. If one party does not perform its obligations, the other party has a right to claim compensation or take other reasonable remedial measures. The liability of the breaching party is equal to the damages suffered by the other party as a result, but will not exceed damages foreseeable at the time the contract was made. Liquidated damages may be provided for in a contract, but a court or arbitral body may reduce or increase them. A party is excused from its contractual responsibilities if it cannot perform due to *force majeure*.

The consent of the other party is required when an assignment is made. If the original contract required government approval, the assignment will also be subject to approval. Parties may by agreement amend a contract, but either party has the right to cancel the contract under certain circumstances. A contract is terminated by certain events, such as performance, mutual agreement, or the order of an arbitration body or court. Certain contractual rights and obligations survive the cancellation or termination of the contract.

Contractual disputes should be settled as far as possible through consultation and mediation by a third party, but the parties may submit a dispute to arbitration or, if the contract has no provisions for arbitration, to a court.

International Practice

As mentioned above, the Foreign Contract Law provides that international **E.11** practice may be applied where Chinese law has no provisions governing certain matters of contract. It appears that, in determining what constitutes international practice, drafters of the Foreign Contract Law relied on the United Nations Convention on Contracts for the International Sale of Goods (hereafter cited as the UN Convention), completed on April 11, 1980. The influence of the UN Convention on the Foreign Contract Law can be seen in the large number of similarities between the two documents. Both the UN Convention and the Foreign Contract Law refer to international practice as a source of law. The Foreign Contract Law refers only to "international practice" and does not define the term, but a Chinese official has quoted with authority the language in the UN Convention as indicative of what the Foreign Contract Law means by this term as follows:

> "a usage of which the parties knew or ought to have known and which in international trade is widely known to, and regularly observed by, parties to contracts of the type involved in the particular trade concerned".[1]

Similarly, both the UN Convention and the Foreign Contract Law limit the damages obtainable for the breach of a contract to those foreseeable at the time of the formation of the contract. Further, both the Convention and the Foreign Contract Law, in three consecutive articles, contain almost identical provisions. These articles concern the obligation of the breaching party to mitigate damages, the payment of interest on payments in arrears, and the excuse for non-performance due to an event classified as a *force majeure*.

It should be noted that there are also certain fundamental differences between the UN Convention and the Foreign Contract Law. First, the UN Convention applies only to the sale of goods, while the Foreign Contract Law applies to contracts of almost all types. Second, the Foreign Contract Law can be seen as a more general and less complex document than the UN Convention. The UN Convention treats in detail the role of offer and acceptance in the formation of contracts, and the effect of delays or errors in the transmission of communications, as well as containing detailed provisions on the obligations of a seller (for example, to deliver conforming goods free from third parties' claims) and the obligations of the buyer (for example, payment of price). Since the Foreign Contract Law requires only a document in writing signed by both parties for the formation of the contract, it does not require detailed provisions concerning these matters such as those contained in the UN Convention.

Standard-Form Contracts

E.12   In China's socialist market economy, most transactions with foreign parties are conducted by state entities and therefore involve the interests of the state. In order to ensure that the state's interests are adequately protected, standard-form contracts are widely used.

China's practice regarding standard-form contracts, however, has been influenced by changes in the country's foreign economic relations over the last 15 years, during which time China's contacts with foreign companies have greatly increased. The monopoly of the former Ministry of Foreign Trade on almost all economic relations with foreign countries has been broken, and other ministries, provinces, and municipalities now have the authority to deal with foreign companies directly. This decentralization of authority has had contradictory effects. In some respects it has resulted in more flexibility in the use of standard forms, since local enterprises may be more willing to negotiate amendments to them. However, it has also reinforced the use of standard forms. Due to the relatively small number of lawyers or legal experts in China and the increasing numbers of entities now involved in foreign trade, the use of standard-form contracts is an important means of protecting China's interests while allowing enterprises to engage in foreign economic relations without full participation by these specialists.

At present, as in the past, the foreigner engaging in business activities in China will invariably meet the standard-form contracts in simple purchase and sales negotiations. In more complex transactions Chinese entities, sometimes those which have only recently engaged in foreign trade, tend to be more flexible. They may have a standard form, but they do not always insist that it be used for the particular transaction if the foreigner has his own standard form. This is most often the case in licensing, joint venture, cooperation, and compensation trade contracts.

The impact of the Foreign Contract Law on the standard-form contracts used by Chinese entities in their economic relations with foreign parties has not been substantial. The standard-form contracts reflect in part international practice, and to a large degree comply with the obligatory provisions of the Foreign Contract Law. In those cases where the Law allows the parties to a contract freedom to stipulate different provisions in the contract, the standard-form contract will reflect the Chinese side's determination of what the two parties should stipulate. Therefore, although the Foreign Contract Law appears to allow more flexibility to foreign enterprises in the negotiation of their contracts with Chinese parties, this may not be so.

The Authority of the Contracting Party

The above-mentioned decentralization of foreign trade in China has also E.13
raised significant questions for foreign companies signing contracts with Chinese enterprises. It has presented foreigners with the problems of choosing among competing Chinese organizations and determining which Chinese entity is the most appropriate one with which to sign a contract. An important part of the answer to such problems is whether the relevant Chinese entities are in fact authorized to engage in the contemplated transaction.

China's new Foreign Trade Law issued May 12, 1994 and effective July 1, 1994 has clarified the criteria a Chinese entity must fulfill to engage in the import or export of goods or technology. In addition to the five criteria listed in Article 9 of the Foreign Trade Law, such as having its own name and organizational structure, the entity must also obtain permission from the State Council's organization in charge of foreign economic and trade matters. A foreign party thus may request the Chinese party to a foreign trade or technology licensing transaction to see this permission or to receive assurances from Chinese lawyers that such permission has been received.

The question of the authority of the contracting party, however, has occurred not only to foreign entities, but also to the Chinese parties themselves. In some cases Chinese enterprises have requested foreign entities to provide written evidence, such as a power of attorney, of the foreigners' authority to conduct negotiations and sign contracts; and certificates of the legal status of the signing parties are among the documents that may be required for approval of a technology transfer contract. Foreign contract negotiators should be aware, therefore, that if they do press the Chinese side for evidence of their authority, the Chinese may well request similar documentation from them.

The Enforcement of Contracts

Under American law a contract is generally considered to be an agreement E.14
between two parties that is enforceable in accordance with its terms. Usually "enforceable" is understood to mean enforcement directly through the courts. However, contracts signed with Chinese entities have not generally been enforceable directly through the courts, but through arbitration. Furthermore, disputes have generally been resolved by conciliation or friendly

discussions prior to arbitration. In fact, non-maritime cases in which a Chinese party to a foreign trade contract has gone to arbitration outside China are still relatively rare. The Foreign Contract Law follows this practice, stating in Article 37 that the parties shall "to the fullest extent possible" settle disputes through consultation or third-party mediation.

Given China's preference for conciliation and arbitration, it is notable that the Foreign Contract Law does allow resort to court and that the Civil Procedure Law of the People's Republic of China has a special chapter dealing with litigation involving foreigners. The Civil Procedure Law allows foreigners to bring contractual disputes to the economic chambers of the people's courts. Article 192 of the Civil Procedure Law provides that disputes involving foreign economic relations, trade, transportation, and maritime matters can be referred to the Chinese courts. Both the Foreign Contract Law and the Civil Procedure Law limit access to the courts in handling such disputes to cases where there is no written agreement between the parties providing for arbitration.[2] Since Chinese entities almost uniformly insist on an arbitration clause in the contracts they sign with foreign parties, resort to the economic courts by foreigners for enforcement of their contracts may not be generally available. Unless the penchant of China's contract negotiators for arbitration clauses declines, the bringing of foreign contractual disputes to court in China will continue to be rare.

It should be noted, however, that although an arbitration clause does generally preclude resort to court, this may not be so in all cases. In some jurisdictions preliminary protective measures, such as an injunction, are available through the courts to parties who have entered into an agreement containing an arbitration clause. It is unclear whether this would be permissible in China under the Civil Procedure Law if the relevant arbitration clause called for arbitration in Stockholm under the Stockholm Chamber of Commerce rules.[3] Some jurisdictions also allow a party to an arbitration agreement to sue in court to have an arbitration award overturned in certain circumstances. In China, Articles 259 and 260 of the Civil Procedure Law provide that such judicial review is not available for arbitration awards rendered by Chinese arbitration organizations except when a court refuses to enforce the award.

While China's policy in favor of arbitration rather than litigation has been consistent over the last 15 years, the provisions in Chinese foreign trade contracts for arbitration have not remained the same. Chinese entities sometimes may agree to alter the standard-form contracts to provide for arbitration in third countries under the rules of foreign arbitral bodies. A review of arbitration clauses in a number of contracts between American and Chinese parties has indicated that Sweden and Switzerland are popular sites for arbitration, that the local arbitration rules of the site of arbitration are often used, and that Chinese entities sometimes request the use of the Arbitration Rules of the UN Commission on International Trade Law (UNCITRAL). More recently, Hong Kong and Singapore have been suggested as appropriate sites for arbitration. In the past, Chinese entities generally opposed a provision for arbitration under the International Chamber of Commerce rules because Taiwan was a member of the Chamber, while China was not. Since China became a member of the Chamber on November 30, 1994, however, this policy should no longer apply.

Governing Law

A familiar problem to lawyers is the choice of law. The standard-form contracts used by Chinese enterprises for purchase and sales as well as licensing transactions have not in the past included any choice of law clause or any other language in the contract which would allow a third party to determine what law should govern the contract. This is still generally the practice, although governing law clauses have appeared in some contracts. Further, Article 5 of the Foreign Contract Law provides that for equity joint ventures, cooperative venture contracts, and contracts for the cooperative exploitation and development of natural resources performed in China, the laws of China are to be applied.

E.15

The absence of a governing law provision in the standard-form contract does not mean that the Chinese party will allow reference to foreign law. On the contrary, the foreigner who demands a clause calling for foreign law as the governing law of the contract will probably be met with a demand by the Chinese party for the use of Chinese law. Where the contracts negotiated with Chinese entities have generally provided for the resolution of disputes in the last resort by arbitration in China, the application of Chinese law to govern the contract is probably inevitable. Since Chinese contracts signed with foreign entities now often contain arbitration clauses calling for arbitration in third countries, the lack of a governing law clause will result, under the Foreign Contract Law, in the application of the law of the country having the "closest connection" with the contract.

If a contract without a choice of law clause were referred to arbitration in a third country, it seems likely that the arbitrators would apply the choice of law rules of the jurisdiction where the arbitration was being held. Since, in many cases, the contracts are negotiated, signed, and largely performed in China, it seems that Chinese law would be applied to interpret the contract by application of the "closest connection" choice of law rule. In fact, it has been suggested that the Chinese desire for the negotiation and signature of contracts in China is related to this rule. However, an increasing number of Chinese entities are now conducting contract negotiations and even signing contracts abroad. In such cases, the results under the choice of law rules turn on the particular facts of each situation.

It is also possible that the law of no one country, but that of the Convention will apply. This can occur in the case of contracts for the sale of goods if both parties agree to the application of the UN Convention. It may also occur when the places of business of both parties to a contract for the sale of goods are in two countries that are signatories to the UN Convention (such as the United States and China) and the parties have not specified any choice of law in the contract.

In some cases foreign parties have been able to have foreign law inserted in the contract as the governing law. This is most often the case in loan, leveraged leasing or other financial transactions. One question which arises in such cases is whether the foreign party should be content with a simple reference to the application of the law of the jurisdiction, or whether it should insist on the application of the substantive, rather than the procedural or choice of law, rules of the jurisdiction. Under the legal concept of *renvoi*, the mere reference to the law of the jurisdiction without further clarification could result in the application merely of the choice of law rules of the jurisdiction which, as noted above in the case of Sweden, could result in the application of Chinese substantive law to interpret the contract.

Commercial Law

E.16 Unlike the United States and many other countries, China does not have a commercial code to comprehensively regulate commercial relations. As China has been pursuing commercial legislation in a piecemeal way and promulgating commercial laws and regulations only when conditions are ripe, the commercial law involving the sale of goods and secured transactions is regulated in such separate laws and regulations as the Foreign Economic Contract Law (FECL), the Economic Contract Law (ECL), the Law of the People's Republic of China on Security (Law on Security), and the Law of the People's Republic of China on Commodity Inspection, etc.

China currently maintains a two-tier system in dealing with domestic sale of goods and foreign-related sale of goods. The ECL, the Regulations on Purchase and Sales Contract for Industrial and Mining Products and the Regulations on Purchase and Sales Contract for Agricultural and Sideline Products form the legal basis to regulate domestic sale of goods, and the FECL is the single most important legislation that deals with foreign-related sale of goods. While the laws regulating the domestic sale of goods have detailed provisions on the quality of the goods, price, packaging, delivery of conforming goods, and liabilities of sellers and buyers for the breach of contract, the FECL is more general and less complex with respect to those provisions.

Under the FECL, a contract for the sale of goods must be in writing in order to be valid and enforceable. A contract is made when the parties have reached agreement on the terms of the contract in written form and have signed it. However, if government approval of the contract is required, the contract is not made until approval is obtained.

Contracts for the sale of goods generally should include the provisions on names, nationalities, main offices or residence of the parties to the contract; the date and place of the signing of the contract; the type of contract and the classification and scope of the objective of the contract; the technical conditions, quality, standard, specifications and quantity of the objective of the contract; the duration, place and method of performance; price conditions, amount of payment, mode of payment and various supplementary costs; whether the contract can be assigned or conditions for the assignment of the contract; compensation for breach of contract and other liabilities; and the method of settlement when disputes arise from the contract and the language(s) used in the contract and its validity.

Contracts are breached when one party does not perform the contract or does not perform the obligations of the contract in accordance with the conditions agreed upon. When one party breaches the contract, the other party has the right to claim compensation for damages or take other reasonable remedial measures. The Chinese law does not allow a non-breaching party to claim consequential damages; its damages are limited to the amount which the party breaching the contract should have foreseen when the contract was made.

For the matters not provided in the contracts for the sale of goods, the **E.17** FECL provides that international practice, which mainly means the United Nations Convention on Contracts for the International Sale of Goods (UN Convention), may be applied to fill the gap. The UN Convention including its complicated and detailed provisions on offer and acceptance, delivery, payment of price, and compensation for damages will apply if the parties to the contracts have not specifically excluded its application and both parties to the contract are located in countries that are signatories to the Convention.

A secured transaction refers to a transaction such as loan, sale, purchase, carriage of goods, and undertaking of processing in which the creditor establishes an interest in personal or real property to secure satisfaction of his rights. The Law on Security has provided five forms of security: guarantee, mortgage, pledge, lien, and earnest money.

Guarantee means the act whereby the guarantor and the creditor stipulate that if the debtor fails to perform his obligations, the guarantor shall preform the obligations or assume liability as stipulated. Guarantee can be divided into ordinary guarantees and joint and several guarantees. The former is a guarantee whereby the guarantor is to bear liability if the debtor fails to perform his obligation while the latter is a guarantee whereby the guarantor and the debtor are jointly and severally liable for the obligation. To establish a guarantee relationship, the guarantor and the creditor are required to conclude a written contract of guarantee to set forth the type and amount of principal obligation guaranteed, the term for the obligor to perform the obligation, the methods of guarantee, the scope of guarantee, the term of guarantee, and other matters.

Mortgage refers to the use by the debtor or a third party of property as security for an obligation without transferring the possession of such property. If the debtor fails to perform his obligation, the creditor shall be entitled to receive payment in priority by converting the property into money or through the proceeds of the auction or selling off of the property. According to Chinese laws, property that can be mortgaged as security includes mainly: buildings and other fixtures to land, machinery, tools of communication and transportation and other property owned by the mortgagor, state-owned land use rights, state-owned machinery, tools of communication and transportation owned by the mortgagor, land use rights to wasteland which have been lawfully contracted for by the mortgagor and on which the party which contracted out the same has consented to a mortgage, and other property that may be mortgaged according to law.

In establishing a mortgage, the mortgagor and mortgagee conclude a written mortgage contract. The contract becomes effective on the date of registration if the mortgage is on land use rights, urban real estate or buildings of township or village enterprises, aircraft, vessel, vehicle, equipment or other movables of enterprises; and on the date of execution of the mortgage contract if the mortgage is on other property. The effective date of the mortgage contract is critical in determining priority in receiving payment when the same property is mortgaged to two or more creditors. For the contract which becomes effective on the date of registration, payment to secured creditors must be made according to the order of precedence of the registration. In case of equal priority, payment is made in proportion to the obligations. For the contract to become effective on the date of execution, if the mortgaged property has already been registered, payment must be made in accordance with the above arrangement. If the mortgaged property has not been mortgaged, payment is made in accordance with the order of precedence of the contracts in becoming effective.

E.18   Pledge is defined as the delivery by the debtor or a third party of the possession of his movable to the creditor, and the use of such movable as security for an obligation. The creditor shall be entitled to receive payment in priority by converting the movable into money or through the proceeds of an auction and selling off of the pledged property. Again, the pledgor and the pledgee are required to conclude a written contract of pledge, and the contract shall become effective at the time of delivery to the creditor of the pledged property. In addition to movables, certain rights may also be pledged. These rights include bill of exchange, checks, promissory notes, bonds, deposit certificates, warehouse receipts, bill of lading, shares and share certificates which may be transferred according to law, exclusive right to use a trademark, patent rights, and property rights among copyrights, which may be transferred according to law, and other rights. It is important to note that the date the pledge contract becomes effective depends on whether it is a bill of exchange, share certificate or intellectual property rights.

A lien refers to a form of security in which the creditor is in possession of a movable of the debtor and is entitled to retain such property in receiving payment in priority by evaluating the property in terms of money or through the proceeds of the auction or selling off of the property when the debtor fails to perform his obligation stipulated in the contract. The creditor has a right of lien if the debtor fails to perform his obligation under a contract of custody, carriage or the undertaking of processing, and other contracts where the law creates a lien. A lien shall be extinguished when there is extinguishment of the obligation or provision of separate security by the debtor and acceptance thereof by the creditor.

Earnest money is defined as a practice where one party gives the other earnest money as security for an obligation. After the debtor has performed his obligation, the earnest money is set off against the price to be recovered. The party providing earnest money is not entitled to demand a refund of the earnest money if he fails to perform the stipulated obligation, while the party receiving the earnest money should refund twice the amount of the earnest money if he fails to perform the stipulated obligation. The contract for earnest money, which must be in writing, becomes effective on the day on which the earnest money is actually delivered.

The amendment of the ECL and FECL and the implementation of the Law on Security on October 1, 1995 has marked a major step toward establishing a commercial law regime to promote the development of the socialist market economy. To facilitate commercial transactions, China still needs to promulgate such laws as agency, contract for sale of goods, etc. As a concrete step, China is reportedly considering consolidating the FECL and the ECL into a single Economic Contract Law that applies to both domestic sale of goods and foreign-related sale of goods.

Companies Law

The Company Law of the People's Republic of China (Company Law) was **E.19** promulgated on December 29, 1993 and became effective on July 1, 1994. This new legislation is a breakthrough in China's economic reforms and provided for the first time a firm legal foundation for the establishment and operation of large and small companies throughout China's "socialist market economy".

When China decided to encourage foreign equity investment in the late 1970s, it passed legislation on equity joint ventures which provided for the establishment of closely-held limited liability companies with foreign investment. Later, in the mid-1980s, it issued legislation allowing wholly foreign-owned enterprises. Many foreign companies have invested in China through such joint ventures or wholly foreign-owned enterprises, but the rapid growth of the Chinese economy over the last decade has created the need for a new legal framework for transforming state-owned enterprises into independent market-oriented entities, for entities selling their shares in China's growing capital markets, for attracting foreign investment, both active and passive, and for the rapidly growing cooperative and private sectors of the Chinese economy.

The Company Law provides for the establishment of two forms of companies, a limited liability company and a joint stock company (also translated as a "company limited by shares"). These two forms are similar to the corporate forms found in many other countries, particularly civil law jurisdictions. Both corporate forms enjoy limited liability and have shareholders and shareholders meetings as well as boards of directors and supervisory boards. The Company Law also provides for a special form of limited liability company for a wholly state-owned entity.

Limited Liability Companies

E.20 The limited liability company under the Company Law is similar to a limited liability company under China's existing legislation on joint ventures and wholly foreign-owned enterprises. The number of shareholders is small, from two to 50 under the Company Law. Capital contributions to the Company can be made in the form of cash, goods, industrial property rights, unpatented technology, and land use rights. Industrial property and unpatented technology, however, generally cannot constitute more than 20 per cent of the registered capital. Further, the Company Law sets certain minimum registered capital requirements. For example, a minimum amount of RMB 500,000 is required for a production Company, RMB 300,000 for a commercial retailing company, and RMB 100,000 for a service company. The Company Law imposes no limitation on foreign ownership in a limited liability company, but it does require that if other laws or administrative regulations require approval by the relevant authorities, then a copy of such approval must be presented when registering the company.

The shareholders hold shareholder meetings which adopt resolutions on the major issues of the company. On certain designated important issues a two-thirds majority vote is required. On other issues the articles of association determine the voting procedures. The board of directors is composed of from three to 13 persons elected by a shareholders' meeting. Directors' terms may not exceed three years, but they may be re-elected. In a limited liability company with a small number of shareholders or of a small scale, an executive director may take the place of the board. The executive director may also hold the position of general manager. The Company Law makes no provisions for the use of proxies at either shareholders' or board meetings.

Stipulations on the labor union differ somewhat from those in the company legislation of many other jurisdictions. The Company Law provides that a company must first obtain the opinion of its labor union and invite the union's representatives to attend meetings at which decisions are made on workers' salaries, benefits, safety and vital interests. The company must also obtain the opinions and suggestions of the labor union and workers in making decisions on major issues in production and operations or in establishing important internal rules.

The Company Law establishes an extensive list of prohibitions to prevent corruption and self-dealing. Certain individuals are not allowed to serve as directors, supervisors or general managers. These include an individual who has served as a director, factory manager or general manager of a bankrupt company who bore "personal responsibility" for the bankruptcy. Such a person cannot serve as a director, supervisor or general manager for a period of three years from the time that the liquidation of the company was completed.

Other provisions of the Company Law prohibit government officials from acting as directors, supervisors or general managers; impose a duty of fidelity to the company and prohibit self dealing, the taking of bribes, unauthorized loans of company funds by directors or general managers, the transfer of corporate funds to an account in the name of a third party, guarantees of personal debts with corporate assets, competition by directors and general managers with the company and contracts between directors or the general manager and the company unless authorized by the articles of association or a shareholders meeting. An obligation of confidentiality is imposed for corporate secrets. Directors, supervisors and general managers who violate these or other provisions of law, administrative regulations or the company's articles of association are liable to compensate the losses caused to the company.

Joint Stock Companies

Under the Company Law, a joint stock company may be established by five E.21 or more promoters, but the majority of them must be residents of China. Capital contributions to a joint stock company are made in the same form as for a limited liability company and the 20 per cent limitation on contributions in the form of intellectual property rights and unpatented technology applies as well. The minimum registered capital requirement is RMB 10 million, but a higher minimum may be established by a law or administrative regulations in certain cases. The establishment of a joint stock company requires the approval of the authorities authorized by the State Council or of the provincial-level People's Government. It is possible to establish a joint stock company by subscription, but in such case the promoters must subscribe to at least 35 per cent of the shares and approval must be obtained from the State Council's securities regulation authorities.

The rules on shareholder meetings are similar to those for a limited liability company. For board meetings, the rules are different. The Company Law requires a quorum of one-half or more of the directors and a simple majority for the adoption of board resolutions. Proxies are specifically authorized, but shareholders of bearer shares who attend shareholders meetings must deposit the shares with the company for a period starting five days before the meeting and ending on the adjournment of the meeting.

The provisions regarding labor and prohibited conduct are generally similar to those for limited liability companies. Those on the supervisory board, however, strengthen the power of the labor union. A joint stock company must establish a supervisory board of three or more supervisors. The supervisors are elected not only by the shareholders meeting, however, but also by the workers. The proportion of supervisors who represent the workers is to be determined in the company's articles of association.

There are no statutory rights of consent or of first refusal concerning the transfer of interests by a shareholder in a joint stock company. Promoters of the company, however, may not transfer their shares in the company for a period of three years from the establishment of the company. In addition, directors, supervisors or general managers of the company may not transfer their shares during their term of office. Finally, the transfer of shares in the company must be made through a securities exchange.

The Company Law also sets forth rules regarding a number of other matters such as the listing of joint stock companies on securities exchanges, the issuance of bonds, financial and accounting matters, mergers and spinoffs, bankruptcy, dissolution and liquidation, branches of foreign companies and legal responsibilities for violation of the Company Law.

Issues of Interest to Foreign Investors

E.22 The Company Law raises a number of issues of concern to foreign investors. The first is how it applies to foreign companies investing in China in the future. The answer is that the effect of the Company law will depend on the form of the future investment, *i.e.* whether in the form of a limited liability company or of a joint stock company. For a foreign invested limited liability company, the new Company Law's only effect, at first glance, would appear to be on issues not covered by existing joint venture and wholly foreign-owned enterprise legislation. Article 18 states, in part, that:

> "this Law applies to limited liability companies with foreign investment, but if the laws regarding Sino-foreign equity joint ventures, Sino-foreign contractual joint ventures and wholly foreign-owned enterprises have other provisions, those other provisions apply."

This rule should result in essentially the same legal regime for the establishment, organization and management of future foreign-invested limited liability companies as for foreign investments under existing legislation.

The other issue for foreign investors is how the Company law will affect existing joint ventures and wholly foreign-owned enterprises. The answer is not altogether clear. Article 229 of the new Company Law states, in part, that:

> "companies registered and established in accordance with a law, administrative regulations, local regulations ... prior to the implementation of this Law are to continue and to be preserved and those that do not completely meet the conditions provided in this Law shall within the stipulated time period reach the conditions provided in this Law."

Since China's existing legislation on joint ventures and wholly foreign-owned enterprises is based on "laws", existing foreign-invested enterprises would seem to have the obligation to conform to the new requirements in the Company Law. It could be argued, however, that Article 18 noted above is intended to apply not only to future investments, but existing investments as well, thereby granting them "grandfather" status even though China's announced policy is to move towards "national treatment" (*i.e.* equal treatment of foreign and local investors) as part of an effort to rejoin GATT.

Although the Company Law does not mention the tax holidays, reductions or other favorable tax treatment enjoyed by the joint ventures and wholly foreign-owned enterprises, it is likely that foreign invested entities established under the Company Law will be interpreted as being "joint ventures" or "wholly foreign-owned enterprises" and therefore subject to the tax treatment under existing legislation on foreign invested entities. However, since under existing joint venture legislation the foreign share in a "joint venture" must generally be at least 25 per cent of the registered capital, the question arises whether joint stock companies or limited liability companies established under the Company Law but with less than 25 per cent foreign ownership will be considered "joint ventures" and enjoy the tax benefits applicable to such entities.

Another major effect of the Company Law on future investment is the opportunity for passive investment in China. Currently, investment in joint ventures or wholly foreign-owned enterprises in China generally involves active investment in a closely-held corporation and an active management role for the foreign partner. The Company Law allows the establishment of joint stock companies that list their shares on securities exchanges. As an increasing number of state enterprises are converted into joint stock companies and listed on China's securities exchanges, foreign investors should have greater opportunities for passive investment in China.

Finally, another aspect of the Company Law of interest to foreign investors in China is its authorization for the establishment in China of branch offices of foreign corporations. Under current law, branch offices of foreign corporations (except for banks) are not allowed by other legislation except the Guangdong Company Regulations. Outside Guangdong, the only presence a foreign corporation may establish on a semi-permanent basis is a representative office, which is severely restricted in the activities it may conduct. The Company Law's provisions on branches leave much to be determined by implementing regulations to be issued by the State Council, but it seems likely that in the future foreign corporations will be able, upon application and approval, to establish branch offices in China to engage in a wider range of activities than they are allowed to conduct through their existing representative offices.

Capital Markets and Securities Law

The emerging security markets in China are a natural outgrowth of Chinese **E.23** economic reforms. Before 1979, enterprises were financed solely through national budget allocations according to priorities set by the state planning authorities. Funds went primarily to state-owned enterprises with dominant positions in the Chinese economy. In return, these enterprises were expected to fulfill their assigned production tasks and turn all profits over to the government. The enterprises were not autonomous and did not have the right to initiate their own development.

Two important steps led the way to reform. First, in order to make the enterprises responsible for their own profits and losses and to raise construction capital to help the enterprises to develop, the State Council issued a directive on March 28, 1987 which allowed state enterprises to issue bonds and debentures subject to approval. It also allowed collective enterprises to issue stock upon approval. The directive did not explicitly prohibit a recognized state-owned shareholding company from issuing stock, and since then a number of state-owned enterprises have sold stock on an internal basis. Second, stock exchanges opened on December 19, 1990 in Shanghai and on July 3, 1991 in Shenzhen. Before 1992, shares on both Shanghai and Shenzhen stock exchanges were available only to Chinese entities and individuals, and traded only in Renminbi (A Shares). In order to attract foreign funds, both Shanghai and Shenzhen municipal governments promulgated administrative rules in late 1991 to allow foreign investors to purchase the special Renminbi denominated shares (B Shares).

Late in 1992, the State Council Securities Commission (Securities Commission) and the China Securities Supervision and Administration Commission (Securities Supervision Commission) were established. The former is in charge of securities markets throughout the country, while the latter is the executive organ of the former for supervision and administration of the specific activities in connection with the issuing and trading of securities.

The process of establishing a securities law system in China began from the local level. In the late 1980s and early 1990s, Shanghai and Shenzhen municipal authorities promulgated a number of rules and regulations on shares issuance, administration of trading and the exchange of securities. In December 1992, the State Council issued a notice to strengthen the administration of security markets. A number of rules and regulations on the national level were also promulgated from 1993, such as the Provisional Rules on Prohibition of Securities Fraud (Securities Fraud Rules), the Prerequisite Clauses of the Articles of Association of Companies Seeking a Listing Outside the PRC, and the Supplementary Provisions on Implementation by Companies Listing in Hong Kong of the "Standards for Companies Listed by Shares Opinion". The Provisional Regulations on Administration of the Issuing and Trading of Shares (Provisional Regulations on Shares), which mainly cover issues of A shares, were promulgated and became effective on April 22, 1993. Effective from July 1, 1994, China's new Company Law also provides stipulations on share issuance, trading and assignment by companies limited by shares. In accordance with the relevant provisions of the Company Law, on December 25, 1995 the State Council promulgated the

State Council Regulations on Listing of Foreign Capital Shares Inside China by Joint Stock Companies (Foreign Capital Shares Regulations) and later their Implementing Rules, which replaced the above mentioned Shanghai and Shenzhen 1991 Administrative Rules. Currently, a national securities law is being drafted and is expected to be promulgated soon.

Issuing of Shares

The issuer of shares must be a company limited by shares that qualifies for the public issuing of shares. To qualify, a company limited by shares must fulfill the following conditions: **E.24**

1. its production and operations conform to the state industrial policies;
2. it issues only one class of common shares and the same shares carry the same rights;
3. the share capital subscribed for by the company's promoters is not less than 35 per cent of the total share capital to be issued by the company;
4. the portion of the total share capital subscribed for by the promoters is not less than RMB 30 million;
5. the portion to be issued to the public is not less than 25 per cent of the total share capital and, of such portion, the share capital subscribed for by the staff and workers of the company does not exceed 10 per cent of the total share capital to be issued to the public (the portion to be issued to the public shall not be less than 10 per cent of the total share capital if the total share capital exceeds RMB 400 million), and
6. the promoters have not committed any serious illegal acts during the last three years.

According to China's Company Law, shares issued to the public may be registered shares or bearer shares, but shares issued by a company to a promoter or organization authorized by the state to make investment or a legal person shall be registered shares and shall bear the name of such promoter, organization or legal person. No separate account with a different name may be opened for such shares, nor may such shares be registered in the name of a representative.

Trading of Shares and Takeover of Listed Companies

Any share trading must be carried out in the securities trading locations where the trading of shares have been approved by the Securities Commission. To apply for its shares to be traded on a securities exchange, a company limited by shares shall fulfill the following conditions: its shares have been issued to the public upon approval by the relevant authorities; its total share capital after issue is not less than RMB 50 million; the number of its individual shareholders holding shares with a face value of RMB 1,000 or more is not less than 1,000, the total face value of shares held by individual shareholders is not less than RMB 10 million; and it has a record of continuous profitability for the last three years. **E.25**

People's Republic of China

The Provisional Regulations on Shares provide that no individual may hold 0.5 per cent percent or more of the outstanding common shares of a listed company. Any excess amount shall be acquired by the company at the lower of the original purchase price and market price upon approval by the Securities Supervision Commission. If within three working days any legal person having direct or indirect holding of outstanding common shares in a listed company reaches 5 per cent of the company's total outstanding common shares, such legal person shall report that fact in writing to the company, the securities trading location and the Securities Supervision Commission, and make an announcement. If the amount of outstanding common shares in a company held by an individual or legal person exceeds the above 0.5 per cent or 5 per cent limit as a result of a reduction in the company's total amount of outstanding common shares, the above limit will not apply during a reasonable period of time.

Disclosure of Information

E.26 Transparency in the financial and securities areas is one of the issues investors trying to make an informed decision of purchase or sale are most concerned about. Full disclosure and fair competition are the basic market principles for healthy securities and financial markets. The Provisional Regulations on Shares provide that a Listed Company shall furnish the Securities Supervision Commission and securities trading locations with the following documents:

1. An interim report to be submitted within 60 days of the end of the first six months of each fiscal year. This report should include the company's financial report; an analysis by the company's management on the company's financial position and operation results; any major litigation involving the company; changes of the outstanding shares of the company; important matters submitted by the company to the consideration of shareholders with voting rights; and other matters that the Securities Supervision Commission requires to be specified.

2. An annual report audited by a registered accountant, to be submitted within 120 days after the end of each fiscal year, which should include a summary of the company; a brief description of the company's main products or services; a summary of the company's industry; a summary of important assets owned by the company such as factories, mines and real property; details of the outstanding shares of the company including a name list of the shareholders holding 5 per cent or more of the company's outstanding shares, and a name list of the 10 largest shareholders; the number of the shareholders in the company; a brief description of the directors, supervisors and senior management personnel of the company, their shareholdings and their remuneration; a table and a brief description of the company and its affiliates; an abstract of financial information regarding the company for the

previous three years or for the period since its establishment; an analysis by the company's management of the company's financial position and operating results; changes of outstanding bonds of the company; any major litigation involving the company; a comparative financial report on the company for the last two years together with attached tables and notes audited by a registered account, and if the list of companies is a holding company, a comparative consolidated financial report for the last two years shall be included as well; and any other matters that the Securities Supervision Commission requires to be specified.

The Provisional Regulations on Shares also require a company to disclose any major event which may have a comparatively large impact on the market value of a Listed Company's shares and which investors are not aware of. All the above information to be disclosed shall be public except the following:

1. trade secrets that are protected and are permitted not to be disclosed by laws and regulations;
2. any non-public information and documents obtained by the Securities Supervision Commission during the course of its investigation of illegal activities, and
3. other information and documents that are not required to be disclosed in accordance with relevant laws and regulations.

Prohibitions

All entities and individuals are prohibited from conducting shares issuance and trading by using inside information in order to obtain profits or reduce losses. According to the Securities Fraud Rules, any of the following acts is considered to be insider trading: **E.27**

1. purchasing, selling, or suggesting others to purchase and/or sell securities by insiders based on inside information;
2. divulging inside information to enable others to buy or sell securities;
3. non-insiders obtaining inside information by improper means and suggesting others to buy or sell securities based on such inside information, and
4. other insider trading acts. Entities and individuals are also prohibited from cheating clients, making false statements, and conducting, by taking advantage of funds and information or by abuse of power, market manipulation to influence securities market prices, creating false information, inducing or causing investors to make decisions without being aware of the true market situation, and disturbing the order of securities markets.

Foreign Capital Shares

Foreign capital shares listed inside China (foreign capital shares) are registered shares denominated in Renminbi that are issued to certain investors for **E.28** trading in foreign currency on stock exchanges in China. Investors who are allowed to buy or sell foreign capital shares are natural and legal persons and other organizations from a foreign country, Hong Kong, Macao, and Taiwan, Chinese citizens who are residing abroad, and other investors as provided by the Securities Commission. A shareholder of the foreign capital shares may appoint a proxy to exercise his shareholder's rights on his behalf, and a beneficial owner of foreign capital shares may register his shares under the name of a nominal holder. Dividends paid and other payments made by the company to its shareholders of foreign capital shares will be calculated and declared in Renminbi and paid in foreign currency, and the dividends and other gains from foreign capital shares may be remitted out of China after payment of tax thereon according to law.

The State has the control over the issues of foreign capital shares. A company which intends to issue foreign capital shares must obtain the approval by the Securities Commission. Where the total par value of the foreign capital shares proposed for issuance exceeds US$30 million, the Securities Commission should report to the State Council for approval. The issuance of foreign capital shares may be for two purposes: to establish a company by means of a share offer for raising capital and to increase a company's capital.

A company which is to issue foreign capital shares is required to disclose information to the public in accordance with relevant laws and other regulations issued by the Securities Supervision Commission as well as the rules in stock exchanges regarding the information disclosure by the listed companies. The company should specify in its articles of association matters such as the place and methods of information disclosure. Except as otherwise provided by the local laws of a foreign country where the shares offer is made, the prospectus provided outside of China to investors should be prepared and provided in accordance with relevant Chinese laws and regulations. As to the fiduciary duties of the company's officials, the Foreign Capital Shares Regulations provide that the directors, supervisors, managers and other senior management personnel such as the company's financial officers, secretary to the board of directors, and persons specified in the articles of association should have an obligation of good faith and diligence to the company.

Foreign capital shares may be traded in stock exchanges in China. Subject to the approval by the Securities Commission, the shares or their derivative forms, such as share warrants and shares depository certificates outside China, may also be circulated and transferred outside China. For the purpose of control, where the number of foreign capital shares held, directly or indirectly, by a single shareholder reaches 5 per cent of the total common shares of a company, such shareholder is required to report to the Securities Supervision Commission, stock exchanges and the company and make an announcement within three working days of the occurrence of the fact, stating the situation and the purpose of his holding the shares. Such a shareholder should also make a similar report and announcement whenever the increase or decrease of his such shares accounts for 2 per cent of the company's total common shares. The shareholder is prohibited from directly or indirectly trading such shares prior to and on the date of submitting the report and making the announcement.

With respect to the issue of voting rights of foreign minority shareholders, the Foreign Capital Shares Regulations only provide that a shareholder of foreign capital shares should have equal rights and obligations with a shareholder of domestic capital shares under the same share category in accordance with the Company Law. Specific matters on the rights and obligations of a shareholder may be stipulated in the company's articles of association. Unlike the previous rules in Shanghai and Shenzhen, the Foreign Capital Shares Regulations provide no specific conditions for securities institutions outside of China to participate in the foreign capital shares business. The Implementing Rules for the Foreign Capital Shares Regulations merely state that securities institutions outside of China may engage in foreign capital shares business as an agent by signing an agent agreement with brokers inside China or in accordance with the rules of stock exchanges in China.

Arbitration and Other ADR Techniques

Arbitration and other Alternative Dispute Resolution techniques are a **E.29** favored means of resolving commercial disputes in the People's Republic of China. Arbitration and other ADR techniques are preferred primarily because they are consistent with China's traditional approach of settling disputes through "negotiation and mediation". Moreover, the skepticism of foreign investors on the fairness and effectiveness of China's judicial system and the inadequacies of the litigation system have also contributed to China's decision to develop a comprehensive and effective ADR mechanism, along with a litigation system, to cope with the fast growing commercial disputes resulting from implementing the reform and the policy of opening to the outside.

Consultation, mediation and arbitration are three major instruments in China's ADR system. Friendly consultation involves negotiations between parties to the dispute in seeking an amicable solution. Chinese law encourages parties to the dispute to use friendly consultation to resolve the dispute or to gain a better understanding of each party's position on the dispute. Friendly consultation is most effective where the disputed issue is simple, the positions of the disputing parties are not far apart and the parties involved share a common desire to maintain a friendly business relationship. Friendly consultation, however, has its limitations, as a party can always walk away from the negotiation and the agreement reached is not enforceable in court if a party refuses to comply with it.

Mediation in the PRC is conducted by people's mediation committees, government departments, arbitration organs and courts. The people's mediation committees are organizations of the masses that resolve civil disputes, commercial disputes and minor criminal cases. The legal departments of the Domestic Commerce Ministry at various levels of governments are government organs in charge of mediation of commercial disputes arising from business transactions between commercial organizations. The Beijing Mediation Center under the China International Chamber of Commerce is responsible for mediating disputes arising from international economic cooperation, trade, finance, investment, technology, insurance, etc.

E.30   A mediation will usually be commenced when mediation organs have received an application for mediation submitted by a party to the dispute. In conducting mediation, mediators are required to follow three fundamental principles: (a) that mediators must act in accordance with the laws and policies of the state; (b) that mediation must be conducted on a voluntary basis, and (c) that mediation is not a prerequisite to a court trial. After investigating the facts and ascertaining each party's liabilities, the mediators should help the parties settle a dispute through reasoning and persuasion. While a mediator should make a settlement proposal in the mediation process, he may not compel any party to accept the proposal. To encourage the parties to make compromises in reaching an agreement, the Rules for Mediation of the Beijing Mediation Center prohibit the parties from using any admission, proposal, and compromise offer made in the mediation process against each other in court after the mediation has failed.

When mediation has been successfully concluded, a mediation agreement should be drawn up and signed by the parties involved. Although mediation agreements generally are not enforceable in a court, a mediation agreement reached in a litigation process could be legally binding provided that it is certified by a court. Moreover, according to the rules governing commercial mediation between commercial organizations, a commercial organization will be subject to administrative disciplinary sanctions for failing to perform a mediation agreement.

Mediation, as a well-received means for resolving disputes, is also used in combination with arbitration which is one of the distinctive features of China's arbitration system. The new Arbitration Law effective September 1, 1995 stipulates that arbitrators shall mediate when both parties voluntarily seek mediation. The Rules of Procedure of the Maritime Arbitration Commission provide that the Maritime Arbitration Commission may endeavor to settle by conciliation any dispute of which it has taken cognizance.

In addition to the process of arbitration, mediation is equally encouraged in the process of civil and commercial litigation in China. The Civil Procedure Law of the PRC provides that:

> "in trying civil cases, the people's courts should stress mediation. When mediation efforts prove to be ineffective, the courts should issue their decisions in a timely manner."

A mediation agreement, put in a written form and signed by a judge, shall have legal binding force on the parties involved once it is delivered with the seal of a people's court affixed to it.

Arbitration in China includes arbitration for disputes involving economic contracts and other disputes over rights and interests of property, arbitration for labor disputes, foreign economic and trade arbitration, and maritime arbitration.

Domestic economic arbitration is governed by the Arbitration Law and conducted by arbitration commissions established in municipalities directly under the central government and in cities where provincial and autonomous region governments are located. The cases handled by the arbitration commissions include contractual disputes and other disputes over rights and interests of property between citizens, legal persons and other organizations having equal civil status.

According to the requirement of the Arbitration Law, an arbitration organ   E.31
shall arbitrate a dispute only when the parties of the dispute have agreed to submit a dispute for arbitration. The agreement to arbitrate must be in writing and be included in a contract in the form of an arbitration clause. The arbitration commissions will turn down an arbitration application for lack of agreement to arbitrate or invalidity of an arbitration agreement. After a decision has been made to accept an application for arbitration, an arbitration tribunal will be set up and an arbitral award will be given based on the investigation of the relevant facts and application of law. When a party involved does not accept an arbitral award, he may seek to set aside the arbitral award in the Intermediate People's Court at the place where the arbitration commission is located within six months following receipt of the written award. If a party fails to perform an arbitral award that he has not sought to invalidate within the prescribed time, the other party may apply to a People's Court for enforcement.

As the Arbitration Law stipulates, arbitration for labor contracts is governed separately by the Provisional Regulations on Management of Labor Disputes in State-Owned Enterprises. The arbitration organs to handle labor disputes are the labor arbitration commissions set up in cities, counties and districts within a city. The cases accepted and heard by the labor arbitration commissions are those related to labor disputes arising out of the performance of labor contracts and disputes resulting from the discharge of employees who have violated discipline. The procedures and rules for labor arbitration are the same as or similar to the procedures and rules provided in the Arbitration Law.

The China International Economic and Trade Arbitration Commission (CIETAC) is the institution to arbitrate disputes arising from international economic transactions. The cases heard and arbitrated by the CIETAC include not only disputes between Chinese and foreign economic entities but also disputes between Chinese economic entities and disputes between foreign economic entities as well.

The arbitral awards rendered by the CIETAC are final and binding on the parties involved. The losing party may seek to set aside foreign-related arbitral awards on the grounds stipulated in the Civil Procedure Law. If the losing party fails to pay an arbitral award within the time fixed by the award, the winning party may seek enforcement of the arbitral award by applying to court in China in accordance with Chinese law and courts in a foreign country that is a signatory to the New York Convention on the Recognition and Enforcement of Foreign Arbitral Awards.

In conclusion, arbitration and other ADR techniques developed in China have provided both domestic and foreign individuals and business entities viable alternatives to resolve disputes arising from economic transactions. The new Arbitration Law has further unified and specialized China's arbitration system by replacing the existing domestic arbitration institutions with local arbitration commissions established in major cities. With China's economic system becoming increasingly market-oriented and with commercial disputes becoming more complicated, it is likely that more rules will be adopted to improve the efficiency of China's ADR system.

Banking and Lending Law

E.32   China's banking system consists of the central bank, commercial banks, state-policy banks, investment companies, and Sino-foreign joint venture banks. The banking system is primarily governed by the Law of the People's Republic of China on the People's Bank of China (the Central Bank Law), the Law of the People's Republic of China on Commercial Banks (the Commercial Bank Law), which constitute the cornerstone of China's new legal framework for banking.

The People's Bank of China (PBOC) is the central bank of the country and is responsible for formulating and implementing state monetary policies and exercising supervision and control over the banking industry under the leadership of the State Council. The main functions performed by the PBOC are to issue Renminbi and control its circulation, to examine and approve the establishment of banking institutions, to supervise and control the financial market, to manage the State foreign exchange and bullion reserve; to manage the state treasury, etc. Under the Central Bank Law, the PBOC is required to report its decisions concerning the annual supply of banknotes, interest rates and foreign exchange rates to the State Council for approval. However, once the State Council has approved the decision, the PBOC enjoys independence in implementing state monetary policies. The PBOC is increasingly employing such international practices as reserve deposits, rediscounts, interest rates, central bank loans and credit limits to stabilize the value of the Renminbi and to prevent inflation rather than relying exclusively on controlling credit.

Commercial banks are enterprise legal persons that receive deposits from the public, make loans, and handle settlement of accounts and other business.

Commercial banks in China include four wholly state-owned banks (the Agricultural Bank of China, the People's Construction Bank of China, the Industrial and Commercial Bank of China, and the Bank of China), a dozen joint stock commercial banks, and thousands of urban and rural coopera- tives. The main functions performed by commercial banks are to grant loans, to handle domestic and international account settlements, to handle discount of negotiable instruments, to issue financial bonds, to buy or sell state bonds, and to provide credit service and guarantee, etc. One significant reform made by the Commercial Bank Law is the separation of policy-oriented banking business from commercial banks. Such separation implies that commercial banks will set their goals to seek profits and increase efficiency instead of performing the impossible dual tasks of making profits and promoting eco- nomic development. Along with the shift of the business goal, commercial banks have been given the right and autonomy to make business decision independently, but are also required to assume their own risks and be re- sponsible for their profits and losses.

State-policy banks are established to carry out the state's industrial and foreign trade policies through providing policy-oriented loans for key state construction projects, the development of agriculture and the export of capital goods. Currently, China has three state-policy banks, namely, the State Development Bank, the Agricultural Development Bank and the Export-Import Credit Bank. State-policy banks do not absorb deposits from the public. Instead, their sources of funds are mainly from financial alloca- tion, central bank reloans, bonds issued to the public, regular sums left in social security funds, and indirect use of post office deposits. The functions performed by state-policy banks are to provide loans to enterprises engaging in capital construction, agricultural development and export of capital goods under the guidance of state industrial policies and economic plans. While policy banks are still expected to maintain a balance or a meager profit in their operations, they will not compete with commercial banks in seeking a high margin of profits.

Foreign banks, branches of foreign banks, wholly foreign-funded banks **E.33** and joint venture banks are permitted to conduct banking business in foreign currency under Chinese law. As of the end of 1995, more than 100 foreign banks had set up branches in Shanghai, Shenzhen, Guangzhou, Tianjin, and 16 other Chinese cities. While all foreign banks are allowed to conduct foreign currency business in certain designated cities, reportedly only a few of them are authorized in limited areas on a trial basis to conduct Renminbi business.

Commercial lending is regulated by the Commercial Bank Law, the Regu- lations on Loan Contracts and a number of regulations promulgated by the State Council, relevant government ministries and local governments. The general principle governing commercial lending is that commercial banks should conduct loan business in accordance with the requirement of the national economy and social development and under the guidance of the industrial policies of the state. This guiding principle is significant as it constitutes a legal basis for the state to require commercial banks to follow the state economic plans, thus setting certain limits on the business autonomy granted to commercial banks in making credit decisions.

As the Commercial Bank Law requires, commercial banks should conduct close investigation on the use of the loans, the capacity of a borrower to repay the loans, and the method of repayment before granting loans. Loans from commercial banks usually require some form of guarantee for loan repayment, but if banks have concluded that a borrower has sound credit standing and the ability to repay the loans, they can waive the guarantee requirement.

In practice, guarantees for borrowing take two forms: credit guarantee and security guarantee. Credit guarantee is usually issued by a financial institution, an enterprise, or other economic entities with sound credit standing and debt servicing capacity. A security guarantee is provided by using marketable assets as security. Assets that the borrower can use as security are materials and property, including marketable securities, building property, machinery and equipment, marketable raw materials, semi-finished and finished products, and other transferable rights and interests. If a borrower fails to repay the loan within the repayment schedule, the guarantor will be responsible for the repayment of the loan principal and interest outstanding in the case of a credit guaranteed loan, and the banks are entitled to priority recovery of the loan principal and interest outstanding by converting the loan security funds or selling off the security in the case of a secured loan.

In making loans to a borrower, commercial banks are required to enter into a written loan contract to define each party's rights and obligations. To constitute a valid legal document, a loan contract should be in written form and contain clauses relating to the type of loan, the use of loan, its amount, the interest rate, the source of repayment, the schedule for repayment, the method for repayment, security provided, and the liability for breach, etc.

E.34   To prevent banks from over-lending, Chinese law has set certain limitations on the lending activities of commercial banks. Commercial banks are required to observe certain capital/debt ratios set by the Commercial Bank Laws in conducting lending. Moreover, commercial banks are prohibited from extending loans to the staff of commercial banks and their relatives or providing secured loans to the staff of commercial banks and their relatives with more favorable terms than those provided for ordinary borrowers. Except for the above limitations and restrictions, commercial banks have autonomy to conduct lending business free from interference from any organization or individual. With the exception that the State Council can require the wholly state-owned commercial banks to make loans to certain special projects, no organizations or individuals can compel commercial banks to make loans or to provide guarantees.

China has taken a decisive step in establishing a modern banking system as evidenced by the promulgation of two major banking laws. However, the reforms undertaken thus far are generally perceived to be not deep enough to transform specialized banks into modern commercial banks. One apparent deficiency of the current banking system is that commercial banks, especially the wholly state-owned commercial banks, are still obliged, both as a matter of law and policy, to continuously "transfuse blood" to inefficient state-owned enterprises to sustain their operations. The lack of freedom for commercial banks to choose their clients makes it extremely difficult for them to operate as modern banks and unrealistic to hold them responsible for their profits and losses. As the goal of the banking reform is to make commercial banks truly independent in business operations, China is expected to resolve this matter by deepening the enterprise reform. It can be predicted that as state-owned enterprises gain more autonomy in making business decisions, commercial banks will be correspondingly granted more autonomy to make credit decisions solely on pure commercial considerations.

Consumer Protection Law

Competition law alone is not sufficient to protect consumers' rights. Free and open competition provides consumers with a variety of products at the lowest prices, because it causes producers in the market to respond to the demands of independent consumers. When buyers do not have sufficient accurate information about the products they are to buy, there is no guarantee that the products bought by consumers will be safe. Although protection of consumer rights is a goal of China's Unfair Competition Law, the major regulations on consumer rights protection are set forth in the Law of the People's Republic of China on Protection of the Rights and Interests of Consumers (Consumer Protection Law), the Product Quality Law of the People's Republic of China (Product Quality Law), other national laws and regulations, and local regulations of almost every province and major city. **E.35**

The Rights of Consumers

The Consumer Protection Law protects the rights and interests of consumers who buy or use commodities, or receive services for consumption purposes in daily life. Such consumers have the right to demand that commodities and services provided by business operators meet the requirements for the protection of their person and property. A consumer also has the right to true information on a commodity or service and thus to require business operators to provide the relevant information on the price, place of origin, producer, use, function, specifications, grade, main ingredients, production date, expiry date, inspection certificate, directions on use, and after-sale service of the commodity, as well as the contents, specifications and fees of a service. A consumer may, on his own, choose a business operator providing commodities or services, choose the type of a commodity or the form of a service and **E.36** is entitled to fair transaction terms and conditions, such as quality guarantee, reasonable price and accurate measures, and to reject coercive acts by business operators. In purchasing and using a commodity or receiving a service, a consumer has the right to have his human dignity, national customs and traditions respected, and is entitled to compensation under the law for harm suffered to his person or property due to the purchase or use of a commodity or the receipt of a service.

The Obligations of Business Operators

E.37 Business operators include producers and sellers of products and service providers who provide commodities or services to consumers. The obligations imposed on business operators are rather strict and comprehensive under Chinese laws.

Ensuring Safety

A business operator shall ensure that the commodities or services provided by it meet the requirements for protection of person and property. The Product Quality Law imposes an "unreasonable danger" standard which requires that no unreasonable danger to person or property exists. For commodities or services that may jeopardize person or property, consumers must be provided with a true statement and a clear warning that explain and indicate the correct methods for use of the commodities or receipt of the services and measures to prevent injury. Moreover, when a business operator finds a commodity or service provided by it to have a serious defect that may cause harm to the person or property even if the commodity or service is used or received correctly, it shall immediately report this fact to the relevant authorities, inform consumers, and adopt measures to prevent injury.

Providing Information

A business operator is required to provide consumers with true information about commodities and services and not conduct misleading, false publicity. It shall clearly indicate its true name and mark, ensure that the actual quality of the commodity or service provided by it is in line with the quality described in its advertisement. Under the Product Quality Law, products or the labels on their packaging shall conform to the following requirements:

1. bear a product quality inspection certificate;
2. display the product name and the producing factory's name and address in Chinese;
3. display the product's specifications, grade, and the names and contents of its major constituents in accordance with the product's characteristics and use;
4. carry the production date, period of safe use or date of expiry for products to be used within a certain period of time, and

5. carry a warning mark or a warning statement in Chinese for products whose improper use is likely to cause the products themselves to be damaged or to endanger the safety of a person or property.

Product labels, however, need not be affixed to unpackaged foodstuffs and other unpackaged products to which it is difficult to affix labels due to the special characteristics of such products.

Conditions of Quality

A business operator is required to ensure that unless a consumer is already aware of the existence of a defect, its commodities or services will have the quality, functions, uses, and date of expiry that they should have during the course of normal use or receipt. To ensure the quality of commodities, strict requirements are imposed on business operators for certain kinds of products. The Implementation Regulations for China's Standardization Law stipulate that the pharmaceutical standards, food hygiene standards, veterinary medicine standards, product standards, safety and hygiene standards for the production, storage, transportation and use of products are mandatory. Under relevant Chinese laws, the production and/or marketing of certain types of foods and cosmetics, fake medicines, and medicines of inferior quality are prohibited.[4]

Warranty Liability

A business operator must provide consumers with a purchase or service voucher in accordance with relevant state regulations or upon the request of the consumer. It shall carry out its responsibilities for the guaranteed repair, replacement and return of its products under state regulations or an agreement it has entered into. The business operator, however, may not set out unfair and unreasonable terms for consumers or alleviate or release itself from civil liability for harm to the lawful rights and interests of consumers by means of standard contracts, circulars, statements or shop notices.

Responsibilities and Liabilities of Business Operators

Each of the following three circumstances constitutes a basis for a consumer to demand from a business operator the repair, replacement or return of the product bought by him and to claim compensation if he suffers losses.   E.38

Except where otherwise provided by the Consumer Protection Law, a business operator providing commodities or services must bear civil liability in accordance with the relevant laws and regulations in any of the following circumstances:

1. where a defect exists in a commodity;
2. where a commodity does not possess functions it should possess, and this is not stated when the commodity is sold;

3. where the commodity standards indicated on a commodity or on the package of such commodity are not met;
4. where the quality condition indicated by way of commodity description, physical sample and so on is not met;
5. where commodities proscribed by formal state decrees are produced or commodities that have deteriorated or expired are sold;
6. where a commodity sold is not adequate in quantity;
7. where the service items and charges are in violation of an agreement;
8. where demands by a consumer for repair, redoing, replacement, return, making up the quantity of a commodity, refund of a commodity price and service fee or claims are subject to deliberate delay or rejected without reason, or
9. other circumstances whereby the rights and interests of consumers are harmed as provided by laws and regulations.

A consumer or other injured party whose person or property is harmed due to a commodity defect may demand compensation from the seller as well as the producer. Where the responsibility lies with the producer or another seller who provided the product to the seller, the seller has the right to recover such compensation from the producer or the other seller. A consumer may also claim compensation from the service provider if its rights and interests are harmed in receiving a service. A producer, however, would not be liable for compensation if it can prove that: (i) it has not put the product into circulation; (ii) the defect causing the harm did not exist when the product was put into circulation, or (iii) the level of science and technology at the time when the product was put into circulation was not sufficient to detect the existence of the defect.

A consumer may choose the following ways to resolve a dispute occurring with a business operator: (i) negotiating a settlement with the business operator; (ii) requesting a consumer association to mediate; (iii) filing a complaint with the relevant administrative authorities; (iv) submitting the dispute to an arbitration organization for arbitration in accordance with an arbitration agreement, and (v) filing legal proceedings with the court.

Liabilities of the business operator include civil, administrative and criminal liabilities. For the consumer or other party's injuries or losses caused by its providing commodities or services, a business operator shall pay the expenses, such as medical expenses, nursing expenses during the treatment, and income lost due to absence from work, expenses for the tools of disabled people and their living subsidies, disability compensation funds, and necessary living expenses for the injured party's dependents. For the consumer's or other party's death caused by its providing commodities or services, the business operator shall bear the expenses such as funeral expenses, death compensation funds and necessary living expenses for the victim's dependents. Administrative liability includes warning, confiscation of the illegal income, fines, suspension of business, and/or revocation of business license. Any business operator may be criminally prosecuted if it has: (a) caused the death or disability of a consumer or other party; or sells products which do not meet state or industry standards for protection of human health, persons or property; (b) mixes improper elements with its products; (c) adulterates its products; (d) passes off fake products or poor quality products; (e) sells expired or deteriorated products; (f) falsifies place of origin, name and/or address of another factory or quality mark; (g) markets or procures products by offering or accepting bribes, and (h) forges inspection data or inspection results.

Consumer Organizations

Consumers have the right to establish social organizations to protect their E.39 lawful rights and interests. Under the Consumer Protection Law, consumer organizations can exercise the following functions:

1. providing information and advice to consumers;
2. participating in the supervision and inspection of commodities and services by relevant administrative authorities;
3. reporting to, inquiring of, or making suggestions to the relevant administrative authorities on issues concerning consumers' lawful rights and interests;
4. handling and conducting investigations and mediation of the consumers' complaints;
5. requiring appraisal departments to appraise the quality of commodities involved in a complaint;
6. assisting injured consumers in filing lawsuits, and
7. revealing and criticizing acts harmful to the lawful rights and interests of consumers through the mass media.

At the same time, in order to keep consumer organizations impartial and independent for the goal of protection of consumers, the Consumer Protection Law prohibits any such organizations from engaging in commodity business or profit-seeking services and from recommending commodities and services to the public for the purpose of profit.

The Consumer Association is now the major consumer association in China. It is a semi-official organization affiliated with the administrative authorities for industry and commerce.

Health, Safety and Environmental Law

China has an extensive and relatively complex legal regime to regulate health, E.40 safety, and environmental protection. While health, safety and environmental laws are mainly promulgated by the National People's Congress, government ministries, agencies and local governments also play an important role in enacting and enforcing the regulations and rules. Chinese law has generally imposed extensive obligations on government organs, public institutions, business entities and individuals to improve health conditions, to ensure safety in production and daily life, and to protect the ecology of the environment. Failure to comply with the laws and regulations can subject an entity or individual to broad administrative, civil, and criminal liabilities.

The health laws consist of a number of laws and regulations governing the prevention and treatment of infectious diseases, frontier health and quarantine, food hygiene, and health of public places, etc.

The Law of the People's Republic of China on the Prevention and Treatment of Infectious Diseases has established a system to prevent, report, control, and eliminate the occurrence of and epidemics of infectious diseases. According to the law, governments at various levels should take necessary measures, including establishing public health facilities to improve the hygienic condition of drinking water, to reduce or eliminate the sources of infectious disease. When an infectious disease occurs, government organs, medical care and health institutions, and anti-epidemic agencies must promptly take preventive measures to control the transmission of the disease.

The Food Hygiene Law of the People's Republic of China has established a system that regulates the hygiene of food, food additives as well as the hygiene of containers, utensils, packaging materials, and equipment used for food. Under the law, the health authority of the State Council is responsible for formulating national hygiene standards for food products. At the same time, local governments are allowed to set local hygiene standards for food production, provided that the national government has not formulated hygiene standards for a food product.

The Frontier Health and Quarantine Law of the People's Republic of China has established the frontier health and quarantine system that requires all persons, means of transportation, transport equipment, and articles such as baggage, goods, and postal parcels that may transmit quarantinable infectious diseases to undergo quarantine inspection upon entering or exiting the country. Without the permission of the health and quarantine inspectors, no person shall be allowed to embark or disembark from any means of transportation, and no articles shall be loaded or unloaded.

The Provision on Sanitation Administration of Public Places has established a sanitation permit system to control the selection of site and the design of newly built, renovated, and expanded construction in public places. To insure sanitation in public places, the regulation has authorized health and anti-epidemic institutions to participate in the selection and design of the newly built, renovated, and expanded construction in public places, and to participate in the examination of the finished building.

Safety legislation regulates safe production, safe transportation, fire prevention, and the handling of fatal accidents to ensure the safety of property and human life.

E.41   The Fire Protection Regulations of the People's Republic of China regulate fire prevention, fire protection organizations, fire fighting, fire supervision, and liabilities for violating the regulations. The regulations provide that the design and construction of new, expanded or reconstructed buildings must conform to the stipulations of the fire prevention code for architectural designs. In building, extending or rebuilding a municipality, the relevant authorities should concurrently plan and build public fire protection facilities, including fire stations, water supply for firefighting, fire service communications, and passageways for fire apparatus. In addition, government organizations, enterprises, and institutions are required to install appropriate types and quantities of firefighting apparatus, equipment and facilities as needed for fire protection.

The regulations governing safety in mines, safety in maritime transportation, and safety in inland water transportation have established systems to ensure the safety of equipment, property and human life. These regulations authorize the competent government departments to administer the safety systems in their respective jurisdictions, to set standards and rules for safe production, and to impose liabilities on those individuals and organizations that have violated the relevant regulations and caused damage to property and human lives. The regulation on the investigation and handling of accidents sets the requirements to preserve accident sites and the procedures for reporting accidents to superior authorities to ensure that the accidents are properly handled.

China's environmental legislation includes the Environmental Protection Law, its Implementation Rules and a large number of laws and regulations with respect to water, noise, and air pollution, marine and mineral resources, the preservation of land, grasslands and fisheries, and water and soil conservation. This comprehensive environmental legislation has resulted in the formation of a series of environmental protection systems, including the environmental administrative system, environmental impact assessment system, (the system for designing, building and putting into operation pollution prevention installations simultaneously with the main project "the three simultaneous measures" system), reporting and registration system, discharge permit system, inspection system and environmental monitoring system.

The environmental responsibility system imposes responsibility on the local people's governments at various levels to take necessary measures to improve environmental protection and be responsible for the environmental quality of the areas under their jurisdiction. The system reflects the understanding that it is inadequate to rely exclusively on the State Environmental Protection Bureau and its local counterparts to carry the burden of protecting the environment. To effectively implement environmental laws and policies, the environmental quality should be one of the criteria to judge the performance of the governments at various levels.

The environmental impact assessment system requires the environmental protection authorities to review and approve an environmental impact assessment for each construction, technical improvement, or development project. An environmental impact assessment must assess the amount of pollutants likely to be produced by the project and the project's likely effect on the environment and stipulate the prevention and control measures that will be implemented in the project.

E.42   As the "three simultaneous measures" system provides, all enterprises must design, build, and commission installations for the prevention and control of pollution at construction projects together with the principal part of the project. Enterprises will not be allowed to start their construction projects until installations for the prevention and control of pollutants have been examined and approved by the competent authorities of environmental protection.

The reporting and registration systems require enterprises and institutions discharging pollutants to report and register with the government authorities in accordance with the relevant provisions issued by the government authorities for environmental protection and administration. The discharge permit system has given the government another tool to control the discharge of pollutants by requiring all enterprises to apply for discharge permits for waste discharge. Government authorities of environmental protection will determine the type, quantity, and concentrations of pollutants that an enterprise may discharge. The system to eliminate and control pollutants within a prescribed time imposes obligations on those enterprises who have caused severe environmental pollution to eliminate and control the pollution within a certain period of time. The discharge fees system imposes a fee payment requirement on all enterprises discharging pollutants into a body of water.

In the process of modernizing its economy, China has been confronted with many of the similar health, safety and environmental problems experienced by the industrialized countries in the early stage of industrialization. The promulgation of health, safety and environmental protection laws and regulations has been instrumental in raising the social awareness of, and curing certain health, safety and environmental problems. However, the existing legal regime for health, safety and environmental protection is far from providing a satisfactory solution to all these problems. In the short run, the focus of health, safety and environmental protection will be on the enforcement of the existing laws and regulations. As the country's economy grows, China is expected to follow the developed countries in setting stricter standards and imposing more severe civil penalties and criminal liabilities to raise health, safety and environmental protection to a higher level.

Employment and Labor Law

E.43   China's employment and labor legislation consists of the Labor Law of the People's Republic of China, the Provisions on Labor Administration in Foreign Invested Enterprises, the Trade Union Law of the People's Republic of China, and a large body of national and local laws and regulations governing different aspects of employment and labor. Compliance with employment and labor legislation, which has become increasingly complex, is a prerequisite for effective operation in China by foreign businesses.

Chinese law provides enterprises and individual economic organizations (employers) inside China with full authority over the hiring and dismissal of their employees. Foreign-invested enterprises are in particular guaranteed managerial autonomy to decide the number, time, condition, and ways of hiring Chinese employees. While foreign-invested enterprises usually hire employees from their Chinese partners in the joint venture or from employment agencies approved by local labor administration authorities, they nevertheless have the right to recruit employees from the community in the area where the ventures are located, and even to conduct the hiring in other regions, provided that they obtain confirmation from the labor administrative authorities of the provincial level government.

Under Chinese law, employers and employees are required to conclude a labor contract to define each party's rights and obligations in establishing an employment relationship. A labor contract may have a fixed term, an open term, or a term determined by job performance. Employers can sign a labor contract with an individual employee or sign a collective labor contract with trade unions which represent the interests of the employees.

A labor contract must contain clauses which address the term of the labor contract, job description, labor protection and work conditions, remuneration, labor discipline, the conditions for termination of the labor contract, and liability for breach of the labor contract. Additionally, a labor contract may stipulate matters concerning preserving confidential information, know-how or technology obtained through employment. A labor contract terminates immediately upon expiration of the contract term or when a condition for termination agreed upon by interested parties arises. A labor contract can be rescinded if the interested parties agree. In the situation where both parties agree to extend, a labor contract can be renewed for an additional term.

An employer may dismiss an employee at any time if the employee has **E.44** failed to meet the recruitment requirements during the probationary period, has seriously violated labor discipline or rules and regulations of the employer, has committed an act of serious dereliction of duty or graft that causes substantial harm to the interests of the employer, or has been convicted of a crime in accordance with the law. Subject to a 30-day written notice, an employer can also rescind a labor contract when an employee has fallen ill or has sustained injuries not relating to work and is not able to perform the original work upon the conclusion of medical treatment, when the employee has been incapable of performing a job and remains incapable after receiving training or being transferred to another post, or when a major change has rendered such contract incapable of being carried out and the parties have failed to reach an agreement on the amendment of such contract after negotiations. In the situation when an employer genuinely needs to reduce the number of his personnel during a period of restructuring or when major production or operational problems arise, the employer shall explain the situation to the trade union or employees 30 days in advance and heed the opinions of the trade union or employees in making a decision to terminate employees. Employers are not allowed to dismiss an employee who has suffered from an occupational disease or has sustained injuries from work and has been confirmed to have lost or partially lost the capacity to work, an employee who is undergoing the required period of medical treatment for an illness or injury, or an employee who is pregnant, in confinement, or nursing.

E.45   Employers have full autonomy in determining remuneration including salaries, wages, bonuses, and subsidies based on the interests, production and operational situation of the employers. Wages and salaries paid by employers to their employees must be above the minimum wage and salary standards set by the provincial level governments. Employers are required to pay wages and salaries to their employees for rest days, holidays, wedding and funeral leaves, as well as during periods when employees take part in social activities in accordance with the law. In addition, employers shall pay labor insurance, medical expenses, pension insurance, unemployment insurance, and certain kinds of government subsidies.

Employers are also required to establish and perfect a system for labor safety and health and to observe the health and safety regulations promulgated by the government on labor protection to ensure safe and civilized production. Labor safety and health facilities for new construction, renovation or extension projects must be simultaneously designed, built and put into production with the main project.

Employees in domestic and foreign-invested enterprises have the right to establish trade unions to represent the interest of the employees. The major functions performed by the trade unions are to sign labor contracts on behalf of employees with the employers, to express opinions on the decisions of such issues as reducing employees and extending working hours, to raise objections to the inappropriate dismissal of employees and other matters.

Labor disputes arising between employers and employees are resolved through mediation, arbitration or legal proceedings. If mediation fails to resolve the dispute, either party may request arbitration by labor arbitration commissions in the area where the employers are located. Neither resorting to mediation nor to arbitration precludes the disputing parties from filing a suit in court.

In January 1996, The Regulations for Administration of the Employment of Foreigners in China (Regulations) was promulgated, and went into effect on May 1, 1996. The Regulations provide that employers recruiting foreign employees must first apply on their behalf for their Employment Permit from the relevant Chinese authorities. The Regulations also stipulate that the position for which a foreigner is hired must be one of special need, for which there is a temporary shortage of suitable candidates inside China and which a foreigner is allowed to take without violating Chinese law.

With the promulgation of the Labor Law and the Provisions on Labor Administration in Foreign Invested Enterprises, the relevant authorities in China are likely to focus on enforcing those laws to make sure the autonomy granted to employers and the rights granted to employees are fully guaranteed.

Foreign Investment Law

As one of the largest host countries of foreign investment in the world, **E.46** China has formed a relatively comprehensive and complex legal regime to encourage foreign investment. This regime allows both direct and indirect investment through equity joint ventures, contractual joint ventures, wholly-foreign owned enterprises, investment companies' representative offices, processing and assembly operations, technology transfer, and other investment vehicles. Central to this legal regime for foreign investment are three foreign investment laws, namely: the Law of the People's Republic of China on Sino-foreign Joint Equity Enterprises (the Joint Venture Law), the Law of the People's Republic of China on Sino-foreign Cooperative Enterprises (the Contractual Joint Venture Law), and the Law of the People's Republic of China on Wholly-Foreign Owned Enterprises (the WFOE Law), and a large body of implementation rules and regulations promulgated by the government ministries and the local governments.

Equity joint ventures are regulated primarily by the Joint Venture Law and the Implementing Regulations for the Joint Venture Law. An equity joint venture is a Chinese legal person established on the basis of a joint venture contract between Chinese and foreign parties and approved by the Ministry of Foreign Trade and Economic Cooperation (MOFTEC) or its local counterparts. An equity joint venture enjoys limited liability.

The establishment of an equity joint venture requires the parties to the joint venture to apply to the examination and approval authority by submitting an application, the joint feasibility study, the joint venture contract, Articles of Association, and other documents. The examination and approval authorities will decide whether to approve the proposed joint venture in three months. A joint venture must register with the local bureaus of the State Administration for Industry and Commerce (SAIC) within one month after approval of the joint venture and a formal business license will be issued after the approval of the application and the payment of a fee.

The parties to the joint venture can make capital contributions to the joint venture in the form of cash, buildings, equipment, technology, materials and the right to use land. If the capital contributions are in a form other than cash, the parties must agree on the appropriate evaluation of the contribution on the basis of fairness and reasonableness or agree to have a third party make the evaluation. Depending on their size and number, the capital contributions must be made within certain periods after the issuance of the business license. An equity joint venture cannot reduce its registered capital and must obtain approval from the examination and approval authorities for increases in the registered capital.

E.47   Joint ventures are required to balance their foreign exchange receipts and expenditures. The Chinese Government encourages joint ventures to export their products to achieve foreign exchange balance.

The board of directors is the highest authority in a joint venture. The appointment of members of the board of directors is generally in proportion to the parties' equity contributions to the joint venture. If a foreign partner appoints a chairman of the board in a joint venture, the Chinese party may appoint the vice chairman and vice versa. The board of directors is required to hold a meeting at least once a year. The quorum for a meeting of the board is at least two-thirds of the members.

Equity joint ventures have full authority over the hiring and dismissal of their employees. Equity joint ventures are required to allocate a certain percentage of after-tax profits to a reserve fund, enterprise expenses fund, and incentive and welfare fund for staff and workers.

Contractual joint ventures are legal entities established between Chinese and foreign parties on the basis of a joint venture contract and approved by the examination and approval authorities. Contractual joint ventures take two different forms. In a "pure" contractual joint venture, the parties make their contributions to the project and bear the risk of loss directly. A "hybrid" contractual joint venture is a separate business entity and the parties to the joint venture are liable to a third party only to the extent of their capital contributions to the entity. The foreign parties' capital contributions to the registered capital generally should not be less than 25 per cent of the total registered capital of the hybrid form contractual joint venture. A hybrid form contractual joint venture would generally qualify as a "legal person" while a pure form contractual joint venture would not.

E.48   The procedures to obtain approval for the establishment of a contractual joint venture are basically the same or very similar to those of equity joint ventures. One difference between the two procedures is that the examination and approving authorities are required to approve the proposed joint venture in 45 days instead of three months after receipt of all the necessary documents.

In addition to the forms of contributions listed above for an equity joint venture, parties to a pure contractual joint venture are allowed to make contributions in currency, in kind, or in rights to industrial property, technology and land use, etc. The most important distinction between a contractual joint venture and equity joint venture is that a foreign party's investment in a contractual joint venture can be repatriated prior to the expiration of the term of the joint venture, provided the joint venture contract stipulates that ownership of all of the assets of the joint venture shall revert to the Chinese party upon expiration of the joint venture term.

Contractual joint ventures may have the same scope of activities as equity joint ventures, but usually have a shorter term. Contractual joint ventures are generally subject to the same foreign exchange laws as equity joint ventures. The law requires that a contractual joint venture have either a board of directors or a joint management office to manage the activities of the joint venture. Another distinctive difference between contractual ventures and equity joint ventures is that the parties in contractual joint ventures may agree on the distribution of profits according to a ratio different from that of the parties' capital contributions.

Wholly foreign-owned enterprises (WFOEs) are entities established under the law of the People's Republic of China on Wholly-Owned Enterprises promulgated in 1986 (the WFOE Law). A WFOE can be a limited liability company or, upon approval, take another form of doing business. Chinese law sets more limitations on a WFOE in that it requires that the enterprises use advance technology and equipment, or that the enterprise export annually products worth 50 per cent or more of its total production.

The procedure for establishing a WFOE is similar to that for equity joint ventures. Prior to filing an application for investment, foreign investors must submit to the local government a report detailing the enterprise's purpose, its scope, scale of business, products, technology and equipment, land use requirements, etc. The local departments for foreign economic relations and trade shall give a reply to the application within 30 days after the report is submitted. The application for establishing a WFOE shall be approved or denied within 90 days after the examination and approval authorities have received the application from the investor. A foreign investor may make capital contributions to a WFOE in the form of foreign currency, machinery, equipment, industrial property, proprietary technology or, upon approval, renminbi profits derived from their other investments in China. Capital contributions are subject to the prescribed debt:equity ratios and reduction of registered capital are prohibited as in the case of equity joint ventures.

WFOEs are permitted to operate for the period provided for in their **E.49** approval. A request for an extension of the term of the operation must be submitted to the examination and approval authorities 180 days prior to its expiration. Under Chinese law, WFOEs are excluded from domestic and foreign trade, insurance, and telecommunications. In addition, the establishment of WFOEs is restricted in public utilities, communications, transportation, real estate, trust and investment, and leasing.

WFOEs are generally subject to the same foreign exchange controls as joint ventures. WFOEs are expected to balance their foreign exchange revenue and expenditure by themselves. The daily operations of a WFOE will be controlled solely by its own management. While the Chinese government or authority shall monitor the activities of a WFOE, the business operation of a WFOE shall not be subject to interference by the government authorities. Unlike equity joint ventures, WFOEs must allocate at least 10 per cent of tax-profits to the reserve fund for a certain number of years.

The major legal basis for investment companies also called "umbrella **E.50** companies" or "holding companies" is the Provisional Regulations on the Establishment of Investment Companies by Foreign Investment which was promulgated and became effective on April 4, 1995 (Investment Company Regulations). Investment companies are limited liability companies and have the status of Chinese legal persons under Chinese law. Foreign investors may establish an investment company in China either in the form of a WFOE or in the form of a joint venture with a Chinese investor.

Foreign investors must meet the following rather strict requirements to establish an investment company:

1. A foreign investor must have good credit standing and the required financial capability. Specifically, it must fulfill one of the following two requirements:
   (a) it has total assets worth no less than US$400 million in the year prior to the submission of its application, has established foreign invested enterprises (FIE) in China with paid-up registered capital of more than US$10 million, and has obtained approval for three or more investment proposals; or
   (b) it has already established 10 or more FIEs engaged in production or infrastructure projects with paid-up registered capital of more than US$30 million;
2. The registered capital of the investment company must be not less than US$30 million; and
3. Where the investment company is to be established in the form of a joint venture, the Chinese party must have good credit standing and the required financial capability and total assets no less than RMB 100 million.

An investment company may invest in sectors such as industry, agriculture, infrastructure and energy that are encouraged by the state and in which foreign investment is permitted. The investment activities of the investment company are not restricted to the place of its registration.

An investment company may also provide services for its invested enterprise, in which the capital contribution by such investment company alone, or together with other foreign investors, should account for more than 25 per cent of the registered capital of the enterprise. The services include:

1. Assisting or acting as an agent in purchasing for production and in selling inside and outside China the products produced by the invested enterprise as well as providing after-sales services;
2. With the consent and under the supervision of the relevant exchange control authority, balancing foreign exchange among the invested enterprises;
3. Assisting in the employment of staff and providing technical training, marketing and consulting services;
4. Assisting in obtaining loans and providing guarantees for the invested enterprise, and

5. Subject to the approval of the People's Bank of China, providing financial support to the invested enterprise. The business between the investment company and its invested enterprises should be conducted as business between independent enterprises.

While an investment company may not act on behalf of its investors to engage in intermediary trading services in China, it may provide consulting services to its investors.

Representative offices and branch offices are two forms of doing business **E.51** widely used by multi-national companies. Representative offices in China are established in accordance with regulations issued by the Chinese government as well as local legislation which supplements the national regulations. Representative offices are permitted only to make business contacts and render services on behalf of their head offices. Branch offices are established by regulations relating to branch offices of foreign banks. The Company Law of the People's Republic of China allows branch offices of foreign companies, but implementing regulations have not yet been issued.

A foreign corporation wishing to establish a representative office must first find a Chinese entity to serve as its sponsor. It must then submit application materials to the local approval authorities. The approval authority will review the applicant's international standing, type of product, know-how or service to be performed in China, and other factors and will approve or reject the application within one month after formal submission.

Processing and assembly arrangements involve the shipment of raw materials or semi-processed goods to a Chinese workshop or factory which then processes or assembles the imported materials or goods and reexports the finished products back to the foreign party. The Chinese party to a processing and assembly operation must have the status of a legal person and must have authority to enter into contracts with foreign partners. The processing and assembly contract must be examined and approved by MOFTEC, the relevant ministry or commission under the State Council or the local government department of foreign economic relations and trade.

Technology transfer is governed by the Provision on the Administration of Technology Import Contracts of the People's Republic of China, its Implementing Regulation, the Foreign Economic Contract Law of the People's Republic of China, and laws and regulations relating to patents, trademarks, copyrights and computer software, etc. Technology transfer contracts must be in writing and be examined and approved by MOFTEC and other agencies authorized by MOFTEC. The examination and approval authorities will make a decision as to whether to approve the contracts in 60 days after receiving the application.

The emphasis of foreign investment legislation in the initial stage of opening to the outside world was to attract the maximum foreign investment to China. The focus of China's foreign investment legislation has now gradually shifted to establishing a rational structure for foreign investment and to utilizing foreign investment to adjust China's industrial structure. One example reflecting this shift of foreign investment policy is the recent promulgation of the Provisional Regulations on Guiding the Direction of Foreign Investment which is intended to channel foreign investment into the industries and areas most in need of foreign capital and technology. By dividing foreign investment into "encouraged", "permitted", "restricted" and "prohibited" projects, the regulations help to make China's investment priorities more transparent, thus making it easier for foreign business to determine a proposed project's chances for approval. Moreover, as China continues its application for the membership in the World Trade Organization, it will likely make further changes to grant foreign invested enterprises the same treatment (*i.e.* "national treatment") enjoyed by domestic invested enterprises.

Tax Laws

E.52 China's current tax regime took shape in the early 1990s. At that time China took two important steps. First, it consolidated the two income tax laws concerning foreign investment and a large body of rulings and regulations into the Income Tax Law of the People's Republic of China for Enterprises with Foreign Investment and Foreign Enterprises in 1991. Second, it unified China's various indirect taxes into a single system with the promulgation of a series of tax regulations concerning turnover and other taxes in 1994. The result of this overhaul of the tax system is a fairly complex and sophisticated tax regime that is compatible with China's economic development and its policy of attracting foreign capital, advanced technology and know-how. Moreover, the tax reform has also laid a solid basis for China to further conform its tax regime to established international practice.

The current tax regime in China has a distinctive feature: it maintains two separate income tax systems, one for domestic invested enterprises and one for foreign invested enterprises. Under China's tax regime, the income of domestic enterprises is taxed under the Provisional Rules of the People's Republic of China on Enterprise Income Tax, while the income of foreign invested enterprises is taxed under the Income Tax Law of the People's Republic of China for Enterprises with Foreign Investment and Foreign Enterprises which extends considerable preferential tax treatment to enterprises. In addition to income tax, both domestic enterprises and foreign enterprises are subject to the same turnover taxes (value added tax, consumption tax, and business tax) and other taxes, including real estate tax, stamp tax, land value-added tax, resource tax, etc. Individuals in China (including foreigners) are subject to individual income tax.

Value added tax (VAT) is a newly-introduced tax that is levied on the value added resulting from production and circulation. The scope of application of the VAT includes all taxable goods and services supplied by all individual enterprises operating in China. VAT is imposed at three rates, namely: the base rate of 17 per cent, a lower rate of 13 per cent, and the zero rate. The 17 per cent rate applies to all sales or import of goods not eligible for the 13 per cent and the zero rate. The 13 per cent rate, as a reflection of preferential state policies toward certain industries, applies to sales or imports of certain daily necessities, public utility products, publications, and certain agricultural products. The zero per cent rate has a narrow scope of application as it applies only to export goods. The VAT regulations also provide VAT exemption for the sale of certain types of goods.

The consumption tax is an excise tax imposed on certain consumer goods and consumer activities. The taxpayers of the consumption tax include individuals and enterprises that manufacture, import consumer goods, provide certain services, or transfer intangible or fixed assets within China. A total of 11 categories of non-necessity and luxury goods are subject to the consumption tax. The tax rates for these goods range from 3 per cent on cars to 45 per cent on high quality cigarettes, reflecting the state's policies to restrain consumption and to employ the "tax lever" to adjust industry structure.

The business tax is levied on all entities and individuals who are located in **E.53** China and provide taxable labor services, assign intangible assets, or sell immovable property. The business tax applies to nine types of business activities that include transportation, construction, postal communication, financial service, and cultural and sports services, etc., with tax rates ranging from 3 per cent to 20 per cent.

The enterprise income tax is levied on income of enterprises from production, business operation, and other sources. The taxpayers of the enterprise income tax are domestic investment enterprises including state-owned enterprises, collectively-owned enterprises, private enterprises, affiliated enterprises, share formulated enterprises, and other organizations with income derived from production, business operations, and other sources. The rate for enterprise income tax is 33 per cent on taxable income.

The income tax for enterprises with foreign investment, foreign enterprises and foreign representative offices is imposed on the income of foreign invested enterprises from production, business operations, and other sources. In addition to income tax, foreign invested enterprises are also subject to turnover taxes composed of VAT, consumption tax, business tax, and other taxes as a result of the unification of turnover taxes for both domestic investment enterprises and foreign invested enterprises. However, to avoid increasing the tax burden for foreign invested enterprises established prior to December 31, 1993, China allows those foreign invested enterprises a refund for the extra tax payments resulting from the newly-introduced turnover taxes for a maximum of five years.

Chinese law offers foreign invested enterprises extensive preferential income tax treatment based on the nature, industry, duration of investment, and location of foreign invested enterprises. As a reflection of China's economic and industrial policies, the income tax law for foreign invested enterprises and local legislation have granted tax exemption and reduction to production enterprises, enterprises adopting advanced technology, export-oriented enterprises, enterprises engaging in agricultural, forestry, animal husbandry, and enterprises reinvesting in China.

E.54   Foreign invested enterprises established in the Special Economic Zones (SEZs), Hainan Province and Shanghai Pudong New Area and foreign invested enterprise engaging in production in Economic and Technological Development Zones are entitled to a reduced rate of 15 per cent on their incomes. Similarly, foreign invested enterprises located in the Coastal Economic Open Zones, and old Urban Districts of cities where SEZs or the Economic and Technological Development are located enjoy a reduced rate of 24 per cent.

Manufacturing enterprises with a term of more than 10 years are eligible for 100 per cent tax exemption for the initial two profit-making years and a 50 per cent reduction in the subsequent three years. Export-oriented, technologically advanced, and enterprises reinvesting in energy, communication, harbor, wharf or other projects encouraged by China enjoy more tax exemption and reduction than other enterprises, and are generally entitled to reduction for local income tax for a longer period of time. Foreign invested enterprises reinvesting their shares of the profits from their other investments in China in a different enterprise for a period of not less than five years are entitled to receive a refund of a certain percentage paid on such reinvested profits.

Foreign invested enterprises are required to adopt an accounting system with the internationally used accrual basis. The accounting system adopted by the foreign invested enterprises must be reported to the competent government authorities and the local financial and tax departments for the record. All accounting records, books and statements are required to be prepared and kept in Chinese, or in both Chinese and another foreign language simultaneously.

The fiscal year of foreign invested enterprises is from January 1 to December 31 and accounting periods are divided into month, quarter and year. Within 15 days after the end of each quarter, the quarterly and annual accounting statements are submitted, separately to the financial departments in charge, the local taxation authority, and the relevant business regulatory department of the enterprises. The annual accounting statements are submitted together with the audit report as compiled by a public accountant certified in China to the original examination and approval authorities within four months after the end of the year. Chinese legislation requires an accountant registered in China to act as the auditor of the joint venture in verifying annual accounting statements.

A Notice issued by the State Council in December 1995 provides that starting from April 1, 1996 customs duties and import value-added tax (VAT) shall be levied on all imported equipment and raw materials based on statutory tax rates. Foreign invested enterprises approved after April 1, 1996 shall pay taxes on equipment and raw materials imported. A grace period of one or two years will be granted to foreign invested enterprises approved before April 1, 1996 so they can still enjoy the preferential treatment of exemption from import taxes.

The establishment of a conventional but sophisticated tax system reflects China's economic transformation to a socialist market economy where it increasingly uses taxation as an "economic lever" to regulate the economy and to reach a balance between using taxation to collect revenue and using taxation to encourage introduction of foreign capital and technology. One remaining problem with China's tax regime is that China still maintains different tax treatment for domestic investment enterprises and foreign invested enterprises and enterprises located in the SEZs and other areas. Once China becomes a member of the World Trade Organization, the income tax treatment for domestic and foreign invested enterprises will probably be unified to meet the requirement of national treatment and to enable all enterprises, foreign invested or domestic invested, to compete on a completely equal footing.

Intellectual Property Law

Intellectual Property Protection

China has made great progress in the area of intellectual property protection   E.55
since 1979. It has issued new legislation regarding patents, trademarks, copyrights, computer software, and trade secrets. It has become a signatory to the Paris Convention, the Patent Cooperation Treaty of the WIPO, the Berne Convention, the Universal Copyright Convention, the Geneva Convention and the Madrid Agreement concerning the International Registration of Marks.

Patents

Patent rights in China are governed by the Patent Law and its implementing   E.56
regulations. The Patent Law protects three separate classes of patents: invention, utility model, and design. An invention comprises any new technical solution regarding a product, a process, or an improvement thereof. A utility model is any new technical solution relating to the shape or structure of a product that is capable of practical use. Design relates to any new shape, pattern, or color of a product or to the combination thereof that creates an aesthetic feeling and that is suitable for industrial application.

The applicant creator of the invention, utility model or design applies for patent protection by filing an application with the Patent Office. The Patent Law adopts a first-to-file system. Pursuant to the Paris Convention, however, if a patent application is filed in China within 12 months after the filing date in another member country of the convention, the prior filing date will be regarded as the priority date in China. Inventions are protected for 20 years from the application filing date, with no renewal term. Utility models and industrial designs are accorded 10 years of protection.

Trade Marks

E.57   The Trade Mark Law provides for a first-to-file system of registration. Therefore, except for "well-known" marks under the Paris Convention, use of a mark is not a prerequisite to registration of a trade mark, but it is required to maintain registration.

An application for trade mark registration must be filed with the Trade Mark Office of the SAIC. Registration of a Chinese version of a foreign-word mark is not mandatory. For marketing purposes, however, it is advisable to develop and register a Chinese version of the foreign-word mark. Since November 1988, China has adopted the International Classification of Goods and Services. From July 1993, applications for service marks also may be filed.

A trade mark registration is valid for 10 years from the date of approval, with a further 10-year renewal term available. The registered trade mark may be canceled, among other things, if it has not been used for a period of three consecutive years or if the quality of the goods to which it is associated has not been maintained. The use requirement is satisfied by use of the mark in media advertising and exhibition as well as actual sale of goods bearing the mark. When a registered trade mark is licensed, a copy of the trade mark license must be submitted to the local SAIC bureau within three months of the execution of such license. The licensor also must file a copy of the license agreement with the Trademark Office. Failure to register a trade mark license may result in cancellation of the registered mark. In addition, the name of the licensee and the place of origin of the goods on which the trade marks are applied must be stated on the goods.

Copyrights

E.58   China enacted the Copyright Law effective June, 1991. Protected subject matter under the Copyright Law covers, among other things, literary works, musical, dramatic and choreographic works, television and video works, product and engineering designs, and computer programs. The implementing regulations under the Copyright Law extend protection to utilitarian articles that have ornamental features, such as jewelry, watches, toys and furniture. Upon China's accession to the Berne Convention in October, 1992, all works originating in a member country of the Berne Convention that were not in the public domain in the country of origin became protected in China. There is no registration requirement for copyright subject matter. Under the Copyright Law, most copyrights are protected for the life of the author plus 50 years. If copyrights are originally vested in a legal person, the duration of protection is 50 years from the date of first publication.

Computer software is protected subject matter under the Copyright Law. The Regulations for the Protection of Computer Software (Software Regulations) provide for details of software protection. Foreign works of software are protected in China in accordance with bilateral or multilateral agreements to which China is a party. For instance, foreign software created by citizens of a member country of the Berne Convention is protected in China. Registration of software is a precondition to the filing of infringement actions with the Chinese courts or administrative departments. The State Copyright Administration is now responsible for administering the registration of copyright in software. The Software Regulations grant an initial term of protection of 25 years from the date of first publication, with an additional 25-year term of protection available upon application. The Software Regulations limit the duration of licensing contracts to 10 years.

Trade Secrets

Trade secrets are protected under the Law of the PRC against Unfair Competition (the Unfair Competition Law). The Unfair Competition Law defines "trade secrets" as technical and economic information which is private and can bring economic benefits to the owner and for which the owner has adopted measures to maintain its confidentiality. Under the Unfair Competition Law, business operators are prohibited from infringing upon trade secrets of another party by theft, inducement, coercion or other illicit means; revealing, using or allowing others to use trade secrets obtained by such means; and revealing, using or allowing others to use trade secrets in breach of an agreement or the confidentiality obligations imposed by another party. If a third party knew or should have known of such acts violating the law, but obtains, uses or reveals trade secrets of others, this also constitutes an infringement. In the event of violation of the Unfair Competition Law, the Administration for Industry and Commerce shall order the infringer to cease the violation and may also impose a fine. The injured party also may seek injunctive relief or damages in court.

E.59

Recent Developments

China's legal framework for the protection of intellectual property is now relatively complete, but China's efforts to implement this legislation have been perceived as inadequate by some foreign countries, particularly in the software, movie and recording industry. In March 1995, the U.S. Trade Representative and the Chinese Foreign Trade Minister signed a letter agreement for rigorous enforcement of Chinese intellectual property laws.

E.60

The action plan under the letter agreement detailed a short-term and long-term strategy of intensive action against counterfeiting. Working conferences under the State Council directed and coordinated the action plan. Enforcement task forces were organized representing authorities responsible for intellectual property protection, including the National Copyright Administration, the SAIC, the Patent Office, police and customs officials. A central-ized copyright verification system was established for audio-visual products and computer software in CD-ROM format. All Chinese producers must show a valid chain of title to obtain government permission to use the work in question. Similarly, the publication of books, periodicals and other printed works requires a publishing license that is dependent on the applicant obtain-ing authorization to publish materials from the relevant intellectual property right holder. A nationwide publicity campaign was conducted to publicize the importance of intellectual property rights. The agreement also provided for the Trademark Office to establish a formal process for the determination of "well-known" status for trademarks.

The U.S. Trade Representative found the implementation of this letter agreement wanting, however, and as a result, another agreement was reached between the Trade Representative and the Chinese Foreign Trade Minister on June 18, 1996. In connection with this latest agreement, China took the following measures:

— it closed entirely or in part 15 factories producing counterfeit com-pact disks, laser disks and CD-ROMs;
— the Ministry of Public Security added intellectual property viola-tions to its "Severe Campaign Against Crime", placing special em-phasis on areas where piracy is serious;
— Chinese customs stepped up border surveillance;
— China established an enforcement verification stystem to prevent piracy, including 24-hour inspectors at every CD factory;
— China agreed to permit greater access to the Chinese market for U.S. movies, music and computer software.

Notes

[1] Zhang Yuejiao, "Law to Guarantee Reliability of Foreign Economic Contracts", *Intertrade*, July 1985, p.66. Ms. Zhang is Deputy Division Chief, Department of Treaty and Law, Ministry of Foreign Economic Relations and Trade. See, also, "The Foreign Economic Contracts Law is a Law that Safeguards and Promotes the Development of Foreign Economic Relations", *Zhongguo fazhi bao*, April 15, 1985, p.3, c.5. For further explanation of the term "international practice" see *China Law and Practice*, May 2, 1988, pp.61–62.
[2] See the Foreign Contracts Law, Art. 38, n.1 and the Law on Civil Procedure of the People's Republic of China, Art. 192.
[3] Art. 194 of the Civil Procedure Law, n.30 states that "a PRC foreign arbitration organization" can apply to a people's court for such protective measures in certain circumstances, but it is unclear whether this applies only to arbitration proceedings in China or to those conducted abroad as well.
[4] The Chinese Food Hygiene Law prohibits the production and marketing of foods in the following categories:

1. foods that can be injurious to human health because they are putrid or deteriorated, spoiled by rancid oil or fat, molded, infested with insects or worms, contaminated, contain foreign matter or manifest other sensory abnormalities;
2. foods that contain or are contaminated by toxic or deleterious substances and can thus be injurious to human health;
3. foods that contain pathogenic parasites, microorganisms or an amount of microbial toxin exceeding the tolerance level prescribed by the state;
4. meat and meat products that have not been inspected by the veterinary health service or have failed to pass such inspection;
5. poultry, livestock, game and aquatic animals that have died from disease, poisoning or some unknown cause, as well as products made from them;
6. foods contaminated by use of filthy or seriously damaged containers or packages, or filthy means of conveyance;
7. foods that impair nutrition or health because they are adulterated or misbranded;
8. foods prepared from inedible raw materials;
9. foods for which the storage time limit has expired;
10. foods of which the sale has been specifically prohibited, for the prevention of diseases or other special reasons, by the health authority of the State Council or by the people's governments of the provinces, autonomous regions, or municipalities directly under the Central Government;
11. foods that contain additives or residues of pesticides that have not been approved for use by the health authority of the State Council; and
12. other foods that do not conform to the standards and provisions for food hygiene.

According to the Regulations on Hygiene Supervision for Cosmetics, no unit or person in the cosmetics business shall be allowed to sell cosmetics of the following kinds:

1. cosmetics produced by an enterprise without a Hygiene License for a Cosmetics Production Enterprise;
2. cosmetics without a quality tag;
3. cosmetics of which the label, the smaller package or the specification sheet does not conform to the rules stipulated in Article 12 of these Regulations;
4. special cosmetics without an approval document;
5. cosmetics that have expired.

And the Chinese Pharmaceutical Administration Law provides that the production and sale of fake medicines are prohibited. A fake medicine has either of the following characteristics:

1. The names of its components are different from those prescribed for it by state pharmaceutical standards or pharmaceutical standards of the relevant province, autonomous region, or municipality directly under the Central Government;
2. the medicine has been produced without being assigned a registration number;
3. the medicine has deteriorated and cannot be used as such; or
4. the medicine has been contaminated.

The production and sale of medicines of inferior quality are prohibited. A medicine of inferior quality has any of the following characteristics:

1. The components of the medicine do not conform in quantity to that required by state pharmaceutical standards or pharmaceutical standards of the relevant

province, autonomous region, or municipality directly under the Central Government;

2. The medicine has passed its expiry date; or
3. The medicine fails to meet the prescribed standards in other respects.

PHILIPPINES

Jacinto D. Jimenez

I. Summary of Business and Political Conditions

Basic Demographic, Political and Economic Information

The Philippines is an archipelago consisting of 7,107 islands. The Philippines   F.01
lies between the southern tip of Taiwan and the northern tip of Borneo and
Indonesia. It is thus strategically located in the center of Southeast Asia.[1] It
has a land area of around 300,000 square kilometers. The area of its territory
is about the same as that of Italy. Luzon and Mindanao, the two largest
islands, consist of 105,000 and 95,000 square kilometers, respectively.[2]

The latest census, which was conducted in 1990, reported a population of
60,703,206.[3] Around 40 per cent of the population belong to the 15 to 40
years age group.[4] Because of the influx to the cities, the 1990 census indicated
that 48.7 per cent of the population are concentrated in the urban areas.[5]

The rate of literacy is 93.5 per cent.[6] Around 28.5 per cent of the population have completed high school education, and 6.4 per cent of the population have obtained a college degree.[7] English is the basic language used in
business, government, education and everyday communication.

The Gross National Product grew at an average rate of 6.2 per cent
annually from 1962 to 1970.[8] World-wide recession in the 1980s did not spare
the Philippine economy. The economic reforms initiated by the Government, which stressed deregulation, liberalization, and privatization, have
reversed the stagnation of the Philippine economy. In 1992, the Gross National Product grew by a modest 0.6 per cent.[9] Investments increased by 7.8
per cent.[10] Inflation was reduced to 8.9 per cent.[11] Exports dipped by 3.4
per cent because of the slow recovery of the global economy.[12] In 1993, the
gross national product grew by 2.3 per cent.[13] Investments increased by
10.5 per cent.[14] Inflation was pared to 7.6 per cent.[15] Exports expanded by

9 per cent.[16] Then in 1994, the gross national product grew by 5.1 per cent.[17] Investments increased by 10.1 per cent.[18] Inflation was pegged at 9 per cent.[19] Exports soared by 19.5 per cent.[20] Thus, the rate of the growth of the economy is accelerating, and inflation has been maintained at a single digit.

General Summary of Political and Governmental System in the Philippines

F.02　The 1987 Constitution sets up a presidential form of government. In accordance with the principle of checks and balances, legislative power is conferred upon Congress, executive power is vested upon the President, and judicial power is lodged in the Judiciary.[21]

Congress consists of two chambers, the Senate and the House of Representatives.[22] The Senate is composed of 24 senators elected on a nation-wide basis.[23] The House of Representatives is composed of 250 congressmen. Two hundred of them are elected by districts, while the remaining 50 are sectoral representatives.[24] The President is elected for a term of six years and is not eligible for re-election.[25]

At the head of the Judiciary is the Supreme Court, which is composed of a chief justice and 14 associate justices.[26] By virtue of the power of judicial review, the Judiciary can pass upon the constitutionality of the acts of Congress and the President.[27] The Constitution assiduously guarantees the independence of the Judiciary. Appointments to the Judiciary are taken from a list prepared by the Judicial and Bar Council.[28] The members of the Judiciary have a fixed tenure and serve until the age of 70.[29] Their salaries cannot be reduced.[30] The budget for the Judiciary cannot be reduced below the amount appropriated for the previous year and shall be automatically released.[31]

The Bill of Rights contains numerous guarantees found in the Constitution of the United States, such as due process, equal protection, security against unreasonable searches and seizures, privacy of communication, freedom of speech and of the press, freedom of religion, and right to form associations.[32]

The Constitution establishes a four-tiered hierarchy of local government units. The local government units are the provinces, cities, municipalities and barangays.[33]

Role of Law in the Past and Future Economic Development of the Philippines

F.03　The laws which regulate commercial activities have been enacted with a twofold purpose, i.e. to encourage business enterprises and to protect the consuming public. Laws have been passed to create an environment under which private enterprise can thrive. Thus, the 1987 Constitution recognizes the indispensable role of the private sector, encourages private enterprise, and provides incentives to needed investments.[34] At the same time, the laws try to insure that the goods and services being offered to the public meet quality standards and protect the public from fraudulent claims and defective products. Since public utilities service basic public needs, the fare they can charge is regulated by different regulatory agencies to insure that they obtain a reasonable rate of return on their investments and that the authorized fare is not unduly burdensome upon the public.[35]

Historical Development of the Legal and Judicial System

Legal System

The Spanish Civil Code, which was based on the Code of Napoleon and was adopted in 1889, was extended to the Philippines, which was then a colony of Spain, by the Royal Decree of July 31, 1889.[36] In 1950, it was replaced by the present Civil Code. Fifty-seven per cent of the provisions of the present Civil Code were taken from the Spanish Civil Code.[37] The Civil Code governs family relations, property, succession, and contracts. Although the Family Code, which was adopted in 1988, superseded the provisions of the Civil Code on family relations, the Family Code was based on the Civil Code. F.04

The Spanish Code of Commerce, which was based on the Code of Napoleon, was extended to the Philippines by the Royal Decree of April 5, 1888.[38] The provisions of the Spanish Code of Commerce governing merchants in general and maritime commerce are still in force.[39]

Upon the signing of the Treaty of Paris at the end of the Spanish-American War, Spain ceded the Philippines to the United States. The United States introduced in the Philippines a new legal system, the Anglo-Saxon common law. The provisions of the Spanish Code of Commerce on companies, negotiable instruments, insurance and insolvency were replaced with new laws patterned after American models.[40]

The legal system of the Philippines is a blending of Spanish laws and American laws adopted to suit the Philippine setting. While the prevailing general principles of contract are taken from civil law, the commercial laws of the Philippines are patterned after American laws.

Judicial System

The first Supreme Court of the Philippines was the Royal Audiencia established by King Philip II on May 5, 1583.[41] It was headed by the Governor- F.04

General. While the Royal Audiencia was principally a judicial body, it also wielded the powers of the Governor General in case of vacancy in the position, and acted as an advisory body to the Governor General on administrative and legislative matters.[42]

On August 5, 1589, King Philip II abolished the Royal Audiencia because of the opposition to it and the prohibitive cost of maintaining it.[43] However, because it played an important though limited role in checking abuses in the colonial administration, on November 26, 1595, King Philip II restored the Royal Audiencia.[44] The Royal Audiencia continued to function until the end of Spanish rule over the Philippines in 1898. Its decisions in certain civil cases were appealable to the Supreme Court of Spain. In 1815, the Governor-General ceased to be a member of the Royal Audiencia. In 1861, its functions were confined to the administration of justice.[45] The Royal Audiencia had its own share of failings, but it laid the foundation for the idea of an institutionalized system for administering justice.

Upon the conclusion of the Spanish-American War, the United States moved swiftly to establish civilian rule in the Philippines. On June 11, 1901, the Philippine Commission enacted Act 136, which established a three-tiered judiciary headed by the Supreme Court. At the bottom of the judicial ladder were the Courts of the Justices of the Peace, which served as trial courts with limited jurisdiction. In the middle were the Courts of First Instance, which were the trial courts with general jurisdiction. President William McKinley appointed three Filipinos and four Americans as the first justices of the Supreme Court. Cayetano Arellano, a Filipino, served as the first chief justice. On December 31, 1935, Commonwealth Act 3 was approved. This law created the Court of Appeals, which was vested with the power to review findings of fact of the Courts of First Instance. This four-tiered judicial structure has remained up to the present.[46]

Current Legal and Judicial Structures for Regulation of Commercial Activities in the Philippines

(a) *Adminstrative Agencies*
Department of Trade and Industry
Board of Investments
Bureau of Export Trade Promotion
Bureau of Patents, Trade Marks and Technology Transfer
Bureau of Product Standards
Bureau of Trade Regulation and Consumer Protection
Philippine Economic Zone Authority

Garments and Textile Export Board
Videogram Regulatory Board
Bangko Sentral ng Pilipinas
Copyright Section, National Library
Insurance Commission
Securities and Exchange Commission
Energy Regulatory Board
Civil Aeronautics Board
Land Transportation Franchising and Regulatory Board
Maritime Industry Authority
National Telecommunications Commission
Bureau of Food and Drugs
Environmental Management Bureau

(b) *Judiciary*
Supreme Court
Court of Appeals
Regional Trial Court
Metropolitan Trial Court, Municipal Trial Court and Municipal
Circuit Trial Court

Role of the Philippines in Global and Regional Trade Forums

With the approval of Resolution No. 97 on December 14, 1994, the Philip-　F.05
pines acceded to the Agreement establishing the World Trade Organization.
The Philippines is active in promoting free trade. It supports the creation
of the ASEAN Free Trade Area, which envisions the adoption of
minimum and uniform tariffs from 0 to 5 per cent by 2003. While the
Philippines endorsed the move to accelerate the pace of the implementation of this Agreement, it spearheaded the move to retain 2003 as the
target date for the inclusion of agricultural products within the coverage
of the ASEAN Free Trade Area. The transition period is needed to
enable its agricultural sector to prepare and adjust to competition in the
region.

The Philippines also endorsed the accord adopted on November 14, 1994
by the Asia Pacific Economic Cooperative to implement free trade in the
Asia Pacific area. Upon the initiative of the Philippines, the Asia Pacific
Economic Cooperation has agreed to recognize the importance of human
resources in achieving economic growth and development. The Philippines is
also promoting the development of small and medium enterprises to make
them competitive in the global market. The Philippines has also joined the
move to exclude agriculture from the scope of free trade in the Asia Pacific
area.

II. Laws and Institutions Affecting Business and Commercial Activities

Competition Law

Criminal Offense

F.06   The penalty of imprisonment from six months and one day to two years and four months or a fine ranging from 200 pesos to 6,000 pesos, or both, shall be imposed upon:

1. Any person who shall enter into any contract or agreement or shall take part in any conspiracy or combination in the form of a trust or otherwise, in restraint of trade or commerce or to prevent by artificial means free competition in the market;
2. Any person who shall monopolize any merchandise or object of trade or commerce or shall combine with any other person or persons to monopolize said merchandise or object in order to alter the price thereof by spreading false rumors or making use of any other artifice to restrain free competition in the market;
3. Any person who, being a manufacturer, producer, or processor of any merchandise or object of commerce or an importer of any merchandise or object of commerce from any foreign country, either as principal or agent, wholesaler or retailer, shall combine, conspire or agree in any manner with any person likewise engaged in the manufacture, production, processing, assembling or importation of such merchandise or object of commerce or with any other persons not so similarly engaged for the purpose of making transactions prejudicial to lawful commerce, or of increasing the market price in any part of the Philippines, of any such merchandise or object of commerce manufactured, produced, processed, assembled in or imported into the Philippines, or of any article in the manufacture of which such manufactured, produced, processed, or imported merchandise or object of commerce is used.

If the offense mentioned in this article affects any food substance, motor fuel or lubricants, or other articles of prime necessity, the penalty shall be that of imprisonment from six years and one day to 10 years, it being sufficient for the imposition thereof that the initial steps have been taken toward carrying out the purposes of the combination. Furthermore, any property possessed under any contract or by any combination mentioned in the preceding paragraphs, and being the subject thereof, shall be forfeited to the Government of the Philippines. Whenever any of the offenses described above is committed by a corporation or association, the president and each one of the directors or managers of the said corporation or association or its agent or representative in the Philippines, in the case of a foreign corporation or association, who shall have knowingly permitted or failed to prevent the commission of such offenses, shall be held liable as principals thereof.[47]

Civil Action

The Regional Trial has the jurisdiction to prevent and restrain violations of the Revised Penal Code 1932, Art. 186.[48] Any person who shall be injured in his business or property by any other person by anything forbidden or declared to be unlawful by the Revised Penal Code 1932, Art. 186, shall recover threefold the damages he sustained, and the costs of suit, including a reasonable attorney's fee.[49] **F.07**

Contract Law

General Principles

A contract is a meeting of minds between two persons whereby one binds himself, with respect to the other, to give something or to render some service.[50] The contracting parties may establish such stipulations, clauses, terms and conditions as they may deem convenient, provided they are not contrary to law, morals, good customs, public order or public policy.[51] The contract must bind both contracting parties; its validity or compliance cannot be left to the will of one of them.[52] Thus, an agreement that a lessee can occupy the leased premises as long as he wants is invalid, for the duration of the lease will depend solely on the will of the lessee.[53] Likewise, a stipulation that the lender can increase the interest at will is void.[54] The determination of the performance of a contract may be left to a third person.[55] However, the determination shall not be obligatory if it is evidently inequitable. In such case, the courts shall decide what is equitable under the circumstances.[56] **F.08**

Contracts take effect only between the parties, their assigns and heirs, except in cases where the rights and obligations arising from the contract are not transmissible by their nature, by stipulation or by provision of law.

If a contract should contain some stipulation in favor of a third person, he may demand its fulfillment provided he communicated his acceptance to the obligor before its revocation. A mere incidental benefit or interest of a person is not sufficient. The contracting parties must have clearly and deliberately conferred a favor upon a third person.[57] A third person who induces another to violate his contract shall be liable for damages to the other contracting parties.[58]

Contracts are perfected by mere consent, and from that moment the parties are bound not only to the fulfillment of what has been expressly stipulated but also to all the consequences which, according to their nature, may exist in keeping with good faith, usage, and law.[59] Real contracts, however, such as deposit, pledge and commodatum are not perfected until the delivery of the object of the obligation.[60]

Essential Requisites

F.09   There is no contract unless the following requisites concur:

1.   Consent of the contracting parties;
2.   Object certain which is the subject matter of the contract, and
3.   Cause of the obligation which is established.[61]

Consent is manifested by the meeting of the offer and the acceptance upon the thing and the cause which are to constitute the contract. The offer must be certain and the acceptance absolute. A qualified acceptance constitutes a counter-offer. Acceptance made by letter or telegram does not bind the offerer except from the time it came to his knowledge.[62] An acceptance may be express or implied.[63] Thus, the payment of the price indicated in a contract implies acceptance of its terms and conditions by the payor.[64] An offer becomes ineffective upon the death, civil interdiction, insanity or insolvency of other party before acceptance is conveyed.[65]

Futhermore, the following cannot give consent to a contract: (a) unemancipated minors; and (b) insane or demented persons, or deaf-mutes who do not know how to write.[66] Contracts agreed to in a state of drunkenness or during a hypnotic spell are voidable; however, contracts entered into by an insane or demented person during a lucid interval are valid.[67]

Furthermore a contract where consent is given through mistake, violence, intimidation, undue influence, or fraud is voidable.[68] In order that mistake may invalidate consent, it must refer to the substance of the thing which is the object of the contract, or to those conditions which have principally moved one or both parties to enter into the contract. Mistake as to the identity or qualifications of one of the parties will vitiate consent only when such identity or qualifications have been the principal cause of the contract.[69] There is no mistake if the party alleging it knew the doubt, contingency or risk affecting the object of the contract.[70] Mutual error as to the legal effect of an agreement when the real purpose of the parties is frustrated, may vitiate consent.[71]

There is violence when in order to wrest consent, serious or irresistible force is employed, and there is intimidation when one of the contracting parties is compelled by a reasonable and well-grounded fear of an imminent and grave evil upon his person or property, or upon the person or property of his spouse, descendants or ascendants, to give his consent. To determine the degree of the intimidation, the age, sex and condition of the person will be borne in mind. A threat to enforce one's claim through competent authority, if the claim is just or legal, does not vitiate consent.[72] Violence or intimidation annuls the obligation, although it may have been employed by a third person who did not take part in the contract.[73]

There is undue influence when a person takes improper advantage of his power over the will of another, depriving the latter of a reasonable freedom of choice. The following circumstances shall be considered: the confidential, family, spiritual and other relations between the parties, or the fact that the person alleged to have been unduly influenced was suffering from mental weakness, or was ignorant or in financial distress.[74]

There is fraud when through insidious words or the machinations of one of the contracting parties, the other is induced to enter into a contract which he would otherwise not have agreed to.[75] Failure to disclose facts, when there is a duty to reveal them, as when the parties are bound by confidential relations, also constitutes fraud.[76]

However the usual exaggerations in trade, when the other party had an opportunity to know the facts, are not in themselves fraudulent.[77] A mere expression of an opinion does not signify fraud, unless made by an expert and the other party has relied on the former's special knowledge.[78] Misrepresentation by a third person does not vitiate consent, unless such misrepresentation has created substantial mistake and the same is mutual.[79] Misrepresentation made in good faith is not fraudulent but may constitute error.[80] In order that fraud may make a contract voidable, it should be serious and should not have been employed by both contracting parties.[81]

All things which are not outside the commerce of men, including future things, may be the object of a contract. Rights which are not intransmissible may also be the object of contracts, as may be services which are not contrary to law, morals, good customs, public order or public policy may likewise be the object of a contract.[82] Impossible things or services cannot be the object of contracts.[83] The object of every contract must be determinate as to its kind. The fact that the quantity is not determinate shall not be an obstacle to the existence of the contract, provided it is possible to determine the same, without the need of a new contract between the parties.[84]

In onerous contracts the cause is understood to be, for each contracting party, the presentation or promise of a thing or service by the other; in remuneratory ones, the service or benefit which is remunerated; and in contracts of pure beneficence, the mere liberality of the benefactor.[85] The statement of a false cause in contracts shall render them void, if it should not be proved that they were founded upon another cause which is true and lawful.[86] Although the cause is not stated in the contract, it is presumed that it exists and is lawful, unless the debtor proves the contrary.[87] Except in cases specified by law, lesion or inadequacy of cause shall not invalidate a contract, unless there has been fraud, mistake or undue influence.[88]

Form

Contracts shall be obligatory, in whatever form they may have been entered into, provided all the essential requisites for their validity are present. However, when the law requires that a contract be in some form in order that it   F.10

may be valid or enforceable, or that a contract be proved in a certain way, that requirement is absolute and indispensable. In such cases, the right of the parties stated in Art. 1357 cannot be exercised.[89]

If the law requires a document or other special form, as in the acts and contracts enumerated in Art. 1358, the contracting parties may compel each other to observe that form, once the contract has been perfected. This right may be exercised simultaneously with the action upon the contract.[90]

The following must appear in a public document:

1. Acts and contracts which have for their object the creation, transmission, modification or extinguishment of real rights over immovable property; sales of real property or of an interest therein are governed by Arts. 1403, no. 2, and 1405;
2. The cession, repudiation or renunciation of hereditary rights or of those of the conjugal partnership of gains;
3. The power to administer property, or any other power which has for its object an act appearing or which should appear in a public document, or should prejudice a third person, and
4. The cession of actions or rights proceeding from an act appearing in a public document.

All other contracts where the amount involved exceeds 500 pesos must appear in writing, even a private one. But sales of goods, chattels or things in action are governed by Arts. 1403 No. 2 and 1405.[91]

Rescissible Contracts

F.11   The following contracts are rescissible:

1. Those which are entered into by guardians whenever the wards whom they represent suffer lesion by more than one-fourth of the value of the things which are the object thereof;
2. Those agreed upon in representation of absentees, if the latter suffer the lesion stated in the preceding number;
3. Those undertaken in fraud of creditors when the latter cannot in any other manner collect the claim due them;
4. Those which refer to things under litigation if they have been entered into by the defendant without the knowledge and approval of the litigants or competent judicial authority, and
5. All other contracts specially declared by law to be subject to rescission.[92]

Rescission shall not take place when the things which are the object of the contract are legally in the possession of third persons who acted in bad faith.[93] Furthermore rescission referred to in nos. 1 and 2 of Art. 1381 shall not take place with respect to contracts approved by the courts.[94] The action for rescission is subsidiary, it cannot be instituted except when the party suffering damage has no other legal means to obtain reparation for the same.[95]

All contracts by virtue of which the debtor alienates property by gratuitous title are presumed to have been entered into in fraud of creditors, when the donor did not reserve sufficient property to pay all debts contracted before the donation. Alienations by onerous title are also presumed fraudulent when made by persons against whom some judgment has been rendered in any instance or some writ of attachment has been issued. The decision or attachment need not refer to the property alienated, and need not have been obtained by the party seeking the rescission.[96] In addition to these presumptions, the design to defraud creditors may be proved in any other manner recognized by the law of evidence.

The following circumstances attending sales have been considered by the courts as badges of fraud:

1. The fact that the consideration of the conveyance is fictitious or is inadequate;
2. A transfer made by a debtor after case has been begun and while it is pending against him;
3. A sale upon credit by an insolvent debtor;
4. Evidence of large indebtedness or complete insolvency;
5. The transfer of all or nearly all of his property by a debtor, especially when he is insolvent or greatly embarrassed financially;
6. The fact that the transfer is made between father and son when there are present other of the above circumstance, and
7. The failure of the vendee to take exclusive possession of all the property.[97]

Rescission shall be only to the extent necessary to cover the damages caused.[98] It creates the obligation to return things which were the object of the contract, together with their fruits, and the price with its interest; consequently, it can be carried out only when he who demands rescission can return whatever he may be obliged to restore.[99] Whoever acquires in bad faith the things alienated in fraud of creditors, shall indemnify the latter for damages suffered by them on account of the alienation, if, for any reason, it should be impossible for him to return them. If There are two or more alienations, the first acquirer shall be liable first, and so on successively.[100]

Voidable Contracts

The following contracts are voidable or annullable, even though there may have been no damage to the contracting parties: **F.12**

1. Those where one of the parties is incapable of giving consent to a contract, and
2. Those where the consent is vitiated by mistake, violence, intimidation, undue influence or fraud.

However, these contracts are binding, unless they are annulled by a proper action in court.[101]

Philippines

The action for the annulment of contracts may be instituted by all who are thereby obliged principally or subsidiarily. However, persons who are capable cannot allege the incapacity of those with whom they contracted; nor can those who exerted intimidation, violence, or undue influence, or employed fraud or caused mistake base their action upon these flaws of the contract.[102]

An obligation having been annulled, the contracting parties shall restore to each other the things which have been the subject matter of the contract and the price with its interest, except in cases provided by law. In obligations to render service, the value of the service shall be the basis for damages.[103] When the defect of the contract consists in the incapacity of one of the parties, the incapacitated person is not obliged to make any restitution except insofar as he has been benefitted by the thing or price received by him.[104]

If the person obliged by the decree of annulment to return the thing cannot do so because it has been lost through his fault, he must return the fruits received and the value of the thing at the time of the loss, with interest from the same date.[105] In addition, if of the contracting parties does not restore what in virtue of the decree of annulment he is bound to return, the other cannot be compelled to comply with what is incumbent upon him.[106]

An action for annulment must be brought within four years. This period shall begin, in cases of intimidation, violence or undue influence, from the time the defect of the consent ceases. In cases of mistake or fraud, it shall begin from the time of discovery of the same. When the action refers to contracts entered into by minors or other incapacitated persons, it shall begin from the time the guardianship ceases.[107]

Ratification extinguishes the action to annul a voidable contract[108] and may be effected expressly or tacitly and may be effected by the guardian of the incapacitated person.[109] It is understood that there is a tacit ratification if, with knowledge of the reason which renders the contract voidable and such reason having ceased, the person who has a right to invoke it should execute an act which necessarily implies an intention to waive his right.[110] Ratification does not require the conformity of the contracting party who has no right to bring the action for annulment.[111]

The action for annulment of contracts is extinguished when the object of the action is lost through the fraud or fault of the person who has a right to institute the proceedings. However, if the right of action is based upon the incapacity of any one of the contracting parties, the loss of the thing shall not be an obstacle to the success of the action, unless the loss took place through the fraud or fault of the plaintiff.[112]

Unenforceable Contracts

F.13   Contracts entered into in the name of another person by one who has been given no authority or legal representation, or who has acted beyond his powers are unenforceable, unless they are ratified as are those that do not comply with the Statute of Frauds as set forth in this number. In the following cases an agreement hereafter made shall be unenforceable by action, unless the same, or some note or memorandum thereof, be in writing, and subscribed by the party charged, or by his agent; evidence, therefore, of the agreement cannot be received without the writing, or a secondary evidence of its contents:

1. An agreement that by its terms is not to be performed within a year from the making thereof;
2. A special promise to answer for the debt, default, or miscarriage of another;
3. An agreement made in consideration of marriage, other than a mutual promise to marry;
4. An agreement for the sale of goods, chattels or things in action, at a price not less than 500 pesos, unless the buyer accept and receive part of such goods and chattels, or the evidences, or some of them, of such things in action, or pay at the time some part of the purchase money; but when a sale is made by auction and entry is made by the auctioneer in his sales book, at the time of the sale, of the amount and kind of property sold, terms of sale, price, names of the purchasers and person on whose account the sale is made, it is a sufficient memorandum;
5. An agreement for the leasing for a longer period than one year, or for the sale of real property or of an interest therein, and
6. A representation as to the credit of a third person.

Contracts where both parties are incapable of giving consent are also unenforceable.[113]

Contracts infringing the Statute of Frauds referred to in no. 2 of Art. 1403, are ratified by the failure of object to the presentation of oral evidence to prove the same, or by the acceptance of benefits under them.[114]

Void Contracts

The following contracts are inexistent and void from the beginning: F.14

1. Those whose cause, object or purpose is contrary to law, morals good customs, public order or public policy;
2. Those which are absolutely simulated or fictitious;
3. Those whose cause or object did not exist at the time of the transaction;
4. Those whose object is outside the commerce of men;
5. Those which contemplate an impossible service;
6. Those where the intention of the parties relative to the principal object of the contract cannot be ascertained, and
7. Those expressly prohibited or declared void by law.[115]

Void contracts cannot be ratified neither can the right to set up the defense of illegality be waived.[116] Furthermore the action or defense for the declaration of the inexistence of a void contract does not prescribe.[117]

When the nullity proceeds from the illegality of the cause or object of the contract, and the act constitutes a criminal offense, both parties being in pari delicto, they shall have no action against each other, and both shall be prosecuted. Moreover, the provisions of the Revised Penal Code relative to the disposal of effects or instruments of a crime shall be applicable to the things or the price of the contract. This rule shall be applicable when only one of the parties is guilty; but the innocent one may claim what he has given, and shall not be bound to comply with his promise.[118] If the act in which the unlawful or forbidden cause consists does not constitute a criminal offense, the following rules will be observed:

1. When the fault is on the part of both contracting parties, neither may recover what he has given by virtue of the contract, or demand the performance of the other's undertaking, and
2. When only one of the contracting parties is at fault, he cannot recover what he has given by reason of the contract, or ask for the fulfillment of what has been promised him. The other, who is not at fault, may demand the return of what he has given without any obligation to comply with his promise.[119]

When money is paid or property delivered for an illegal purpose, the contract may be repudiated by one of the parties before the purpose has been accomplished, or before any damage has been caused to a third person. In such cases, the courts may, if the public interest will thus be subserved, allow the party repudiating the contract to recover the money or property.[120] When the agreement is not illegal *per se* but is merely prohibited, and the prohibition by the law is designed for the protection of the plaintiff, he may, if public policy is thereby enhanced, recover what he has paid or delivered.[121]

Commercial Law

Sales

F.15 By the contract of sale one of the contracting parties obligates himself to transfer and deliver the determinate thing, and the other to pay therefore a price certain in money or its equivalent.[122] The thing must be licit and the vendor must have a right to transfer the ownership of it at the time it is delivered.[123] A thing is determinate when it is particularly designated or physically segregated from all others of the same class. The requisite that a thing be determinate is satisfied if at the time the contract is entered into, the thing is capable of being made determinate without the necessity of a new or further agreement between the parties.[124] Things having a potential existence may be the object of the contract of sale. The efficacy of the sale of a mere hope or expectancy is deemed subject to the condition that the thing will come into existence. The sale of a vain hope or expectancy is void.[125] The goods which form the subject of a contract of sale may be either existing goods, owned or possessed by the seller, or goods to be manufactured, raised, or acquired by the seller after the perfection of the contract of sale, in this Title called "future goods". There may be a contract of sale of goods, whose acquisition by the seller depends upon a contingency which may or may not happen.[126]

The fixing of the price can never be left to the discretion of only one of the contracting parties. However, if the price fixed by one of the parties is accepted by the other, the sale is perfected.[127] In order that the price may be considered certain, it is sufficient that it be so with reference to another thing certain, or that the determination thereof be left to the judgment of a special person or persons. Should such person or persons be unable or unwilling to fix it, the contract shall be inefficacious, unless the parties subsequently agree upon the price. If the third person or persons acted in bad faith or by mistake, the courts may fix the price.[128] Gross inadequacy of price does not affect a contract of sale, except as it may indicate a defect in the consent, or that the parties really intended a donation or some other act or contract.[129] The price of securities, grain, liquids, and other things shall also be considered certain, when the price fixed is that which the thing sold would have on a definite day, or in a particular exchange or market, or when an amount is fixed above or below the price on such a day, or in such an exchange or market, provided the said amount be certain.[130] The vendor is bound to transfer the ownership of and deliver, as well as warrant, the thing which is the object of the sale.[131]

The thing sold shall be understood as delivered, when it is placed in the control and possession of the vendee.[132] When the sale is made through a public instrument, the execution thereof shall be equivalent to the delivery of the thing which is the object of the contract, if from the deed the contrary does not appear or cannot clearly be inferred. With regard to movable property, its delivery may also be made by the delivery of the keys of the place or depository where it is stored or kept.[133] It may also be made by the mere consent or agreement of the contracting parties, if the thing sold cannot be transferred to the possession of the vendee at the time of the sale, or if the latter already had it in his possession for any other reason.[134]

With respect to incorporeal property, the provisions of the first paragraph of Art. 1498 shall govern. In any other case where the said provisions are not applicable, the placing of the titles of ownership in the possession of the vendee or the use by the vendee of his rights, with the vendor's consent, shall be understood as a delivery.[135]

In a contract of sale, unless a contrary intention appears, there is:

1. An implied warranty on the part of the seller that he has a right to sell the thing at the time when the ownership is to pass, and that the buyer shall from that time have and enjoy the legal and peaceful possession of the thing, and
2. An implied warranty that the thing shall be free from any hidden faults or defects, or any charge or encumbrance not declared or known to the

buyer.[136] The vendee is bound to accept delivery and to pay the price of the thing sold at the time and place stipulated in the contract.[137]

Secured Transactions

F.16 By guaranty a person called the guarantor binds himself to a creditor to fulfill the obligation of the principal in case the latter should fail to do so. If a person binds himself solidarily with the principal debtor, the contract is called a suretyship.[138] A guaranty cannot exist without a valid obligation. Nevertheless, a guaranty may be constituted to guarantee the performance of a voidable or an unenforceable contract. It may also guarantee a natural obligation.[139] A guaranty may also be given as security for future debts, the amount of which is not yet known. There can be no claim against the debtor until the debt is liquidated. A conditional obligation may also be secured.[140] A guarantor may bind himself for less but not more than the principal debtor both as regards the amount and the onerous nature of the conditions. Should he have bound himself for more, his obligations shall be reduced to the limits of that of the debtor.[141] The guarantor cannot be compelled to pay the creditor unless the latter has exhausted all the property of the debtor, and has resorted to all the legal remedies against the debtor.[142]

This excussion shall not take place:

1. If the guarantor has expressly renounces it;
2. If he has bound himself solidarily with the debtor;
3. In case of insolvency of the debtor;
4. When he has absconded or cannot be sued within the Philippines unless he has left a manager or representative, or
5. If it may be presumed that an execution on the property of the principal debtor would not result in the satisfaction of the obligation.[143]

The guarantor who pays for a debtor must be indemnified by the latter. The indemnity comprises:

1. The total amount of the debt;
2. The legal interests thereon from the time the payment was made known to the debtor, even though it did not earn interest for the creditor;
3. The expenses incurred by the guarantor after having notified the debtor that payment had been demanded of him, and
4. Damages, if they are due.[144]

The guarantor who pays is subrogated by virtue thereof to all the debts which the creditor had against the debtor. If the guarantor has compromised with the creditor, he cannot demand of the debtor more than what he has really paid.[145] If the guarantor should pay without notifying the debtor, the latter may enforce against him all the defenses which he could have set up against the creditor at the time the payment was made.[146]

The guarantor, even before having paid, may proceed against the principal debtor:

1. When he is sued for payment;
2. In case of insolvency of the principal debtor;
3. When the debtor has bound himself to relieve him from the guaranty within a specified period, and this period has expired;
4. When the debt has become demandable, by reason of the expiration of the period for payment;
5. After the lapse of ten years, when the principal obligation has no fixed period for its maturity, unless it be of such nature that it cannot be extinguished except within a period longer than ten years;
6. If there are reasonable grounds to fear that the principal debtor intends to abscond, or
7. If the principal debtor is in imminent danger of becoming insolvent.

In all these cases, the action of the guarantor is to obtain release from the guarantee or to demand a security that shall protect him from any proceedings by the creditor and from the danger of insolvency of the debtor.[147]

When there are two or more guarantors of the same debtor and for the same debt, the one among them who has paid may demand of each of the others the share which is proportionally owing from him. If any of the guarantors should be insolvent, his share shall be borne by the others, including the payee in the same proportion. This provision shall not be applicable unless the payment has been made by virtue of a judicial demand or unless the principal debtor is insolvent.[148]

The obligation of the guarantor is extinguished at the same time as that of the debtor, and for the same cause as all other obligations.[149] Thus, an increase in the amount of the debt secured by the guaranty made without the consent of the guarantor is a material change in the principal contract and discharges the guarantor from all liabilities.[150]

If the creditor voluntarily accepts immovable or other property in payment of the debt, the guarantor is release, even if the creditor should afterwards lose the same through eviction.[151] An extension granted to the debtor by the creditor without the consent of the guarantor extinguishes the guaranty.[152] Furthermore, the guarantors, even though they be solidary, are released from the obligation whenever by some act of the creditor they cannot be subrogated to the rights, mortgages, and preferences of the latter.[153]

The guarantor may set up against the creditor all the defenses which pertain to the principal debtor and are inherent in the debt except for those that are purely personal to the debtor.[154]

The rules applicable to pledge and mortgage are:

1. That they be constituted to secure the fulfillment of a principal obligation;

2. That the pledgor or mortgagor be the absolute owner of the thing pledged or mortgaged, and
3. That the persons constituting the pledge or mortgage have the free disposal of their property, and in the absence thereof, that they be legally authorized for the purpose.[155]

In addition, a public utility which will pledge or mortgage its properties must obtain the approval of the appropriate government agency regulating it.[156]

The creditor cannot appropriate the things given by way of pledge or mortgage, or dispose of them. Any stipulation to the contrary is void.[157] Thus, a stipulation that if the mortgagor fails to pay the mortgagee for his indebtedness the mortgagee will become the owner of the property mortgaged, is void.[158]

A pledge or mortgage is indivisible.[159] Thus, if several properties were pledged or mortgaged, if only a part of the debt has been paid, all the properties remain liable for the balance.[160]

To constitute the contract of pledge, the thing pledged must be placed in the possession of the creditor or of a third person by common agreement.[161] All movables which are within commerce may be pledged, provided they are susceptible of possession.[162] Incorporeal rights, evidenced by negotiable instruments, bills of lading, shares of stock, bonds, warehouse receipts, and similar documents may also be pledged. The instrument proving the right pledged shall be delivered to the creditor, and if negotiable, must be endorsed.[163] A pledge shall not take effect against third persons if a description of the thing pledged and the date of the pledge do not appear in a public investment.[164]

However, if the thing pledged is returned by the pledgee to the pledgor, the pledge is extinguished.[165] A statement in writing by the pledgee that he renounces or abandon the pledge is also sufficient to extinguish the pledge. For this purpose, neither the acceptance by the pledgor nor the return of the thing pledged is necessary.[166]

Sale of Thing Pledged

F.17 The creditor to whom the credit has not been satisfied in due time may proceed before a notary public to the sale of the thing pledged. This sale shall be made at a public auction and with notification to the debtor and the owner of the thing pledged in a proper case, stating the date and the place the sale is to be held. If at the said auction the thing is not sold, a second one with the same formalities shall be held. If at the second auction there is no sale either, the creditor may appropriate the thing pledged.[167]

The sale of the thing pledged shall extinguish the principal obligation, whether or not the proceeds of the sale are equal to the amount of the principal obligation, interest and expenses. If the price of the sale is more than said amount, the pledgor shall not be entitled to the excess unless it is otherwise agreed. If the price of the sale is less, the creditor shall not be entitled to recover the deficiency, notwithstanding any stipulation to the contrary.[168]

Personal property is recorded in the Chattel Mortgage Register as a security for the performance of an obligation.[169] Although the subject matter of a chattel mortgage is supposed to be personal property, the constitution of a chattel mortgage or real properties, such as a building or machinery bolted to the ground, has been considered as valid between the parties on the basis of estoppel.[170] If the chattel mortgage is not registered, it is binding between the parties. The mortgagee has the right to demand its registration.[171] Should the property which is the subject of a chattel mortgage be situated in a province or city different from that where the mortgagor resides, the chattel mortgage must be registered with the register of deeds, in both places.[172] If the subject matter of the chattel mortgage is a motor vehicle, to be valid against third parties it must also be registered with the Land Transportation Office.[173] No mortgage on a vessel of domestic ownership shall be valid against any person other than the mortgagor and a third person having actual knowledge of it until the mortgage is recorded in the office of the Philippine Coast Guard of the port of registration of the vessel.[174] No mortgage on a civil aircraft of Philippine registry shall be valid against any person other than the mortgagor and any person having actual knowledge thereof until it is recorded in the office of the Air Transportation Office.[175]

The mortgagor and the mortgagee must subscribe an affidavit to be appended to the chattel mortgage and recorded with it stating that the mortgage is made for the purpose of securing the obligation specified in the chattel mortgage and for no other purpose and that the same is a just and valid obligation and not entered into for the purpose of fraud.[176] The absence of an affidavit of good faith renders a chattel mortgage invalid against third parties.[177] Since the mortgagor and the mortgagee are required to swear that the chattel mortgage is being executed to secure a just and valid obligation, a chattel mortgage cannot be executed to secure a future indebtedness.[178]

While a chattel mortgage over real properties is valid between the parties on the basis of estoppel, for purposes of foreclosure the procedure for the foreclosure of a real estate mortgage should be followed.[179] Although the Chattel Mortgage Law 1906, section 14 provides that in cases of foreclosure, the sale may be held by public auction, the parties may stipulate that it will be by private sale.[180]

If the proceeds of the sale result in a deficiency, the creditor may sue the debtor to recover the deficiency.[181] However, in case of a chattel mortgage constituted on personal property which was sold in installment to secure the payment of the price, the seller cannot recover any deficiency in case of foreclosure, even if there is any stipulation to the contrary.[182]

Land may be mortgaged to a foreign creditor. However, in the case of foreclosure, the foreign creditors are disqualified to bid in the sale.[183] Foreigners are disqualified from owning land in the Philippines.[184] A real estate mortgage is valid between the parties even if it is not registered, but registration is required to make it binding on third parties.[185] A real estate mortgage may be foreclosed judicially[186] or extrajudicially.[187] If the foreclosure was made judicially, as a rule the mortgagor cannot redeem the property.[188] If the foreclosure was made extrajudicially, the mortgagor can redeem the property within one year.[189] The redemption period is counted from the date of the registration of the sale and not from the date of the sale.[190] However, if the mortgagee is a bank, whether the foreclosure was made judicially or extrajudicially, the mortgagee has the right to redeem the property within a period of one year.[191]

By the contract of antichresis, the creditor acquires the right to receive the fruits of an immovable of his debtor, with the obligation to apply them to the payment of the interest, if owing, and thereafter to the principal of his credit.[192] The amount of the principal and of the interest shall be specified in writing. Otherwise, the contract of antichresis shall be void.[193] The debtor cannot reacquire the enjoyment of the immovable without first having totally paid what he owes the creditor.[194] Moreover, the creditor may foreclose on the property given in antichresis either judicially or extra judicially.[195]

A trust receipt transaction is any transaction by and between an entrustee and an entruster whereby the entruster, who owns or holds absolute title or security over certain specified goods, documents or instruments, releases the same to the possession of the entrustee upon the latter's execution and delivery to the entruster of a trust receipt wherein the entrustee binds himself to hold the designated goods, documents or instrument in trust for the entruster and to sell or otherwise dispose of the goods, documents or instruments with the obligation to turn over to the entruster the proceeds thereof to the extent of the amount owing to the entruster or as appears in the trust receipt if they are unsold or not otherwise disposed of, in accordance with the terms and conditions specified in the trust receipt.[196] A trust receipt is a security agreement. The entruster does not become the real owner of the goods covered by the trust receipt. The entruster cannot therefore compel the entrustee to accept the goods in payment of his indebtedness.[197]

Companies Law

F.18   A corporation is an artificial being created by operation of law, having the right of succession and the powers, attributes and properties expressly authorized by law or incident to its existence.[198] It has a juridical personality separate and distinct from that of its stockholders[199]. However, its separate juridical personality will be disregarded when it is used to defeat public convenience, justify wrong, protect fraud or defend crime.[200]

Incorporation

F.19   The shares of stock corporations may be divided into classes or series of shares or both, any of which classes or series of shares may have such rights, privileges, or restrictions as may be stated in the articles of incorporation. The power to classify shares of stock is subject to the following restrictions:

1. No share may be deprived of voting rights except those classified and issued as preferred or redeemable shares;
2. Banks, trust companies, insurance companies, public utilities and building and loan associations shall not be permitted to issue no-par value shares of stock;
3. Preferred shares of stock may be issued only with a stated par value;
4. Shares without par value may not be issued for a consideration less than five pesos per share.[201]

Any group of not less than five but not more than 15 persons, all of legal age, and a majority of whom are residents of the Philippines, may form a private corporation. Each of the incorporators of a stock corporation must be a subscriber of at least one share of the capital stock of the corporation.[202]

At least 25 per cent of the authorized capital stock as stated in the articles of incorporation must be subscribed at the time of incorporation, and at least 25 per cent of the total subscription must be paid upon subscription. In no case shall the paid-up capital be less than 5,000 pesos.[203]

Directors and Officers

Directors are elected from among the stockholders and may hold office for one year and until their successors are elected and qualified.[204] Every stock-holder entitled to vote shall have the right to vote in person or by proxy. He may vote such number of stock for as many persons as there are to be elected or may cumulate said shares and give one candidate as many votes as the number of directors to be elected multiplied by the number of his shares may equal, or may distribute them on the same principle among as many candidates as he shall see fit.[205] Every director must have at least one share of the capital stock and a majority of the directors must be resident in the Philippines.[206]

In the absence of any provision in the by-laws fixing their compensation, the directors shall not receive any compensation except for reasonable *per diems*. Such compensation may be granted to the directors by the vote of the stockholders representing at least a majority of the outstanding capital stock. In no case shall the total yearly compensation of the directors exceed 10 per cent of the net income before income tax of the corporation during the preceding year.[207]

Any director may be removed from office by a vote of the stockholders holding at least two-thirds of the outstanding capital stock. Removal may be with or without cause, but removal without cause may not be used to deprive minority stockholders of the right of representation.[208]

Officers should be elected by the board of directors and not by the stockholders.[209] The president must be a director and the corporate secretary

F.20

must be a resident and citizen of the Philippines. Any two or more positions may be held by the same person, except that no one shall act as president and secretary or as president and treasurer at the same time.[210]

The officers cannot grant themselves compensation.[211] Their compensation must be fixed by the board of directors if it is not provided in the by-laws.[212] Furthermore, the officers hold office at the will of the board of directors and are removable anytime except when the exercise of this power is limited by a provision in the contract with a particular officer.[213]

A director or officer may be held personally liable in the following instances:

1. He assents to a patently unlawful act of the corporation;
2. He is guilty of bad faith or gross negligence in directing affairs;
3. He is guilty of conflict of interest, resulting in damages to the corporation, its stockholders or other persons;
4. He consents to the issuance of watered stock or having knowledge thereof, does not forthwith file with the corporate secretary his written objection thereto;
5. He agrees to hold himself personally and solidarily liable with the corporation;
6. He is made by a specific provision of law personally liable for his corporate action.[214]

Thus, the officers who fraudulently collected the payment for the account of corporate debtors which had been previously assigned to the bank and failed to remit the payment to the bank were guilty of bad faith and could be held personally liable by the bank.[215] The same holds true of the directors who dismissed in bad faith and without just cause the general manager who tried to implement remedial measures to stop anomalies.[216]

When a director or officer acquires any interest adverse to the corporation in respect of any matter which has been reposed in him in confidence as to which equity imposes a disability upon him to deal in his own behalf, he must account for the profits which otherwise would have accrued to the corporation.[217] In addition a director by virtue of his office acquires for himself a business opportunity which should belong to the corporation, he must account to the corporation for all profits he obtained, unless his act is ratified by a vote of the stockholders representing at least two-thirds of the outstanding capital stock. This rule applies even if the director risked his own funds in the venture.[218]

A contract of the corporation with one or more of its directors or officers is voidable at the option of the corporation unless the following conditions are present:

1. The presence of such director in the board meeting in which the contract was approved was not necessary to constitute a quorum for such meeting;

2. The vote of such director was not necessary for the approval of the contract;
3. The contract is fair and reasonable under the circumstances, or
4. In the case of an officer, the contract with him has been previously authorized by the board of directors.

Where any of the first two conditions is absent, such a contract may be ratified by the vote of the stockholders representing two-thirds of the out-standing capital stock, provided that full disclosure of the interest of the director is made at the meeting and that the contract is fair and reasonable under the circumstances.[219] The same rule applies in the case of contracts between corporations with interlocking directors when the interest of the interlocking director in one corporation exceeds 20 per cent of the outstanding capital stock and is merely nominal in the other corporation.[220]

With reference to the third condition above, a director of a corporation which manufactures white cement could not enforce a five-year distributorship agreement with the corporation which provided for a fixed selling price to him, because the contract was not fair, since the price of cement was not stable and was expected to rise.[221]

Stockholders

Stocks shall not be issued for considerations less than the par or issued price thereof. Consideration for the issuance of stock may be any of the following: **F.21**

1. Actual cash paid to the corporation;
2. Property, tangible or intangible, actually received by the corporation and necessary or convenient for its use and lawful purposes and a fair valuation equal to the par or issued value of the stock issued;
3. Labor performed for or services actually rendered to the corporation;
4. Previously incurred indebtedness of the corporation;
5. Amounts transferred from unrestricted retained earnings to stated capital, or
6. Outstanding shares exchanged for stocks in the event of reclassification or conversion.[222]

Subject to the provisions of the contract for subscription, the board of directors may at any time declare due and payable to the corporation unpaid subscriptions to the capital stock and may collect the same or such percentage of said unpaid subscription, as it may deem necessary.[223] The board of directors may, by resolution, also order the sale of delinquent stocks.[224]

All stockholders shall enjoy the pre-emptive right to subscribe to all issues or disposition of shares of any class in proportion to their respective shareholdings.[225] This includes the offering of the authorized but unissued capital stock for subscription. However, the stockholders shall have no pre-emptive right in the following instances:

1. The right is denied by the articles of incorporation;
2. The shares are being issued in compliance with laws requiring stock offerings or minimum stock ownership by the public;
3. The shares are being issued in good faith, with the approval of the stockholders representing at least two-thirds of the outstanding capital stock, in exchange for property needed for corporate purposes;
4. The shares are being offered in good faith, with the approval of the stockholders representing at least two-thirds of the outstanding capital stock in payment of a previously incurred debt.[226]

Stockholders may vote in person or by proxy in all meetings of stockholders. Proxies shall be in writing signed by the stockholders and filed before the scheduled meeting with the corporate secretary. Unless otherwise provided in the proxy, it shall be valid only by the meeting for which it is intended. No proxy shall be valid or effective for a period longer than five years at any one time.[227]

Holders of non-voting shares of stock are entitled to vote on the following matters:

1. Amendment of the articles of incorporation;
2. Adoption and amendment of by-laws;
3. Sale, lease, exchange, mortgage, pledge or other disposition of all or substantially all of the corporate property;
4. Incurring, creating or increasing bonded indebtedness;
5. Increase or decrease of capital stock;
6. Merger or consolidation of the corporation with another corporation or other corporations;
7. Investment of corporate funds in another corporation or business, or
8. Dissolution of the corporation.[228]

Stock corporations are prohibited from retaining surplus profits in excess of 100 per cent of their paid-in capital stock and must declare the excess as dividends except in the following instances:

1. When it is justified by definite corporate expansion projects or programs approved by the board of directors;
2. When the corporation is prohibited under any loan agreement with any financial institution or creditor, whether local or foreign, from declaring dividends without its consent, and such consent has not yet been secured, or
3. When it can be clearly shown that such retention is necessary in the corporation, such as when there is a need for special reserve for probable contingencies.[229]

The records of all business transactions of the corporation and the minutes of any meeting shall be open to inspection by any director or stockholder at reasonable hours on business days. They may demand in writing a copy of excerpts from the records or minutes at their own expense. Inspection may be refused if the person demanding to examine and copy excerpts from the records and minutes has improperly used any information secured through any prior examination of the records or minutes or was not acting in good faith or for a legitimate purpose in making his demand.[230] Thus, a corporation may refuse to allow a stockholder who purchased one share of stock purposely to be able to pry into transactions entered into by the corporation before he became a stockholder, because he was not acting in good faith.[231]

Any stockholder of a corporation shall have the right of dissent and to demand payment of the fair value of his shares in any of the following instances:

1. In case any amendment to the articles of incorporation has the effect of changing or restructuring the rights of any stockholders or class of shares, or of authorizing preferences in any respect superior to those of outstanding shares of any class, or of extending or shortening the term of corporate existence;
2. In case of sale, lease, exchange, transfer, mortgage, pledge or other disposition of all or substantially all of the corporate property and assets;
3. In case of merger or consolidation,[232] and
4. In case the corporation invests its funds in any other corporation or business or for any purpose other than the primary purpose for which it was organized.[233]

No payment shall be made to any dissenting stockholder unless the corporation has unrestricted retained earnings in its books to cover such payment.[234] The reason for this requirement is that the capital stock of the corporation is a trust fund for the benefit of its creditors.[235]

The right of the stockholders to bring a derivative suit is recognized in the Philippines. The following are the requisites for the filing of a derivative suit:

1. There must be a cause of action which call for such kind of relief, such as, when the directors waste or dissipate the corporate funds, fraudulently dispose of corporate property, or perform *ultra vires* acts;
2. The complaining stockholder must exhaust all remedies within the corporation by applying for redress to the board of directors and the stockholders as a body, unless to do so is excused;
3. The stockholders must have been such at the time the acts complained of occurred unless the acts continue and are injurious to the stockholder, or affect him especially in some other way, and
4. The action must be brought in the name and for the benefit of the corporation.[236]

Thus, if the directors are the very ones to be sued or hold complete control over the corporation, there is no need to apply to them for redress before filing a derivative suit.[237] The fact that the shareholding of the suing stockholder is insignificant does not preclude him from filing a derivative suit, since he is not suing on his own behalf but on behalf of the corporation.[238] The majority stockholders and directors cannot dismiss a derivative suit filed by a stockholder. Otherwise, his right to file a derivative suit will be rendered nugatory.[239]

A corporation may be dissolved voluntarily or involuntarily.[240] Voluntary dissolution of a corporation may be brought about in the following instances:

1. Vote of a majority of the board of directors and resolution of the stockholders representing at least two-thirds of the outstanding capital stock, where no creditors are affected;[241]
2. Judgment dissolving the corporation upon petition of a majority of the board of directors and resolution of the stockholders representing at least two-thirds of the outstanding capital stock, where the rights of creditors may be prejudiced, or[242]
3. Amendment of the articles of incorporation shortening the corporate term.[243]

Involuntary dissolution of a corporation may occur in the following instances:

1. Expiration of the corporate term in the articles of incorporation;[244]
2. Failure to organize and commence transaction of its business within two weeks from the date of incorporation;[245]
3. Judgment in a *quo warranto* case filed by the government, or[246]
4. Petition by a minority stockholder for misuse or non-use of the corporate franchise.[247]

Foreign Corporations

F.22   No foreign corporation can transact business in the Philippines unless it first obtains a license to do business.[248] A foreign corporation transacting business in the Philippines without a license shall not be permitted to maintain or intervene in any action in any court or administrative agency of the Philippines but may be sued before the courts and administrative agencies of the Philippines.[249] However, if a party is aware that a foreign corporation is transacting business without a license, contracted with it and reaped the benefits of the contract, he will be estopped from questioning the legal capacity of the foreign corporation to sue him in the Philippines.[250] A contract entered into by a foreign corporation transacting business in the Philippines without a license is valid as the law considers the imposition of a penalty and the denial of access to the courts and administrative agencies of the Philippines as sufficient sanctions.[251]

There are several ways in which a foreign corporation can establish its economic presence in the Philippines.

1. It can set up a branch in the Philippines by obtaining a license to transact business here.

2. It can establish a domestic subsidiary. In case the foreign corporation decides to organize a domestic subsidiary, its liability to creditors will be limited to its subscription in the capital stock of the domestic subsidiary. In addition, it will not be subject to the requirement to deposit securities with the Securities and Exchange Commission to answer for claims of domestic creditors. This requirement applies only to foreign corporations licensed to transact business in the Philippines.

3. It can enter into a joint venture with a domestic corporation by forming a new corporation.

4. It can acquire shares of stock in an existing corporation. By following this route, the foreign corporation will readily enjoy several advantages. First, the domestic corporation is already a going concern. It has generated goodwill for its business. It has a marketing force that will be immediately available to market new products to be introduced by the foreign corporation.

5. It may merge with a domestic corporation.[252]

6. It may simply enter into a technology transfer arrangement. In this way, the foreign corporation does not assume the risk that the domestic corporation might fail. Even if the domestic corporation is not reaping profits, it will still have to pay royalties for the technology being supplied to it.

7. It may enter into a management contract with a domestic corporation.[253] As in the case of the technology transfer arrangement, here the foreign corporation is shielded from the risk of the failure of the domestic corporation.

Capital Markets and Securities Law

Any corporation desiring to issue commercial paper shall apply for registration with the Securities and Exchange Commission.[254] **F.23**
The following specific debt instruments are exempt *per se* from registration:

1. Evidence of indebtedness arising from interbank loans;
2. Evidence of indebtedness issued by the national and local governments;
3. Evidence of indebtedness issued to the Bangko Sentral ng Pilipinas under its open market or rediscounting operations;
4. Evidence of indebtedness issued by the Bangko Sentral ng Pilipinas, Development Bank of the Philippines, Land Bank of the Philippines, Government Service Insurance System, and the Social Security System;
5. Evidence of indebtedness issued to primary lenders, provided all such evidence of indebtedness shall be held on to maturity and shall neither be negotiated nor assigned to anyone other than the Bangko Sentral ng

Pilipinas, and the Development Bank of the Philippines. With respect to private development banks in connection with their rediscounting privileges;

6.   Evidence of indebtedness the total outstanding amount of which does not exceed five million pesos and issued to not more than ten primary lenders other than primary institution lenders, which shall be payable to a specific person and not to bearer and shall neither be negotiated nor assigned but held on to maturity;
7.   Evidence of indebtedness denominated in foreign currency, or
8.   Evidence of indebtedness arising from *bona fide* sale of goods or property.[255]

Commercial papers issued by any financial intermediary authorized by the Bangko Sentral ng Pilipinas to engage in quasi-banking functions are also exempt from registration.[256] The authority to issue commercial paper is valid for a period of 365 days, but the renewal thereof may be for a period shorter than 365 days.[257]

In the event that the commercial paper issuer fails to pay in full any commercial paper upon demand on stated maturity date, the authority to issue commercial paper is automatically suspended. Whenever necessary to implement the monetary and credit policies promulgated from time to time by the Monetary Board of the Bangko Sentral ng Pilipinas, the Securities and Exchange Commission may suspend the authority to issue commercial paper, reduce the authorized amount thereunder, or schedule the maturities of the registered commercial paper to be issued.[258] Furthermore, the Securities and Exchange Commission may, on its own motion or upon verified complaint by any aggrieved party, issue a cease and desist order if the violation of the rules and regulations may cause great or irreparable injury to the investing public or may amount to palpable fraud or violation of the disclosure requirements of the Revised Securities Act and of the rules and regulations.[259]

Any corporation desiring to issue long-term commercial papers, *i.e.* evidence of indebtedness with a maturity period of more than 365 days, shall apply for registration.[260] Long-term commercial papers shall be registered under any of the following conditions:

1.   The amount of long term commercial papers applied for is covered by the following collaterals which are not registered and which shall be maintained at their respective values at all times indicated in relation to the face value of the long-term commercial paper issue:
    (a) Securities listed in the stock exchange of a current market value of 200 per cent;
    (b) Registered real estate mortgage of an appraised value of 150 per cent;
    (c) Registered chattel mortgage on heavy equipment, machinery and similar assets acceptable to the Securities and Exchange Com-

mission and registrable in the appropriate government agency of an appraised value of 200 per cent;

2. The registrant meets such standard as may be prescribed by the Securities and Exchange Commission on the following complimentary financial ratio for each of the immediate past three fiscal years:
   (a) Ratio of the total cash, marketable securities, current receivables to the total of current liabilities;
   (b) Debt to equity ratio, with debt referring to all kinds of indebtedness, including guarantees;
   (c) Ratio of net income after taxes to net worth;
   (d) Net profits to sales ratio, and
   (e) Such other financial indicators as may be referred by the Securities and Exchange Commission.
3. The recomputed debt to equity ratio of the appellant based on the required financial statements shall not exceed 4:1 provided that the authorized short-term commercial papers do not exceed 300 per cent of net worth.[261]

The following long-term debt instruments are exempt *per se* from registration:

1. Evidence of indebtedness arising from interbank loan transactions;
2. Evidence of indebtedness issued by the national and local government;
3. Evidence of indebtedness issued by government instrumentalities the repayment and servicing of which are fully guaranteed;
4. Evidence of indebtedness issued to the Bangko Sentral ng Pilipinas under its open market or rediscounting operations;
5. Evidence of indebtedness issued by the Bangko Sentral ng Pilipinas, Philippine National Bank, Development Bank of the Philippines, and Land Bank of the Philippines.
6. Evidence of indebtedness issued to primary institution lenders, provided all such evidences of indebtedness shall be held on to maturity and shall neither be negotiated nor assigned to anyone other than the Bangko Sentral ng Pilipinas, and the Development Bank of the Philippines with respect to private development banks in connection with their rediscounting privileges;
7. Evidence of indebtedness the total outstanding amount of which does not exceed 15 million pesos and issued to not more than 15 primary lenders other than primary institutional lender, which shall be payable to specific persons and not to bearer, and shall neither be negotiated nor assigned but held on to maturity, provided that the aggregate amount of fifteen million pesos shall include outstanding short-term commercial papers, provided, further, that in reckoning compliance with the number of primary lenders, holders of short-term commercial papers exempt from registration shall be counted.

8. Evidence of indebtedness denominated in foreign currencies, and
9. Evidence of indebtedness arising from bona fide sale of goods or property.[262]

The following long-term commercial papers are also exempt from registration:

1. Long-term commercial papers issued by a financial intermediary authorized by the Bangko Sentral ng Pilipinas to engage in quasi-banking functions, and
2. Long-term commercial papers fully secured by debt instruments of the national government and the Bangko Sentral ng Pilipinas physically delivered to the trustee in the trust indenture.[263]
3. Conditions of Authority to Issue Long-Term Commercial Papers:
   (a) During the effectivity of the underwriting agreement, should the issuer fail to pay in full any interest due on, or principal of long term commercial paper upon demand on stated maturity date, the authority to issue long-term commercial papers shall be automatically suspended.
   (b) Upon the expiration of the underwriting agreement, it is the responsibility of the issuer to notify the Securities and Exchange Commission that it failed to pay the full interest due on or principal of long-term commercial paper upon demand at stated maturity date and has accordingly automatically suspended the issuance of its long-term commercial papers.
   (c) Whenever necessary to implement the monetary and credit policies promulgated from time to time by the Monetary Board of the Bangko Sentral ng Pilipinas, the Securities and Exchange Commission may suspend the authority to issue long-term commercial papers reduce the authorized amount thereunder, or schedule the maturities of the registered long-term commercial paper to be issued.[264]

The Securities and Exchange Commission may on its own motion or upon verified complaint by an aggrieved party issue a cease and desist order if the violation of the rules and regulations may cause great or irreparable injury to the investing public or will amount to palpable fraud or violation of the disclosure requirement of the Revised Securities Act and of the rules and regulations.[265]

Revised Securities Act

F.24 As a rule, no securities shall be sold to or offered for sale or distribution to the public within the Philippines unless such securities shall have been registered.[266]

The requirement of registration shall not, however, apply to any of the following classes of securities:

1. Any security issued or guaranteed by the government of the Philippines or by any political subdivision or agency thereof or by any of its public instrumentality;
2. Any security issued or guaranteed by the government of any country with which the Philippines maintains diplomatic relations, or by any state, province or political subdivision thereof;
3. Any security issued or guaranteed by any banking institution authorized to do business in the Philippines as a financial institution licensed to engage in quasi-banking;
4. Any security issued by a building and loan association, non-stock savings and loan association, or similar institution;
5. Certificates issued by a receiver or by a trustee in bankruptcy approved by the courts;
6. Any insurance or endowment policy or annuity contract issued by a corporation subject to supervision by the Insurance Commission;
7. Any security covering any right or interest in real property, where the sale or transfer is subject to supervision by the Housing and Land Use Regulatory Board;
8. Pension plans subject to regulation by the Bureau of Internal Revenue or the Insurance Commission.

Other securities may be exempted by the Securities and Exchange Commission if it finds registration is not necessary in the public interest and for the protection of investors.[267] The requirement of registration shall not apply to the sale of any security in any of the following transactions:

1. Any judicial sale or sale by an executor, administrator, guardian or receiver in insolvency or bankruptcy;
2. Sale by or for the account of a pledge holder, or mortgage or any other similar lien holder selling in the ordinary course of business to liquidate a *bona fide* debt;
3. An isolated transaction;
4. The contribution by a corporation of securities to its stockholders or other security holders;
5. The transfer or exchange by one corporation to another corporation of their securities in connection with a consolidation or merger;
6. The issuance of bonds or notes secured by mortgage upon real estate or tangible personal property, where the entire mortgage together with all the bonds or notes are sold to a single purchaser at a single sale;
7. The issue and delivery of any security in exchange for any other security of the same issuer pursuant to a right of conversion;
8. Broker's transactions executed upon customer's orders but not those made upon the solicitation by brokers of such orders;
9. Subscription for shares of the stocks of the corporation prior to incorporation to comply with the requirements of the law, and

10. The exchange of securities by the issuer with its existing security holder exclusively.

Other transactions may be exempted by the Securities and Exchange Commission if its finds that registration is not necessary in the public interest for the protection of the investing public by reason of the small owner involved or the limited character of the public offering.[268]

Any person acquiring a security the registration of which contains an untrue statement and who suffers damage may sue the following:

1. Every person who signed the registration statement;
2. Every person who was a director of or partner in the issuer;
3. Every person who is named in the registration statement as being or about to become a director or partner in the issuer and whose written consent thereto is filed with the registration statement;
4. Every person whose profession gives authority to a statement made by him who prepared or certified any part of the registration statement or of report used in connection with it;
5. Every underwriter with respect to such security.[269]

It is unlawful for any person, directly or indirectly, to perform any of the following:

1. For the purpose of creating a false or misleading appearance of active trading in any security:
   (a) To effect any transaction in such security which involves no change in the beneficial ownership thereof;
   (b) To enter an order for the purchase of such security with the knowledge that an order of substantially the same size and price for the sale of such security will be entered;
   (c) To enter any order for the sale of such security with the knowledge that an order of substantially the same size, time and price for the purchase of such security will be entered;
2. To effect a series of transactions in securities that does any of the following:
   (a) Raises the price for the purpose of inducing the purchase of a security by others;
   (b) Depresses the price for the purpose of inducing the sale of a security by others;
   (c) Creates active trading for the purpose of inducing such sale.
3. To induce the purchase or sale of any security by the circulation of information that no price of such security is likely to rise or fall because of market operations conducted for the purpose of raising or depressing the price of such security;
4. To make, for the purpose of inducing the purchase or sale of such security, any statement which is false or misleading with respect to any

material fact, and which he knew or had reasonable ground to believe was false or misleading;

5. For a consideration received, to induce the purchase or sale of any security by the circulation of information to the effect that the price of any such security is likely to rise or fall because of the market operations of anyone conducted for the purpose of raising or depressing the price of such security, or

6. To effect any series of transactions for the purchase or sale of any security for the purpose of fixing the price of such security.[270]

It is unlawful for any person by the use of any facility of any exchange:

1. To effect a short sale or to use any stop-loss order in contravention of such rules and regulations as the Securities and Exchange Commission may prescribe;

2. To use in connection with the purchase or sale of any security, any manipulative or deceptive device or contrivance;[271]

3. To adopt and enforce artificial measures of price control without the prior approval of the Securities and Exchange Commission;[272]

4. To employ any device, scheme, or artifice to defraud;

5. To obtain money or property by means of any untrue statement of a material fact or any omission to state a material fact to make the statement made not misleading;

6. To engage in any act, transaction, practice or course of business which operates as a fraud or deceit upon another person;

7. To describe a security to a second person without purporting to offer it, for a consideration from any other person unless he concurrently discloses the source of the consideration or the nature of or reason for his employment, or if the second person or his agent in the transaction is identified, that information is known to the second person,[273] or

8. To sell or buy a security if he knows a fact of special significance that is not generally available unless the insider proves that the fact is generally available or that the other party knows it.[274]

Arbitration Law

There are two ways by which an agreement to submit a dispute to arbitration **F.25** may arise. First, the parties to a contract may stipulate in advance that any controversy that may arise between them shall be settled by arbitration. Second, even when there is no such previous agreement, the parties may agree to submit to arbitration a controversy between them after it has arisen.[275] An agreement to submit a controversy to arbitration must be in writing and signed by the parties and their agents.[276] If a case is filed in court despite an agreement to arbitrate, the court should not entertain the case.[277] An agreement to arbitrate may be waived.[278] Thus, a defendant in a lawsuit who answered the complaint and sought affirmative relief from the court cannot belatedly invoke the arbitration clause after losing the case.[279]

If in the agreeemeent, a provision is made for the method of appointing the arbitrator or arbitrators, such method shall be followed.[280] However, a stipulation giving one of the parties the power to choose more arbitrators than the other is void.[281]

The Regional Trial Court shall appoint the arbitrator or arbitrators in the following instances:

1. No method for appointing arbitrators is provided in the agreement to arbitrate;
2. The parties are unable to agree upon a single arbitrator;
3. An arbitrator appointed by the parties unwilling or unable to serve, and his successor has not been appointed in the manner in which he was appointed;
4. Either party fails or refuses to name his arbitration within fifteen days after receipt of the demand for arbitration;
5. The arbitrator appointed by each party or appointed by one party and by the proper court shall fail to agree upon a third arbitrator.[282]

Any person appointed to serve as an arbitrator must be of majority age, in full enjoyment of his civil rights and must know how to read and write. A person is disqualified to serve as an arbitrator in the following cases.

1. He is related by blood or marriage within the sixth degree to either party to the contrary;
2. He has a financial, fiduciary or other interest in the controversy or in the result of the proceeding;
3. He has any personal bias, which might prejudice the right of any party to a fair and impartial award.[283]

Thus, lawyers and the employees of a party are disqualified from serving as arbitrators.[284]

The award of the arbitrators has the effect of *res judicata* upon the parties.[285]

Within one month after the award has been made, any party to the controversy may apply to the Regional Trial Court for an order confirming the award. The court must confirm the award in the absence of a ground to vacate, modify, or correct it.[286] In spite of a stipulation that the award of the arbitrators shall be final, the Regional Trial Court must vacate the award upon proof of the existence of any of the following grounds:

1. The award was procured by corruption, fraud or other undue means;
2. There was evident partiality or corruption of the arbitrators;
3. The arbitrators were guilty of misconduct in refusing to postpone the hearing upon sufficient cause shown, or in refusing to hear evidence pertinent and material to the controversy; that one or more of the

    arbitrators was disqualified to act as such and wilfully refrained from disclosing such disqualification or of any other misbehavior by which the rights of any party have been materially prejudiced, or

4. The arbitrators exceeded their powers or so imperfectly executed them that a mutual, final and definite award upon the subject matter submitted to them was not made.[287]

Likewise, the Regional Trial Court must modify or correct the award in any of the following cases:

1. There was an evident miscalculation of figures, or an evident mistake in the description of any person, thing or property referred to in the award;
2. The arbitrators have awarded upon a matter not submitted to them, not affecting the merits of the decision upon the matter submitted, or
3. The award is imperfect in a matter of form not affecting the merits of the controversy, and if it had been a commissioner's report, the defect could have been amended or disregarded by the court.[288]

Banking and Lending Law

Only entities duly authorized by the Monetary Board of the Bangko Sentral ng Pilipinas may engage in banking.[289]   **F.26**

Domestic Banks

Domestic banks must be organized in the form of a stock corporation.[290] The Securities and Exchange Commission cannot register the articles of incorporation of any bank unless they are accompanied by a certificate of authority issued by the Monetary Board.[291]

    At least 70 per cent of the voting stock of any domestic bank must be owned by citizens of the Philippines.[292] Furthermore, the total stock which any corporation may own in a domestic bank must not exceed 20 per cent of the voting stock. If a corporation is wholly owned or the majority of the voting stock is owned by one person or persons related to each other within the third degree of consanguinity or affinity, that corporation may not more than 20 per cent of the voting stocks.[293] In addition any person or persons related to each other within the third degree of consanguinity shall not own more than 20 per cent of the voting stock of the bank.[294]

    At least two-thirds of the members of the board of directors must be citizens of the Philippines.[295] The Monetary Board may pass upon and review the qualificiations of persons who are elected or appointed directors and officers and disqualify those found unfit.[296]

Foreign Banks

The Monetary Board may authorize foreign banks to operate in the Philippines through any of the following modes of entry: **F.27**

Philippines

1. Acquiring, purchasing or owning up to 60 per cent of the voting stock of one existing domestic bank;
2. Investing in up to 60 per cent of the voting stocks of one new banking subsidiary incorporated under the laws of the Philippines, or
3. Establishing branches with full banking authority.[297].

In approving the application of foreign bank the Monetary Board must:

1. Ensure geographic representation and complementation;
2. Consider strategic trade and investment relationship between the Philippines and the country of incorporation of the foreign bank;
3. Study the demonstrated capacity, global reputation for financial innovation and stability in a competitive environment of the appellant;
4. See to it that reciprocity rights are enjoyed by Philippine banks in the country of the appellant, and
5. Consider willingness to fully share the technology.

Only those among the top 150 foreign banks in the world or of the top five banks in their country of origin will be allowed to incorporate a subsidiary or establish branches.[298]

Foreign banks are allowed to establish branches within five years from the effectivity of R.A. 7721, 1994. During this period, six new foreign branches are allowed entry upon the approval of the Monetary Board. An additional four foreign banks may be allowed on the recommendation of the Monetary Board, upon the approval of the President as national interest may require,[299] but the number of branches for each new foreign bank cannot exceed six.[300] Foreigners may become members of the board of directors of a bank to the extent of the foreign participation in its equity.[301]

Investments

F.28 Commercial banks may invest in warehousing companies, leasing companies, storage companies, safe deposit box companies, companies engaged in the management of mutual funds but not in the mutual funds themselves, bank, and other similar activities as the Monetary Board may declare appropriate. The total investment shall not exceed 25 per cent of the net worth of the bank, and the investment in any one enterprise shall not exceed 15 per cent of the net worth of the bank.[302]

The Monetary Board may authorize a commercial bank to operate under an expanded commercial banking authority and by reason thereof, exercise the powers of an investment house, invest in the equity of a non-allied undertaking, or own majority or all of the equity in a financial intermediary other than a commercial bank. The total investment in equities must not exceed 50 per cent of the net worth of the bank. The equity investment in any one enterprise must not exceed 15 per cent of the net worth of the bank and, the equity investment in a single non-allied enterprise must not exceed 35 per cent of the total equity in the enterprise.[303]

Lending

The purpose of all loans shall be stated in the contract between the bank and the borrower. If the funds have been employed without the approval of the bank for another purpose, the bank may terminate the loan and demand immediate repayment.[304] Before granting a loan, banks must exercise proper caution to ascertain that the debtor is capable of fulfilling his commitments to the banks.[305] Furthermore banks shall grant loans only in the amounts and for the period of time essential for the effective completion of the operations to be financed.[306] Except as the Monetary Board may otherwise prescribe, the total liabilities of any person to a commercial bank for money borrowed shall at no time exceed 15 per cent of the unimpaired capital and surplus of such bank, excluding the following loans:

1. Loans secured by obligation of the Bangko Sentral ng Pilipinas or of the Philippine Government;
2. Loans fully guaranteed by the Philippine Government as to the payment of the principal and interest;
3. Loans covered by hold-out on or assignment of deposits maintained in the lending bank and held in the Philippines;
4. Loans and acceptances under letters of credit to the extent covered by margin deposits;
5. Other loan or credits which the Monetary Board may from time to time specify as non-risk assets, and
6. Liabilities secured by shipping documents, warehouse receipts or other similar documents transferring or securing title covering readily marketable, non-perishable staples, which must be fully coverd by insurance and must have a market value equal to at least 125 per cent of such liabilities.[307]

Loans against real estate security may not exceed 70 per cent of the appraised value of the real estate security,[308] and loans on the security of chattels may not exceed 50 per cent of the value of the security and the title to the chattels must be free from all encumbrances.[309] No commercial bank may make any loan on the security of shares of its own capital stock unless such security be necessary to prevent loss upon a debt previously contracted in good faith.[310]

Directors or Officers of banks may not become guarantors, indorsers or surety for loans from the bank except with the written approval of the majority of the directors of the bank excluding the director concerned. The outstanding credit accomodation which a bank may extend to each of its stockholders owning 2 per cent or more of the subscribed capital stock, its directors, or its officers, shall be limited to an amount equivalent to the respective outstanding deposits and book value of the paid-in capital contribution in the bank.[311]

The amortization schedule of bank loans are adapted to the nature of the operations to be financed. In the case of loans with maturities of more than two years, provisions are made for periodic amortization payments, but such payments must be made at least annually. When the borrowed funds are to be used for purposes which do not initially produce revenues adequate to cover regular amortization payments, the bank may permit the initial amortization payment to be deferred but in no case may the initial amortization date be later than three years from the date on which the loan is granted.[312]

Consumer Protection Law

F.30 If a consumer product is found to be injurious, unsafe or dangerous, an order may be issued for its recall, prohibition, or seizure from public sale or distribution.[313]

Any consumer product offered for importation will be refused admission if it:

1. Fails to comply with an applicable consumer product quality and safety standard or rule;
2. Is or has been determined to be injurious, unsafe and dangerous;
3. Is substandard, or
4. Has a material defect.[314]

The State ensures the safety and quality of food, drugs, cosmetics and devices, and regulates their production, sale, distribution and advertisement to protect the health of the consumer.[315] It also adopts measures designed to protect the consumer against substances other than food, drugs, cosmetics and devices that are hazardous to his health and safety.[316]

The State protects the consumer against deceptive, unfair and unconscionable sales acts and practices.[317] An act or practice is deemed deceptive whenever the producer, manufacturer, supplier or seller, through concealment, false representation or fraudulent manipulation, induces a consumer to enter into a sale or lease transactions of any consumer product or service.[318] An act or practice is deemed unfair or unconscionable if the producer, manufacturer, distributor, supplier or seller, takes advantage of the consumer's physical or mental infirmity, ignorance, illiteracy, lack of time or the general conditions of the environment or surrounding, to induce him to enter into a sales or lease transaction grossly inimical to the interest of the consumer or grossly one-sided in favor of the producer, manufacturer, distributor, supplier or seller.[319]

Warranties

F.31 For the warrantor of a consumer product to meet the minimum standard for warranty, he shall:

1. Remedy such consumer product within a reasonable time and utmost charge in case of a defect, malfunction, or failure to conform to such written warranty, and
2. Permit the consumer to elect whether to ask for a refund or replacement without charge of such product or part, where after reasonable number of attempts to remedy the defect or malfunction, the product continues to have the defect or to malfunction.[320]

The seller and the consumer may stipulate on the period within which the express warranty shall be enforceable. If the implied warranty on merchantability accompanies an express warrant, both will be of equal duration. Any other implied warranty shall not be less than 60 days nor more than one year following the sale of new consumer products.[321]

In every contract for the supply of service to a consumer, there is an implied warranty that the services will be rendered with due care and skill and that any material supplied in connection with such services will be reasonably fit for the purpose for which it is supplied.[322] When the consumer makes known to the seller the particular purpose for which the services are required, there is an implied warranty that the services supplied and any material supplied with them will be reasonably fit for that purpose or are of such a nature or quality that they might reasonably be expected to achieve that result, unless the consumer does not rely on the seller's skill or judgment.[323]

The State enforces compulsory labelling and fair packaging to enable the consumer to obtain accurate information as to the nature, quality and quantity of the contents of consumer products and to facilitate his comparison of the value of such products.[324] In addition the State protects the consumer from misleading advertisements and fraudulent sales promotion practices.[325]

Liability for Products and Services

Any manufacturer, producer, and any importer is liable for redress, inde- **F.32** pendently of faults for damages caused to consumers by defects resulting from design, manufacturer, construction, assembly and erection, formulas and handling and making up, presentation or packing of their products, as well as for the insufficient or inadequate information on the use and hazards thereof.[326]

The service supplier is liable for redress, independently of fault, for damages caused to consumers by defects relating to the rendering of the services, as well as for insufficient or inadequate information on the fruition or hazards thereof.[327]

The supplier of durable or nondurable consumer products are jointly liable for imperfections in quality that render the products unfit or inadequate for consumption which they are designed or decrease their value, and for those resulting from inconsistency with the information provided on the container, packaging, labels or publicity messages, or advertisements.[328]

Environmental Law

F.33   Ambient air quality standards which prescribe the maximum concentration of air pollutants permissible in the atmosphere consistent with public health, safety and general welfare have been established. Factors such as local atmospheric conditions, location and land use, and available technology were considered when setting these standards.[329]

National emission standards for use and existing stationary and mobile sources of pollution have also been established. Such factors as type of industry, practicable control technology available, location and land use, and the nature of pollutants were taken into consideration when these were set.[330]

Appropriate standards for community noise levels have been established[331] as have standards for noise-producing equipment such as construction equipment, transportation equipment, stationary engines, and electrical or electronic equipment and such similar equipment or contrivances. The magnitude and condition of use, the degree of noice reduction achievable through the application of the best available technology provided on the container and the cost of compliance were taken into consideration.[332]

Regarding water quality management the National Pollution Control Commission, in coordination with appropriate government agencies, classifies Philippine waters according to their best usage. The National Pollution Control Commission takes into account the following:

1.   The existing quality of the body of water at the time of classification;
2.   The size, depth, surface area covered, volume, direction, rate of flow, gradient of stream, and
3.   The most beneficial uses of said bodies of water and lands bordering them for residential, agricultural, commercial, industrial, navigational, recreational and aesthetic purpose.[333]

The Commission also prescribes quality and efficient standards taking into consideration such factors as:

1.   The standard of water quality or purity according to beneficial use;
2.   The technology relating to water pollution control.[334]

The production, utilization, storage and distribution of hazardous, toxic and other substances such as radioactive materials, heavy metals, pesticides, fertilizers, and oils, and the disposal, discharge and dumping of untreated waste water, mine tailings and other substances that may pollute any body of water of the Philippines resulting from the normal operations of industries, water-borne sources, and other human activities, as well as those resulting from accidental spills and discharge are regulated by appropriate government agencies.[335]

The Housing and Land Use Regulatory Board formulates and recommends to the National Environmental Protection Council a land use scheme.[336] In the location of industries, factories, plants, depots and similar establishments, the social, economic, geographic and significant environmental impact of the said establishments are taken into consideration.[337]

The Department of the Environment and Natural Resources has established a system of rational exploitation of fisheries and aquatic resources, a system of rational exploitation and conservation of wildlife resources, and a system of rational exploitation of forest resources.[338] In addition, the Department of Energy is responsible for an energy development program encouraging therein the utilization of invariant sources such as solar, wind and tidal energy.[339] The National Water Resources Board prescribes measures for the conservation and improvement of the quality of Philippine water resources ancd provides for the prevention, control and abatement of water pollution.[340]

The gainful exploitation and rational and efficient utilization of mineral resources is the responsibility of the Department of the Environment and Natural Resources.[341]

The preparation and implementation of waste management programs is required of all provinces, cities and municipalities. The Department of the Interior and Local Government promulgates guidelines for the formulation and establishment of waste management program.[342] Solid waste disposal is by sanitary landfill, incineration, composting and other methods as may be approved by competent government authority.[343] The dumping or disposal of solid wastes into the sea and any body of water, including shorelines and river banks, where these wastes are likely to be washed into the water is prohibited.[344] Waste water from manufacturing plants, industries, community or domestic sources is treated either physically, biologically, or chemically prior to disposal in accordance with the rules and regulations promulgated by the proper government authority.[345]

Employment and Labor Law

Conditions of Employment

The normal hours of work of any employee cannot exceed eight hours a day.[346] Rest periods of short duration during working hours are counted as hours worked.[347] Every employee has to be paid a night shift differential of not less than 10 per cent of his regular wage for each hour of work performed between 10 o'clock at night and six o'clock in the morning.[348] Employees may work longer than eight hours a day provided that they are paid for the overtime work an additional compensation equivalent to their regular wage plus at least 25 per cent.[349]

F.34

Each employee must be given a rest period of not less than 24 hours after every six consecutive normal work days.[350] Every worker must be paid his regular daily wage during regular holidays, except in retail and service establishments which regularly employ less than ten workers.[351] Workers who have rendered at least one year of service shall be entitled to a yearly incentive leave of five days with pay.[352]

The minimum wage for agricultural and non-agricultural employees and workers in every region is prescribed by the Regional Tripartite Wages and Productivity Boards,[353] and all employers are required to pay all their rank-and-file employees a thirteenth month pay not later than December 24 every year.[354]

Regarding the employment of women, they cannot be employed:

1. In any industrial undertaking between 10 o'clock at night and six o'clock in the morning of the following day;
2. In any commercial undertaking between midnight and six o'clock in the morning of the following day, or
3. In any agricultural undertaking at nightime unless she is given a period of rest of not less than nine consecutive hours.[355]

Employers must give a pregnant employee who has rendered service of at least six months for the last 12 months, maternity leave of at least two weeks prior to the expected date of delivery and four weeks after normal delivery or abortion with full pay based on her regular or average weekly wages. Maternity leave has to be paid by the employer for the first four deliveries of any employee.[356]

It is unlawful for any employer to discriminate against any woman employee with respect to terms and conditions of employment on account of her sex.[357] It is also unlawful for an employer to require as a condition of employment or continuation of employment that a woman employee shall not get married.[358]

Regarding the employment of minors, children below 15 years of age may not be employed except:

1. When a child works directly under the sole responsibility of his parents or legal guardian and where only members of the employer's family are employed.
2. When a child's employment or participation in public entertainment or information through cinema, theater, radio or television is essential.[359]

Within the above criteria, the following conditions also apply:

1. The employment must not endanger the child's life, safety, health and morals.
2. The employment must not impair the child's normal development.
3. The parent or legal guardian must provide the child with primary and secondary education.[360]

In no case is the employment of a person below 18 years of age in an undertaking which is hazardous or deleterious allowed.[361]

Termination of Employment

In the case of regular employment, the employer shall not terminate the **F.35**
services of an employee except for a just cause or when authorized by the
Labor Code of the Philippines 1979. An employee who is unjustly dismissed
from work shall be entitled to reinstatement without loss of seniority rights
and other privileges and to his full backwages, inclusive of other benefits,
computed from the time his actual reinstatement.[362]

Probationary employment cannot exceed six months unless it is covered
by an apprenticeship agreement stipulating a longer period. The services of a
probationary employee may be terminated for a just cause or for failure to
qualify as a regular employee in accordance with reasonable standards made
known by the employer to the employee at the time of his engagement. An
employee who is allowed to work after a probationary period shall be considered a regular employee.[363]

An employer may terminate an employment for any of the following
causes:

1. Serious misconduct or willful disobedience by the employee of the
   lawful orders of his employer or representative in connection with his
   work;
2. Gross and habitual neglect by the employee of his duties;
3. Fraud or wilfull breach by the employee of the trust reposed in him by
   his employer or duly authorized representative;
4. Commission of a crime or offense by the employee against the person
   of his employer or any immediate member of his family or his duly
   authorized representative, and
5. Other causes analogous to the foregoing.[364]

In order to terminate employment, the employer must furnish the employee with a written notice stating the particular acts or omission constituting the grounds for his dismissal.[365]

The employee may answer the allegations in the notice within a reasonable
period from receipt of it. The employer must afford the employee ample
opportunity to be heard and to defend himself with the assistance of his
representative, if he so desires.[366] The employer must then immediately notify
an employee in writing of a decision to dismiss him stating clearly the reasons
for it.[367]

The employer may terminate the employment of an employee due to the
installation of labor saving devices, redundancy, retrenchment to prevent
losses, or the closing or cessation of operation of the establishing by serving
a written notice on the workers and the Department of Labor and Employment at least one month before the intended date. In the case of termination
due to the installation of a labor saving device, the employee affected is be
entitled to a separation pay equivalent to at least one month's pay or to at
least one month pay for every year of service, whichever is higher. In the case

of termination to prevent losses in cases of closure or cessation of operation of the establishment, the separation pay must be equivalent to one month pay or at least one-half month pay for every year of service, whichever is higher.[368]

An employer may terminate the services of an employee who has been found to be suffering from any disease and whose continued employment is prohibited by law or is prejudicial to his health and the health of his co-employees. He shall be paid separation pay equivalent to at least one month's pay or one-half month pay for every year of service, whichever is greater.[369]

An employee may terminate without just cause the employer-employee relationships by serving a written notice on the employer at least one month in advance. The employer upon whom no such notice was served may hold the employee liable for damages.[370]

An employee may terminate the relationship without serving any notice on the employer for any of the following just causes:

1. Serious insult by the employer on the honor and person of the employee;
2. Inhuman and unbearable treatment accorded the employee by the employer or his representative;
3. Commission of a crime or offense by the employer or his representative against the person of the employee or any of the immediate members of his family, and
4. Other causes analogous to any of the foregoing.[371]

The factors affecting retirement are as follows:

1. Any employee may be retired upon reaching the retirement age established in the collective bargaining agreement or other applicable employment contract.
2. In the absence of a retirement plan or other agreement, an employee may retire upon reaching the age of 60 years or more, if he has served at least five years in the establishment.
3. In the absence of a retirement plan or other agreement, an employee shall retire upon reaching the age of 65 years.[372]

In the absence of a retirement plan or agreement, an employee who retires shall be entitled to retirement pay equivalent to at least one-half month pay for every year of service.[373]

Foreign Investment Law

Investment without Incentives

Foreign Investments Negative Lists: List A

F.36 Foreign ownership is limited by the 1987 Constitution and specific laws in the following areas:

1. *No Foreign Equity*
   (a) Mass media
   (b) Services involving the practice of licensed professions
   (c) Retail trade
   (d) Cooperatives
   (e) Private security agencies
   (f) Small-scale mining
   (g) Rice and corn industry except as authorized by the National Food Authority
2. Up to 75 per cent Foreign Equity
   Private recruitment, whether for local or overseas employment;
3. Up to 30 per cent Foreign Equity
   Advertising
4. Up to 40 per cent Equity
   (a) Exploration, development and utilization of natural resources (full foreign participation is allowed through financial or technical assistance agreements with the President)
   (b) Ownership of private lands
   (c) Operation and management of public utilities
   (d) Ownership and establishment of educational institutions
   (e) Financing companies
5. Variable Foreign Equity Limitation
   Construction

Foreign Investments Negative Lists: List B

Foreign ownership is limited to 40 per cent for reasons of security, defense, **F.37** risk of public health and morals, and protection of small and medium-scale enterprises:

1. Manufacture, repair, storage, or distribution of firearms, ammunition, lethal weapons, military ordinance, explosives, pyrotechnics and similar materials, unless the manufacture or repair is specifically authorized with a substantial export component to a non-Philippine national by the Secretary of National Defense.
2. Manufacture and distribution of dangerous drugs.
3. All forms of gambling.
4. Night clubs, bars, beer houses, dance halls, sauna and steam bathhouses and massage clinics.
5. Domestic enterprises with paid-in capital of less than $200,000 but domestic enterprises with a paid-in capital of at least $100,000 shall be allowed non-Philippine nationals if they involve advanced technology as determined by the Department of Science and Technology or directly employ at least 50 employees.

Philippines

Any non-Philippine national may do business or invest in a domestic enterprise or in an export enterprise up to 100 per cent of its capital subject to the following conditions:

1. It is investing in areas outside the Foreign Investments Negative Lists.[374]
2. The country or state of the applicant allows Filipino citizens and corporations to do business therein.[375]

Applications for registration must be filed with the Securities and Exchange Commission in the case of foreign corporations and domestic corporations or partnerships.[376] In the case of single proprietorships, the application shall be filed with the Bureau of Domestic Trade and Consumer Protection.[377]

A non-Philippine national may be granted incentives under the Omnibus Investments Code 1987 on the following conditions:

1. It will engage in a pioneer project defined in the investment priorities plan submitted by the Board of Investments to the President every year, or it will export at least 70 per cent of its total production, which may be reduced by the Board of Investments in meritorious cases under such conditions or limited incentives as the Board of Investments may determine;
2. At least 60 per cent of its capital will be transferred to citizens of the Philippines within 30 years from the date of registration or such longer period as the Board of Investments may require taking into account the export potential of the project, but a registered enterprise which exports 100 per cent of its production need not comply with this requirement.
3. The pioneer area it will enjoy is one that is not within the activities reserved by the 1987 Constitution or other laws of the Philippines to Philippine citizens or corporations owned or controlled by Philippine citizens.[378]

For six years from commercial operation for pioneer firms and four years for non-pioneer firms, new registered firms shall be fully exempt from income tax. The exemption may be extended for another year in the following cases:

1. The indigenous raw materials used in the manufactured product must at least be 50 per cent of the total cost of raw materials for the preceding years prior to extension unless the Board of Investments prescribes a higher percentage.
2. The ratio of the total imported and domestic capital equipment to the number of workers for the project does not exceed US $110,000 to one worker.
3. The net foreign exchange savings or earnings amount to at least US $500,000 annually during the first three years of operation.

In no case shall the registered pioneer firm have the benefit of this incentive for a period exceeding eight years.[379]

For the first year from registration, a registered enterprise is allowed additional deduction from taxable income of 50 per cent of the wages corresponding to the increment in the number of direct labor for skilled and unskilled workers if the project meets the prescribed ratio of capital equipment to number of workers set by the Board of Investments. This additional deduction is doubled if the activity is located in a less developed area.[380] The importation of breeding stocks and genetic materials for ten years from registration or commercial operation is exempt from all taxes and duties.[381] A tax credit equivalent to the value of the taxes and custom duties that would have been waived on the breeding stocks and genetic materials had these been imported is given for their purchase from a domestic producer.[382] The customs procedure for the importation of equipment, spare parts, raw materials and supplies, and exports of processed produce have been simplified.[383] Furthermore, the period of use of consigned machinery, equipment and spare parts is unrestricted provided a re-export bond is posted.[384]

Foreign nationals may be employed in supervisory, technical or advisory positions for five years from registration, extendible fees limited periods subject to the discretion of the Board of Director. The president, treasurer and general manager are not subject to this limitation.[385]

A tax credit is granted for the taxes and customs duties paid on the supplies, raw materials and semi-manufactured products used in the manufacture of export products.[386] Export-oriented enterprises also have access to the use of manufacturing and trading bonded warehousing system.[387] Exports are exempted from wharfage dues and any export tax, duty, import and fee for five years.[388]

Supplies and spare parts imported from consigned equipment or imported by a registered enterprise with a bonded manufacturing warehouse are exempt from customs duties and taxes provided at least 70 per cent of production is exported.[389]

Special Economic Zones

Special economic zones have been established in the Philippines.[390] **F.38**

Any person or any form of business orgnization, regardless of nationality, control or ownership of the capital may apply for registration as an Export or Free Trade Enterprise within a Special Economic Zone in any sector of industry, international trade and commerce, except duty free retailing and wholesale trading of imported finished products for the purpose of supplying the domestic market. If the area of investor is within Lists A and B of the Foreign Investments Act 1991, the applicable nationality requirements must be observed.[391]

The following rights and guarantees apply to firms operating as an Export or Free Trade Enterprise in a Special Economic Zone:

1. Foreign investments may be repatriated completely in the currency in which the investment was originally made and at the rate of exchange prevailing at the time of repatriation.
2. Profits may be remitted outward.
3. Such a sum as may be necessary to meet the payments on foreign loans and foreign obligations arising from technological assistance contracts may be remitted at the rate of the exchange prevailing at the time of remittance.
4. The property of the enterprise may not be expropriated except for public use or in the interest of national welfare or defense and upon payment of just compensation.
5. The property of the enterprise may not be requisitioned except in the event of war or national emergency. Just compensation shall be paid.[392]

Merchandise, raw materials, supplies, articles, equipment, machinery, spare parts and wares of every description brought into the restricted area by an Export or Free Trade Enterprise are not subject to customs duties, national taxes, and local taxes.[393] Export and Free Trade Enterprises are exempt from all national and local taxes.[394] In lieu of paying taxes, they pay 5 per cent of the gross income earned within the Special Economic Zone.[395] Export and Free Trade Enterprises are also exempt from wharfage dues.[396] In addition, Export and Free Trade Enterprise are granted incentives under the Omnibus Investment Code 1987.[397]

Tax Law

Income Tax

F.39 As a general rule, non-resident alien individuals and foreign corporations that are not engaged in trade or business in the Philippines are taxed on a gross basis on items of income derived from sources within the Philippines,[398] while non-resident alien individuals and foreign corporations engaged in trade or business in the Philippines are taxed on all income from sources within the Philippines regardless of whether or not such income is effectively connected with the Philippine trade or business.[399] Resident alien individuals, however, are taxed like citizens of the Philippines on a net basis on income derived from the Philippines or abroad.[400]

For income tax purposes, a corporation includes partnerships, no matter how created or organized, joint stock companies, joint accounts, associations or insurance companies.[401] However, general professional partnerships which are formed for the purpose of exercising a common profession, and joint ventures or consortiums formed for the purpose of undertaking construction projects or engaging in petroleum, coal, geothermal and other energy operations pursuant to an operating or consortium agreement under a service contract with the Government are not treated for income tax purposes as corporations.[402]

Domestic corporations are generally subject to income tax at the rate of 35 per cent of net income derived from sources worldwide.[403] Foreign corporations doing business in the Philippines and resident foreign corporations are also subject to income tax at the rate of 35 per cent of net income but only on income derived from Philippine sources.[404]

Thus, both a branch and a subsidiary are subject to an income tax based on net income at the rate of 35 per cent. However, a branch is subject to tax only on income derived from Philippine sources, while a Philippine subsidiary is subject to tax on income derived from sources worldwide. A branch is allowed as deduction from gross income a ratable part of expenses, losses or other deductions of its head office which are effectively connected with its business or trade in the Philippines. No such deduction is allowed to a subsidiary with respect to expenses, losses and other deductions of its parent, although its parent's home country may allow some form of tax credit for Philippine taxes paid by the subsidiary. Branch profit remittances are generally subject to a 15 per cent final withholding tax on net profits after tax,[405] while dividends paid by the subsidiary to the parent company will generally be subject to a 35 per cent final withholding tax. The tax on the dividends may be reduced to 15 per cent if the country in which the parent company is domiciled grants a credit for tax deemed paid in the Philippines equivalent to the 20 per cent difference between the regular 35 per cent rate and the preferential 15 per cent rate.[406] This tax-sparing device has been applied for the benefit of corporations residing in the Cayman Islands,[407] Bermuda,[408] Liechtenstein,[409] Hongkong,[410] Switzerland,[411] the Bahamas,[412] and the Republic of Vanuatu.[413] If the parent company resides in a country with which the Philippines has a double taxation treaty, the preferential rates imposed on dividends under such treaty shall apply.

Both a branch and a subsidiary are subject to final tax on the following income:

1. Interest on Philippine currency bank deposits and yield or any other monetary benefit from deposit substitutes and from trust fund and similar arrangements and Philippine-source royalties at a rate of 20 per cent.[414]
2. Net capital gain derived from the sale of shares of stock[415] not listed in the stock exchanges at a rate of 10 per cent of the gain not over 100,000 pesos and at a rate of 20 per cent on excess.
3. Net capital gain derived from the sale of shares of stock listed in the stock exchanges at a rate of 0.5 per cent.
4. Dividends received from a domestic corporation are exempt from tax.[416]

International air carriers and foreign companies engaged in international shipping are subject to a tax of 2.5 per cent of their gross Philippine billings.[417] Foreign mutual life insurance companies are taxed at 10 per cent of their gross investment income derived from Philippine sources,[418] except with respect to interest on Philippine currency bank deposits any yield or any other monetary benefit from deposit substitutes and trust fund and similar arrangements and Philippine-sourced royalties, which are subject to a 20 per cent final tax. Offshore banking units[419] and foreign currency deposit units[420] are exempt from taxes on offshore income, *i.e.* income from foreign currency transactions with non-residents, offshore banking units and local commercial banks, including branches of foreign banks authorized to transact business with offshore banking units and foreign currency deposit units, while on-shore income (*i.e.* interest on foreign currency loans granted to residents other than offshore banking units, foreign currency deposit units or local branches of foreign banks authorized to transact business with offshore banking units) is subject to a 10 per cent final tax. All other income of offshore banking units and foreign currency deposit units are subject to the regular 35 per cent corporate income tax rate.

Foreign corporations not doing business in the Philippines, non-resident foreign corporations, are generally subject to a final withholding tax of 35 per cent of their gross income derived from Philippine sources.[421] However, non-resident cinematographic film owners, lessors or distributors are subject to a final tax of 25 per cent on gross income derived from Philippine sources;[422] non-resident owners of vessels chartered by Philippine Nationals where the charter has been approved by Maritime Industry Authority are subject to a final tax of 4.5 per cent;[423] and non-resident lessors of aircraft, machinery and other equipment are subject to a final tax of 7.5 per cent.[424]

Interest on foreign loans paid to non-resident foreign corporations are subject to a final tax of 20 per cent.[425] Dividends paid to such corporations are generally subject to a 35 per cent final tax which may be reduced to 15 per cent under the tax-sparing provision of the National Internal Revenue Code.[426] Finally, non-resident foreign corporations are subject to the 10 per cent/20 per cent capital gains tax on net gains received from the sale of shares held as capital asset and not traded through the stock exchanges.[427] If the shares are traded in the stock exchanges, the tax is 0.375 of 1 per cent, which will be increased to 0.5 of 1 per cent beginning May 28, 1995.[428]

Individual taxpayers are divided into two main groups, namely: citizens and residents, and non-resident aliens.

Citizens and residents who earn compensation income are subject to graduated income tax rates of from zero to 35 per cent on gross income derived from all sources.[429] Citizens and residents who earn business income or income derived from the exercise of a profession are subject to graduated income tax rate of from 3 per cent to 35 per cent on net income derived from all sources.[430] Non-resident citizens, including those earning compensation or business income, are subject to a preferential graduated rate of one to three percent on foreign source income.[431] While citizens and residents in general are allowed only certain basic and personal exemptions from their gross income, only those who earn business income or income derived from the exercise of a profession taxpayers are allowed itemized deductions referred to as direct costs from their gross income. In lieu of the itemized deductions, the taxpayers may opt for a straight deduction equivalent to 40 per cent of gross receipts.[432]

Non-resident aliens engaged in trade or business in the Philippines are taxed in the same manner as residents and citizens but only on income derived from sources within the Philippines.[433] Non-resident aliens not engaged in the conduct of trade or business in the Philippines, are generally subject to a final withholding tax of 30 per cent on all income derived from sources within the Philippines.[434] As part of an incentive to certain foreign companies to establish their business in the Philippines, a 15 per cent tax on salaries, wages, annuities, compensation, remuneration and other emoluments of aliens employed by regional or area headquarters,[435] offshore banking units[436] and petroleum service contractors and subcontractors[437] is imposed.

The National Internal Revenue Code 1977 imposes final taxes at reduced rates on certain types of income earned by individual taxpayers as shown in the following table.[438]

Income	Citizens and Residents	Non-Resident Aliens (engaged in trade or business)
I. (a) interest from Philippine currency bank deposit (b) yield, monetary benefit from deposit substitutes (c) trust funds and similar arrangements (d) royalties (e) prizes of more than 3,000 pesos (f) other winnings	20%	20%
II. Dividends	Exempt	30%
III. Sale of shares (a) Not traded through stock exchanges (b) Traded through stock exchanges	gain not exceeding 100,000 gain in excess of 100,000	10% 20%
IV. Sale of real property classified as capital asset	0.375 of 1% of gross selling price (to be increased to 0.5 of 1% in 1995)	5% of gross selling price

Philippines

Value Added Tax

F.40 Taxpayers engaged in business in the Philippines are generally subject to either the Value Added Tax (VAT) or a percentage tax in addition to the income tax at various rates depending on the nature of the taxpayer's business. A taxpayer who is subject to the percentage tax is exempt from the VAT and vice versa.

The VAT system of taxation was introduced on a limited basis on January 1, 1988 under Executive Order No. 273. Generally, it covered only movable and tangible properties. On May 5, 1994, Republic Act No. 7716, known as the Expanded VAT Law, which is intended to widen the coverage of the VAT to include the sale and lease of real property under certain conditions and intangibles such as intellectual property, was enacted. The Supreme Court upheld the constitutionality of the Expanded VAT Law.[439]

As is typical in the VAT system of taxation, a VAT-registered person is subject to an output VAT at specified rates on its sales of goods or services. A uniform 10 per cent rate is applied on all sales of goods and services. The taxpayer may credit against such output VAT an input VAT passed on to it on its purchases of goods and services from another VAT-registered person. Any excess of input VAT over the output VAT may be carried over to succeeding taxable periods or, income cases, claimed as a tax credit or refund.[440] The option to claim a tax credit or refund is available where the input VAT is attributable to a zero-rated or effectively zero-rated sale or incurred in its purchase of capital goods except automobiles, aircraft and yachts.

Certain sales are subject to a zero-rated VAT.[441] Thus, a zero-rated seller is still entitled to claim a refund or tax credit of the input VAT incurred on its purchases of goods and services which are attributable to its zero-rated sales. Exempt taxpayers, on the other hand, are not subject to the output VAT and are thus not allowed to recognize input VAT on their purchases on which a refund or tax credit of input VAT may otherwise be taken.[442] They may, however, treat the input VAT as part of the cost of operations for income tax purposes.

The following taxpayers previously subject to the percentage tax are now subject to VAT by virtue of the Expanded VAT Law: hotels and motels; restaurants, refreshment parlors and other eating places; transportation contractors; holders of legislative franchises; finance companies, and insurance companies.[443]

Accounting Rules

F.41 All persons required by law to pay taxes must keep a journal and a ledger or their equivalents. Those whose quarterly receipts do not exceed 3,000 pesos may use a simplified set of bookkeeping records.

Those whose gross quarterly earnings exceed 25,000 pesos must also have their books of account audited yearly by an independent certified public accountant.[444] Those keeping books of accounts may also keep subsidiary books.[445] All books of accounts must be preserved for a period of three years from the last date for filing a tax return.[446]

Intellectual Property Laws

Patents

Any invention of a new and useful machine, manufactured product or sub-   **F.42**
stance, process, or an improvement of any of the foregoing is patentables.[447]
An invention cannot be patentable if it is contrary to public order or morals, or to public health or welfare, or if it constitutes a mere idea, scientific principle or abstract theorem not embodied in an invention as specified in the Patent Law 1947, section 7, or any process not directed to the making or improving of a commercial product.[448]

Any new, original and ornamental design for an article of manufacture and any new model of implement or tools or of any industrial product, or of part of the same, which does not possess the quality of invention, but which is of practical utility by reason of its form, configuration, construction or composition, may be protected by the author thereof, the former by a patent for a design and the latter by a patent for a utility model, in the same manner and subject to the same provisions and requirements as related to patents for inventions in so far as they are applicable, except as otherwise provided in the law.[449]

The making, using, or selling of a patented machine, article or product and the using of a patented process without the authorization of the patentee constitutes infringement of the patent for an invention.[450] Infringement of a design patent or of a patent for utility model shall consist in unauthorized copying of the patented design or utility model for the purpose of trade or industry in the article or product and in the making, using or selling of the article or product copying the patented design or utility model.[451]

Copyright

The rights granted by the Decree on Intellectual Property 1972, from the   **F.43**
moment of creation, subsist with respect to any of the following classes of works:

1. Books, including composite and cyclopedic works, manuscripts, directories, and gazetteers;
2. Periodicals, including pamphlets and newspapers;
3. Lectures, sermons, addresses, dissertations prepared for oral delivery;
4. Letters;
5. Dramatic or dramatic-musical compositions, choreographic works and entertainments in dumb-show, the acting form of which is fixed in writing or otherwise;
6. Musical compositions, with or without words;

7. Works of drawing, painting, architecture, sculpture, engraving, lithography, and other works of art, models or designs for works of art;
8. Reproductions of a work of art;
9. Original ornamental designs or models for articles of manufacture, whether or not patentable, and other works of applied art;
10. Maps, plans, sketches, and charts;
11. Drawings or plastic works of a scientific or technical character;
12. Photographic works and works produced by a process analogous to photography, lantern slides;
13. Cinematographic works and works produced by a process analogous to cinematography or any process for making audio-visual recordings;
14. Computer programs;
15. Prints, pictorial illustratins advertising copies, labels, tags, and box wraps;
16. Dramatizations, translations, adaptations, abridgements, arrangements and other alterations of literary, musical or artistic works or of works of the Philippine Government as herein defined, which shall be protected as provided in section 8 of this Decree;
17. Collections of literary, scholarly, or artistic works or of works referred to in section 9 of this Decree which by reason of the selection and arrangement of their contents constitute intellectual creations, the same to be protected as such in accordance with section 8 of this Decree, and
18. Other literary, scholarly, scientific and artistic works.[452]

Copyright consists in the exclusive right:

1. To print, reprint, publish, copy, distribute, multiply, sell and make photographs, photo-engraving, and pictorial illustrations of the work;
2. To make any translation or other version or extracts or arrangements or adaptations thereof; to dramatize it if it be a non-dramatic work; to convert it into a non-dramatic work if it be a drama; to complete or execute it if it be a model or design;
3. To exhibit, perform, represent, produce, or reproduce the work in any manner or by any manner or by any method whatever for profit or otherwise; if not reproduced in copies for sale, to sell any manuscript or any record whatsoever thereof;
4. To make any other use or disposition of the work consistent with the laws of the land.[453]

Trade Marks

F.44 The owner of a trade mark, trade name or service mark used to distinguish his goods, business or services from the goods, business or services of others has the right to register the same on the principal register, unless it:

1. Consists of or comprises immoral, deceptive or scandalous matter; or matter which may disparage or falsely suggest a connection with persons, living or dead, institutions, beliefs, or national symbols, or bring them into contempt or disrepute;
2. Consists or comprises the flag or coat of arms or other insignia of the Philippines or any of its political subdivisions, or of any foreign nation, or any simulation thereof;
3. Consists of or comprises a name, portrait, or signature identifying a particular living individual except by his written consent, or the name, signature, or portrait of a deceased President of the Philippines, during the life of his widow, if any, except by the written consent of the widow;
4. Consists of or comprises a mark or trade name which so resembles a mark or trade name registered in the Philippines or a mark or trade name previously used in the Philippines by another and not abandoned, as to be likely, when applied to or used in connection with the goods, business or services of the applicant, to cause confusion or mistake or to deceive purchasers; or
5. Consists of a mark or trade name which, when applied to or used in connection with the goods, business or services of the applicant is merely descriptive or deceptively misdescriptive of them, or when applied to or used in connection with the goods, business or services of the applicant is primarily geographically descriptive or deceptively misdescriptive of them, or is primarily merely a surname;
6. Except as expressly excluded above, nothing shall prevent the registration of a mark or trade name used by the applicant which has become distinctive of the applicant's goods, business or services. The Director may accept as *prima facie* evidence that the mark or trade name has become distinctive, as applied to or used in connection with the applicant's goods, business or services, proof of substantially exclusive and continuous use thereof as a mark or trade name by the applicant in connection with the sale of goods, business or services for the five years next preceding the date of the filing of the application for its registration.[454]

Any person who uses, without the consent of the registrant, any reproduction, counterfeit, copy or colorable imitation of any registered mark or trade name in connection with the sale, offering for sale, or advertising of any goods, business or services on or in connection with which such use is likely to cause confusion or mistake or to deceive purchasers or others as to the source or origin of such goods or services, or identity of such business; or reproduce, counterfeit, copy or colorably imitate any such mark or trade name and apply such reproduction, counterfeit, copy, or colorable imitation to label, signs, prints, packages, wrappers, receptacles, or advertisements intended to be used upon or in connection with such goods, business or services, is liable to a civil action by the registrant for any or all of the remedies provided.[455]

III. General Considerations in Negotiating Business Transactions in the Philippines

Cultural Factors and Business Negotiations

F.45   To enter into a lasting and fruitful business relationship with Filipino businessmen, it is necessary to understand the cultural traits of the Filipinos.

The Filipinos trace their origins to the Malayan stock. They have been exposed to Chinese, Spanish, and American influence. The result is a cultural blend which is distinctly Filipino.

Filipinos are by nature friendly, cheerful and hospitable. The typical Filipino business executive is highly educated. He may have studied commerce, economics, business management, or law. Frequently, he may have completed graduate studies abroad. While the typical Filipino business executive may have been exposed to Western ways, he has integrated Western influence and Filipino values.

The Filipino values harmonious personal relationships. He maintains emotional relationships not only with his immediate family but with an expanded group that includes remote relatives, friends, and the baptismal and wedding sponsors of his children.

To avoid embarrassing another party with whom he is dealing, the Filipino will resort to euphemisms. He will not openly criticize the position the other person has taken. Instead, he will announce that he wishes to be clarified on certain points. If he cannot accommodate the position the other party has taken, the Filipino will not declare that he does not like the idea. Instead, he will offer some excuse why it is beyond his power to accede to it. Filipinos prefer to settle a dispute by mediation rather than confrontation. If a Filipino gets embroiled in a dispute with another party, he will not approach the other party directly to settle it. To avoid unpleasantness, he will look for an intermediary who is acceptable to the other party to straighten out the dispute. It is only after the intermediary has paved the way that he will personally approach the other party. He will refer to the dispute as a simple case of a misunderstanding. In negotiating with a Filipino, verbal clashes should be avoided. Speaking in anger and adopting a domineering attitude will yield negative results. It will be more productive to present one's position in the tone of a request. One should refrain from expressing impatience.

In the final analysis, a lasting business relationship must be based on fairness and mutual respect. A lopsided agreement bears within it the seeds of its own destruction.

Role and Competence of Local Counsel

Local counsel who will be involved in negotiating a commercial contract **F.46** must possess an excellent grasp of the field of law involved in the contract. He must be kept abreast of the latest amendments to the law, administrative regulations, administrative rulings, and jurisprudence. If negotiation of a commercial contract will involve different fields of law like a corporation law, taxation and finance, a law office will usually assign a team of lawyers composed of experts in the various fields of law involved. However, an expert in a given field of law should also have a good working knowledge of the other branches of law so that he may have a comprehensive viewpoint. In addition, a lawyer must be management oriented. He must be familiar with financing, production, marketing and human resources. He must have a good grasp of the financial, economic, and social environment within which business firms have to operate.

As international barriers are being knocked down, local counsel must be knowledgeable in cross-border transactions. He must be familiar with joint ventures, license agreements, loan syndications, project finance, and build-operate-and-transfer projects.

Local counsel can help build the cultural gap when a foreign client negotiates with a Filipino businessman. Local counsel can brief him on the background of the Filipino businessmen and give him advice on the suitability of the prospective business partner.

In the negotiation of a commercial contract, it is the role of the local counsel to see to it that it complies with the local laws. Local law or regulations may require that certain contracts like technology transfer arrangements be governed by Philippine law. Even in those instances where the partner may stipulate that their contract be governed by foreign law, under the Civil Code 1950, Art. 17, Philippine laws which are prohibitive and which have for their object public order, public policy and good customs shall not be rendered ineffective by the laws of a foreign country. If the commercial contract has to be submitted for approval by an administrative agency or has to be registered with a government registry, the local counsel must see to it that the contract complies with the requirements for approval or registration.

In some cases, there may be a need to restructure the proposed commercial contract between the partner to comply with the law. Competent local counsel can restructure the agreement so that the partner can still achieve his objective within the framework of the law. In other cases, local counsel can advise the partner on how he can save taxes by restructuring the agreement. In negotiating commercial contracts, local counsel must appreciate the viewpoint of the other party. He must be able to address the legitimate concerns of the other party. A one-sided contract is an open invitation to trouble. To some extent there must be a system of checks and balances in the commercial contract.

Local counsel must see to it that there is no ambiguity in the provisions of a commercial contract and that it accurately embodies the intention, understanding and expectations of the parties. This will minimize if not prevent disputes later on. He must be creative and resourceful. In many instances, he will have to offer alternative texts and formulas to meet the objections of the other party. He should try to foresee what contingencies might happen and define the rights and obligations of the parties in case such contingencies happen.

The commercial contract should contain a mechanism for resolving disputes like negotiation, mediation and arbitration. Usually, the parties prefer to have their disputes resolved by arbitration rather than litigation. Arbitration is usually speedier and less expensive than litigation. Parties will more readily accept the award of an impartial arbitrator than the decision of a judge in the country of one of the parties.

Local counsel must see to it that the provision for arbitration is clear and valid. The provision for arbitration should define what rules will govern the arbitration, how the arbitrators will be chosen, where the arbitration will be held and what language will be used. Usually, the parties prefer to have the arbitration be governed by international rules like the rules of the International Chamber of Commerce and that the arbitration be held in a neutral country.

In making a decision whether or not to litigate a client will usually consider the importance of the case, the chances of success, the amount of expenses involved and the duration of the litigation. Here the client will usually rely greatly on the advice and evaluation of legal counsel. However, legal counsel must recognize his limitations and should refrain from making business decisions for clients.

The legal aspects may be only one of the factors to be considered in making a business decision. A course of action a client intends to take may be legal but may be fraught with legal risks. All that a legal counsel can do is to give advice on the legal risks involved. Should the client decide to assume such risks, legal counsel should try to reduce the risks.

Government Resources and Business Assistance Program

F.47   The Department of Trade and Industry has established several offices to assist investors, exporters, and entrepreneurs.

The one Stop Action Center helps investors get all the necessary information and documentation in one physical location. Representatives of different agencies involved in processing investments are housed under one roof. The center disseminates information on investment laws and opportunities, provides advice on registration requirements, and facilitates applications for investment incentives, and employment of foreign nationals.

The Bureau of Export Trade Promotion provides expert information on such matters as export procedure and documentation, buyer linkages, financing, sources of raw materials, and statistics. It also assists exporters on export-related problems and trade complaints.

The One Stop Export Documentation Center facilitates exports by eliminating bottlenecks. It brings under one roof representatives of various offices involved in the application, processing and approval of export documents.

The Bureau of Small and Medium Business Development is involved in the promotion and development of small and medium enterprises. It helps them obtain credit, counsels them in investments, trains them for productivity and profitability and provides them with consultancy services.

In addition, there is the Small Business Guarantee and Finance Corporation which guarantees loans to qualified small enterprises.[456] Government financial institution are required to develop credit facilities which offer preferential and simplified credit schemes to exporters.[457]

Practical Considerations in Negotiating Specific Business Transactions in the Philippines

Sale of Goods Transactions

As a rule, only the warranties against eviction and against hidden defects are implied in a contract of sale.[458] In the sale of second-hand goods, there is no implied warranty.[459] If the buyer wants the seller to warrant other matters, such as the merchantability, quality, and fitness of the goods for a particular purpose or to warrant that second-hand goods are free from hidden defects, an express stipulation is required.   F.48

In the absence of a stipulation to the contrary, the expenses for the execution and registration are borne by the seller.[460] Since the cost of the documentary stamps and the expenses of registration in the sale of real property are substantial, the seller usually requires the buyer to shoulder these items or to share one-half.

Joint Ventures

The specific contributions of the parties should be specified, such as cash, equipment, technology, marketing know-how and management.   F.49

If a minority partner in a joint venture does not have enough votes to legally veto the decisions of the majority, he may insist that a super-majority be required for major decisions, such as amendment of the articles of by-laws, sale of the major assets of the joint venture, increasing the capital block, merger or consolidation, expansion into a different line of business.

Philippines

An agreement should be made regarding the distribution of the executive offices such as chairman of the board, president, general manager, treasurer, and comptroller, and the seats in the board of directors.

To prevent the entry of a new partner who is not acceptable to the others, the joint venture agreement should grant the other partners the right of pre-emption should any partner desire to sell his shares of stocks or to look for a buyer acceptable to them who will match the terms and conditions of the offer of the selling partner.

The joint venture agreement should contain provisions for resolving continuing deadlocks among the partners such as mediation, arbitration, and buy-out arrangements.

Technology Transfer Arrangement

F.50 The main concern in technology transfer arrangement is to see that it does not contain any provision prohibited by and contains all the provisions required by the Department Order Nol. 5, Series of 1988, as amended by Department Order No. 6, Series of 1992.

Production and Manufacturing Agreements

F.51 The owner of the formula or the products under a production and manufacturing agreement usually requires the party who will manufacture the products to keep his trade secrets confidential.

To insure the products manufactured meets his quality standards, the owner of the formula or process usually requires the party who will manufacture the products to buy the materials only from sources approved by it.

Distribution Arrangement

F.52 The distribution arrangement should provide that the relationship between the parties is that of buyer and seller rather than that of principal and agent. The distributor has to pay for the goods whether or not he is able to resell them, resells them in its own name, and is free to fix the resale price. Otherwise, the seller will be deemed as doing business in the Philippines and will have to get a license if it is a foreign corporation.[461]

The distributor usually asks for exclusivity for its protection while the manufacturer usually refuses to tie itself down to one distributor. A possible solution is to grant exclusivity subject to the condition that the distributor will meet a certain volume of sales. It will lose its exclusivity if it fails to meet this goal.

Employment

F.53 Managerial and technical employees may be required to sign an undertaking that they will keep the trade secrets of the employer confidential.

The same employees may be required not to engage in a competing line of business or to work for a competitor for a limited period after they cease to be employed.

Loan Agreements

In huge loans, the representations, warranties and covenants of the borrower **F.54** will be of great concern to the lenders. Another serious concern of the lender is the enumeration of the events of default.

The lender may require that a voting trust be executed in favor of its representative who will then be elected to the board of directors, so that the lender can be kept informed about the operations of the borrower. The lender may also be required that it be consulted if there will be a change in the controlling interest on the top management of the borrower. In addition, the lender may require that its prior approval be obtained before the borrower declares any dividend.

Notes

[1] Fund for Assistance to Private Education, *The Philippine Atlas.* (1975), Vol.1, p.3.
[2] *Ibid.*, p.15.
[3] National Statistics Office, *1990 Census of Population and Housing; Report No. 3 Socio-Economic and Demographic Statistics*, p.1.
[4] *Ibid.*, p.5.
[5] *Ibid.*, p.XXVI.
[6] *Ibid.*, p.47.
[7] *Ibid.*, p.59.
[8] *Ibid.*, p.1.
[9] National Economic and Development Authority, *Performance of the Economy for 1992*, p.3.
[10] *Ibid.*, p.7.
[11] *Ibid.*, p.11.
[12] *Ibid.*, p.5.
[13] National Economic and Development Authority, *The 1993 Socio-Economic Report*, p.2.
[14] *Ibid.*, p.3.
[15] *Ibid.*, p.4.
[16] *Ibid.*, p.3.
[17] National Economic and Development Authority, *The President's 1994 Socio-Economic Report*, p.7.
[18] *Ibid.*, p.8.
[19] *Ibid.*, p.12.
[20] *Ibid.*, p.7.
[21] 1987 Constitution, Art. VI, s.1; Art. VII, s.1; and Art. VIII, s.1.
[22] *Ibid.*, Art. VI, s.1.
[23] *Ibid.*, Art. VI, s.2.
[24] *Ibid.*, Art. VI, s.5(1).
[25] *Ibid.*, Art. VII, s.4.
[26] *Ibid.*, Art. VIII, ss.1 and 4(1).

27 *Ibid.*, Art. VIII, s.5(2)(a).

28 *Ibid.*, Art. VIII, s.9.

29 *Ibid.*, Art. VIII, s.11.

30 *Ibid.*, Art. VIII, s.10.

31 *Ibid.*, Art. VIII, s.3.

32 *Ibid.*, Art. III, s.s.1, 2, 3, 4, 5 and 6.

33 *Ibid.*, Art. X, s.1.

34 *Ibid.*, Art. X, s.1.

35 Public Service Act 1936, s.16(c).

36 *Benedicto v. De La Rama* [1903] 3 Phil. 34 at 36.

37 Code Commission, *Report on the Proposed Civil Code of the Philippines*, p.9.

38 Tolentino, *Commentaries and Jurisprudence on the Commercial Laws of the Philippines* (8th ed. 1958), Vol.1, p.3.

39 Agbayani, *Commentaries and Jurisprudence on the Commercial Laws of the Philippines* (1992 ed), Vol.1, p.7.

40 *Ibid.*, p.3.

41 Blair and Robertson, *The Philippine Islands* (1903), Vol.V, pp.274–318 and Vol.VI, pp.35–44.

42 Paño and Martinez, *The Supreme Court of the Philippines* (1988) pp.3–4.

43 Paño and Martinez, *Justice and Freedom* (1988), p.2.

44 Blair and Robertson, *op. cit.*, Vol.IX, pp.189–195.

45 Paño and Martinez, *Justice and Freedom*, pp.2–3.

46 Judiciary Reorganization Act 1983, ss. 3, 9, 13, 19, 25 and 32.

47 Revised Penal Code 1932, Art. 186.

48 Act 3247, s.4.

49 *Ibid.*, s.6.

50 Civil Code 1950, Art. 1305.

51 *Ibid.*, Art. 1306.

52 *Ibid.*, Art. 1308.

53 *Encarnacion v. Baldomar* [1946] 77 Phil. 470 at 472–473; *Puahay Lao v. Suarez* [1968] 22 SCRA 215 at 218.

54 *Philippine National Bank v. Court of Appeals* [1991] 196 SCRA 536 at 545; *Philippine National Bank v. Court of Appeals* [1994] 238 SCRA 20 at 26.

55 Civil Code 1950, Art. 1309.

56 *Ibid.*, Art. 1310. 57 *Ibid.*, Art. 1311.

58 *Ibid.*, Art. 1314. 59 *Ibid.*, Art. 1315.

60 *Ibid.*, Art. 1316. 61 *Ibid.*, Art. 1318.

62 *Ibid.*, Art. 1319. 63 *Ibid.*, Art. 1320.

64 *American President Lines, Ltd. v. Klepper* [1960] 110 Phil. 243 at 247; *Villonco Realty Co. v. Bormaheco, Inc.* [1975] 65 SCRA 352 at 364.

65 Civil Code 1950, Art. 1323.

66 *Ibid.*, Art. 1327. 67 *Ibid.*, Art. 1328.

68 *Ibid.*, Art. 1330. 69 *Ibid.*, Art. 1331.

70 *Ibid.*, Art. 1333. 71 *Ibid.*, Art. 1334.

72 *Ibid.*, Art. 1335. 73 *Ibid.*, Art. 1336.

74 *Ibid.*, Art. 1337. 75 *Ibid.*, Art. 1338.

76 *Ibid.*, Art. 1339. 77 *Ibid.*, Art. 1340.

78 *Ibid.*, Art. 1341. 79 *Ibid.*, Art. 1342.

80 *Ibid.*, Art. 1343. 81 *Ibid.*, Art. 1344.

82 *Ibid.*, Art. 1347. 83 *Ibid.*, Art. 1348.

84 *Ibid.*, Art. 1349. 85 *Ibid.*, Art. 1350.

86 *Ibid.*, Art. 1353. 87 *Ibid.*, Art. 1354.

88 *Ibid.*, Art. 1355. 89 *Ibid.*, Art. 1356.

90 *Ibid.*, Art. 1357. 91 *Ibid.*, Art. 1358.

[92] *Ibid.*, Art. 1381.   [93] *Ibid.*, Art. 1385
[94] *Ibid.*, Art. 1386.   [95] *Ibid.*, Art. 1383.
[96] *Ibid.*, Art. 1387.
[97] *Oria v. McMicking* [1912] 21 Phil. 243 at 250–251; *Orsal v. Alisbo* [1959] 106 Phil. 655 at 659.
[98] Civil Code 1950, Art. 1384.
[99] *Ibid.*, Art. 1385.   [100] *Ibid.*, Art. 1388.
[101] *Ibid.*, Art. 1390.   [102] *Ibid.*, Art. 1397.
[103] *Ibid.*, Art. 1398.   [104] *Ibid.*, Art. 1399.
[105] *Ibid.*, Art. 1400.   [106] *Ibid.*, Art. 1402.
[107] *Ibid.*, Art. 1391.   [108] *Ibid.*, Art. 1392.
[109] *Ibid.*, Art. 1394.   [110] *Ibid.*, Art. 1393.
[111] *Ibid.*, Art. 1395.   [112] *Ibid.*, Art. 1401.
[113] *Ibid.*, Art. 1403.   [114] *Ibid.*, Art. 1405.
[115] *Ibid.*, Art. 1409.   [116] *Loc. cit.*
[117] *Ibid.*, Art. 1410.   [118] *Ibid.*, Art. 1411.
[119] *Ibid.*, Art. 1412.   [120] *Ibid.*, Art. 1414.
[121] *Ibid.*, Art. 1416.   [122] *Ibid.*, Art. 1458.
[123] *Ibid.*, Art. 1459.   [124] *Ibid.*, Art. 1460.
[125] *Ibid.*, Art. 1461.   [126] *Ibid.*, Art. 1462.
[127] *Ibid.*, Art. 1473.   [128] *Ibid.*, Art. 1469.
[129] *Ibid.*, Art. 1470.   [130] *Ibid.*, Art. 1472.
[131] *Ibid.*, Art. 1495.   [132] *Ibid.*, Art. 1497.
[133] *Ibid.*, Art. 1498.   [134] *Ibid.*, Art. 1499.
[135] *Ibid.*, Art. 1501.   [136] *Ibid.*, Art. 1547.
[137] *Ibid.*, Art. 1582.   [138] *Ibid.*, Art. 2047.
[139] *Ibid.*, Art. 2052.   [140] *Ibid.*, Art. 2053.
[141] *Ibid.*, Art. 2054.   [142] *Ibid.*, Art. 2058.
[143] *Ibid.*, Art. 2059.   [144] *Ibid.*, Art. 2066.
[145] *Ibid.*, Art. 2067.   [146] *Ibid.*, Art. 2068.
[147] *Ibid.*, Art. 2071.
[148] *Ibid.*, Art. 2073; *Sadaya v. Sevilla* [1967] 19 SCRA 924 at 930–931.
[149] Civil Code 1950, Art. 2076.
[150] *Philippine National Bank v. Veraguth* [1927] 50 Phil. 253 at 256–257; *Philippine National Bank v. Court of Appeals* [1987] 147 SCRA 273 at 276.
[151] Civil Code 1950, Art. 2077.
[152] *Ibid.*, Art. 2079; *Radio Corporation of the Philippines v. Roa* [1935] 62 Phil. 211 at 217; *Yulo v. Chua Chuco* [1950] 87 Phil. 448 at 454; *Valencia v. Leoncio* [1956] 99 Phil. 638 at 642.
[153] Civil Code 1950, Art. 2080.
[154] *Ibid.*, Art. 2081.
[155] *Ibid.*, Art. 2085.
[156] Public Service Act 1936, s.20(g); *Zamboanga Transportation Co., Inc. v. Public Utility Commission* [1927] 50 Phil. 237 at 240.
[157] Civil Code 1950, Art. 2088.
[158] *Hechanova v. Adil* [1986] 144 SCRA 450 at 453.
[159] Civil Code 1950, Art. 2089.
[160] *Dayrit v. Court of Appeals* [1970] 36 SCRA 548 at 560.
[161] Civil Code 1950, Art. 2093.
[162] *Ibid.*, Art. 2094.
[163] *Ibid.*, Art. 2095; *Caltex (Philippines), Inc. v. Court of Appeals* [1992] 212 SCRA 448 at 464.
[164] Civil Code 1950, Art. 2096; *Caltex (Philippines), Inc. v. Court of Appeals* at 460.
[165] Civil Code 1950, Art. 2110.

[166] *Ibid.*, Art. 2111.
[167] *Ibid.*, Art. 2112.
[168] *Ibid.*, Art. 2115; *Manila Surety and Fidelity Co. v. Velayo* [1967] 21 SCRA 515 at 918.
[169] Civil Code 1950, Art. 2140.
[170] *De Jesus v. Gevan Bee Co., Inc.* [1941] 72 Phil. 464 at 467; *Navarro v. Pineda* [1963] 9 SCRA 631 at 636; *Tumalad v. Vicencio* [1971] 41 SCRA 143 at 152; *Makati Leasing and Finance Corporation v. Wearever Textile Mills, Inc.* [1983] 122 SCRA 296 at 301.
[171] Civil Code 1950, Art. 2125; *Filipinas Marble Corporation v. Intermediate Appellate Court* [1986] 142 SCRA 180 at 191–192.
[172] Chattel Mortgage Law 1906, s.4; *Chua Guan v. Samahang Magsasaka, Inc.* [1935] 62 Phil. 472 at 481; *Malonzo v. Luneta Motor Co.* [1956] 52 O.G. 5566 at 5569.
[173] Land Transportation and Traffic Code 1964, s.5(e); *Borlough v. Fortune Enterprises, Inc.* [1957] 100 Phil. 1063 at 1068; *Aleman v. De Catera* [1961] 1 SCRA 776 at 780; *Montano v. Lim Ang* [1963] 7 SCRA 250 at 256; *Uy v. Zamora* [1965] 13 SCRA 508 at 511.
[174] Ship Mortgage Decree 1978, s.3.
[175] Civil Aeronautics Law, 1952, s.38.
[176] Chattel Mortgage Law 1906, s.6.
[177] *Giberson v. A. N. Jureidini Bros., Inc.* [1922] 44 Phil. 216 at 219; *Benedicto v. F. M. Yap Tuo and Co.*, [1923] 46 Phil. 753 at 756; *Philippine Refining Co. v. Jarque* [1935] 61 Phil. 229 at 232.
[178] *Belgian Catholic Missionaries, Inc. v. Magallanes Press, Inc.* [1926] 49 Phil. 647 at 655–656; *Jaca v. Davao Lumber Co.* [1982] 113 SCRA 107 at 127.
[179] *Manarang v. Ofilada* [1958] 99 Phil. 108 at 112.
[180] *Philippine National Bank v. De Poli* [1923] 44 Phil. 763 at 771; *Philippikne National Bank v. Manila Investment and Construction, Inc.* [1971] 38 SCRA 462 at 466.
[181] *Bank of the Philippine Islands v. Olutanga Lumber Co.* [1924] 47 Phil. 20 at 22; *Garrido v. Tuason* [1968] 24 SCRA 727 at 730; *Philippine National Bank v. Manila Investment Construction, Inc.* at 467; *Bicol Savings and Loan Association v. Guinhawa* [1990] 188 SCRA 642 at 647.
[182] Civil Code 1950, Art. 1484; *Filipinas Investment and Finance Corporation v. Ridad* [1969] 30 SCRA 564 at 569.
[183] R. A. 133 1947, s.1.
[184] 1987 Philippine Constitution, Art. XII, s.7.
[185] *Mobil Oil Philippines, Inc. v. Diocares* [1969] 29 SCRA 656 at 660; *Tan v. Valdehueza* [1975] 66 SCRA 61 at 65.
[186] Rules of Court, r. 68, ss.1 and 2.
[187] Act 3135 1924.
[188] *Government Service Insurance System v. Court of First Instance of Iloilo* [1989] 775 SCRA 19 at 24.
[189] Act 3135 1924, s.6.
[190] *Rosario v. Tayug Rural Bank, Inc.* [1968] 22 SCRA 1220 at 1225; *General v. Barrameda* [1976] 69 SCRA 182 at 189; *Gorospe v. Santos* [1976] 69 SCRA 191 at 206.
[191] General Banking Act 1949, s.78.
[192] Civil Code 1950, Art. 2132.
[193] *Ibid.*, Art. 2134.
[194] *Aldea v. Fuentes* [1913] 24 Phil. 303 at 308; *Macapinlac v. Gutierrez Repide* [1922] 43 Phil. 770 at 786.
[195] *Pardo de Tavera v. El Hogar Filipino, Inc.* [1939] 68 Phil. 712 at 716.
[196] Trust Receipts Law 1973, s.4.

197 *Vintola v. Insular Bank of Asia and America* [1987] 150 SCRA 578 at 584; *Vintola v. Insular Bank of Asia and America* [1988] 159 SCRA 140 at 144.
198 Corporation Code 1980, s.2.
199 Civil Code 1950, s.44(3).
200 *Koppel (Philippines), Inc. v. Yatco* [1946] 77 Phil. 496 at 505.
201 Corporation Code 1980, s.6.
202 *Ibid.*, s.10.
203 *Ibid.*, s.13.
204 *Ibid.*, s.23.
205 *Ibid.*, s.24.
206 *Ibid.*, s.23.
207 *Ibid.*, s.30.
208 *Ibid.*, s.28.
209 Securities and Exchange Commission, Opinion dated February 24, 1970.
210 Corporation Code 1980, s.25.
211 Securities and Exchange Commission, Opinion dated September 8, 1975.
212 Securities and Exchange Commission, Opinion dated July 15, 1953.
213 *Gurrea v. Lezana* [1958] 103 Phil. 553 at 562.
214 *Tramat Mercantile, Inc. v. Court of Appeals* [1994] 238 SCRA 14 at 19.
215 *Consolidated Bank & Trust Corporation v. Court of Appeals* [1991] 197 SCRA 663 at 670.
216 *Benguet Electric Cooperative, Inc. vc. National Labor Relations Commission* [1992] 809 SCRA 55 at 66.
217 Corporation Code 1980, s.31.
218 *Ibid.*, s.34
219 *Ibid.*, s.32.
220 *Ibid.*, s.33
221 *Prime White Cement Corporation v. Intermediate Appellate Court* [1993] 220 SCRA 103 at 112–113.
222 Corporation Code 1980, s.62.
223 *Ibid.*, s.67.   224 *Ibid.*, s.68.
225 *Ibid.*, s.39.   226 *Loc. cit.*
227 *Ibid.*, s.58.   228 *Ibid.*, s.6.
229 *Ibid.*, s.43.   230 *Ibid.*, s.74.
231 *Gonzales v. Philippine National Bank* [1983] SCRA 489 at 495.
232 Corporation Code 1980, s.81.
233 *Ibid.*, s.42.
234 *Ibid.*, s.82.
235 *Boman Environmental Development Corporation v. Court of Appeals* [1988] 167 SCRA 540 at 548.
236 Agbayani, *Commentaries and Jurisprudence on the Commercial Laws of the Philippines*, Vol.3, 1993 ed., p.567.
237 *Evangelista v. Santos* [1950] 86 Phil. 387 at 394.
238 *San Miguel Corporation v. Kahn* [1989] 176 SCRA 447 at 463.
239 *Comnart (Phils.), Inc. v. Securities and Exchange Commission* [1991] 198 SCRA 73 at 80.
240 Corporation Code 1980, s.117.
241 *Ibid.*, s.118.
242 *Ibid.*, s.119.
243 *Ibid.*, s.120.
244 *Ibid.*, s.11.
245 *Ibid.*, s.22.
246 Rules of Court, r. 66, s.
247 *Financing Corporation of the Philippines v. Teodoro* [1953] 93 Phil. 678 at 680.

[248] Corporation Code 1980, s.123.
[249] *Ibid.*, s.133.
[250] *Merrill Lynch Futures, Inc. v. Court of Appeals* [1992] 211 SCRA 824 at 836; *National Sugar Trading Corporation v. Court of Appeals* [1995] 246 SCRA 465 at 469–470.
[251] *Home Insurance Co. v. Eastern Shipping Lines* [1988] 123 SCRA 424 at 438–439.
[252] Corporation Code 1980, s.132.
[253] *Ibid.*, s.44.
[254] New Rules on Registration of Short-Term Commercial Papers, s.3.
[255] *Ibid.*, s.4.   [256] *Ibid.*, s.5.
[257] *Ibid.*, s.11.   [258] *Ibid.*, s.12.
[259] *Ibid.*, s.19.
[260] New Rules on the Registration of Long-Term Commercial Papers, s.4.
[261] *Ibid.*, s.3.   [262] *Ibid.*, s.7.
[263] *Ibid.*, s.8.   [264] *Ibid.*, s.11.
[265] *Ibid.*, s.17.
[266] Revised Securities Act 1982, s.4.
[267] *Ibid.*, s.5.   [268] *Ibid.*, s.6.
[269] *Ibid.*, s.12.   [270] *Ibid.*, s.26.
[271] *Ibid.*, s.27.   [272] *Ibid.*, s.28.
[273] *Ibid.*, s.29.   [274] *Ibid.*, s.30.
[275] *Chung Fu Industries (Phils.), Inc. v. Court of Appeals* [1992] 206 SCRA 545 at 552.
[276] Arbitration Law 1953, s.4.
[277] *Bengson v. Chan* [1977] 78 SCRA 113 at 119; *Chung Fu Industries (Phils.), Inc. v. Court of Appeals* at 552; *Toyota Motors Philippines Corporation v. Court of Appeals* [1992] 216 SCRA 236 at 246; *Puromines, Inc. vs. Court of Appeals* [1993] 220 SCRA 281 at 291; *Associated Bank v. Court of Appeals* [1994] 233 SCRA 137 at 145; *La Naval Drug Corporation v. Court of Appeals* [1994] 236 SCRA 78 at 91.
[278] *Coquia v. Fieldmen's Insurance Co., Inc.* [1968] 26 SCRA 178 at 183.
[279] *Compagnie de Commerce et de Navigation D'Extreme Orient v. Hamburg Amerika Packetfacht Acton-Gessellschaft* [1917] 36 Phil., 590 at 634.
[280] Arbitration Law 1953, s.8.
[281] Civil Code 1950, Art. 2045.
[282] Arbitration Law 1953 s.8.
[283] *Ibid.*, s.10.
[284] *Degra v. Reyes*, CA-G. R. No. 38203-R, October 20, 1966.
[285] Civil Code 1950, Arts. 2037 and 2043.
[286] Arbitration Law 1953, s.23.
[287] *Ibid.*, s.24; *Linte Law Union v. Rock Insurance Co., Ltd.* [1921] 42 Phil. 548 at 554–555; *Robinson, Fleming and Co. v. Cruz and Tan Chong Soy* [1926] 49 Phil. 42 at 50; *De Lopez v. Fajardo* [1957] 101 Phil. 1104 at 1109; *United CMC Textile Workers Union v. Clave* [1982] 115 SCRA 894 at 903; *Chung Fu Industries (Phils.), Inc. v. Court of Appeals* [1992] 206 SCRA 545 at 553–555.
[288] Arbitration Law 1953, s.25.
[289] General Banking Act 1949, s.2.
[290] *Ibid.*, s.7.   [291] *Ibid.*, s.9.
[292] *Ibid.*, s.12.   [293] *Ibid.*, s.12-B.
[294] *Ibid.*, s.12-D.   [295] *Ibid.*, s.13.
[296] *Ibid.*, s.9-A.
[297] R. A. 7721 1994, s.2.
[298] *Ibid.*, s.3.   [299] *Ibid.*, s.6.
[300] *Ibid.*, s.4.   [301] *Ibid.*, s.7.
[302] General Banking Act 1949, s.21-A.
[303] *Ibid.*, s.21-B.   [304] *Ibid.*, s.77.

[305] *Ibid.*, s.76.   [306] *Ibid.*, s.75.
[307] *Ibid.*, s.23.   [308] *Ibid.*, s.78.
[309] *Loc. cit.*   [310] *Ibid.*, s.24.
[311] *Ibid.*, s.83.   [312] *Ibid.*, s.79.
[313] Consumer Protection Act 1992, Art. 10.
[314] *Ibid.*, Art. 15.   [315] *Ibid.*, Art. 20.
[316] *Ibid.*, Art. 42.   [317] *Ibid.*, Art. 48.
[318] *Ibid.*, Art. 50.   [319] *Ibid.*, Art. 52.
[320] *Ibid.*, Art. 68(d).   [321] *Ibid.*, Art. 68(e).
[322] *Ibid.*, Art. 69(a).   [323] *Ibid.*, Art. 69(b).
[324] *Ibid.*, Art. 74.   [325] *Ibid.*, Art. 108.
[326] *Ibid.*, Art. 97.   [327] *Ibid.*, Art. 99.
[328] *Ibid.*, Art. 100.
[329] Philippine Environment Code 1977, s.3.
[330] *Ibid.*, s.4.   [331] *Ibid.*, s.5.
[332] *Ibid.*, s.6.   [333] *Ibid.*, s.15.
[334] *Ibid.*, s.18.   [335] *Ibid.*, s.19.
[336] *Ibid.*, s.23.   [337] *Ibid.*, s.24.
[338] *Ibid.*, ss.26, 28 and 30.
[339] *Ibid.*, s.36.   [340] *Ibid.*, s.39.
[341] *Ibid.*, s.40.   [342] *Ibid.*, s.43.
[343] *Ibid.*, s.45.   [344] *Ibid.*, s.49.
[345] *Ibid.*, s.50.
[346] Labor Code of the Philippines 1974, Art. 83.
[347] *Ibid.*, Art. 84.   [348] *Ibid.*, Art. 86.
[349] *Ibid.*, Art. 87.   [350] *Ibid.*, s.91.
[351] *Ibid.*, s.94.   [352] *Ibid.*, s.95.
[353] *Ibid.*, s.99.
[354] Memorandum Order no.28 1986.
[355] Labor Code of the Philippines 1974, s.130.
[356] *Ibid.*, s.133.
[357] *Ibid.*, s.135.
[358] *Ibid.*, s.136.
[359] Special Protection of Children against Child Abuse, Exploitation and Discrimination Act 1992, s.12.
[360] Department of Labor and Employment, Department Order No. 18, s.3.
[361] Labor Code of the Philippines 1974, s.139(c).
[362] *Ibid.*, s.279.
[363] *Ibid.*, s.281.
[364] *Ibid.*, s.282.
[365] Rules to Implement the Labor Code, Book VI, r. XIV, s.2.
[366] *Ibid.*, s.5.
[367] *Ibid.*, s.6.
[368] Labor Code of the Philippines 1974, Art. 283.
[369] *Ibid.*, Art. 284.
[370] *Ibid.*, Art. 285(a).
[371] *Ibid.*, Art. 285(b).
[372] *Ibid.*, Art. 287; Rules to Implement the Labor Code, Book VI, r. II, ss.3 and 4.
[373] Labor Code of the Philippines 1974, Art. 287.
[374] Foreign Investments Act 1991, ss.5, 6 and 8, as amended by Republic Act No. 8179 1996.
[375] Implementing Rules and Regulations of Republic Act No. 7042, r. IV, s.1.
[376] Foreign Investments Act 1991, s.5.
[377] *Loc. cit.*

Philippines

378 Omnibus Investment Code 1987, Art. 32.
379 *Ibid.*, Art. 39(a); 1995 Investment Priorities Plan, p.7.
380 Omnibus Investment Code 1987, Art. 39(b).
381 *Ibid.*, Art. 39(i).   382 *Ibid.*, Art. 39(j).
383 *Ibid.*, Art. 39(f).   384 *Ibid.*, Art. 39(g).
385 *Ibid.*, Art. 39(h).   386 *Ibid.*, Art. 39(k).
387 *Ibid.*, Art. 39(l).
388 *Ibid.*, Art. 39(n); 1995 Investment Priorities Plan, p.8.
389 Omnibus Investment Code 1987, Art. 39 (m).
390 Special Economic Zone Act 1995, s.5.
391 Rules and Regulations to Implement Republic Act No. 7916, r. III, s.1.
392 *Ibid.*, r. II, s.1.
393 *Ibid.*, r. XV, s.1.
394 *Ibid.*, r. XV, s.2.
395 Special Economic Zone Act 1995, s.24.
396 Rules and Regulations to Implement Republic Act Nol 7916, r. XV, s.4.
397 Special Economic Zone Act 1995, s.23.
398 National Internal Revenue Code 1977, ss.22(b) and 25(b)(1).
399 *Ibid.*, ss.22(a) and 25(a)(1).
400 *Ibid.*, s.21(a).
401 *Ibid.*, s.20(b).
402 *Loc. cit.*
403 *Ibid.*, s.24(a).
404 *Ibid.*, s.25(a)(1).
405 *Ibid.*, s.25(a)(5), id.
406 *Ibid.*, s.25(b)(5)(B).
407 BIR Ruling No. 208-89 dated September 28, 1989.
408 BIR Ruling No. 111-88 dated March 19, 1988.
409 BIR Ruling No. 009-85 dated January 21, 1985.
410 BIR Ruling No. 045-85 dated March 22, 1985; BIR Ruling No. 094-83 dated June 1, 1983; BIR Ruling No. 100-83 dated June 9, 1983; BIR Ruling No. 126-83 dated July 8, 1983.
411 BIR Ruling No. 178-85 dated October 4, 1985.
412 BIR Ruling No. 113-84 dated June 29, 1984.
413 BIR Ruling No. 046-83 dated March 21, 983.
414 National Internal Revenue Code 1977, s.24(e)(1) and 25(a)(6)(A), NIRC.
415 *Ibid.*, s.24(e)(2), 25(a)(6)(C) and 124-A.
416 *Ibid.*, s.24(e)(4) and 25(a)(6)(D).
417 *Ibid.*, 25(a)(2).   418 *Ibid.*, 25(a)(3).
419 *Ibid.*, 25(a)(4).   420 *Ibid.*, s.25(a)(6)(B).
421 *Ibid.*, s.25(b)(1).   422 *Ibid.*, s.25(b)(2), id.
423 *Ibid.*, s.25(b)(3), id.   424 *Ibid.*, s.25(b)(4), id.
425 *Ibid.*, s.25(b)(5)(A), id. 426 *Ibid.*, s.25(b)(5)(B).
427 *Ibid.*, s.25(b)(5)(C), NIRC. 428 *Ibid.*, s.124-A, id.
429 *Ibid.*, s.21(a), id.   430 *Ibid.*, s.21(f), id.
431 *Ibid.*, s.21(b), id.   432 *Ibid.*, s.29, id.
433 *Ibid.*, s.22(a)(1)   434 *Ibid.*, s.22(b)
435 *Ibid.*, s.22(c)   436 *Ibid.*, s.22(d)
437 *Ibid.*, s.22(e)
438 *Ibid.*, s.21(c)(1), (c)(2), (d)(2), (e)
439 *Tolentino v. Secretary of Finance* [1994] 235 SCRA 630.
440 *Ibid.*, s.106   441 *Ibid.*, s.100(2)
442 *Ibid.*, s.103.   443 *Ibid.*, s.102.
444 *Ibid.*, s.232(a).   445 *Ibid.*, s.233.

446 *Ibid.*, s.235.   447 Patent Law 1947, s.7.

448 *Ibid.*, s.8.   449 *Ibid.*, s.55.

450 *Ibid.*, s.37.   451 *Ibid.*, s.60.

452 Decree on Intellectual Property 1972, s.2.

453 *Ibid.*, s.5.

454 Trademarks Law 1947, s.4.

455 *Ibid.*, s.22.

456 Magna Carta for Small Enterprises 1991, s.11.

457 Export Development Act 1994, s.16(f).

458 Civil Code 1950, Art. 1547.

459 *Moles v. Intermediate Appellat Court* [1989] 169 SCRA 777 at 785.

460 Civil Code 1950, Art. 1487.

461 Implementing Rules and Regulations of Republic Act No. 7042, r. I, s.1(f)(3).

SINGAPORE

Christopher J. Murphy

I. Summary of Business and Political Conditions

Basic Demographic, Political and Economic Information

The Republic of Singapore is located in Southeastern Asia approximately 137   G.01
kilometers north of the equator between the southern tip of West Malaysia
and Indonesia.[1] Singapore has a total land area of 622.6 square miles[2] with a
population of 2,904,468 (July 1995 est.).[3] In addition to its natural demographic makeup, Singapore is blessed by its topographic dimensions. With
193 kilometers of coastline,[4] primarily lowland terrain[5] and a relatively mod-
erate climate[6] Singapore enjoys a pleasant living and working environment.
Singapore is ideally located with a domestic environment that is inviting for
international trade, commerce and travel. As such, it has become a focal point
of Southeast Asian trade with interest increasing as 1997 approaches for
Hong Kong. Singapore enjoyed significant economic growth in the 1980s but
experienced a downturn at the beginning of the 1990s.[7] By the end of 1992
with inflation under control and the rebound of the United States' economy
beginning to take effect, the Singapore economy also began to improve.[8]

Recent figures indicate fundamental adjustments have taken effect to provide for stable sustainable economic growth through the end of the century.
Singapore's 1994 gross domestic product was $57 billion (est. $19,940 per
capita) with a growth rate of 10.1 per cent.[9] Despite its significant growth
rate, Singapore has been able to maintain low rates of inflation (3.6 per cent)
and unemployment (2.6 per cent).[10] The manufacturing, financial services and
computer components industries have led the recovery.[11]

The national financial indicators of Singapore are solid and positive. Singapore has exports of $96.4 billion[12] and imports of $102.4 billion.[13] 1994
revenues are estimated at $11.9 billion with overall expenditures of $10.5
billion.[14] Its currency is the Singapore dollar (S$) which is broken down into

405

one hundred cents. The government's fiscal year is April 1 to March 31. And, as a developing nation, Singapore is the beneficiary of foreign economic aid aggregating over $1 billion.

Singapore has an excellent physical plant capable of supporting further growth. As a result of thoughtful long-term planning, Singapore's infrastructure is second to none in the region. It has 2,796 kilometers of paved highway,[15] 38.6 kilometers of 1.000-meter gauge railroads and the deepsea port of Singapore.[16] Singapore has 10 usable airports with Changi airport as the regional international air hub.[17] Currently, Changi airport bridges a total of 108 international cities with more than 2,100 flights on 58 airlines every week.[18]

General Summary of Political and Governmental Systems in Singapore

G.02 In order to understand Singapore today, and particularly its political system, one must place it in recent historical context. Singapore was founded as a British trading post on the Straits of Malacca in 1819 by Sir Thomas Stamford Raffles.[19] Raffles is credited with much of the island's early and continuing economic success.[20] Raffles was then Lieutenant-Governor of the Bencoolen in the service of the Honorable East Indian Company. In 1826, after significant negotiations with the Dutch regarding the overall colonization of the Malay Archipelago, Malacca and Singapore became known as the Straits Settlements under an independent Indian Presidency which included Calcutta, Madras and Bombay.[21]

In 1867, following the demise of the East Indian Company, Singapore was recomposed as an independent British colony under the Crown.[22] This status, subject to brief interruptions, lasted until 1959 when Singapore was granted internal self-government.[23] Thereafter, Singapore attempted to merge unsuccessfully with Malaysia.[24] On December 22, 1965, the Singapore Legislative Assembly enacted the Singapore Independence Bill and a Constitutional Amendment creating a parliamentary system of government with a largely ceremonial presidency.[25] Subsequently, the Constitution has been amended to expand its coverage.[26]

The political structures and participants in Singapore have remain relatively constant. The President is elected by the Parliament for a four year term.[27] The President in turn appoints a member of Parliament to serve as Prime Minister.[28] The President then, with the advice of the Prime Minister, appoints the Attorney General.[29]

The Parliament is a unicameral body consisting of 81 members each elected for five-year terms from 42 single-member constituencies and 13 multi-racial group constituencies.[30] Parliament meets at least once a year to deliberate on bills which if passed by a simple majority and approved by the President are published in the official *Gazette*.[31]

Historical Development of the Legal and Judicial System

The political participants in Singapore's government have remained constant since independence in 1965. The ruling party is the People's Action Party (PAP). Lee Kuan Yew, currently Senior Minister in the government, was the Prime Minister from 1965 until elections in 1990 when Goh Chok Tong was appointed by President Ong Teng Cheong.[32] The next elections are scheduled for August 31, 1996.

There are five major political parties in Singapore. They are the PAP, the Worker's Party (WP), the Singapore Democratic Party (SDP), the National Solidarity Party (NSP), and the Barisan Sosialis Socialist Front (BS).[33] The PAP currently holds 77 seats, the SDP 3, and the WP have 1.[34] The Cabinet has 13 ministries, as follows: defense, law, foreign affairs, national development, education, environment, communications and information, home affairs, finance, labor, community development, trade and industry, and health.[35]

The Singapore Judiciary is encapsulated in the Supreme Court and the Subordinate Courts. The Chief Justice and an unspecified number of other Judges are appointed by the President on the advice of the Prime Minister.[36] Thereafter, in order of priority are the vice-presidents of the Court of Appeal, the judges of the High Court, ranked respectively by appointment.[37] The Supreme Court consists of the High Court (unlimited jurisdiction), the Court of Appeal (hears appeals from the High Court), and the Court of Criminal Appeal (hears appeals from the High Court in criminal matters).[38] Only the High Court and Court of Appeal have jurisdiction over commercial law matters.[39] The Subordinate Courts (*i.e.* District, Magistrates, Coroners', Juvenile and Small Claims) generally handle claims for amounts less than $10,000 and domestic matters.[40]

Historical Development of the Legal and Judicial System in Singapore

Due to its colonial past and its necessary connection with Malaysia and other neighbors in the region, Singapore has had a somewhat complicated legal past. In addition, the recent geopolitical history of Southeast Asia has made economic and political stability in Singapore even more remarkable. However, because of its dependence on international trade and investment, stability and predictability have been the cornerstones of its success. **G.03**

As will be discussed below, Singapore has been struggling with the structure of its legal system for many years. In keeping with its cultural and political traditions, it has taken a long-term approach to development. As a result, Singapore has relied almost exclusively on the English common law and statutory regimes. However, as with other former colonies such as Canada, New Zealand, and India, the continuing legal system of the United Kingdom was eventually replaced to accommodate local demands and culture.

Singapore

Perhaps the most difficult task any lawyer faces when attempting to discern the applicable law in Singapore is the history of the legal system. Because Singapore was a British colony, its legal roots are in the English common law.[41] The entire common law, as of the Straits Settlements in 1826, was "received" into the colony.[42] Therefore, English Acts and cases decided before 1826 are the law of Singapore while post-1826 English cases have highly persuasive value, through 1993, but are not binding.[43]

S.5 The Civil Law Act

G.04   Only English cases that have not been replaced by Singapore law remain with respect to the commercial law.[44] This concept is well known to the common law trained lawyer. The main problem in the commercial law context, until its repeal in 1993, was found in the Civil Law Act, section 5 (hereinafter "Civil Law Act s.5" or "s.5").[45] It is worth stating and explaining Civil Law Act s.5 at this point for subsequent understanding.

> 5(1)   Subject to the provisions of this section, in all questions or issues which arise or which have to be decided in Singapore with respect to the **laws of partnerships, corporations, banks and banking, principals and agents, carriers by air, land and sea, marine insurance, average, life and fire insurance, and with respect to mercantile law generally,** the law with respect to those matters to be administered shall be the same as would be administered in England in the like case, at the corresponding period, if such question or issue had arisen or had to be decided in England, unless in any case other provision is or shall be made by any law having force in Singapore. [emphasis added]

The section continued by excluding specific English laws, international treaties to which Singapore was not a signatory and subject to modifications "as the circumstances of Singapore may require."[46] Plainly stated, no section in the commercial law of Singapore has caused more discussion or confusion.

The debate began with the question of whether "received" the applicable English law into Singapore or whether English law was applicable by "reference only" for the enumerated categories. The reception approach was the simpler and more popular.[47] It required only that one determine whether an issue fell into one of the nine enumerated areas of s.5 and, if it did, the applicable English law was used.[48] Under the reference approach, a judge would determine whether the issue of law fell under one of the categories and then transport him or herself to England and decide the question as if in England with the entire body of English law available.[49] For various reasons, simplicity chief among them, Singapore judges routinely applied the reception approach.[50] Therefore, the choice of law test under 5 could be described as follows:

"An English statute is applicable in Singapore by virtue of s.5 of the Civil Law Act when:

1. it pertains to any of the enumerated categories, and
2. no express provision is made otherwise, and
3. there is no Singapore statute corresponding to that English Act;
4. the English statute is not made for the purpose of giving effect to a treaty to which Singapore is not a party, and
5. the English statute does not regulate the exercise of any business or activity by providing for:
   (a) registration, or
   (b) licensing, or
   (c) imposition of penalties, or
   (d) any other means of control.

Given that the requirements 1 to 5 are satisfied, the [English] statute will be applicable in Singapore, subject to any modifications and adaptations that may be necessary due to local circumstances."[51]

Section 5 was the law of Singapore until repealed by the enactment of the Application of English Law Act (AELA) in 1993.[52] However, section 5 remains applicable to "any proceedings instituted or any cause of action accruing" before the enactment of the AELA.[53] There is also an ever growing body of local statutory and independent case law which is slowly replacing the need for reliance on English precedent.[54] Due to inapplicability and understandable resentment towards the importation of English statutes, the Singapore Government sought to clarify which laws, primarily commercial, are received as the law of Singapore and repealed all non-listed but potentially applicable English law.[55]

The Application of English Law Act 1993

The AELA begins by declaring that "[t]he common law of England (including the principles and rules of equity), so far as it was part of the law of Singapore immediately before the commencement of this Act, shall continue to be part of the law of Singapore."[56] Although subject to varying interpretation, this provision can generally be thought of as creating a cut-off date with respect to reception of new English common law and equity in Singapore.[57] The section concludes by stating that "[t]he common law shall continue to be in force in Singapore, as provided in subsection (1), so far as it is applicable to the circumstances of Singapore and its inhabitants and subject to such modification as those circumstances may require."[58] One commentator has asserted that this provision provides an escape from English statutory changes to the common law or equity that might otherwise undermine the intention of the AELA to completely break with English law.[59]

G.05

Singapore

The AELA then enacts the specific English commercial statutes that are listed in the three Schedules of the Act, unless inconsistent with Singapore law after the AELA.[60] The First Schedule, Part II, enacts 13 English statutes with identified exceptions. The statutes enacted are as follows:

Statute	Application
Mercantile Law Amendment Act 1856[61]	Sections 3 and 5.
Policies of Assurance Act 1867[62]	The whole except section 8.
Factors Act 1889[63]	The whole except the amendment to section 9 by the Consumer Credit Act 1974.
Partnership Act 1890[64]	The whole
Marine Insurance Act 1906[65]	The whole
Third Parties (Rights against Insurers) Act 1930[66]	The whole
Corporate Bodies' Contracts Act 1960[67]	The whole
Misrepresentation Act 1967[68]	The whole
Unfair Contract Terms Act 1977[69]	Part I (except section 1(1)(c) and (3)(b) and the amendment to that section by the Occupiers' Liability Act 1984) and Part III.
Sale of Goods Act 1979[70]	The whole except sections 22 and 25(2).
Supply of Goods and Services Act 1982[71]	The whole except Part II.
Minor's Contracts Act 1987[72]	The whole except sections 1(b) and 4(1).
Carriage of Goods by Sea Act 1992[73]	The whole.

It should be noted that this list may be subject to revision as Singapore enacts local law to replace each of the preceding. It is also important to consult the ever-growing body of Singapore common law for guidance. The legislature made some minor amendments to Part II of the First Schedule which are reflected in Part III. The Second Schedule of the AELA lists amendments to the Civil Law Act in the area of the Statute of Frauds and other statutes with less commercial application.[74]

In 1989 Singapore significantly restricted the right of appeal from the Supreme Court to the Privy Council Judicial Committee in London.[75] Currently, only civil cases and very few criminal cases are eligible for appeal to the Privy Council.[76] As for commercial law, assuming parties to a civil dispute are permitted to continue their appeal to London, they must have agreed in writing to such action prior to "hearing of the case."[77] Therefore, if parties to a contract wish to have the right to appeal decisions of a Singapore court regarding a contract to the Privy Council, they must expressly provide for such right of appeal in the contract itself.[78] There appears to be little doubt that the right of appeal to the Privy Council will be completely abolished in the future.[79]

Current Legal and Judicial Structure for Regulation of Commercial Activities in Singapore

Singapore maintains a large formal governmental structure for attracting, assisting, and regulating foreign and domestic business. A major part of that structure is the establishment of various Statutory Boards. The Statutory Boards are overseen by the appropriate government Ministry to implement the policies of the government. Statutory Boards maintain offices in Singapore and throughout the world with the main goal of attracting foreign investment while protecting the country's natural assets.

G.06

Role of Singapore in Global and Regional Trade Forums

Singapore is a member of most of the regional and world trade and development organizations. In particular, the Association of Southeast Asian Nations (ASEAN) which provides preferential trading arrangements for thousands of items. Of more recent interest is Singapore's membership in the Asian Pacific Economic Council (APEC) which is a regional policy discussion and cooperation organization.

G.07

On the international level, Singapore participates in many international trade organizations. Perhaps of greatest importance is Singapore's membership in the General Agreement on Tariffs and Trade (GATT) and its newest progeny the World Trade Organization (WTO). As a member of the GATT, Singapore enjoys and provides preferences to products from developed countries under the Generalized System of Preferences (GSP) and from developing countries under the Global System of Trade Preferences (GSTP).[80] However, Singapore has taken the role of observer only in the General Agreement on Trade in Services (basic telecommunications) (GATS).[81] In order to be in compliance with certain agreed upon provisions of the GATT, Singapore is in the process of changing certain domestic commercial laws. In addition, Singapore participates in many other international organizations.[82]

It is also important to point out that a "growth triangle" has begun to develop in the immediate vicinity of Singapore. The "triangle" consists of Singapore, the Riau Islands of Indonesia, and the Malaysian state of Johor.[83] The governments of these states are cooperating to provide complimentary goods and services to potential investors and existing businesses.[84]

II. Laws and Institutions Affecting Business and Commercial Activities

Competition Law

G.08 Singapore has no former legal regime in the area of competition or antitrust.[85] Neither does it maintain any government price controls.[86] Takeovers and Mergers are governed by the Companies Act and its supplementing code which are discussed in greater detail below.[87] The few industries that are not subject to free competition are those of "natural monopolies" which are maintained by quasi-governmental organizations (*i.e.* public utilities, postal services, and telecommunications).[88]

In 1992, the Singapore government took steps toward privatizing the Singapore telephone company and separating it from the regulatory Telecommunications Authority.[89] However, the telephone company will maintain a 15-year monopoly for "basic" services and a five-year monopoly for mobile communications.[90] According to the U.S. Office of the United States Trade Representative, these restrictions effectively restrict market access for potential competitors in the lucrative telecommunications market.[91]

Contract Law

G.09 English common law is the applicable law of general contracts in Singapore although this is called into question with the passage of the AELA.[92] The law of the sale of goods is discussed extensively in the following section. Section 5 of the Civil Law Act made English "mercantile law generally" applicable in Singapore until the enactment of the AELA.[93] Therefore, great care should be undertaken to independently determine whether Singapore has replaced the applicable statutory or common laws in this area.

Formation

G.10 Under the English common law, a contract begins with an offer which is capable of being accepted.[94] This is contrasted with options and advertisements which are characterized as open-ended offers and invitations for offers, respectively.[95] An acceptance must not be conditional or introduce new terms in which case it will be treated as a counteroffer. Neither can the offer require silence as a form of acceptance.[96] An acceptance is binding once it is known to the offeror.[97] Likewise, a revocation is only enforceable once it comes to the knowledge of the other party.[98] The legal relationship that exists from discussion between parties is construed narrowly in the common law to permit non-binding negotiations.[99] The courts will review the facts surrounding the parties negotiations in determining whether the parties intended a binding contract.[100]

Under the common law, courts will not endeavor to determine whether the consideration for the contract is adequate, unless it is illegal.[101] While the common law requires privity for enforcement of a contract; consideration for the contract may come from a third party.[102] In addition, the common law does not enforce contracts in which the consideration is a prior act or forbearance.[103] The exception to this is if the act or forbearance was done prior to the offer being made.[104] In addition, the common law does not recognize "natural affection" as a valid form of consideration.[105] At the moment, it remains unclear whether the doctrine of accord and satisfaction is applicable in Singapore.[106] However, the doctrine of promissory estoppel is applicable to contractual relationships to prevent one party from denying the other benefits which were given under the contract by enforcing terms in the contract.[107]

Terms

The courts of Singapore follow the common law tradition by finding a G.11 difference between conditions and warranties in contracts.[108] The courts will also inquire as to whether a breach of the terms of the contract are material and fashion a proportional remedy.[109] The express terms of a contract in Singapore have been narrowly construed.[110] Likewise, the courts will not generally imply terms into a contract unless it is necessary to fulfill the intentions of the parties or it is a customary term.[111]

Extrinsic evidence will not be allowed to interpret a written contract expect where offered to contest the validity of the contract itself.[112] Similarly, courts are reluctant to hear evidence of "collateral contracts" which are offered to supplement the agreement of the parties. However, where the court finds that the collateral agreement was intended to induce the other party to enter the main contract it will consider it along side the written agreement.[113] The law in the area of limitation of liability by contract has been uncertain. The caselaw holds that broad release clauses are suspect and will not provide a "safe harbor" for the careless.[114]

Void and Voidable

Contracts governed by the law of Singapore may be voidable until action is G.12 commenced after which they may be deemed void if induced through fraud, misrepresentation, duress, coercion or undue influence. The common law defines fraud as a knowingly or recklessly false misrepresentation.[115] However, the standard of proof in a case attempting to establish fraud is high.[116] The common law requires that the fraud alleged have been a factor which induced the agreement in order to be actionable.[117] Fraud is defined as knowledge of the person making the representation that the statement is false.

Singapore

Conversely, innocent misrepresentation does not require knowledge of the falsity of the statement.[118]

With the passage of the Misrepresentation Act, received by the AELA, English law creates the cause of action of negligent misrepresentation but does not require proof of the existence of a duty to inform.[119] The effect of these different levels of misrepresentation is that recession of the entire contract will probably not be available for innocent misrepresentation. [120] However, both recession and damages may be available for negligent misrepresentation or fraud.[121]

In addition, contracts may be voided upon proof of duress, coercion or undue influence. Duress and coercion which required proof of physical violence have been eliminated for the most part due to difficulties of proof and expanded relief under the theory of undue influence.[122] In this regard, the doctrine of undue influence typically puts the onus on the party initiating the agreement to prove that it was properly negotiated.[123]

A mistake by one or both of the parties to a contract may void the agreement.[124] The variations on the issue of mistake, whether by one party or both, will determined the remedy.[125] However, the common law will not excuse a party who is careless when signing a contract.[126]

Although there is some debate about the age of majority in Singapore, contracts with minors are void under the common law, unless it is for the minor's benefit.[127] Likewise, contracts that are illegal under English or Singapore law are void.[128] Where there is a non-competition clause in a contract, the courts will hold it void due to the public policy against restraint of trade.[129]

Performance and Discharge

Discharge of a contract in Singapore takes place upon frustration, performance or breach by one or both of the by the parties to the agreement. In the area of frustration due to impossibility of performance, the Law Reform (Frustrated Contracts) Act 1943 is the governing law in Singapore.[130] *Force majeure* clauses will also be enforced when the non-performance of a party is due to circumstances beyond his or her control.[131]

Contracts may be divided into two types. Those that require a one time completion and those that can be broken down into more than one part. Contracts that require a one time performance must be completed in their entirety on time,[132] unless excused by substantial performance.[133] Those that can be divided[134] are more likely to occur in the sale of goods area discussed below.

Finally, there are essentially two actionable types of breach under the common law. The first for refusal to complete the contract as agreed and the second for disability to perform. Under refusal to perform, the common law permits the innocent party to treat the contract as having been discharged.[135] The innocent party in a disability breach can obtain the same type of relief.[136]

The repudiating party can assert the defense that the breach was not material or "fundamental" in an attempt to mitigate damages or other remedies.[137]

Remedies

As in the preceding areas, the rules governing the award of damages, specific relief or injunction are those of the English common law. With respect to damages, the courts of Singapore apply the rule of *Hadley v. Baxendale*.[138] Namely, that damages are determined as those that flow from the breach and would have been reasonably contemplated by the parties at the time they entered the contract.[139]

In the case of contractual liquidated damages and penalty clauses, the English courts have endeavored to compare the nature of the damage provisions to the actual damages suffered to deny enforcement of penalties for breach.[140] However, the English courts have distinguished the situation of deposit forfeiture from penalty by characterizing a deposit as "a guarantee that the contract shall be performed".[141] In the area of nominal damages and damages for inconvenience, where no amount is written down or easily calculated, the Singapore courts will award damages.[142] In some cases the courts of Singapore may even go further.[143]

Specific performance may be granted in cases where damages are not easily ascertained such as land sale contracts and executory contracts.[144] The courts will not require specific performance when there are uncertainties in the contract itself, if the plaintiff has delayed in bringing the action or committed some type of fraud or if such award would require continuing court supervision.[145] In addition, the English courts will not award specific performance of a part of a contract[146] unless it can be severed.[147]

Injunctive relief can be either temporary or permanent. In the case of a temporary or interlocutory injunction, the requesting party is required to prove that its *prima facie* case demonstrates a great likelihood of success and that the court must maintain the *status quo* until the case may be heard.[148] Affirmative or mandatory injunctions are also available in Singapore under the applicable English common law.[149] However, such relief will be subject to review at the request of relevant parties.[150]

Commercial Law

Singapore has recently become a signatory to the United Nations Convention on Contracts for the International Sale of Goods.[151] The Convention serves as a default legal scheme in transactions for the international sale of goods by defining buyers' and sellers' rights and duties when such terms are absent from the parties' agreement. It should be noted that parties to an international goods transaction must expressly opt out in order to avoid its application.

G.13

Singapore

In order to determine the applicable law to the sale of goods in Singapore s.5 of the Civil Law Act re-emerges as does the AELA after 1993.[152] There is little Singapore law, statutory or common law, in this area primarily because of s.5. As a result there is some dispute and uncertainty about what law will be applied in particular circumstances.[153] However, the main English statute governing the sale of goods is the Sale of Goods Act which was specifically made applicable in the First Schedule of the AELA, as previously described.[154] The Sale of Goods Act provides that common law cases apply where they do not conflict with the Act.[155]

The legal requirements for the formation of a contract for the sale of goods[156] in Singapore should be familiar to most common law trained lawyers.[157] Despite a few departure points peculiar to Singapore law, the concepts of offer, acceptance, and consideration[158] are prerequisites to the formation of an enforceable contract.[159] Worthy of note here is the fact that married women are free to enter contracts[160] and that corporations may enter *ultra virus* contracts.[161] Finally, so long as the price can be discerned from the conduct of the parties[162] there are few other required formalities. However, it is highly recommended that parties wishing to avoid the uncertainties of an oral agreement reduce the terms to writing.[163]

Parties bargaining under the commercial law of Singapore do so within the basic principle of "freedom of contract".[164] That is, the parties are free to negotiate the terms of their deal so long as they do not violate the fundamental law of contracts.[165] However, it should be noted that the courts will not supply any essential terms that may have been omitted which may nullify the contract.[166] Therefore, once again the parties should reduce their negotiations and final deal to writing. Nonetheless, the Sale of Goods act will imply certain non-essential terms as to title,[167] description,[168] and quality.[169]

The next issue that arises in the sale of goods context is the legal transfer of title after the contract has been entered. If the goods are specifically identified[170] title is transferred at the time the parties specify.[171] If the goods are not specifically identified (*i.e.* site unseen) they must be determined before title may pass.[172] When the parties have not stated when title to goods is to pass the law will attempt to carry out the intent of the parties.[173] The Sale of Goods Act and the Unsolicited Goods and Services Act provide additional rules for the transfer of title to goods if the contract contains conditions precedent[174] or the goods were not requested by the buyer.[175]

The seller may also reserve the right to transfer title until a condition has been met by the buyer (*e.g.* payment) under what is known as a *Romalpa* clause.[176] The parties can and should contemplate allocation of the risk of the transfer of the goods in their contract. Unless otherwise agreed, the seller assumes the risk until title transfers to the buyer.[177]Should the transaction fail to be completed for reasons beyond the parties' control their performances may be excused under the doctrine of "frustration".[178] Finally, in the situations where non-owners such as agents are transferring title, the buyer may be required to answer to the party who has title at a later time[179] or may take the goods with good title if received as a *bona fide* purchaser without notice.[180]

For the most part, the duties of the seller and the buyer in a contract for the sale of goods under Singapore law are those of the reasonable businessperson under the circumstances. This includes delivery, acceptance or rejection, and payment. As previously mentioned, the parties are free to conclude their own terms under the doctrine of the "freedom of contract". Generally, it is the duty of the seller to deliver the goods at a reasonable time, place, and method or pursuant to the contract.[181] Once delivered, the buyer has the right to inspect the goods[182] to see that they conform to the contract prior to acceptance.[183] The buyer may then reject[184] the goods or keep them and sue for damages[185] if the seller has tendered non-conforming goods unless the nonconformity is considered *de minimis*. The buyer simultaneously has the duty to make payment.[186] The seller retains a lien on any portion of the goods for which payment has not been received.[187]

The parties to the contract for the sale of goods may seek redress for failures to perform. The seller has a statutory right to sue for damages for the buyer's failure to make payment on the date prescribed in the contract,[188] for wrongful rejection of the goods,[189] or for specific performance of ascertained goods.[190] The buyer has the right to sue the seller for non-delivery,[191] specific performance of the contract,[192] or for breach of warranties under the terms of the contract or implied by law.[193]

Companies Law

All but a few forms of business in Singapore are open to foreign and domestic business people. The main administrative authority over business conducted in Singapore is the Registrar of Businesses which regulates pursuant to the Business Registration Act.[194] Most, but not all parties intending to do business in Singapore must register.[195] The Registrar of Businesses accepts filing fees, reviews all legally required papers, and performs all on-going regulatory functions related to businesses.[196] The main choices of business form include sole proprietorship, partnership, corporation, branch, and representative offices.[197] Each entity has its advantages and disadvantages depending on the objects of the party wanting to conduct business in Singapore. The main features of each will be discussed below.   **G.14**

Sole Proprietorships

An individual desiring to operate as a sole proprietor in Singapore must submit the following information to the Registrar of Businesses: (1) business name; (2) nature of the business; (3) principal place of business; (4) individuals in management and sole proprietor's name, addresses, nationality, etc.;   **G.15** and (5) date of commencement of business.[198] The sole proprietor must then pay the annual fee and, if approved, will receive a registration certificate and be entitled to conduct business using the term "trading as".[199] However, the sole proprietor will remain personally liable for all debts whether personal or business.[200]

Partnerships

G.16   The law of partnership ("Partnership Act") in Singapore is received from the United Kingdom through s.5 of the Civil Law Act and the AELA.[201] The Partnership Act requires that there be a business engaged in between persons[202] directed toward making a profit.[203] Those wanting to establish a partnership in Singapore may do so for a time certain or for an indefinite life.[204] There must be at least two partners but not more than 20.[205] The Partnership Act states the following test for determining whether a partnership exists:

1.   The use of commonly owned property in a business;
2.   The sharing of profits and losses is *prima facie* evidence of a partnership;
3.   Other evidence such as the partnership agreement and actions;
4.   Mere installment payments of a debt does not make a lender a partner.[206]

The partnership must be registered with the Registrar of Businesses, discussed above, pursuant to s.5 of the Business Registration Act.[207] The partnership is also governed by the agreement between the partners which may be oral or written.[208] The typical partnership agreement describes the partners' business, important dates, capitalization, remuneration, liabilities, partner changes,[209] administration and dissolution, to name the more common.[210]

As with any business entity in Singapore involving the participation of more than one person, certain rights and duties are bestowed upon the partners. Usually, the partnership agreement, if well drafted, will address most situations in accordance with the law at the time. However, where the agreement has "gaps" or is contrary to the law, the Partnership Act will be applied by the courts.[211]

Disputes often arise in the areas of relations with third parties and among partners. Generally, all partners are agents of the firm and the other partners.[212] The partnership[213] and the partners will be jointly and severally liable[214] for all acts of a partner taken within the scope of the partner's authority.[215]

Similarly, partners have rights and obligations among and between themselves and the partnership.[216] Chief among a partner's obligations is the equitable obligation to act in "good faith" when involved in firm matters.[217] The Partnership Act specifically obligates a partner to account for benefits derived from firm business[218] and from competing business in which the partner has an interest.[219] Firm decisions are typically controlled by majority decision unless the partnership agreement provides otherwise.[220] Partners have the right to inspect the books of the partnership personally or through a representative.[221]

Both partner and the firm may invoke the jurisdiction of the courts to enforce rights and compel fulfillment of obligations by appropriate means which may include injunction, civil action, and appointment of a receiver.[222] The partnership may be dissolved by one of following happenings: (1) natural expiration[223]; (2) upon notice[224]; (3) death of a partner[225]; (4) bankruptcy of a partner[226]; (5) placement of a charging order upon a partner's interest[227]; (6) illegality of the partnership[228]; (7) expulsion of a partner[229]; and (8) other reasons.[230] The firm assets and liabilities will thereafter be divided according to contributions and liabilities.[231] Finally, third parties (*e.g.* creditors) are permitted to petition for dissolution of a partnership if it has (1) ceased doing business in Singapore; (2) it is unable to pay it debts; or (3) a court finds that it should be terminated.[232]

Companies

The Companies Act of 1984 (hereinafter Companies Act) governs the incorporation and operation of Singapore companies.[233] The history of the Companies Act is important to understanding its interpretation and application. The Singapore Companies Act is modeled after the Malaysian Companies Act 1965 which is drafted after the Australian Uniform Companies Acts and the British Companies Act of 1948.[234] When ruling on the application of the Singapore Companies Act, Singapore Courts often rely on Australian and English case law and common law to provide legal analysis.[235] Two complementary pieces of legislation, the Companies Regulations 1984 and the Companies (winding-up) Rules 1969, fill out the statutory legal regime over companies in Singapore.[236]

G.17

Limited and Unlimited Liability Companies

The Companies Act provides three options for promoters and incorporators. Companies can be: (a) share or stock corporations; (b) guarantee corporations, and (c) unlimited companies.[237] The first two forms of corporate entity are limited liability and carry the suffix "limited" ("ltd") or "berhad" ("bhd").[238] Limited and unlimited companies may be freely converted from one to another, assuming they meet the requisite qualifications with the Registry of Companies.[239] Most foreign investors would want the limited share company as the preferred investment vehicle in Singapore.[240]

Public and Private Companies

Share companies may be either public or private.[241] A public company raises capital by issuing shares on the Singapore Stock Exchange (SSE).[242] A company that fails to meet the requirements for being private is a public company.[243] A private company is one that has articles of association which: (a) restrict share transfers; (b) has no more than 50 members; (c) prohibits public purchase of its shares or debentures, and (d) prohibits public solicitation for money.[244] A private company may be deemed an exempt private company if it has no more than 20 members and none of its shares are held by a corporation.[245] The advantage to being an exempt private corporation is that less disclosure is required to the Registrar of Companies.[246]

Holding and Subsidiary Companies

Singapore recognizes holding companies, subsidiaries and groups or related corporations.[247] Of note in this area is that subsidiaries of subsidiaries are the parent corporation. In addition, any allotment of shares to a subsidiary is void, and a company may not be a member of its holding company.[248]

Incorporation

The persons who organize a company in Singapore are called "promoters".[249] The promoters must reserve a corporate name,[250] submit the memorandum and articles of incorporation[251] along with the capital registration fee,[252] and then wait for the certificate of incorporation[253] from the Registrar of Companies.[254] Once incorporated the corporation becomes an independent legal entity[255] providing limited liability to its members[256] until such time as it is legally terminated.[257]

The liability protection provided by a corporation for its members and directors may be challenged under the doctrine of "lifting the [corporate] veil" either by statute or common law. If challenged by statute, there are four grounds available. Those are:

1. fewer than two members;[258]
2. company name on commercial documents;[259]
3. unauthorized officer contracting,[260] and
4. fraudulent corporate dealings with third parties.[261]

The corporate veil may also be "lifted" by a court to determine if the corporate controllers are enemies of Singapore during a time of war, residency of the corporations controllers is outside Singapore or the corporation is being used by its controller(s) to perpetrate a fraud.[262] The final and separate grounds for attacking the corporate shield is if the corporation is part of a larger group of companies. In this case, certain reporting requirements may come into play for the entire group not just the technically Singapore corporation.[263]

Participants and Management

During the life of the corporation, the participants (*i.e.* directors, officers, and members) will be governed by the memorandum and articles of incorporation and the Companies Act as interpreted and enforced by the Singapore courts. The memorandum which must be filed with the Registrar of Companies must contain certain information. Namely, the corporate name, goals, share issue and price information, members' liability, subscribers' information, and agreement of subscribers to the incorporation.[264]

As the memorandum is the organic document of the corporation it is intended to be difficult to change.[265] As a result, the memorandum is often unnecessarily long and detailed with respect to the objects[266] and powers[267] of the company in order to avoid potential attacks from those claiming an action is *ultra vires*.[268] In comparison, the articles of association which govern the daily corporate affairs[269] are easily changed[270] assuming there is not an attempt to deliberately interfere with the rights of the minority.[271]

The members of a Singapore corporation may either be human or corporate. If the company is a wholly owned subsidiary it will be excused from the rule that its shares must be held by two or more members.[272] Every fully paid-up member has the right to vote at meetings,[273] enforce the memorandum and articles,[274] and inspect corporate books and registers.[275] The corporation must give adequate notice[276] of annual meetings.[277] The members will then vote[278] on resolutions[279] presented. Minority members who believe they have been treated unfairly due to majority oppression can appeal to the courts for relief.[280] However, shareholders may not sue on behalf of the corporation to enforce rights not being advanced, in their opinion, by management or the board of directors.[281] Finally, a Singapore company is required to maintain registers of all members,[282] directors and officers,[283] debt[284] and liens on company property.[285]

The members of the corporation will generally elect the board of directors at the annual meeting.[286] In order to be eligible to serve as director of a Singapore corporation one must be an adult natural person.[287] A Singapore corporation must have at least two directors with one whom is a Singapore resident.[288] The board of directors is given complete control over the company's affairs[289] in those areas which the memorandum of incorporation dictates.[290]

A director's payment may be set by the board itself, the general membership or the incorporating documentation.[291] A director of a Singapore company has the duty to act as a fiduciary by holding the company's interests above the director's own[292] and the statutory duty of disclosing anything that might give the appearance of being a conflict of interest.[293] A director may be removed,[294] resign[295] or reach the maximum age limit of 70.[296]

Capital

Singapore corporations may be capitalized through debt or equity vehicles. A share certificate is *prima facie* evidence of ownership[297] and may be transferred.[298] Shares may be ordinary[299] or preferred.[300] Dividends may only be paid out of profit, not ordinary corporate capital.[301] The company may also issue debentures to creditors[302] or give secured (fixed) and unsecured (floating) liens (charges) which have relative priorities in the event of a bankruptcy or winding up.[303] Liens must be registered with the Registry of Companies within 30 days.[304]

Winding Up

Dissolution of a Singapore corporation can be accomplished by the court,[305] the corporation or its creditors.[306] If the corporation's solvency is in issue, the directors will be required to make a declaration[307] regarding the corporation's ability to pay its debts over the next year.[308] If the corporation is able to pay its debts the winding up will be left to the corporation's members. The creditors of the corporation may oppose this and request appointment of a liquidator.[309] Claims in a winding up will be paid out according to the statutory priorities.[310] Finally, the company is dissolved when the liquidator obtains an order of dissolution from the court.[311] It should be noted that many of these provisions have been recently modified by the passage of the Bankruptcy Act.

Branch and Representative Offices

G.18 A foreign company may register a Singapore branch office rather than forming a Singapore entity.[312] The branch must be registered before doing business in Singapore.[313] A branch must have two Singaporean agents, pay a capital registration fee, and file annual audited accounts.[314] A less formal entity still is the representative office which is licensed by the Trade Development Board.[315]

Capital Markets and Securities Law

G.19 The applicable laws for securities regulation in Singapore are the Companies Act[316] and the Securities Industry Act.[317] Other applicable law can be found in the Banking Act,[318] the Insurance Act,[319] and the Futures Trading Act.[320] This section will focus on the Companies and Securities Industry Acts.

Solicitation

G.20 A Singapore corporation may solicit capital by issuing shares or borrowing directly. Share solicitation may be accomplished by direct allotment, share sales, insider sales, or private placement.[321] If the shares are being offered to the public a prospectus[322] must be prepared and filed with the Registry of Companies.[323]

The information that must be disclosed in the prospectus is carefully prescribed in the Companies Act.[324] Additional disclosure is required for direct borrowing from the public.[325] Corporations may be exempted from the disclosure requirements upon approval from the Registrar of Companies if such disclosure would be over burdensome or is a subsequent issue to insiders.[326]

The prospectus must be signed by all the directors.[327] Directors may face criminal[328] or civil[329] penalties and liabilities for willfully or negligently signing a prospectus that contains false or misleading information. However, in order to sustain and recover on a misrepresentation or fraud cause of action, a plaintiff must prove reliance and actual damages as a result of the misrepresentation.[330] Strict liability may be imposed under the English Misrepresentation Act.[331] Shareholders could also potentially sue for breach of contract, breach of statutory duty,[332] and recission of the share issue altogether depending on the court's chosen remedy.[333]

Stock Listings

There are three stock exchanges on which public companies shares may be listed and traded. They are the Singapore Stock Exchange (SES) or the "big board", the Stock Exchange of Singapore Dealing and Automated Quotation System (SESDAQ),[334] for smaller and emerging companies, and the Central Limit Order Book International (CLOB International) for Malaysian and Hong Kong companies. The exchanges are established under the legislative authority of the Securities Industry Act with the approval of the appropriate Minister.[335]

G.21

The SES is operated by the Stock Exchange of Singapore Limited under its policies and rules. The Securities Industry Act requires that anyone dealing in securities be licensed, unless specifically exempted by the statute.[336] There are two types of licenses. There is the dealer's license which is issued to securities trading companies[337] and the representative's license issued to those who work for securities trading firms.[338] Stockbroker companies must own a share of the Stock Exchange Limited in order to qualify for a seat on the Exchange in order to conduct floor trading. These organizational functions and general oversight are conducted by the Committee of the Exchange (Exchange) which is authorized pursuant to the rules of the Exchange.

In order to be listed for trading, a company must meet the criteria of the Exchange which are set out on its Listing Manual.[339] The minimum requirements are: (1) S$4,000,000 (S$15 million in practice)[340] original shareholder capitalization; (2) at least 25 per cent or S$1.5 million, the greater of the two, of the original shareholder capital must be held by no fewer that 500 shareholders, and (3) a three-year pretax profit record of S$1 million each year or a total of S$7.5 million over the same period.[341] Additional criteria for listing include a good prospective outlook, and a stable management team.[342] The company must also include information about corporate control, the directors and managers, and corporate assets in its organic documents and a prospectus to the satisfaction of the Exchange.[343] Once approved for listing and payment of the appropriate fee,[344] the company may commence trading on the Exchange subject to ongoing disclosure and reporting requirements.[345] Debentures may also be listed subject to similar requirements.[346]

There are specific settlement rules implemented by the Exchange regarding securities trade contracts, delivery and settlement. The stockbroker is a fiduciary liable to the client to inform, consult, and advise accordingly and may be sued in tort for breach of the duty.[347] Conversely, the stockbroker house has a lien over securities it purchases for clients until settlement and delivery.[348]

The SESDAQ's governing entity is the Central Depository Pte Ltd (CDP) which is a subsidiary of the Stock Exchange of Singapore, Ltd.[349] The rules for listing on the SESDAQ are more relaxed but as a minimum require a three-year profitable financial record and at least 500,000 shares or 15 per cent of paid-up capital.[350] Trading on the SESDAQ is computer automated but must be conducted through Participants who are approved SESDAQ members.[351]

Insider Trading

G.22   Insider trading is defined as trading by or on the advice of a director, officer, employee, substantial shareholder or professional advisor and their immediate families.[352] A person becomes potentially liable for a criminal offense or civil liability if he or she uses "special confidential information."[353] Other types of securities trading behavior prohibited by Singapore law include use of information for personal gain to company detriment,[354] sham securities transactions,[355] market rigging activities,[356] or schemes to defraud others.[357] Damages are available to compensate persons impacted by such violations upon agreement of the Attorney General to prosecute.[358]

Takeovers

G.23   Takeovers in Singapore are governed by the Companies Act and the Singapore Code on Takeovers and Mergers (Code).[359] The Code is enforced by the Securities Industry Council.[360] Compliance with the Code is required if the suitor is attempting to control 25 per cent or more[361] of the target corporation either directly or indirectly.[362] Once it is determined by the suitor that it will be able to make a good faith offer the details must be published in a Singapore newspaper.[363] The offeror must then give notice to the target company not before 28 days or after 14 days prior to the proposed takeover date.[364] The notice must be filed with the Registry of Companies.[365] The target company must formally reply within 14 days of receipt of the notice.[366] Thereafter, the offer must be made within three days and remain open for 21 days.[367] The offer may be modified if the suitor gives notice to the target and the public and files documents indicating the changes with the regulatory entities.[368] If there are dissenting shareholders but the suitor has been able to acquire at least 90 per cent of the target corporation, the Companies Act may be invoked to buy those shareholders out.[369] Once completed the securities will be delisted.[370] It should be noted that partial takeovers (*i.e.* less than 100 per cent) are discouraged.[371]

Arbitration and Other ADR Techniques

Arbitration

Domestic arbitration in Singapore is covered by the Arbitration Act.[372] Singapore has recently enacted the International Arbitration Act (hereinafter   **G.24** "IAA") to govern international commercial arbitration and enforcement.[373] The IAA adopts the UNCITRAL Model Law on International Commercial Arbitration (hereinafter "Model Law") and the Convention on the Recognition and Enforcement of Foreign Arbitral Awards Concluded at New York (hereinafter "New York Convention") into the law of Singapore, with few modifications. The following will briefly summarizes the basic provisions of each as adopted by the IAA.

Part II of the IAA sets out the specific application of the Model Law in Singapore. To begin, the Model Law is adopted in its entirety, except for Chapter VIII.[374] The IAA then sets forth the basic jurisdiction of the document indicating that it will only apply if the arbitration is international.[375] International is explained to mean:

1. one party has its place of business outside Singapore;
2. either the place of arbitration or a "substantial part of the obligations" at issue are outside Singapore, or
3. the parties have expressly agreed that the "subject-matter of the arbitration agreement relates to more than one country."[376] The IAA then permits the Singapore courts to stay domestic legal proceedings if satisfied that the arbitration agreement is not voidable (*i.e.* against public policy[377]).[378]

The IAA then continues by describing the domestic Singapore players in international arbitration. First, the High Court is designated as the competent court with respect to Article 6 functions.[379] Second, the Chairman of the Singapore International Arbitration Centre, or the appointee of the Chief Justice of the Supreme Court of Singapore shall be the competent authority under article 11.[380] Third, the parties may choose the number of arbitrators but if they fail to specify there will be one arbitrator appointed.[381]

The IAA then provides the parties to the dispute with a four-month conciliation procedure permiting the arbitrator to serve as conciliator.[382] If the conciliation attempt fails and the arbitration goes forward, the IAA then confers on the arbitrators the power to make and enforce orders in aid of the proceedings such as, discovery, collection of evidence, interim injunctions, and even goes as far as permitting the tribunal to turn itself into an "inquisitorial process" if it is necessary.[383] Thereafter, the IAA recognizes the arbitral award as having the same effect as a Singapore judgment and provides for the power to enforce and tax the judgment.[384] Finally, with respect to the award, the IAA provides that an award may be set aside by the High Court of Singapore if obtained by "fraud or corruption" or "a breach of the rules of natural justice" prejudicing one of the parties.[385]

The IAA also relieves arbitrators of any liability as a result of negligence or "mistake in law, fact or procedure."[386] One final note in this area must be made with respect to foreign individuals serving as arbitrators or representing clients in arbitrations that take place in Singapore. Several years ago in the High Court case of *Builders Federal (Hong Kong) Ltd. and Joseph Gartner & Co. v. Turner (East Asia) Pte. Ltd.*, a New York law firm was prohibited from representing its client in a Singapore arbitration as an unauthorized practice of law under the Legal Profession Act.[387] Therefore, counsel are advised to consult with Singapore counsel as early as possible if Singapore is a potential situs for arbitration.

Enforcement of Foreign Judgments and Awards

G.25   The third part of the IAA enacts the New York Convention. This area of private international law is not new in Singapore. While the IAA repeals the Arbitration (Foreign Awards) Act[388] its continues the principles of that Act through the New York Convention adoption in the present Act retroactively to 1986.[389]

The New York Convention, as implemented in the IAA, provides that "mere" presentation of a duly authenticated foreign award in a Singapore court will be accorded *prima facie* evidentiary standing with respect to the validity and enforceability of the award in Singapore.[390] However, the foreign award may be challenged on several grounds. The enforcement of the award may be challenged on the basis that the agreement itself fails for reasons of incapacity or legal invalidity.[391] Alternatively, the arbitration itself may be contested at the enforcement stage for not following correct procedures or violation of the laws underwhich the tribunal was created.[392] Finally, the enforcement action may be contested by asserting the non-binding effect of the award, the inability to submit the issues decided to a similar Singapore court or on the basis that enforcement would violate Singapore public policy.[393]

Banking and Lending Law

G.26   The Singapore banking sector has been open to foreign entry since the 1960s in order to promote Singapore as one of the major financial centers of Asian currency.[394] Singapore's high quality infrastructure, geographic location, and political stability coupled with tax incentives and banking secrecy laws have placed it among the world's most important financial centers.[395]

Banking Law

The statutory legislation covering banking law in Singapore is titled the Banking Act.[396] The Singapore banking sector is licensed by the Monetary Authority of Singapore (MAS) under the auspices of the Ministry of Finance and functions as the central bank. The currency issuing authority lies with the separate Board of Commissioners of Currency. More specifically, the MAS regulates banks, finance companies, insurance companies, securities dealers, and exchange activities.[397] The Banking Act was amended in 1993 to liberalize some of the rules and regulations regarding capital requirements, credit exposure, secrecy, stored value cards, and the powers of the MAS.[398]

G.27

Singapore permits three types of commercial banks. First, the Full License which provide the deposit and lending facilities primarily to Singapore residents.[399] Second and third, are the Restricted Banks and Offshore Banks which are the branch offices of foreign banks operating in Singapore.[400] Foreign bank branch offices are generally restricted to one office in Singapore and are not permitted to handle consumer type domestic activities except through their special Asian Currency Units (ACU).[401] In addition, the Singapore government has a moratorium on new full licenses and permits foreign banks to own no more than 40 per cent of the equity in local banks.[402] The ACU may handle common domestic banking activities but is prohibited from involvement in the Singapore dollar market.[403]

Other regulated financial institutions include merchant banks, finance companies, and the government owned and operated Post Office Savings Bank (POSB). The POSB channels domestic savings into primarily government projects and corporations.[404] In addition, the currency and precious metals futures market in Singapore is operated by the Singapore International Monetary Exchange (SIMEX).[405]

Lending Law

Singapore has a great deal of local capital which its banking institutions leverage through various financial vehicles. Domestically, banks grant overdraft protection, personal and real property loans, business capital and guarantees.[406] Financial institutions are particularly well prepared to service the financial needs of the international business community.

G.28

Singapore banks and other financial institutions are fully capable of completing complex financial transactions through letters of credit, bills discounting, trust and acceptance financing, international trade guarantees, repurchases and currency swaps.[407] Interest and exchange rates are free floating in Singapore.[408] However, once again Singapore banks are discouraged from providing Singapore dollar facilities for non-Singaporeans.[409]

Negotiable Instruments Law

G.29   The Bills of Exchange Act[410] together with the common law form the basis for law in Singapore relating to transferable and non-transferable financial instruments (*i.e.* bills of exchange, checks, promissory notes, bearer debentures, Treasury bills, warrants, etc.). The Bills of Exchange Act covers creation, acceptance, and the rights and liabilities of parties dealing in such instruments. There are no prescribed forms for bills of exchange or promissory notes however, certain customary styles have developed.[411]

Bearer instruments are payable to the person tendering it for payment while instruments that specify the payee are payable to order documents.[412] When the instrument is presented for payment, the drawee, the payee, and third parties may contest the payment recipient. On the other hand, the Bills of Exchange Act provides protection for holders in due course who receive a financial instrument in good faith and without notice of its defects.[413] The Notice of Dishonour is available for issuers of instruments that wish to stop payment.[414] In addition, the Bills of Exchange Act provides for the rights and liabilities of the parties after the instrument has been created through to final discharge or cancellation.[415]

Consumer Protection Law

G.30   The legal regime covering consumer goods in Singapore can be found primarily in the Sale of Food Act[416] and the Sale of Drugs Act.[417] Also, the Consumer Protection (Trade Descriptions and Safety Requirements) Act must be consulted as many of its provisions overlap with the preceding Acts.[418] Of particular interest here are the provisions appointing the Director of Consumer Protection and the powers conferred to enforced information on labeling which coordinates with the previous Acts.[419] These provisions establish minimum standards for the quality and labeling of governed goods and sanctions for violations. Import licenses may be required for products such as live animals, meats, certain plants, and sweeteners.[420]

Additionally, the Price Control Act[421] appoints a Price Controller who is given the responsibility of establishing maximum prices and charges on certain domestic consumer items. Local counsel should be consulted if a party seeks to sell consumer products in Singapore. This section is merely intended to identify areas for consideration by those considering doing business in Singapore.

Health, Safety and Environmental Law

Health Law and Safety Law

G.31   The government of Singapore has provided the main impetus for establishing health and safety standards in the workplace.[422] The Ministry of Labor is charged with carrying out the policies enunciated primarily in comprehensive the Factories Act.[423] The Factories Act mainly covers workers and employers of companies with more than 10 employees however, the Act itself is quite detailed and should be reviewed for application to specific situations.[424] It has been estimated that the Factories Act covers approximately 40 per cent of the Singapore workforce.[425]

The Factories Act creates standards for cleanliness, space, safety and other work conditions to protect against accidents and injuries.[426] If accidents occur, they must be reported to the Chief Inspector of Factories.[427] Other provisions require use of protective gear, removal of hazardous substances, and reduction of noise and other irritants as well as medical supervision of employees in these types of environments.[428] Workers and employers are also required to form safety committees and employ competent safety personnel in factories that have more than 50 employees.[429] Penalties for offenses may include fines of up to S$25,000 and/or imprisonment for up to one year.[430]

Various other Acts and Regulations cover specific industries and materials. The Singapore Port Regulations cover dock work and vehicle activities, including handling of hazardous materials.[431] The Building Control Regulations and Petroleum Acts, enforced by the Fire Safety Bureau, regulate the work environment of dangerous activities and oil storage and transportation.[432] The Radiation Protection Regulations are enforced by the Ministry of Health to protect workers handling radioactive materials.[433] The Public Utilities Regulations and the Electrical Workers and Contractors Licensing Act are designed to cover electrical installations.[434] Finally, the Hydrogen Cyanide (Fumigation) Act 1974 protects those workers employed in the fumigation industry.[435]

Environmental Law

Though highly industrialized, Singapore has maintained a high standard of environmental quality by creating and enforcing strict regulations to govern use and disposal of industrial pollutants.[436] In this regard, Singapore can be thought of as promoting a policy of "sustainable development".[437] The two main laws are the Clean Air Act[438] and the Water Pollution Control and Drainage Act.[439] Singapore has also been on the forefront of efforts to encourage regional partners to improve the environment.

G.32

The Clean Air Act applies to facilities that emit air pollutants.[440] Violators are subject to sanctions, under government discretion, that range from reduction and modification of emissions to total dismantling.[441] In addition, Singapore is a signatory to the Montreal Protocol on Substances That Deplete the Ozone Layer which controls chloroflourocarbon emissions.[442] Thus far, Singapore has exceed the reduction requirements but may find it difficult to completely eliminate such emissions by the 1999 closing date.[443]

The Water Pollution Control and Drainage Act which governs emissions into inland waters is supplemented by the Prevention of the Pollution of the

Sea Act 1973[444] which covers Singapore's coastal waters. The Minister of the Environment is given the responsibility for enforcement of these Acts.[445] The Acts provide for mandatory fines when violations are discovered but significantly exempt certain government activities such as the disposal of sewage.[446] There is also substantial discretion with respect to dumping as the government sees fit.[447]

Employment and Labor Law

G.33   During the late 1950s and early 1960s, Singapore suffered greatly from the withdrawal of the British military and basic questions which are described above regarding its political future. As a result, there was a great deal of civil unrest and labor strikes. The strikes essentially shut the country's production down. In order to quell this unrest and with recognition of the poor conditions underwhich the Singapore labor force had worked in the past, the government of Singapore imposed strike breaking legislation with counterbalancing requirements for employer contributions to a social welfare fund for workers and better working conditions. Specifically, Singapore workers were given maximum work hours and vacation leave rights. Currently, the National Wages Council, composed of representatives from government, trade unions, and management organizations, establishes flexible wage guidelines.[448]

As of 1994, the labor force of Singapore numbered 1,649 million.[449] This can be broken down by sector as follows: service industries 33.5 per cent, manufacturing 25.6 per cent, commerce 22.9 per cent, construction 6.6 per cent, and other 11.4 per cent.[450] The government of Singapore discourages the hiring of unskilled foreign labor particularly in the construction industry by imposition of a levy on the employer. Countries singled out as "non-traditional labor" include the Philippines, Sri Lanka, Indonesia, and Thailand.[451]

Employers must obtain employment passes for foreign workers from the Immigration Department.[452] Employment passes may be obtained for periods of between one to three years and usually take two to four weeks to issue.[453] Foreign workers making under S$1,500 will be issued a Work Permit from the Ministry of Labor.[454]

There is not space available to delve into all the laws in Singapore effecting employment, however, the following are the principle local legislation:

- The Employment Act;
- The Industrial Relations Act;
- The Central Provident Fund Act;
- The National Servicemen (Employment) Act.[455]

- The Factories Act;
- The Workmen's Compensation Act;
- Trade Unions Act;

Under the Singapore Employment Act of 1985 all employees are covered by the Employment Act except executives, managers, seamen, security guards, and domestic servants.[456] The Employment Act provides for a variable probationary period, termination notice requirements, restricted weekly work hours, paid leave, and other benefits.[457] Employers are required to pay for worker's compensation insurance.[458] The Central Provident Fund Act requires both employers and employees to contribute to the Fund based on a statutory schedule.[459] In addition, the Skills Development Levy Act requires employers to pay 1 per cent of monthly pay for workers making less than S$750.[460] No payroll taxes are required however, the employer must keep the Singapore tax authorities informed of hiring, annual pay, and termination of employees pursuant to the Singapore Income Tax Act.[461]

Foreign Investment Law

Singapore has aggressively pursued foreign investment form its first days of independence in 1965.[462] Free trade, liberal foreign ownership rules, tax incentives, and availability public and private domestic capital are significant factors that have contributed to the success of Singapore in attracting foreign investment. The government efforts have been coordinated by the well-known Economic Development Board.[463] The Economic Expansion Incentives (Relief from Income Tax) Act of 1967 is the guiding legislation with respect to the foreign investment area.[464]   **G.34**

Singapore has given priority to investment in high technology and related support sectors. The government is attempting to encourage current investors to automate, update, and evolve Singapore operations through incentives.[465] The incentives can be broken down into the two main categories of financial and tax savings.

Financial Incentives

The government of Singapore offers its financial incentives through various agencies. The most commonly encountered agencies are: the Economic Development Board (EDB), the Singapore Trade Development Board (TDB),[466] the National Productivity Board (NPB), The Science Council of Singapore (SCS), and the Monetary Authority of Singapore (MAS).[467] As an overview, some of the programs offered under the EDB are described below.   **G.35**

As a "rule of thumb" each requires at least 30 per cent equity participation in order to be eligible for the described grants and loans. The Local Enterprise Finance Scheme (LEFS), the Small Industries Technical Assistance Scheme (SITAS), and the Business Development Scheme (BDS) are designed to provide start-up capital, external technical expertise, and foreign market research resources, respectively, for Singapore businesses.[468] Other forms of assistance are not limited to the size of a Singapore company. The Product Development Assistance Scheme (PDAS), the Automation Leasing Scheme (ALS), and the Initiatives in New Technology Scheme (INTECH) are available to encourage new or improved product lines with new technologies and a higher skilled workforce to match.[469]

The remaining government programs provide financing, training, and research assistance. They are: the Equity Participation Scheme, the Venture Capital Programme, the Capital Assistance Scheme (CAS), the Market Development Assistance Scheme (MDAS),[470] the Training Grant Scheme,[471] the Research and Development Assistance Scheme (RDAS),[472] and the Export Bills Rediscounting Scheme.[473] Each program has different goals, criteria, and targets for development. However, the Singapore government attempts to make them as complementary and accessible to foreign investors as local citizens in the overriding effort to encourage foreign investment.

Tax Incentives

G.36   Singapore also offers numerous tax incentives in the form of concessions and exemptions for foreign investors. These incentives are targeted to new and continuing business location activities in the trade and financial service sectors. The main programs are described below.

Companies involved in technology service and manufacturing activities can obtain an income tax exemption on profits for a period of between five and ten years under the Pioneer Enterprise status.[474] Specific service industries covered include, engineering, computers, entertainment, publishing, education, medical, agriculture, business, international trade related activities, capital fund activity, and mass transit, to name the most common.[475] Companies making additional capital investments after the expiration of their pioneer status may apply for Post-Pioneer Status to receive reduced taxation of profits at 10 per cent for another five years or longer.[476]

Alternatively, Singapore offers tax exemption on up to 50 per cent of capital expenditures, distributable as a tax exempt dividend, for projects or services in the high technology sector.[477] In an effort to encourage the location of companies' headquarters in Singapore, the concessionary rate of 10 per cent is applicable to income received from overseas subsidiaries for a period of up to 10 years.[478] In order to qualify, a company must maintain at least two of its administration, raw materials sourcing, research and development, technical support, overall management structure, and financial affairs in Singapore.[479] In addition, the company must spend S\$2,000,000 annually, have at least five senior management people in Singapore and maintain three operating companies.[480] Once again, tax exempt income may be distributed tax-free to shareholders.[481] On-going tax deductions and depreciation allowances are available for research and development activities and associated costs.[482]

Companies engaged in services offered outside Singapore may also obtain tax preferences. The eligible services are construction, engineering, consultancy, procurement, telecommunications, professional, and education.[483] Approved companies receive 90 per cent of their qualified income tax exempt and available for tax-free distribution for a period of five years or longer.[484]

Other forms of tax incentives in Singapore focus on specific industries. For instance, a venture capital investment that sustains losses after two years of involvement in Singapore may be permitted to deduct losses from the sale of shares or investment liquidation.[485] Income from offshore banking, insurance, and futures activities may be eligible for a 10 per cent income tax rate.[486] Offshore syndication activities may be tax exempt if more than 50 per cent of the members are Asian and most of the work is done in Singapore.[487] Financial Funds managed from Singapore may be taxed at the lower 10 per cent rate on income from management.[488] Other specifically recognized industries include shipping on Singapore registered vessels (tax exempt), oil trading activities (10 per cent), commodities trading (10 per cent), and currency hedging operations of multinational corporations (10 per cent).[489]

Tax Law

The laws of taxation affecting Singapore income can be found in the Income   G.37
Tax Act.[490] English caselaw is applicable, where appropriate, to provide guidance in interpreting the Income Tax Act.[491] Certain business activities are also exempt from income tax pursuant to the Economic Expansion Incentive (Relief from Income Tax) Act.[492] As the laws governing income taxation are constantly amended. This section is as up-to-date a possible however, the practitioner is advised to contact professionals qualified to render tax advice on specific issues.

Income tax in Singapore is assessed on an annual basis. Income tax is impose on income from activities derived from the following sources:

1. gains or profits from any trade, business, profession or vocation;
2. gains or profits from employment;
3. dividends, interest or discounts;
4. pensions, charges or annuities;
5. rents, royalties, premiums and any profits arising from property, and
6. any gains or profits of an income nature not covered by the above.[493]

Singapore does not tax capital gains unless they are recategorized under one of the preceding categories.[494]

In determining whether income is derived from "trade", the courts will consider the facts of the particular transaction (*i.e.* subject matter, ownership, number of transactions, alteration, disposition, and motive).[495] The term "business" is designed to cover a broader set of dealings than trade.[496] The words "profession or vocation" indicate personal services of an intellectual nature.[497] Income from "employment" is taxable if it takes the form of wages, salary, leave pay, fees, commissions, bonuses, gratuities, or other fringe benefits.[498] However, reimbursements are not taxed.[499] "Dividends" are defined as sums paid to shareholders based on their holdings but are only taxable if received in Singapore.[500] "Interest" is taxable if received in or derived from Singapore.[501] "Discounts" are a term of art used to describe discounting of bills of exchange before they reach maturity.[502] "Pensions" derived from Singapore are taxable unless paid to a resident of Singapore.[503] A "charge" is income received pursuant to a court order.[504] An "annuity" is an annual contractual payment.[505] Finally, "income from property" is profits arising from use, exploitation, or other fees paid on real or personal property derived from Singapore.[506]

The corporate tax rate in Singapore is 27 per cent with additional reductions expected to 25 per cent in the future.[507] A corporation is considered resident if its "control and management" takes place in Singapore.[508] A non-resident company is treated the same as a resident company unless it enjoys the protection of a double taxation treaty or its status is that of a representative office.[509] Trustees of trusts are generally taxed at the 27 per cent rate.[510] However, a partnership is not generally subject to taxation on income.[511] Finally, Singapore introduced a Goods and Services Tax (GST) of 3 per cent in 1994.[512]

Singapore has double taxation treaties with the following countries: Australia, Bangladesh, Belgium, Canada, The People's Republic of China, Denmark, Finland, France, Germany, India, Israel, Italy, Japan, Korea, Malaysia, Netherlands, New Zealand, Norway, Philippines, Sri Lanka, Sweden, Switzerland, the Republic of China (Taiwan), Thailand, and the United Kingdom.[513] Taxable income received from a treaty country provides tax credits to the entity receiving such income in Singapore.[514] Other forms of double taxation relief are available for Commonwealth countries, Indonesia, the United States, Middle Eastern countries and non-treaty countries.[515] Singapore permits exemptions from income taxation for certain individuals, institutions, non-residents, and certain activities which are beyond the scope of this work.[516]

Generally, deductions are allowed for expenses incurred in the production of income.[517] Such expenses include but are not limited to interest, rent, repairs, bad debts, pension contributions, and other areas the government wishes to provide incentives.[518] Capital expenditure and "wear and tear" allowances or depreciation against income may be permitted for industrial buildings,[519] plantations,[520] and equipment.[521] Finally, the government provides incentives, including "double deductions" particularly in new industries and those promoting high technology manufacturing and services, as described in the Foreign Investment section of this work.[522]

Taxable or "chargeable" income[523] is calculated by determining the recipient's gross or "statutory" income,[524] taking into account exemptions and allowances, and subtracting deductions and "personal reliefs" (i.e. public policy deductions for contributions such as pension funding). Thereafter, tax is levied at the applicable rate which is between 3.5 and 33 per cent for individuals (depending on residence status) and a flat 27 per cent for regular taxable corporate income.[525] Taxes are required to be withheld and paid to the Comptroller of Income Tax on payments to nonresidents.[526]

Singapore imposes three other types of taxes. Income from rental property is taxed on the value of the property at the rate of 16 per cent or 4 per cent, if owner occupied.[527] Stamp duties are imposed on certain documents (*e.g.* affidavits, mortgages, insurance policies) at flat rates or percentages of value depending on the particular documents.[528] And finally, estate tax is levied upon the death of the owner of property situated in Singapore at 5 per cent for the first S$10 million and 10 per cent thereafter.[529]

The Comptroller may disregard transactions or entities which in his or her opinion are unnatural or a sham.[530] If the assessed entity disputes the tax imposed by the Comptroller, it has 30 days to object.[531] If the parties cannot reach agreement, the dispute can be appealed to the Board of Review.[532] Thereafter, questions of law and facts may be appealed to the Singapore courts.[533]

Accounting Rules

As previously discussed, Singapore requires complete record keeping and independent auditing.[534] Fortunately, the local accounting profession is well trained and populated. The profession is formally governed by the Accountants Act which established the Institute of Certified Public Accountants of Singapore.[535] The Institute establishes standards and procedures which are mandated by both the Accountants Act and the Companies Act.[536]   **G.38**

Accounting principles are established by the Institute and published in the Statements of Accounting Standards.[537] The Standards cover financial and income statements.[538] The Standards are based on the International Accounting Standards and therefore tend to provide optional methods of reporting.[539] Finally, disclosure requirements for the foreign investor are limited to the name of the holding company, disclosure of directors share holdings, significant intercompany transactions, and directors' compensation from subsidiaries.[540]

Intellectual Property Law

Singapore is a signatory to the General Agreement on Tariffs and Trade as revised by the Uruguay Round Agreement on Trade-Related Aspects of Intellectual Property (hereinafter TRIPs) which includes trademarks, patents, and copyrights.[541] As such, Singapore is under a binding obligation to amend and modify its domestic intellectual property laws and regulations to comply with the requirements of TRIPs by the end of 1995. These provisions are enforceable through the World Trade Organization's dispute settlement mechanism. Therefore, changes in the domestic intellectual property laws of   **G.39**

Singapore may be forthcoming that were not ascertainable at the time of writing.

Trade Marks

G.40 The Trade Marks Act (Cap.206),[542] modeled after the English Trade Marks Act 1938, and the Trade Marks Rules 1968 (S46/1968) are the statutory regimes that cover trade marks in Singapore. The Trade Marks Act provides the legal rules and the Trade Marks Rules provide the procedure applicable to trade marks.[543] The common law, primarily English cases, supplies the persuasive precedent governing trade mark litigation.[544]

In order to be registerable, a proposed trade mark must be both distinctive[545] and in use or be intended for use.[546] Trade marks that are likely to confuse consumers will not be registered.[547] Trade marks which have been approved for registration must be advertised as such in the *Government Gazette* and are thereafter subject to challenge.[548] A registered trade mark is initially valid for seven years renewable for 14 year periods.[549] A trade mark may be challenged for non-use after a period of five years.[550]

The use of trade marks may be licensed.[551] Unauthorized use of a registered trade mark is subject to legal action for infringement[552] and "passing-off".[553] Likewise, trade mark counterfeiting is an actionable offense under the Trade Marks Act.[554] Finally, it should noted that amendments were passed in 1991 to strengthen and broaden the coverage of the Trade Marks Act to include service industries.[555]

Patents

G.41 Singapore recently passed its first patent law which came into effect in February, 1995.[556] Previously, Singapore relied upon registration in England through the United Kingdom Patents Act.[557] The new Patent Act provides for registration in Singapore and a 20 year exclusivity period.[558] Compulsory licensing and government use are areas of concern and are believed to be inconsistent with the TRIPs Agreement which requires compliance by January 1, 1996.[559] Singapore was not a signatory to the Paris Convention for the Protection of Industrial Property.[560]

Copyrights and Designs

G.42 Singapore's current statutory copyright regime was introduced in the Copyright Act 1987 and 1994 amendments and Regulations.[561] The Copyright Act affords protection to: (i) literary works; (ii) musical works; (iii) artistic works; (iv) dramatic works; (v) sound recordings; (vi) cinematographic works; (vii) broadcasts; (viii) cable programs; and (ix) publishers' rights.[562] These specific areas of coverage under the Copyright Act are more broadly divided into the categories of author's works and entrepreneurial rights.[563]

Copyright protection for authors' works extends for the life of the author plus 50 years.[564] Protection for entrepreneurial works exists for 50 years after the first date of publication, except for published works which are only protected for 25 years.[565] Copyrighted material is protected under the Act by conferring on the owner the cause of action for infringement[566] as limited by statutory defenses.[567] Available remedies include injunction,[568] including *Anton Piller* Orders,[569] and damages.[570] With respect to "moral rights", as identified in 6*bis* of the Berne Convention, Singapore has only indirect protection.[571]

Singapore has made special concessions to the U.S., the U.K., and Northern Ireland under the Copyright Act 1987 through regulation promulgated by the Minister in order to apply the Copyright Act to works originating in those countries.[572] Although Singapore is now a member of the World Intellectual Property Organization, it has not become a signatory to the Universal Copyright Convention or the Berne Convention for the Protection of Literary and Artistic Works. Regardless, it has even greater binding and enforceable obligations under the TRIPs agreement which must be implement by January 1, 1996. However, the United States remains skeptical with respect to Singapore's 1994 amendments to the Copyright Act which, in the U.S. view, significantly weaken Singapore's obligations to protect textile designs.[573]

As an aside, computer software programs have had coverage problems from a characterization standpoint. However, under the TRIPs agreement, all types of computer programs, source documents, source codes and object codes, must be protected by January 1, 1996.[574] Also, semiconductor works are protected under the United Kingdom Designs (Protection) Act.[575]

Trade Secrets

Trade secrets and "know-how" are not afforded statutory protection in Singapore. However, the common law applies the law of confidence and Singapore is obligated under the TRIPs Agreement to provide protection to undisclosed secret information, misappropriation of information, and unfair commercial use of information provided to member governments.[576] **G.43**

III. General Considerations in Negotiating Business Transactions in Singapore

Cultural Factors and Business Negotiations in Singapore

While Singapore has a diverse population the majority culture is Chinese. In **G.44** this respect, the Malaya and other minorities sometimes feel dominated by the majority. Therefore, when approaching a Singaporean to investigate opportunities or negotiate transactions, it is important to understand his or her specific background. However, as has been noted earlier, the Singapore culture has come a long way in a relatively short period of time with stability. The people of Singapore have had to make some sacrifices with respect to individual freedoms and government control in return for substantial economic growth. This is a trade-off that has been accepted with the view toward a full blossoming of society in the future.

There have been pressures on the government in the past to change the way it does business but those have been summarily rejected. The bottom line remains, the system, though authoritarian, serves the people's needs and produces tangible results. Therefore, a foreign business person approaching the Singapore business culture must understand the need for structure and efficiency in negotiations and on-going relations.

Also, the foreigner should not be surprised if the government appears to be an important player in Singapore business life. The Singapore government has played an active and apparently successful role in the lives of each Singaporean through the Central Provident Fund and used that capital to leverage the economic well-being of the entire city-state. And, for the most part, it seems to have worked very well. Senior Minister, Lee Kuan Yew, has been quoted as saying, "I have no idea whether [a western-type of political culture] will come, because the culture is the other way. It may never come."[577]

Role and Competence of Local Counsel

G.45   Naturally, the best way to have the local culture on your side when attempting to establish a presence in Singapore, or anywhere else for that matter, is to obtain the advice and counsel of someone who is a part of the culture. That is part of the valuable role local counsel plays. There are also more practical reasons. Chief among them is the concern foreign counsel should have about the appearance of practicing in Singapore without a license. That is, foreign lawyers present in Singapore may only advise clients on foreign or international legal matters.[578] Any practice that borders on advice regarding Singapore law must be referred to local counsel. In addition, while foreign lawyers have opened offices in Singapore, they must restrict their practice accordingly and are not permitted to form partnerships with Singaporean lawyers to practice Singapore law.[579]

Singapore has a unified Bar. That is, there is no distinction between barristers and solicitors, as in England. However, the training is very similar for obtaining "qualification".[580] The basic law governing the profession is the Legal Profession Act.[581] The Law Society also imposes standards of practice and discipline for violations for the protection of the public.[582] The concept of legal malpractice exists by establishing a "general community" standard of care[583] for the profession. On the other hand, the legal privilege enjoyed by the profession includes protection of attorney-client communications related to the giving of legal advice.[584] These latter factors should provide confidence to the non-Singaporean client.

The Singapore government has recently moved to limit the number of students entering the legal profession fearing that too many bright minds are being drained from other less populated professions.[585] As such, the government has increased the standards and reduced the number of overseas graduates permitted to enter the legal market in the years to come.[586]

Government Resources and Business Assistance Programs

Many of the government resources have been identified in the preceding **G.46** sections of this work, particularly in the section on foreign investment.[587] However, it should be noted that overseas offices of the Singapore government and particular agencies such as the Trade Development Board are available for assistance throughout the world. In addition, the Economic Development Board operates the Venture Capital Club which is designed to bring Singapore businesspeople together with potential foreign partners.[588]

Practical Considerations in Negotiating Specific Business Transactions in Singapore

Sale of Goods Transactions

As stated previously, Singapore is an open and inviting trading environment, **G.47** particularly in the sale, processing, and transport of goods. It should be reiterated at this point that Singapore has recently adopted the United Nation Convention on Contracts for the International Sale of Goods.[589] As such, parties negotiating a contract for the sale or transaction of goods are reminded that they must expressly opt out of the Convention in order to avoid its application.

Aside from the strictly legal requirements discussed above, there are certain practical considerations that must be taken into account when doing business in Singapore. Chief among the considerations are import restrictions, duties, documentation and storage. The following list of items are the most currently available. Therefore, it is necessary to check a particular product's treatment at the time of negotiations and shipment.

First, import licenses are required for rice, sewing machines, firearms, pharmaceuticals, transmitters, meats, coffee, and various publications.[590] Second, duties are imposed on liquor, tobacco, petroleum, automobiles, cosmetics, and furniture, unless exempted by international agreement.[591] Third, documentation, customs declarations, and invoices on international goods may be processed electronically through the Trade Development Board's TradeNet service.[592] Fourth, Singapore maintains five ocean and one air based free-trade zones.[593] These zones are protected by high levels of security and have large capacities.[594] Re-export is permitted without the requirement of added local content however, it is suggested that a local customs agent be employed to assist with clearance procedures.[595]

Joint Ventures

G.48 Singapore does not have a specific legal regime for joint ventures because of its open economic and legal environment, except for shipping and retail companies.[596] Rather the general laws must be reviewed for applicability.[597] Also, if the parties agree, they may make a non-Singapore law govern their agreement.[598]

Joint ventures in Singapore may take the form of corporations or partnerships.[599] Foreign corporate joint venture participants tend to prefer the corporate entity unless the purpose of the joint venture is temporary.[600] Foreign members of an unincorporated joint venture are taxed at the corporate rate of 27 per cent of its share of income while a member of an incorporated joint venture is tax on dividends received.[601] In addition, transfer pricing issues should be considered when planning a joint venture.[602]

Technology License Arrangements

G.49 Due to the absence of restrictions on foreign investing in Singapore, no particular government approval is required for technology licensing.[603] However, an investor should keep in mind the government incentives for conducting research and development in Singapore.[604] In addition, an investor should obtain advice on royalty payments which may be subject to withholding taxes.[605]

Production and Manufacturing Arrangements

G.50 Once again, Singapore does not require any restrictions in production or manufacturing beyond applicable domestic law.[606] That is parties are free to negotiate the express terms of an agreement whether labor, distribution, or technology transfer.

Distribution Agreements

G.51 Particular consideration should be given to the area of agency and distribution contracts for reasons of tax attribution. That is, whether a Singapore agent is dependent or independent may have an impact on the taxation of the foreign entity or investor.[607] Singapore does not impose special penalties by law for early termination of distribution or agency agreements. The parties agreement will control unless it is found to be oppressive for reasons of public policy under general contract and employment laws.

Employment Agreements

Singapore does not impose any special requirements on employment con-   G.52
tracts, other than what is required by local law, as outline above.

Loan Agreements

The potential investor should be aware of the lucrative Singapore govern-   G.53
ment loan programs available for selected businesses. However, because the private lending environment is so international, the lending standards and practices do not differ greatly from those of the West. The reader should refer to the Foreign Investment section above for specific information regarding preferred investment industries and loans available from government agencies. In order to qualify, a certain amount of domestic ownership or employment may be required in the proposed enterprise.

Notes

[*] The author has made every attempt to locate the most recent citations for Singapore law. However, due to the evolving nature of the law in Singapore and the lack of access to the most recent revised editions, there may be instances where the citation is slightly outdated. The reader should verify the citation with the legislation list included and check sources independently.

[1] KPMG Peat Marwick, *Investment in Singapore* (1991) p.11 (hereinafter "*Investment*").

[2] Central Intelligence Agency *The World Fact Book*, (1995), p. 379 (hereinafter "*World Fact Book*").

[3] *Ibid.* The following breakdown provides further detail of the population of Singapore as of 1995: Population growth rate: 1.06%; Birth rate: 15.93 births/1,000 population; Death rate: 5.35 deaths/1,000 population; Infant mortality rate: 5.7 deaths/1,000 live births; Life expectancy at birth: total population 76.16 years male 73.28 years female 79.25 years; Net migration rate: 0 migrant(s)/1,000 population; Total fertility rate: 1.87 children born/woman; Nationality: noun Singaporean(s); adjective Singapore; Ethnic divisions: Chinese 76.4%, Malay 14.9%, Indian 6.4%, other 2.3%; Religions: Buddhist (Chinese), Muslim (Malays), Christian, Hindu, Sikh, Taoist, Confucianist; Languages: Chinese (official), Malay (official and national), Tamil (official), English (official); Literacy: age 15 and over can read and write (1990 est.); total population 89% male 95% female 83% ; Labor force: 1,649,000 by occupation: financial, business, and other services 33.5%, manufacturing 25.6%, commerce 22.9%, construction 6.6%, other 11.4% (1990).

[4] *Ibid.*, p.379.

[5] *Ibid.*, p.379. Singapore has undulating plateaus providing natural water catchment. *Ibid.*

[6] *Ibid.* Singapore's climate can be described as tropical; hot, humid, rainy; no

Singapore

pronounced rainy or dry seasons; thunderstorms occur on 40% of all days (67% of days in April). Therefore, Singapore is fortunate not to have significant variances in climate, unlike other Southeast Asian neighbors, making it more conducive to year-round business.

7 *Ibid.*, p.379.

8 *Ibid.*, p.379.

9 *Ibid.*, p.379.

10 *Ibid.*, p.379.

11 *Ibid.*, p.379.

12 *Ibid.*, p.379. (f.o.b., 1994); computer equipment, rubber and rubber products, petroleum products, telecommunications equipment. Partners: Malaysia 19%, US 19%, Hong Kong 9%, Japan 7%,Thailand 6%.

13 *Ibid.*, p.379. (c.i.f., 1994) aircraft, petroleum, chemicals, foodstuffs. Partners: Japan 22%, Malaysia 16%, US 15%, Saudi Arabia 4%, Taiwan 4%.

14 *Ibid.*, p.379.

15 See World Wide Web (http://www.doc.gov.bem.sing) UNITED STATES DEPARTMENT OF COMMERCE, BIG EMERGING MARKETS (1995). The Singapore government tightly controls Singapore's vehicle population through high taxes. Despite the high costs of vehicle ownership demand exceeds supply.

16 *Ibid.*

17 *See*, World Wide Web (http://www.doc.gov.bem.sing) UNITED STATES DEPARTMENT OF COMMERCE, BIG EMERGING MARKETS (1995).

18 *Ibid.*

19 LePoer, Federal Research Division, Library of Congress, *Singapore: A Country Study*, xxi (2d ed. 1991).

20 *Ibid.*

21 Woon, *Commercial Law of Singapore* (1986), p.5. *See update*,Woon, *Basic Business Law in Singapore* (Prentice Hall, 1995). *See also*, Rutter, *The Applicable Law in Singapore and Malaysia* (1989), p.108, discussing the 1824 British-Dutch Treaty and the British Act transfering Singapore to the East Indian Company (5 Geo. IV c.108).

22 *Ibid.*

23 *Ibid.*, p.6. (The Imperial Japanese Army invaded Singapore for three years beginning on February 15, 1942. The British put Singapore and Malaya under British Military rule until Malaya was detached in 1948 under the Malayan Union. Singapore was officially separated from the Straits Settlements and became a Crown Colony in 1946. Straits Settlements (Repeal) Act 1946 (9 & 10 Geo. 6 c.37); Straits Settlements (Repeal) Order in Council, 1946 SR & O 1946, No 462; Singapore Colony Order in Council, 1946 SR & O 1946, No. 464; State of Singapore Act, 1958; Singapore (Constitution) Order in Council [1958] UK SI 2156 (No 1956)).

24 LePoer, *op. cit.*, p.53. Singapore, Malaysia, Sabah and Sarawak signed the Malaysian Agreement to form the Federation of Malaysia on July 9, 1963. *Ibid.*, p.55. Thereafter, Singapore became an automomous state with its own constitution within Malaysia on September 16, 1963. *Ibid.*, p.180. Apparently, Malaysian leaders, fearful of Singaporean Chinese domination, formally opposed such a merger when the Malayan parliament voted 126 to 0 on August 9, 1965 to remain a separate nation. Immediately thereafter, Lee Kuan Yew, head of the People's Action Party, declared Singapore to be an independent state. *Ibid.*, p.57.

25 *Ibid.*, pp.180–181.

26 *Ibid.*, p.180. The amendments which require a two-thirds vote of Parliament are summarized as follows: to permit appeal to the Judicial Committee of the British Privy Council in London (1966), *see also, Robins v. National Trust Co Ltd* (1927) 1 MLJ 1; creation of the office of Vice President and liberalization of citizenship requirements (1968); establishment of the Supreme Court as the highest court of

appeal (1969); protection of the sovereignty of Singapore by prohibiting merger or other de-nationalization (1972); and finally, an amendment creating a Fundamental Liberties section of the Constitution in Part IV, Articles 9–16 (1978). *Ibid.*

27 *Ibid.*

28 *Ibid.*, pp.181–182.

29 *Ibid.*

30 *Ibid.*, p.177. In 1984, the Parliamentary Elections Act was amended to permit appointment of up to three non-constituency members if opposition parties fail to get at least three seats. *Ibid.*, p.179.

31 *Ibid.*, p.182. All bills are examined by the Presidential Council for Minority Rights which determines whether the legislation discriminates against any group under the mandate of the Constitution. *Ibid.* Acts of Parliament are cited by their "short titles" and Chapter ("Cap."). *See also,* Woon, *op. cit.,* p.278 for a comprehensive discussion of researching Singapore legislation.

32 *World Fact Book, op. cit.,* p.380. President Ong was elected by 59% margin. Lee Hsien Loong is Deputy Prime Minister and son of Lee Kuan Yew.

33 *Ibid.*, p.380.

34 *Ibid.*, p.380.

35 LePoer, *op. cit.,* p.179.

36 *Ibid.*, p.184. The Prime Minister is required to consult with the Chief Justice on appointments to the Supreme Court. *Ibid.* The organic act of the Supreme Court is the Supreme Court of Judicature Act, January 9, 1970. Woon, *op. cit.,* p.14. *See also,* the Supreme Court of Judicature Act (Cap. 322 Rev.Ed 1985) and the Supreme Court of Judicature (Amendment) Act 1993, No. 17.

37 Supreme Court of Judicature (Amendment) Act 1993, s.3.

38 LePoer, *op. cit.,* p.184.

39 *Ibid.*, p.14. *See also,* the Supreme Court of Judicature (Amendment) Act, s.10 (*in personam* jurisdictional requirements).

40 *Ibid.*, p.16. *But see,* Thorpe, "Some Practical Points About Starting a Business in Singapore" 27 Creighton L. Rev. 1052 (1994)(the subordinate courts have jurisdiction to handle cases up to a value of S$50,000). *See generally,* The Subordinate Courts Act (Cap. 321).

41 Woon, *op. cit.* p.8. Letters Patent were granted to Singapore and Malacca with the 1826 Straits Settlements. These superceded the East Indian Company's Charter and are therefore referred to as the Second Charter. *Ibid.*

42 *Ibid.* The only reservation was that the common law be modified to as not to "work oppressively on the native inhabitants." *Ibid. See also generally,* Rutter, *op. cit.,* p.96, *discussing, Ong Cheng Neo v. Yeap Cheah Neo* (1872) 1 Ky 326.

43 Woon, *op. cit.,* p.9. Likewise, other Commonwealth countries' (*i.e.* Canada, Australia, Hong Kong, *et al.*) case law can be reviewed and argued as providing guidance on the proper application of law where Singapore has none. *Ibid.*

44 *Ibid.*

45 Civil Law Ordinance No. IV of 1878, s.6; Civil Law Act (Cap. 43), s.5(1) (Singapore Statutes, 1985 Rev. Ed., see now 1988 Rev. Ed.); Hickling (1979) 21 Mal LR 351, p.362). Rutter, *op. cit.,* p.172–173.

46 Civil Law Act, ss.2, 3.

47 Woon, *op. cit.,* p.12.

48 *Ibid.* This approach was utilized by the Privy Council in *Shaik Sahied bin Abdullah Bajerai v. Sockalingam Chettiar* (1933) AC 342. *See also,* Rutter, *op. cit.,* p.186–190 which discusses *Sockalingam* and two additional cases on point, *Ngo Bee Chan v. Chia Teck Kim* (1912) 2 MC 25 and *Seng Djit Hin v. Nagurdas Purshotumdas & Co* (1921) 14 SSLR 181, [1923] AC 444 (PC).

49 Woon, *op. cit.,* p.11, *citing Seng Djit Hin.*

50 *Ibid.*, p.13. *See also,* Phang, "Theoretical Conundrums and Practical Solutions in

Singapore Commercial Law: A Review and Application of the Civil Law Act" 17 Anglo-Am. L.Rev. 251–294 (1988).

[51] Woon, *op. cit.*, p.13.
[52] No.35 of 1993; *see also*, (Cap. 7A 1994 Rev.Ed) (hereinafter "AELA").
[53] AELA, s.6.
[54] Rutter, *op. cit.*, p.580–582.
[55] AELA, s.5.
[56] AELA, s.3(1).
[57] Phang, "Cementing the Foundations: The Singapore Application of English Law Act 1993" 28:I U.B.C. L. Rev. 205, 234 (1994).
[58] AELA, s.3(2).
[59] Phang, *op. cit.*, note 57, p.239.
[60] AELA, s.4.
[61] 19 & 20 Vict. c.97.
[62] 30 & 31 Vict. c.144.
[63] 52 & 53 Vict. c.45.
[64] 53 & 54 Vict. c.39.
[65] 6 Edw. 8 c.41.
[66] 20 & 21 Geo. 5 c.25.
[67] 8 & 9 Eliz. 2 c.46.
[68] c.7.
[69] c.50.
[70] c.54.
[71] c.29.
[72] c.13.
[73] c.50.
[74] AELA, Second Schedule.
[75] Phang, *op. cit.*, note 57, p.234. *See also supra*, note 26 which describes the Constitutional amendment which created the right of appeal to the Privy Council. Appeals were narrowed by the Internal Security (Amendment) Act (No. 2 of 1989) and the Judicial Committee (Amendment) Act (No. 21 of 1989).
[76] Rutter, *op. cit.*, pp.238–240 which descibes the cases where appeals are permitted and under what circumstances.
[77] *Ibid.*, p.240.
[78] *Ibid.*
[79] *Ibid.*, p.248, *citing* "Singapore Appeals to the Judicial Committee of the Privy Council — An Endangered Species?", (1985) 27 Malay L.R. 284, p.308. For a general discussion on the abolition of appeals from Malyasia to the Privy Council on January 1, 1985, *see ibid.*, (Chapter 19) 498–520.
[80] Price Waterhouse, *Doing Business in Singapore* (1993), p.47 [hereinafter "*Doing Business*"].
[81] United States Trade Representative, *Report on Non-Tariff Barriers* (1995), p.278 [hereinafter "*Report*"].
[82] Member of: AsDB, ASEAN, C, CCC, COCOM (cooperating), CP, ESCAP, G-77, GATT, IAEA, IBRD, ICAO, ICC, ICFTU, IFC, ILO, IMF, IMO, INMARSAT, INTELSAT, INTERPOL, IOC, ISO, ITU, LORCS, NAM, UN, UNAVEM II, UNCTAD, UNIKOM, UNTAC, UPU, WHO, WIPO, WMO.
[83] *Doing Business*, p.211, Appendix XVIII.
[84] *Ibid.*
[85] *Ibid.*, p.53.
[86] *Ibid.*
[87] *See* below.
[88] *Doing Business*, p.53.

89 *Report*, p.278.
90 *Ibid.*
91 *Ibid.*
92 Sinnadurai, *Law of Contract in Malaysia and Singapore Cases and Commentary* (2nd Ed. 1987), p.1.
93 *See, discussion* above.
94 *Halsbury's Laws of England* (4th ed.).
95 Sinnadurai, *op. cit.*, pp.23–24.
96 *Fraser v. Everett* (1889) 4 Ky 512; *Lee Seng Heng v. Guardian Assurance Co Ltd* [1932] MLJ 17 (the postal rule).
97 *Parke and Francis v. Ng Eng Kiat* [1953] MLJ 214.
98 *Dunmore v. Alexander* (1830) 9 Sh 190.
99 *Guha Majumder v. Donough* (1974) 2 MLJ 114; *Yap Eng Thong v. Faber Union Ltd* (1973) 1 MLJ 191.
100 *Lim Keng Siong v. Yeo Ah Tee* (1983) 2 MLJ 39; *Choo Tiong Hin v. Choo Hock Swee* [1959] MLJ 67 (contractual intentions).
101 *Bainbridge v. Firmstone* (1880) 1 P & D 2; 112 ER 1019, *see also, Chappell & Co. Ltd v. Nestle Co Ltd* [1960] AC 87.
102 *Kepong Prosepecting Ltd v. Schmidt* (1968) 1 MLJ 170 (privity).
103 *Roscorla v. Thomas* (1842) 114 ER 496; *Re McArdle, Decd* (1951) 1 Ch 669.
104 *Lampleigh v. Braithwait* (1615) 80 ER 255; *Pao On v. Lau Yiu Long* [1980] AC 614.
105 *Bret v. JS and his wife* (1600) 78 ER 987.
106 *Koh v. Koh* (1965) 1 MLJ 99 (permitting accord and satifaction); *but see, D & C Builders Ltd v. Rees* (1966) 2 QB 617 (disallowing accord and satisfaction).
107 *Bank Negara Indonesia v. Philip Hoalim* (1973) 2 MLJ 3.
108 *Eastern Supply Co v. Kerr* (1974) 1 MLJ 10.
109 Sinnadurai, *op. cit.*, p.155.
110 *Baker v. Asia Motors Co Ltd* [1962] MLJ 171.
111 9 *Halsbury's Laws of* England (4th edition) paragraph 356. For Singapore case law, *Sino-British Engineering Corporation (Malaya) Ltd v. Ma Namazie Ltd* [1949] MLJ 212; *see also, Pasuma Pharmacal Corpn v. McAlister & Co Ltd* (1965) 1 MLJ 221; *but see, Soon Nam Co Ltd v. Archynamics Architects* (1979) 1 MLJ 212.
112 12 *Halsbury's Laws of England* (4th edition) paragraphs 1478–1498.
113 *Teo Siew Peng v. Guok Sing Ong* (1983) 1 MLJ 132; 9 *Halsbury's Laws of England* (4th ed.) paragraph 334 ff.
114 *Sze Hai Tong Bank Ltd v. Rambler Cycle Co Ltd* [1959] MLJ 200. *But see*, Sinnadurai, *op. cit.*, pp.158–209 stating that Unfair Contract Terms Act 1977 may be applicable to "exemption clauses" pursuant to s.5 Civil Law Act.
115 *Derry v. Peek* (1889) 14 App Cas 337.
116 *Tan Chye Chew v. Eastern Mining & Metals Co Ltd* (1965) 1 MLJ 201.
117 *Horsfall v. Thomas* (1862) 1 H & C 90.
118 *Chan Chor Tng v. Housing & Urban Development Co (Pte) Ltd* (1981) 2 MLJ 298.
119 *Misrepresentation Act 1967, s.2(1). See also, Mahn Singh v. Guan Soon Transport Co Ltd* [1955] MLJ 51.
120 *Malayan Miners Co (M) Ltd v. Lian Hock & Co* (1966) 2 MLJ 273 (innocent misrepresentation remedy is damages not recission).
121 *Senanayake v. Annie Yeo* (1965) 2 MLJ 241.
122 Sinnadurai, *op. cit.*, pp.215, 256; *see also, Maria Chia Sook Lan v. Bank of China* (1976) 1 MLJ 245.
123 *Lloyds Bank v. Bundy* [1975] QB 326; *but see, National Westminister Bank Plc v. Morgan* (1985) 1 All ER 821.

[124] *Seck v. Wong & Lee* [1940] MLJ Rep 146.

[125] Sinnadurai, *op. cit.*, pp.283–285.

[126] *Serangoon Garden Estate Ltd v. Marian Chye* [1959] MLJ 113.

[127] Employment Act, s.12; *see also, Re Oie Tiong Ham* [1928] SSLR 56.

[128] *Aroomoogum Chitty v. Lim Ah Hang* (1894) 2 SSLR 80.

[129] *Thomas Cowan v. Orme* [1961] MLJ 41; *see also, Framroz v. Mistri* [1932] MLJ 96 (trade secrets).

[130] *See also,* Law Reform (Frustrated Contracts) Ordinance 1959; *Chan Buck Kia v. Naga Shipping & Trading Co Ltd* [1963] MLJ 159.

[131] *Hong Guan & Co Ltd v. R Jumabhoy & Sons Ltd* [1960] MLJ 141 (rejecting *force majeure* defense).

[132] *Himatsing & Co v. Joitaram* (1970) 2 MLJ 246 (time of the essence contract).

[133] *Building & Estates Ltd v. Connor* [1958] MLJ 173.

[134] *Tong Aik (Far East) Ltd v. Eastern Minerals & Trading Ltd* [1963] MLJ 322 (payment required upon individual deliveries).

[135] *Wong Poh Oi v. Gertrude Guok* (1966) 2 MLJ 134.

[136] *Allen v. Robles* (1969) 1 WLR 1193.

[137] *Bunge Corporation, New York v. Tradex Export SA, Panama* (1981) 1 WLR 711.

[138] (1854) 9 Ex 341.

[139] *Bulsing Ltd v. Joon Seng & Co* (1972) 2 MLJ 43.

[140] *Export Credit Guarantee Department v. Universal Oil Products Co* (1983) 2 All ER 205.

[141] Sinnadurai, *op. cit.*, p.672, *citing, Howe v. Smith* (1884) 27 Ch D 89.

[142] *Hilborne v. Tan Tiang Quee, Chung v. Tan Tiang Quee* (1972) 2 MLJ 94 (nominal damages); *Hong Leong Co Ltd v. Pearlson Enterprises Ltd (No 2)* (1968) 1 MLJ 262.

[143] *Fox v. Ek Liong Hin Ltd* [1957] MLJ 1 (injury to reputation).

[144] Sinnadurai, *op. cit.*, pp.763–764, *citing,* Jones and Goodhart, *Specific Performance* (1986) and *Decro-Wall International SA v. Practitioners in Marketing Ltd SA* (1971) 1 WLR 361.

[145] Sinnadurai, *op. cit.*, p.764, *citing,* Chitty, *Contracts* (25th ed.), chap. 27 and *Re Schwabacher* (1908) 98 LT 127, 128; *Waring & Gillow v. Thompson* (1912) 29 TLR 154; *Ryan v. Mutual Tontine Association* (1893) 1 Ch 116.

[146] *Ryan v. Mutual Tontine Association* (1893) 1 Ch 116, 123.

[147] *Odessa Tramways Co v. Mendel* (1878) 8 Ch D 235; *Ailion v. Spiekermann* (1976) 1 All ER 497.

[148] *Holiday Inn Inc v. Hotel Enterprises Ltd* (1976) 1 MLJ 213.

[149] *Redland Brick Ltd v. Morris* [1970] AC 652.

[150] *Regent Oil Co Ltd v. JT Leavesley (Lichfield) Ltd* (1966) 1 WLR 1210 (injunction dissolved).

[151] The Sale of Goods (United Nations Convention) Act (No. 14 of 1995).

[152] *See discussion above.*

[153] Woon, *op. cit.*, p.114 (applicability of the Unfair Contract Terms Act 1977 and Supply of Goods and Services Act 1982). Rutter, *op. cit.*, p.467. *But see,* Ricquier, "United Kingdom Sale of Goods Act 1979 and its Applicability in Singapore" 22 MLR 145 (1980)).

[154] U.K. Sale of Goods Act 1979 which repealed the 1893 version and as adopted by the AELA after 1993 [hereinafter "SGA"]. *See also,* Sinnadurai, *op. cit.*, p.196, n.1A for a detailed discussion of the applicability of the Act in Singapore. *See also,* The Merchant Shipping Act 1995 (No. 19 of 1995) (Cap. 179 of the 1985 Rev. Ed.); and The Regulation of Imports and Exports Act 1995 (No. 24 of 1995).

[155] Woon, *op. cit.*, p.114.

[156] SGA, s.61(1) (goods are defined as all movable property except money and causes of action).

[157] SGA, s.2(1).

[158] SGA, s.2(1) (consideration must be money).

[159] Woon, *op. cit.*, pp.115–121. For a detailed discussion of these concepts under the Sale of Goods Act, as applicable to Singapore.

[160] Women's Charter (Cap. 47).

[161] Companies Act (Cap. 185), s.25 [hereinafter "CA"].

[162] SGA, s.8(1).

[163] Evidence Act (Cap. 5), s.94 (inadmissibility of parol evidence); The Statute of Frauds 1677, s.17 (unenforceability of oral agreements over a certain amount) not be applicable after the AELA and replaced by specific local provisions; *see*, Woon, *op. cit.*, pp.120–121 for a more detailed discussion.

[164] SGA, s.55(1); *see also*, Woon, *op. cit.*, p.124 which suggests that parties, goods, delivery, price and payment be covered in any basic contract.

[165] *See*, U.K. Unfair Contract Terms Act 1977. Applicable by the AELA.

[166] Woon, *op. cit.*, p.124.

[167] SGA, s.12(1), (2).

[168] SGA, ss.13 (sale by description), 15 (sale by sample).

[169] SGA, ss.14, 15 (*caveat emptor*); s.14 (merchantability and fitness for a particular purpose). *But see*, Unfair Contract Terms Act, s.6 for treatment of nonconsumers.

[170] SGA, s.61(1).

[171] SGA, s.17.

[172] SGA, s.16.

[173] SGA, s.18.

[174] SGA, s.61(5).

[175] Unsolicited Goods and Services Act 1971, s.1 which may not be applicable after 1993.

[176] SGA, s.19; *see also, Aluminium Industrie Vaasen B.V. v. Romalpa Aluminium Ltd* (1976) 1 WLR 676.

[177] SGA, s.20.

[178] Frustrated Contracts Act (Cap. 33) which may not be applicable after 1993.

[179] SGA, s.21 which codifies the *nemo dat* rule that one can only transfer the title one has. *See*, Woon, *op. cit.*, p.141.

[180] Factors Act 1889, s.2.

[181] SGA, ss.27 (seller's general duty), 29(3) (reasonable time), 29(1) (seller's place of business or residence), 32(2) (third party delivery), 31(1) (installments).

[182] SGA, s.34.

[183] SGA, s.35(1) (buyer's delay or conduct indicia of acceptance).

[184] SGA, s.30.

[185] SGA, s.36.   [186] SGA, s.28.

[187] SGA, s.39.   [188] SGA, s.49.

[189] SGA, s.50.   [190] SGA, s.52.

[191] SGA, s.51.   [192] SGA, s.52.

[193] SGA, s.53.

[194] Business Registration Act (No. 36 of 1973), s.5 [hereinafter BRA].

[195] Woon, *op. cit.*, p.21. "Business includes every form of trade, commerce, craftsmanship, calling, profession and any activity carried on for the purposes of gain." It specifically excludes certain types of employment such as hawkers, home craftsmen, taxi drivers, trishaw drivers, farmers and the like. In addition, persons holding office, employees of another, and traditional professionals (*i.e.* doctors and lawyers). *Ibid.*, p.21 to 22.

[196] *Invesment*, p.33.

[197] Png, "Going International in Singapore" in *Counseling Emerging Companies in Going International* (ABA 1994), p.653.

[198] Woon, *op. cit.*, p.22.

[199] *Ibid.*, pp.23–24.
[200] *Ibid.*, p.24.
[201] *Above*, I regarding the Civil Law Act, s.5(1) and the AELA. *See also generally*, Partnership Act of 1890 (UK) [hereinafter "PA"].
[202] Woon, *op. cit.*, p.29 (corporations may be partners).
[203] PA, s.1.
[204] Woon, *op. cit.*, pp.25–26.
[205] CA, s.17 which requires incorporation for businesses with more than 20 members. For a discussion of who may be counted as a partner (*e.g.* salaried partners, sleeping partners, etc.) *see*, Woon, *op. cit.*, pp.26–27.
[206] Woon, *op. cit.*, pp.26–27.
[207] BRA, s.5.
[208] Woon, *op. cit.*, p.28.
[209] PA, s.24(7) which requires unanimous consent for admission of new partners in the absence of agreement otherwise.
[210] Woon, *op. cit.*, pp.28–29.
[211] *Ibid.*, p.28.
[212] PA, s.5.
[213] The Rules of the Supreme Court of Singapore provide that a firm may be sued. Woon, *op. cit.*, p.36.
[214] Partnership Act, ss.9 (contracts and debts), 12 (errors and ommissions).
[215] Woon, *op. cit.*, pp.31–34.
[216] *Ibid.*, p.37.
[217] *Ibid.*
[218] PA, s.29.
[219] PA, s.30.
[220] Woon, *op. cit.*, p.38. The following partnership acts require unanimous consent: (1) amendment of rights and duties; (2) change of business; (3) new partner; and (4) removing a partner.
[221] PA, s.24(9). Woon, *op. cit.*, p.43.
[222] Woon, *op. cit.*, pp.43–46.
[223] PA, s.32(a) (fixed term), (b) (single enterprise).
[224] PA, s.32(c).
[225] PA, s.33(1).
[226] Woon, *op. cit.*, p.47.
[227] PA, s.33(2).
[228] PA, s.34.
[229] PA, s.25 this must be in the partnership agreement.
[230] Woon, *op. cit.*, p.48.
[231] PA, ss.39 (net due), 44 (final accounting), 36(1) and 38 (post-dissolution liability), 40(return of contribution).
[232] Woon, *op. cit.*, pp.49–50, *citing*, Companies Act, 350.
[233] *Ibid.*, p.53.
[234] *Ibid.*
[235] *Ibid.*
[236] *Ibid.*
[237] CA, s.17(2).
[238] CA, s.27(7).
[239] CA, s.30.
[240] *Investment*, p.34.
[241] CA, ss.4 (any company that is not a private company is a public company), 18(1)(private company).

[242] *Investment*, p.34.
[243] CA, s.4.
[244] CA, s.18(1).
[245] CA, s.4.
[246] Woon, *op. cit.*, p.55.
[247] CA, ss.5 (holding companies), 6 (subsidiaries), and 21 (related companies).
[248] Woon, *op. cit.*, p.55.
[249] *Ibid.*, p.56.
[250] CA, s.27(10). The reservation is good for two months. The name may not be "undesirable", duplicative, likely to be mistaken for another corporation, or prohibited by the Minister. CA, s.27(1).
[251] CA, s.19 (declaration of compliance and certificate of indentity must be filed by a director or the secretary and officers, repectively); *see also,* the Companies Regulations 1984 for applicable forms.
[252] Company Registration Fees based on share capitalization: S$0 − S$100,000 is S$1,200; S$100,001 − S$1,000,000 is S$1,200 + S$400 for each additional S$100,000; S$1,000,001 and up is S$4,800 + S$300 for each additional S$1,000,000 up to a maximum of S$35,000. *Doing Business*, Appendix XIII, p.190 (1993).
[253] CA, s.398.
[254] See, Woon, *op. cit.*, p.57 for a discussion of the reasons the Registrar of Companies may refuse to register a corporation.
[255] *Ibid.*, p.58, *citing, Salomon v. A. Salomon & Co. Ltd.* [1897] AC 22.
[256] CA, s.22(3).
[257] CA, s.241.
[258] CA, s.42.
[259] CA, s.144(2)(c) (romanized lettering on documents obligating the corporation).
[260] CA, ss.25(2)(b), 406.
[261] CA, s.401.
[262] Woon, *op. cit.*, p.61.
[263] *See generally,* CA, s.235.
[264] CA, s.22(1).
[265] CA, s.26.
[266] Woon, *op. cit.*, pp.65–66.
[267] CA, ss.23, 24.
[268] CA, s.25.
[269] *See,* CA, the Fourth Schedule.
[270] CA, s.37.
[271] *Allen v. Gold Reefs of West Africa Ltd* (1900) 1 Ch 656; CA, s.216.
[272] Woon, *op. cit.*, p.72.
[273] CA, s.180.
[274] CA, s.39.
[275] CA, ss.40, 203.
[276] CA, s.177(2) (14 days notice required).
[277] CA, s.175(1).
[278] CA, s.181 (proxies).
[279] CA, s.184 (ordinary and special resolutions and voting margins).
[280] CA, s.216.
[281] Woon, *op. cit.*, p.102, *citing, Foss v. Harbottle* (1843) 2 Hare 461.
[282] CA, s.190.
[283] CA, s.173; *see also,* CA, ss.164 (directors' holdings), 88 (substantial shareholders).
[284] CA, s.93.
[285] *Ibid.*

Singapore

286 CA, s.150.
287 CA, s.145(2). *See also*, CA, s.147 regarding directors' share qualification requirements.
288 CA, s.145(1).
289 CA, s.151, *but see*, CA, s.159.
290 CA, ss.160, 161 which expressly prohibits the board of directors from deciding issues regarding dissolution or shares issues, respectively.
291 Woon, *op. cit.*, p.91.
292 Woon, *op. cit.*, pp.91–92.
293 CA, ss.156, 162, 163, 165.
294 CA, s.152.
295 CA, s.145(5) which provides the limitations on resignation.
296 CA, s.153(2).
297 CA, s.123.
298 CA, s.121.
299 CA, s.74.
300 CA, s.75.
301 CA, s.403. *But see*, Woon, *op. cit.*, pp.96–97.
302 Woon, *op. cit.*, p.98.
303 Woon, *op. cit.* pp.98–99.
304 CA, s.131.
305 Bankruptcy Act (No. 15 of 1995) [hereinafter "BA"], ss.3, 74. The High Court has jurisdiction and can issue a stay of proceedings.
306 CA, s.247; *see also*, BA, s.57 (involuntary proceedings).
307 CA, s.293 places a high burden on directors making a declaration regarding the company's solvency.
308 CA, s.293.
309 CA, s.254(1) (grounds for a winding up petition).
310 CA, s.327; *but see also*, BA, ss. 90, 99 for priorities and preference actions in bankruptcy.
311 CA, s.275; *see also*, BA s.124 (effect of discharge).
312 CA, s.379.
313 *Investment*, p.41.
314 *Ibid.*, p.42.
315 Png, *op. cit.*, p.653.
316 *See generally*, CA.
317 The Securities Industry Act (Cap. 289, 1985 rev. ed.), some references by Woon are to the 1973 Act [hereinafter "SIA"].
318 Banking Act (Cap. 19, 1985 rev. ed.).
319 Insurance Act (Cap. 142, 1985 rev. ed.).
320 Futures Trading Act (Cap. 116, 1985 rev. ed.).
321 Woon, *op. cit.*, pp.196–197.
322 CA, s.47 (any notice or similar inducement for the purchase of shares or debt).
323 CA, s.50.
324 CA, s.45.
325 Woon, *op. cit.*, pp.200–201.
326 CA, ss.46, 47.
327 CA, s.50(2)(b).
328 CA, s.401.
329 CA, s.55.
330 *See, Hedley Byrne & Co. Ltd. v. Heller & Partners Ltd.* [1964] AC 465.
331 Woon, *op. cit.*, p.204; *but see also*, the AELA.
332 CA, s.45.
333 Woon, *op. cit.*, pp.204–205.

334 est. 1986.
335 SIA, s.[5].
336 SIA, s.[2].
337 SIA, s.[14].
338 SIA, ss.[2, 10].
339 *Investment, citing,* Securities Exchange of Singapore, Listing Manual and Corporate Disclosure Policy [hereinafter "Listing Manual"].
340 *Doing Business* (Supp. 1993), p.9.
341 *Ibid.*
342 *Investment,* p.39.
343 *Ibid.*
344 *Ibid.,* p.40: S$500 for every S$1 million of each class listed with a minimum of S$2,000 and a maximum of S$20,000.
345 *Ibid.*
346 *Ibid.* (S$750,000 minimum with 100 holders subject to a deed of trust)
347 *Hedley Byrne & Co. Ltd v. Heller & Partners Ltd* [1964] AC 465.
348 Woon, *op. cit.,* p.214.
349 *Investment,* p.41.
350 *Doing Business,* pp.54–55.
351 *Investment,* p.41.
352 CA, s.158.
353 This term has been defined to mean information not publically available. Woon, *op. cit.,* p.215.
354 CA, s.157(2).
355 SIA, s.[84].
356 SIA, s.[85].
357 SIA, ss.[86, 87].
358 SIA, s.[94].
359 CA, ss.213, 213(17); *see generally,* Bennett, "Securities Regulation in Singapore" 12 Pac.Basin L.Rev. 1, 12–13 (1993), *citing,* Code (1985 rev. ed.). *See also,* East Asian Executive Reports, "Singapore Amends Code On Takeovers and Mergers" (Dec. 1985), p.20.
360 Bennett, *Loc. cit.*   361 CA, s.213(3).
362 CA, s.213.   363 CA, s.213(9).
364 CA, s.213(4)(a).   365 CA, s.213(8)(I).
366 CA, s.213(5).   367 CA, s.213(6).
368 CA, s.214.   369 CA, s.215.
370 Woon, *op. cit.,* p.223, *citing,* Listing Manual, r.601(7).
371 *Ibid.,* p.221.
372 Arbitration Act (Cap. 10 1985 rev. ed.).
373 International Arbitration Act (No. 23 of 1994) [hereinafter "IAA"].
374 IAA, s.3(1).   375 IAA, s.5(2).
376 IAA, ss.5(2)(a), (b), (c).
377 IAA, s.11.   378 IAA, s.6.
379 IAA, s.8(1).   380 IAA, s.8(2).
381 IAA, s.9.   382 IAA, s.16.
383 IAA, s.12.   384 IAA, ss.18–21.
385 IAA, s.24.   386 IAA, s.25.
387 Lowenfeld, "Singapore and the Local Bar: Aberration or Ill Omen?" 5 J.Int'l Arb.71–73 (1988).
388 IAA, s.36.
389 IAA, s.28.
390 IAA, s.30.
391 IAA, ss.31(2)(a), (b).

Singapore

392 IAA, ss.31(2)(c), (d), (e).
393 IAA, ss.31(2)(f), (3), (4).
394 *Investment*, p.85.
395 *Ibid.*
396 Banking Act (Cap 19); *see also*, Banking (Amendment) Act (No. 28 of 1993).
397 *Investment*, p.85.
398 Boxall and McCracken, "Singapore Banking (Amendment) Act 1993" 5 J. Banking & Fin. Law and Prac. (1994), p.75 (12% capital adequacy ratio and transaction secrecy relaxation).
399 *Investment*, p.86.   400 *Ibid.*
401 *Ibid.*   402 *Report*, p.279.
403 *Investment*, p.87.   404 *Ibid.*
405 *Ibid.*, pp.89–90.   406 *Ibid.*, pp.87–88.
407 *Ibid.*, pp.88.   408 *Ibid.*
409 *Ibid.*
410 Bills of Exchange Act (Cap. 28); *see also* Bills of Exchange (Amendment) Act (No. 34 of 1992).
411 Woon, *op. cit.*, pp.154, 157.
412 Bills of Exchange Act, ss.7, 34.
413 Bills of Exchange Act, s.29.
414 Woon, *op. cit.*, p.166.
415 *Ibid.* pp.168–173.
416 (No. 12 of 1973).
417 (Cap. 167, 1970 ed.).
418 (No. 18 of 1975).
419 *Ibid.*, s.5 and Part III.
420 *Doing Business*, p.55.
421 Campell and Wolff, *Legal Aspects of Business Transactions and Investment in the Far East* (Kluwer 1989), pp.65, 69.
422 Ono, *Profile on Occupational Safety and Health in Singapore* (International Labor Organization 1991), p.1.
423 Factories Act (No. 6 of 1973).
424 Factories Act, Part II.
425 Ono, *Loc. cit.*
426 Factories Act, Parts IV, V.
427 *Ibid.*, Part V.
428 *Ibid.*, Part VII.
429 *Ibid.*
430 Ono, *op. cit.*, p.4.
431 *Ibid.*
432 *Ibid.*
433 *Ibid.*, p.5.
434 *Ibid.*
435 *Ibid.*
436 *See generally*, Smith, *Singapore: A Model of Urban Environmentalism in Southeast Asia*, (Note) 16 Hastings Int'l & Comp. L. Rev. (1992).
437 *Ibid.*, p.140.
438 Clean Air Act (No. 29 of 1971); *see also*, Clean Air (Amendments) Act.
439 Water Pollution Control and Drainage Act (No. 29 of 1975).
440 Clean Air Act, s.5(1).
441 Clean Air Act, ss.5, 6.
442 Montreal Protocol on Substances That Deplete the Ozone Layer, *opened for signature* September 16, 1987, 26 I.L.M. 1541 (entered into force January 1, 1989).

[443] Smith, *op. cit.*, p.128.
[444] Prevention of Pollution of the Sea Act (Cap. 243 of the 1985 Rev. Ed.), Civil Liability (Oil Pollution) Act 1973 (No. 43 of 1973). *See also*, Merchant Shipping (Oil Pollution) Act (Cap. 180 of the 1985 Rev. Ed.)
[445] Smith, *op. cit.*, p.130.
[446] *Ibid.*
[447] *Ibid.*, p.131.
[448] *Investment*, p.77.
[449] *World Factbook*, p.380.
[450] *Ibid.*, p.380.
[451] *Investment*, p.83; *see also* Employment of Foreign Workers Act (No. 21 of 1990).
[452] *Investment*, p.79.
[453] *Ibid. See also,* Thorpe, *op. cit.*, p.1064, n.276 *citing*, Price Waterhouse, *Investment Regulations Around The World: Singapore* 255, 256 (1983) (proof of Singaporean workers may be required).
[454] *Investment*, p.79.
[455] *Ibid.*, p.83.
[456] Thorpe, *op. cit.*, p.1064.
[457] *Investment*, pp.79–81 (probation — one to six months; termination notice — one to three months; work hours — 44 hours per week, one day of rest each week, one hour for lunch, and overtime provisions; annual vacation leave — 7 days first year and one additional day up to 14 days each year thereafter, plus 11 public holidays; medical — 14 to 60 days, maternity leave — 8 weeks; National Military Service Leave — usually two to three weeks but no more than 40 days).
[458] *Ibid.*, p.81 (Workers' Compensation Act).
[459] Thorpe, *op. cit.*, p.1065, n.287 which indicates that contributions by both employees and employers based on monthly earnings by are as follows: under S$50 — none; S$50 to S$200 — 20% (employer); S$200 to S$363 — 20% (employer) and 7% (employee); over S$363 — 22% (employer) and 23% (employee).
[460] *Investment*, p.82; *see also* The Skills Development Levy (Amendment) Act (No. 19 of 1992).
[461] *Investment*, pp.83–84.
[462] Lim and Fong, *Foreign Direct Investment and Industrialisation in Malaysia, Singapore, Taiwan and Thailand*, (OECD, Development Center, Paris, 1991), p.51.
[463] Png, *op. cit.*, p.653 (the EDB is described as the country's "business architect" with respect to foreign investment).
[464] Asher, Rolt, Ariff and Khan, *Fiscal Incentives and Economic Management in Indonesia, Malaysia and Singapore* (Asian-Pacific Tax and Investment Research Centre, Singapore, 1992), p.106; *see also* Economic Expansion Incentives (Relief from Income Tax)(Amendment) Act (No. 41 of 1993).
[465] Png, *Loc. cit.*, p.653.
[466] *See generally*, Trade Development Board (Amendment) Act (No. 16 of 1992).
[467] *Investment*, p.21.
[468] *Ibid.*, pp.22–24.
[469] *Ibid.*, pp.24–27.
[470] Administered by the Trade Development Board. *Ibid.*, p.29.
[471] Administered by the Skills Development Fund under the NPB. *Ibid.*, p.30; *see also* The Skills Development Levy (Amendment) Act (No. 19 of 1992).
[472] Administered by the National Science & Technology Board. *Investment*, p.30.
[473] Administered by the Monetary Authority of Singapore. *Ibid.*, p.31.
[474] *Ibid.*, p.15.
[475] *Ibid.*, pp.15–16.

476 *Ibid.*, p.16. *See also*, Png, *op. cit.*, p.654.
477 *Investment*, pp.16–17 (Investment Allowance Incentive). *See also*, Png, *op. cit.*, p.654.
478 *Investment*, p.16.
479 *Ibid.*, pp.17–18 (Operating Headquarters Incentive).
480 *Ibid.*, p.18.
481 *Ibid.*
482 Png, *op. cit.*, p.654.
483 *Investment*, p.18.
484 *Ibid.*, p.19.
485 *Ibid.*
486 *Ibid.*
487 *Ibid.*, p.20.
488 *Ibid.*
489 *Ibid.*, pp.20–21.
490 Income Tax Act (Cap. 141); *see also*, Income Tax (Amendment) Act (No. 11 of 1994) and Income Tax (Amendment) Act (No. 32 of 1995) and The Goods and Services Tax Act of 1993 (Cap. 117A).
491 Woon, *op. cit.*, p.251. *But see*, AELA.
492 Economic Expansion Incentives (Relief from Income Tax) Act (Cap. 135).
493 Income Tax Act, s.10(1).
494 *Investment*, p.46.
495 Woon, *op. cit.*, pp.252–253.
496 *Ibid.*, p.253.
497 *Ibid.*
498 Woon, *op. cit.*, p.254.
499 *Ibid.*
500 *Ibid.*, p.255.
501 Income Tax Act, s.12(6).
502 Woon, *op. cit.*, p.255.
503 *Ibid.*, p.259.
504 *Ibid.*, p.256.
505 *Ibid.*
506 *Ibid.*
507 *Doing Business* (Supp. 1993), p.33, Appendix XVIII.
508 *Investment*, p.46.
509 *Ibid.*
510 *Doing Business* (Supp. 1993), p.20.
511 *Investment*, p.46.
512 *Doing Business* (Supp. 1993), p.33, Appendix XVIII.
513 *Ibid.*, p.181.
514 Png, p.657.
515 *Doing Business*, pp.100–101.
516 Income Tax Act, s.13.
517 Income Tax Act, s.14(1).
518 Woon, *op. cit.*, pp.261–262.
519 Income Tax Act, s.16.
520 Income Tax Act, s.18.
521 Income Tax Act, s.19.
522 *Investment*, p.51, *citing*, Income Tax (Amendment) Act 1989.
523 Income Tax Act, s.38.
524 Income Tax Act, s.35.
525 *Doing Business* (Supp. 1993), p.20.
526 *Investment*, p.57.

[527] *Ibid.*, p.60. *But see, Doing Business* (Supp. 1993), p.21 (one time 25% tax rebate for commercial and industrial property income).

[528] *Investment*, pp.60–62.

[529] *Ibid.*, p.63.

[530] Woon, *op. cit.*, p.270.

[531] *Ibid.*

[532] Income Tax Act, s.79.

[533] Income Tax Act, s.81.

[534] *Doing Business,* pp.96–97.

[535] *Ibid.*, p.98.

[536] *Ibid.*

[537] *Ibid.*, p.100.

[538] *Ibid.*, p.101–102.

[539] *Ibid.*, p.105.

[540] *Ibid.*, p.105–6.

[541] General Agreement on Tariffs and Trade-Related Aspects of Intellectual Property Rights, Annex I.C. to the Marrakesh Agreement Establishing the World Trade Organization.

[542] *See also,* Trade Marks (Amendment) Act (No. 7 of 1992).

[543] Woon, *op. cit.*, p.224.

[544] *Ibid.*

[545] Trade Marks Act, s.10(2).

[546] Trade Marks Act, s.11(1), *see also,* Trade Marks Act, s.11(7)(a) (registered trademarks intended for assignment).

[547] Trade Marks Act, s.23.

[548] Trade Marks Act, s.18.

[549] Trade Marks Act, ss.32, 34.

[550] Trade Marks Act, s.40.

[551] Trade Marks Act, s.30.

[552] Trade Marks Act, s.45.

[553] Trade Marks Act, s.53. *See also, Erven Warnink B.V. v J. Townend & Sons (Hull) Ltd* [1979] AC 731.

[554] Trade Marks Act, s.69.

[555] *Report*, p.277.

[556] Patents Act (No. 21 of 1994). *See also,* Patents (Amendment) Act (Cap. 221 of the 1995 Rev. Ed.) (No. 40 of 1995).

[557] Registration of United Kingdom Patents Act (Cap. 271).

[558] Patents (Compulsory Licensing) Act (Cap 221) (1968).

[559] *Report*, p.278.

[560] TIAS 6923.

[561] Copyright Act (Cap. 63); *see also,* Copyright (Amendment) Act (No. 14 of 1994).

[562] Copyright Act, ss.27, 87–91.

[563] Wei, *The Law of Copyright in Singapore* (Singapore National Printers, 1989), p.39.

[564] Copyright Act, s.28(2).

[565] Copyright Act, ss.92–95.

[566] Wei, *op. cit.*, pp.103–152.

[567] *Ibid.*, pp.153–200.

[568] *Ibid.*, pp.201–210.

[569] *Anton Piller K.G. v. Mfg. Processes Ltd.* [1976] Ch. 55. *See generally,* Wei, *op. cit.*, pp.203–210.

[570] Wei, *op. cit.*, pp.211–228.

[571] *Ibid.*, p.268.

[572] *Ibid.*, p.75.

[573] *Report*, p.278.

Singapore

574 TRIPs, art. 10.
575 United Kingdom Designs (Protection) Act (Cap. 339). This Act may not be applicable pursuant to the AELA.
576 TRIPs, art.39.
577 Thorpe, *op. cit.*, p.1051, *citing*, Economist, "Freedom and Prosperity: Yes, They Do March Together, but Sometimes Out of Step" June 29, 1991, p.18.
578 *Report*, p.279.
579 *Ibid.*
580 Lin, *The Law of Advocates and Solicitors in Singapore and West Malaysia* (Butterworths 1991), p.10.
581 (Act 166 of 1976) Singapore Academy of Law (Amendment) Act (No. 34 of 1995) (Cap. 294A of 1989; Cap 208 of 1985 Rev. Ed.; and Cap. 322 of the 1985 Rev. Ed.) *See also*, The Legal Aid and Advice Act (No. 20 of 1995) (Cap. 160 of the 1985 Rev. Ed.).
582 Lin, *op. cit.*, p.8.
583 *Ibid.*, pp.170–182.
584 *Ibid.*, pp.251–258.
585 Thorpe, *op. cit.*, p.1055.
586 *Ibid.*, n.193.
587 *See above*, Part II.
588 *Doing Business*, p.33.
589 *See above.*
590 *Doing Business*, p.66.
591 *Ibid.*
592 *Ibid.*, p.67.
593 *Ibid.*
594 *Ibid.*
595 *Ibid.*, p.68.
596 Campell and Wolff, *op. cit.*, p.74.
597 Dobkin, *International Technology Joint Ventures in Countries of the Pacific Rim* (Butterworth 1988), p.155.
598 *Ibid.*
599 *Doing Business*, p.85.
600 *Ibid.*
601 *Ibid.*, p.150.
602 Dobkin, *op. cit.*, pp.161–162.
603 Campell and Wolff, *op. cit.*, pp.69–70.
604 Shahbaz, "Joint Ventures, ASEAN and the Global High Technology Industry" 18 T. Marshall L. Rev. 327, 370 (Note) (1993).
605 Campell and Wolff, *op. cit.,* p.71.
606 *Ibid.*, p.68.
607 *Ibid.*, p.69.

SOUTH KOREA

Joseph S. Cha

I. Summary of Business and Political Conditions

Basic Demographic, Political and Economic Information

The Korean Peninsula, which contains both South Korea and North Korea,   H.01
extends for nearly 600 miles south of Manchuria and separates the sea of
Japan from the Yellow Sea. South Korea (hereinafter Korea) occupies 38,000
square miles of the southern portion of the Korean Peninsula, compared to
the 47,300 square miles occupied by North Korea in the north. Only about
one-fifth of the land, primarily the rice-growing river valleys and coastal
river basins, is arable and the entire Peninsula is quite mountainous. Korea's
relative lack of natural resources, as well as its close proximity to China —
Beijing is 500 miles to the west — and Japan, which lies 150 miles to the
south-east, has had a significant effect upon the social and economic development of the nation, particularly during the last two centuries. As of mid-
1994, the estimated population of South Korea was approximately 45.5
million, and it is estimated that the country's population will grow to about
54 million by the year 2020.

For nearly a thousand years before its partition after World War II, Korea
was an autonomous ethnic, cultural, linguistic, and political entity. Because
of the extreme isolationism of its last ruling dynasty, traditional Korea did
not establish formal relations with any country other than China until it was
forced to do so in the last quarter of the 19th century. Prior to the 20th
century, Korea's dominant ideological tradition emphasized the subordina-
tion of individual interests to those of the group and an authority structure of
ranked status and power. Even today, differences in rank and prestige are
constantly emphasized through language and behavior and are reinforced
through the internal structures of the family, schools, business firms, and
even social or sports clubs.

South Korea

Individualism also plays a significant and dynamic role in the Korean ideology. In contrast to other Confucian-based societies, Korean ideological tradition did not necessarily assign a priority to the demands of the state over individual moral imperatives, particularly with regard to family issues. Good government was defined by adherence to the universal right to benevolent rule, and the duties that are required of individuals are contingent on the proper fulfillment of that right. Each individual recognizes his duty to serve his superior loyally and faithfully, however he is also inclined to judge his superior's behavior on moral grounds and is highly sensitive to the issue of whether or not he is being treated fairly.

In addition to the ideological and religious elements within the Korean society, its history of chronic poverty, foreign occupation, political oppression, and limited social mobility has had a dynamic effect on the ambitions of modern Koreans. Two recent historical events, in the form of the separate occupations of Korea first by Japan and then the United States during the first part of this century have had profound effects on Korean development during the last 40 years. Moreover, traditional affiliations of a rural society had been upset by the ravages of war and the great migrations to the urban areas have forced individuals to rely on their own wits and resources and to decide their own destinies.

Korea's period as a Japanese colony, and the imposition of the "Japanese system", during the first part of the 20th century intensified Korean patriotism and also helped stimulate the nation, in a remarkably short period of time, out of its previous ways of thinking and acting and into a new period of modernization, industrialization, and urbanization. Due to the relative abundance of agricultural land and natural resources in Korea, economic development was focused on the production of crude and semi-processed agricultural and mineral products for export within the Japanese empire. But the Japanese also devoted capital equipment and human resources toward industrializing the Korean economy during this period with the result that the contribution of the manufacturing sector to Korean net commodity product rose from an average of 3.5 per cent during 1910–1915 to 22 per cent in 1940.

The period between 1945 and 1960 was marked by heavy American military and economic involvement in the domestic economy. The principal objective of Korea's foreign economic policy during that period was to maximize the inflow of economic and military aid from public sources and capital inflows from private sources were not encouraged. The United States and, to a much less degree, the United Nations provided virtually all resource inflows during this time, largely in the form of grant assistance. The massive inflow of foreign assistance before and during the Korean War was essential to the survival of South Korea as an independent country. Continuation of a high level of economic assistance for the decade after the war probably was the reason that the economy was able to achieve even the meager 1.5 per cent per annum growth rate in per capita income during that period.

Without even the minimal economic growth achieved during the 1950s, the standard of living of the Koreans would have remained desperate, political unrest would have continued, and the country would have been unable to lay the foundations for subsequent economic growth. As late as 1961 Korea continued to suffer from almost all the difficulties facing any typical developing country today. Korea's gross national product per capita in current prices in that year was a meager $87. The country, already over-populated, was experiencing an annual population growth rate of 3 per cent, and there was widespread unemployment and underemployment. Domestic savings were negligible and the nation had no significant exports to offset a chronic balance of payments deficit.

Sustained economic development did not get under way until after General Park Chung Hee came to power in 1961 as a result of a military coup. President Park imposed on the country a developmental strategy of modernization through planned growth and combined it with a determination to maintain a strong military posture against the danger of renewed attack from North Korea. Military standards of discipline and achievement were transferred to the bureaucracy and production, the value of exports, employment, and wages began to rise significantly and continued to progress well into the 1970s. Major institutions, such as commercial banks, were "nationalized" in order to effect the government's economic plans. **H.02**

After 1961 the Korean government began to promote inflows of foreign resources of all kinds. As a result, a rapidly increasing diversification of sources of foreign influence has characterized the development of Korea over the last three decades. Moreover, as import substitution opportunities began to falter, the nation began to adopt measures that mobilized domestic and foreign resources to achieve rapid economic development through export-oriented industrialization. Fiscal and monetary reforms were enacted to increase public and private savings, a uniform exchange rate was adopted, and by 1966 exporters virtually operated under a free-trade regime and were paying no more than world market prices for domestic and foreign inputs. Korean exporters also enjoyed access to private loans from the United States, Japan, and Western Europe, primarily in the form of suppliers' credits of one type or another.

As a result of the foregoing policies, the average annual rate of growth in the index of manufacturing output rose to 24 per cent between 1965 and 1975 (compared to 11 per cent during the previous 10 year period) and the shares of exports in gross manufacturing output rose from roughly 6 per cent in 1965 to almost 25 per cent by 1975. By 1975, Korea was a major exporter in a number of traditional and relatively new industrial sectors and grew into the world's 12th largest trading nation by the end of the last decade. Korea's per capita GNP rose an impressive 8.5 per cent per annum from 1980–92, and exports rose at an average annual rate of 11.9 per cent (same as the PRC) during the same period. Most forecasts of economic growth for Korea in the near future anticipate gains exceeding those of most other economies in the region, although export growth has been slowing somewhat in the last few years. Korea has expanded its export base, and is no longer as dependent on exports to the United States and within the region.

Like Japan, Korea has overcome its relatively poor endowment of natural resources by successfully implemented a strategy of export-led industrialization. Korea has been heavily influenced by the successes and practices of the Japanese and, due to the long period of occupation and involvement in the economy, the policies of the United States. Long-term development plans for Korea call for a continuing decline in the agricultural sector of the economy with corresponding increases in manufacturing, social overhead, and services. Within the manufacturing sector the shift from light to heavy industry is expected to continue with the output composition therein changing drastically to emphasize machinery, electronics, automobiles, and industrial chemicals. Employment shares in the economy as a whole will continue to shift from the agricultural sector to the manufacturing sector and, within the manufacturing sector, further shifts will lead to an increase the share of employment in electronics and reduction of employment in such traditional areas as textiles.

II. Laws and Institutions Affecting Business and Commercial Activities

Competition Law

Anti-Dumping

H.03　Anti-dumping duties have generally not been imposed by Korea with frequency in the past, but as import tariffs have been coming down, the Korean government is becoming more assertive about protecting its local industries from unfair trade by foreign countries. The Customs Act[1] provides the framework for imposing anti-dumping duties in accordance with GATT Article VI and Anti-Dumping Code.[2] The basic rule on anti-dumping is that if the import price is lower than its normal value (thus constituting dumping) and the dumping causes or threatens to cause material injury to a domestic industry that is deemed to require protection, an anti-dumping duty may be imposed up to the amount of difference between the normal value and dumping price (Customs Act, Art. 10(1)). As such, in order to determine dumping this four-pronged test consisting of dumping, material injury, causation, and necessity of protection must be satisfied.

First, in determining dumping, the normal value is ordinarily defined as the ordinary transaction price of like goods or similar goods in the exporting country, and imported price is the price paid or to be paid (Enforcement Decree (E.D.) of Customs Act, Art. 4-6(1)). Second, material injury is defined as material injury to a domestic industry, a clear and imminent threat of material injury or material retardation of the establishment of a domestic industry,[3] and the determination must have a basis in substantial evidence including import quantity, price, market share, real or potential effect on domestic industry, increase in rate of dumping, etc. (E.D. of Customs Act, Art. 4-7). Third, it must be established that the dumped imports caused the material injury. Although there is no accepted rule, the causation would be determined by looking into factors showing injury beyond the mere entry of dumped imports.[4] The fourth prong is a policy consideration analyzing the necessity of protecting a domestic industry. Some factors to be considered are impact on domestic industry, domestic price, exports and related domestic industries, effectiveness of other protections for the domestic industry, whether merchandise is a promoted item, and other public interest.[5]

The anti-dumping procedure in Korea begins with a complaint filed with the Korea Trade Commission (KTC). The KTC then initiates an investigation and within a month decides whether to proceed with the complaint or turn down the complaint for reasons such as insufficient evidence to presume the existence of dumping or material injury, the dumping margin or injury is minimal, petitioner not qualified to bring the complain, or other special reasons.[6] Once the KTC decides to go ahead with the investigation, a two step investigation begins.

In the preliminary investigation stage the Customs Administration investigates dumping and the KTC investigates whether the dumping causes or threatens material injury to a domestic industry or materially retards a domestic industry.[7] Based on this preliminary investigation, the Ministry of Finance and Economy (MOFE) may impose provisional measures or require a deposit of security, or terminate the investigation for a negative report.[8] Provisional anti-dumping duties may be imposed for up to four months if it is deemed necessary to prevent injury during the period of investigation and there is sufficient evidence of dumping and substantial damage (Customs Act, Art. 10(2) and E.D. of Customs Act, Art. 4-10). At this point, some negotiation with the government may be possible in that the exporters may offer an undertaking to the MOFE.[9] The exporter can propose to revise the imported price to eliminate damage caused by the dumping; if the proposal is accepted by MOFE, the exporter must submit a written promise (Customs Act, Art. 10(3) and E.D. of Customs Act, Art. 4-11).

The main investigation by the KTC and the Customs Administration is completed within three months, and if material injury and dumping are found, the MOFE may impose anti-dumping duties within one month. The anti-dumping duty is usually calculated as the difference between the normal value and dumping price. In determining this difference or margin, however, comparison should be made at the same time and transaction step and adjustments must be made for differences in physical characteristics, quantity, conditions of sale, and differences in assessment (E.D. of Customs Act, Art.

4–6(5)). In calculating the relevant prices, Korea applies the accumulated average method.[10] The MOFE's imposition of anti-dumping duty may be appealed to the courts and also to the World Trade Organization dispute settlement mechanism.[11]

Safeguard Measures for the Protection of Domestic Industries

H.04 The Foreign Trade Act (FTA)[12] further regulates international trade by providing that if a domestic industry is seriously injured by increased imports of particular goods, increase in the trade and supply of distribution services or by infringement on intellectual property rights, the relevant domestic industry can request an investigation by the KTC (FTA, Art. 32). Upon finding of serious injury, the KTC can order limits on the quantity of such imports, adjust the customs tariff, suspend or prohibit importation, or other appropriate measures (FTA, Art. 34). Provisional measures are also possible if the domestic industry would potentially be damaged irrevocably during the period of investigation (FTA, Art. 35). Also, under the Technology Development Promotion Act,[13] domestic technology infant industries may be temporarily protected for up to five years from foreign investment and competition.

Monopoly Regulation and Fair Trade

H.05 The Monopoly Regulation and Fair Trade Act (MRFTA)[14] aims to promote competition and prevent market domination by regulating market-dominating activities, corporate acquisitions and combinations, collaborative activities, unfair trade practices, and international contracts (MRFTA, Art. 1). The Fair Trade Commission (FTC) enforces provisions of the MRFTA by conducting investigations, ordering corrective measures, and imposing penalties and sanctions (MRFTA, Art. 49).

Under the MRFTA, prohibited unfair trade practices include discrimination, eliminating competitors, coercing a competitor's customer, utilizing an unreasonable bargaining position, dealing on terms and conditions that unreasonably restrict business activity, and deceptive and misleading advertising and use of trademark (Art. 23). Fixing resale prices are also prohibited (MRFTA, Art. 29). Collaborative activities, which include agreements on fixing prices, fixing sales terms, restricting production, shipment or sale, restricting sales territory, restricting new establishment or expansion, restricting kind or size of sales, establishing a firm for collaborative undertaking, and restricting other businesses are also prohibited unless approved by the FTC for enumerated conditions. (MRFTA, Arts. 19, 21 and 22.) The FTC can order corrective measures and impose penalties for non-compliance, and impose surcharges for engaging in unfair trade practices or collaborative activities.

The domestic parties of an international agreement or contract, including joint ventures, are required to report the transaction to the FTC within 30 days (MRFTA, Art. 33). Provisions constituting collaborative activity, resale price fixing, and unfair trade practice are prohibited unless the FTC finds that the effect of such clauses are negligible or for other reasons acceptable (MRFTA, Art. 32). The specific unfair clauses for a joint venture include requiring raw materials to be provided by the foreign partner, requiring exports to be approved by the foreign partner, and having exports exported through the foreign partner.[15] The FTC may order corrective measures to omit the offending clauses (MRFTA, Art. 34). It may be advisable to enter into agreements using the Standard Joint Venture Agreement and Standard Technical License Agreement published by the Office of Fair Trade, as it would avoid the examination for unfair clauses by the FTC. Mandatory reporting is no longer required for technology transfer agreement as a voluntary validation system has replaced reporting. The FTC, nevertheless, has authority to investigate technology transfer agreements and impose monetary sanctions for MRFTA violations.

In addition, the MRFTA prohibits market-dominating entrepreneurs, who are defined as entrepreneurs whose domestic supply of a particular product exceeds 50 million Won, from price fixing, exercising control over sales, business interference, obstructing competitors, substantially hindering competition, or eroding consumer interests (MRFTA, Art. 3). The FTC can take appropriate measures, including price reduction and ordering the cessation of unreasonable activities, for violations (MRFTA, Art. 5). Non-compliance with FTC orders can result in the imposition of surcharges based on the entrepreneur's market-dominating activities (MRFTA, Art. 6).

Trade Secrets

The Unfair Competition Prevention Act (UCPA)[16] was recently amended   **H.06** to regulate the unauthorized use of trade secrets. A trade secret is defined as a method of production, sale, or information concerning technology or management beneficial to business activities unknown to the public because of efforts to keep secret. Its infringing acts include acquiring a trade secret by theft, deception or assault; disclosing such secret to a third party; utilizing or disclosing trade secret with knowledge of unfair acquisition or gross negligence; or utilizing or disclosing trade secret by one under obligation to keep secret for purpose of obtaining unjust profits or injuring the trade secret holder (UCPA, Art. 2). The remedies available for infringement are injunctive orders, compensation for damages, and restoration of reputation (UCPA, Arts. 4 to 6 and 10 to 12). The limitations in a trade secret action are that only Paris Convention member country business and individuals may claim under the UCPA and the availability of remedies will lapse unless exercised within one year of discovering the infringing act (UCPA, Art. 14).

Contract Law

H.07 The domestic contract laws of Korea, as is with other civil law countries, are part of the Civil Code[17] section on obligations. To any given contractual transaction, the applicable contract law depends on the expressed or implied intention of the parties, but if not specified, the law of the place where contractual relationship arose, the place of offer, or domicile of the offeror will apply (Conflict of Laws Act,[18] Art. 11). Although parties are generally free to agree to contract provisions, it should be noted that with certain types of international contracts the government oversees the contract by requiring reports to the Fair Trade Commission by the domestic party and by ordering correction of unreasonable provisions. Also, even when foreign law applies to a contract, provisions contrary to Korean good customs and social order will not be given effect (Conflict of Laws Act, Art. 5).

Generally, a contract comes into effect and becomes binding after an offer is made and accepted. An offer must be accepted within the stipulated period or within a reasonable time if the period is not stipulated (Civil Code, Arts. 527, 528 and 529). An acceptance is effective upon dispatch, but if an acceptance is sent before the expiration of the stipulated period and is calculated to arrive within that period but arrives late, the acceptance is not effective if the offeror immediately sends notice of the lateness (Civil Code, Art. 528). The offeror, however, may treat the delayed acceptance as a new offer (Civil Code, Art. 528). An acceptance is not always necessary as a contract may be effective based on an implied acceptance that hinges on the occurrence of a certain event if that is the manifestation of intent or is customary (Civil Code, Art. 532). Also, where two offers by the same parties regarding the same content are simultaneously dispatched, a contract may be formed when each receives the offer (Civil Code, Art. 533). An acceptance with conditions or modifications is considered a rejection and a counter-offer (Civil Code, Art. 534).

In other formation issues, the capacity to contract is limited by an age of majority, which is 20, and for the feeble-minded and spendthrifts, but a foreigner who takes legal actions in Korea and is incompetent under foreign law is deemed competent if competent under Korean law (Conflict of Laws Act, Art. 6). Faults in contracting, such as mistake, fraud, duress, and undue influence, all render a contract voidable. In Korea, there is also no formal requirements for a valid contract.

A contract of gift becomes binding when the donor manifests an intent to gratuitously transfer property and the donee accepts (Civil Code, Art. 554). The contract of gift, however, can be rescinded if the contract is not in writing or if the financial status of the donor has changed to such an extent that the donor's living conditions would be severely affected by performance (Civil Code, Arts. 555 and 557). As for unjust enrichment issues, an unjustly enriched party who benefits from another and causes loss is required to return the benefits or its value (Civil Code, Arts. 741 and 747). If the obligor renders performance in error, the obligee is again required to return, but if there was bad faith, the obligor may not demand return (Civil Code, Art. 743).

After a contract comes into effect, if the time for performance is stipulated for one party, it is presumed that this is the time for performance for the other party (Civil Code, Arts. 585). Performance may be refused in a bilateral contract until the other party tenders performance when due or if there is reason to believe the other party will not perform (Civil Code, Art. 536). If performance becomes impossible because of the obligee or because of the obligee's delay in accepting performance, the obligor is entitled to counter-performance (Civil Code, Art. 538). If one of the parties to a bilateral contract cannot perform due to neither of the parties' fault, however, the other party will not be entitled to performance (Civil Code, Art. 537). A third party who is the direct beneficiary of performance may demand performance directly from the obligor and such rights cannot be extinguished by the parties to the contract (Civil Code, Arts. 540 and 541).

Additionally, if one party does not perform when due, the other party may demand performance within a reasonable period and may rescind the contract if no performance is forthcoming (Civil Code, Art. 544). If the obligor manifests an intent not to perform, however, no demand is required for recession (Civil Code, Art. 544). If the objective of the contract is unattainable unless performed at a specific time period and one party does not perform during this period, the other may rescind without making a demand (Civil Code, Art. 545). If performance becomes impossible due to actions of the obligor, the obligee may also rescind the contract (Civil Code, Art. 546). Any right of future recession or the right of rescission may be effected by manifestation of intention to the other party, and if several persons constitute the other party, the rescission is indivisible and must be effected against all (Civil Code, Arts. 543 and 547). After rescission, each party is liable to restore each other to their original position (Civil Code, Art. 548).

The obligor is responsible for damages caused by delay in performance if rendered after a fixed period or after demand is made, and the obligee may be liable for delay in accepting performance (Civil Code, Arts. 387, 392 and 400). If performance is not voluntarily forthcoming, a request may be made for compulsory performance from the court as long as the nature of the obligation permits or the obligee can refuse performance and claim damages (Civil Code, Arts. 389 and 395). Damages can be claimed for failure to perform as long as the obligor was at fault (Civil Code, Art. 389). Damages are limited to ordinary damages recoverable in money (Civil Code, Arts. 393 and 394). In determining damages fault may be taken into consideration (Civil Code, Art. 396). The interest recoverable for non-performance of a monetary debt is the legal rate (six per cent for commercial transaction debts) or a reasonable agreed rate (Civil Code, Art. 397). The parties can agree to liquidated damages, but if found unreasonable, the court has discretion to reduce damages (Civil Code, Art. 398). The obligee may revoke and be returned to the original state if the obligor acts to prejudice the property right (Civil Code, Art. 406).

H.08   If there are several obligees or obligors, each has rights and duties in equal proportion, unless otherwise agreed (Civil Code, Art. 408). If the obligations are indivisible, each obligor can demand performance on behalf of the other obligors, and the obligors can render performance to any obligee (Civil Code, Art. 409). For joint and several obligations, where each of several obligors can perform the entire obligation, performance by one obligor discharges the other obligors, an obligee may demand performance from one or all (simultaneously or in succession, in whole or in part) which is effective against all; one joint obligor's avoidance of obligation does not affect the others; and a novation or set-off for one joint obligor extinguishes other obligor's obligation, but a release affects only that joint obligor's share (Civil Code, Arts. 413 to 419).

Claims may be assigned unless contrary to the nature of the claim or agreed otherwise (Civil Code, Art. 449). An assumption of an obligation by a third party contracting with the obligee is possible to discharge the obligation of the original obligor unless it is against the will of the obligor or the nature of the obligation, and an assumption of debt by a third person in a contract with the obligor is effective when the obligee gives consent (Civil Code, Arts. 453 and 454). In assigning claims and assuming obligations, however, the rights of third parties are not affected.

The discharge of an obligation can take different forms. One obvious way to discharge an obligor from liability for default is performance (Civil Code, Art. 461). The performance must strictly follow the obligation, but if the obligee had previously refused tender or an act by the obligee is required for performance, notification of performance and request for acceptance is sufficient (Civil Code, Art. 460). The obligor may be liable for performance effected earlier than the time for performance (Civil Code, Art. 468). Performance by a third person is possible, but may be precluded if the nature of the obligation or the agreement does not permit. In other methods of discharge, a deposit of the subject matter of the obligation at the deposit office when an obligee refuses or is unable to accept performance relieves the obligation (Civil Code, Arts. 487 and 488). A set-off of similar obligations when both become due is possible to extinguish both parties' obligations up to the corresponding amount (Civil Code, Art. 492). A set-off requires manifestation of intent without conditions or time limits (Civil Code, Art. 493). An obligation is extinguished by novation when the essential elements of the original obligation are modified or when the obligee manifests intent to the obligor to release the obligor from the obligation (Civil Code, Arts. 500 and 506). Finally, when a right and its corresponding obligation become vested in one person the obligation is discharged (Civil Code, Art. 507). Unless discharge is effected by performance, however, third party rights may be unaffected.

Commercial Law

Sales of Goods

Korea has not acceded to the United Nations Convention on Contracts for   H.09
the International Sale of Goods and, as a result, the applicable law depends on
specific contractual provisions or upon the place of contracting. On most
matters the contractual provisions are applicable, but the Civil Code
and Commercial Code supply specified rules when there are no specific
provisions.

According to the Civil Code, a sale becomes effective when one party
agrees to transfer and another party agrees to purchase goods (Art. 563). The
obligation of the parties once there is a contract for sale is that the seller will
transfer the property right to the buyer and the buyer will pay the price of the
property to the seller (Civil Code, Art. 568). If the purchase price is required
to be paid simultaneously with the delivery of the subject matter of the sale,
payment is to be tendered at the place of delivery (Civil Code, Art. 586). An
option contract for sale becomes effective when the optionee expresses an
intention to conclude the sale (Civil Code, Art. 564).

For commercial transactions, special rules apply for formation of the
contract. An offer made face-to-face lapses if not immediately accepted and
for other situations, if a period is not specified for acceptance, the offer lapses
if not accepted within a reasonable period (Commercial Code, Arts. 51 and
52). Under the Commercial Code, when a merchant receives an offer relating
to his business from a regular business partner, however, the merchant will be
deemed to have accepted the offer unless a notice of rejection is dispatched
without delay (Art. 53).[19] It should be noted that all companies are considered merchants for such purposes (Commercial Code, Art. 5).

Upon the sale of goods, several warranties attach to the transaction unless
agreed otherwise. If the object of the sale did not initially belong to the seller,
the seller is under an obligation to acquire ownership and transfer to buyer,
otherwise the buyer may rescind the contract and collect damages if buyer
was not aware the object did not belong to the seller (Civil Code, Arts. 569
to 571). If the seller is unable to acquire and transfer a part of the property
right or if the contracted quantity is short or has been lost, the buyer may
demand reduction of the purchase price in proportion or rescind the contract, and also claim damages (Civil Code, Arts. 572 to 574). If the buyer was
unaware of defects in the subject matter of the sale, within six months of
discovery, the buyer may rescind the contract if the objective of the contract
is unattainable, but otherwise the buyer may only be entitled to damages
(Civil Code, Arts. 580 and 582). The same rule applies if the subject matter of
the sale was specified in kind and afterwards defects are found in the designated subject matter, but the buyer may demand delivery of non-defective
goods without having to rescind or claim damages (Civil Code, Art. 581).

South Korea

Disclaimers by the seller for the above warranties are not applicable for liability arising from facts known by the seller but not disclosed, or with respect to any right the seller created in favor of or assigned to a third person (Civil Code, Art. 584). Between merchants, when taking delivery, the buyer must immediately examine the goods after delivery and immediately dispatch notice of defect or deficiency, otherwise the buyer foregoes the right to rescind, demand reduction in price, or to claim damages (Commercial Code, Art. 69). A similar immediate notice is required for defects not immediately discoverable once the defect is discovered (Commercial Code, Art. 69).

Between merchants, the Commercial Code provides for additional rules. If the buyer refuses or is unable to take delivery, the seller may deposit the goods with a competent authority or after notice sell at auction (Commercial Code, Art. 67). If performance is required at a specific time or period for attaining the object of the contract and one party allows this time period to lapse, the other party is deemed to have rescinded the contract unless performance is immediately demanded (Commercial Code, Art. 68). If the buyer does rescind the contract for good cause, the goods must be held in custody or deposited with a competent authority at the seller's expense, but if the goods are susceptible to loss or deterioration, the buyer must sell at auction with permission of the court (Commercial Code, Art. 70). If a claim becomes due, the obligee may retain chattel obtained through commercial transactions with the obligor until performance is forthcoming (Commercial Code, Art. 58). A merchant has a duty to hold goods at the expense of the offeror, even if he rejects the offer (Commercial Code, Art. 60).

Carriage of Goods

H.10   Regarding transactions for the sale of goods, a discussion of carriage of goods and documentary transfers may be important for international transactions. Korea's banks have adhered to the Uniform Customs and Practice for Documentary Credits, but those provisions apply to transactions between member country companies only if incorporated in the documents. The Commercial Code, nevertheless, sets out some basic rules if not specifically provided in the documents.

A carrier is required to furnish a bill of lading upon demand by the consignor and if a bill of lading is made, a demand for delivery must be accompanied by the bill of lading as it may be transferred by endorsement (Commercial Code, Arts. 128 to 130). Matters relating to carriage are to be governed by provisions of the bill of lading and the disposition of goods made according to the same provisions (Commercial Code, Arts. 131 and 132).

If goods are lost, in whole or in part, and not due to the consignor's fault, the carrier cannot demand freight and if pre-paid, must refund the amount (Commercial Code, Art. 134). If loss is due to the consignor's fault or because of the nature of the goods, however, the carrier can claim the full freight amount (Commercial Code, Art. 134). In general, a carrier is not relieved of liability for damages, loss, or delay unless the carrier proves exercise of due care with regard to receipt, delivery, custody, and carriage of the goods by the carrier, forwarding agent, and any employees (Commercial Code, Art. 135). With valuable instruments, money, and other valuables, the carrier is liable only if the consignor expressly noted their description and value (Commercial Code, Art. 136). Damages are determined by value at the time when the goods should have been delivered in the case of total loss, and value at the time of delivery for partial loss (Commercial Code, Art. 137). If loss, damage, or delay is caused intentionally or by gross negligence, the carrier is liable for all damages (Commercial Code, Art. 137). Another remedy available is that the consignor may demand the discontinuance carriage and return of goods, but in such a case the carrier may demand freight for the portion of the carriage already concluded (Commercial Code, Art. 139).

A consignee has the same rights as the consignor and has the duty to pay freight and other expenses to the carrier (Commercial Code, Art. 140). If a consignee cannot be ascertained, the carrier may deposit the goods with a competent authority and also sell the goods by official auction if the known consignor or holder of the bill of lading does not give instructions as to disposal (Commercial Code, Art. 142). If the consignor, the holder of the bill of lading, and the consignee are all unascertainable, the carrier must give public notice and a period of at least six months to claim before selling the goods by official auction (Commercial Code, Art. 144). The liability of the carrier ends when the delivery has been effected without any reservation and freight is paid, unless there is defect not immediately discoverable (Commercial Code, Art. 146).

Secured Transactions

Under Korean laws and customs, security for transactions comes under two categories: personal and real. Although most of these security mechanisms are used in connection with loan agreements, they may be flexible enough to cover credit sales. The personal security that is applicable for securing payment would be by assigning a surety. A surety is liable for the obligation when the principal defaults, including interest on the principal obligation, penalty, compensation for damages, and other charges incidental to the principal obligation (Civil Code, Arts. 428 and 429). Creation of a surety is possible by mere agreement.

H.11

As to real rights, the types available for goods is a pledge and *yangdo tambo* (security by transfer of title). As a traditional pledge would not be commercially practicable because it requires possession of the good by the creditor, a modified pledge based on carriage bills (bill of lading and waybills), warehouse bills, or industrial rights may prove effective. Under each of these circumstances, the possession of a document by the creditor becomes analogous to holding the goods since the documents give rights to posses-sion.[20] The formalities required are agreement and delivery of the document, and the possession of the document ensures priority over other creditors.

The *yangdo tambo* is not enumerated under Korea laws, but is a long recognized custom and established by case law.

> "[A] *yangdo tambo* involves the transfer in trust of the title of the collateral from the debtor (or a third party surety) to the creditor, on a condition that the title will be returned to the debtor (or a third party real surety) upon payment of the loan."[21]

The creation is simple and the consequence is that the creditor has priority to the collateral.

Companies Law

H.12 The presence of a foreign company in Korea can take many different forms depending on the extent of contact and investment. It may try to test the waters by establishing a liaison or branch office, or set up a full-fledged company by means of a joint venture or a wholly-owned subsidiary.

Generally, under the Commercial Code a foreign company that intends to conduct business in Korea must appoint a representative, establish a business office, effect same registration as a branch office of a domestic company of the same nature, and simultaneously effect registration of the proper law on which it had been incorporated (Commercial Code, Art. 614). If the foreign office in Korea is the principle office or its chief object is to engage in business in Korea, the office must comply with the same provisions as a company incorporated in Korea, but in any case, a foreign company (includ-ing liaison and branch offices) is deemed to be a company formed in Korea of the same nature insofar as the application of other laws is concerned (Com-mercial Code, Arts. 617 and 621). The courts can order dissolution of such foreign business offices for the same reasons as a domestic company (Com-mercial Code, Art. 619).

Liaison and Branch Offices

H.13 A liaison office is a preliminary presence of a foreign corporation and is established by reporting to the Bank of Korea.[22] It is a not a legal entity and as long as its activities are merely preliminary and not income-producing, it is not subject to Korean taxes.[23] As a consequence, legal acts of the liaison office cannot be conducted in the firm's name and the firm's function is basically limited to information gathering and promotion for the home of-fice.[24] The activities are limited to simple purchase and storage of assets not for sale, advertisement, public relations, information processing, market sur-vey or other preparatory and auxiliary business activities.[25] The liaison office may only conduct such work for the home office otherwise it would be a taxable act.

A branch office, on the other hand, is an entity capable of conducting business in Korea. As a legal entity, a branch office can conduct activities in its own name and is more flexible than a liaison office in that it can remain tax-free by only engaging in non-taxable activities or conducting profit-making and taxable activities, such as trading, sales, and service activities with the exception of manufacturing and certain other specific exceptions.[26] The choice to establish a liaison office or a branch office may depend on other tax issues such as permanent establishment status.

As with a liaison office, only reporting to the Bank of Korea is required for establishment of a branch office, but approval by the MOFE is necessary if the branch wants to repatriate funds; the approval usually requires at least 50 million Won capital or three years of operating history.[27] The branch needs to keep within the bounds of approved activities as only profits from such activities may be repatriated. In addition, a branch office is a taxable presence and must be recorded as a legal entity with the commercial record-ing office and with the appropriate tax office as well as receiving approval from the Bank of Korea.[28]

Although liaison and branch offices may have advantages over subsidiaries and joint-ventures in that a corporation need not be incorporated and main-tained in Korea, a drawback is that these entities are not separate legal entities with limited liability and the overseas foreign company may be liable for claims beyond the branch office's assets.[29]

Corporations

A corporation is a legal person and comes into existence upon registration of incorporation at the site of its principle office (Commercial Code, Arts. 171 and 172). The Commercial Code enumerates four types of corporate forms: general partnership (*hapmyong-hoesa*), limited partnership (*hapcha-hoesa*), stock corporation (*chusik-hoesa*), and private limited corporation (*yuhan-hoesa*) (Commercial Code, Art. 169). As foreign companies cannot engage in the two types of partnerships because of legal or practical reasons,[30] the foreign company is limited to forming a stock corporation or a private limited corporation. In joint ventures and wholly-owned subsidiaries of foreign companies, the stock corporation is the most commonly used. It should be noted that after completing incorporation, the new entity needs to register with the local tax office, report and register with the MOFE as a foreign-invested enterprise, and obtain the applicable licenses and registra-tions required to conduct business.

H.14

Stock Corporations

The formation of a stock corporation requires at least seven promoters to prepare and notarize the articles of incorporation (Commercial Code, Arts.

H.14

288 and 289). The formation capital must be at least 50 million won and the amount of shares, which must be equal, must be at least 5,000 won (Commercial Code, Art. 329.) For a stock corporation, the transfer of shares cannot be prohibited or restricted and the liability of shareholders is limited to the value of shares (Commercial Code, Arts. 331 and 335).

During incorporation all of the shares can be bought by the promoters or a subscription of shares can be made (Commercial Code, Arts. 301 to 307). After capital contribution is made, a constituent meeting must be called to appoint directors and auditors (Commercial Code, Arts. 296 and 312). For promotive companies, the directors apply to the court to appoint an inspector to inquire into the incorporation and for subscriptive companies, the directors and auditors investigate the incorporation (Commercial Code, Arts. 298 to 300). The registration of the incorporation must be effected within two weeks of inquiry by inspector for a promotive company or the termination of the constituent meeting or alteration for a subscriptive company (Commercial Code, Art. 317). In connection with the incorporation promoters and officers are jointly and severally liable for neglecting to perform duties and for failing to complete incorporation (Commercial Code, Art. 326).

The total number of shares at the time of incorporation must be at least one-fourth the total authorized and matters such as class, number of shares, number and amount of shares above par value must be determined with the consent of all the promoters or be provided for in the articles of incorporation (Commercial Code, Arts. 289 and 291). The company can also issue different classes of shares with respect to profits, interest, surplus assets, voting, and can provide for the conversion of shares from one class to another according to the articles of incorporation (Commercial Code, Arts. 344, 346 and 370). The board of directors usually determines issuance of new shares, the class and number, issue-price, method on take, and matters on transfer of pre-emptive rights to new shares (Commercial Code, Art. 416). A stock company may invite subscription for debentures, but the total amount may not exceed twice the stated capital and reserve funds (Commercial Code, Arts. 469 and 470). The stock company is generally restricted from acquiring its own shares (Commercial Code, Art. 341).

The general meeting of shareholders adopts resolutions on matters provided in the Commercial Code or the articles of incorporation and must be convened at least once a year at the principle office or adjacent locality with at least two weeks written notification (Commercial Code, Arts. 361 to 365). The board of directors or shareholders with at least five per cent share can convene a meeting (Commercial Code, Art. 362). Most resolutions are adopted by a majority of votes with majority quorum, unless the articles of incorporation provide otherwise, and each shareholder has one vote per share of voting stock (Commercial Code, Arts. 368 and 369). Certain matters such as the alteration of the articles of incorporation and reduction of stated capital are effected by resolution of the general meeting by a two-thirds majority vote (Commercial Code, Arts. 433 to 435 and 438).

At least three directors are to be appointed at the general meeting by majority vote (no cumulative voting) for a term not exceeding three years and, in the same way, directors may be removed from office (Commercial Code, Arts. 382 to 385). In joint ventures, the foreign shareholder nominated directors cannot exceed the foreign shareholder's equity per centage and may not have the tie-breaking vote.[31] The meeting of board of directors is convened by giving a week's notice or by consent, and the resolutions are adopted by majority vote and majority quorum (Commercial Code, Arts. 390 and 391). The powers of the board of directors include "administering the affairs of the company, the appointment of or removal of a manager, and the establishment, change or discontinuance of a branch" (Commercial Code, Art. 393). An auditor is also appointed at general meetings, but shareholders with more than three per cent of voting shares may not vote in appointing the auditor (Commercial Code, Art. 409). Directors are required to prepare financial statements consisting of a balance sheet, profits and loss statement, and statement of disposition of unappropriated retained earnings or a statement of treatment of deficit, and a business report (Commercial Code, Arts. 447 and 447–2). The documents are presented to the auditors at least six weeks prior to the general meeting and the auditor makes an auditing report (Commercial Code, Arts. 447–3 and 447–4). The auditor reports on the functions of the directors, examines proposals and documents submitted to the general meeting, and states opinions on actions that may violate law, violate the articles of incorporation, or are seriously unreasonable (Commercial Code, Arts. 412 and 413). Under the Act Concerning External Audit of Joint Stock Corporation,[32] stock corporations with stated assets above a certain amount are subject to external auditing and the company must select and appoint an auditor within four months from the start of each business year. Both directors and auditors are jointly and severally liable for contravention of law or the articles of incorporation, or for neglecting to perform duties.

Corporations are generally permitted to merge, and upon merger the **H.15** execution of the articles of incorporation and other acts must be jointly effected by the organizing committees appointed by each of the companies (Commercial Code, Arts. 174 and 175). For effecting merger of companies, a written agreement must be prepared and approved by a two-thirds majority of shareholders at the general meeting (Commercial Code, Art. 522). If one of the companies is to remain after the merger, a general meeting needs to be convened or if a new company is to be incorporated through the merger, the merger must be registered within two weeks at the locality of principle office and within three weeks at the locality of each branch and also register the alteration and dissolution (Commercial Code, Arts. 523, 524, 526 and 528). Within six months of the merger, an action for nullification of the merger may be bought by a shareholder, director, auditor, liquidator, administrator in bankruptcy, or by creditors who disapprove of the merger (Commercial Code, Art. 529). Large conglomerates' corporate combinations and mergers are further scrutinized by the Monopoly Regulation and Fair Trade Act, which takes into account anti-trust issues. As with other extraordinary acts, mergers involving a foreign-invested corporation requires approval of the MOFE.

The courts can order the dissolution of any type of corporation when the object of the company is illegal, the company fails to commence business one year after incorporation or discontinues business for a year or longer, or when the director or a member administering affairs of the company commits acts in violation of laws or the articles of incorporation that does not make it permissible to continue the company (Commercial Code, Art. 176). A stock corporation may additionally be dissolved for expiration of the duration of the company or other reasons specified in the articles of incorporation, by merger, by order or judgment of court, or by a two-thirds majority resolution of a general meeting of shareholders (Commercial Code, Art. 520). Shareholders with 10 per cent or greater outstanding shares may demand dissolution when a deadlock in the affairs of the company is causing irreparable injury to the company or when the managing or disposing of the company's property is grossly improper and the existence of the company is in danger (Commercial Code, Art. 520). Public notice and notices to shareholders are required for dissolution (Commercial Code, Art. 521). Upon dissolution of the company, creditors are given peremptory notice by public notice and by individual notice to known creditors; unknown creditor's claim must be presented within a fixed period or be excluded, but known creditors will not be excluded nevertheless (Commercial Code, Art. 535). The remaining assets are distributed among shareholders in proportion to the number of shares (Commercial Code, Art. 538).

Private Limited Company

H.16 Although most foreign-invested enterprises are incorporated in the form of stock corporations and usually only because stock corporations are considered more prestigious, a private limited company may have advantages. A private limited company is characterized by the ability to restrict the transfer of shares by requiring a resolution of general meeting or other measures, to adopt resolutions of directors by written consent, and by the fact it is excepted from the requirement of going public under the Capital Markets Promotion Act (Commercial Code, Arts. 553 and 556). The liability of shareholders, as with a stock corporation, is limited to the amount of contribution (Commercial Code, Art. 553).

In incorporating a private limited company, two or more members draft the articles of incorporation and registration is to be effected two weeks from completing the capital contribution (Commercial Code, Arts. 543 and 549).

The total membership of a private limited company may not exceed 50 and the total capital must be at least 10 million won consisting of equal units of contribution worth at least 5,000 won (Commercial Code, Arts. 545 and 546). The maintenance of the corporation is similar to that of stock corporations with certain exceptions. One difference is that a private limited company may not issue bonds or debentures.

Capital Markets and Securities Laws

Securities Laws

The Securities Exchange Act (SEA)[33] defines securities as government bonds, municipal bonds, specially issued bonds, corporate bonds, certificates of contribution, stock certificates, certificates issued by foreign governments or corporations, or other certificates and instruments (SEA, Art. 2). The Ministry of Finance and Economics, the Korea Securities Exchange Commission (SEC), Korea Securities Supervisory Board, and the Korea Stock Exchange enforces the SEA. Registration with the SEC is required for listing on the securities market, making public offerings, merging with a listed company, transacting over-the-counter, and inviting subscriptions of securities (SEA, Art. 3).

H.17

In order to initiate a public offering or secondary distribution of securities, registration must be filed with the SEC disclosing information depending on the type of securities being offered (SEA, Art. 8). The SEC reviews the registration and if amendments are not needed for incomplete or inaccurate filings, the registration statement will be accepted and becomes effective as of the date of its submission (SEC, Arts. 9 and 11). The issuer of the securities must prepare and publicly make available a prospectus based on the information given at registration, but the effective registration does not guarantee accuracy of the information by the SEC (SEC, Arts. 9 and 12). The issuer is liable for false statements and omission of material facts in the registration statement or in the prospectus and the injured party may recover the difference between the amount actually paid and either the market price or the price at which the securities were disposed (SEC, Arts. 14 and 15). After distribution of the securities, the issuer must file a report to the SEC (SEC, Art. 17).

When a tender offer is made for a listed corporation or registered corporation, a statement must be filed with the SEC setting forth the period of purchase, purchase price, and method of payment, and takes effect 10 days after receipt by the Committee (SEA, Art. 21 and Enforcement Decree of SEA,[34] Art. 10). The tender offer must be transmitted to the issuer of securities prior to the time statement takes effect, a pubic notice posted and copy submitted to the Stock Exchange (SEA, Art. 22). No purchases are allowed through a tender offer until the statement takes effect and public notice is posted (SEA, Art. 23). During the tender offer period, the tender offeror may not purchase the same securities except by means of the tender offer and the SEC can order conditions and methods of the tender offer purchase (SEA, Art. 23). Proxy solicitation is regulated by requiring reference documents prior to or concurrent with the solicitation that enables the solicitee to clearly state positions with respect to every agenda discussed at the shareholders meeting, and by requiring a submission of the documents to the Security Supervisory Board (E.D. of SEA, Art. 85).

Insider trading is restricted by prohibiting officers, employees, or major stockholders (more than 10 per cent share) from gaining short-swing profits by selling stock within six months of purchasing or by purchasing stock within six months of selling (SEA, Art. 188). The company or the SEC may request remittance of profits to the company and if the corporation does not claim after 30 days of a stockholder's request, the stockholder can also claim the profits on behalf of the corporation (SEA, Art. 188(3)). The same individuals, and also including persons in contact with the corporation, are prohibited from disclosing important non-public information and from using or having another use the information for buying or selling securities issued by the corporation (SEA, Art. 188-2). The SEA also prohibits certain unfair trading activities, including market manipulation and fixing prices, by requiring compensation for losses as a result of such activities (SEA, Art. 105).

Capital Markets

Investing in the Korea Stock Market

H.18   Investing in the Korean stock market by foreigners (which for securities law purposes are defined as domestic companies with more than half the capital owned by a foreigner, foreign incorporated companies, or companies practically controlled by either of the former) is currently possible with certain limitations. In addition to special investment trust funds, investment companies such as the Korea Fund and the Korea-Europe Fund and convertible funds, investors may invest directly in listed corporations. According to the Regulation of Trading of Securities by Foreigners, foreigners who register with the Securities Supervisory Board and open accounts with securities companies may acquire shares in listed, and now unlisted, companies up to an aggregate of 18 per cent (Arts. 4, 5, 9, 16 and 20). There is no restriction on the remittance of dividends or the sale proceeds of shares. It is expected that foreigners will soon be able to buy up to an aggregate of 25 per cent of a company's equity and by 1999 the ceiling may be lifted altogether, but majority control by foreigners will probably not be possible and there will be capital outflow restrictions.

Ownership of shares by foreigners are further restricted by the requirement of making transactions through the exchange market, having transactions made by a securities company reported to the Securities Commission, other restrictions by the SEC, and by the target company's articles of incorporation (SEA, Art. 203 and E.D. of SEA Art. 87-2).

Engaging in Securities Business

Foreign securities firms and financial institutions are allowed to open **H.19** branches in Korea and engage in securities business. After obtaining a license from the MOFE, any licensed stock corporation with at least 50 billion won capital is allowed to engage in the securities business, but not less than 50 per cent of the stated capital or voting power must be owned by Korean nationals or domestic corporations (SEA, Art. 28 and E.D. of SEA Art. 14). Foreign securities companies are specifically permitted to establish branch offices in Korea by obtaining a license from the MOFE and satisfying other requirements of a foreign branch office (SEA, Art. 28-2). The criteria for being granted a license are reciprocity, international reputation, business fund, and transactions in the region (E.D. of SEA, Art. 17-2). The requirement of a two-year of operating history as a foreign securities representative office is no longer required. Foreign securities firms may also set up second or third branches in the Korean provinces if the firm has been penalty-free and has had no operating losses for two years.

Arbitration and Other ADR Techniques

Arbitration

Commercial arbitration is well-recognized in Korea as a method of settling **H.20** disputes and as a result the rules are fairly clear and established. Commercial arbitration in Korea is regulated by the Arbitration Act (AA)[35] and implemented by the Korean Commercial Arbitration Board (KCAB) under its Korean Commercial Arbitration Rules (KCAR).[36] Arbitration agreements are effective upon agreement through a specific arbitration agreement, arbitration clauses, or agreements through exchanges of correspondence (AA, Art. 2). The parties are bound by an arbitration award unless the arbitration is invalid or loses effect (AA, Art. 3). The specifics of arbitration for the most part are determined by terms of the arbitration agreement, but if not specified in the arbitration agreement, certain matters are provided for in the Arbitration Act.

The KCAB is the only approved institutional arbitral body in Korea and can arbitrate any commercial disputes pursuant to the Arbitration Act.[37] Arbitration proceedings with the KCAB begin when a party initiates arbitration by filing the agreement to arbitrate, a written request for arbitration, documentary evidence supporting claim, and if request is made by an agent, a power of attorney. The request is served and the other party has 30 days to file an answer. Three arbitrators are selected and the procedure is determined by commercial arbitration rules (AA, Arts. 4 and 7). After the arbitrator hears the parties, an award is made upon a majority concurrent vote within three months of commencement (AA, Arts. 8 and 11). A copy of the written award signed by the arbitrators, the text of arbitration award and summary of reasons is served on the parties, an original copy is submitted to the applicable court, and if any act necessary for the award cannot be performed by the arbitrators, the court can act upon request (AA, Arts. 9 and 11).

The following arbitration clause is recommended by the KCAB:

> "All disputes, controversies, or differences which may arise between the parties, out of or in relation to or in connection with this contract, or for the breach thereof, shall be finally settled by arbitration in Seoul, Korea, in accordance with the Commercial Arbitration Rules of the Korean Commercial Arbitration Board and under the laws of Korea. The award rendered by the arbitrator(s) shall be final and binding upon both parties concerned."[38]

The KCAB's judgment and other valid arbitration awards have the same effect as a final and conclusive court judgment (AA, Art. 12). An action of cancellation can be brought for violating the Arbitration Act or arbitration agreement, if the parties were without capacity, the award includes an illegal act, the parties were not heard or the award does not include a reason, or for other reasons that would require canceling a court judgment (AA, Art. 13 and Code of Civil Procedure,[39] Art. 4-9). The action for cancellation must be brought within 30 days of discovering the cause of cancellation or within five years of the judgment of execution of the arbitration award (AA, Art. 16).

As Korea acceded to the United Nations Convention on Recognition and Enforcement of Foreign Arbitral Awards ("New York Convention") with reservations requiring reciprocity and limiting application to those of commercial nature, Korea has undertaken to apply the Convention to differences arising out of commercial legal relationships and to recognize and enforce awards made in another contracting state.[40]

Mediation and Conciliation

H.21   Before the KCAB proceeds with arbitration, or even if there is no valid arbitration agreement, parties have the option of submitting the dispute to the intermediation services of the KCAB (KCAR, Art. 9). In fact, most disputes that are submitted to the KCAB, including disputes involving foreign parties, are settled by intermediation.[41] Intermediation is effective because the KCAB can influence the local party to cooperate and enforce decisions through administrative sanctions.[42] Generally, the KCAB acts to assist the parties settle the agreement on their own in the process of mediation and does not necessarily make recommendations as to an appropriate settlement.[43]

Conciliation and statutory mediation are other methods of dispute resolution widely applied in Korean disputes. Basically, an impartial third party provides facilities for settlement and negotiation.[44] Several statutes provide for mandatory or voluntary conciliation or mediation for disputes including, but not limited to, the Civil Conciliation Act, Environmental Injuries Dispute Adjustment Act, Labor Dispute Adjustment Act, the Insurance Business Act, Copyright Act, Consumer Protection Act, and Securities Transaction Act.[45] In these conciliation or mediation proceedings, a judge may act as a conciliator or mediator or there may be provisions for the establishment of a conciliation or mediation committee. If mediation or conciliation is not successful, many of the statutes provide for compulsory arbitration to settle the matter.

Banking and Lending Law

Banking Law

Under the Banking Act,[46] establishment of a foreign bank branch requires **H.22** application to the Bank Supervisory Board (BSB) of the Bank of Korea, which in turn makes recommendation to the Monetary Bank to authorize the branch (Art. 37-2). In practice, a letter of intent is first filed with the BSB to establish an office and then upon the BSB's positive determination, an invitation is extended to make a preliminary application to the Monetary Board through the BSB.[47] The criteria for approval of preliminary application are contribution to the Korean economy, international credit worthiness, reciprocity, economic and trade relationship with the foreign country, and domestic financial money capacity.[48] After this preliminary approval, an almost perfunctory final application is filed. A license to engage in the banking business is the result of final approval, but subsequent acts such as mergers, dissolution, amendment of articles of association, or opening or closure of a bank branch, also requires authorization from the Monetary Board through the BSB (Banking Act, Art. 9).

Banking Business

The Banking Act specifically provides that authorized foreign bank branches **H.23** shall be regarded as a "banking institution" under the Banking Act and thus amenable to all its provisions and also the Bank of Korea Act (Banking Act, Arts. 1, 1-2 and 37-3). According to Article 30 of the Conflict of Laws Act, however, the extra-national relations of foreigners in Korea and of Korean nationals abroad, the affairs and effect of banking business are to be governed by the law of the country the bank belongs.

Banking institutions are allowed to engage in any activity related to the banking business, including commercial banking and long-term finance

(Banking Act, Arts. 18 to 21). In conducting its banking business, banking institutions must maintain a total amount of capital equivalent to at least one-twentieth of its outstanding shares (Banking Act, Arts. 15 and 16). When profits are disposed, at least 10 per cent must be credited to the reserve fund until the fund equals the total capital (Banking Act, Art. 17-2). For banking institutions that are joint ventures with foreign countries, the normal requirement that an individual shall not own or control more than 8 per cent of the total shares and requirement of at least 100 billion won total capital does not apply (Banking Act, Art. 17-3). The repatriation of profits and liquidation proceeds are guaranteed.

As to specific business transactions, investment in securities with maturities exceeding three years cannot exceed 100 per cent of shareholder's equity, loans to government agencies must be fully guaranteed by the government for principal and interest, trust business must be kept separate from banking business, and business other than banking business must be authorized by the Monetary Board (Banking Act, Arts. 22 to 25). Also, the total amount of debentures may not exceed five times the shareholders' equity (Banking Act, Art. 26). In other banking regulations, the Monetary Board controls activities of banks by fixing maximum interest rates, placing ceiling on outstanding loans and rate increases, approving large loans, issuing regulations on maximum maturities of loans, restricting loans to the same business group, and requiring banking institutions to hold or withdraw deposits with the Bank of Korea Monetary Stabilization Account (Banking Act, Arts. 30 and 30-2). Although for most transactions foreign banks are afforded national treatment, they are restricted from issuing corporate bonds, foreclosing on real estate held as collateral, must separately capitalize each branch, are unable to receive government deposits, although not prohibited, and indirect aggregate limits are imposed on foreign currency loans.[49]

Banking institutions are required to publish a balance sheet, a profit and loss statement, and consolidated financial statements on forms provided by the BSB within three months of the end of each fiscal year, and after each month, the banking institution must submit a report outlining its operation and a general balance sheet (Banking Act, Arts. 35 to 37). Banking institutions may be periodically examined by the BSB and may be required to submit statistical data and other required information to the Research Department of the Bank of Korea (Banking Act, Arts. 32 and 37(3)). The Monetary Board has the power to terminate authorization if the foreign bank branch merges or is sold, dissolves or terminates banking business, cancels its banking license, is bankrupt, a disciplinary action is bought for unlawful conduct or unsound management practices, or business is suspended or discontinued (Banking Act, Art. 37-4). The branch is required to maintain all or part of its assets in Korea and, in case of liquidation or bankruptcy, claims of Korean citizens and foreigners with domicile or residency in Korea are to be settled first.

Foreign Exchange

According to the Foreign Exchange Control Act (FECA)[50] the engagement   H.24
in foreign exchange and money changing business, and concluding contracts
with foreign banking institutions regarding foreign exchange require permits
from the MOFE (FECA, Arts. 7 to 9). Foreign exchange bank branches of
foreign country banks must supply funds for carrying on business only from
funds that the head office supplies to the branch by selling foreign currency
to the Bank of Korea, funds transferred from reserve funds, or funds that the
branch obtains by selling foreign currency to the Bank of Korea (ED of
FECA, Art. 14).

Lending Law

Debt financing of foreign businesses in Korea is a possibility that is not well   H.25
developed. Although a foreign subsidiary in Korea may theoretically borrow
money from a Korean bank and other domestic sources, in practice this is
very difficult as the amount of capital available is limited and lending requires
mortgages of real estate or chattel for security.[51] Recently, however, foreign
companies with 50 per cent or more foreign capital were granted credit
guarantees as domestic companies, possibly resolving the problem of lack of
collateral. A subsidiary of a foreign corporation may be able to borrow from
a Korean branch of a foreign bank by providing a guarantee or comfort letter
to the main bank office overseas.[52] Other possible sources of capital for
foreign business are short-term finance companies, insurance companies,
merchant banking institutions, and venture capital companies.

Loans from offshore foreign banks or foreign investors are limited because of the government's concern about its account surplus and possible
inflationary pressures, and is usually only approved for foreign-invested
businesses involved in high technology manufacturing.[53] By 1997 it is expected that high technology businesses will be able to borrow up to 75 per
cent of its capital from overseas sources and even other manufacturing businesses will be able to borrow up to 50 per cent.

Consumer Protection Law

Enacted to protect the rights and interests of consumers, the Consumer   H.26
Protection Act (CPA)[54] applies to many activities of businesses and it is likely
that a foreign company conducting business in Korea would run into its
provisions (Art. 1). Businesses, including manufacturers, importers, sellers,
and those who furnish services, are under a duty to take measures necessary
for protection of consumers, cooperate with policies for consumer protection,[55] and are prohibited from dealing in goods or services that may be
dangerous (CPA, Arts. 15 and 16). Businesses are required to establish
and operate an organization to handle consumer complaints and settle

compensation for damages. Also, businesses are required to submit operational records on the protection of consumers to the appropriate agency (Enforcement Decree of CPA, Art. 16).[56]

The rights of consumers include being protected against injury and danger from goods and services; a right to information about goods and services; a right to choose the place, price, and conditions of consumption; the right to express opinion of enterprisers; the right to obtain just compensation for damages according to prompt and fair procedures; a right to consumer education; and the right to organize consumer interest groups. In order to facilitate the protection of consumers, the Korea Consumer Protection Center and the Consumer Dispute Mediation Committee were established (CPA, Arts. 21, 26 and 34). The Consumer Protection Center settles complaints, redresses damages, and conducts investigations and tests on standards, quality, and safety (CPA, Art. 28). The Consumer Dispute Mediation Committee mediates and decides on consumer disputes (CPA, Art. 34). Contravention of the CPA may be punishable by imprisonment up to one year and fines of up to 10 million won.

Health, Safety and Environmental Law

Environmental Law

H.27   In the past few years Korea has enacted and updated several laws setting standards for environmental protection. The Basic Environmental Policy Act[57] (BEPA) provides the framework for legal enforcement and applies to foreign investment in Korea in that it obliges all enterprisers to take measures for environmental protection (BEPA, Art. 5). Its Enforcement Decree[58] provides standards for air pollution levels, water quality, and acceptable noise levels. Other statutes that apply are the Liability for Environment Improvement Expenses Act,[59] which imposes environmental improvement charges from building and facility owners for causing environmental pollution; the Environmental Pollution Damage Dispute Adjustment Act,[60] which provides for mediation, conciliation, and arbitration for disputes caused by environmental pollution damages; the Natural Environment Preservation Act,[61] which obligates businesses to takes measures for preventing natural environment damages and for restoration of damaged sites; the Noise and Vibration Regulation Act,[62] which regulates noise and vibration from factories, including installation of preventive facilities; the Water Environment Preservation Act,[63] which regulates emission facilities and installation of preventive facilities; and the Sea Pollution Prevention Act,[64] which prohibits oil discharges and requires installation of preventive equipment according to Annexes I, II, and V of the MARPOL Protocol of 1978 Relating to the International Convention for the Prevention of Pollution from Ships.

Under these laws, Korea has undertaken to protect its environment by maintaining standards and prohibiting certain processes and substances. The methods of enforcement include effluent charges, improvement orders, shutdown or lockout, and criminal sanctions.[65] As the Ministry of Environment enforces environmental laws predominantly by administrative guidance, foreign-invested businesses should not be too concerned about sanctions. Criminal sanctions, in fact, have been known not to be imposed for accidental pollution, but only for intentional acts. The immediate impact of these laws is that the foreign company investing in manufacturing facilities would have to coordinate activities with the Ministry of Environment. Specifically, under the Environmental Impact Assessment Act private project planners are required to prepare environmental impact statements and consult with the Ministry of Environment on issues concerning the natural environment, living environment, and the socio-economic environment.[66]

A company, however, may be held responsible for clean-up costs and environmental improvement in the area as "[a] successor-in-interest or an assignee of shares of a company is responsible for any emission charges incurred by the company" and "purchaser of the assets of a company is responsible for emission charges incurred by the seller if the purchaser is deemed to have purchased all of the existing business from the seller."[67] Parent companies of subsidiaries, however, are not liable for environmental pollution.

In addition, the Environment Improvement Charge System introduced in 1992 levies charges against facilities that fall within certain categories based on the facility's potential for pollution.[68] Another impact of the environmental movement is that under the Foreign Capital Inducement Act, projects highly prone to pollution may not be induced because they are classified as prohibited projects and in order to determine polluting potential, the Ministry of Environment is consulted in evaluating the project.[69] Environmental technology, however, may be induced with tax exemptions and other benefits incident to high technology. Certain hazardous chemicals may be prohibited from manufacture and trade under the Act Relating to Transboundary Movements of Wastes and Their Disposal.[70]

Industrial Injury

The Industrial Safety and Health Act (ISHA),[71] an act that applies to all businesses, was enacted to "maintain and promote the safety and health of employees by preventing industrial accidents through establishing standards on industrial safety" (Arts. 1 and 3). The general obligations of the employer are to observe industrial safety standards, maintain and promote health and safety, comply with industrial accident prevention policies, and take measures for safety and health (ISHA, Art. 5).

Specifically, the employer must attach safety marks on harmful or dangerous facilities with emergency instructions, keep employees informed of the

H.28

contents of ISHA, and prepare safety and health management rules (ISHA, Arts. 11, 12 and 20). The employer must also appoint enumerated safety and health managers and an industrial health doctor, establish and operate an industrial safety and health committee, and conduct health and safety education (ISHA, Arts. 13 to 19 and 31). Provisions are further made for prohibition on contracting harmful work, prohibiting the manufacture of certain hazardous chemicals, self-inspection of machines and facilities, and evaluation of the working environment. In addition to enforcement, the Ministry of Labor (MOL) can order safety and health evaluations and improvement plans (ISHA, Arts. 49 and 50).

To further protect workers, under the Industrial Injury Compensation Act (IICA),[72] the MOL carries on industrial injury insurance business with the business owners as the insured to protect workers (IICA, Arts. 1 and 6). The insurance provides for medical care, recuperative benefits, disability benefits, survivor's compensation, injuries or disease compensation annuity, and funeral expenses (IICA, Art. 9). The IICA applies to all businesses and working places, and premiums are collected from the insured businesses to cover expenses of the MOL (IICA, Art. 19). Every insurance year the insured businesses are required to report and pay premiums to the MOL based on an amount calculated by multiplying the applicable premium rate, which is determined and classified by the MOL based on the business category and injury rates, with the total wages to all workers (IICA, Arts. 21, 23 and 25).

Employment and Labor Law

Employment Contracts

H.29   A contract of employment becomes binding when one party agrees to render services and the other agrees to pay for the services (Civil Code, Art. 655). Certain aspects of the employment agreements are regulated by the Labor Standards Law (LSL)[73] and agreements that do not meet its standards are null and void (LSL, Art. 20).

The employment agreement is not to exceed one year, the employer must specifically set out wage, working hours and other conditions, and the employer cannot insert provisions for penalty or liquidated damages for non-performance, off-set wage with advance, require compulsory savings deposit, nor dismiss or impose punitive measures without justification (LSL, Arts. 21, 22, 24 to 27). Either parties to the contract can give notice of rescission with one month notice and can also rescind the contract if an unavoidable situation arises, but if due to the fault of one of the parties, that party may be liable for damages (Civil Code, Arts. 660 and 661). There is an implication of renewal if an employee continues working after the expiration of the employment period (Civil Code, Art. 662). The employer may not assign rights in the contract without consent of the employee and the employee may not allow a third party to perform the contracted service without the employer's consent (Civil Code, Art. 657).

In the situation that a foreign worker will be employed, the Immigration Control Act (ICA)[74] requires that the foreign employee receive temporary employment qualification (ICA, Art. 18). After being granted the temporary employment qualification, the foreign employee may only work at the designated working place (ICA, Art. 18). Those who employ foreigners must report the fact to the immigration office within 15 days and notify of discharge, disclose whereabouts if it becomes unknown, report important changes in the employment contract, and report violations of the ICA by the foreign worker (ICA, Art. 19).

Labor Standards

The Labor Standards Law provides the minimum standards for employment   H.30
in Korea (Art. 2). The minimum wage for employers with 10 or more employees, which may apply to all enterprises and workplaces in the future, is determined yearly by the Minimum Wage Counsel. The standard working hours are not to exceed eight hours a day or 44 hours a week, with exceptions for certain businesses and if by mutual agreement (LSL, Arts. 42 and 47-2). Workers are entitled to a day off per week, a day per month leave, and 10 days vacation per year, all with pay (LSL, Arts. 45, 47 and 48). For overtime, night-time, or holiday work, the employee is entitled to time and a half (LSL, Art. 46). The employer must also establish a retirement allowance that is not less than 30 days average wage per year for the consecutive years employed at the company (LSL, Art. 28).

The Employment Equality Act (EEA)[75] codifies equal opportunity for women by enumerating that equal wages must be paid for work of equal value, that there be no discrimination in training, assignment and promotion, and that a contract cannot stipulate marriage, pregnancy, or childbirth as a cause for retirement (Arts. 6, 6-2, 7 and 8). The EEA provides that leave be granted for child-care and that facilities be provided for child-care and, under the LSL, women are also entitled to 60 days maternity leave with pay and employers must provide a place for nursing (LSL, Arts. 60 and 61).

The LSL provides standards for child labor in that those under 13 are prohibited from being employed and that if an employee is under 18, the employer must keep a copy of the minor's census register testifying to the minor's age and written consent from the parents (Arts. 50 and 52). Minors are prohibited from immoral and dangerous work, night work, and may not work more than seven hours a day or 42 hours a week (LSL, Arts. 51, 55 and 56).

As for compensation for accidents in the course of employment, the employer is required to provide medical care and incidental expenses for occupational injury or disease and the employer is responsible for 60 per cent of an employee's wage during medical leave (LSL, Arts. 78 and 79). In addition, the employer is responsible for survivor's compensation and funeral expenses (LSL, Arts. 82 and 83).

The Labor Management Council Act (LMCA)[76] requires that a Labor Management Council be established in each business or workplace with the power to decide conditions of employment and that a Grievance Committee also be established to hear and handle employee grievances (Arts. 4 and 24). The Council is composed of an equal number of members representing employees and employer, not less than three and no more than 10, and the Council is to meet every three months (LMCA, Arts. 6 and 11). The Council consults on the improvement of productivity, promotion of employee welfare, employee education and training, prevention of labor disputes, handling employer grievances, improvement of safety, health and working environment, improvement of labor management and operation, and other matters concerning labor-management cooperation (LMCA, Art. 20). The employer and employees are to observe Council decisions in good faith, and the employer is under a further duty to report and explain the company's general management, production and manpower plans, and financial conditions (LMCA, Arts. 21 and 23).

Labor Unions

H.31 Under the Labor Union Act (LUA),[77] employees have a right to freely organize and join labor unions, which are defined as organizations formed by employees for maintaining and improving conditions of employment (LUA, Arts. 3 and 8). The establishment of labor unions and the initiation of labor disputes in foreign-invested businesses require the submission of a report to the Minister of Labor (Temporary and Special Act Concerning Labor Unions and Mediation of Labor Disputes in Foreign-invested Enterprises (Special Act),[78] Arts. 4 and 5). Collective bargaining agreements, which are not to exceed one year, are to be negotiated by labor union representatives with authority and employers are under a duty not to refuse or neglect the conclusion of a collective bargaining without justification (LUA, Arts. 33 and 35).

An employer is under a duty not to engage in unfair labor practices, which includes dismissing or sanctioning for joining or organizing labor unions, requiring as a condition of employment that the employee not join or withdraw from a specific labor union or join a specific labor union, rejecting or neglecting collective negotiations without just cause, controlling or interfering in the formation or operation of a union or subsidizing expenses for labor union operations, and dismissing or sanctioning for joining a justified collective action or for reporting or testifying before a labor committee (LUA, Art. 39).

In addition to the general allowance for voluntary reconciliation between employees and employers, the Labor Disputes Adjustment Law (LDAL)[79] provides for conciliation by named conciliators, mediation as a next step, and finally arbitration. Arbitration can be imposed by the Labor Committee, by both parties' request, or by one party's request according to a collective bargaining agreement. Decisions adopted through conciliation, mediation, and arbitration have the same effect as a collective bargaining agreement. The LDAL provides for certain restrictions during a labor dispute: a labor union can act only upon majority vote; acts of violence and subversion, intervention by a third party and hiring or replacing an employee during period of dispute are prohibited; and lockouts are possible only after the labor union commences action in the labor dispute and the employer reports to the administrative agency (Arts. 11 to 17). The Special Act also establishes a council on mediation for settling disputes with foreign-invested businesses.

One complaint of foreign investors in Korea is that foreign employers are subject to external pressures to reach settlements that are unreasonable. It should be noted that, as with recent disputes involving Citibank, compulsory arbitration is not subjective and favors the foreign party in many cases. In line with the Government's fair treatment of labor, the Ministry of Labor has a special desk for foreign firms.

Foreign Investment Law

The Foreign Capital Inducement Act (FCIA)[80] is the basic legal framework   **H.32** for investing in Korea. The law is encompassing in that it covers loans from foreign sources, equity investments (foreign direct investment in the form of joint ventures or wholly-owned subsidiaries), and technology licensing and transfer. Since its inception in 1966, the FCIA has shifted its emphasis from loans to equity investments to technology transfers and the areas available for foreign investment have expanded to most manufacturing sectors and also to several service industries, such as insurance and brokerage, advertising, motion picture production, rental and distribution, trading concerns, freight forwarding and brokerage, and securities business.[81] The law guarantees overseas remittance of earned capital, guarantees the property right of the foreign-invested property in accordance with Korean laws, and affords national treatment with regard to business activity and tax exemptions (FCIA, Arts. 4 to 6).

Foreign Investment

Foreign investment can be induced under the FCIA by Korean nationals,   **H.33** Korean juridical persons, or non-residents through a resident agent (FCIA, Arts. 3 and 18-2). Foreign investment is restricted according to a negative list separated into restricted and prohibited activities (FCIA, Art. 9). Under Attachment 1 of the FCIA Regulations, the prohibited businesses include legislative administration, foreign affairs, defense and public activities, postal activities, central banking, and administration and regulation of certain government activities, and Attachment 2 restricts foreign investment in certain agricultural activities, mining of hard coal, publishing, utilities, certain wholesale and retail activities, transport and communications, certain finance, insurance, real estate and business services, and certain heath and social work. For the restricted business, the foreign investment may be limited to joint ventures where the foreign interest is less than 50 per cent. Other restrictions on foreign investment are that certain small- and medium-sized businesses may be limited to joint ventures where foreign equity does not exceed 50 per cent.[82] Certain foreign investment may be rejected for reasons relating to security of the state and nationals, maintenance of public order and the protection of good morals and customs, fulfillment of duties related to international peace and safety, and protection of the national health and the preservation of the environment (FCIA, Art. 9 and Enforcement Decree of FCIA,[83] Art. 7(2)).

As a first step, foreign investment requires approval from the MOFE, but for non-negative list industries it is sufficient to merely report the investment to the Bank of Korea, Korea Development Bank, or the Industrial Bank of Korea by filing a report including tradename and nationality of the foreign investor, amount, method, and rate of investment of a foreign investor, the project to be operated, and other important matters (FCIA, Art. 7 and ED of FCIA, Art. 9-2). After approval or reporting, the foreign investor must complete payment of the investment award within two years and then register with the registry of foreign-invested enterprises with the MOFE (FCIA, Arts. 11 to 12). Contracts that have been granted approval for remittance of funds previously are not affected by the FECA, but payments and transactions dealing with foreign currency may require a permit from the MOFE. The remittance of foreign funds, receipt of overseas funds, and currency transactions are regulated by the Foreign Exchange Control Act.

After foreign investment, the disposition of foreign capital, additional foreign investment, changes in the scope of business, and acquiring of stock or shares of another enterprise all require notification to the MOFE (FCIA, Art. 13). The foreign investor may also not use the invested funds for non-approved activities (FCIA, Art. 13-2). The MOFE may investigate the status of the foreign investment and its use and may make requests for correction if illegal or unjust acts are discovered (FCIA, Art. 39). The MOFE may cancel approval of a foreign investment if the subject matter of the investment is not paid in the two years, the foreign-invested enterprise discontinues or does not conduct business for two years, correction orders are not complied with, for other causes, or if the foreign investor requests (FCIA, Art. 18).

Technology Inducement

H.34   Currently, the focus of the FCIA is in its technology inducement provisions. Although there are three channels for introducing technology, the FCIA, Foreign Exchange Control Act, and the Technical Services Business Promotion Act (TSBPA), the FECA is seldom used because there are no tax benefits or exemptions and is short-term (three years or less) and the TSBPA is also seldom used because it is applicable only for government introduction of a particular technology for governmental purposes. As such, the FCIA is the important channel for foreign investors. Technology is introduced through a technology inducement agreement, which is a contract for the purchase of industrial or other technology from a foreigner by a Korean national.

Approval is required for technology inducement and the criteria for approval are that the royalty should be paid in foreign currency, the term of the agreement should be three years or longer, but not longer than 10, and the technology should be sufficiently sophisticated (FCIA, Art. 23).[84] The introduction of technology will be prohibited if it merely takes advantage of an exclusive sales right, merely sells raw materials, parts or accessories, or if it is contrary to the FCIA or other laws and regulations (ED of FCIA, Art. 24). Royalties may be fixed or floating and demanded with an initial lump-sum fee, but royalties in excess of 5 per cent net sales are seldom approved by the government except for very advanced technology.[85] Unfair trade practices that are restricted in relation to technology inducement agreements are practices that place "restrictions on the export of products manufactured by using the licensed technology, and require[s] that the licensee cease using unpatented licensed technology upon termination of the license".[86]

Tax Exemption and Benefits

Under the FCIA there are several articles pertaining to reduction or exemption from various taxes, including income, corporation, acquisition, property, and gross land taxes, for projects that involve highly advanced technology or is located in a Free Export Zone (FCIA, Art. 14). Upon specific application to the MOFE, income or corporation tax may be exempted for three years in proportion to foreign investment in the enterprise and, for highly advanced technology investments, an additional 50 per cent reduction after the initial three years (FCIA, Art. 14(2)). Income or corporation tax from dividends on shares or stock acquired may be reduced by 50 per cent for the three years (FCIA, Art. 14(3)). Income, property, and gross land taxes on property acquired or possessed by the foreign-invested enterprise may be reduced by 50 per cent for three years, but if property is acquired for original business purpose before the regular tax exemption period, the acquisition, property, and gross land tax may be reduced 50 per cent for five years (FCIA, Art. 14(4)). If capital goods need to be imported for the project (not as subject matter of investment), customs duties, special consumption tax, and value added tax may be reduced by 50 per cent (FCIA, Art. 15). If the foreign investor's capital increases, the exemption and reduction provisions are to apply *mutatis mutandis* (FCIA, Art. 16).

In order to qualify for the high technology tax exemption, the technology is required to be sufficiently advanced in that it is essential for the national

H.35

economy and difficult to develop independently in Korea (FCIA, Art. 24 and ED of FCIA, Art. 24-2). Although foreign-invested enterprises located in metropolitan areas could not qualify for the deductions and exemptions, the rule was recently lifted. The tax exemptions and reductions are all subject to retroactive collection for cancellation of approval, de-registration, non-compliance with conditions of approval, transfer of stock or shares, discontinuance of business, or if foreign capital is used for purposes not approved (FCIA, Art. 17).

Another benefit available to high technology investment is that manufacturers may be entitled to lease land free for five years for factory construction and renew at below market lease rates after the initial five years. The high technology investments may also allowed to finance the investments from long-term loans from overseas. Under the FCIA, approval is required from the MOFE for loan contracts by Korean residents or companies from a foreign national and also for disposition of the foreign capital (FCIA, Arts. 19 to 20). In granting approval, the MOFE looks at the investment plan and contents of the contract, sale, details and procurement scheme of the required domestic and foreign capital, and the operational plan (ED of FCIA, Art. 21). The contract must be enforced by the borrower within six months of approval; non-enforcement is cause for cancellation of approval (FCIA, Arts. 19(3) and 22).

Acquiring Land

H.36 Related to the issue of foreign capital inducement is the acquiring of land by foreigners. The Act Concerning Land Acquisition and Management of Alien (Alien Land Act)[87] recently permitted foreigners to acquire real rights and rights of lease in land, as long as there is reciprocity in the foreigners home country (Alien Land Act, Arts. 3 and 4). Upon application to and approval by the Minister of Construction, branch offices and juridical persons established under Korean law can acquire rights in land needed for the business purpose and for residence of employees (Alien Land Act, Arts. 6 and 7). Such land includes land less than 660 m² to build a residential house, commercial land less than 165 m², and land to carry on a manufacturing business (ED of Alien Land Act,[88] Arts. 3 and 6). The Minister of Construction advises on the use of land, must be consulted on change of use, and can even order disposal for land not used for the proper business reasons (Alien Land Act, Arts. 9 to 11).

Tax Law

H.37 Taxation is one of the important issues to be considered when doing business anywhere. The important applicable taxes for foreign business enterprises in Korea would be the corporation tax, value-added tax (VAT), customs tax, inhabitant tax, acquisition tax, registration tax, property tax, and global land tax.[89] The national tax system includes separate statutes while the Local Tax Act[90] is all encompassing (29 types). The Ministry of Finance and Economy has broad general jurisdiction and the Office of National Tax Administration has primary jurisdiction over tax collection. An opposition to tax assessment and decisions are filed with the district tax office. Appeals are made to the National Tax Tribunal of the MOFE, then to the high court for tax matters, and finally to the Supreme Court.

The Tax Exemption and Reduction Act (TERA)[91] enumerates the cases and requirements for exemption or reduction in addition to the specific tax laws. The TERA has provisions for special cases involving small and medium enterprises, development of technology and manpower, foreign capital earning business, for promoting investment, industrial structure adjustments, balanced development among areas, support of public utilities, certain special cases of capital gains taxes, and for stability of national living. The Act provides for zero tax rate, exemptions for VAT, and reductions on customs for certain goods.

Corporate Tax

The Corporate Tax Act (CTA)[92] provides that domestic corporations, a corporation having its head or principal office in Korea, and foreign corporations with income accruing from domestic sources are liable for corporate tax (Art. 1). The general tax rate is 18 per cent for the first 100 million Won and 32 per cent for income exceeding 100 million Won (CTA, Art. 22). If there is a treaty between Korea and a foreign country to prevent double taxation, the government may adjust the calculation of income for a branch office of a foreign corporation or a foreign legal corporation outside the country according to the treaty (CTL, Art. 20-2).

For domestic corporations, which includes foreign-invested domestic corporations, the tax base is the amount of business income after deducting accrued deficit amounts for the past five years, non-taxable income, and enumerated income deductions (CTA, Art. 8). The income is calculated by deducting the total pecuniary loss from the total pecuniary receipts (CTA, Art. 9). The CTA enumerates in detail the scope of deductions, non-taxable income, pecuniary loss, and pecuniary receipts. A domestic corporation is also responsible for taxes on liquidation income, which is the amount remaining after deducting the aggregate paid-in capital or investments and surplus from the value of residual assets of the liquidated company (CTA, Art. 43).

For foreign corporations with a business place in Korea (a concept similar to "permanent establishment") or with real estate income in Korea, the corporate tax basis is the amount remaining after deducting accrued deficits, non-taxable income, and income accruing from navigation of vessels and aircrafts from domestic sources of income (CTA, Art. 53). For such corporations the tax basis is the amount of income from domestic sources and the tax rate is the same as for domestic corporations (CTA, Art. 53). Income from domestic sources that forms the taxable basis includes income from interest, dividends, income, real estate, lease of chattel, accruing from business operated in Korea, services, capital gains, forest income, compensation related to intellectual property, and income from the sale of stock (CTA, Art. 55).

A business place in Korea includes fixed places for conducting business, including branches, stores, workshops, building and construction sites and mines, and the scope of a fixed place includes providing service through an employee more than six months of the year (CTA, Art. 56). Even if there is no domestic business place, if the foreign company conducts business through one authorized to conclude contracts on behalf of the company, such as an agent, the foreign company will be deemed to have a domestic business place (CTA, Art. 56). Specifically, the fixed place does not include places for simple purchase of assets, storage of assets not purported for sale, place used for advertisement, public relations, information processing, market survey or other preparatory and auxiliary business activities, and only for having others process its assets (CTA, Art. 56).

H.38   The practical consequence of being deemed to have a business place is that the total profits of an overseas supplier earned from sales to Korean buyers are subject to Korean corporate income tax.[93] Although this foreign entity may be able to deduct the tax amounts as a foreign tax credit or foreign income exception, it may be worthwhile to establish mechanisms to overcome being taxed in Korea. It is stated that the "primary tax planning consideration is to preclude the sales income of the selling entity from being taxed in Korea as business income".[94] The idea is to use two corporate entities, one for sales and another for the Korean office. In such a method, the sales office is only taxed on the commission to the offer agency, and the Korean office is not taxed because the activities are merely preparatory and auxiliary to the sale. The two offices should be managed independently, as the tax authorities can disregard the separate offices if the commercial reality is that the two offices are in fact one.

For royalties related to high technology, if there is a business place where the licensed technology is effectively connected, the royalties must be included in the gross income, but if there is no permanent establishment, the corporate tax rate or rate under a treaty is withheld.

A person is required to withhold corporate tax and remit to the government for income from domestic sources paid to a foreign corporation that is not substantially related or is not returned to the domestic place (CTA, Art. 59). Domestic corporations and foreign corporations with a business place in Korea are not subject to withholding taxes, with the exception of certain enumerated creditable withholding, but a foreign company without a business place is subject to a final withholding tax.

A special surtax is applicable on gains from the transfer of rights, stocks or investment certificates relating to land, buildings or real estate (CTA, Art. 59-2). The tax rate is 40 per cent for transfers before registration and 25 per cent in other cases (CTA, Art. 59-4). Also, for issues of transfer pricing, the current market price is used.

Income Tax

According to the Income Tax Act (ITA),[95] residents (defined as those domiciled or having residence for a year or longer in Korea) and non-residents are liable for income tax, and residents, non-residents, domestic corporations, and foreign corporations are liable to pay income tax withheld at the source of income (ITA, Art. 1).

    The tax base for residents is the global income, which includes interest income, dividend, real estate, business, wage and salary after deductions, retirement income, transfer income, and forest income (ITA, Art. 15). Non-residents are liable for tax only with respect to income derived from sources within Korea, as defined in the CTA. If Korea is the domestic place of business, then global taxation is applied on aggregate domestic source of income. If there is no domestic place of business, then withholding of tax method is applied to each domestic source of income. If there is an applicable bilateral treaty, however, the treaty applies.

    The income tax rates are 10 per cent for the first 10 million won taxable, 20 per cent for the next 20 million won, 30 per cent for the next 30 million won, and 40 per cent for taxable income exceeding 60 million won.

H.39

Value-Added Tax

The Value-Added Tax Act (VAT Act)[96] imposes VAT on the supply of goods or services, including royalty for technology, and importation of goods transactions and on those who independently supply goods on a business basis (VAT Act, Arts. 1 and 2). The VAT tax rate is 10 per cent and the tax base is determined by the actual amount of payment or otherwise the current market rate (VAT Act, Arts. 13 and 14). The VAT payable is the amount computed by deducting the tax amount from the goods, services, or imports used or to be used for that business (input tax amount) from the tax amount on the goods, services, or imports supplied by that business (output tax amount) (VAT Act, Art. 17). An input tax amount that exceeds the output tax amount is refundable (VAT Act, Art. 17). A zero tax rate applies to goods or services supplied outside of Korea, to international navigational services, and those earning foreign currency, and a tax exemption applies for certain necessary and socially redeeming goods, services, and imports (VAT Act, Arts. 11 and 12).

H.40

Customs Tax

Another important tax consideration is the customs tax. The Customs Act[97] provides that customs duties are levied on importers for all imported

H.41

goods based on quantity and price at the time of import declaration according to the Tariff Schedule, with exemptions and abatements in certain instances (Customs Act, Arts. 3, 4, 6, 7 and 9). As the basis of the customs duty is the price and quantity of the imported goods, the price of goods must normally be declared on the import declaration, accompanied by data on determination of dutiable value (Customs Act, Arts. 9 and 9-2).

The dutiable value is normally determined by the transactional value adjusted by commissions or brokerage, packing costs, cost of goods and services supplied for purpose of transacting, amount paid for intellectual property rights, amount reverted that accrued from resale, disposal or use, and freight and transportation costs that are actually paid or have to be paid (Customs Act, Art. 9-3). If the actual transactional value cannot be determined, then the Customs Act provides for other methods of valuation: based on the transactional value of identical goods, transactional value of similar goods, unit price at which imported goods, identical goods, or similar goods are sold domestically, computed value based on raw materials, processing, profits and expenses, or based on a reasonable basis (Customs Act, Arts. 9-4 to 9-8).

The importer, or anyone required to pay customs duties, upon making a declaration of import, must make a declaration on payment of customs duties and pay that duty within 15 days (Customs Act, Art. 17). Besides the normal exemption and abatement provisions for diplomats, academic research, government procurement, etc., the Customs Act provides exemptions and abatements for raw materials for manufacturing vessels that are navigating overseas, for goods geared toward preventing environmental pollution, goods to be re-exported, raw materials for manufacturing export goods, and for goods that are re-imported (Customs Act, Arts. 27 to 34). The customs duty may be paid in installments for up to five years for certain goods (Customs Act, Art. 36). For raw materials to be exported within a year and six months, customs can be postponed with security and the customs paid may be refunded upon request by the importer.[98]

Local Tax

H.42　Under the Local Tax Act, local governments may impose and collect ordinary taxes and objective taxes in accordance with its provisions (Art. 2). The four levels of local government taxes include Special City taxes and Direct Control City taxes, Provincial taxes, Shi/Kun taxes, and Ku taxes. These include ordinary taxes such as acquisition, registration, resident, automobile, farmland, etc., taxes and objective taxes such as city planning, public facilities, business office, regional development, etc., taxes. One notable local tax is that for incorporation, which includes registration and inhabitant taxes.

Intellectual Property Law

As of 1986, Korea gave into international pressures and modernized intellec- **H.43**
tual property laws and enhanced the standards of protection to international
levels. Besides the specific intellectual property laws, the first line of defense
against intellectual property infringement is the Foreign Trade Act, which
provides that no trader, trade agent, or consignor shall infringe on intellectual
property rights and that the Ministry of Trade, Industry and Resources can
take corrective measures after an investigation (FTA, Art. 44). What this
means is that the import or export of goods that violates intellectual property
rights is prohibited.

Patents (Including Utility and Design)

As to international treaties, Korea has acceded to the Paris Convention, the **H.44**
Budapest Treaty, and the Patent Cooperation Treaty. As a result, Paris
Convention member country businesses and individuals are afforded prospective protection of patents in Korea under reciprocal conditions afforded
Korean nationals in the foreign country. Retroactive protection may be
provided for by bilateral treaties as they exist with the United States, European Community, and Japan, but other World Trade Organization member
country patent-holders may claim under the most-favored-nation clause.[99]
Also, an international application under the Patent Cooperation Treaty may
be made to the Administrator of the Patent Administration by nationals,
foreigners with domicile or place of business in Korea, or one represented by
either of the former.

The Patent Act[100] provides that anyone who makes an invention capable
of industrial application may obtain a patent and has exclusive rights for a
term of 15 years with extensions of five years for certain patents, including
pharmaceuticals and agrochemicals (Arts. 29 and 88). Specifically, the
Patent Act's protected works include products and processes, including
pharmaceutical drugs, chemicals, agrochemicals, and plants among others. In
line with international standards, if is likely the patent term will soon be
extended to 20 years. The Utility Model Act[101] provides that devices that
relate to shape, structure, or industrially applicable articles may be registered
and enjoy exclusive rights to commercial use for a term of 10 years (Arts. 4,
22 and 23). The Design Act[102] provides for registration and exclusive use of
any design able to be utilized in the industry for a term of 10 years (Arts. 5
and 40).

A patent for the three types intellectual property rights may not be
granted if the invention is not novel in that it is publicly known or worked in
Korea or the invention is described in a Korean or foreign publication, or
that it is not inventive in that the invention can easily, or very easily in
the case of utility models, be made by a person with ordinary skill in the

pertinent art or if it is identical to a prior patent application. Particularly relating to utility models and designs, certain designs similar to national symbols, designs against public order or good morals, and those which might cause confusion with articles connected with another business are not registerable (Design Act, Art. 6). Also, inventions against public morality are prohibited.

The patent rights come into force upon registration and only the first applicant is entitled to obtain a patent and its exclusive rights. For foreign patent applications given effect in Korea, the date of filing in the foreign country is deemed the date of filing in Korea under the several statutes. The exclusive rights to a patent, however, do not extend to uses for research or experiment, identical products existing in Korea at the time the patent application was filed, and for cars, vessels and airplanes (including machinery and instruments) passing through Korea.

H.45   Patent rights, and the rights to obtain a patent, are transferable, and the patentee may grant exclusive or non-exclusive rights to the invention, but if there are joint owners, the consent of all is required. For patents obtained by employees in the course and scope of the business of the employer, the employer has a non-exclusive license on the patent right, but the invention itself belongs to the employee. After four years of granting a patent, non-exclusive compulsory licenses may be available if the invention is not worked for three years or more unless due to *force majeure*, is not commercially worked on a reasonable scale for three years without justification, domestic demand is not being satisfied, or the patent holder unjustly refuses to grant license and is necessary for public interest. Mediation and arbitration are provided for determining compulsory licensing. A patent may even be canceled for such reasons.

The remedies available to a patent holder for infringement are demand for prohibition and prevention of infringing measures, damages in the amount of lost profits due to the infringement, and criminal sanctions. The infringing activities are defined as manufacturing, transferring, leasing, importing, or commercially demonstrating objects exclusively used in manufacturing the patented subject matter or used exclusively for the patented process. Infringement actions and other procedures relating to patents by persons without domicile in Korea or a place of business in Korea requires representation by a patent agent. A separate patent court is slated to be established in March of 1998.

It has been noted, however, that for process patents there may be problems with enforcement. In *Chevron Research Co. v. Jin Heung Fine Chemical Co.* "[t]he court did not recognize the principle that an owner of a dependent patent is not free to use that patent when such a dependent patent is an improvement of an exiting pioneering patent."[103] Enforcement in general seems to be the problem in Korea as it is difficult to prove infringement in Korea as evidence must be gathered by the plaintiff and the assistance of a private investigator is prohibited.[104] Injunctive remedies are time-consuming, requiring a few months, and a deposit of security is required.[105] The damages are sometimes inadequate as they are based on profits earned by the infringer or reasonable royalty, rather than the actual loss due to infringement.[106]

Trade Mark

The Trade Mark Act (TMA)[107] provides that any person who uses or intends   **H.46** to use a trade mark in Korea is entitled to register the trade mark and has exclusive rights to use that trade mark for the designated goods for 10 years periods that can be renewed indefinitely (Arts. 3, 42 and 50). It is important to note that rights under the TMA require registration. The registerable trade marks include combinations of symbols, color schemes, letters or devices (TMA, Art. 2).

Unregisterable marks include generic names conventionally used for the type of good, a name that indicates only origin, quality or geography, which is a common surname, is a simple and common mark, or is a mark that does not show ownership (TMA, Art. 6). Other reasons for not being able to register marks include the same reasons as unpatentable designs; marks falsely representing relationship with or is likely to libel or insult states, races, organizations, religions; marks similar to well-known marks indicating state or public organizations; a mark likely to injure public order or morals; those similar to honorary medals or certificates; relating to renowned persons; identical or similar to a trade mark already registered; similar to a trade mark conspicuously known to others as the goods of another; or likely to cause confusion with the goods or business of another (TMA, Art. 7). Enforcement and remedies available for infringement are similar to the measures available for patent infringement.

In other enforcement measures, the Unfair Competition Prevention Act (UCPA)[108] regulates unfair trade practice relating to trade mark infringement. Unfair trade practices include causing confusion of one's goods with another, causing confusion as to commercial facilities or activities, or causing misconception of the place of origin (UCPA, Art. 2). The remedies available for infringement are injunctive orders, compensation for damages and restoration of reputation, and it is possible for the damaged party to request seizure and destruction of counterfeit goods in addition to orders for ceasing infringing activities (UCPA, Arts. 4 to 6 and 10 to 12). The provisions of the UCPA, however, extend only to injured parties with residence or business office in a foreign country that is a party to the Paris Convention.

Copyright

The Copyright Act[109] provides that works of foreigners are entitled to pro-   **H.47** spective protection under the treaties acceded to by Korea only if published after the effective date of accession (which is July 1, 1987 under the Universal Copyright Convention) and if reciprocity exists with the copyright holder's country (CA, Art. 3). Korea has joined the Universal Copyright Convention

(UCC) and Geneva 71 Convention, and is expected to join the Berne Convention, but with limitations or exception to the retroactivity clause. The Copyright Act provides protection for linguistic and artistic works, musical works, theatrical works, architectural works, photographic works, visual works, maps and diagrammatic works, and computer program works (CA, Art. 4).

Publication by foreigners residing in Korea, works first published in Korea, or works published in Korea within 30 days after foreign publication are also entitled to protection of the Copyright Act (CA, Art. 3). The Copyright Act affords protection, regardless of registration, for life plus 50 years or 50 years for anonymous or pseudonymous works and works created by organizations (CA, Arts. 36 to 38). The author has the right to reproduce work, publicly perform work, broadcast, exhibit, distribute, and prepare derivative works (CA, Arts. 16 to 21). The author's property rights may be transferred in whole or in part, but unlike patents, copyrights for work made in the course of employment and under the employer's direction belong to the employer (CA, Art. 41).

The copyright holder may also establish a publishing right. Unless otherwise agreed, the publishing right holder has a duty to publish to work within nine months and the right lasts for three years (CA, Arts. 55 and 56). Derivative works are protected as independent works and neighboring rights, which includes stage performances, recordings and broadcasts, are protected for 50 years (CA, Arts. 5, 61 and 70).

Acts of infringement of a copyright include importing goods for distribution and local distribution of infringed products (CA, Art. 92). In determining compensation, the infringer's profits are deemed to be the copyright holder's damages, but if estimation is difficult the Copyright Act provides for a statutory quantity (CA, Arts. 93 to 94). Other remedies include injunctive orders and claims for restoration of reputation (CA, Arts. 91 and 95).

Software and Semiconductor Circuit Layout

H.48 According to the Computer Program Protection Act (CPPA)[110] programs by foreigners are protected according to treaties that Korea has acceded to, but if the programs are created by a foreign legal person with principle office in Korea or are first published in Korea, it is protected by the CPPA as long as there is reciprocity (CPPA, Art. 3). As such, businesses of UCC member countries are afforded protection. Although registration is not required for protection, the Federation of Korea Information Industries handles software registration.

The program copyright lasts for 50 years from the time the program is created and no formal procedures are required (CPPA, Art. 8). The CPPA's protection probably extends to the object and source code as the definition of a computer program is a series of instructions or commands used, directly or indirectly, for obtaining a certain result from an information processor (Art.

2). The program author has the right to decide disclosure, the right to indicate real name or pseudonym, the right to maintain the identity of the title, contents and form of program, and the right to reproduce, adapt, translate, distribute and publish the program (CPPA, Art. 8). In particular, a license to use a computer program does not include the right to transfer the right to a third person without the consent of the copyright holder. Derivative programs are protected as independent programs.

The Semiconductor Chip Layout-Design Protection Act[111] protects foreign chip designs, but Korea has not acceded to any international treaties. The right to exclusive commercial use for 10 years is created by registering the design. The Act provides for compulsory "non-exclusive license if the Minister finds that the awarding of the non-voluntary license is necessary for national security, to protect free competition, or to prevent an abuse of the layout-design rights."[112]

Notes

[1] The Customs Act, Law, No. 1976 (November 29, 1967), last amended by Law No. 4743 (March 24, 1994).

[2] Hyung Jin Kim, "The Current Korean Anti-Dumping System" (1993) 21 Kor. J. Comp. L. 1 at p.2.

[3] *Ibid.*, p.9.

[4] *Ibid.*, p.13.

[5] *Ibid.*, p.14.

[6] Young Moo Shin, Dook Sik Kim and Sung Geun Kim, "Recent Korean Anti-Dumping Cases Against Foreign Companies" pp.2–3 (The International Association of Korean Lawyers, 1993 San Francisco Conference).

[7] *Ibid.*, p.3.

[8] *Ibid.*, p.4.

[9] *Ibid.*, p.5.

[10] Hyung Jin Kim, *op. cit.*, p.9.

[11] *Ibid.*, p.6.

[12] Foreign Trade Act, Law No. 3895 (December 31, 1986), amended by Law No. 4573 (August 5, 1993).

[13] Technology Development Promotion Act, Law No. 2399 (December 28, 1972), last amended by Law No. 4148 (December 30, 1989).

[14] Monopoly Regulation and Fair Trade Act, Law No. 3320 (December 31, 1980), last amended by Law No. 4513 (December 8, 1992).

[15] Chang Hee Lee and Byung Kook Min, "Legal Aspects of Establishing a Business Presence in the Republic of Korea" (1990) 3 Transnational Lawyer 39 at pp.68–69.

[16] Unfair Competition Prevention Act, Law No. 911 (December 30, 1961), last amended by Law No. 4478 (December 31, 1991).

[17] Civil Code, Law No. 471 (February 22, 1958), last amended by Law No. 4199 (January 13, 1990).

[18] Conflict of Laws Act, Law No. 966 (January 15, 1962).

[19] Commercial Code, Law No. 1000 (January 20, 1962), last amended by Law No. 4470 (December 31, 1991).

20 *See* Yoon Chick Kwack, Allan, Hiscock and Rebuck, *Credit and Security in Korea* (1973).

21 Chang Hee Lee and Byung Kook Min, *op. cit.*, pp.72–73.

22 Sang-Hyun Song, "Foreign Investment in Korea under the Foreign Capital Inducement Act and the Foreign Exchange Control Act" in *Korean Law in Global Economy*, Vol.II, §7(a)(i), p.11 (unpublished New York University School of Law class materials compiled by Professor Sang-Hyun Song 1995). *See also* Tae Hee Lee, "Doing Business in Korea" (1991) 13 Comp. Yearbook of Int'l Bus. 180.

23 Sang-Hyun Song (foreign investment), *op. cit.*, pp.11–12. "Non-income-producing activities may include purchasing goods, storing or displaying goods not for sale, conducting advertising or public relations, collection and supply of information, market research, having materials processed by others, and similar liaison activities of a preliminary or auxiliary nature, for its home office and other branches of the same corporate entity." *Ibid.*, (citing Corporation Tax Law Art. 56(4)).

24 *See* Tae Hee Lee, *op. cit.*, p.180.

25 Corporate Tax Act, Law No. 1964 (November 29, 1967), last amended by Law No. 4664 (December 31, 1993) Art. 56, para. 4.

26 *Ibid.*

27 Sang-Hyun Song (foreign investment), *op. cit.*, pp.13–14.

28 Tae Hee Lee, *op. cit.*, p.13. *See* Com. Code Art. 614, paras. 1–2.

29 Chang Hee Lee & Byung Kook Min, *op.cit.*, p.46.

30 Commercial Code, Article 173 provides that a company cannot be a member with unlimited liability of another company.

31 Chang Hee Lee and Byung Kook Min, *op. cit.*, p.66.

32 Act Concerning External Audit of Joint Stock Corporation, Law No. 3297 (December 31, 1980), last amended by Law No. 4680 (December 31, 1993).

33 Securities Exchange Act, wholly amended by Law No. 2920 (December 22, 1976), last amended by Law No. 4701 (January 5, 1994).

34 Enforcement Decree of the Securities Exchange Act, wholly amended by Presidential Decree No. 8436 (February 9, 1977), last amended by Presidential Decree No. 14229 (April 30, 1994).

35 Arbitration Act, Law No. 1767 (March 16, 1966), amended by Law No. 4541 (March 6, 1993).

36 Sang-Hyun Song, "Alternative Dispute Resolution Procedures in Korea" in *The Korean Law in Global Economy*, Vol.1, §6(b), p.3 (unpublished New York University School of Law class materials compiled by Professor Sang-Hyun Song 1995).

37 *Ibid.*, p.5.

38 *Ibid.*, p.11.

39 Code of Civil Procedure, Law No. 547 (April 4, 1960), last amended by Law No. 4561 (June 11, 1993).

40 Han-Gak Jang, "Republic of Korea" (1990) 14 Maritime Lawyer 321 at 321 n.2. *See also* Young June Mok, "The Principle of Reciprocity in the United Nations Convention on the Recognition of Enforcement by Foreign Arbitral Award of 1958" (1989) 21 Case Western Reserve J. of Int'l L. 123 at pp.151–157.

41 Sang-Hyun Song (dispute resolution), *op. cit.*, p.6.

42 *Ibid.*, "The administrative sanctions appear to be severe enough to persuade many Korean respondents in the international commercial claims to honor their obligations." *Ibid.*

43 *Ibid.*, p.42.

44 *Ibid.*, p.33.

45 *Ibid.*, pp.33–34.

46 Banking Act, Law No. 19 (May 5, 1950), last amended by Law No. 4468 (December 31, 1991).

47 KPMG Sang Tong & Co., *Banking in Korea* (1992), pp.106–107.

48 *Ibid.*, p.107.

49 *Ibid.*, pp.98–99.

50 Foreign Exchange Control Act, wholly amended by Law No. 4447 (December 27, 1991).

51 Song (foreign investment), *op. cit.*, p.11.

52 *Ibid.*

53 *Ibid.*

54 Consumer Protection Act, wholly amended by Law No. 3921 (December 31, 1986).

55 The MOFE establishes consumer protection policy on a year to year basis (Enforcement Decree of CPA Art. 3).

56 Enforcement Decree of the Consumer Protection Act, wholly amended by Presidential Decree No. 12121 (April 1, 1987), amended by Presidential Decree No. 13870 (March 6, 1993).

57 Basic Environmental Policy Act, Law No. 4257 (August 1, 1990), last amended by Law No. 4492 (December 31, 1991).

58 Enforcement Decree of the Basic Environmental Protection Act, Presidential Decree No. 13303 (February 2, 1991), last amended by Presidential Decree No. 14255 (May 4, 1994).

59 Liability for Environment Improvement Expenses Act, Law No. 4493 (December 31, 1991), last amended by Law No. 4714 (January 5, 1994).

60 Environmental Pollution Damage Dispute Adjustment Act, Law No. 4285 (August 1, 1990).

61 Natural Environment Preservation Act, Law No. 4492 (December 31, 1991).

62 Noise and Vibration Regulation Act, Law No. 4259 (August 1, 1990), last amended by Law No. 4654 (December 27, 1993).

63 Water Environment Preservation Act, Law No. 4266 (August 1, 1990), last amended by Law No. 4782 (August 3, 1994).

64 Sea Pollution Prevention Act, wholly amended by Law No. 4365 (March 8, 1991).

65 Tae Hee Lee and Sugayan, "Environmental Law of South Korea" in *International Environmental Law and Regulation* (1992) p.S.Kor-9.

66 Korean Ministry of Environment, "National Report of the Republic of Korea to the Commission on Sustainable Development" in *The Present Condition Global Environmental Measures* (1994) pp.219–220.

67 Tae Hee Lee and Sugayan, *op. cit.*, p.S.Kor-27.

68 Korean Ministry of Environment, *op. cit.*, pp.218–219.

69 *Ibid.*, p.222.

70 Act Relating to Transboundary Movements of Wastes and Their Disposal, Law No. 4534 (December 8, 1992).

71 Industrial Safety and Health Act, wholly amended by Law No. 4220 (January 13, 1990), last amended by Law No. 4622 (December 27, 1993).

72 Industrial Injury Compensation Act, Law No. 1438 (November 5, 1963), last amended by Law No. 4641 (December 27, 1993).

73 Labor Standards Law, Law No. 286 (May 10, 1953), last amended by Law No. 4220 (January 13, 1990).

74 Immigration Control Act, Law No. 4522 (December 8, 1992), last amended by Law No. 4592 (December 10, 1993).

75 Employment Equality Act, Law No. 3989 (December 4, 1987), last amended by Law No. 4126 (April 1, 1989).

76 Labor Management Council Act, Law No. 3348 (December 31, 1980), last amended by Law No. 3968 (November 28, 1987).

77 Labor Union Act, Law No. 1329 (April 17, 1963), last amended by Law No. 3966 (November 28, 1987).

[78] Temporary and Special Act Concerning Labor Unions and Mediation of Labor Disputes in Foreign Invested Enterprises, Law No. 2192 (January 1, 1970), last amended by Law No. 3691 (December 31, 1983).

[79] Labor Disputes Adjustment Law, Law No. 1327 (April 17, 1963), last amended by Law No. 3967 (November 28, 1987).

[80] Foreign Capital Inducement Act, wholly amended by Law No. 3691 (December 31, 1983), amended by Law No. 4584 (December 10, 1993).

[81] Tae Hee Lee, *op. cit.*, p.175.

[82] Chang Hee Lee and Byung Kook Min, *op. cit.*, p.62.

[83] Enforcement Decree of the Foreign Capital Inducement Act, wholly amended by Presidential Decree No. 11460 (June 30, 1984), last amended by Presidential Decree No. 14178 (February 28, 1994).

[84] Chun Wook Hyun, "Legal Aspects of Technology Licensing in the Republic of Korea" (1988) 27 Columbia J. of Trans. Law 53 at 60.

[85] Tae Hee Lee, *op. cit.*, p.178.

[86] *Ibid.*

[87] Act Concerning Land Acquisition and Management by Aliens, Law No. 4726 (January 7, 1994).

[88] Enforcement Decree of the Act Concerning Land Acquisition and Management by Aliens, Presidential Decree No. 14233 (April 30, 1994).

[89] Sang-Hyun Song (foreign investment), *op. cit.*, p.9. In tax planning it is advisable to consult guidelines as there are always notices one is not aware that may seriously affect business prospects.

[90] Local Tax Act, Law No. 827 (December 8, 1961), last amended by Law No. 4720 (January 7, 1994).

[91] Tax Exemption and Reduction Act, wholly amended by Law No. 4666 (December 31, 1993), last amended by Law No. 4744 (March 24, 1994).

[92] Corporate Tax Act, Law No. 1964 (November 29, 1967), last amended by Law No. 4664 (December 31, 1993).

[93] Chang Hee Lee & Byung Kook Min, *op. cit.*, pp.57–58.

[94] Sang-Hyun Song (foreign investment), *op. cit.*, p.18.

[95] Income Tax Act, Law No. 2705 (December 24, 1974), last amended by Law No. 4661 (December 31, 1993).

[96] Value-Added Tax Act, Law No. 2394 (December 22, 1976), last amended by Law No. 4743 (March 24, 1994).

[97] Customs Act, wholly amended by Law No. 1976 (November 29, 1967), last amended by Law No. 4743 (March 24, 1994).

[98] Special Act Relating to Refundment of Customs, etc. on Raw Materials for Export, wholly amended by Law No. 3747 (August 7, 1984), last amended by Law No. 4667 (December 31, 1993) Arts. 5, 10.

[99] Sang-Hyun Song and Seong-Ki Kim, "The Impact of Multilateral Trade Negotiations on Intellectual Property Laws in Korea" (1994) 13 UCLA Pac. Basin L.J. 118 at p.123.

[100] Patent Act, Law No. 2505 (February 8, 1973), last amended by Law No. 4594 (December 10, 1993).

[101] Utility Model Act, wholly amended by Law No. 4209 (January 13, 1990), last amended by Law No. 4596 (December 10, 1993).

[102] Design Act, wholly amended by Law No. 4208 (January 13, 1990), last amended by Law No. 4595 (December 10, 1993).

[103] Judgment of Apr. 19, 1985 (*Chevron Research Co. v. Jin Heung Fine Chemical Co.*) Taepopwon [Supreme Court], 83 Hu 85, 1985(1) Popwon Kongbu 732 (Korea) (cited in Sang-Hyun Song and Seong-Ki Kim, *op. cit.*, p.131).

[104] Sang-Hyun Song and Seong-Ki Kim, *op. cit.*, p.133.

[105] *Ibid.*

[106] *Ibid.*

[107] Trademark Act, wholly amended by Law No. 4210 (January 13, 1990), last amended by Law No. 4597 (December 10, 1993).

[108] Unfair Competition Prevention Act, Law No. 911 (December 30, 1961), last amended by Law No. 4478 (December 31, 1991).

[109] Copyright Act, wholly amended by Law No. 3916 (December 31, 1986), last amended by Law No. 4717 (January 7, 1994).

[110] Computer Program Protection Act, Law No. 3920 (December 31, 1986), last amended by Law No. 4541 (March 6, 1993).

[111] Semiconductor Chip Layout-Design Protection Act, Law No. 4526 (December 8, 1992).

[112] Enforcement Decree of the Semiconductor Integrated Circuit Layout-Design Act, Presidential Decree No. 13972 (1993) art. 6 (cited in Sang-Hyun Song and Seong-Ki Kim, *op. cit.*, p.129).

TAIWAN

Gregory Klatt

I. Summary of Business and Political Conditions

Basic Demographic, Political and Economic Information

Taiwan is an island lying 160 kilometers off the south-east coast of China.   I.01
Long governed as a dependency of imperial China, Taiwan gained provincial
status in 1887. After being defeated in the Sino-Japanese War (1894–1895),
China ceded control of Taiwan to Japan. Japan imposed reformist yet repres-
sive colonial rule on Taiwan and exploited the island's natural resources to
fuel its imperialistic expansion efforts.

In 1911 Nationalist forces under the command of Generalisimo Chiang
Kai-shek overthrew the Chinese imperial government and established the
Republic of China (ROC). Control of Taiwan was returned to China in 1945,
after Japan's defeat ended the Second World War. Four years later the
Communist takeover of the Chinese mainland forced the Nationalists to
relocate the ROC government to Taiwan. Since 1949 the Nationalists have
controlled Taiwan, the small islands of Quemoy and Matsu lying within
artillery range of the mainland coast, and several other small islands in the
South China Sea.

Thereafter known as the Government of the Republic of China *on Taiwan*, the Nationalist government continued to be widely recognized as the
sole legitimate government of China. This changed in 1971, however, when
the ROC was ejected from the United Nations and the People's Republic of
China (PRC) allowed to enter. By 1979, most nations, including the United
States, recognized the PRC as the sole legitimate government of China,
including Taiwan.

Yet the ROC government remains firmly in control of Taiwan, and it is
unlikely that Taiwan will be militarily or politically reunited with China in

the foreseeable future. At the dawn of the 21st century, Taiwan is an integral player in the world economy and one of the most successful democracies in Asia. Most developed nations have substantial economic ties with Taiwan and hence a vested interest in maintaining stability in the region. The United States, for historical and political reasons, maintains especially close ties with Taiwan under a thick veneer of unofficiality. Consequently Taiwan, economic powerhouse and *de facto* nation, promises to play an important role in the 21st century.

Geographic and Demographic Information

I.02   Taiwan straddles the Tropic of Cancer some 160 kilometers off China's south-eastern coast. The island is oblong shaped, measuring 377 kilometers (245 miles) from north to south and up to 142 kilometers from east to west. Taiwan's land area, including the 13 smaller islands of the Taiwan Group, is nearly 36,000 square kilometers. Mountains cover some 64 per cent of the island, foothills 11 per cent, alluvial plains 24 per cent, and urban or industrial areas the remainder. The Central Mountain Range, containing some of the highest peaks in Asia outside of the Himalayas, divides Taiwan along a roughly north-south meridian. To the west, mountains gently slope into foothills and extensive alluvial plains. To the east, peaks plunge steeply into the Pacific Ocean, forming one of the most rugged and majestic coastlines in Asia. Taiwan's population, agriculture, and industry are concentrated on the western coastal plains. The climate is generally subtropical, and typhoons frequently impact the island during the summer. With the exception of now denuded forests and fisheries, Taiwan has few natural resources.

Taiwan's population is fast approaching 25 million. The descendants of Polynesian and Malay settlers have inhabited the island for thousands of years, but after centuries of conflict and intermarriage with ethnic Chinese immigrants, these "aboriginal" peoples are now few in number and largely restricted to the island's most remote mountain areas. Today almost all Taiwanese are ethnic Chinese. Mandarin (*guo yu*) is the official language of the ROC, but a derivative of the Min dialect (*Minnan hua*), commonly referred to as "Taiwanese" (*Taiwan hua*), is widely spoken. A variety of other Chinese dialects are spoken in the homes of more recent immigrants. Tens of thousands of non-Chinese, mainly foreign business professionals and immigrant laborers, also reside on Taiwan. English is compulsory in primary and secondary school, yet relatively few people outside the higher levels of government, commerce and academia master the language.

Prior to 1945, nearly all the Chinese on Taiwan were descended from rice farmers and fishermen who began immigrating in significant numbers from Fujian and Guangdong in the 17th century. Between 1945 and 1950, several million more ethnic Chinese fleeing from the civil war and turmoil on the mainland relocated on Taiwan. Many of these so-called "mainlanders" (*wai sheng ren*) were government officials, landlords, and businessmen from every province of China; over 500,000 were members of the Republic of China's armed forces. After relocation of the ROC government to Taiwan in 1949, the "mainlanders" controlled not only the central government, but also the provincial government and all levels of local government. This bred resentment among the "Taiwanese" (*ben sheng ren*), the descendants of pre-20th century immigrants. Tensions between "mainlanders" and "Taiwanese" have been greatly reduced, however, by the passage of time, intermarriage, and democratization of Taiwan's social, political, and economic institutions.

Many people in their twenties and thirties think of themselves first as *Taiwan ren*, or a "person from Taiwan", which denotes an identity *vis à vis* the rest of the world regardless of one's *wai sheng* or *ben sheng* heritage. While on a different and higher level, ethnic Chinese on Taiwan think of themselves as being Chinese (*zhong guo ren*).

Political and Economic Information

Although the government of the ROC is structured as a constitutional democracy with attributes of both presidential and parliamentary systems, Jiang Jie-shi (more commonly known in the West as Chiang Kai-Shek) and the Nationalist Party (*Guoming Dang*) ruled Taiwan with an iron fist for decades following the relocation of the ROC government to the island in 1949. The constitution was suspended and the national legislature frozen in its pre-1949 state.   I.03

Martial law was finally lifted only after political and economic conditions on Taiwan had stabilized. Political reforms throughout the late 1980s and early 1990s have since moved Taiwan well on its way toward full democracy. Recently Taiwan made headlines worldwide with the first popular election of a chief executive in Chinese history. While the Nationalist Party still dominates national, provincial, and local politics, the Democratic Progressive Party (*Minjin Dang*) is a viable opposition party and commands a sizable minority in the national legislature.

Under the Constitution of 1946, chief executive power may reside in either the president or the premier. At present, the two offices share power. The government is divided into five organs, or *yuan*. Executive power resides in the Executive Yuan, which administers through eight ministries and two commissions, namely the Ministry of Interior, Ministry of Foreign Affairs, Ministry of National Defense, Ministry of Finance, Ministry of Justice, Ministry of Education, Ministry of Economic Affairs, Ministry of Communications, Overseas Chinese Commission, and Mongolian & Tibetan Affairs Commission. Primary legislative authority resides in the Legislative Yuan. The Judicial Yuan supervises the courts and has limited power to make laws applicable to the judiciary. The Control Yuan is charged with supervising the conduct and operations government officials and agencies. The Examination Yuan administers civil service exams and other national examination systems.

Taiwan's post-war economy has been characterized by rapid growth and change. Taiwan's gross domestic product (GDP) grew at an annual rate of 9.1 per cent between 1950 and 1990, and is now the fourth largest in Asia, behind Japan, China and South Korea.[1] In 1992, Taiwan's GDP was $206.5 billion, up 13 per cent in nominal terms and 6.7 per cent in real terms from 1991.[2] By 1994, Taiwan's GDP topped $240 billion.[2a] At present, Taiwan has the fifth highest standard of living in Asia, surpassed only by that of Japan, Australia, Hong Kong, and Singapore, and its per capita income is comparable to that in many southern European countries.[3] In 1992, Taiwan's per capita gross national product (GNP) was $9,895, up 12.3 per cent in nominal terms from 1991.[4] The economy is predicted to grow at slightly less impressive but robust rates well into the next century.

Once agrarian-based, Taiwan's economy is now dominated by the service and manufacturing industries, with foreign trade related activity accounting for three-quarters of Taiwan's GDP. Taiwan was ranked the world's fourteenth largest trading nation in 1991. Although the state actively manages and regulates many areas of economic activity, the 1993 World Competitive Report ranked Taiwan as the third most open economy among the world's newly industrialized countries.[4a]

Small- or medium-sized, family owned and operated businesses form the backbone of Taiwan's economy. These businesses are characteristically headed by highly entrepreneurial risk takers who have proven adapt at meeting the challenges and exploiting the opportunities created by economic globalization. Due to the limited size of these enterprises, however, they have generally not been able to take advantage of economies of scale or develop product image like the large conglomerates of Japan, Korea, and Hong Kong.

State-run enterprises — most importantly monopolies in alcohol and tobacco, sugar, transportation, ship building, telecommunications, petroleum, steel, fertilizer, and banking — are responsible for nearly one-third of Taiwan's gross domestic product. Although Taiwan has embarked on an ambitious program to privatize its state-run enterprises, results thus far have been less than satisfactory.

No discussion of Taiwan's economy would be complete without mention of the recent explosion of trade with mainland China. Although the government strictly forbids direct trade with China, indirect trade is believed to have grown at an annual rate of 36 per cent since 1987 and is now estimated to account for 10 per cent of Taiwan's foreign trade. The government recently relaxed restrictions on indirect trade with China, and it will be forced to set parameters for direct trade after China takes control of Hong Kong in 1997.

Historical Development of the Legal and Judicial System in Taiwan

The history of Taiwan's legal and judicial system can be divided into two periods: the traditional period, starting with the advent of Chinese imperial system and ending just before the collapse of the Qing dynasty in the late 19th century; and the modern period, starting in the late Qing era and continuing through today's rapid reforms.   I.04

The law of Imperial China was shaped by two philosophies, Legalism and Confucianism. Legalism, pre-eminent during the Qin dynasty (221–206 BC), was founded on a belief in the rule of law. Legalist believed that social and political order was dependent on the law, under which all men should be treated equally. They believed social order could only be fostered and maintained through widespread knowledge and severe penal sanctions for violation of the law. The law was to be imposed from the top down, however, so it is more accurate to describe Legalism as being based on a belief in "rule by law," not the "rule of law".[5] Confucianism, by contrast, emphasized moral education and the example of virtuous leaders as foundations of social and political order. Confucianism, which became dominant during the reign of Emperor Wu-ti of the Western Han dynasty (approximately 140–86 BC), placed a premium on strict observance of hierarchical relationships as necessary for the maintenance of social harmony.[6] Law was seen as an instrument for the preservation of hierarchical relations and social harmony. Rights and duties, rewards and punishments all depended on social status. For this reason, Confucianism has been described as a system of "rule of personality".

Imperial legal codes focused on criminal and public law; private law was given little attention. Consequently, civil disputes were resolved through informal means according to custom and tradition. Without the rule of law to ensure observance of private rights and obligations, the stability of business relations traditionally depended on personal ties of blood, friendship, and association; a tradition of no small importance in modern Taiwanese business circles.

China was forced to confront the inadequacies of its legal system as a result of contact with the West in the 19th century. Western powers were able to extract grants of extraterritorial rights from the Qing government based on the argument, backed up by superior military might, that China's "primitive" legal system did not afford adequate protection to the property or person of foreign merchants and officials. Soon afterwards the Qing government launched a program to modernize the Chinese legal system. Foreign laws were studied in detail. New codes were drafted, based largely on the laws of Japan, an East Asian country that had successfully transformed itself into a modern nation capable of defending itself from foreign powers. Japan had based its modern codes on the civil law systems of continental

Europe, particularly Germany, as the piecemeal nature of the common law did not lend itself to translation or wholesale adoption.

The pace of legal reform slowed during the turmoil of the 1911 Revolution and the war with Japan, but never completely stopped. By the end of World War II, the government had codified all the major civil, commercial, and criminal laws necessary for the governance and welfare of a modern state. Legal reform in the post-war period has focused on implementation of existing laws and changes and innovations necessitated by experience and the modernization of Taiwan's society and economy. Post-war legal reforms have been heavily influenced by American law, especially those laws directly affecting commercial transactions in Taiwan.

The government has come to view law as an important tool of economic and social policy. Most notably, the government has embarked on ambitious programs to modernize Taiwan's commercial law in order to foster the development of Taiwan as a regional center for banking and finance, shipping and transportation, telecommunications and media operations, and bioengineering, just to name a few of the economic sectors targeted thus far. As in the 19th century, the goal is to achieve economic and political parity with the West and Japan.

Role of Taiwan in Global and Regional Trade Forums

I.05 Taiwan's ability to participate in global and regional trade forums is greatly hampered by China's insistence on non-recognition of the ROC. China has firmly refused to let Taiwan participate in UN organizations in any form. Taiwan was allowed to maintain its seat on the Asian Development Bank (ADB), however, under the name of "Taipei, China". And Taiwan was able to join the Asian-Pacific Economic Cooperation (APEC) under the name of "Chinese Taipei". Taiwan has lobbied heavily to join the General Agreement on Tariffs and Trade (GATT) since the early 1980s. While Taiwan has yet to be granted full membership in the GATT as a result of China's steadfast resistance, it has been granted observer status, and prospects for full membership can only improve as Taiwan's role in the world economy expands.

Current Legal and Judicial Structure for Regulation of Commercial Activities in Taiwan

I.06 The Constitution of 1946 is the supreme law of Taiwan. Any law in conflict with the Constitution is null and void.[7] Legislation, second in authority to the Constitution, is passed by the Legislative Yuan and promulgated by the President.[8] Treaties have the force of legislation.[9] Government agencies are authorized by legislation to enact rules and regulations in their particular areas of competence and authority.[10] Any rule or regulation in conflict with the Constitution or valid legislation is likewise null and void.[11] Judicial precedent has no binding force under Taiwan law, yet as in most civil law counties, judges feel obligated to follow the decisions of higher courts.

Taiwan has a four-tiered court system consisting of the Council of Grand Justices, charged with interpreting the Constitution and providing authoritative interpretations of legislation and regulations; the ROC Supreme Court, the highest court of appeal for all civil and criminal cases excluding questions of constitutional and administrative law; the Taiwan High Court, an intermediary court of appeal for all cases but those involving national security or foreign relations, over which the High Court enjoys primary jurisdiction; and numerous District Courts, the court of first instance in most cases. The Administrative Court, established at the same level as the Supreme Court, provides judicial review of administrative rules and actions. The Commission on the Discipline of Public Functionaries, also on parity with the Supreme Court, tries actions for impeachment of public officials brought by the Control Yuan.

The laws affecting commercial transactions in Taiwan are concentrated in the Book on Obligations of the ROC Civil Code, the ROC Company Law, and the ROC Law of Negotiable Instruments. The ROC government has also passed a wide range of statutes dealing with specific commercial practices and markets, the Fair Trade Law and the Securities and Exchange Law being just two examples. These statutes are usually supplemented by agency enacted rules and regulations. While Taiwan has developed an extensive body of modern commercial law, many laws and regulations are not strictly enforced or are ignored in practice.

II. Laws and Institutions Affecting Business and Commercial Activities

Competition Law

The basic provisions of Taiwan's competition law and unfair trade law are contained in the ROC Fair Trade Law (FTL), promulgated in 1991 and enforced as of February 4, 1992. The FTL replaces an array of antiquated laws — some adopted prior to World War II — which were designed to meet the special needs of Taiwan's wartime and post-war economy. These laws, and the interventionist or protectionist policies behind them, became outmoded as Taiwan's economy matured.[12]

The FTL, enacted "to maintain order in transactions, to protect the interests of consumers, to ensure fair competition, and to promote the stability

I.07

and prosperity of the national economy", regulates monopolies, mergers and combinations, concerted actions, and unfair trade practices.[12a] The FTL is applicable to activities that take place or have an effect in Taiwan, and so may apply to foreign firms that conduct business in Taiwan but do not maintain a permanent presence there. Government agencies are subject to the FTL under a market-participation test.[13] The FTL is only intended to prohibit practices which have a *net* effect of reducing competition.[14] Consequently, the FTL embodies a "rule of reason" approach that permits enforcement authorities to take into account the intent, effect, and reasonableness of regulated practices in determining whether they should be prohibited.[15] Importantly, the FTL does not apply to acts "performed by an enterprise in accordance with other laws".[15a] As this would render the FTL ineffective in many instances, the government is considering amending a wide range of laws to incorporate the FTL's provisions.

The ROC Fair Trade Commission (FTC), formed under the Executive Yuan, has primary responsibility for implementing the FTL. The FTC is comprised of nine presidential-appointed commissioners who sit for three-year, renewable terms. Commissioners have expertise in such areas as law or economics and function as independent administrators, with the exception of the chairman, a cabinet level official answerable to the legislature.[15b] The FTL authorizes the FTC to promulgated rules and regulations, investigate violations of the FTL, issue a wide range of administrative orders, and impose fines for violation of the FTL or failure to comply with its orders.[15c]

Antitrust Law

Monopolies

I.08   The primary focus of the FTL's competition provisions is monopoly regulation. The FTL defines "monopoly" as a condition where an enterprise does not face competition or, by virtue of market share, is able to exclude competitors from a particular market.[15d] The scope of the market in question is a function of market structure, that is, the relevant product market and geographic market.[16] The FTL also regulates oligopolies, defined as a condition where two or more enterprises do not compete with each other in pricing and whose relations, taken as a whole, create a "monopoly" as defined above.[16a]

In determining whether an enterprise is a "monopoly", the FTC must consider the enterprise's market share and ability to control market prices, the availability of substitute products or services in the given market; the existence of barriers to market entry by other enterprises; and import and export conditions.[17] Article 10 of the FTL requires the FTC publishes the names of monopolistic and oligopolisitc enterprises, but this may be discontinued under pending amendment to the FTL.

The FTL does not prohibit the mere possession of monopoly power. Rather, monopolies are prohibited from engaging in unfair practices that

exclude competitors, engaging in improper pricing practices, securing preferential treatment from other enterprises without proper cause, engaging in
improper pricing practices, and engaging in any conduct which constitutes an
abuse of market position.[18] Violation of the FTL's monopoly provisions are
punishable by up to three-years imprisonment and fines of up to NT$1
million per offense.[19] Injured parties may also recover damages, but the FTL
does not contain any provision for the recovery of punitive damages.[20]

Mergers and Combinations

The FTL regulates the formation of monopolies through pre-transaction   **I.09**
notification and approval requirements. Specifically, the FTC must be notified and its approval secured where an enterprise intends to merge with
another enterprise; acquire more than one-third of the voting shares or
capital of another enterprise, acquire or lease more than half of another
enterprise's business or assets, engage in prolonged joint operations with
another enterprise or manage another enterprise at that enterprise's request,
or directly or indirectly control the operations or personnel of another
enterprise.[21] Because the FTL is only intended to regulate combinations that
will have a significant effect on the market in question, FTC notification and
approval is required only where the combined enterprise will control one-
third of the relevant market; one of the enterprises to be combined already
controls one-quarter of the relevant market; or one of the enterprises to be
combined had sales in excess of a threshold set by the FTC.[22] Failure to
comply with the FTL's notice and approval provisions may result in forced
divestiture, suspension or cessation of business operations, and fines of up to
NT$1 million per violation.[23]

The FTC decides whether to approve a proposed combination using a
cost-benefit analysis. The FTC may permit combinations where the benefits
to the national economy outweigh the costs of restricted competition.[24] This
cost-benefit analysis is in tension with the FTL's market share analysis for
determining the existence of a monopoly.[25] It remains to be seen how the
FTC will balance the competing interests represented by these tests.

Concerted Actions, Vertical Restraints, and Exclusionary Practices

The FTL contains several provisions designed to curtail business practices   **I.10**
that restrain free trade. Specifically, competing enterprises are generally
prohibited from acting in concert to set prices or restrict "quantities, technology, products, equipment, trading counterparts or trading territories".[26] Exceptions are provided for concerted action that the FTC has approved as
beneficial to the national economy and the public interest, including the
creation of industry standards, joint research and development, market spe-
cialization, overseas ventures, importing ventures, production limits neces-

sary to protect hardship industries, and cooperation among small- and medium sized enterprises.[27] FTC approval is granted for three years and may be renewed for another three on a showing of good cause.[28] Violation of the FTL's concerted action provisions is punishable by up to three years imprisonment and fines of up to NT$1 million per offense.[29] Injured parties may recover damages.[30]

The FTL also specifically prohibits exclusionary practices including coercive boycotting, unjustified discriminatory treatment, unfair inducements, and tying arrangements.[31] The FTL also prohibits enterprises from acquiring trade secrets through improper means.[32] Violation of these prohibitions is punishable by up to two years imprisonment and fines of up to NT$500,000 per offense.[33] Injured parties may also sue for damages.[34]

Unfair Trade Law

I.11   The FTL's unfair trade provisions are designed to protect business goodwill and prevent consumer confusion. Specifically, the FTL prohibits the misuse of publicly recognized trademarks, business names, service marks, and other commercial symbols.[35] Each offense is punishable by up to three years imprisonment and a fine of up to NT$1 million. False advertising and misrepresentations likely to mislead the public are also prohibited, as are false statements likely to harm the business of another enterprise.[36] Pyramid schemes, once rampant in Taiwan, are subject to special regulation and, if participants earn income mainly from introducing others to join the scheme, prohibited outright.[37] Lastly, the FTL contains a blanket prohibition against deceptive or unfair practices likely to cause market disruption.[38] More specific protection of consumer interests is provided under the Consumer Protection Law (CPL), as discussed below. Violators of the FTL's unfair trade provisons are subject to administrative fines and imprisonment, as well as being liable to injured parties for damages.[39]

Contract Law

I.12   Taiwan's domestic law of contracts is derived from the Book on Obligations of the ROC Civil Code and numerous cases applying and interpreting the code's broadly worded provisions. As in all civil law countries, *mutual agreement* is central to Taiwan's contract law. This doctrine also finds expression in Taiwan's conflict of laws provision governing contracts, under which the intent of the contracting parties, either expressed or implied, determines the law governing the contract.[40] If the parties do not evidence a specific intent, however, then the law governing the contract is either the law of the place where the contract was formed, the place of offer, the domicile of the offeror, or the place of performance, depending on the circumstances.[41] The ROC courts will not give effect to any provision of foreign law that is "contrary to the public order and good morals".[42]

Contract formation requires manifestation of the parties' express or implied intent to form a contract and agreement on the contract's essential terms.[43] A contract may also be formed by receipt of a deposit in partial payment of the contract amount.[44] An offer remains open, unless the offeror expressed a contrary intent at the time of offer, until it is revoked, rejected, or expires.[45] A face-to-face offer must be accepted immediately.[46] Other offers must be accepted before expiration of a reasonable period of time, or the time stipulated.[47] Acceptance may be in the form of an agreed upon act.[48] Acceptance may also be in the form of some other act where custom or the nature of the contract so dictate, or where the offeror has waived notice of acceptance.[49] Delayed acceptance is binding if the offeree was not at fault for the delay, unless the offeror provides timely notice thereof.[50] Late acceptance is deemed a new offer.[51] Likewise, an acceptance proposing the addition, deletion, or modification of terms is deemed a new offer.

The terms of performance are generally set by the parties. The place of performance, if not specified by the parties, operation of law, or custom, and not ascertainable by reference to the nature of the contract or the surrounding circumstances, is generally deemed to be the place of the creditor's domicile.[52] If the parties have set the time of performance, the creditor may not demand early performance; the debtor, however, may tender performance early, unless either party has expressed a contrary intent.[53] If the parties have not set the time of performance, and it is not ascertainable by operation of law or reference to the nature of the contract or the surrounding circumstance, the creditor may demand performance and the debtor may tender performance at any time.[54] If performance is contingent on the existence of pre-conditions, and those pre-conditions have not been satisfied by the agreed upon time for performance, the debtor is not required to perform.[55] The costs of performance, unless set by the parties or by law, are the debtor's responsibility.[56] However, if the creditor increased the costs of performance by virtue of changing domicile or any other act, the creditor is responsible for the increased costs.

Parties are required to perform in honesty and good faith.[57] The object of performance is not required to be something that can be valued in money, but may take the form of a forbearance or payment in kind.[58] Substitute performance is effective, subject to the creditor's approval.[59] If the debtor fails to satisfy the substituted obligation, the original obligation revives, unless the parties have agreed otherwise.[60] If the contract provides for a choice among several forms of performance, the debtor has the right of choice, upon timely notice to the creditor, unless otherwise provided for by law or contract.[61] A party to a contract may refuse to perform, subject to the aforementioned restrictions of honesty and good faith, until the other party performs.[62] If one party has performed in part, however, the other party cannot refuse to perform, unless doing so would not be a breach of honesty and good faith. If, on the other hand, a decline in a party's financial condition after formation of the contract casts doubt on that party's ability to perform, the other party may refuse to perform until the problematic party actually performs or provides security for its performance.[63]

If performance of a contract is impossible, the contract is deemed void.[64] Parties are relieved from any duty to perform to the extent they are not responsible for the impossibility.[65] If a party has a choice among several forms of performance, and one form was impossible from the beginning or becomes impossible, that party, if not responsible for the impossibility, is relieved from the duty to perform to the extent of the impossibility.[66] If, through no fault of the parties, it becomes impossible for one of the parties to perform, the other party is relieved from the duty to counter-perform to the extent of the impossibility.[67] However, a party that knew or had the means of knowing of the impossibility of full or partial performance at the time the contract was formed is liable to the misled party.[68] Lastly, injured parties have subrogation rights against innocent parties that recover from third parties.[69]

The rules governing multi-party transactions can be divided into two categories: those governing multi-party contracts, and those governing transfers of rights and obligations. Disputes in multi-party contracts usually revolve around who is entitled to performance. In the case of a contract that provides for performance for the benefit of a third party, both the third party and promisee can demand performance.[70] If the third party declares the intention not to take advantage of the contract, the parties may modify or cancel the contract, and the third party loses all contractual rights. The promisor is liable for the third party's failure to perform.[71] All defenses arising under the contract are available to the promisor against the third party beneficiary.[72]

Parties to multi-party contracts may be subject to joint and several liability.[73] Creditors and debtors of the same divisible obligation possess equal shares of rights and liabilities, unless otherwise provided for by law or the parties' agreement.[74] Joint liability adheres where the parties expressly accept joint liability, or where the case law so indicates.[75] Joint debtors who satisfy an obligation enjoy the right of contribution against the non-performing joint debtors. Each joint debtor, however, is individually liable for costs and damages caused by that debtor.[76]

Creditors are allowed to assign claims to a third party, subject to notice to the original debtor, unless the nature of the claim does not permit transfer; the parties have agreed to the contrary; or the claim in not subject to judicial attachment.[77] The creditor's tender of a deed of transfer to the debtor is considered due notice.[78]

Debtors may assert not only the defenses available against the third party assignee, but also the defenses that would have been available against the creditor absent the assignment.[79] Debtors may transfer obligations to third parties, subject to the creditor's approval.[80] The third party assuming an obligation may present all the defenses available to the original debtor against the creditor.[81] Several of the aforementioned articles also provide rules for the treatment of set-offs in multi-party contract scenarios.

Parties can terminate contract obligations in several different ways. Tender of performance to the creditor or its qualified representative extinguishes an obligation.[82] If the creditor has defaulted or is impossible to ascertain, the debtor may terminate the obligation by depositing a sum equal in value to the obligation with the appropriate institution or the court.[83] Of course, a creditor may always release a debtor from its obligation.[84] Parties may also set-off similar obligations owed to each other.[85] And contract rights and obligations may be terminated if they become vested in the same person.[86]

A party will be held in default if it does not tender performance within the agreed-upon time.[87] If the time of performance is not specified, a debtor who receives notice from the creditor demanding performance will be held in default if it does not tender performance within the time set forth in the demand notice. Likewise, a creditor who refuses the debtor's performance will be held in default.[88]

Parties injured by default have a range of remedies available. Injured parties must generally be restored to their pre-injury condition.[89] Injured parties are entitled to damages if their prior condition cannot be restored without great difficulty.[90] Courts will only award damages for actual injury and lost profits, the latter defined as that profit normally expected in the course of ordinary business or according to projections, preparation, or other special circumstances.[91]

If a debtor fails to perform in full or in part, the creditor may apply to the court for an order of compulsory execution and sue for damages.[92] Where the claimant contributed to its damages, the court may reduce the damages or grant no damages at all.[93] The court also has discretion to reduce damages if the injury complained of was not caused intentionally or through gross negligence, or reparation would seriously threaten the responsible party's livelihood.[94]

The other main remedies available are recision, preservation, and liquidation damages. If a party fails to perform within a reasonable period after the other party gives notice, the other party may rescind the contract.[95] The other party's exercise of its right of recision does not extinguish its right to damages.[96] To preserve its interests, a creditor may exercise any right of the debtor that the debtor fails to exercise on its own behalf, excepting those rights that are by nature personal to the debtor.[97] In addition, a creditor may petition to the court to enjoin the debtor from performing an act that is likely to be prejudicial to the creditor's interests, provided that the recipient of the act to be enjoined knew of the surrounding circumstances.[98] An injured party may also sue for liquidation damages if the contract so provides.[99] The injured party may also sue for damages, unless the parties agreed to the contrary.[100]

Commercial Law

Sales Law

I.13   Taiwan, not being a member of the United Nations, is not a party to the UN Convention on Contracts for the International Sale of Goods. Furthermore, Taiwan does not have a statutory equivalent to the United States' Uniform Commercial Code. Consequently, the law governing a sales contract depends on the contract's provisions or place of formation.[101] If not otherwise provided for by the parties or operation of law, the specific rules governing sales transactions set forth in the Book of Obligations of the Civil Code apply.

For the Civil Code's sales provisions to apply, the contract must be a "contract of sale" as defined in the Code. A "sale" is defined as a contract wherein the parties agree that one party will transfer its rights over a property to the other in exchange for the other's payment of a price.[101a] The existence of a sale is not dependent on completion of the formalities of transferring ownership registration.[102] Rather, a contract of sale is formed when the parties agree upon the object of sale and sales price.[103]

The Code sets forth several gap-filling provisions that enable courts to enforce sales contracts despite the ambiguity of certain terms. For example, the sales price, if not set by the parties, may be inferred from the surrounding circumstances.[104] If the parties agreed to set the price according to the market, the price is deemed to be the market price as of the time and place of performance unless otherwise provided for by contract. And if the price is set according to weight, the weight is deemed not to include the weight of the packaging unless otherwise provided for by contract or custom.[105]

The profits and risks of the object (or right to possession) sold pass to the buyer at the time of delivery unless otherwise provided for by contract. However, if the buyer requests that the seller deliver the object sold to a location other than where, based on the Codes provisions governing performance, the object would normally be delivered, the risks pass to the buyer when the seller delivers the object to the entity entrusted with its transport to the specified location.[106]

The costs of performance are borne by the parties equally unless otherwise provided for by law, contract, or custom.[107] Subject to the same qualifications, the seller bears the costs of transferring the right sold, transporting the object sold to the place of performance, and delivery, and the buyer bears the costs of taking delivery, forwarding the thing sold to a place other than the place of performance, and registering ownership. In addition, the buyer is obligated to reimburse the seller for necessary costs the seller incurs in relation to object sold after the risks have passed to the buyer but prior to actual delivery.[108] The seller is liable, however, to the buyer for damages resulting from the seller's unwarranted deviation from the buyer's forwarding instructions.[109]

The formation of a sales contract creates certain rights and obligations in the parties. The seller is required to deliver the object sold and cause the buyer to acquire its ownership (or cause the buyer to acquire the right sold).[110] The seller must also extend several warranties. Specifically, the seller must warrant that the right or object sold is free from any third party rights enforceable against the buyer.[111] The seller of a right or claim is required to warrant that the right or claim actually exists.[112] The seller of a right must warrant any defects in the right sold unless the buyer had notice thereof.[113] The seller of a claim, however, is not required to warrant the debtor's solvency, and any warrant so extended is only presumed to warrant the debtor's solvency as of the time of the claim's transfer.[114] The seller must further warrant that the thing sold has the promised qualities and is free from any defects in quality which may impair or destroy its value, or is fit for the purposes of the sales contract.[115] An agreement disclaiming the seller's liability for defects is void if the seller intentionally concealed the defect from the buyer.[116] In addition, the courts generally will not give effect to contract language disclaiming the above described quality and performance warranties.[117]

The buyer is required to pay the agreed upon sales price to the seller and to accept delivery of the object sold.[118] However, the buyer may refuse to pay the sales price to the extent it has good reason to believe that a third party may assert rights which may deprive the buyer of its rights, unless the seller has provided adequate security.[118a] The buyer is also obligated to inspect the thing delivered to him without delay and notify the seller of any defects unless they could not have been discovered immediately.[119] If the required notice is not given, the buyer is deemed to have accepted the thing delivered unless the defect could not have been discovered by ordinary examination. The buyer is also required to preserve perishable goods it has rejected as defective if the seller does not have an agent at the place of delivery.[119a] If the buyer fails to preserve such goods, the defect is presumed not to have existed at the time of delivery.

If the seller fails to perform its duties under the warranties of ownership and freedom from third party claims described above, the buyer can seek specific performance, sue for damages, or employ any of the other remedies that the Code provides for non-performance of obligations in general.[120] If the seller fails to perform its duties under the quality warranties described above, the buyer has the option to ask for a reduction in price or to rescind the contract.[120a] Recision is not available, however, where it would constitute an obvious unfairness to the seller.[120b] If the thing sold does not have a certain quality that the seller warranted, or if the seller intentionally concealed the defect, the buyer may demand compensation for non-performance, instead of seeking a reduction in price or recision.[121] Similarly, if the thing sold is designated only as to its kind and the thing delivered is defective, the buyer may ask the seller to deliver a defect-free replacement instead of seeking a reduction in price or recision.[122] The seller is not responsible, however, for quality defects of which the buyer had notice or, if the seller has not warranted that the thing sold is free from quality defects, defects which the buyer would have discovered if not for its own gross negligence.[123]

Secured Transactions

I.14   Financing in Taiwan, both short- and long-term, is largely asset based. Consequently, Taiwan has relatively comprehensive laws governing security agreements. It does not, however, have a comprehensive system for floating charges and liens like the United States' Uniform Commercial Code.

Credit transactions in Taiwan are usually documented by a basic financing agreement, promissory note(s), and other documentation of registration required to create security interests over the assets securing the extended credit. Credit agreements in Taiwan usually cover the same issues that such agreements in developed countries address.

Common security devices in Taiwan include real estate and chattel mortgages, trust receipts, pledges, and assignments/endorsements of negotiable instruments.[124] Non-residents are barred from holding security interests in Taiwan mortgages or trust receipts.[124a]

Real estate and chattel mortgages are created by execution and registration of the mortgage agreement. Mortgaged chattel must also be affixed with a plaque identifying it as such. Land and buildings are often owned separately, and are subject to being mortgaged separately. Chattel mortgages are commonly used to secure financing for equipment purchases. A mortgage creates a security interest in favor of the mortgagee in priority to other creditors and later mortgages. If the mortgagor defaults, the mortgagee can foreclose and dispose of the mortgaged property through private sale or public auction.[124b]

Trust receipts are created by execution and registration of a trust agreement. Trust receipts give the trustor ownership and the right of repossession. Foreclosure and sale procedures are similar to those for mortgages.[124c]

Creation of a pledge requires execution of a pledge agreement and transfer of possession of the pledged property. Pledges are most often used to create security interests in assets whose ownership is evidenced through stocks, bonds, and similar inidicia, such that "transfer of possession does not interfere with the benefits of ownership".[125] Pledges may also be used to establish a security interest in inventory.[126] Foreclosure and sale procedures are similar to those for mortgages.[127]

An assignment of rights is created by execution of an assignment agreement and notification of the debtor. Although possible, assignments are rarely used in Taiwan to create security interests in receivables.[128] Instead, such security interests are more often created by the endorsement of a post-dated check or promissory note.[129] Post-dated checks are the most popular of the two forms, stemming from the fact that dishonoring a post-dated check used to be a *per se* criminal offense.[130] Today, however, promissory notes may be preferable, among other reasons,[131] because of the expedited collection procedures available under the Law on Negotiable Instruments.[132]

Companies Law

Basic rules governing the formation, organization, operation, and dissolution of Taiwan businesses are set forth in the Company Law.[133] The Ministry of Economic Affairs (MOEA) has primary authority to regulate Taiwan companies under the Company Law. The MOEA is now considering amending the Company Law to shed some of its more paternalistic provisions, especially those pertaining to disposition of earnings and reorganizations, and bring the law up to date with modern developments and conditions.   **I.15**

The Company Law authorizes four forms of business organization: unlimited companies,[134] a form of incorporated partnership; unlimited companies with limited liability shareholders,[135] akin to limited liability partnerships; limited companies,[136] a form of closely held, limited liability company; and companies limited by shares,[137] the Taiwan equivalent of limited liability "corporations".[138] The first two forms — rarely used in practice since they subject owners to double taxation on company earnings — are not discussed further in this chapter.

General Provisions

Several of the Company Law's provisions are applied to both limited companies and companies limited by shares. The promoters of either must first secure a Certificate of Incorporation (company license) from the MOEA or its designated agent, and a Certificate of Business Registration (business license) from the appropriate tax authority, before the company is recognized as a legal entity.[139] To be issued a company license, promoters must submit the company's articles of incorporation, proof of deposit of the company's authorized capital, and a "clean" opinion from an independent auditor. A company's articles of incorporation serve as both its organic law and bylaws, and as such are typically more detailed than those of foreign companies. Minimum capital requirements are set by the MOEA, and additional amounts may be required in certain industries.[140] Business may not be conducted in a company's name until the above registration requirements have been satisfied.[141] Company names must be registered with the MOEA, but protection of company and trade names is best effected through the Fair Trade Law.   **I.16**

Responsibility for company management lies with a company's board of directors. Responsibility for day-to-day operations, however, is usually delegated to one or more appointed managers, all of whom must be Taiwan residents.[142] Shareholders must approve the appointment, removal, and terms of employment of company managers.[143] An individual may be disqualified from serving as a company manager based on a recent bankruptcy or past criminal convictions for fraud, embezzlement, or wrongful business conduct.[144]

At the end of each fiscal year a company's board of directors must submit numerous records to the shareholders for approval or acceptance, including an operations report, balance sheet, statement of inventory, income statement, statement of cash flows, and any proposed resolutions concerning the distribution of dividends or apportionment of losses.[145] Any material misrepresentation in reporting may lead to the imposition of criminal sanctions.[146] The MOEA is authorized to inspect a company's records at any time to ascertain its business and financial conditions, and to determine whether it has complied with the above reporting requirements.[147] Interference with government inspectors is punishable by administrative sanctions.

The Company Law contains several provisions limiting corporate action in order to protect creditors. Generally, a company may not conduct business outside the scope of activities authorized in its articles of incorporation.[148] Specifically, a company may not be an unlimited liability shareholder in another company or a partner in a partnership; invest more than the equivalent of 40 per cent of its own paid-in capital in another limited liability company unless authorized to do so in its articles of incorporation; or extend loans to shareholders or third parties (including other corporations) unless there is a business purpose for doing so.[149] Creditors must beware, however, that a company's guarantee will not be valid against the company unless it is authorized to act as a surety or guarantor in its articles of incorporation.[149a]

Limited Company

I.17 A limited company must have at least five and no more than 21 shareholders.[150] At least half of a limited company's shareholders must be ROC nationals domiciled in Taiwan, and these shareholders must provide at least half of the company's initial paid-in capital. The liability of limited company shareholders is limited to their capital contributions.[151]

Instead of issuing shares, a limited company issues scrip indicating each shareholder's capital contribution.[152] Shareholders have one vote each, unless the company's articles of incorporation provide for voting power to be allocated in proportion to each shareholder's capital contribution. Shareholder resolutions generally require majority approval, but important changes may only be approved at a meeting of a super-majority or all shareholders, depending on the nature of the proposed action.[153] Majority approval is required for any transfer of shares, and dissenting shareholders have first refusal rights.[154]

A limited company must have at least one and not more than three directors.[155] At least one active director must be an ROC national domiciled in Taiwan. A director must secure approval from all shareholders to transfer any part of his or her shares in the company.[156]

Company Limited by Shares

A company limited by shares must have at least seven initial shareholders,   I.18
half of whom must be Taiwan residents.[157] These promoters may pay the company's authorized capital in installments, but the first installment must be at least one-quarter of the authorized total.[158] If the company's authorized capital exceeds a certain ceiling, it must "go public"; that is, it must offer a certain amount of its shares to the public and comply with the registration and reporting requirements set forth in the securities laws.[159]

A company limited by shares will usually issue only one class of common stock.[160] It may issue special stock, however, if its articles of incorporation so authorize.[161] A company limited by shares is generally prohibited from buying back its common stock short of a registered and approved reduction in paid-in capital.[162] It may buy back its special stock, however, using the proceeds of new issues.[163] When making a new issue, the company must set aside 10 to 15 per cent of the shares for purchase by its employees.[164]

Share transfers may not be restricted in the articles of incorporation of a company limited by shares.[165] Shareholders, however, are free to contract transfer restrictions among themselves. Promoters are specifically barred from transferring their shares for one year after the company is incorporated.[166]

A company's board of directors is responsible for managing the company's business and finances.[167] Board decisions are effected through resolutions, which must receive majority approval at a meeting of a quorum of directors to be binding on the company.[168] A company's founding directors must elect a chairman, who is empowered to convene board meetings.[169] Directors must attend board meetings in person.[170] A director who is unable to attend in person may appoint a proxy, but the proxy must be another director, and a director may serve as a proxy for only one other director. A large board may appoint managing directors, who are authorized to convene meetings among themselves and act in the capacity of the board of directors when the full board is not in session.[171]

The powers of directors are constrained in several important ways. First, shareholders must approve directors' salaries.[172] Second, a director is required to disclose his interests in a company upon election to its board, and must retain at least half of his equity interest in the company as of the date of his election throughout his term or be immediately dismissed from office.[173] Third, directors must execute their duties with due care.[174] Fourth, directors are prohibited from voting, either in their personal capacity or as proxies, on resolutions in which their interests may be adverse to those of the company.[175] Lastly, and perhaps most importantly, directors must act in accordance with the law, regulation, the company's articles of incorporation, and shareholder resolutions.[176] The Company Law provides for derivative suits against directors who have breached any legal or fiduciary duty to the company or shareholders.[177] Derivative suits have been relatively rare to date,[178] but may increase in frequency as direct foreign investment in Taiwan's public companies increases.

Directors are also constrained through the independent auditing of elected shareholder representatives, called "supervisors". A company must have at least one "supervisor", and at least one supervisor must be a Taiwan resident.[179] In the case of multiple supervisors, each supervisor has a duty to act in the company's best interests independent of the other supervisors.[180] Supervisors have blanket authority to inquire into the status of a company's financial and operational conditions, inspect the company's books, records, and documents, and demand reports from the board of directors.[181] Supervisors also have an affirmative duty to investigate all statements and records submitted by the board at shareholders' meetings.[182] If a supervisor becomes aware of any board action contrary to the law, regulations, or the company's articles of incorporation, he is required to demand the board to cease the offensive act.[183] Directors may not interfere with a supervisor's execution of his duties, and must immediately report any material losses or damages the company is in danger of suffering.[184] Supervisors represent the company in derivative suits against directors.[185]

Ultimate authority for decision-making lies with a company's shareholders. Shareholders wield their authority through resolutions, which must be passed by a majority vote at a shareholders meeting.[186] Shareholders must attend meetings in person, but a shareholder who is unable to attend a meeting may appoint a proxy by executing a power of attorney prepared by the company for that purpose.[187] A quorum requires the presence, in person or by proxy, of shareholders owning at least half of a company's issued and outstanding shares.[188] Majority approval during a meeting of a super-quorum of shareholders is required for major corporate decisions, including merger, dissolution, sale of substantially all assets, and major acquisitions.[189] A company may not vote its own shares, and company-owned shares are not counted in calculating a quorum.[190]

I.19   Shareholder power is constrained in two important ways. First, a shareholder may not vote, either his own shares or as a proxy, on a resolution concerning a matter in which the shareholder's interests may be adverse to those of the company.[191] Second, a shareholder resolution approving action contrary to the law, regulation, or the company's articles of incorporation is null and void, and any shareholder may petition the court to revoke the offending resolution.[192]

The board of directors is required to call a shareholders' meeting at least once six months after the close of each fiscal year.[193] Special meetings may be called at any time with appropriate notice. Besides the board of directors, any shareholder may submit a resolution for shareholder approval, but only shareholders owning at least three per cent of a company's issued and out-standing shares may call for a special shareholder meeting.[194]

Shareholder approval is required for distributions of dividends and em-ployee bonuses.[195] For this reason, and also for cultural reasons, most compa-nies pay out dividends and bonuses only once a year.[196] Dividends must be distributed *pro rata*.[197] Bonuses must be paid in accordance with the terms set forth in a company's articles of incorporation.

Dividends and bonuses may only be paid out of company earnings in excess of capital reserve requirements. Capital reserves accrue from stock premiums, retained earnings, profits from the sale of capital assets, capital contributions, and merger generated gains.[197a] Ten per cent of net profits must be set aside until the reserve equals the company's total authorized capital.[198] Reserves must first be used to cover any current or accrued losses.[198a] Only after covering all losses and building up the required reserve may a company use *additional* net profits to pay out dividends and employee bonuses.[199] A limited exception is provided for situations where a payment of dividends and bonuses is necessary to maintain a company's stock price.

Corporate reorganization requires court approval.[199a] A company may be dissolved by shareholder resolution or court order.[200] The court may order a company dissolved if it has not conducted business for six months or there is evidence of illegal activity.[201] Dissolution does not require shareholder ap-proval if the pre-condition(s) for dissolution identified in the company's articles of incorporation are present.[202]

Foreign Companies

All the forms of business enterprise set forth in the Company Law are available to foreigners. Furthermore, the government encourages certain categories of foreign investment by exempting approved foreign-invested companies from the provisions of the Company Law designed to preserve local control and promote diversification of ownership.[203] On the other hand, the government specifically bars or restricts foreign investment in certain industries it considers of strategic significance[204] and several other more broadly defined categories of enterprise.[205] In order to conduct business in Taiwan, a foreign company must be recognized by the MOEA as duly organized and engaged in business in its home country, under Company Law art. 371.

Foreign companies are also free to enter joint venture arrangements with Taiwan companies as Taiwan law neither defines nor provides special rules applicable to "joint ventures". Joint venture agreements are viewed as private contracts and do not trigger any registration requirement as in many devel-oping nations. The only limits on joint ventures are those applicable to foreign investment in general.[206]

The company limited by shares is the most popular form of enterprise among foreign investors, in part because until recently a company wishing to

I.20

avail itself of the incentives provided under the Statute for Upgrading Industry[207] (SUI) had to be organized as such. Many foreign companies maintain a less formal — and therefore less expensive — presence in Taiwan in the form of liaison, representative, or branch offices. A foreign company's choice of form for its Taiwan operations depends on the scope and intensity of the activities it intends to conduct locally, as well as issues of head firm liability and taxation.

Liaison and Representative Offices

I.21 A foreign firm that only requires the services of a local representative to perform liaison functions — such as inspecting shipments or conducting market surveys — may establish a liaison office, the least formal foreign commercial presence in Taiwan. A liaison office is not a legal entity, and the head firm's Taiwan representative may not perform juristic acts on its behalf. A liaison office is created simply by securing a tax unified number — used for withholding purposes — from the local tax authorities. Besides being simple to establish, a liaison office has the advantage of not exposing its head firm to the jurisdiction of the Taiwan courts or tax authorities.

A firm requiring a local representative capable of performing juristic acts on its behalf but not intending to conduct business in Taiwan may establish a representative office under article 386 of the Company Law. A so-called "386 office" is not a legal entity and is not allowed to engage in profit-seeking activities. To establish a 386 office, a foreign company must secure the above-described recognition from the MOEA and a tax number from the tax authorities.[208] While establishing a 386 office exposes the head firm to the jurisdiction of Taiwan courts, it does not create Taiwan tax liability for the head office (unless, of course, the 386 office engages in profit-seeking activities). Consequently, the 386 office is well suited for firms that source in Taiwan, but may not be suitable for firms that wish to conduct local marketing or sales activities.

Branch Offices

I.22 A foreign firm that wishes to conduct business in Taiwan but not create a separate legal entity for that purpose may establish a branch office. Branches may engage in profit-seeking activities,[209] including manufacturing.[210] Branches have been far more popular among foreign finance and trade enterprises than foreign manufacturing firms because until recently branches engaged in manufacturing were not eligible for the investment incentives otherwise available to companies under the SUI.

To establish a branch office, a foreign company must be recognized by the MOEA as described above and remit sufficient capital to meet applicable minimum capital requirements and fund the branch's operations.[211] The foreign firm is also required to appoint an agent to represent the company in all legal and non-legal matters, and to serve as the "responsible person" for the branch's activities in Taiwan.[212] Once formed, the branch must secure a branch company license from the local authorities before conducting business and is required to secure a business license form the tax authorities.[213] Once established, a branch must maintain separate books and is subject to local taxation on income generated in Taiwan. A branch must also submit annual financial and operating reports[214] to its head office for shareholder approval.[214a]

Capital Markets and Securities Law

Capital Markets

The Taiwan Stock Exchange (TSE), formed in 1962, is Taiwan's only public securities exchange. The TSE did not play a significant role in Taiwan's capital markets until the late 1980s, when the doubling of the stock index from 1985 to 1986 attracted individual investors in droves. Rampant speculation ensued, launching the index from 1,000 to over 12,000 points in four very active years of trading. The bubble burst in late 1990, however, with trading volumes plummeting and the index crashing to just over 2,500. The TSE has since regained some of its former vibrancy, but the index is not expected to approach its 1990 zenith for some time.   **I.23**

An over-the-counter (OTC) market in government bonds and shares in privatized enterprises has existed since the early 1950s. An OTC market for corporate securities did not exist until 1988, however, when the securities laws were revised to authorize and regulate over-the-counter transactions.

Securities Law

The Securities and Exchange Law (SEL), promulgated in 1968 and comprehensively amended in 1988, is the primary statute regulating Taiwan's capital markets and market participants. The SEL is modeled on the United States' Securities Act of 1933 and Securities Exchange Act of 1934, and to a somewhat lesser degree Japan's Securities Exchange Law of 1948.[215]   **I.24**

The SEL is administered by the Ministry of Finance through the Securities and Exchange Commission (SEC).[216] The SEC regulates the issuing, offering, and trading of securities and supervises the financial reporting of public companies.[217] The SEC, like its U.S. counterpart, has broad rulemaking authority and enforcement power, with a variety of remedial measures and administrative penalties at its command.

The SEL defines "securities" to include any government bonds, corporate stocks, and corporate bonds issued by public offering, and any other securities the MOF may designate.[218] To date the MOF has designated foreign government bonds, corporate stocks, and corporate bonds issued by public offering as securities. Importantly, the MOF has indicated that some foreign investment contracts may be equivalent to securities. Certificates of payment, options, and warrants relating to the foregoing securities are also considered securities subject to the SEL's provisions.[218a]

The SEL prohibits fraudulent acts and misrepresentations in the public offering, issuance, or trading of securities.[219] The filing or publishing of false or misleading information in company financial reports is also prohibited. Sellers and purchasers of securities injured by violation of the above prohibitions may recover "any and all damages" from the offending party. The courts, however, have construed the SEL's anti-fraud provisions narrowly, and few defendants have been held liable despite recurring market scandals.[220]

Companies must secure approval from, or have an effective registration statement filed with, the SEC before issuing securities to the public.[221] Issuers, underwriters, their employees and retained professionals are liable for misrepresentations of material fact and omissions of material fact in public offering materials.[222] The SEL, like its U.S. models, provides for a defense of "due diligence".

The SEL does not contain an express private placement exception. The SEL defines "public offering" to mean any offer of securities to "nonspecific persons".[223] However, the SEC has not further defined "nonspecific persons", and there is no well-developed judicially recognized private placement exception.[224] Furthermore, SEC rules generally require SEC approval or pre-registration for almost all security offerings.[225] Nonetheless, issuers can and do avoid all but the SEL's anti-fraud provisions if they refrain from making any general solicitations and only make offers to wealthy, knowledgeable persons in a directed fashion, preferably through a licensed intermediary.[226]

The SEL regulates tender offers through provisions modeled after those of the U.S. Williams Act of 1968.[227] Any person who acquires more than ten per cent of a public company's total issued shares must report the size of their holdings, purpose of acquisition, and sources of funding, as well as any other information the SEC may require, within ten days of the acquisition.[228] In addition, the SEC's prior approval is required for any public tender offer made outside the TSE or the OTC market.[229]

The SEL addresses the problems of insider trading — rampant in Taiwan's stock market — in two respects. First, the SEL provides a mechanism whereby issuers and shareholders can force corporate insiders[230] to disgorge short-swing profits.[231] Second, the SEL prohibits certain insiders[232] from trading on information which may materially affect the market price of listed shares.[233] To date only a handful of criminal and civil suits have been filed under the SEL's insider trading provisions.[234]

The SEL also addresses the problems of manipulative trading practices. Specifically, the SEL prohibits phantom trading in any listed security,[235] trading or colluding to trade in order to manipulate the market price of any listed security, and disseminating false rumors in order to manipulate the market price of any listed security.[236] In addition, the SEL contains a catch-all provision prohibiting any manipulative act that affects the market price of any listed security. Violation of the above prohibitions is punishable by up to seven years imprisonment and a fine of up to NT$750,000.[236a]

Foreign Market Participation

The SEL expressly forbids foreign nationals from owning the publicly traded **I.25** shares of Taiwan companies.[237] Qualified foreign institutional investors, however, are eligible to apply to for approval to invest directly in securities traded on the TSE or in the OTC market.[238] In order to ensure domestic control of Taiwan's publicly owned companies, no foreign institution may own more than 7 per cent of the total issued shares of any domestic company, and collective foreign institutional ownership may not exceed 15 per cent.[239] These ownership restrictions, as well as stringent restrictions on foreign remittance and use of invested funds, have dampened foreign interest in Taiwan's securities market.[240] Indirect investment in Taiwan's stock market is becoming increasingly popular, however, as numerous funds comprised of Taiwan stocks are being listed on overseas exchanges. Foreign companies may have their shares traded in Taiwan through convertible bonds or Global Depository Receipts sponsored by Taiwan companies.[241]

Foreign securities firms are allowed to participate in Taiwan's capital markets through several channels. First, the SEC allows foreign securities firms to apply to open branch offices. Applicants must met stringent capital and experience criteria, including paid-in capital of $2 billion and $20 billion in total assets, membership on the New York, London, and Tokyo stock exchanges, and employment of at least two brokers with more than ten years of foreign exchange experience.[242] At present only two foreign securities firms operate branch offices in Taiwan.

Second, foreign securities firms are allowed to enter into joint ventures with Taiwan securities firms. No foreign firm may own more than a 10 per cent interest in any joint venture, however, and aggregate foreign ownership cannot exceed 40 per cent.[243]

Finally, foreign securities firms may own up to 49 per cent interests in Taiwan securities investment trust enterprises (SITEs),[244] which manage Taiwan's mutual fund market. Foreign firms may also own interests in securities investment consulting enterprises (SICEs),[245] which offer investment advice concerning domestic and foreign securities. There are no limits on foreign ownership of SICEs.

Arbitration and Other ADR Techniques

The Chinese have a long tradition of resolving disputes through non- **I.26** confrontational means in order to preserve social harmony and maintain long-term relationships. This tradition continues to dominate dispute resolution in modern Taiwan despite rapid industrialization and the resulting disruption of traditional relationships.[246] Most petty civil and criminal claims are settled informally, and mediation through community leaders predominates in rural Taiwan.[247] The law also provides for court-supervised mediation.[248]

Commerical Arbitration

I.27   Commercial arbitration, especially as a mean of resolving transnational commercial disputes, has a much shorter history in Taiwan. As in many countries, the judiciary and legislature resisted commercial arbitration as an infringement on government sovereignty. Resistance relaxed, however, after the international community's 1958 ratification of the Convention on the Recognition and Enforcement of Foreign Arbitral Awards.[249] The ROC Statute for Commercial Arbitration [SCA] was enacted soon afterwards.[250]

The SCA sets forth rules to govern all commercial arbitration in Taiwan, including arbitration of labor disputes[251] and certain claims arising under the securities laws.[252] The statute adopts the contract theory of arbitration, as evident in its choice of law provisions. The parties to an arbitration agreement are free to choose rules other than those contained in the SCA to govern the arbitration process.[253] The parties to a transnational arbitration agreement are free to choose the law governing the arbitration agreement[254] and any claims arising out of the underlying contractual relationship.[255] Finally, the parties may request an arbitration to be decided on equitable principles rather than legal rules.

An agreement to arbitrate must be in writing to be enforceable.[255a] While the SCA does not define "in writing", the courts have taken a rather restrictive view.[256] Consequently, it is recommended that both parties to an agreement to arbitrate execute an express arbitration agreement.[257] In addition, the arbitration agreement must provide for an odd number of arbitrators.[258]

The existence of an enforceable agreement to arbitrate is crucial in two instances. First, if one party to an arbitration agreement attempts to bring suit against the other, the party being sued can have the court refer the parties to arbitration.[259] Second, a party to an arbitration agreement can petition the court for interim measures to preserve the assets of the other party pending arbitration.[260] In both scenarios, the arbitration agreement must encompass the controversy in question to be given effect.[260a]

The parties are free to choose the number of arbitrators — with the above-mentioned proviso that there be an odd number of arbitrators — and the manner of appointing arbitrators.[261] If an arbitration agreement does not provided for the number or manner of appointment of arbitrators, the SCA provides for three arbitrators, each party appointing one and the parties' arbitrators appointing the third.[262] If the parties cannot agree on a tribunal, they may petition the court to appoint arbitrators as-needed. Arbitrators are subject to the highest standards of professionalism and impartiality but are not subject to any nationality restrictions.[263]

Since Taiwan has not ratified the New York Convention on Foreign Arbitral Awards nor adopted its provisions through legislation, the SCA governs recognition and enforcement of both domestic and foreign arbitration awards. The SCA treats foreign awards differently from domestic awards in several important respects. For example, to be enforceable, a domestic award must identify the parties, their counsel, the material facts of the dispute, and the tribunal's reasoning of decision.[264] Foreign awards are not subject to these requirements unless the arbitration agreement identifies Taiwan law as governing the arbitration.[265]

The court must refuse *ex officio* to enforce an award that directs a party to perform an illegal act or pertains to a matter outside the scope of the arbitration agreement.[266] In addition, a party may challenge an award based on the invalidity of the arbitration agreement; unfairness of the proceedings; partiality, misbehavior, or disqualification of an arbitrator; the tribunal's lack of jurisdiction; falsification of evidence; or a judicial change in the substantive law governing the dispute.

Foreign awards are subject to special enforcement requirements mirroring those contained in Article 5 the New York Convention. Specifically, a foreign award will not be enforced if the underlying claim was not subject to arbitration under the law governing the dispute; the award is not final under the law governing the arbitration; there were irregularities in the arbitration panel or procedure; or the award violates public policy.[267] The SCA also allows the court to deny recognition if the country in which the award was rendered does not recognize awards rendered in Taiwan. This reciprocity requirement is largely chimerical insofar as it is discretional and the Taiwan courts view arbitration as a private and not a judicial process.[268] Moreover, awards rendered in the United States are generally enforceable under treaty.[269]

An arbitration award cannot be executed until a Taiwan court has issued an execution order.[269a] A limited exception exists for a domestic awards where the arbitration agreement provides for execution without court order and the claim underlying the award is for cash or cash substitutes, a fixed amount of securities, or specified movable property.

Commercial Arbitration Associations

The SCA authorizes chambers of commerce and industrial associations to   I.28
form commercial arbitration associations.[269b] The ROC Commercial Arbitration Association [CAA] was formed in 1955 as Taiwan's first private arbitration association. No other associations have formed, and the CAA has been largely ignored as a venue for alternative dispute resolution. This is changing, however, as Taiwan businesses increasingly incorporate arbitration

agreements into their domestic and transnational contracts. At present, the CAA has several hundred registered arbitrators and handles dozens of arbitrations annually.

Banking and Lending Law

I.29   Although banking institutions of one form or another have existed in Taiwan for centuries, banks in the modern sense did not exist until the Japanese took control of the island in the early part of the 20th century. The Japanese government formed Taiwan's first modern banks to facilitate exploitation of the island's resources by Japanese industry. The Nationalist government inherited these instruments of Japanese colonialism in the retrocession of 1945. Taiwan's banks remained largely under provincial control, however, until the Nationalists retreated to Taiwan in 1949.

China's banking system was in complete disarray after the Communist takeover of the mainland. The Nationalist government, after relocating to Taiwan, was forced to rely on Taiwan's existing banking system to implement national monetary policy.[270] Only after a ten-year regrouping period did the government allow the Central Bank of China (CBC) to resume full operations. The government also established the China Development Company at this time to facilitate industrialization of Taiwan's economy. Other banks were allowed to resume operations in the following years, and several new banks were allowed to open. A handful of foreign banks were also allowed to set up small-scale operations. Yet government banking policy remained conservative and protectionist.

The Banking Law,[271] the primary statute governing Taiwan's banking industry, was enacted when Taiwan's economy was based on agriculture. For various economic, social and political reasons beyond the scope of this discussion, the Banking Law remained largely unchanged for decades. Reform was not forthcoming until it had became patently obvious that Taiwan's archaic banking system was stymieing economic growth and preventing effective use of the island's burgeoning foreign exchange holdings. Privately owned credit and investment companies partially filled the gaps, but poor regulation and even poorer management often resulted in great losses to investors and periodically threatened economic instability.

After taking tentative steps toward rationalizing Taiwan's banking law in the 1970s, the government embarked on an intensive program to liberalize and internationalize Taiwan's entire banking system in the 1980s. The Banking Law was substantially amended in 1989. Further revisions followed in 1992, and additional amendments are under discussion. Legislation to create an offshore banking center in Taiwan was passed in 1983. And foreign banks have been given greater access to Taiwan's financial markets. The government's goal, besides reforming the banking system to meet current financial service needs, is to foster the development of Taiwan as a regional financial center.

Domestic Banks

The Banking Law identifies four categories of banking institutions: I.30

1. commercial banks, the main component of Taiwan's banking system, which provide traditional deposit and credit services and an increasingly broad range of other banking services;
2. savings banks, authorized to accept savings deposits and extend medium- to long-term credit;
3. specialized banks, which provide loans to specific industries or commercial sectors; and
4. investment trust companies, created to pool capital for commercial investment. The government encourages the conversion and consolidation of investment trust companies and savings banks into commercial banks with trust and savings departments.

Nearly all of Taiwan's banks are government owned. A handful of privately owned banks were allowed to open in the 1960s and 1970s, but the moratorium on the establishment of new commercial banks was not lifted until the 1989 amendments. While several dozen new privately owned commercial banks have been charted since then, they still do not account for a significant portion of Taiwan's banking business.

The Ministry of Finance (MOF) has primary authority to regulate Taiwan's banking industry and exercises that authority through its Monetary Affairs Department.[271a] The MOF has delegated most of its examination authority to the CBC and mainly concerns itself with regulating the chartering and dissolution of banks. This is changing, however, as Taiwan's banking industry expands and the Monetary Affairs Department, elevated to bureau status in 1991, gets more staffing and experience.

The MOF maintains stringent requirements for privately owned commercial banks. For example, individuals and legal entities are prohibited from owning more than 5 per cent of a new bank's total shares directly or 15 per cent through affiliates.[272] New banks must be capitalized at NT$10 billion (approximately US$400 million).[273] Bank managers must have substantial experience in banking or finance. And banks are required to adhere to international capital reserve standards.[274] These requirements, with the exception of the capital reserve standards, are significantly more restrictive than those in most developed countries.

Internationalization

The Offshore Banking Act (OBA) was enacted in 1983 to foster the development of an offshore banking center in Taiwan. The OBA authorizes qualified I.31

Taiwan banks to establish offshore banking units (OBUs) in Taiwan. Approved OBUs enjoy exemptions or special treatment in relation to foreign exchange controls, interest rate regulations, taxes, and capital reserve requirements.[275] Offshore banking has yet to flourish in Taiwan, in part because Singapore, Hong Kong, and offshore banking centers in other regions offer stiff competition to any newcomers, in part because Taiwan has not done enough to make itself attractive to potential offshore banking customers.

Foreign banks, by contrast, have met with more success in penetrating Taiwan's financial markets. The Banking Law authorizes the MOF to allow foreign banks to establish branches in Taiwan as needed to facilitate economic development and international trade.[275a] Under MOF regulations, foreign banks are initially limited to one branch each, usually either in Taipei or Kaohsiung, but may apply to establish additional branches after five years.[276] Foreign head banks must remit US$2 million as operating capital for each Taiwan branch.[277] Managers of foreign bank branches are also subject to educational and experience requirements more stringent than those for domestic bank managers.[278] Due mainly to intensive lobbying by American banking interests, restrictions on the establishment of branches by foreign banks have been relaxed and such branches are now allowed to offer many of the same services as their Taiwan counterparts. Restrictions on foreign investment in Taiwan banks have also been lifted. It will still be many years, however, before foreign banks have complete access to Taiwan's financial markets.

Consumer Protection Law

I.32   Consumer protection languished in Taiwan for decades as policymakers focused on the country's economic development. The tide began to change in 1980 with formation of the Consumers Foundation, a private non-profit organization dedicated to a progressive consumer rights agenda. The Foundation's intensive lobbying efforts paid off in 1994 with passage of the Consumer Protection Law (CPL). Enacted to "protect the rights and interests of consumers, promote the safety of national consumption and living, and enhance the quality of national consumption and living", the CPL is the first legislation of its type in Taiwan's history.

The CPL requires businesses, including non-profit enterprises, to ensure that the goods or services they provide do not pose a danger to the health or safety of consumers or third parties.[279] Goods or services are considered dangerous, and therefore defective, if they do not met normal, reasonable expectations of safety.[279a] Businesses are required to recall goods or cease providing services upon the discovery of potential defects if prompt action will not ameliorate the danger.[280] If particular goods or services are inherently dangerous, conspicuous warning of the danger and, if applicable, explanation of emergency treatment procedures must be displayed on the goods or in connection with the services in question.[281]

An injured consumer or third party may file a complaint directly with the offending business, a consumer protection group, or a local government consumer service center.[282] Businesses are required to respond to consumer complaints within 15 days. Every business in the chain of production and distribution of defective goods or services that cause injury may be held jointly and severally liable for compensatory and punitive damages.[283] Once a dispute goes to court, plaintiffs have the burden of proving the existence of the defect, damages, and causation.[284] Businesses may petition for a reduction in punitive damages based on a showing of non-negligence.[285] Distributors may avoid liability altogether based on a showing of "due care".[286] Furthermore, a showing that the goods or services met then current technological or professional standards will relieve every business in the chain of production and distribution from liability.[287] Businesses may not be held liable on the basis of remedial measures or subsequent improvements in safety.

In addition to ensuring consumer safety, the CPL attempts to protect the rights and interests of consumers with respect to so-called "adhesion" contracts. Standard form contracts must be based on the principles of equality and reciprocity.[288] Consumers must be given reasonable time to review standard contracts in order for such contracts to be enforceable.[289] Ambiguous terms will be interpreted in favor of consumers. Terms that violate the principles of good faith and fairness are null and void.[290] In addition, government agencies are authorized to publish standard form contracts,[291] and contracts that do not conform to government standards are also null and void.[292]

The CPL also seeks to protect consumers in respect to special methods of sale. Consumers who have purchased goods through mail order or as the result of a door-to-door sale have seven days to return the goods and demand a full refund without cause. Contracts containing terms contrary to the above provision are null and void. Installment sales agreements must be in writing and contain the downpayment amount, rate of interest, and total finance charges.[293]

The CPL addresses the problems of exaggerated and fraudulent advertising by requiring enterprises to ensure the accuracy of advertising and to deliver on all promises made in advertising.[294] An advertiser who publishes advertising which it knows or had reason to know contains misleading information is jointly and severally liable for any resulting injury.[295]

Qualified consumer interest groups are recognized as legal entities under the CPL, and, subject to certain limitations, are given standing to sue on behalf of consumers[296] Consumer groups are also authorized to conduct surveys and tests, publish reports, educate consumers and enterprises, mediate consumer disputes, and lobby the government for legislation or administrative action.[297] The CPC is charged with accrediting consumer groups, and qualified groups are eligible to receive government financial support.[298]

Taiwan

The CPL is enfored at the local level. Local governments are required to establish consumer service centers to advise and educate consumers and businesses about their rights and duties under the CPL.[299] Consumer service centers are also required to investigate violations of the CPL and may issue administrative orders to business to recall defective goods or cease providing defective services.[300] In addition, consumer service centers are required establish mediation committees and mediate consumer disputes upon request.[301]

The CPL is administered at the national level by the Consumer Protection Commission (CPC). Formed in July of 1994, the CPC is charged with formulating consumer protection policy and supervising local government enforcement of the CPL, but is not an enforcement agency itself.[302] The CPC promulgated enforcement rules for the CPL on the same day it was formed. The Consumer Foundation has complained that the CPC has been rather lax in executing its duties.[303] This laxity probably reflects the continued dominance of commercial interests in government policy.

Foreign Investment Law[304]

I.33 Foreign direct investment in Taiwan is regulated by either the Statute for Investment by Foreign Nationals ("SIFN") or the Statute for Investment by Overseas Chinese, depending on the identity of the investing party.[305] Investments in Taiwan under either one of these statutes must be approved by the Investment Commission of the Ministry of Economic Affairs.[306] The Investment Commission may condition its approval of an investment project on, for example, an agreement by the foreign company to limit its market share in Taiwan (at least with regard to investments in certain restricted industries).[307]

Foreign investors are allowed to invest cash (remitted in foreign exchange), raw materials, machinery and equipment, technical know-how or patent rights to establish a new enterprise, expand an existing enterprise, to extend loans, to purchase stock or bonds of an existing enterprise or to furnish technical know-how or patent rights as capital stock.[308] Foreign investments under the SIFN require approval of a foreign investment application by Investment Commission which requires, among other things, a description of the investment plan and certain background information regarding the foreign investor.[309] Investment in certain industries may require separate applications for approval to the competent authority regulating the said industry. In practice, not all foreign investment is effected through an application and approval by the Investment Commission. For example, where the structure of the investment is such that it will not be positively affected by the advantages of foreign investment approval or where the investment is in certain restricted industries (see below), the foreign investor may elect not to file an application.

Once approved, foreign investment projects are entitled to certain privileges. These include:

1. repatriation of investment principal after a one-year holding period, and unlimited repatriation of dividend earnings so long as the dividends do not exceed the annual net profit or the accumulated profit as shown on the corporation tax return of the Taiwan company (note that non-approved foreign investing entities may only repatriate up to US$20 million per year and non-approved individuals may only repatriate up to US$5 million per year unless they receive special Central Bank of China approval to remit out greater amounts;[310]
2. exemption from Taiwanese nationality and domicile requirements for the chairman, at least one supervisor, and over one-half of the shareholders of the corporation;[311]
3. ability of the company to be 100 per cent foreign owned via exemption from the aforesaid nationality and domicile requirements for over one-half of shareholders;[312]
4. reduction in the dividend withholding tax from either 25 or 35 per cent to 20 per cent;
5. guarantee against government expropriation for 20 years, provided foreign shareholding exceeds 45 per cent;[313]
6. exemption from the requirement that 10 per cent to 15 per cent of any issuance of new shares be reserved for subscription by the employees of the company.[314]

Foreigners are not permitted to invest in certain industries in Taiwan. These include the following:

1. agriculture, animal husbandry, and hunting;
2. forestry;
3. fishing;
4. certain chemical production (nitroglycerine, alcohol, CFC's, HCFC's, trichloroethane, tetrachloromethane, gun powder, fulminating mercury, and other firing agents);
5. military equipment production (gun barrels, swords, firearms, ammunition, military instruments, other weapons);
6. certain transportation services (bus, taxi, car rental, trucking);
7. communications (phone and mail service);
8. real estate; and
9. radio and television broadcasting.[315]

In addition, foreigners may face restrictions when investing in the following:

1. producing certain types of chemicals (pesticides, herbicides, toxic substances, medicines)
2. mining;

3. petroleum production and refining;
4. electricity production;
5. railway, air, and sea transport;
6. banking and finance;
7. insurance; and
8. legal and medical services.[316]

The list of industries in which foreign investors face restrictions is likely to change, though. In an effort to qualify to join the World Trade Organization, the Investment Commission of the Ministry of Economic Affairs has proposed opening up certain industries to foreign investment, including oil refining, rail transport, and power generation.[317]

Foreign Investment in Securities

I.34   Foreign investment in Taiwanese securities is regulated under the Regulations Governing Investment in Securities by Overseas Chinese and Foreign Nationals and Relevant Foreign Exchange Remittance Procedures (the "Investment Regulations") promulgated in accordance with the SIFN.[318] As a precursor to the Investment Regulations, regulations were promulgated in May of 1983 permitting foreign investment in the ROC securities but only indirectly through the purchase of beneficiary certificates issued by collective investment schemes known as Securities Investment Trust Enterprises (SITEs).[319] The Investment Regulations were later promulgated to permit direct investment in Taiwanese securities by Qualified Foreign Institutional Investors (QFIIs) and were amended in March of 1996 to permit direct investment by individual and corporate investors.[320]

The Investment Regulations permit investment by QFIIs, SITEs or corporate and individual investors not residing in Taiwan in listed and over-the-counter (OTC) stocks, listed and OTC beneficiary certificates, government and corporate bonds, financial bills and other securities as may be approved by the Taiwanese securities and exchange commission (the SEC).[321] No single foreign investor may own more than 7.5 per cent of the outstanding shares of a listed or OTC traded company and the collective shareholding of foreign investors in a listed or OTC traded company may not exceed 20 per cent of the outstanding shares.[322] Previously QFIIs were required to invest between a minimum of US$5 million and a maximum of US$200 million. However, pursuant to a series of letter rulings by the Ministry of Finance in early 1996 the minimum investment requirement for QFIIs has been dropped and the investment ceiling for individual QFIIS has been raised to US$400 million.[323] Pursuant to a May 10, 1996 Ministry of Finance letter ruling, individual investors may invest up to US$5 million in Taiwanese securities and corporate investors may invest up to US$20 million. Income and dividends from foreign investment in Taiwanese securities may generally be remitted out of Taiwan at any time but said income and dividends must be realized.[324]

1. SITEs: SITEs may be established by qualifying fund management institutions and banks pursuant to the Rules for the Administration of Securities Investment Trust Enterprises ("SITE Regulations").[325] SITEs must be organized in the form of a company limited by shares and must have a minimum paid-in capital of three hundred million NT dollars.[326]

2. QFIIs: QFIIs include qualified banks, insurance companies, fund management and other investment institutions approved by the SEC pursuant to an investment permit application. The SEC reviews each QFII application and approved or disapproves each application after consultation with the CBC.

3. Individual and Corporate Investors: Individual and corporate investors must appoint an agent to be their representative within Taiwan for the purposes of filing tax returns and paying taxes. Documents evidencing the appointment of such an agent must be submitted for examination and approval.[327]

QFIIs and non-resident foreign individual and corporate investors may not, inter alia: (1) trade securities on margin; (2) engage in short selling; (3) extend loans or provide collateral; or (4) engage in other activities which are prohibited by the SEC.[328]

Taxation

There are currently no taxes assessed in Taiwan on capital gains from investments in securities. However, securities transaction tax ("SST") and dividends tax will be assessed as discussed below.   I.35

1. SST: Under the Statute for Securities Transaction Tax, any and all transfers of ROC securities will be subject to SST which is assessed as 0.3 per cent of the transaction price of the shares and should be withheld from the purchase price by the buyer on behalf of the seller and reported to the tax office no later than the second day after the transfer of the shares. In practice if the transfer price is lower than the book value of the shares, the tax office may assess the SST on the basis of the book value of the shares. In addition, SST will not be assessed for share transactions where SST would be less than NT$1 (i.e. transactions where the greater of the transaction price or the book value of the shares is less than NT$333).

2. Dividends Tax: Distributions of cash and stock dividends are treated as income of the recipient shareholder. Withholding tax will be assessed on both cash and stock dividends on the amount of the dividend, which tax will, in nearly all cases, be withheld by the distributing company at the time of distribution of the dividend. Dividends will be withheld at rates specified in the Standards of the Withholding Tax Rate for Each Type of Income (the Withholding Tax Standards) of

between 15 per cent and 35 per cent depending on the status of the investing shareholder.

Under Article 16 of the Statute for Upgrading Industry, when a company distributes newly issued shares in lieu of undistributed earnings which are reinvested in upgrading machinery or equipment or in the research and development of designated technologies, withholding tax on the dividends may be deferred until subsequent transfer of the shares. Tax will be withheld upon transfer of the shares following initial distribution at the current applicable withholding tax rate based on the status of the shareholder at the time of distribution and will be assessed on the par value of the shares. Where new shares are issued based on a recapitalization of a company's capital reserve no withholding tax will be assessed either on the distribution or upon the subsequent transfer of the shares.

Tax Laws and Accounting Rules

I.36   Taxation of both individual and business income in Taiwan is governed by the Income Tax Law.[329] Tax rates are fixed by the Statute for Income Tax Rates, reenacted annually to effect rate changes. Unlike the Internal Revenue Code of the United States, Taiwan's incolme tax laws are rather straightforward and leave little room for manipulation or evasion.

Primary responsibility for tax policy and implementation of the Income Tax Law lies with the Ministry of Finance. The MOF directly administers tax collection in Taipei and Kaohsiung, while the Taiwan Provincial Government is responsible for collection in other areas.

Taxation of Individuals

I.37   Individuals are subject to taxation on all income generated in Taiwan.[329a] Since Taiwan companies and other business entities "headquartered" in Taiwan are taxed on world-wide income,[330] individuals with overseas investments generally invest in their own name, thus avoiding Taiwan taxation of foreign generated income. The Ministry of Finance is considering amending the Income Tax Law to tax individual world-wide income, but such a provision would be almost impossible to enforce, especially with the offshore banking centers of Hong Kong and Singapore only a few hours' flight away.

Taiwan tax law generally does not distinguish between ordinary income and capital gains, with two important exceptions. Gains from the sale of securities are exempt from income taxation and have been since 1990.[331] And gains from the sale of land are taxed at lesser rates than ordinary income under the Land Tax Law.[332]

Residence status determines how an individual will be taxed. Residents pay income tax at graduated rates and enjoy personal exemptions and deductions, with tax payments due on March 15 of each year.[333] Non-residents generally pay a flat tax without exemptions or deductions, with taxes either withheld at the source or due before the non-resident departs Taiwan, depending on the non-resident's length of stay.[334]

Resident individuals may deduct sizable personal exemptions for themselves and dependents.[335] Special exemptions are provided for pensions, grade school teacher salaries, death or disability compensation, and income derived from certain artistic endeavors.[336] Resident wage earners may also claim itemized deductions or a standard deduction.[337] Itemized deductions include, with limits, charitable contributions, insurance premiums, uncompensated medical expenses, mortgage interest, losses on the sale of real estate, and income from savings. A special deduction is also granted for disabled dependents.

Taxation of Business Enterprises

The Income Tax Law provides different treatment for foreign and domestic **I.38** companies. Profit-seeking enterprises organized under Taiwan law — whether or not foreign-owned — are taxed on world-wide income, while enterprises organized under foreign law are only taxed on income generated in Taiwan.[338] Note, however, that domestic enterprises are credited for income taxes paid to foreign tax authorities.

Enterprises are taxed on net income, calculated by deducting costs, expenses, losses and taxes from gross income. Capital gains are treated the same as ordinary gains, with the two exceptions described above. Income, deductions and tax credits must be calculated according to the accounting rules set forth in the Auditing Criteria for Business Income Tax Returns.

Enterprises may deduct ordinary and necessary business expenses, including interest and royalty payments, uncompensated casualty losses, rental payments, and salary expenses.[339] Pension expenses, entertainment expenses, charitable contributions, bad debt expenses, capital losses and inventory write-downs may also be deducted within limits.[340] Organization expenses and refurbishing costs, on the other hand, must be capitalized.[341]

Depreciation expense is also deductible.[342] Enterprises are generally free to use the straight-line method, declining-balance, or service-hour method to calculate depreciation. The service lives of various assets are set forth in the Auditing Criteria. Equipment and machinery purchased for use in research and development, experimentation, energy conservation or quality control may be depreciated in two years. Accelerated depreciation is also allowed for machinery and equipment purchased by enterprises in certain targeted industries.[343] Intangibles, including goodwill, may be amortized, and depletion of natural resources gives rise to a depletion allowance.[344]

Enterprises with especially good tax records may be allowed to carry losses forward for five years, but no carry-backs are allowed.[345] Tax credits are afforded for income taxes paid to foreign tax authorities and investment in automation or pollution control equipment, research and development, personnel training, or international brand name development.[346] Additional credits and incentives are available to qualified enterprises under the Statute for Investment of Foreign Nationals and the Statute for Upgrading Industry.[347]

Value-Added Tax

I.39 Enterprises are subject to an European style value-added tax (VAT) imposed under the Business Tax Law (BTL).[348] A tax is levied on the value added to goods or services at each stage of production and distribution, including import-related transactions.[349] An importer, however, may deduct the amount of VAT paid on imports in calculating the VAT due on the sale of those imports, and an importer who regularly accounts for this credit in calculating the VAT due on the sale of imported goods may defer paying the import VAT until it has calculated its total liability under the BTL.[350] The BTL also provides exemptions for certain export-related transactions and commercial activities the government views as serving the public interest.[351] And to encourage foreign companies to use of Taiwan as a regional operations center, the BTL also exempts sales of derivatives, corporate bonds, and bank debentures, as well as foreign exchange calls.[352]

Tax Treaties

I.40 Taiwan's ability to conclude international tax treaties is retarded by its lack of international diplomatic status. To date Taiwan has concluded tax treaties with only four countries: Singapore, South Africa, Indonesia and Paraguay.[353] Taiwan is currently negotiating tax treaties with several other countries, including the United States, but the success of these negotiations is far from certain given the Chinese government's sensitivity to Taiwan's diplomatic efforts.

Intellectual Property[354]

Background

I.41 Taiwan's intellectual property laws were first promulgated during the period before 1949 when the Republic of China governed both Taiwan and the mainland of China. The copyright law was first promulgated and implemented on May 14, 1928, and the trademark law followed shortly thereafter on May 6, 1930 (implemented January 1, 1931). The Republic of China's patent law was passed on May 29, 1944, although it was not implemented until January 1, 1949.[355]

When the Republic of China moved its government to Taiwan in 1949, it brought these laws with it. However, enforcing the intellectual property rights created under these laws was not a priority of the government. The protection afforded by these laws was also relatively weak by comparison to the protection afforded under the laws of other industrialized countries. Under pressure from the United States, Taiwan began revising its intellectual property laws in 1985. New trademark and copyright laws were promulgated in 1985, and a new patent law was enacted in 1986.[356] As its economy increasingly turned to a high technology base, and as the United States continued to exert pressure for more reform, Taiwan further revised all of these laws.[357] The protection afforded under Taiwan's intellectual property laws is now comparable to that which can be obtained in other industrialized nations.

Patents

Taiwan is not a member of any international patent treaty, such as the Paris Convention or the Patent Cooperation Treaty, with respect to patents. The latest amendments to Taiwan's patent law (the Patent Law) were made on January 21, 1994, with an effective date of January 23, 1994. These amendments were an attempt by Taiwan to meet the requirements of the TRIPS (Trade Related Aspects of Intellectual Property Rights) agreement, and instituted for the first time in Taiwan a system of reciprocal priority rights similar to those provided for under the Paris Convention. Thus, a foreign national may claim priority from a patent application filed within one year prior to the filing of an application in the Republic of China, if the foreign applicant's home country has completed an agreement with the Republic of China, or if the Republic of China becomes a member of an international convention such as the World Trade Organization of which the foreign applicant's home country is also a member.[358]

I.42

The Patent Law provides for three different categories of patents: invention patents, new utility model patents, and new design patents.[359] Invention patents and utility model patents protect the useful features of an article or a process, while design patents protect the shape, pattern, color or configuration of an object.[360] The different types of patents also provide different periods of protection: 20 years for invention patents, 12 years for utility models, and 10 years for design patents[361]; however, an extension of the term of a patent may be obtained if the subject matter of the patent concerns a pharmaceutical or pesticide invention.[362]

An ROC patent grants the patentee the exclusive right to preclude other persons from manufacturing, selling, using or importing a patented article in the territory of the Republic of China.[363] The patentee of a manufacturing process has the exclusive right to preclude others from using the process and from using, selling or importing articles made through the direct use of that process without the consent of the patentee.[364] However, the provisions barring importation of patented articles or articles made through a patented process currently apply only to ROC citizens or to foreign patentees whose home countries have signed an agreement with Taiwan for reciprocal protection.[365] The ROC Patent Office may grant a compulsory license under a patent to a third party without the consent of the patent holder in certain situations, such as where an applicant for a compulsory license has failed to reach a licensing agreement with the patentee under reasonable commercial terms, where a patentee refuses to license underlying technology to the owner of a reinvention patent, or where the owner of a patent on a product refuses to grant a license to the owner of a patented manufacturing process which produces that product.[366]

In Taiwan, patents are enforced through the judiciary. Both civil and criminal lawsuits may be instituted against an infringer.[367] In a civil proceeding, a patentee may recover damages or obtain an order to enjoin or prevent infringement.[368] The remedies available in a criminal case, on the other hand, include fines, detention, and/or prisons sentences.[369]

Trade Marks

I.43   Taiwan's trade mark system is similar to that of many other industrialized nations. A trade mark in Taiwan may consist of any word, drawing, or symbol which is sufficiently distinctive to identify the source of the goods on which the mark is used.[370] Protection can also be obtained for service marks, collective marks, and certification marks.[371] Service marks must be capable of distinguishing the services provided by a business, while collective marks must be able to distinguish a particular organization or association.[372] The most recent amendments to the Trade Mark Law were promulgated on December 22, 1993. These amendments instituted the international classification of goods and services, used by virtually all other industrialized countries, as the system for classifying the goods and services listed in trademark registrations.[373] Both civil and criminal remedies are also now available under the present law.[374]

In order to obtain protection under Taiwan's Trade Mark Law, a trademark must be registered.[375] The prior use of a trade mark in Taiwan will not by itself accord the right to exclude others from fusing the same mark for the same or similar goods. However, such prior use may give the prior user a limited right to continue using the trade mark, even if someone else obtains a registration on that mark.[376] Foreign applicants from virtually all countries may file trade mark applications in Taiwan.[377] The Trade Mark Office will even accept trade mark applications from mainland China.[378]

The owner of a registered trade mark has the right of exclusive use of that trade mark in connection with the goods which are included in the registration.[379] The use of an identical or similar mark on the same or similar goods may also be punished.[380] If a trade mark owner begins using a mark on goods which are similar to those listed in the owner's trade mark registration, or begins using a similar mark on the same or similar goods, the trade mark owner should apply for an associated trade mark.[381] Such an associated trade mark registration will help to prevent others from obtaining a trade mark for the similar mark or for the same mark on similar goods.

A trade mark registration remains in force for ten years from the date of registration.[382] The term of a registration may be extended for additional ten-year periods by applying to renew the registration during the year before it expires.[383] The term of a trade mark registration will only be renewed with respect to the goods designated in the trade mark registration on which the trade mark has been actually used prior to filing the renewal application.[384] A renewal application will be denied if the trade mark has not been used during the three years prior to the application for renewal.[385] The owner or licensee of a registered trade mark in Taiwan, including a foreign trade mark owner or licensee, may enforce that trade mark.[386] Both civil and criminal penalties are available against infringers.

Copyright

Taiwan's Copyright Law protects literary, academic, scientific, artistic, and **I.44** other creative works.[387] Such works may enjoy both economic rights and moral rights.[388] Certain typeset, rearranged, and photocopied versions of works which do not otherwise qualify for copyright protection can also be registered for plate-right protection.[389] Taiwan is not a member of the Berne Convention or any other international copyright treaty. Therefore, foreign authors are only entitled to copyright protection in Taiwan if works produced by ROC nationals are entitled to copyright protection in the foreign author's home country according to a treaty, agreement, law, regulation, or the customary practice of that country, *or* the work is first published in Taiwan, or is published in Taiwan within 30 days after being published outside of Taiwan, as long as the foreigner's home country accords similar protection to ROC nationals.[390] Copyright protection based on reciprocity is currently available to nationals of the U.S., U.K., Hong Kong, and Switzerland.[391] Citizens of South Korea and Spain who reside in Taiwan may also receive copyright protection under ROC law.[392]

An author is entitled to copyright protection upon the completion of a work.[393] An "author" is defined in the copyright law as the person who creates a work.[394] Unlike the situation in many countries, an employee is presumed to be the author of a work created within the scope of the employee's job unless the employee and employer agree otherwise.[395] No further steps are required to perfect the copyright in that work, although registration may be required for the works of some foreign authors.[396] In order to enforce a copyright, it is advisable to register the copyright with the Copyright Office. The Copyright Office will register information as to authorship, the ownership of the economic rights to a work (economic rights are explained in detail below), the date of first public release, and/or the date of the first publication of a work.[397]

Taiwan recognizes two separate categories of copyright rights: moral rights and economic rights.[398] The moral rights of an author under the Copyright Law include the right to publicly release a work, the right to have the author's name indicated or not indicated on the work, and the right to maintain the integrity of the work.[399] The economic rights inherent in a copyright include the exclusive rights to do the following: (1) reproduce a work (2) publicly recite an oral or literary work; (3) publicly broadcast a work; (4) publicly present an audiovisual work; (5) publicly perform an oral, literary, musical, dramatic, and/or choreographic work; (6) publicly exhibit the original of an artistic or photographic work which has not been published; (7) adapt a work, create a derivative work, and/or compile the work into a compilation; and (8) rent a work to others.[400]

The term of the economic rights in a work is the life of the author plus 50 years after the author's death.[401] However, if a work is first publicly released between the 40th year and the 50th year after the death of an author, then the economic rights will last for 10 years from the time of public release of the work.[402] If the work is a joint work, then the term will last for 50 years from the death of the last surviving author.[403] If the author is a company or other organization, then the term of the copyright will be 50 years from the time of public release of the work.[404] However, if the work is not released during the first 10 years after the completion of the work, then the 50 year term will be calculated from the time of the completion of the work.[405] The economic rights in photographic works, audiovisual works, sound recordings, and computer programs, however, are 50 years from the first public release of such works, notwithstanding any of the foregoing provisions.[406]

If a copyright is infringed, the copyright holder may collect damages or seek other remedies in a court of law. Damages may be collected for the infringement of either moral rights or economic rights.[407] The owner of a copyright or a plate-right may, in addition, obtain an injunction to halt an infringement or to prevent an infringement.[408] An order to destroy infringing articles and/or articles which were solely used for committing an infringement can also be obtained.[409] A convicted infringer can further be forced to publish the judgment against him or her in newspapers or magazines, at the infringer's expense.[410] Civil damages may be obtained against anyone who intentionally or negligently infringes another person's economic rights in a work or who infringes another's plate-rights.[411] If more than one person is involved in an act of infringement, each person may be held jointly and severally liable for such damages.[412]

Trade Secrets and Know-How

I.45   Know-how, including technology, business information, and other commercially useful knowledge, may also be protected as a trade secret. Taiwan promulgated a Trade Secrets Law in mid-1996, however trade secrets may also be protected under contract law, criminal law, or the new Fair Trade Law. A party to a contract may be contractually bound not to disclose a trade secret, and such a clause can be enforced through an injunction.[413] In addition, damages for a trade secret violation may be obtained if the amount of actual damages suffered as a result of the disclosure of the trade secret can be proven.[414] Liquidated damages, if provided for in a contract, may also be obtained for a trade secret violation, provided that such damages are reasonable.[415] Taiwan's criminal code further provides that a person who is required by law or by contract to maintain the confidentiality of commercial or industrial secrets obtained through employment may be punished if that person discloses such secrets without permission and without reason.[416]

Notes

[1] *Taiwan Business: The Portable Encyclopedia for Doing Business with Taiwan* 5 (1994).

[2] *Ibid.*

[2a] Directorate-General of Budget, Accounting & Statistics, Executive Yuan, ROC, 1995, Statistical Yearbook of the ROC 159 (1995).

[3] *Ibid.*, at 6.

[4] *Ibid.*

[4a] Cited in *ibid.*

[5] Hungdah Chiu & Jyh-pin Fa, "Taiwan's Legal System and Legal Profession", in *Taiwan Trade and Investment Law* 21 (Mitchell A Silk ed., 1994).

[6] *Ibid.*, at 22.

[7] ROC Constitution Art. 171, para. 1.

[8] *Ibid.*, Art. 170.

[9] Chiu & Fa, *above* n.5, at 26.

[10] *See* Standard Law on Enacting National Statutes and Regulations Art. 7.

[11] *Ibid.*, Art. 172.

[12] *See* Lawrence S. Liu, "Unfair Competition", *Taiwan Trade and Investment Law*, *above* n.5, at 603–605.

[12a] FTL Art. 1.

[13] Draft Guidelines for Application of the Fair Trade Law to Governmental Enterprises (1995).

[14] Liu, *above* n.12, at 606.

[15] *Ibid.*

[15a] See Art. 46.

[15b] See Art. 28.

[15c] See Arts. 25–27, 41, 43, 48.

[15d] FTL Art. 5.

[16] *See* Enforcement Rules of the Fair Trade Law, Art. 5 (1992) [hereinafter FTL Enforcement Rules].

[16a] FTL Art. 5.

[17] *Ibid.*, Art. 3.

[18] These rather vague prohibitions, based on Article 86 of the Treaty Establishing the European Economic Community, 298 U.N.T.S. 11 (1958) (commonly known as the Treaty of Rome), are probably best interpreted in light of continental authorities. Lawrence S. Liu, "In the Name of Fair Trade: A Commentary on the New Competition Law and Policy of Taiwan, The Republic of China", 27 Int'l Law. 145, 150 (1993).

[19] FTL Art. 35.
[20] *Ibid.*, Art. 31.
[21] *Ibid.*, Art. 6.
[22] The sales threshold is currently set at NT$2 billion.
[23] *Ibid.*, Arts. 13, 40.
[24] *See* FTL Enforcement Rules, Art. 13.
[25] Liu, *above* n.12, at 608.
[26] *Ibid.*, Art. 7
[27] *Ibid.*, Art. 14.
[28] *Ibid.*, Art. 15.
[29] *Ibid.*, Art. 35.
[30] *Ibid.*, Art. 31.
[31] *Ibid.*, Art. 19.
[32] The recently enacted Trade Secrets Law contains additional prohibitions on engaging in or utilizing the spoils of industrial espionage.
[33] *Ibid.*, Art. 36.
[34] *Ibid.*, Art. 31.
[35] *Ibid.*, Art. 20.
[36] *Ibid.*, Arts. 21, 22.
[37] *Ibid.*, Art. 23.
[38] *Ibid.*, Art. 24.
[39] *Ibid.*, Arts. 31, 35, 37.
[40] *See* Law Governing the Application of Laws to Civil Matters Involving Foreign Elements, Art. 6 (1953).
[41] *Ibid.*
[42] *Ibid.*, Art. 25.
[43] If the parties have not agreed on all of the contract's non-essential terms, the court has wide discretion to gap-fill. Civil Code [Civ. C.] Art. 153.
[44] *Ibid.*, Art. 248.
[45] *Ibid.*, Arts. 154–58, 182.
[46] *Ibid.*, Art. 156.
[47] *Ibid.*, Arts. 157, 158.
[48] *Ibid.*, Art. 166.
[49] *Ibid.*, Art. 161.
[50] *Ibid.*, Art. 159.
[51] *Ibid.*, Art. 160.
[52] *See Ibid.*, Art. 314. If the debtor is obliged to deliver an object, the place of performance, in the absence of the aforementioned determiners, is deemed to be the place where the object was located at the time the contract was formed.
[53] *Ibid.*, Art. 316.
[54] *Ibid.*, Art. 315.
[55] Pitman B. Potter, "Contract and Sales Law", *Taiwan Trade and Investment Law*, *above* n.5, at 446 (citing Case No. 455 (1957), 1 *Professional Volume of Judicial Interpretations of Civil and Criminal Law* 463 (Ts'ai Tun-ming ed., 1982)).
[56] *Ibid.*, Art. 317.
[57] *Ibid.*, Art. 219. According to Potter, this is one of the most often cited provisions of the Book on Obligations, and is used as a catch-all where other provisions do not provide an adequate basis for the imposition of liability on non-performing parties. *See* Potter, *above* n.55, at 447.
[58] *Ibid.*, Arts. 199, 200.
[59] *Ibid.*, Art. 319.
[60] *Ibid.*, Art. 320.
[61] *Ibid.*, Arts. 208, 209.
[62] *Ibid.*, Art. 264.
[63] *Ibid.*, Art. 265.
[64] *Ibid.*, Art. 246.
[65] *Ibid.*, Art. 225.

[66] *Ibid.*, Art. 211. [67] *Ibid.*, Art. 266.
[68] *Ibid.*, Art. 247. [69] *Ibid.*, Art. 225.
[70] *Ibid.*, Art. 269. [71] *Ibid.*, Art. 268.
[72] *Ibid.*, Art. 270.
[73] *See* Civ. C. Arts. 271–293.
[74] *Ibid.*, Art. 271. It is important to note, however, that the benefits and liabilities of a contract will fall on individual parties in circumstances not covered by contract or the rules of joint and several liability under discussion. *Ibid.*, Art. 279.
[75] *See also* Potter, *above* n.55, at 451.
[76] *Ibid.*, Art. 280.
[77] *Ibid.*, Arts. 294, 297. [78] *Ibid.*, Art. 297.
[79] *Ibid.*, Art. 299. [80] *Ibid.*, Arts. 300–302.
[81] *Ibid.*, Art. 303. [82] *Ibid.*, Art. 309.
[83] *Ibid.*, Arts. 326, 327. [84] *Ibid.*, Art. 343.
[85] *Ibid.*, Art. 334. [86] *Ibid.*, Art. 344.
[87] *Ibid.*, Art. 229. [88] *Ibid.*, Art. 234.
[89] *Ibid.*, Art. 213. [90] *Ibid.*, Art. 215.
[91] *Ibid.*, Art. 216. [92] *Ibid.*, Art. 227.
[93] *Ibid.*, Art. 217. [94] *Ibid.*, Art. 218.
[95] *Ibid.*, Art. 254. [96] *Ibid.*, Art. 260.
[97] *Ibid.*, Art. 242. [98] *Ibid.*, Art. 244.
[99] *Ibid.*, Art. 250. [100] *Ibid.*, Art. 251.
[101] Since Taiwan is still active within the International Chamber of Commerce, contracts may incorporate ICC rules governing documentary credits.
[101a] Civ. C. Art. 345.
[102] Potter, *above* n.55, at 461.
[103] Civ. C. Art. 345.
[104] *Ibid.*, Art. 346. [105] *Ibid.*, Art. 372.
[106] *Ibid.*, Art. 374. [107] *Ibid.*, Art. 378.
[108] *Ibid.*, Art. 375. [109] *Ibid.*, Art. 376.
[110] *Ibid.*, Art. 348. [111] *Ibid.*, Art. 349.
[112] *Ibid.*, Art. 350. [113] *Ibid.*, Art. 351.
[114] *Ibid.*, Art. 352. [115] *Ibid.*, Art. 354.
[116] *Ibid.*, Art. 366.
[117] Potter, *above* n. 55, at 463.
[118] Civ. C. Art. 367.
[118a] *Ibid.*, Art. 368. [119] *Ibid.*, Art. 356.
[119a] *Ibid.*, Art. 358. [120] *Ibid.*, Art. 353.
[120a] *Ibid.*, Art. 359. [120b] *Ibid.*
[121] *Ibid.*, Art. 360. [122] *Ibid.*, Art. 364.
[123] *Ibid.*, Art. 355.
[124] Personal and corporate guarantees are also used in Taiwan, but give rise to legal complexities best explored in another forum. For a discussion of these issues, see McGowan, "Banking, Credit, and Finance: The Transactional Aspects", in *Taiwan Trade and Investment Law, above* n.5, at 381–84.
[124a] *Ibid.*
[124b] *Ibid.*
[124c] *Ibid.*
[125] *Ibid.*, at 380.
[126] *Ibid.*
[127] *Ibid.*
[128] *Ibid.* at 381.
[129] *Ibid.*

[130] Creditors preferred to receive this form of security agreement because of the leverage the threat of imprisonment provided.

[131] Imprisonment for dishonored checks became so common in the 1980s as to create a *de facto* debtors' prison in Taiwan. This created so many social problems that the government determined to decriminalize check bouncing absent a showing of an intent not to pay at the time the check was drafted.

[132] (Amended 1987).

[133] (Amended 1990).

[134] *See* Company Law Arts. 40–97.

[135] *See Ibid.*, Arts. 114–127.

[136] *See Ibid.*, Arts. 98–113.

[137] *See Ibid.*, Arts. 128–356.

[138] *Ibid.*, Art. 2.

[139] *Ibid.*, Art. 6.

[140] *Ibid.*, Art. 100, 156. The MOEA sets minimum capital requirements for all companies by regulation. Specialized agencies may set additional requirements for companies in the industries they regulate. For example, the Board of Foreign Trade BOFT sets additional capital requirements for import/export companies.

[141] *Ibid.*, Art. 19.

[142] *Ibid.*, Art. 29. Companies formed under the aegis of foreign investment approval, see *below* note 203 and accompanying text, commonly sponsor the applications of foreign managers for resident visas and alien resident certification.

[143] *Ibid.*

[144] An individual is also disqualified if under indictment for or convicted of treason. *Ibid.*, Art. 30.

[145] *Ibid.*, Art. 20.

[146] *Ibid.*, Art. 20.

[147] *Ibid.*, Arts. 20, 21.

[148] *Ibid.*, Art. 15.

[149] *Ibid.*, Arts. 13, 15.

[149a] *Ibid.* Art. 16.

[150] *Ibid.*, Art. 98.

[151] *Ibid.*, Art. 99.

[152] *Ibid.*, Art. 104.

[153] *Ibid.*, Art. 113.

[154] *Ibid.*, Art. 111.

[155] *Ibid.*, Art. 108.

[156] *Ibid.*, Art. 111.

[157] *Ibid.*, Art. 128.

[158] *Ibid.*, Art. 156.

[159] *Ibid.* The MOEA sets the amount of authorized capital triggering the "go public" requirement by regulation.

[160] Lawrence S. Liu, "The Legal Framework for Foreign Investment", in *Taiwan Trade and Investment Law, above* n.5, at 159.

[161] *Ibid.*, Art. 156.

[162] *Ibid.*, Art. 167.

[163] *Ibid.*, Art. 158.

[164] *Ibid.*, Art. 267.

[165] *Ibid.*, Art. 163. In practice, shareholders can and do contract among themselves to restrict transfers. Liv, *above* n. 5 at 160.

[166] Company Law, Art. 163. This prohibition is intended to protect both creditors and non-insider shareholders from promoter fraud.

[167] *Ibid.*, Art. 202.

[168] *Ibid.*, Art. 206.

[169] *Ibid.*, Arts. 203, 208.

[170] *Ibid.*, Art. 205.

[171] *Ibid.*, Art. 208.

[172] *Ibid.*, Art. 196.

[173] *Ibid.*, Art. 197.

[174] *Ibid.*, Art. 192.

[175] *Ibid.*, Art. 206.

[176] *Ibid.*, Art. 193.

[177] *Ibid.*, Arts. 212–215.

[178] Liu, *above* n.160, at 163.

[179] *Ibid.*, Art. 216.

[180] *Ibid.*, Art. 221.

[181] *Ibid.*, Art. 218.

[182] *Ibid.*, Art. 219.

[183] *Ibid.*, Art. 218-2. [184] *Ibid.*, Art. 218-1.

[185] *Ibid.*, Art. 213. [186] *Ibid.*, Art. 174.

[187] *Ibid.*, Arts. 174, 177. [188] *Ibid.*, Art. 174.

[189] *Ibid.*, Arts. 185, 316. Other corporate acts requiring super-majority approval, including the distribution of dividends and bonuses, are detailed in Company Law, Arts. 209, 240, 241, and 277.

[190] *Ibid.*, Arts. 179, 180. [191] *Ibid.*, Arts. 178, 179.

[192] *Ibid.*, Art. 191. [193] *Ibid.*, Art. 170.

[194] *Ibid.*, Art. 173. [195] *Ibid.*, Art. 240.

[196] The MOEA is considering amending the Company Law to allow for interim and multiple distributions of dividends.

[197] *Ibid.*, Art. 235.

[197a] *Ibid.*, Art. 238.

[198] *Ibid.*, Art. 237.

[198a] *Ibid.*, Art. 239.

[199] *Ibid.*, Art. 232.

[199a] *Ibid.*, Art. 282.

[200] *Ibid.*, Arts. 10, 316.

[201] *Ibid.*, Art. 10.

[202] Sue H. Su, "Dissolution under Articles of Incorporation", *Lee & Li Bulletin*, May 1995, at 6.

[203] Specifically, companies formed under the aegis of foreign investment approval [FIA] are exempted from the Company Law's employee subscription provision (Art. 267), "go public" requirement (Art. 156), and the nationality or residence restrictions for shareholders (Arts. 98, 128), board chairmen (Art. 208), and supervisors (Art. 216). Statute for Investment of Foreign Nationals, Art. 18 (amended 1996) [hereinafter SIFN].

[204] The Executive Yuan prohibits or restricts foreign investment in some 55 categories of business by negative listing.

[205] Foreign investment is prohibited in any enterprise that threatens public safety, violates public morals, or causes a high level of pollution. SIFN Art. 5. Prior approval is required for foreign investment in public utilities, finance and insurance companies, and media enterprises. *Ibid.*

[206] *See below* nn.304–17 and accompanying text.

[207] SUI Art. 3 (prior to 1995 amendments) (Taiwan).

[208] Company Law Art. 386.

[209] Company Law Art. 1. *See also Ibid.*, Arts. 371, 372, 375, 386.

[210] SIFN Art. 6

[211] *Ibid.*, Art. 372.

[212] *Ibid.* In practice, the branch manager usually serves in both capacities.

[213] *See also* Income Tax Law Art. 17 (amended 1995); Business Tax Law Art. 70 (1995).

[213a] Company Law Art. 371.

[214] Operating reports must conform with the requirement of article 66(2) of the Business Accounting Law (amended 1988).

[214a] Company Law Arts. 20, 377.

[215] *See* In-Jaw Lai, "Securities Regulation", in *Taiwan Trade and Investment Law*, *above* n.5, at 326–27.

[216] *See* SEL Art. 3; Organic Law of the Securities Exchange Commission of the Ministry of Finance (1984).

[217] *See also* SEL, Arts. 2, 6, 25, 36, 38, 39.

[218] *Ibid.*, Art. 4.

[218a] *Ibid.*, Art. 6.

[219] *Ibid.*, Art. 20.

220 Lai, *above* n.215, at 337.
221 *Ibid.*, Art. 22.
222 *Ibid.*, Art. 32.
223 *Ibid.*, Art. 7.
224 Jeffrey H. Chen & Jack J. T. Huang, "Taiwan's Evolving Stock Market: Policy and Regulatory Trends", 12 UCLA Pac. Basin L. J. 34, 50 (1993).
225 SEL, Arts. 17, 22. *See* Guidelines Governing the Issue and Offer of Securities by Issuers (amended 1995).
226 *See* Chen & Huang, *above* n.224, at 50–51.
227 Brian W. Semkow, *Taiwan Financial Markets* 179 (1992).
228 SEL, Art. 43-1.
229 *See* Regulations Governing Tender Offers for Securities of Public Companies (1995).
230 Corporate "insiders" include directors, managerial and supervisory personnel, and ten percent shareholders of the issuer. SEL, Art. 157.
231 *Ibid.*, Art. 157.
232 "Insiders" for the purposes of Article 157-1 include directors, managerial and supervisory personnel, ten per cent shareholders of equity shares, any person who has learned material information due to any professional or control relationship with the issuer, and any person who has learned information from any of the aforementioned persons.
233 *Ibid.*, Art. 157-1.
234 *See* Lai, *above* n.215, at 339–43.
235 That is, "failing to deliver securities or tender the purchase price under a transaction made and accepted on the stock exchange, in a manner that may disrupt the market," or "falsifying a transaction through the stock exchange without actually transferring rights in the securities". SEL, Art. 155.
236 *Ibid.*, Art. 155.
236a *Ibid.*, Art. 171.
237 *Ibid.*, Art. 128.
238 *See generally* Regulations Governing Investment in Securities and Repatriations by Overseas Chinese and Foreign Nationals (amended 1995) [hereinafter QFII Regulations].
239 QFII Regulations, Art. 14. The SEC is authorized to adjust these foreign ownership limits in light of domestic economic and financial conditions. *Ibid.*, Art. 4.
240 *See* Chen & Huang, *above* n.224, at 41–44; *see also* Semkow, *above* n.227, at 182–183.
241 *See* Guidelines Governing the Issue and Offer of Foreign Securities by Issuers (1994).
242 *See* Criteria for the Establishment of Securities Firms (amended 1995); *and* Guidelines for Review of Applications by Foreign Securities Firms to Establish Brach Offices (amended 1995).
243 *See* Criteria for the Establishment of Securities Firms.
244 *See* Regulations Governing the Administration of Securities Investment Trust Fund Enterprises (1983).
245 *See* Regulations Governing the Administration of Securities Investment Consulting Enterprises (1983).
246 For a brief discussion of traditional Chinese values that continue to influence modern attitudes toward dispute resolution in Taiwan, see Nigel N. T. Li, "Dispute Resolution", in *Taiwan Trade and Investment Law*, above n.5, at 645.
247 *See* Statute for Rural Mediation (1982).
248 *See* Code of Civil Procedure [C. Civ. Proc.] Arts. 403–436-7.
249 Convention on the Recognition and Enforcement of Foreign Arbitral

Awards, done at New York, June 10, 1958, 330 U.N.T.S. 3 [hereinafter New York Convention].

249a SCA art. 5.

249b Art. 5.

250 The SCA was enacted in 1961 and amended to better conform with international norms regarding the recognition and enforcement of foreign arbitral awards in 1982 and 1986. Further revision is now under discussion to bring the SCA up to date with international developments. "Taiwan: Officials Now Search for Merits of Commercial Arbitration", *China Economic News Service*, Apr. 12, 1994, available in LEXIS, News Library, TXTNWS File.

251 *See* Law Governing the Handling of Labor/Management Disputes, Arts. 23–36 (1988).

252 *See* SEL, Arts. 166–70.

253 For example, the parties to an arbitration agreement are free to choose rules for arbitration procedure established by the International Chamber of Commerce (ICC Rules) or the United Nations Committee on International Trade Law (UNCITRAL Rules).

254 There is conflicting authority regarding whether the SCA's provisions governing recognition of arbitration agreements apply where the parties identify another body of law as governing the arbitration agreement. *See* Li, *above* n.92, at 653.

255 *See* Law Governing Choice of Law on Civil Matters Involving Foreign Elements, Art. 6.

255a SCA Art. 1.

256 In 1978, for example, the ROC Supreme Court held that an arbitration clause appearing on a bill of lading was only "an expression of the unilateral intention of the carrier, not a mutual agreement of the parties . . ." Judgment of the Supreme Court, 1978 Tai-Shang 3762, quoted in Chun Li, "Arbitration and Enforcement of Foreign Awards in Taiwan", *East Asian Executive Reports*, Jan. 15, 1993, at 9.

257 The Commercial Arbitration Association of the Republic of China recommends the following standard arbitration clause:

> All disputes, controversies or differences which may arise between the parties out of, in relation to, or in connection with this contract or for the breach thereof shall be finally settled by arbitration in Taipei, Republic of China, in accordance with the Commercial Arbitration Rules of the Commercial Arbitration Association of the Republic of China and under the laws of the Republic of China. The award rendered by the arbitrator(s) shall be final and binding on the parties concerned.

Paiff Huang, *Taiwan*, 14 Mar. Law. 347, 349 (1990).

258 SCA Art. 12.

259 *Ibid.*, Art. 3.

260 *Ibid.*, Art. 27.

260a Choosing a legal regime other than the SCA to govern the arbitration agreement should not affect the availability of the remedies otherwise available under SCA Arts. 3 and 27. The Taiwan courts will recognize an arbitration agreement governed by the law of another jurisdiction if it is valid under both the SCA and the law of the named jurisdiction. *See* Li, *above* n. 246, at 655–656.

261 SCA Art. 12.

262 *Ibid.*, art, 4.

263 *Ibid.*, Art. 5.

264 *Ibid.*, Art. 19.

265 Li, *above* n. 256, at 657.

266 SCA Art. 23.

267 *Ibid.*, Art. 32.

268 *See* Li, *above* n. 256, at 658.

269 Treaty of Friendship, Commerce, and Navigation, Nov. 30, 1948, U.S.–ROC, 63 Stat. 1299, 25 U.N.T.S. 69 (continued in force by virtue of the Taiwan Relations Act. 22 U.S.C. 1301–16 (1979)).

269a SCA Art. 21.

269b *Ibid.*, Art. 5.

270 For example, in 1949 the crippled Central Bank of China authorized the Bank of Taiwan to issue the New Taiwan Dollar to serve as the *de facto* national currency.

271 (Amended 1996).

271a Banking Law Arts. 19, 45.

272 The MOF is authorized to set ownership limits under Banking Law, Art. 25.

273 The MOF is authorized to set minimum paid-in capital requirements under Banking Law Art. 23.

274 Bank for International Settlements, Committees on Banking Regulation and Supervisory Practices, "Proposals for International Convergence of Capital Requirements and Capital Standards" (1988) 27 Int'l Legal Materials 530. *See* Banking Law, Arts. 44, 50.

275 OBA Arts. 5, 11–20.

275a *Ibid.*, Art. 118.

276 *See* Guidelines for Foreign Banks to Establish Branches and Representative Offices.

277 *Ibid.*

278 *See* Addendum to Guidelines of Qualifications for Responsible Persons of Banks.

279 Consumer Protection Law Enforcement Rules, Art. 5 (1994) [hereinafter CPL Enforcement Rules].

279a CPL Art. 7.

280 CPL, Art. 10.

281 *Ibid.*, Art. 7.

282 *Ibid.*, Art. 43.

283 *Ibid.*, Arts. 8, 9, 51.

284 *Ibid.*, Art. 6.

285 *Ibid.*, Art. 7.

286 *Ibid.*, Art. 8.

287 *Ibid.*, Art. 5. This "state of the art" defense is crucial to the continued vigor of Taiwan's hi-tech industries, pharmaceutical companies, and service providers.

288 *Ibid.*, Art. 11.

289 CPL.

290 *Ibid.*, Art. 12.

291 For example, the Ministry of Finance recently published mandatory terms for credit card agreements.

292 *Ibid.*, Art. 17.

293 *Ibid.*, Art. 21.

294 *Ibid.*, Art. 22.

295 *Ibid.*, Art. 23.

296 *Ibid.*, Arts. 27, 28, 49–54.

297 *Ibid.*, Arts. 28, 29.

298 *Ibid.*, Arts. 32.

299 *Ibid.*, Art. 42.

300 *Ibid.*, Art. 36.

301 *Ibid.*, Arts. 33, 44, 45.

302 *Ibid.*, Arts. 40, 41.

303 *See, e.g.* "Taiwan: Consumers' Foundation Blasts Ineffective Government Com-

mittee" *China Economic News Service*, Reuter Textline, January 12, 1995, available on LEXIS.

[304] The author gratefully acknowledges the assistance of Michael Fedrick and Andrew Ruff in preparing this section relating to foreign investment regulation in Taiwan.

[305] Szczepanski, *Op. cit.* at 48–6. The SIFN was promulgated in July 1954 and was last amended in May 1989. The Legislative Yuan is currently considering an amended draft of this statute which would limit some of the privileges and election available under current law.

[306] Liu, Lawrence S., *Op. cit.* at TAI2-48.

[307] *Ibid.*

[308] SIFN, Art. 3.

[309] SIFN, Art. 8.

[310] SIFN, Art. 13.

[311] SIFN, Art. 18.

[312] *Ibid.*

[313] SIFN, Art. 16.

[314] SIFN, Art. 18.

[315] "List of Prohibited and Restricted Industries for Investment by Overseas Chinese and Foreign Nationals", promulgated by the Investment Commission of the Ministry of Economic Affairs in September, 1995 (provided by Mr. William W. L. Chen, Saint Island International Patent and Law Offices).

[316] *Ibid.*

[317] "Taiwan Opens 'Restricted' Industries to Foreigners," *Japan Economic Newswire*, August 11, 1995.

[318] Regulations Governing Investment in Securities by Overseas Chinese and Foreign Nationals and Relevant Foreign Exchange Remittance Procedures promulgated December 28, 1990, last amended March 3, 1996. Promulgated pursuant to SIFN, Art. 13(4).

[319] Investment in SITE issued beneficiary certificates continued to be permitted under the Investment Regulations, article 2(1). SITE establishment and operation is regulated under the Securities Investment Trust Regulations (last amended March 1, 1996).

[320] Investment Regulations, Art. 2.

[321] *Ibid.*, Art. 4.

[322] *Ibid.*, Art. 5.

[323] Note that the specific investment quota of a given QFII will be determined by the SEC in consultation with the Central Bank of China (the CBC) based upon the QFIIs application for an investment permit. Investment Regulations, Art. 11.

[324] Investment Regulations, Arts. 8 & 13.

[325] SITE Regulations, Art. 5. Promulgated May 26, 1983 amended September 2, 1991.

[326] *Ibid.*, Art. 4.

[327] Investment Regulations, Art. 6.

[328] *Ibid.*, Art. 18.

[329] (Amended 1995).

[329a] Income Tax Law Arts. 2, 8.

[330] Income Tax Law Art. 3. *See* "Taxation of Business Enterprises".

[331] *Ibid.*, Art. 4–1.

[332] Arts. 28–39-2 (amended 1994).

[333] Income Tax Law Art. 71.

[334] *Ibid.*, Art. 2.

[335] *Ibid.*, Art. 17.

[336] *Ibid.*, Art. 4.

[337] *Ibid.*, Art. 17.

[338] Foreign companies that do not maintain an agent or fixed place of business in

Taiwan are taxed via withholding at the source of income. Income Tax Law Art. 73. The MOF sets withholding rates by regulations. *See* Standards on Withholding Tax Rates for All Types of Income (amended 1989).

339 *Ibid.*, Arts. 29, 30, 35, 71, 72.

340 *Ibid.*, Arts. 32, 33, 35, 37, 49, 71.

341 *Ibid.*, Art. 34.

342 *Ibid.*, Art. 37.

343 SUI, Art. 5.

344 Income Tax Law Arts. 38, 53.

345 *Ibid.*, Art. 39.

346 *See* Regulations Governing Investment Tax Credits for Company Research and Development, Personnel Development and Training, and Establishment of International Brand Image (amended 1995).

347 See "Foreign Investment Law".

348 The VAT was enacted in 1986 to replace the Gross Business Receipt Tax, which was highly criticized as inefficient and inequitable. *See* Ching-Chang Yen, "Business (Value Added) Tax", in *Taiwan Trade and Investment Law*, above n.5, at 511.

349 BTL, Art. 1.

350 *Ibid.*, Art. 41.

351 *Ibid.*, Arts. 7, 8.

352 *Ibid.*, Art. 8.

353 Sophia Yeh, "Tax Treaties Update", *Lee and Li Bulletin*, May 1995, at 21; Baker & McKenzie, *Taiwan: A Legal Brief* 68 (Keye S. Wu *et al.* eds., 1995).

354 The section on intellectual property was adapted from materials prepared by Michael Fedrick, Esq., of Baxter Healthcare Corporation in Glendale, California. Mr. Fedrick is the author of the chapter on Taiwan's intellectual property laws which appears in Gutterman & Brown, *Intellectual Property Laws of East Asia*, published by Sweet & Maxwell in 1997.

355 "Taiwan", Int'l Fin. L. Rev. 26–29, (1992) ("Ideas In The Making Supplement").

356 *Ibid.*

357 *Ibid.*

358 Patent Law, Art. 4.

359 *Ibid.*, Art. 2.

360 *Ibid.*, Arts. 20, 97 and 106.

361 *Ibid.*, Arts. 50, 100 and 109.

362 *Ibid.*, Art. 51.

363 *Ibid.*, Art. 56.

364 *Ibid.*

365 *Ibid.*

366 *Ibid.*, Arts. 78 and 80.

367 *Ibid.*, Arts. 88 and 131

368 *Ibid.*, Art. 88.

369 *Ibid.*, Arts. 123–130.

370 Trademark Law, Art. 5.

371 *Ibid.*, Arts. 72–74.

372 *Ibid.*, Arts. 72 and 74.

373 *Ibid.*, Art. 35; Enforcement Rules of the Trademark Law, Table of Classification of Goods and Services (amended 1994).

374 *Ibid.*, Arts. 61–65.

375 *Ibid.*, Art. 2.

376 *Ibid.*, Art. 23.

377 Communication with Mr. Johnny Yang, Taiwan International Patent and Law Office, October 27, 1995.

378 "Taiwan Approves First Chinese Trademark", *Reuters World Service*, June 16, 1994.

379 Trademark Law, Art. 21.

380 *Ibid.*, Art. 62, para.1, s.1; Communication with Mr. Johnny Yang, Taiwan International Patent and Law Office, October 27, 1995.

381 *Ibid.*, Art. 22.

382 *Ibid.*, Art. 24.

383 *Ibid.*, Art. 25.

384 *Ibid.*

385 *Ibid.*

386 Trademark Law, Arts. 61, 69 and 70.

387 Copyright Law, Art. 3, para.1, s.1.

388 *Ibid.*, para.1. s.3.

389 Copyright Law, Art. 79.

390 *Ibid.*, Art. 4.

391 Fu, Jacqueline C., "Legal Protection for Computer Software: Taiwan," Presentation to the Inter-Pacific Bar Association in San Francisco, May, 1995; Wang & Young, "Taiwan's New Copyright Regime: Improved Protection for American Authors and Copyright Holders," 27 Int'l Law (1993); Yang, S. T., "Copyright Protection in Taiwan," *Intellectual Property Practice in Taiwan*, published by Taiwan International Patent and Law Office (1995).

392 *Ibid.*

393 Copyright Law, Art. 13.

394 *Ibid.*, Art. 3.

395 *Ibid.*, Art. 11.

396 Paul Hayden, "Ministry Proposes Bill to Amend the Copyright Act," 8 *World Intellectual Property Report* 296 (1994).

397 Copyright Law, Art. 74.

398 *Ibid.*, Art. 3, para.1, s.3.

399 *Ibid.*, Arts. 15–17.

400 *Ibid.*, Arts. 22–29.

401 *Ibid.*, Art. 30.

402 *Ibid.*

403 Copyright Law, Art. 31.

404 *Ibid.*, Art. 33.

405 *Ibid.*

406 Copyright Law, Art. 34.

407 *Ibid.*, Arts. 85 and 88.

408 *Ibid.*, Art. 84.

409 *Ibid.*

410 Copyright Law, Art. 89.

411 *Ibid.*, Art. 88.

412 *Ibid.*

413 Szczepanski, Steven Z., *Eckstrom's Licensing in Foreign and Domestic Operations*, Vol.3A, Rel. no.43, pp.48-20 and 48-22, September 1995; Communication with Mr. William W. L. Chen Saint Island International Patent and Law Offices, December 4, 1995.

414 *Ibid.*

415 *Ibid.*

416 Criminal Code, Article 317; Terrence F. MacLaren, ed., *Worldwide Trade Secrets Law*, Vol.2, Rel. no.1, p.C2-3, November, 1994.

* The author would like to note that any errors or omissions are his own responsibility and not that of the publisher.

THAILAND

Bentley J. Anderson

I. Summary of Business and Political Conditions

Basic Demographic, Political and Economic Information

Thailand is located in South-East Asia, bordered by Cambodia to the south-east, by Laos to the north-east, Myanmar (formerly Burma) to the north and west, and by Malaysia to the south. The country has extensive coastline, facing the Andaman Sea on the west coast, and the Gulf of Thailand on the east, which it shares with Cambodia and Malaysia. Thailand is made up of four distinct geographical regions. The northern quarter of the country is mountainous and forested. The north-east, which has provided refuge for both Cambodians fleeing the civil war in that country and the Khmers Rouges after the Vietnamese invasion of Cambodia in 1979, is semi-arid with poor soil. The central region, where Ayuthya, the former capital of Thailand, is located, is a vast alluvial plain. Finally, the southern quarter of Thailand is a narrow peninsula with a tropical climate. This region of Thailand provides most of the mineral wealth of the country.

Thailand has a population of approximately 60 million. The main ethnic group is the Thai, although Bangkok, the capital of Thailand, has a substantial Chinese minority. There are also Lao, Malay, and Cambodian minorities, as well as various ethnic groupings, referred to generically as "hilltribes", which continue to inhabit the mountainous north-western quarter of the country. Over 90 per cent of the population of Thailand is Buddhist, although the Malay minority in Thailand is overwhelmingly Muslim.

Thai is the national language of Thailand. There are various regional dialects of Thai, which developed from the ancient South-East Asian

J.01

559

languages of Pali and Sanskrit. The Thai alphabet also developed from these languages. English is spoken in areas frequented by tourists, in certain business circles in the capital, and by many Thai attorneys, but is otherwise not widely used.

The present form of government in Thailand, established in 1932, is a constitutional monarchy, in which the king is the Head of State and the chief of the armed forces. The present king, King Bhumibol Adulyadej, also known as King Rama IX of the Chakri Dynasty, ascended to the throne in 1946. There has been a substantial amount of political uncertainty and instability in Thailand since 1932: there have been nine successful and nine abortive *coups d'etat*, 15 constitutions, and 17 general elections since that year. Moreover, the Thai military, which was responsible for most of these uprisings, continues to play a critical role in the Thai political scene.

Under the present constitution, promulgated in 1979, the executive powers of the King are exercised by the Prime Minister and a Council of Ministers. The Constitution provides for a Parliament comprised of two houses: a lower house (Assembly), elected by universal suffrage, and an upper house (Senate) whose members are appointed by the King on the recommendation of the Prime Minister. Twelve ministries make up the executive branch of the Thai government and are responsible for determining and applying national policies in their respective areas. The ministries of greatest importance for purposes of commercial and financial transactions are the Ministry of Industry, which develops and implements national manufacturing and mining policies; the Ministry of Commerce, which regulates external and internal trade; and the Ministry of Finance, which supervises the Bank of Thailand (the central bank) and the stock exchange, the Securities Exchange of Thailand, which was established in 1975 and is located in Bangkok.

The Thai economy is well-diversified. A significant number of industrialized nations, including the U.S. and the members of the European Union, continue to import the main commodities produced by Thailand, including rice, jewelry and processed food. Thailand has also been quite successful at exporting high-tech and capital intensive goods such as computers, computer peripherals and parts, integrated circuits, and electric appliances. Indeed, since 1987 the electronics industry, broadly defined to include everything from the production of air conditioners to the manufacture of semiconductors, has been one of the fastest growing sectors of the Thai economy. This has taken place, in substantial part, as a result of massive foreign investment in this sector. For example, several large American multinational corporations, including Advanced Micro Devices, AT&T, and IBM, in addition to Japanese firms such as Sony, Hitachi, Toshiba, and NEC, have all made major investments in Thailand since 1987. The development and stability of the Thai economy has also been assisted by the indirect linkage of the Thai currency, the baht, to the U.S. dollar.

No discussion of the Thai economy would be complete without noting the important role played by the substantial ethnic Chinese minority in the economic development of the country. There has always been a sizeable ethnic Chinese community in Thailand. Before the Second World War, the Chinese were mostly merchants, shopkeepers and importers. Because of the growing threat to the Chinese of Thai nationalism, however, the Chinese gradually began to assimilate into Thai society, adopting Thai names, such as Sophonpantich and Tejapaipul, and becoming citizens of the country. The Chinese also began to diversify into manufacturing, banking, and insurance. At present, several large Thai conglomerates, such as Siam Motors, are controlled by ethnic Chinese families, as are four of the largest banks in Thailand (Bangkok Bank, Bangkok Metropolitan Bank, Thai Farmers Bank, and Bank of Ayudhya).[1]

In some respects the economy of Thailand is a model for other developing nations.[2] In the 1960s, the economy was based on the export of agricultural commodities such as rice, rubber and teak. With the assistance of the government, the Thai economy became more diversified in the 1970s, particularly in the manufacturing sector. Between 1975 and 1985, for example, the contribution to gross domestic product (GDP) made by agriculture decreased from 30 per cent to 23 per cent, while the contribution made by manufacturing rose from 18 per cent to 21 per cent. This trend has continued as the government has increased its efforts to encourage foreign investment. The manufacturing sector in Thailand is now the largest in South-East Asia.[3] **J.02**

However, although the Thai economy is relatively developed, it has not yet reached the level of economic development or performance attained by the Newly Industrialized Countries (NICs), such as Taiwan, Singapore, and Hong Kong, against which Thailand must compete for foreign investment and export markets. For example, despite Thailand's high literacy rate (93 per cent), the Thai labor force is not as well-educated or as well-trained as the workers of other member states of the Association of South East Asian Nations (ASEAN), such as Singapore and Malaysia. In addition, the infrastructure of Thailand remains relatively undeveloped, and electricity in the areas outside of the two main cities, Bangkok and Chiang Mae, is in short supply. Bangkok is also considered by the World Health Organization to be one of the most polluted cities in the world. Hence, regardless of its deserved reputation as a liberal, semi-industrialized economy that favors private enterprise and foreign investment, there are numerous serious challenges which Thailand must overcome before it reaches the level of economic development that its chief competitors, such as Korea and Taiwan, have attained.[4]

Historical Development of the Thai Legal System[5]

Thai history is usually divided into three distinct periods: the Sukhothai period (1250 to 1350), the Ayuthya period (1350 to 1767) and the Bangkok period (1767 to date). The history of the Thai people is characterized by a steady geographic progression southward from the region of present-day **J.03**

Thailand

Yunnan Province in China, along the Chao Phraya river to Bangkok, the capital. The constant but gradual movement south of the Thai was brought about because of numerous wars that the Thai fought with the peoples of bordering states, including the Mongols, Khmer and the Burmese. After 1767, the capital moved to Bangkok, where it has remained.

There is no written evidence of a Thai legal system prior to 1285. It is known, however, that in that period the king was an absolute monarch, and the final arbiter of disputes, including questions arising over the ownership of property. Gradually, the Thai developed several bodies of law which formed the basis for the Thai legal system. First, the Thai came to rely on a corpus of unwritten principles based on the so-called Code of Manu, a body of Hindu jurisprudence known to the Thais as the *Dhammasattham*. These principles provided the framework for civil relations, in addition to the first recorded set of criminal laws. The Thais also developed a set of natural law principles, the *thammasat*, from the neighboring Mon ethnic group. The *thammasat* was based on Hindu principles that had been interpreted and recorded by the Mon and the Thais, both of whom were overwhelmingly Buddhist. Members of the royal court also began to collect the recorded decisions of the Thai monarchs, as they were called upon to resolve disputes.

After the capital of Thailand moved from Ayuthya to Bangkok (1767), the king, Rama I of the present Chakri dynasty, established a committee to compile and revise the laws prevailing in the former Ayuthya period. The resulting code, the "Law of the Three Great Seals", included the rules of evidence, ordeals by fire and water, and "the law of husband and wife". The king's principal motivation in ordering this compilation was to harmonize the salient features of traditional Thai law. In particular, the king sought to remove, to the extent possible, inconsistent king-made decisional law that had accumulated over several centuries. Although the compilation was considered completed in 1805, the Law of the Great Seals retained the inconsistencies and lack of uniformity that had characterized Thai law in the pre-Bangkok period.

In the nineteenth century, trade relations began to develop between Thailand and several Western nations, including Great Britain, France and the United States. Disputes between individual traders or trading companies and the Thai Government usually resulted in the foreign trader refusing to submit to the application of Thai law in a Thai court. Part of the hostility expressed by Westerners to the Thai legal system was based on the confusing set of principles and harsh punishments that made up Thai law. As a result, treaties entered into between Thailand and foreign nations, such as the Bowring Treaty of 1855, which opened Thailand to trade with Great Britain, usually contained an extraterritoriality clause pursuant to which foreign nationals in Thailand would be subject only to the extraterritorial application of their national law.

Concerned with the implications to Thailand's sovereignty arising from extraterritorial application of law, King Chulalongkorn (Rama V) ordered a comprehensive reform of the Thai legal system. The king's motivation was his belief that only by demonstrating that Thailand was a "civilized country" could he support abrogation of the extraterritorial rights enjoyed by foreign nationals in Thailand. As part of his Chakri Reformation, the king ordered that several Western bodies of law, particularly the German and French civil codes, be introduced and applied to the codification of Thai law. The resulting code, produced during his reign and including the Penal Code of 1908, the Codes of Procedure, the Laws of Evidence of 1895, and the Transitory Civil Procedure Code of 1896, reshaped the Thai legal system. Later, in June of 1932, after the absolute monarchy was abolished and the present constitutional monarchy was created, the government promulgated the complete Civil and Commercial Code (the Code), which continues to provide the basis for existing Thai laws in the commercial field. Although the Code was drawn from the laws of countries with primarily civil (*i.e.* codified) legal systems, such as the French, German, Japanese and Swiss legal systems, the drafters of the Code also incorporated elements from the common law system of Great Britain, and the traditional laws of Thailand.

Thai Participation in Global and Regional Trade Organizations

Thailand is a member of the major international and regional organizations, **J.04** including the United Nations and the new World Trade Organization (WTO), which replaced the General Agreement on Tariffs and Trade (GATT). From a Thai perspective, perhaps the most important organization of which Thailand is a member is the Association of South-East Asian Nations (ASEAN). ASEAN was founded in 1967 by Indonesia, Malaysia, the Philippines, Singapore, and Thailand with the objective of increasing economic cooperation in, among other fields, food production, industry and commerce, shipping and telecommunications. Thailand has made use of its membership in ASEAN to argue successfully in favor of reduced tariffs on numerous exports from Thailand to industrialized countries, including rice and textile products, and to increase the volume of exports to fellow ASEAN nations. At the same time, Thailand has adroitly avoided playing a leading role in any of the problematic diplomatic issues that ASEAN has been called on to resolve, such as the military presence of Vietnam in Cambodia.

Thailand is also a member of a number of multilateral economic and trade organizations, including the ASEAN Free Trade Area (AFTA), a free trade zone made up of the members of ASEAN;[6] the Asia-Pacific Economic Cooperation (APEC) group, which founded in 1991 and includes nations on both sides of the Pacific Ocean; and the East Asian Economic Caucus (EAEC), which was established in 1990 following the breakdown of the Uruguay Round of the GATT.[7] Thailand is also a signatory to the ASEAN

Preferential Trading Agreement, which ensures reciprocal trade treatment of member-states of ASEAN. Finally, Thailand is a member of the Generalized System of Preferences (GSP), pursuant to which developing nations, such as Thailand, receive exemptions from or preferential treatment regarding tariffs.

The Current Thai Legal and Judicial System in the Regulation of Commercial Activities

J.05   The supreme law of Thailand is the Constitution, which was enacted in 1979. The Constitution is supplemented by Acts and the various Codes, which are promulgated by the legislative branch of the Thai government (Assembly and Senate); administrative rules and decrees, including decrees issued by the King; and laws promulgated by local administrative entities, such as municipal ordinances. At various times in this century, and as recently as 1991, the military has assumed control of the government of Thailand, and the Constitution has been suspended. In such instances, the military has typically governed through a National Executive Council or a similar body. The councils in turn have issued pronouncements which have been treated as equivalent to acts or code provisions promulgated by the executive or legislative organs of government.

Thailand has a three-tiered judicial system made up of the Supreme Court (*Sarn Dika*), the Court of Appeals (*Sarn Uthorn*), and the provincial Courts of First Instance (*Sarn Chunton*). There are also separate Juvenile, Tax, and Labor courts, although no separate courts exist for determining administrative law issues. All cases in Thailand are determined by judges; there is no provision for jury trial in Thai law.

The main source of law governing commercial transactions in Thailand is the Code, which is divided into three Books. Book I, entitled "General Principles", provides definitions and presumptions inherent in defining the scope of commercial legal principles. Book II addresses the topic of "Obligation", and contains critical provisions concerning the general rights and obligations of parties to a contract, and the remedies of the parties in the event of a default or breach. Finally, Book III ("Specific Contracts") begins by defining the elements of the sales contract, and then discusses specific types of contracts by subject matter, such as contracts for the "Hire of Services", the "Carriage of Goods", and contract principles underlying "Mortgages". The provisions of the Code governing the law of contract are supplemented by other Code provisions addressing the law of partnerships and companies. However, other legal issues relevant to undertaking commercial transactions in Thailand, such as tax and bankruptcy law issues, are governed by different statutes, including the Revenue Act and the Bankruptcy Act of 1940, respectively.

II. Laws and Institutions Affecting Business and Commercial Activities

Competition Law

Thailand is a relatively open economy, based on capitalist principles. Con-   J.06
sistent with these values, there are two statutes which are designed to prevent
the creation or development of monopolies and other anti-competitive forms
of business. The older of these statutes, the Trade Association Act B.E. 2509
(1966), is aimed expressly at preventing restraints of trade. Section 4 of the act
defines a trade association as "an institution formed ... in order to promote
business without seeking profit or income for distribution". Trade Association Act at section 4. Section 6 of the statute provides further that "persons
engaged in business shall be prohibited from joining together to promote
business except in the form of a trade association under this Act." Other
provisions of the act make clear that no actions may be taken by private
businesses to "depress or increase the price of merchandise or service charges,
or upset prices or merchandise or service charges", *Ibid.* at section 22(2), or
"to increase, reduce, or restrict the quantity or production of any merchandise or service". *Ibid.* at section 22(4). Finally, section 22(5) of the act prohibits any action that tends to "destroy normal business competition". *Ibid.* at
section 22(5).

The Trade Association Act is supplemented by another, more recent
statute, the Price Control and Anti-Monopoly Act B.E. 2522 (the Price
Control Act). The Price Control Act is the broadest form of anti-competitive
trade practices legislation in Thailand. In brief, the act establishes a Central
Board, made up of the Minister of Commerce, the Under-Secretary of State
for Commerce, and four to eight other members appointed by the Minister
of Commerce. The Central Board has one task: to determine if goods in a
particular sector of the economy are being monopolized. To make this
determination, the Central Board may consider any or all of the following
factors:

1. The number of producers and sellers in that sector;
2. The variety of similar types of goods;
3. Whether there have been any abrupt or rapid changes in the quantities
   of the particular goods on the market;
4. The ease with which new production may be introduced into the
   marketplace;
5. Whether the same price is being charged for similar or identical goods;
6. Whether the major producers of a given product are experiencing
   declining market share;
7. Whether the market share of individual producers remains stable;

8. Whether different prices are being charged for the same goods in different locations without an adequate economic justification.

The Central Board is free to consider other factors as it deems appropriate in conducting its investigation.

If the Central Board determines that monopolization of a given commodity or good exists, it may declare the business to be a "controlled business". This determination requires the manufacturer or producer to report regularly to the government on the quantity, storage, manufacturing costs, expenditures, methods of production, and distribution methods used for all controlled goods. In this manner, the government restricts the ability of the monopolist to recover the maximum price that it could charge in the market for that good.

The existence of anti-competitive legislation in Thailand does not compel the conclusion that no monopolies or other anti-competitive forms of organization exist. On the contrary, the Thai government itself, like the governments of many other developing and developed nations, has tended to operate monopolistic entities in several sectors of the economy, such as telecommunications, domestic air transportation, cigarette production, and several forms of public transportation, including the railways and municipal bus lines. Moreover, through the guidelines under which the Board of Investment grants promoted status to foreign investment projects, such as exemptions from the payment of income tax, or the exclusive right to develop land in a given area, the government creates circumstances that would make it difficult for a competitor to enter the market.

Contract Law

J.07 The Code provides general principles governing all commercial transactions, and specific sections governing contract formation. Under Thai law, all contracts, regardless of whether they are concerned with matters of a civil or commercial nature, are subject to the general law of obligations set forth in Book II of the Code. In addition, Book III of the Code provides supplementary rules governing commercial transactions. The contracts expressly included in Book III are sales contracts, leases, installment contracts, and contracts for the provision of services.

The principles governing the formation of a contract illustrate the interplay between various sections of the Code, and the necessity of reviewing several Code provisions in order to determine the validity of a given juristic act. In general, Thai law recognizes the formation of an enforceable contract where:

1. two or more parties declare their intention to form a contract, establishing enforceable duties to perform (Book I, section 112); and

2. the object of the contract is not expressly prohibited by law or is contrary to public policy (Book I, section 113); and
3. the contract is in the form prescribed by law (Book I, section 115), and
4. the contract complies with the requirements of all juristic acts, such as the demonstrated capacity of the parties to the contract. Book I, section 116.

The contract itself must identify the parties, demonstrate that all parties to the contract have mutually assented to its terms, and it must be based upon a legitimate and lawful object.

In Thai law, the act of contracting is referred to as effecting a "juristic act", which in turn is defined by section 112 of the Code as a "voluntary lawful act, the immediate purpose of which is to establish between persons juristic relations to create, modify, transfer, preserve, or extinguish rights". More-over, a statement of offer or acceptance is referred to as a "declaration of intention". A juristic act is effected, and the contractual relation is estab-lished, when the declaration of intention embodying acceptance is duly received by the party who has issued the declaration of intention embodying the offer. Book III, section 361. If, prior to the offer, no time has been established for receipt of acceptance of the offer, the promisor may fix a reasonable time and notify the promisee to state definitely within that time period whether he or she will complete the performance. *Ibid.* at section 454. If the promisee does not give a definite answer within that time, the promise lapses. *Ibid.*

A declaration of intention may not be voided on the ground that the declarant did not intend to be bound by his expressed intention, unless the "hidden intention" was known to the other party. Book I at section 117. A declaration will be voided, however, if made under a mistaken belief as to an essential element of the juristic act, unless the mistake resulted from the gross negligence of the person making the declaration, in which case the declarant cannot assert the invalidity of the assertion. *Ibid.* at section 119. A declara-tion would be voidable, for example, if it was made under a mistake as to the quality of the goods being sold, if the complainant can demonstrate that the quality of the purchased items was considered essential to the transaction. Also, if the declaration of intention was procured by fraud or duress, the declaration is voidable. *Ibid.* at section 120. For purposes of voiding a decla-ration, duress must be such that the declarant must hold a well founded fear of personal and imminent harm or injury to his person, or to his family or to his property. *Ibid.* at section 126. When an act is deemed to be void, it is considered to have been void *ab initio*, and the parties are restored to the condition in which they had been prior to the act. *Ibid.* at section 135.

There is a critical distinction under Thai law between the terms "sale" and "agreement to sell". The term "sale" is defined as the completed transaction of sale, *i.e.* the exchange of consideration for property, Book III at section 453, while an "agreement to sell" is essentially an agreement to complete a sale at a later date.[8] Any property is sellable, as long as the property has a determinable value and is capable of being owned.[9] Thus, Thai law allows for the sale of a variety of personal rights, such as options on the purchase of stock.[10] However, the Code expressly prohibits the sale of certain rights and property, including the sale of property in the public domain or belonging to the Crown; the right to receive a pension; or a temple and the land on which the temple is located.[11]

Thai law also requires that certain contracts for sale be in writing. If the object of the sale is immovable property, for instance, then the contract must be in writing, and the sale must be registered with the "competent official" in order to be valid. Book III at section 456. The failure to adhere to these requirements nullifies the contract for sale. *Ibid*. At the same time, the Code provides exemptions from the writing requirement. For example, if "earnest", a term defined in the Code as money or property given as proof of the existence of the contract and as security for the performance of the contract, *Ibid*. at section 337, is provided for the contract, or if there is part performance of the contract, then the agreement need not be in writing. *Ibid*. at section 456.

J.08   The Code expressly provides for the passing of title to goods purchased pursuant to a valid contract. As a general proposition, ownership of the property that is the subject of the sale passes to the purchaser from the moment in which the contract for sale is formed. *Ibid*. at section 458. If the contract is subject to a condition or a time clause, however, title to the property does not pass until the condition is fulfilled, or the time to perform has passed. *Ibid*. at section 459. Of course, in each transaction the parties retain the ability to determine the time at which title to goods shall pass.

Every seller of goods has three obligations under Thai law, regardless of whether such obligations are stated expressly in the parties' agreement. First, the seller must deliver to the purchaser the property sold. *Ibid*. at section 461. Delivery is made by any act "which has the effect of putting the property at the disposal of the purchaser". *Ibid*. at section 462. This includes delivering the property to a carrier. *Ibid*. at section 463. The seller must also deliver the property in a defect-free condition. *Ibid*. at section 472. If the property is defective in a manner that tends to diminish its value, its fitness for ordinary use, or its fitness for the purposes for which the property was purchased under the contract, the seller is liable regardless of whether he was aware of the defect. *Ibid*. at section 472. This does not mean, however, that the seller has no defenses to otherwise strict liability for the sale of defective goods. On the contrary, if the seller can prove that the purchaser knew of the defect at the time of the sale, or would have known of the defect through the exercise of ordinary care and scrutiny; or if the defect was apparent at the time of delivery, and the buyer accepted the property without reservation; or if the seller had sold the property at a public auction, then the seller is not liable for defects in the property. *Ibid.* at section 473(1)–(3). In the event that the seller cannot avail himself of these defenses, the purchaser may refuse to accept the goods and compel the seller to deliver goods that strictly comply with the purchaser's original request. *Ibid.* at section 465. The purchaser may also withhold the entire price or a part thereof if a defect is discovered on inspection of the goods, unless the seller provides the purchaser with "security". *Ibid.* at section 488. The purchaser also has the option of accepting the nonconforming goods. *Ibid.* However, if the purchaser accepts the goods, the "proportionate price" must be paid to the seller. *Ibid.*

Thai law also imposes certain duties on the purchaser of goods under a valid sales contract. First, the purchaser must accept delivery of the property sold if non-defective goods are delivered. *Ibid.* at section 486. Second, the purchaser must pay the price set forth in the contract on receipt of the goods, or at another time if the contract so provides. *Ibid.* However, if the contract provides only a date for delivery of the goods, the Code specifically provides that payment is presumed to be due on the same date. *Ibid.* at section 490.

Commercial Law

The Law of Juristic Acts

The first book of the Code provides an overlay of principles applicable to all   J.09
commercial transactions in Thailand. In general, the creation of all valid legal relationships among individuals, from the formation of a valid contract to the registration of a company with the relevant ministry, are considered "juristic acts" under Thai law. Book I of the Code provides a body of principles governing all juristic acts. Specifically, in order to be valid, it must be demonstrated for each juristic act that:

1. the parties possessed the capacity to commit the act;
2. the parties declared their intent to enter freely into the act, and
3. the form of the act is acceptable (*e.g.* the contract is in writing, if required by a specific Code provision).

Book I, sections 112–132. Any juristic act may be declared void or voidable depending on the method in which the act was committed. A void act is null and cannot be ratified. *Ibid.* at section 134. In contrast, a voidable act can be ratified by the parties and will be deemed to be valid from the date of the act. *Ibid.* at section 140. As mentioned above, these basic principles govern all juristic acts, including the formation of contracts. Consequently, parties seeking to demonstrate the validity of a contract must demonstrate that they have satisfied both the specific rules of contract formation and the general principles governing valid juristic acts.

Thailand

Creation and Perfection of Security Interests

J.10   The creation, perfection and enforcement of security interests in property are governed by the terms of the Civil and Commercial Code. Under the Code, the technical requirements for the creation of a security interest depend on the type of property. The Code classifies property into three types: immovable property; tangible movable property; and intangible movable property. Under sections 100, 108, and 109, immovable property is defined as land or structures fixed to land, including any rights arising from ownership of the land. Certain types of property, including "ships or vessels of six tons and over, steam launches, or motor boats of five tons and over", and "beasts of burden", also fall within the category of immovable property. *Ibid.* at section 703(1). The security interest in immovable property is a mortgage, which is defined as:

> "a contract whereby a person, called the mortgagor, assigns a property to another person, called the mortgagee, as security for the performance of an obligation, without delivering the property to the mortgagee."

Ibid. at section 702. Under section 703, any immovable property may be subject to a mortgage. The mortgage is created pursuant to a written document that must describe the immovable property. *Ibid.* at section 704. The mortgage obligation must be paid in installments, unless the agreement provides to the contrary. *Ibid.* at section 713. Additionally, in order to be effective, the mortgage must be registered with the local branch of the Land Office, which is referred to in the Code as the "competent official." *Ibid.* at section 714. The failure to register the mortgage renders the security interest invalid with respect to third persons, although the underlying contract would remain valid as between the mortgagor and mortgagee.

The second form of security interest in immovable property is the sale with the right of redemption. In this transaction, the buyer and seller enter into a contract "whereby the ownership of the property sold passes to the buyer subject to an agreement that the seller can redeem the property." *Ibid.* at section 491. The seller may redeem the property at anytime within the period stated in the contract, although the redemption period is deemed to have lapsed after 10 years if the right to redemption is not exercised within that time. *Ibid.* at section 494(1). The parties may agree to a shorter redemption period in their agreement. *Ibid.* If the seller redeems the property, the title to the property is deemed never to have passed to the buyer. *Ibid.* at section 492.

There are several means by which security interests are created in tangible movable property under the Code. The most common form is the pledge, defined as "a contract whereby a person, called the pledgor, delivers to another person, called the pledgee, a movable property as a security for the performance of an obligation". *Ibid.* at section 747. The pledge is made to secure the performance of an obligation and the payment of interest and compensation in the event that the pledgor fails to perform the obligation. *Ibid.* at section 748. The Code allows the property to be held in escrow by a third person. *Ibid.* at section 749. The pledge may be made orally or in writing, although if the pledged property consists of a right under a "written instrument", the pledge must be made in writing and the pledged property must be delivered to the pledgee. *Ibid.* at section 750. The pledgee must also formally notify the pledgor of the creation of the security interest in the pledged property. *Ibid.* The pledge may also be made on the basis of an after-acquired property clause in the agreement, allowing the pledge to secure continuing transactions. Because the pledgee retains possession of the collateral pending satisfaction of the obligation, the pledgee has responsibility for the safe-keeping of the collateral, and if the property is damaged or destroyed while in the custody of the pledgee the pledgee must restore the property or provide the pledgor with compensation. *Ibid.* at sections 759, 760.

In addition to the pledge, tangible movable property may be conveyed   J.11 subject to a redemption agreement or pursuant to a conditional sale. A redemption agreement for the sale of tangible movable property takes substantially the same form as the redemption agreement discussed above for the sale of immovable property. A conditional sale is a straightforward conveyance of property made on the condition that the price be paid in full over time. The seller technically retains ownership of the property, and if the obligation is not satisfied pursuant to the terms of the sales contract, the seller may recover the property. A security interest in intangible movable property is created in similar fashion as a security interest in tangible movable property. There is no separate provision in the Code for the creation of a security interest in intellectual property. Thus, the pledge of a patent or copyright would be created pursuant to section 750.

The priority of security interests in either immovable or movable property is determined by the date of perfection. In the event of a default (as defined in the parties' agreement), the secured party's remedies depend on the type of property pledged as collateral. If the secured party has retained the property pursuant to a pledge agreement, the secured party must notify the pledgor prior to selling the property at a public sale, which takes the form of an auction. *Ibid.* at section 764. It is not necessary for the pledgee to file suit in court in order to obtain a judgment prior to effecting such a disposition of the pledged property. In the event that the sale realizes more than the amount of the debt, the pledgee must pay over to the pledgor such surplus. *Ibid.* at section 767. The pledgor remains responsible for any deficit. *Ibid.*

If the collateral consists of property purchased on the basis of a conditional sale, the seller — as owner of the property — may dispose of the property in any way he or she sees fit. Where the collateral is immovable property secured by a mortgage, the secured party must initiate a court action in order to obtain a judgment against the obligor. *Ibid.* at section 728. The mortgagee may then attach the property and hold a public sale to dispose of it. *Ibid*. Any amount recovered from the sale in excess of the amount that was owed must be paid by the mortgagee to the mortgagor. *Ibid*. at section 732. The mortgagor is not, however, liable for any shortfall in the net proceeds from the sale of the immovable property. *Ibid*. at section 733.

Bankruptcy

J.12 Bankruptcies under Thai law are governed by the Bankruptcy Act of 1940. As a threshold matter, the object of Thai bankruptcy law is to terminate the business operations of the bankrupt entity, marshall the bankrupt's assets, and sell off the assets in order to satisfy the bankrupt's outstanding obligations. Under the act, any debtor or entity or person domiciled in Thailand, or any person who "earns his living therein", is subject to the jurisdiction of the court, in the event that a petition is filed seeking a determination that the debtor is insolvent. Bankruptcy Act at section 7. Significantly, the broad definition of natural and juristic persons susceptible of the court's bankruptcy jurisdiction includes foreign businesses incorporated outside of Thailand which operate in the Kingdom under the terms of the Alien Business Law, in addition to locally-incorporated Thai branches of foreign corporations.

In the event that a bankruptcy petition is filed, a presumption of insolvency exists:

1. If the debtor transfers property or rights in management of his property to others for the benefit of all his creditors whether such be done within or without the Kingdom.
2. If the debtor transfers or passes over his property with dishonest or fraudulent intent whether such be done within or without the Kingdom.
3. If the debtor transfers his property or creates any right over such property which, if the debtor were a bankrupt, would be deemed an act of preference to a creditor whether such act be done within or without the Kingdom.
4. If the debtor does any of the following in order to avoid payment of his debt, or in order to prevent a creditor from receiving payment of the debt:
   (a) leaves the Kingdom, or, having previously left, remains outside the Kingdom.
   (b) leaves the premises on which he has resided, or conceals himself in any premises, or absconds, or closes his place of business.
   (c) fraudulently removes property out of the jurisdiction of the court.
   (d) consents to judgment ordering the payment of money which he should not pay.

Ibid. at section 8(1)–(4(a)–(d)). The debtor is also considered to be insolvent if he informs the court, or any creditor, "that he cannot pay his debts". *Ibid.* at section 8(6)–(7). A creditor may institute a bankruptcy proceeding against the debtor if the debtor becomes "insolvent", as defined above, and the creditor(s) determine that the debtor's total obligations amount to, in the case of a natural person, more than 50,000 baht, and in the case of a juristic person, 500,000 baht. *Ibid.* at section 9(2). The petition is then filed with the court. All courts empowered to hear civil matters may accept a bankruptcy case; no special bankruptcy courts exist under Thai law.

If the court admits the petition, a date is selected for a hearing, and a copy of the petition is served on the debtor. Any creditor may also request that the court issue an order that the bankrupt be detained in order to be questioned and his property seized if the creditor believes, and has evidence, that the debtor has or is about to leave the country; has concealed, transferred or fraudulently removed property that should be considered part of the bankrupt estate; or has committed a fraud against one or more of its creditors. *Ibid.* at section 16. The court may also grant an *ex parte* request by a creditor seeking temporary control of one or more of the debtor's assets; in order to grant such a request, the court may order the petitioning creditor to provide security for the asset(s). *Ibid.* at section 17.

After filing the request for bankruptcy, and in the absence of an emergency order, the court issues an order to control the debtor's property. The order also dictates the appointment of the "official receiver", who conducts an investigation to determine the identity and location of all of the debtor's property, and then collects such property for disposition by the court in the event that the petition is accepted by the court. *Ibid.* at section 22. Property seized by the receiver pursuant to the court order of appointment may not be sold or otherwise disposed of until the court adjudicates all issues arising from the debtor's status. *Ibid.* at section 19. The court's order controlling the debtor's property renders all transactions by the debtor involving such property null and void. *Ibid.* at section 24.

After the court has issued an order controlling the property, the receiver conducts a meeting with the debtor for purposes of compiling all necessary information regarding the debtor's business and assets. *Ibid.* at section 30. The debtor is obligated to attend this meeting, and to submit responses under oath to all of the receiver's inquiries. *Ibid.* The receiver then conducts a meeting with the creditors. The purpose of the meeting is to determine whether an order for composition (see below), allowing the debtor's business to continue in operation while satisfying the obligations to the creditors, should be granted, or "whether the court should be asked to adjudge the debtor a bankrupt". *Ibid.* at section 31. The creditors, who may act through the medium of a committee headed by one or more individual creditors, *Ibid.* at section 37, then vote on how the petition should be resolved.

If the creditors vote that the court should declare the debtor a bankrupt, a hearing date for consideration of the petition is elected by the court. At the hearing on the petition, the court accepts evidence from both the creditors and the debtor. If the petitioning creditor(s) cannot prove the factual assertions contained in their petition, the court may deny the petition. Similarly, if the debtor can demonstrate his ability to pay his debts in full, or that there are other grounds not justifying the bankruptcy petition, then the court may deny the petition.

If the court grants the bankruptcy petition, the receiver undertakes the management of the bankrupt's business and assets, the collection of the bankrupt's accounts, and the settlement of the bankrupt's debts. *Ibid*. at section 61. The debtor is obligated to assist the receiver in the collection and disposition of assets. *Ibid*. at section 65. The receiver then sets the amount that the debtor requires for the maintenance of himself and his family. *Ibid*. at section 67(1).

Anytime after the court adjudges the debtor to be a bankrupt, the bankrupt may apply to the court for an order from the court discharging him from the bankruptcy. *Ibid*. at section 68. The court may take a number of factors into account in considering whether to grant the bankrupt's application, including any explanation or account rendered by the receiver, the record made on the basis of the public examination of the bankrupt's assets, and any explanation offered by the bankrupt under oath, as the court may require, or by the creditors or their representatives. *Ibid*. at section 70. The court is specifically prohibited from discharging the bankrupt if there is evidence that the bankrupt committed fraud. *Ibid*. at section 71. In addition, the Bankruptcy Act states that if any of a number of facts are shown to be true, including the fact that the total number of assets on hand is not more than 50 per cent of the total unsecured obligations of the debtor, or the fact that the bankrupt continued to carry on business "after knowing that he was bankrupt", the court may elect from a number of options, including, *inter alia*, refusing to discharge the bankrupt, or staying the discharge from bankruptcy for a period "of not less than two years". *Ibid*. at sections 72, 73.

On the other hand, if the court grants the motion to discharge the bankrupt, the bankrupt is released from liability for the repayment of all obligations, except for any taxes owed to the government, or for any debts which can be shown to have arisen from the fraud or dishonesty of the debtor. *Ibid*. at section 77(1)–(2). The bankrupt must also continue to assist the receiver in the collection and disposition of assets pending the final distribution to creditors. *Ibid*. at section 79. The discharge order does not, however, relieve any partner(s) of the bankrupt from liability for any joint obligations, or any other person who had joint responsibility with the bankrupt for the control of the assets, or any guarantor of the bankrupt. *Ibid*. at section 78.

Composition

J.13   The bankruptcy process set out in the act is distinct from another procedure, composition, which is available only to juridical persons under the act. *Ibid*.

at section 45. The goal of composition, in contrast to bankruptcy, is to ensure that the debtor remains in business while, at the same time, satisfying its obligations. A composition proposal may be submitted by the debtor to the court anytime before a bankruptcy petition has been filed against him. *Ibid.* Under section 63 of the act, the debtor may also file a composition proposal after the court has made an adjudication that he or she is bankrupt. *Ibid.* at section 63. However, if the court, during the pendency of the composition petition, determines that the debtor has breached the terms of the petition, or that the composition cannot be resolved as stated, the court may terminate the composition petition and adjudge the debtor to be bankrupt. *Ibid.* at section 60.

Under composition, the debtor and creditor(s) develop a plan for the repayment of debt that allows the debtor to remain in business. The act states that the purpose of composition is to allow the debtor "to come to a settlement for the satisfaction of his debts by payment of a part or in any other matter[.]" *Ibid.* As with a bankruptcy filing under chapter 11 of the United States Bankruptcy Code, any composition plan must be approved by the court in order to be effective. Thus, the debtor must submit a list of debts to the receiver, as well as a plan for the repayment of the obligations, the necessary security, if any, intended to guaranty the repayment of the debts, and other information. At that point, the receiver calls a meeting of the creditors, who, acting as a group, may elect to accept or reject the plan proposed by the debtor. *Ibid.* A vote in favor of accepting the plan does not, in itself, bind the creditors to the plan; rather, upon notification by the creditors of their acceptance, the receiver or the debtor must apply to the court for an order affirming the repayment plan. *Ibid.* at section 49. A necessary pre-requisite to the acceptance of the plan by the court is the completion of a public investigation of the debtor's assets and financial condition. *Ibid.* at section 51. The court must also consider the objections of any creditors who have not joined the group accepting the debtor's repayment plan. *Ibid.* at section 52. If the court approves the repayment plan, the order is published in the government *Gazette*. *Ibid.* at section 55. Moreover, if the court accepts the plan, the plan is binding on all creditors of the debtor, unless the creditor can demonstrate that the debt owed to that particular creditor falls within a narrow category of obligations which may not be discharged through bankruptcy, such as liability for unpaid taxes and debts arising from fraudulent conduct by the debtor. *Ibid.* at section 77.

Companies Law

Civil and Commercial Code

The first several Books of the Code represent an attempt to provide a com- J.14
prehensive set of rules governing the law of contracts, in general, and the law

of sales contracts, in particular. The Code also provides, however, along with the Public Companies Act of 1978, the basic principles of corporate law in Thailand. In addition, it is important to note that, despite the existence of certain restrictions on share ownership of entities chartered in Thailand, as well as restrictions on certain industries in which these organizations may operate, the basic forms of enterprise available to foreigners are the same as those for Thai citizens. It is also possible for companies or limited partnerships chartered in other jurisdictions to transact business in Thailand. However, these entities must take one of three specific forms and usually must comply with extensive registration requirements imposed by the Ministry of Commerce.

Limited Liability Company

The limited liability company is formed by filing two sets of documents. The Memorandum of Association describes the business purposes and capital of the company. The Memorandum states the name of the proposed company, which must end with the word "limited", the corporate purpose(s) for which the company was organized, and the address of the registered office of the company. Book III at section 1098(1)–(6). The Memorandum must also state that the liability of the shareholders is limited, identify the total capital of the company and the number of shares into which it is divided, and the names, addresses and occupations of the promoters. *Ibid*. The Memorandum must also identify the number of shares, if any, subscribed by the promoters. *Ibid*. The Articles of Association, which are adopted pursuant to a shareholders' meeting required by the Code to be called after the initial subscription of shares, set out the operational regulations and by-laws pursuant to which the company will be managed.

The promoters are required to file the Memorandum of Association with the Registrar of Partnerships and Companies, the Ministry of Commerce, or with a Provincial Registration Office if the head office of the company is located outside of Bangkok. As mentioned above, once the shares are subscribed, the promoters are required to call a statutory meeting of subscribers to adopt the Articles of Association, to elect the first board of directors, and to make other necessary preliminary decisions (such as appointing an accountant). Presently, there are no nationality or residency requirements on directors of private companies.

The Code contains specific provisions on the liability of promoters of limited liability companies. For example, the promoters of the company remain jointly and severally liable for all obligations of the company not approved by the statutory first meeting of the shareholders. *Ibid*. at section 1113. However, even if the obligation(s) incurred or disbursement(s) made by the company are approved at the first meeting of the shareholders, the promoters remain liable until the company is registered. *Ibid*. Shareholders of a private company are liable only to the extent of the unpaid contribution for the shares for which they subscribed. *Ibid.* at section 1096. Directors may make calls on the shareholders for any unpaid contribution for shares already subscribed. *Ibid.* at section 1120.

Limited liability companies are managed by the directors, subject to the control of the shareholders, and in accordance with the company's "regulations" (by-laws and articles). *Ibid.* at section 1144. Unless the regulations of the company state otherwise, the directors may delegate any other powers to managers, or to committees consisting of all members of the board of directors. *Ibid.* at section 1164. All acts taken by the directors are valid even if it is subsequently discovered that a director was not validly appointed or certified. *Ibid.* at section 1166. Relations between the directors, the company and third persons are governed by the principles of agency law.

A limited liability company is dissolved pursuant to its specific organizational structure or purpose. If the company was formed for a specific purpose, and that purpose has been accomplished, the company is dissolved. *Ibid.* at section 1236(3). The company can also be terminated by the expiration of the time period during which the company was to operate. *Ibid.* at section 1236(2). In addition, the shareholders of the company can promulgate a specific resolution to dissolve the company. *Ibid.* at section 1236(4). Dissolution can also take place through bankruptcy of the company, by a court order if the company fails to file the statutory report with the government, or if the company fails to hold the required shareholder meeting. *Ibid.* at section 1237(1). A court order dissolving the company may also issue if the petitioning person can demonstrate that the business of the company can be carried on only at a loss and there is no prospect for improvement in the financial status of the company, *Ibid.* at section 1237(3), or if the number of shareholders drops below seven. *Ibid.* at section 1237(4). The liquidation of the company is carried out pursuant to the terms of the Bankruptcy Act of 1940, and by sections 1247–73 of the Code.

Under Thai law, a limited liability company can be formed under either the Code or the Public Companies Act of 1978. A public company is a limited liability company chartered under the Public Company Act of 1978. The term "public company" does not refer to public ownership of the shares of the company, or to the fact that its shares are traded on the Securities Exchange of Thailand or another securities exchange. Rather, the distinction has to do with the ability of the company to issue debentures and offer its shares to the public through the medium of a public offering without first obtaining government approval. A private company, for example, in order to undertake a public offering of securities or to issue debentures, must seek and obtain the permission of the Securities Exchange of Thailand. A public company, on the other hand, need not obtain prior approval of that body.

The ability freely to issue shares to the public is one of the only advantages of the public company. Indeed, because of the numerous restrictions imposed on public companies that are not imposed on private companies, the overwhelming majority of business organizations incorporated in Thailand are private companies. For example, a public company must have on its formation (by filing the Articles of Association and the Memorandum of Association) more than 100 shareholders, of which natural persons must hold at least 50 per cent of the issued shares. Moreover, each natural shareholder must not own more than 0.6 per cent of the total number of authorized shares. The remaining shareholders must not own more than 10 per cent of the remaining authorized shares. Finally, all shares of a public company must be paid in at formation, and directors must themselves be shareholders.

Partnerships

J.15   Thai law recognizes both "ordinary" and limited partnerships. Ordinary partnerships, in turn, fall into one of two categories: registered or unregistered. Every type of partnership is governed by the Code, which provides the rules which must be followed in establishing an ordinary or limited partnership. (Unless otherwise noted, in the following discussion the principles applicable to ordinary partnerships are applicable to both registered and unregistered ordinary partnerships.)

Ordinary and Limited Partnerships

J.16   The Code provides certain common characteristics of both ordinary and limited partnerships. For example, both types of partnerships are characterized essentially as contracts for the sharing of profits between two or more persons, with each partner making a specified contribution of assets to the partnership. *Ibid.* at section 1012. In an ordinary partnership, each partner may contribute money, property or services, *Ibid.* at section 1012; in a limited partnership, each partner — either the limited or general partner — may contribute only cash or property. *Ibid.* at section 1083. There is no provision under Thai law for the contribution of services to a limited partnership.

Each type of partnership is formed by the execution of a partnership agreement. There is no specific requirement that the agreement be in writing. Indeed, the agreement governing an ordinary partnership may be oral or in writing, or made by the conduct of the parties. However, in the overwhelming majority of cases the partners enter into a formal, written partnership agreement, and, given the flexibility of the Code in this area, it makes no legal or business sense to operate without one.

Unless the agreement specifies otherwise, no change in the original contract of partnership or in the nature of the business may be made without the unanimous consent of the partners. *Ibid.* at section 1032. The business may be managed by each of the partners subject to the rule that no partner may enter into a contract to which another partner objects. *Ibid.* at section 1033. If it is agreed that partnership matters are to be decided by majority vote, each partner has one vote, regardless of the contribution(s) made to the partnership by that partner. *Ibid.* at section 1034. Alternatively, the partners may agree that the business shall be managed by several managing partners, subject to the rule that no managing partner may do anything to which another managing partner objects. *Ibid.* at section 1035. Relations between the managing partners are governed by the Code provisions on the law of agency. No new partner may be added to the partnership without the consent of all partners, unless the partnership agreement provides otherwise. *Ibid.* at section 1040.

Each partner shares in the profits and losses of the partnership in proportion to his contribution to the partnership. *Ibid.* at section 1044. A partner is entitled to his share in all partnership transactions, regardless of his participation or assistance. *Ibid.* at section 1048. However, if the partnership is unregistered, a partner cannot acquire rights against a third party to a failed transaction in which his name did not appear. *Ibid.* at section 1049. If, on the other hand, the partnership is registered, each partner acquires rights against third parties despite the fact that the partner had nothing to do with the failed transaction. *Ibid.* at section 1065.

For an unregistered partnership, there is no organizational requirement beyond formation of an agreement among the partners. In order to create a separate juridical personality under Thai law, however, the partnership must be registered. The registration entry must contain the name of the partnership, the purpose for which the partnership was organized, the principal office and other locations where the partnership will carry on business, and the full names, addresses and occupations of each partner. *Ibid.* at section 1064(1)–(6). If all partners are not going to manage the partnership, then the names of the managing partners, together with the restrictions, if any, on the authority of the managing partners, must also be filed. *Ibid.*

The key distinction between an ordinary partnership (registered or unregistered) and a limited partnership is that a limited partner's liability is limited to the amount that each such partner contributes to the partnership. *Ibid.* at section 1077(1). However, as with the Uniform Limited Partnership Law of the United States, each limited partnership must have one or more general partners, who each have unlimited joint and several liability for the debts and obligations of the limited partnership. *Ibid.* at section 1077(1). The limited partnership must, however, be managed by the general partner(s), *i.e.* the person(s) with unlimited liability. *Ibid.* at section 1087.

As mentioned above, the contributions of limited partners must be in money or other property, *Ibid.* at section 1083; there is no provision in the Code for a contribution of services by a limited partner. In addition, no dividend or interest may be paid to a limited partner unless there are partnership profits, and then only after any losses incurred by the partnership have first been fully satisfied. *Ibid.* at section 1084. One advantage of possessing a limited partner's interest is that such interest may be freely transferred without the consent of the other limited partners or the general partner(s). *Ibid.* at section 1091.

Thailand

A limited partnership registration must contain the partnership's name, the purpose for which the limited partnership was formed, the address of the principal business office, and the location of any branch offices. *Ibid*. at section 1078(1)–(7). The registration entry must also state that the partnership has limited liability, and must contain the names, addresses, occupations, and contributions of the limited partners. *Ibid*. The names, addresses, and occupations of the general partners must also be reported, in addition to the restrictions, if any, on the authority of the general partner(s) to bind the partnership. *Ibid*. A limited partnership is deemed to be an ordinary partnership until it registers with the government. *Ibid*. at section 1079. Thus, until registration, all partners are considered to possess unlimited personal liability for all of the obligations of the partnership.

An ordinary partnership is dissolved upon the occurrence of any of the following:

1. any cause for dissolution specified in the partnership agreement;
2. the expiration of the time set forth in the partnership agreement for the duration of the partnership;
3. the undertaking for which the partnership was formed has been accomplished;
4. if the partnership agreement provides for an unlimited duration, the notice given by any partner at least six months in advance of his intention to terminate the partnership at the end of a particular financial year of the partnership, or
5. the death, bankruptcy, or incapacitation of any partner.

Ibid. at section 1055(1)–(5). If the partnership is registered, then in the event of the bankruptcy of one of the partners, the remaining partners may purchase the shares of the bankrupt partner, and the partnership may continue to exist. *Ibid*. at section 1072. A partnership may also be dissolved by order of court obtained after a showing that:

1. one or more partners willfully or through gross negligence violated an essential term of the partnership agreement; or
2. the partnership business can only be carried on at a loss and there is no prospect of improvement; or
3. for any other reason that would make the operation of the partnership at a profit impossible.

Ibid. at section 1057(1)–(3). At the same time, the non-petitioning partners may request an order of the same court expelling the petitioning partner as an alternative to dissolution of the partnership. *Ibid*. at section 1058. In contrast, none of the above-listed conditions causes a limited partnership to cease unless such condition is expressly provided in the limited partnership agreement. *Ibid*. at sections 1092–94. For example, under the Code the heirs of a deceased or incapacitated limited partner become partners in place of that partner. *Ibid*. at section 1093.

Foreign Companies

An entity chartered in another jurisdiction but doing business in Thailand   J.17
can be deemed to be foreign under two distinct conditions. Specifically, the
company can fall within the definition of alien under section 3 of the Alien
Business Law of November 24, 1972 B.E. 2515 (1972), or if the company
operates branches or agencies chartered in another jurisdiction but is carrying on business in the Kingdom.

Section 3 of the Alien Business Law defines a foreign or alien entity as "a
natural or juridical person who is not of Thai nationality", and which is:

1. a juridical person of which half or more of the capital is owned by an
   alien business or businesses; or
2. a juridical person of which half or more of the shareholders, partners,
   or members are aliens, irrespective of the amount invested by such
   aliens; or
3. a limited partnership or registered ordinary partnership whose managing partner or manager is an alien.

The Alien Business Law divides the economy into three sectors or "classes"
in which foreign natural or juridical persons may (or may not) operate.
Businesses listed on Schedules A and B of the statute, including a variety of
agricultural and service businesses, are closed to foreigners. Thus, aliens may
engage in the businesses listed on Schedules A and B of the act only with the
issuance of a Royal Decree exempting them from the act's prohibitions.
Foreign nationals may, however, engage in businesses listed on Schedule C if
they first procure a license issued at the discretion of the Director-General of
the Department of Commercial Registration. However, in view of the fact
that the government has established a policy of not issuing licenses unless
it can be demonstrated that a Thai firm is not competent to conduct the
business, the ability to obtain a license and operate even a Class C business is
doubtful.

Companies chartered in the United States may be able to obtain a license
by making use of the Treaty of Amity and Economic Relations Between the
United State of America and the Kingdom of Thailand, which provides that
a Thai company, the majority of shares of which are owned by Americans, or
a branch office of an American company can operate in the following sectors:

1. real estate;
2. communications;
3. transportation;
4. fiduciary functions;
5. banking, including taking deposits;
6. natural resources, and
7. agricultural resources.

In order to register a Thai company under the auspices of the treaty, the
applicant must prove that a majority of the shares of the company are owned

by American natural or juridical persons. It is possible to convert a company formed under the Treaty from American to Thai ownership by conveying the requisite number of shares.

A company incorporated outside Thailand may establish a branch office to conduct business in Thailand. The branch office is treated as the same legal entity as its head office, and the acts of the head office are viewed as the acts of the branch office. There are no specific provisions under Thai law for the creation of the branch office. However, in order to be established as a branch office, a foreign company must file a series of documents with the Ministry of Commerce and appoint a branch manger with powers of attorney to act for the head office. The documentation required includes the Certificate of Incorporation, Articles and Memorandum of Association (Bylaws), an affidavit from a director describing the scope of the branch offices's competence, and a Power of Attorney in favor of the local manager. As the head office is responsible for the liabilities of the branch office, the power of attorney granted to the local manager should be restricted. However, the Ministry of Commerce requires that it be broad enough to enable the manager to do all that may be required to manage the branch office. All such documents must be notarized and authenticated by a Thai Embassy or Consulate. The intended business activities of the branch office will determine which specific laws and which particular Ministry will have oversight of its operations. However, in general the same licenses and registration requirements with which Thai companies must comply must also be satisfied by a foreign branch office.

A sub-class of the branch office is the representative office. A representative office may carry on more restricted activities than the branch office: its primary function is to provide a liaison between the head office and the foreign company's operations or interests in Thailand. A representative office does not conduct business in Thailand, and generates no income. Thai law recognizes three different types of representative offices. First, an "International Business Office" is restricted to performing international business activities, which are defined as:

> "seeking a source of goods or services in Thailand for purchase or utilization by the head office, checking and controlling quality and quantity of goods purchased or contracted to be manufactured in Thailand by the head office, giving advice in respect of goods sold to agents or consumers in Thailand by the head office, and disseminating information concerning goods or new services of the head office and reporting on business developments in Thailand to the head office."

It is also possible to form a "Foreign Bank Representative Office", or a "Financial, Securities, or Credit Foncier Representative Office" for foreign companies carrying on those businesses in Thailand.

Joint Ventures

The term "joint venture" is undefined in Thai law. Generally, joint ventures **J.18** in Thailand take the form of a Thai limited liability company with a contractual shareholders' agreement which controls the relationship and shareholdings of the different shareholding parties. Often both parties contribute capital, with one providing technological know-how and the other such benefits as basic production facilities, local marketing expertise, and Thai national status.

A joint venture may be incorporated or unincorporated. A corporate joint venture requires the incorporation of an entity formed specifically to conduct the business of the venture. An unincorporated joint venture, on the other hand, allows each party to maintain a separate identity within the venture. This form of organization is based on the contractual relationship between the parties and, under Thai law, is not regarded as a separate legal entity. An unincorporated form would most often be used where the proposed venture, such as a construction project, is limited in scope and duration.

A joint venture agreement is considered to be a private contract and is not registered with the government. However, any resulting Thai limited liability company or partnership must obtain certain registrations and licenses according to the nature of the business activity undertaken and the particular form or structure which the joint venture adopts. If a joint venture agreement provides for other, ancillary agreements, such as agreements for the use of trade marks, or for the management of the project, they should be submitted to the Bank of Thailand in order to obtain approval, if necessary, for the remittance of consultant fees or royalties abroad.

Mergers

Mergers are governed by Book III, sections 1238–1243 of the Code. These **J.19** provisions, however, provide only a passing treatment of the issue. Under Thai law, a merger is referred to as an "amalgamation", and requires only that each company pass a special resolution approving the merger. Book III at section 1238. A special resolution, as that term is defined in the merger section of the Code, is one that is passed in two successive general meetings of the shareholders, held within six weeks of each other, by a minimum of a three-fourths vote in the first meeting and by at least a two-thirds vote in the second meeting. The resolution must then be registered with the Ministry of Commerce within 14 days of the second vote, and the details of the amalgamation published in a local newspaper and to the company's creditors. *Ibid.* at section 1240. A creditor has six months in which to raise and file an objection to the merger, and the creditor's claim must be satisfied or must receive security for the obligation owing before the merger can be completed. *Ibid.* If there is no objection to the amalgamation after six months, the merger is completed by registering the new company. *Ibid*. at sections 1240–41. The new company must have the equivalent share capital as the previous companies, and it must retain the same rights and privileges to its shareholders and be subject to the same liabilities as each of the former entities. *Ibid*. at section 1242.

Capital Markets and Securities Law

J.20   Since its founding in 1974, the Stock Exchange of Thailand (SET) has been vibrant, and its recent performance has underscored this trend. At present, the SET is ranked by the International Finance Corporation, an affiliated agency of the World Bank, as among the 20 largest capital markets in the world in terms of total market capitalization, total value of securities traded, and the number of domestic companies listed on the exchange.[12] The volatility of the market has also been recently demonstrated through losses across the board amounting to approximately 25 per cent decline in the relative values of the stock prices of Thai companies.[13] In large part, this was due to the decline of the U.S. dollar, the leading currency to which the baht is tied. Investors, including many from developed nations, were concerned that the Thai government would increase interest rates to attract the capital needed to sustain the same level of growth in the Thai economy.[14] This decline, however, was followed by a slow but steady movement upward, which was highlighted by several large public offerings of new securities on the SET. Among others, Bangkok Bank, one of the largest commercial banks in Thailand, Thai Telephone and Telecommunications, Ltd, and Electricity Generating Company, Ltd all had successful offerings in 1994.[15]

The Securities Exchange of Thailand Act

J.21   The SET was established and is regulated pursuant to the Securities Exchange of Thailand Act B.E. 2517 (1974). Under that act, the SET is the sole entity that may operate a securities market in Thailand. The SET is under the policy direction of a Board of Directors, which is subject to the direction of the Ministry of Finance. Membership on the SET is limited to securities companies licensed by the Ministry of Finance to engage in the securities business as stock brokers (see below). Only members of the exchange may trade directly on the SET, although non-members may trade for customers through members of the exchange. Trading takes place on the three boards established by the SET, on the basis of an auction. The Main Board consists of trades in even blocks of securities. The Special Board is designed to accommodate trading in odd or especially large blocks of securities. Shares owned by non-Thai nationals may only be traded on the Foreign Board. Citizens of Thailand may finance up to 30 per cent of their purchases through margin loans from their brokers; foreign purchasers, however, are not permitted to purchase securities on margin. Significantly, the SET also has prohibited short selling of securities.

Members of the SET may trade two types of securities on the SET. "Listed" securities are those issued by a company listed on the SET. In order to be listed on the SET, a company must have a registered share capital in excess of 20 million baht. In addition, the initial public offering of shares by a listed company must be subscribed by at least 300 "small shareholders", who are defined in the act as shareholders who each own at least 10,000 baht worth of shares; each individual small shareholder's holdings, however, cannot equal more than 0.5 per cent of the total share capital of the company. Small shareholders must also own in the aggregate at least 30 per cent of the paid-in capital of the company.

The SET also provides for the trading of securities issued by an "authorized" company. An authorized company must have a registered share capital of at least 10 or 20 million baht, depending on whether the company is newly incorporated. In addition, the authorized company must have at least 50 small shareholders, who own in the aggregate at least 20 per cent of the company. Finally, the authorized company must also convince the SET that it has already established a stable financial record. Alternatively, if the authorized company lacks an adequate record, it must demonstrate to the SET that it has sufficient potential to provide an adequate return on investment for its small shareholders.

Securities Firms

The regulation of securities firms is conducted pursuant to the Act on the Undertaking of Finance Business, Securities Business, and Credit Foncier Business, promulgated in 1979. The term "securities business" is defined under this statute in the following manner: **J.22**

1. Business of brokerage for buying and selling of securities;
2. Business of trading in securities;
3. Business of providing investment advice;
4. Business of managing sales of securities;
5. Business of investment management, and
6. Other types of business concerning securities as prescribed in ministerial regulations.

Act on the Undertaking of Finance Business, Securities Business, and Credit Foncier Business at section 7. The terms "securities" is defined to include all common forms of securities, including:

1. Treasury bills;
2. Bonds, bills, or other commercial instruments;
3. Shares or debentures, certificates representing the rights to shares or debentures, certificates representing the rights to buy shares or

debentures, or certificates evidencing the subscription for shares or debentures;

4. Certificates representing the rights to dividends or interests from securities, and

5. Instruments or evidences representing the rights to the property of investment plans issued by a person who engages in the business of investment management, whether locally or abroad.

Under the Act, all securities companies are required to be limited liability companies which have obtained a license from the Ministry of Finance to carry on a securities business. *Ibid.* at section 4. Moreover, every securities company must include the term "securities company" in its name, and the term "limited" at the end of its name. *Ibid.* at section 40. In order to obtain the appropriate license from the Ministry of Finance, the securities company must demonstrate that it has satisfied all of the capitalization requirements imposed by the Ministry after reviewing the application. *Ibid.* at section 42. The capitalization of the securities company cannot be changed without the prior permission of the Ministry.

The Securities Act imposes numerous obligations on the conduct of the securities business. The purpose of the legislation is to protect consumers (those purchasing securities from brokers). For example, the Act prohibits securities companies from committing "any act which may mislead its customers or the public in matters concerning price, value or nature of the securities involved". *Ibid.* at section 43(2). Also, securities companies are barred from purchasing securities in advance of their public issuance, unless authorization is obtained from the Minister of Finance. *Ibid.* at section 43(4). Securities companies are additionally prohibited from engaging in any other forms of business except the securities business. *Ibid.* at section 43(6). Finally, securities companies may not employ as a broker any person who has not been approved to occupy such employment by the Bank of Thailand. *Ibid.* at section 44.

Banking and Lending Law

J.23 The first bank in the modern sense established in Thailand was the Hongkong and Shanghai Banking Corporation, which opened an office in Bangkok in 1888. Reflecting the regional interests of the chief colonial powers, England and France, in the Southeast Asian region, this institution was followed by the The Chartered Bank in 1894, and the Banque de l'Indochine in 1897.[16] Five Thai-owned banks were founded before 1942, when the central bank, the Bank of Thailand, was founded. Prior to the founding of the Bank of Thailand, the Ministry of Finance had the responsibility of printing money.

There are four major statutes regulating the banking sector of the Thai economy. As mentioned above, the Bank of Thailand Act, passed in 1942, established the Kingdom's central bank. The Savings Bank Act established the national network of savings institutions, such as the Thai Savings Bank, which accept deposits. Third, the Industrial Finance Corporation of Thailand Act created the chief governmental development bank, which provides medium- to long-term financing for industrial development projects. Finally, the Commercial Banking Act of 1962 opened the Thai market to commercial banking. At present there are six commercial banks incorporated in Thailand, the largest of which are Bangkok Bank, Krung Thai Bank, Siam Commercial Bank, and Thai Farmers Bank. In addition, in the commercial banking sector, there are 17 branch offices and 32 representative offices of foreign banks, including the Chase Manhattan Bank, the Bank of America, and the Bank of Tokyo.[17]

Commercial Banking Act of 1962

The Commercial Banking Act of 1962 superseded the previous legislation, **J.24** promulgated in 1954. In brief, the law sets out the conditions for establishing a commercial bank in Thailand. Under the reforms enunciated in the 1979 commercial banking act, "commercial banking" is defined as:

> "the business of accepting deposits of money subject to withdrawal on demand or at the end of a specified period and on employing such money in one of several ways, such as:
>   (a)   granting of credits;
>   (b)   buying and selling of bills of exchange or any other negotiable instrument; [or]
>   (c)   buying and selling of foreign exchange."

Commercial Banking Act at section 4. A bank established pursuant to the act must be in the form of a limited public company, and it must be licensed by the Ministry of Finance. No one individual or juristic person may hold more than 5 per cent of the shares of the bank. *Ibid.* at section 5.bis. For purposes of identifying shareholders, the 1979 amendments to the Commercial Banking Act clarified that the definition of "person" used in the statute expressly includes entities such as partnerships and limited partnerships organized under the Code, as well as individuals. *Ibid.* Any transfer that would result in such a person owning more than 5 per cent of the shares of a commercial bank under the act is invalid. *Ibid.* at section 5ter. Each commercial bank is also required to have at least 250 "shareholders who are natural persons". *Ibid.* at section 5cinque. The bank must affirm the content of its shareholder base prior to each distribution of dividends to ensure that no violations of the prohibitions imposed by the act have occurred. *Ibid.* at section 5septem. The act also requires that any foreign bank seeking to establish a branch office in Thailand first obtain a license from the Ministry of Finance. *Ibid.* at section 6. In contrast to the branch office, in order to create a representative office in Thailand, the foreign enterprise must obtain a license from the Bank of Thailand. *Ibid.* at section 7.

Thailand

The activities of all commercial banks are regulated by the central bank. The Bank of Thailand, for instance, establishes the level of cash reserves that each commercial bank must maintain. *Ibid.* at section 10(1). Reserves maintained by a commercial bank are a function of the bank's total assets, with a minimum of 5 per cent of funds kept as reserves. *Ibid.* Under section 10 of the act, each bank may include in calculating its total assets any cash and deposits with the Bank of Thailand. Part of these reserves must be deposited with the Bank of Thailand. The central bank also establishes the rate of interest that banks may charge on borrowed funds, and the rate that banks can pay on deposited funds. *Ibid.* at section 14(1)–(2). Perhaps most importantly, prior to the relatively recent foreign exchange reform that the government undertook with the guidance of the Internal Monetary Fund, Thai commercial banks acted as agents of the Bank of Thailand in scrutinizing and approving foreign exchange transactions.

There are a number of restrictions on practices in which a commercial bank may engage. For example, no commercial bank is permitted to grant credit to or provide a guaranty on behalf of any of its directors. *Ibid.* at section 12(2). In addition, there is a prohibition on the purchase by a commercial bank of any "immovable property" unless it is for the purpose of opening a branch or another form of physical expansion. *Ibid.* at section 12(4)(a). Finally, no commercial bank organized under Thai law may purchase or hold more than 10 per cent of the shares of a limited liability company, *Ibid.* at section 12(5), or any shares in another commercial bank. *Ibid.* at section 12(6).

Exchange Control Laws

J.25 The chief legislation on the control of currency and foreign exchange in Thailand are the Exchange Control Act B.E. 2485 (1942), the Royal Decree Amending the Exchange Control Act B.E. 2486 (1943), Ministerial Regulation No. 13 of 1954, and Ministerial Regulation No. 20, 1991. The legislation has grown considerably more liberal since 1990, when the Government, motivated by the need to maintain a flexible exchange control system to support the dynamic and rapidly growing Thai economy, accepted in principle the dictates of Article VIII of the Articles of Agreement of the International Monetary Fund. Under that provision, Thailand is moving toward the elimination of all restrictions on the importation and export of currency, regardless of purpose. Due to the Government's action, beginning in 1991, the Thai government implemented three rounds of foreign exchange deregulation. Although certain restrictions remain on some transfers of funds, the government intends to achieve the complete liberalization of all foreign exchange regulations over the next three years.[18]

In broad form, the government's actions have eliminated, in most cases, the requirement that the foreign entity obtain prior Government approval for the repatriation of capital out of Thailand. For example, the export of dividends or earnings payable in U.S. dollars or other forms of foreign exchange may now be made without approval of the Bank of Thailand. However, the central bank must nonetheless approve the repatriation of amounts in excess of US$10 million if such funds are intended for investment outside of Thailand, or if such funds are intended to be a loan to an overseas subsidiary of a company chartered in Thailand.

There is no restriction on the amount of foreign exchange that may be brought into Thailand. The importer of such currency, however, has 15 days from the date of importation to convert the funds to baht, or to deposit the funds into a foreign currency account maintained at a commercial bank in Thailand. If the entity importing the currency deposits or sells to the commercial bank the equivalent of US$5,000 or more per day, that person must complete the requisite control forms. The forms must be completed for record-keeping purposes only, however, and do not require prior government approval of the transaction.

As mentioned above, government approval must be obtained for a narrow set of transactions. For example, any foreign currency account opened by a foreign national at a Thai commercial bank cannot, without prior government approval, maintain a balance greater than US$500,000, if the depositor is a natural person, and US$5 million in the event the depositor is a juristic person. Second, the proceeds from the sale of items exported from Thailand must be collected within 180 days of the date of export. The proceeds must then be deposited with, or sold to, a commercial bank within 15 days from the date that the person acquired the funds.

Government approvals must also be maintained for various types of import transactions. Thus, although a person importing goods into Thailand no longer needs to obtain government approval prior to paying for such goods, the Thai commercial bank acting as the agent for the government must collect documentary evidence that the funds were allocated to the purchase of imports. If the value of the goods exceeds 500,000 baht, the importer must then submit a report with the bill of lading to the customs officer at the place of importation detailing the foreign exchange transaction.

The value of the Thai currency, the baht, is set each day by the central bank. The value of the baht is not pegged to any particular currency, but is, rather, fixed to the value of a basket of hard (*i.e.* Western and Japanese) currencies. However, because the commercial banks are not required to follow the rate established by the Bank of Thailand, a relatively fluid currency market has developed.

Consumer Protection Laws

Consumer protection legislation in Thailand is sparse. Most of the legislation **J.26** that exists is outdated and intended to apply only to the rationing of goods during national emergencies. For instance, the Act Controlling

Thailand

Consumer Goods and Things During Critical Situations, passed in 1945, allows the government to control the distribution of goods in order to assure an adequate supply to the public. Under this statute, the government may impose rationing of the good if it determines that such protection is necessary. Additionally, under the Act for the Control of Consumer Goods (1952), the government may limit the distribution of certain goods throughout the country, or in one particular region of Thailand, if it determines that such restrictions are for the benefit of the Kingdom as a whole.

The chief modern consumer protection legislation is the Consumer Protection Act of 1979, the focus of which is the correct labeling of goods. The act creates a Consumer Protection Committee which considers grievances brought by the public due to misfeasance or improper labelling by the seller of a consumer good. The Committee is expressly empowered, among other things, to confiscate and destroy any goods that are deemed to be dangerous to the public; to post public notices identifying the sellers distributing goods considered to be dangerous to the public; and to compel sellers to provide an explanation as to what particular goods are considered dangerous. These obligations have their basis in all Thai consumers' rights to protection, which the act defines as follows:

1. Right to correct and sufficient information concerning goods or services;
2. Right to freedom of choosing goods or services;
3. Right to satisfaction in the use of goods and services, and
4. Right to compensation in the event a consumer is injured as a result of damage inflicted by a defective good.

Another important component of the act is the creation of two ad hoc committees: one committee focuses on fair trade practices in advertising, and one addresses such practices in trade labeling. The advertising committee was created to ensure that no advertisement would use any statement in the description of the origins, condition, quality, or characteristics of the good which are "unfair to consumers" or which would cause damage to society as a whole. Unfair statements under the act are those that:

1. Falsify or exaggerate (but not ones which the public will recognize as obviously untrue);
2. May mislead the public regarding the essence of the goods;
3. Directly or indirectly encourage a violation of law to occur, or
4. May cause "disunity" or disruption among the Thai populace.

There are also prohibitions on advertisements that would cause injuries or other hazards to public health, or advertisements that would be considered, or are found to be, a nuisance.

The primary task of the second ad hoc committee is the fair labelling of consumer goods sold or distributed in Thailand. Under the Consumer

Protection Act, the Ad Hoc Committee on Trade Labels may declare that certain goods are "controlled" on the ground that they pose a threat to the public due to poor labelling. The committee identifies controlled goods on the basis of several factors, including whether the goods cause or could cause bodily injury, and whether the public would benefit from improved or new labels on the goods, particularly if the public would benefit from labels that provide more information. The committee also ensures that all labels contain accurate descriptions of the goods and their contents. In this regard, the committee scrutinizes closely those goods which may possibly mislead consumers into believing that certain goods contain elements which they do not, in fact, contain. The committee may conduct an examination of any good which the committee believes contains a misleading or incomplete label. If the examination conducted by the committee results in a finding that the label is misleading, and a hazard to the health of Thai consumers, the committee may forbid the sale of all such goods, or order the producer to modify the label on the goods to reflect their actual contents. The committee may also permanently prohibit the sale or destroy the goods if, in the opinion of the committee, such actions are in the public good.

Foreign Investment Law

The legal framework for foreign investment in Thailand is set forth in the **J.27** Promotion of Investment Act B.E. 2520 (1977). The Act established the Board of Investment (BOI), which promotes and regulates foreign investment in the Kingdom. The members of the BOI are the Prime Minster, who acts as Chairman, the Minister of Industry, who acts as Vice-Chairman, a secretary-general, who is charged with the day-to-day administration of the BOI, and 10 other "competent persons". Promotion of Investment Act at section 6. Through its chief agency, the Office of the Board of Investment, *Ibid.* at section 11, the BOI has broad discretionary authority to provide incentives to foreign investors. In contrast to the foreign investment legislation in many other developing nations, the Promotion of Investment Act authorizes the BOI to "promote" investments (*i.e.* grant incentives) on a case-by-case basis. Thus, the type and the number of incentives that the BOI is likely to grant depend on the subject matter of the investment, and whether the BOI is attempting to encourage investment in the area in which the investment is to be made.

The BOI has issued guidelines outlining the areas that it seeks to promote. The Act provides a nebulous set of criteria that the BOI will employ to review applications for investment promotion. After stating that the proposed investment must be "one which is economically and technologically sound", the Act provides that incentives will be granted after the BOI has considered:

1. the existing number of producers and production capacity in the king-dom and the size of production capacity to be created under promo-tion compared with demand estimates;
2. the potential for which the investment project seeking promotion will expand the market, and support the production of the commodities or products produced or assembled in the kingdom;
3. the quantity and proportion of the resources available in the kingdom, including the capital, raw or essential materials and labor or other services utilized;
4. the amount of foreign currency which may be saved or earned for the kingdom;
5. the suitability of the production or assembly processes; and
6. the requirements which the Board deems necessary and appropriate.

Ibid. at section 18. The specific sector in which the foreign investment is to be made is also a critical factor in the BOI's determination of whether to grant promotion status. The Promotion of Investment Act contains a lengthy schedule listing the particular commodities and types of goods that are subject to promoted status by the BOI.

Special requirements are imposed on applications for promoted status where the investment will be made through a joint venture. For example, if the purpose of the joint venture is to produce goods or other items for domestic sale (*i.e.* in Thailand), Thai nationals must own 51 per cent of the registered capital of the joint venture. If, on the other hand, the purpose of the venture is to export at least 50 per cent of the venture's production from Thailand, then foreign persons may own the majority of the registered capital of the entity. Moreover, foreign nationals may own up to 100 per cent of the registered capital of the venture if between 80 per cent and 100 per cent of the production of the joint venture is exported.

If the BOI decides to promote the project, it may offer one or more of a variety of benefits, including the relaxation on the number of foreign em-ployees that the enterprise may have in Thailand, *Ibid*. at section 25; the right to own land, which is critical since non-Thai nationals are not otherwise permitted to own land in Thailand, *Ibid*. at section 27; and limited protection for the products to be assembled or produced in Thailand, through the reduction or elimination of tariffs on goods that are produced and exported. *Ibid*. at section 41. The BOI also offers various guaranties to foreign inves-tors, including the guaranty that the Government will not nationalize the assets of the foreign investment project, *Ibid*. at section 43, and the guaranty that the Government will not join with any domestic or foreign competitor in the industry in which the foreign investment is made. *Ibid*. at section 44.

The BOI is also authorized to issue numerous types of tax incentives. The BOI applies particular criteria to determine whether a foreign investment project is eligible for tax incentives. These criteria include the geographic location of the project; the foreign exchange earnings that the project is likely to generate for the kingdom; the extent to which raw materials can be supplied from local (Thai) sources; the number of Thai employees that the project will utilize; and the specific type of goods to be produced. The incentives range from the exemption or reduction of import duties on machinery, raw materials, and other items that are necessary for the production of the goods, to indirect measures such as allowances to carry forward losses longer than the period permitted under the Revenue Code. As an example, under the *New Criteria for Granting Tax and Duty Privileges for Promoted Projects*, effective from April 1, 1993, the BOI will offer no exemption on corporate income tax for investments made in Bangkok, Samut Prakan, and several other locations in "Zone 1", which contains the most developed areas in the country. For the same investment in "Zone 2" locations, however, the BOI will provide an exemption on corporate income tax for up to three years, as well as other incentives, such as reductions or exemptions on the payment of duty from the importation of raw materials. As with other incentives, the failure to observe all of the requirements imposed by the BOI as conditions precedent to promoted status entitles the agency to revoke the rights and privileges that the investors received. Promotion of Investment Act at section 54.

To assist foreign investors in the application process, the BOI has established so-called "Investment Service Centers", known colloquially as "one-stop service centers". The purpose of these agencies is to assist investors in completing applications for related licenses and permits, such as for the employment of foreign nationals and for any necessary building permits. The centers also give tax advice and counsel on the repatriation of foreign exchange and other currency matters.

Tax Law

Revenue Code of Thailand

The primary law on taxation in Thailand is the Revenue Code B.E. 2481   **J.28**
(1983). The Revenue Code contains sections addressing both the taxation of individuals and corporations. Tax matters are also affected by a number of other statutes, such as the Investment Promotion Act (discussed below) and the Industrial Estate Authority of Thailand Act, if the entity being taxed is involved in importing or exporting manufactured or agricultural goods. Under these and other tax provisions, persons are either taxed because they are natural or juristic persons, or on the basis of a particular transaction.

Corporate Taxation Under Thai Law

The key distinction between the entities paying corporate tax is whether the   **J.29**
enterprise operates "on-shore" (*i.e.* domestically), or is chartered "off-shore". A company or partnership chartered in Thailand pays tax in a

number of forms, including taxes on its income and taxes in the form of withholding charges. Corporate tax is also paid by all companies, foundations, partnerships, associations, and registered partnerships that are chartered in foreign jurisdictions but which "carry on business in Thailand". Revenue Code at section 76bis. Under that section, the phrase "carrying on business in Thailand" has a broad definition:

> "If a juristic company or partnership incorporated under a foreign law has in Thailand for carrying on its business an employee, a representative or a go-between and thereby derives income or gains in Thailand, such juristic company or partnership shall be deemed to be carrying on business in Thailand[.]"

Ibid. Excluded from this definition is an independent sales agent, as long as the entity can demonstrate that the agent does not solely act for the foreign company, and that payments for any goods purchased in Thailand are paid directly by the purchaser to the foreign manufacturer or distributor. However, section 70 of the Revenue Code states that foreign juristic entities, such as corporations and partnerships, that do not carry on business in Thailand, but which receive income from a source in Thailand, including any royalty, rent, interest, dividends, or other similar payments, are liable to pay withholding tax under the Revenue Code. *Ibid.* at section 40.

Any enterprise carrying on business in Thailand must pay tax on its net profits, if any, derived from the income the entity earns in Thailand. At present, the rate that all such corporations must pay is 30 per cent on net profits earned in any given tax year. The Revenue Code does not impose a separate tax on capital gains derived from the sale of assets. The tax year is any 12 month period selected by the taxpayer, as long as the same period is used consistently. In the event that the enterprise fails to file a return, the income tax rate is 5 per cent of the firm's gross receipts or total sales, with no allowance for deductions, if any.

The Revenue Code allows the firm to apply generally accepted accounting principles in order to determine annual income tax liability. Income includes any gain earned by the firm, regardless of source or form. All expenses incurred in earning income are deductible from income to determine net profit. Such expenses include business expenses, bad debts, and depreciation. In the absence of records identifying the expenses that the firm has incurred, the firm may elect to apply a standard deduction to determine its income tax liability. The extent of the standard deduction depends on the type of business operated by the taxpayer. A service business, for example, may apply a deduction of 30 per cent of its income. Taxpayers with income from the rental of real property, however, may elect to deduct only 10 per cent of their income. Moreover, if reasonable efforts have been undertaken to recover bad debts, such obligations can be written off by the taxpayer.

There are five types of depreciation of company or partnership assets allowed under the Revenue Code. For example, there is a 5 per cent depreciation allowance for all "permanent buildings", such as company offices. For temporary buildings, the code permits a full 100 per cent depreciation. The code also permits depreciation of varying amounts up to one hundred percent for intangible assets such as patents, trademarks and goodwill. The Revenue Code prescribes the use of a straight-line method of depreciation. Additionally, any losses incurred by the enterprise in one year may be carried forward for a maximum of five consecutive years. All such losses may be set off against income, regardless of its source.

In addition to the tax that the enterprise must pay on its net profits, each entity is subject to withholding tax for its employees and for the tax on profits remitted from Thailand. Withholding tax is payable on the salary of each of its employees. The employer is obligated to pay the tax and file a return within seven days after the end of the month in which the tax has been deducted. The so-called profit remittance tax is levied at the rate of 20 per cent of the net amount remitted. The off-shore office receiving the profits is obligated to pay the tax on the remitted income.

Corporate income tax is payable twice each year. The first installment must be paid within two months of the close of the first half of the taxpayer's tax year. At that time, 50 per cent of the tax due from the taxpayer's estimated net profits must be paid. If the taxpayer's calculations produce a shortfall of 25 per cent or more in estimated tax, the taxpayer must pay a penalty of 20 per cent of the difference between what is owed and what was paid. The annual return must be filed within 150 days from the close of the taxpayer's tax year. If the taxpayer misses the filing deadline, the Ministry levies a surcharge of 12 per cent of the amount that is ultimately due from the taxpayer.

Thailand also imposes a value added tax (VAT). The VAT is a broad-based consumption tax that must be collected and remitted to the Government by almost all manufacturers, importers, and retailers. The key criterion in payment of the VAT is whether the taxpayer sells goods in the normal course of its business. The term "sale" includes any "disposition, conveyance, or transfer of tangible or intangible property having a monetary value". Businesses providing services must also pay VAT: a service is any act which results in "a benefit other than a sale." The only taxpayers exempt from the collection and remittance of the VAT are firms with less than 600,000 baht in revenue on an annual basis, and which produce or deal in certain types of goods, such as particular types of medicines and chemical products, newspapers and magazines, and services provided by libraries, museums and zoos.

Finally, if the taxpayer is classified as a "trader", the enterprise must pay an additional "business tax" on gross monthly receipts. A trader is defined in the Revenue Code as a person carrying on a "business". A "business", in turn, is defined as "engaging in business, trade, industry, agriculture, production, importing, exporting or in the rendering of services for gain". *Ibid.* at section 77. As the language used in the statute demonstrates, this definition expands the total number of enterprises liable to pay business tax. The tax levied under the business tax provisions of the code, however, depends on the type of business that the taxpayer is engaged in. The Revenue Code contains a schedule identifying the types of businesses liable for the payment of business tax, and the rates at which such tax must be paid. A firm selling securities, for instance, must pay one-tenth of one per cent (0.1 per cent) of its gross monthly receipts as business tax. An enterprise that operates a restaurant, on the other hand, must pay between 2 per cent and 15 per cent of gross monthly receipts, depending on the type of enterprise. The determination of the amount liable under the business tax provisions is also important for determining the amount that each enterprise must pay under the Municipal Revenue Act of 1954. Under that statute, each taxpayer liable for the payment of business tax is also subject to a municipal tax of a flat 10 per cent of the business tax payable by that taxpayer.

International Tax Treaties

J.30   Thailand is a signatory to approximately 30 tax treaties.[19] In general, these treaties are aimed at preventing double taxation. Whether the terms of a particular tax treaty apply in a given situation depends on the specific facts of the matter. However, in the main, these treaties share certain common characteristics. It is clear, for example, that in order to receive protection under one of the treaties the taxpayer must demonstrate that it maintains a permanent establishment (or, in the case of an individual, permanent residency) in the foreign nation. The term "permanent establishment" is generally defined as a fixed site for carrying on business in that location, such as an office, factory, or warehouse. The term also typically includes a branch office. The critical inquiry is, therefore, whether the taxpayer carries on business in Thailand. Another common characteristic is that each treaty provides a mechanism whereby the taxpayer receives credit or other similar relief in one country for the payment of taxes in the other jurisdiction.

Arbitration and Other ADR Techniques

J.31   The Thais have a long history of using alternative dispute resolution methods to avoid litigation of matters in court. Under Thai law, there are two means by which disputes may be arbitrated. First, under the Civil and Commercial Code, the parties to a pending court action may, with the approval of the court, assign one or more particular issues to an arbitrator for resolution. Code at sections 21–222. Second, the parties may decide to avoid the judicial process and seek arbitration of the entire dispute under the auspices of the Arbitration Act B.E. 2530 (1987).

The guidelines established by the Arbitration Act for the resolution of disputes are similar to those found in many developing and developed nations. Under Thai law, any agreement to arbitrate a matter must be in writing. The parties are free to select in their agreement the arbitrator(s) that will preside over the proceeding, and the jurisdiction of the arbitral panel so assembled. Arbitration Act at section 5. The Arbitration Act also provides that each party may, within "a reasonable time" (unless a time is specified in the parties' arbitration agreement), select one arbitrator, who then together appoint a third person as a co-arbitrator. *Ibid.* at section 11. The parties also have complete freedom to select the procedural and substantive law that will govern the arbitration. Among other bodies of law, the parties may elect to apply the arbitration principles of the International Chamber of Commerce, the Thai Chamber of Commerce (also known as the Board of Trade), or the rules established by the Economic and Social Commission for Asia and the Pacific (ESCAP). The rules on arbitration promulgated by the United Nations Committee on International Trade Law (UNCITRAL) have not been adopted by statute in Thailand, and, therefore, are only applicable in the event that the parties specifically agree to the application of such principles.

There are a number of circumstances under which a court may intervene in an arbitration conducted under the Arbitration Act. Under section 10 of the act, for example, a party to an arbitration agreement may bring a motion before a court of competent jurisdiction to dismiss a lawsuit filed in contravention of the agreement to arbitrate. *Ibid.* at section 10. Also, a court may appoint an arbitrator where one or more parties has failed to satisfy its obligation to select an arbitrator. *Ibid.* at section 13. Thai courts are also empowered to provide the crucial decisive vote in the event that the panel of arbitrators reach a stalemate. *Ibid.* at section 16. An arbitrator may submit to the court any procedural or evidentiary issue for determination and resolution. *Ibid.* at section 18. Awards issued by a competent arbitral panel are considered final and binding on all parties, and courts in Thailand are barred from reviewing the award.

Arbitral awards issued in Thailand may be enforced through various means. First, the award may be enforced as a judgment under Thai law. This is a problematic process under the terms of the Arbitration Act, since that statute allows a judge to refuse to enforce the award if the court determines that it was not within the scope of the arbitration clause in the parties' contract, or if the judge otherwise determines that the award is "illegal". Thailand is, however, a signatory to the New York Convention on the Recognition and Enforcement of Foreign Arbitral Awards. Thus, the prevailing party may seek to enforce and execute an arbitration award under that treaty, which provides relatively transparent procedures for the enforcement of awards. Significantly for foreign investors, the Government of Thailand is not a signatory to the Convention for the Settlement of Investment Disputes Between States and Nationals of Other States,[20] pursuant to which a substantial body of law on the resolution of foreign investment disputes has developed.

Intellectual Property Laws

J.32 The protection of intellectual property, particularly intellectual property developed outside of the country, has been a consistent problem for Thailand. For several years, Thailand has been characterized by widespread piracy of property protected by international intellectual property conventions. Persistent avoidance of these obligations eventually led the U.S. government, through its Office of the U.S. Trade Representative, to place Thailand on a "priority watch list" of nations that it considered to be responsible for the most egregious violations of intellectual property rights.[21] Most of these violations occurred in the pharmaceutical, electronics and video areas.[22]

Thailand has recently taken several steps to improve enforcement and protection of intellectual property rights. For example, the Government last year enacted a new copyright law, and in the last half decade has revamped both its patent and trademark legislation. These legislative changes were made in response to pressure from several Western nations, particularly the U.S.[23] Through these recent enactments, Thailand does not pose the same degree of risk to the foreign investor interested in technology transfers that it once did. Moreover, because Thailand is a signatory to the General Agreement on Tariffs and Trade (GATT), as well as the new agreement on the creation of the World Trade Organization (WTO), the recent Agreement on Trade-Related Intellectual Property Rights (TRIPs)[24] will be binding on the Kingdom. This is not to say, however, that technology transfers transactions are now risk-free in Thailand; on the contrary, as with other areas of Thai legislation, the issue that remains to be resolved is the extent to which Thai courts and the government will uphold and enforce this new legislation.

Patent Act B.E. 2521 (1979); Patent Act (No. 2) B.E. 2535 (1992)

J.33 The issuance, protection and enforcement of patents in Thailand are governed by two statutes, the Patent Act B.E. 2521 (1979), and the Patent Act (No. 2) B.E. 2535 (1992). Under these statutes, there are four requirements for patentability. First, the invention must be "novel", which means that the specifications and dimensions of the invention must not have been disclosed within or outside of Thailand prior to application in the Kingdom. A patent pending in a foreign jurisdiction for more than 12 months is considered to have been disclosed and, thus, not protected. Second, the invention must be a discovery of a new or improved product or process. Third, the invention must have an industrial application. Finally, the invention must fall within the category of matters eligible for patent protection. Under the revised statutes, patents may not be issued for scientific or mathematical principles, computer programs, methods of diagnosis or treatments of sicknesses and diseases, and several other classes of inventions which are considered to be contrary to public policy.

A patent application is filed at the Patent Office, which is part of the Patents and Trade Mark Division of the Department of Intellectual Property, Ministry of Commerce. The applicant must be the inventor, and also a Thai national or a citizen of a country that permits reciprocal rights to Thai nationals to submit patent applications. The application itself must contain the title of the invention; a brief statement of the nature and purpose of the invention; a clear and concise claim of patentability; and any other information that the Ministry may require. Patents issued by the Patent Board are valid for 20 years. It should be noted, however, that Thailand is not a signatory to the major international convention on the treatment of patents, the Paris Convention for the Protection of Industrial Property.[25]

The owner of a patent has several rights. Among others, the owner has the exclusive right to own and use the patented invention in Thailand. The patent owner also has the exclusive right to use the phrase "Thai Patent". Patent Act (1992) at section 37. The unauthorized manufacture of a product that is patented, or the unauthorized application of a process that is patented, gives rise to a potential penalty of two years in prison and payment of a fine of up to 400,000 baht, or both. Also, section 86 of the Patents Act (1992) states that the person that sells or offers to sell the product made may be subject to a penalty of up to two years in prison and a fine of 20,000 baht. The new patent legislation fails to provide, however, any mechanism to ensure "pipeline protection" — protection of the invention between the time that the patent is granted and the product is ready for the market. For certain products, such as pharmaceuticals, pipeline protection is critical, and its absence from Thailand's new legislation leaves a significant lacuna.

The patent owner's rights may be transferred pursuant to an enforceable license agreement. To be enforceable, the license agreement must be in writing. Moreover, the agreement may not impose conditions or restrictions on the license arrangement that would have the effect of "damaging" the development of industry, manufacturing, agriculture or commerce. Finally, the license agreement must be registered with the Ministry of Commerce. *Ibid.* at section 41. The new patent legislation also retains the right to obtain a compulsory license. A person may apply for a compulsory license as long as the patented product has not been produced or sold in Thailand, *Ibid.* at section 46(1), or, if the product is sold in Thailand, it is marketed at "an unreasonably high price." *Ibid.* at section 46(2). Thus, the new legislation compels the patent owner to "work" the patent (*i.e.* produce the good), since that is the only means of avoiding the issuance of a compulsory patent.

Thai Trade Mark Act B.E. 2534 (1991)

The new Thai Trade Mark Act became effective on February 13, 1992. The   J.34
act replaced prior legislation that dated to 1931, with subsequent revisions in

Thailand

1961. That legislation was based on the English Trade Mark Act of 1919. The new act incorporates the terms of the International Classification System under the Nice Convention, promulgated by the World Intellectual Property Organization (WIPO), for the classification of goods and services for purposes of registration. In addition, under the new act, unlike prior Thai statutes, protection is offered to trade marks, service marks, certification marks, or collective marks. The act defines a trade mark as a device or signal that is used in connection with goods for the purpose of communicating to the public that a particular company is the owner of the mark, or its agent. A service mark is used to identify the source of the provider of the service. A certification mark is a mark used in order to certify the origin of the goods, or the condition or level of quality of the goods containing the mark. A collective mark is defined as any mark used by a group of entities to identify to the public their relationship or connection.

The statutory pre-requisites to registration are that the mark: (1) be distinctive; (2) not be prohibited under the Act; and (3) not be so similar to another mark as to create confusion among or mislead the public.

The mark itself may be in any of the following forms:

1. The name of a person or company presented in a special manner;
2. any word or words having descriptive characteristics;
3. invented letter(s), numeral(s), or word(s);
4. invented picture(s); and
5. a signature.

Certain items are expressly excluded from receiving trade mark protection, including any depiction of the royal coat of arms or crests; the official flags of Thailand; any photographs of the royal family; or the emblem utilized by the Red Cross.

Protection of a mark under Thai law is made by registering the mark with the Ministry of Commerce. To be valid, the registration must be made by a resident Thai agent. The registration is made on official forms supplied by the Ministry of Commerce, together with a sample of the mark. The application must also specify the type of good or goods with which the applicant hopes to identify the mark.

Whether the mark is accepted by the Ministry depends upon whether the application satisfies the criteria outlined above. If the criteria are not satisfied, the Ministry will reject the application. If, on the other hand, the Ministry finds that the mark satisfies these criteria, then the mark is advertised in the government *Gazette*, and the applicant pays the required publication fees. If no objection is received within 90 days, the mark is registered on the payment of the registration fee. A registered trade mark is valid for 10 years, and can be-renewed for separate 10 year periods.

The registration of a trade mark entitles its owner to its exclusive use within Thailand. Non-use of the trade mark, however, is a sufficient basis for the cancellation of the mark. In this context, the owner may demonstrate through the use of evidence that it has used the mark either in Thailand or outside of the country. If the proponent of cancellation can demonstrate that the mark has not been used within three years of registration, the Ministry may cancel the mark. In addition, any member of the public may bring an action for cancellation of the mark on the basis that it is contrary to public policy or good morals.

Like patents, marks recognized under the Trade Mark Act may be transferred or licensed. The license or conveyancing document must be in writing and must be registered with the Ministry. The application to register the license or other agreement must identify the terms of the arrangement between the licensor and the licensee, and must describe the mark to be licensed.

Both the Thai civil and criminal law provide remedies for infringement of a registered trade or other mark. Under the Trade Mark Act, for example, an imitation of a registered trade mark is considered an infringement of that mark, entitling the owner of the mark to bring criminal charges which could subject the offender to up to two years imprisonment and a fine of up to 200,000 baht, or both. *Ibid.* at section 109. The act also allows the owner of the mark to bring an action for "passing-off" against any person who characterizes or describes its own goods as manufactured or distributed by the trade mark owner. *Ibid.* at section 46.

Copyright Act B.E. 2536 (1994)

Copyrights have two sources of protection in Thailand. First, Thailand is a   J.35
signatory to the Berne Convention for the Protection of Literary and Artistic Works (the Berne Convention).[26] As a result, a copyright belonging to a person who is a national of a signatory state to the convention receives as much protection as a Thai copyright protected under Thai law. Second, the Copyright Act of 1994 provides protection for copyrights of works created in Thailand. The works eligible for protection under Thai law include:

1. literary works;
2. dramatic works;
3. artistic works;
4. musical works;
5. audio-visual works;
6. cinematographic works, and
7. television and broadcasting works.

Included in the definition of "literary works" are computer programs, which are defined as instructions (or a set of instructions) used in conjunction with a computer in order to cause the computer to perform any function. No distinction is made regarding the type of program. Additionally, the act provides for the protection of "performer's rights". This term includes the version, edition or performance of any "actor, musician, singer or dancer, and a person who displays postures, sings, speaks, dubs or performs follow-ing a script or in any other manner". The protected performance must take place in Thailand or in a nation that is a signatory to the Berne Convention. The prior Thai legislation contained no provisions for the protection of such rights.

There is no registration requirement for the protection of a copyright under Thai law. Rather, in order to receive protection, the work must have received its first publication in Thailand or in a nation that is a signatory to the Berne Convention. Alternatively, the work must have been published in Thailand or in a signatory to the Berne Convention within 30 days from the date of first publication of the work outside of these jurisdictions. The Act states that any copying or modifying of the protected work, or publication or use of the copyrighted material in an advertisement without prior permis-sion, are infringements of the act. The Act excepts from the definition of infringement the use of the copyrighted work in research or academic study, public comment or criticism, or reporting through the mass media. However, if an infringement is shown to have occurred, the offender is subject to both civil and criminal penalties.

A copyright may be transferred or assigned under Thai law. An assign-ment of the copyright must be in writing. A license agreement, on the other hand, may be in writing or done orally. Even though the owner of the copyright may assign his rights in the work, the Copyright Act permits the owner to prohibit the assignee from distorting or modifying the work in any manner that would cause injury to the reputation of the author. section 15.

Trade Secrets

J.36   In broad terms, the term "trade secret" describes proprietary information which gives its owner an advantage or the opportunity to gain an advantage over competitors. A trade secret may take the form of a formula, a pattern, or a compilation of information, such as a list of customers. Unlike other nations in Southeast Asia, particularly Malaysia, which has a substantial case law on the topic of trade secrets, Thai law does not recognize the existence of a right to confidentiality in intellectual property. As a result, the owner of a trade secret may obtain protection for such property only through a contrac-tual agreement. However, section 324 of the Penal Code of Thailand pro-vides that:

> "whoever, by reason of his functions, profession, or calling or trust, having known or acquired a secret concerning industry, discovery or scientific invention, discloses or makes use of such secret for the benefit of himself or any other person, shall be punished with imprisonment not exceeding six months or a fine not exceeding one thousand baht, or both."

The threat of criminal sanctions notwithstanding, a non-Thai company employing Thais should endeavor to enter into agreements with those employees to protect any confidential proprietary information that the company may seek to protect. Moreover, as a natural consequence of the absence of any positive or decisional law on trade secrets, the right to transfer or license a trade secret is subject to the terms of the contract governing the relationship between employer and employee.

The present state of Thai law with respect to trade secrets may, however, be subject to modification in light of the recent passage of the TRIPs legislation. Under the TRIPs agreement, to which Thailand is a signatory, trade secrets receive protection as long as the information:

1. is secret in the sense that it is not, as a body or in the precise configuration and assembly of its components, generally not known among or readily accessible to persons within the circles that normally deal with the kind of information in question;
2. has commercial value because it is secret; and
3. has been subject to reasonable steps under the circumstances, by the person lawfully in control of the information, to keep it secret.[27]

Civil and Commercial Code

Section 420 of the Civil and Commercial Code allows a person to claim   J.37
compensation (damages) from any person who commits a "wrongful act". The term "wrongful act" is defined to include any contravention of "the rights of another person". As discussed above, Thai law recognizes the existence of property rights in certain forms of intellectual property. Thus, the unauthorized use of a patent, trade mark or copyright could be considered a violation of section 420. The existence of a claim for violation of a trade secret would, however, depend on the terms contained in the contract creating the right(s).

III. General Considerations in Negotiating Business Transactions in Thailand

The Possible Structures of Commercial Transactions in Thailand

The structure that a commercial transaction takes depends, in the main, on   J.38
the goals of the foreign investor and his or her Thai counterpart. If the foreign person seeks merely to buy goods from or sell goods to a Thai organization, then awareness of the formal restrictions imposed by Thai law would be critical. In this regard, the foreign entity would want to review the

Code for the scope of protection available to persons entering into contracts that will be governed by Thai law. It would also be important to identify the restrictions, if any, on the export of goods to be manufactured or foreign currency derived from the goods manufactured in Thailand. It would also be important to investigate the relevant Thai laws on the means of protecting any technology that the foreign investor will transfer in order to manufacture the goods.

Consideration of a more substantial investment in Thailand gives rise to additional sources of concern. For example, subject to the restrictions contained in the Alien Business Law, the foreign investor may desire some sort of long-term relationship to secure the production of goods for distribution by a Thai firm. In this event, the foreign investor, and its Thai partner, must consider the appropriate form that the production arrangement should take. It might be most advantageous to enter into a joint venture with the Thai partner for the production of the goods. If a joint venture is advisable, depending on the circumstances, then it may also be worthwhile submitting a request to the BOI for preferential treatment in the form of concessions on or exemptions from the payment of taxes. The benefits offered by the BOI, in turn, will likely depend on the proportion of the enterprise's production that will be exported, and the number of Thais that will be employed. It may also be advisable for the foreign investor to establish a wholly-owned subsidiary. This will avoid the problem of seeking out and obtaining a qualified Thai partner, and will also obviate the need to conduct a review of the credit history, tax liabilities, or contingent obligations of an existing Thai firm that the foreign investor could purchase as a vehicle to enter the Thai market. In sum, the form that the commercial relationship will take depends on the goals of the foreign investor, and the position and status of the Thai partner or co-investor. Moreover, as with most other issues involving the interpretation of Thai law, the emphasis on the use of the Thai language in negotiations and documentation will compel the foreign enterprise to retain a Thai attorney.

The Legal Profession in Thailand

J.39   The legal profession in Thailand is regulated by the Board of the Attorney Council pursuant to the terms of the Lawyers Act of 1985. The Attorney Council is made up of a representative of the Ministry of Justice, a representative of the Thai Bar Association, the President of the Thai Attorney Council and 23 members elected by attorneys throughout Thailand. Admission to practice law in Thailand is restricted to Thai nationals; the Alien Business Law expressly excludes from the list of professions in which foreign nationals may work "giving service in legal working or law suit". Licenses to practice law are issued by the Thai Attorney Council, which has taken the place of the Thai Bar Association. In order to practice, the applicant for a license must possess a law degree from a recognized university, and must successfully complete a one-year training program administered by the Thai Attorney Council. There is no requirement that the applicant work as a clerk for a designated period. Moreover, Thailand has a "fused" bar: there is no distinction in Thailand between barristers and solicitors. Foreign lawyers have no right to appear in an action filed in a Thai court. The fact that the official language of all Thai legal proceedings is Thai also severely limits the opportunities that a foreign lawyer has to advise a client on Thai law, or appear in a Thai court. The requirement that all legal proceedings and documentation be in Thai also means that retaining a Thai attorney is an indispensable part of doing business in Thailand.

Cultural Factors and Business Negotiations

As with business dealings in other nations, foreign businessmen face a variety of non-legal concerns in attempting to enter the Thai marketplace. Perhaps the most important concern of any foreign businessman in Thailand is the ability to communicate. In and around the capital, Bangkok, a fair number of persons can be found who speak English. Employees of government agencies that deal frequently with foreign businessmen, such as the Board of Investment's One Stop Service Center, typically speak English. It is also not difficult to find attorneys in Bangkok who speak English. Outside of Bangkok, however, it may be much more difficult to communicate with Thais (unless the businessman speaks Thai). J.40

In their business dealings, Thais favor the development of long-term relationships, based on mutual trust and close personal relationships.[28] The emphasis on these values may explain the success of the Japanese as foreign investors in Thailand, since the Japanese also tend to prefer long-term perspectives on their investments. The key to developing trust in establishing a business relationship is to ensure that local (Thai) needs are satisfied, even if the price that the foreign manufacturer or distributor asks is slightly above the price that another supplier has set.[29] In building a relationship based on trust, necessary emphasis must be placed on meeting the initial supply and delivery dates.[30] In the end, the development of a personal relationship with a Thai purchaser may increase the price of the good as much as ten percent above the market price.

The emphasis on the development of personal relationships in Thailand is also seen in the attitude toward employees. Thai nationals are rarely, if ever, fired from their jobs.[31] In part, this is due to the prevailing attitude among Thais that the company is a large family. The management is also expected to demonstrate, as part of its familial duty, its concern with the home life of its employees.[32] This expectation can create problems for the foreign enterprise operating in Thailand, since in most Western nations underperforming employees can be terminated by the employer (after observing various forms of administrative requirements).

Foreign businessmen should also not lose sight of another important and prevalent problem in Thailand, corruption.[33] Local business dealings, in particular, are characterized by corruption, typically requiring the foreign company seeking a license, for example, to bribe a local official or policemen. The Bangkok police force has been described as "notoriously corrupt".[34] The political scene is also rife with corruption; in the last general election, the party that won, the Chart Thai (Thai Nation) party, distributed 50 baht bank notes in the countryside to assure the rural vote.[35] In the capital, sitting members of parliament offered to defect from their party for ten million baht.[36] Moreover, the government of the U.S. recently denied requests for visas made by two members of the Chart Thai party, who the U.S. believes are involved in drug trafficking.[37] Nor was the previous ruling party, the Democrat Party, which possessed a reputation as being relatively clean, above corruption. Shortly before the general election, the Democrat Party was rocked by allegations of corruption surrounding ten persons who were given deeds by the party as part of the land reform program that the party had initiated. After review by local authorities, it was discovered that the property that the ten had been given was located in Phuket, a well known holiday resort, and that the land was intended for development. The Thai military, despite their self-professed image as the savior of Thai politics, is also rumored to have made millions from weapons sales to the Khmers Rouges fighting in Western Cambodia, which Cambodian forces paid for with licenses issued to companies controlled by members of the Thai military to harvest Cambodia's teak forests.

For the foreign businessman, the extent of corruption in Thailand poses several difficult questions. First, the bribe or other incentive may be the only means to secure the necessary approval to complete the project for which the investment in Thailand has been made. The bribe may mean the difference between obtaining the contract that the foreign businessman has been sent to secure, or the protection from competitors that the foreign enterprise needs in the first few months that it operates in Thailand. In this regard, corruption can be a very real problem. Widespread corruption also poses the threat that, if caught, the foreign enterprise will be subject to criminal prosecution in its home jurisdiction. This is true for U.S. firms, for instance, which are barred from undertaking criminal activity (such as bribing officials of a foreign government) pursuant to the Foreign Corrupt Practices Act. Finally, there is no security in acceding to the demands of corrupt government officials; there is nothing to prevent such officials from playing off the foreign business person against the local competitor by asking for the highest price for the license that each company is willing to pay.

Notes

1. Patrice Renard et al., *Sales and Distribution Guide to Thailand* 19 (1993).
2. Among other examples, Thailand has been suggested as a model for the development of the economy of Vietnam. See Camelia Ngo, "Foreign Investment Promotion: Thailand as a Model for Economic Development in Vietnam", *16 Hastings Int'l & Comp. L. Rev.* 67 (1992).
3. World Bank, *Trends in Developing Economies 1994* 481 (1995).
4. For recent appraisals of the Thai economy, see *Thailand's Industrialization and its Consequences* (Medhi Krongkaew ed. 1995); Robert J. Muscat, *The Fifth Tiger: A Study of Thai Development Policy (1994)*; *The Thai Economy in Transition* (Peter G. Warr ed. 1993).
5. See generally, David M. Engel, *Law and Kingship in Thailand During the Reign of King Chulalongkorn* (1975).
6. The Conference Board, *The Southeast Asian Boom* 6 (1994).
7. Henrik Hansen, "Malaysia Proposes Asian Trading Blocs", *East Asian Exec. Rep.*, January 5, 1991, at 4.
8. Prapone Sataman & Paichitr Bunyapan, *Annotation on the Civil and Commercial Code on Sale* 47–69 (1st ed. 1983).
9. *Ibid*. at 40.
10. *Ibid*.
11. *Commercial, Business and Trade Laws* section A.2, at 18 (Montri Hongskrailers ed. 1984).
12. International Finance Company, *Emerging Stock Markets Factbook* 22 (1995).
13. *Ibid*. at 212–13.
14. *Ibid*. at 213.
15. *Ibid*.
16. Paul Sithi-Amnual, *Finance and Banking in Thailand: A Study of the Commercial System, 1888–1963*, 23–24 (1964).
17. In addition to the commercial banking sector, numerous "credit foncier" operations exist in Thailand. These institutions lend money primarily to lower income consumers, at rates slightly higher than the prevailing market rates. The credit foncier entities are regulated under the terms of the Act on the Undertaking of Finance Business, Securities Business, and Credit Foncier Business, promulgated in 1979.
18. Baker & McKenzie, "Thailand", of *Doing Business in Asia* Paras. 55-002, at 81,102 (CCH 1995).
19. Baker & McKenzie, *Thailand: A Legal Brief* 40 (1990).
20. Done at Washington, D.C., Mar. 18, 1965, 17 U.S.T. 1270, T.I.A.S. No. 6090, 575 U.N.T.S. 159 [entered into force October 14, 1966]). The treaty created the International Centre for the Settlement of Investment Disputes (ICSID).
21. U.S. General Accounting Office, *U.S. Trade Representative: Investigations of Foreign Country Practices* 10 (1994).
22. *Ibid*. at 11. For a discussion of the conflict between American pharmaceutical manufacturers and the Thai government, see Stefan Kirchanski, Note, "Protection of U.S. Patents Rights in Developing Countries: U.S. Efforts to Enforce Pharmaceutical Patents in Thailand", 16 *Loy. L.A. Int'l & Comp. L.J.* 569 (1994); Thomas N. O'Neill, III, Note, "Intellectual Property Protection in Thailand: Asia's Young Tiger and America's 'Growing' Concern", 11 *U. Pa. J. Int'l Bus. L.* 603 (1989).

Thailand

23 Julie S. Park, Note, "Pharmaceutical Patents in the Global Arena: Thailand's Struggle Between Progress and Protectionism", 13 *B.C. Third World L.J.* 121, 123–24 (1993).

24 "Final Act Embodying the Results of the Uruguay Round of Multilateral Trade Negotiations", done at Marrakech, Morocco, April 15, 1994 [hereinafter "TRIPs Agreement"], reprinted in *The Results of the Uruguay Round of Multilateral Trade Negotiations — The Legal Texts 2–3* (1994).

25 Paris Convention on the Protection of Industrial Property, March 20, 1883, as revised, 21 U.S.T. 1583, T.I.A.S. No. 6923, 823 U.N.T.S. 305.

26 Berne Convention for the Protection of Literary and Artistic Works, September 9, 1886, revised at Paris, July 24, 1971, J.O.F. 28 Aug. 74, 1974 R.T.A.F. 51.

27 TRIPs Agreement, above n.24 at Art. 39(2).

28 Renard, above n.1, at 1.

29 *Ibid.*

30 *Ibid.* at 2.

31 *Ibid.*

32 *Ibid.*

33 In a survey of local managers of foreign businesses operating in Asia, who were asked to rate the level of corruption in the nations in which they were based, Thailand finished behind China, India, Indonesia, and the Philippines. "Hard Graft in Asia", *Economist*, May 27, 1995, at 61.

34 Gregory J. Koebel, Note, "Protection of Intellectual Property Rights in Singapore and Thailand: A Comparative Analysis", 13 *Brook. J. Int'l L.* 309, 329–30 (1987).

35 "Hucksters on the hustings", *Economist*, June 24, 1995, at 36. The winner in Thailand's last general election, the current premier, Banharn Silpa-archa, is referred to as "Mr. ATM" from his rumored exploits in past elections. "Jam Today", *Economist*, August 26, 1995, at 30.

36 "Jam Today", above note 35.

37 "Thailand's Quick Change", *Economist*, July 8, 1995, at 29; "Thailand's New Premier Could Upset U.S. Ties", *N.Y. Times*, July 14, 1995, at A3 (discussing one of the persons allegedly involved in the drug trade).

VIETNAM

Per Bergling

I. Summary of Business and Political Conditions

Basic Demographic, Political and Economic Information

Vietnam has a population of approximately 73.1 million people,[1] growing at
rate of about 2.1 per cent per year. There are 32.7 million people in the labor
force, with 65 per cent engaged in agriculture; 35 per cent in industry and the
service sectors;[2] and 25 per cent unemployed.[3] About eight out of every 10
people live in rural areas,[4] and about 80 per cent of the population is under
the age of 40.[5] 88 per cent of the people are literate.[6] Vietnam has a GNP per
capita of US$220[7] and the average worker makes about US$30.00 in wages
per month.[8]

K.01

As a result of economic reforms initiated in 1987, known as *doi moi*
(renovation), Vietnam has increasingly modified its economy from a centralized planned economy to a market oriented economy based on supply
and demand, and experiencing relatively high growth rates. In 1992, Vietnam
had a real growth rate of GDP of 8.3 per cent.[9] The annual growth rate
between 1986 and 1990 was 3.9 per cent,[10] in 1990 it was 5.1 per cent; 1991 it
was 6 per cent and in 1992 it was 8.3 per cent.[11] The projected annual GDP
growth rates through to 1998 average about 8.4 per cent.[12]

Vietnam's overall trade with the world is still relatively small but growing
rapidly. In 1990, for example, the value of its exports was US$1.57 billion.[13]
From 1988 through to 1993, however, exports increased at an average rate of
about 30 per cent per year.[14] Today, Vietnam is the world's third largest
exporter of rice (behind Thailand and the U.S.), growing from zero in 1988
to two million tons (earning $420 million) in 1992.[15] Its principal exports
include, crude oil, rice, marine products, coffee, coal, rubber, handicrafts and

wood products. Vietnam's chief markets for its exports are Japan (42 per cent) and Hong Kong (11.4 per cent); Philippines (8 per cent); and Thailand (6.7 per cent).[16] The value of Vietnam's imports was US$1.84 billion in 1990.[17] Vietnam's chief imports are fuel, capital equipment, vehicles, fertilizers and consumer goods.[18] Vietnam's main import suppliers in 1990 were: Japan (23.2 per cent); the Federal Republic of Germany (16 per cent); Hong Kong (14.8 per cent); and France (10 per cent).[19] As of May 1993, Vietnam reported registered investment capital of $6 billion since 1988, with the following leading investors (in US dollars): Taiwan ($1.1 billion), Hong Kong ($854 million), Australia ($680 million), France ($548 million), and Japan ($453 million).[20]

Vietnam is one of the latest of the former socialist economies to open up to foreign trade and investment, but is now experiencing rapid economic growth and has managed to attract substantial investments from abroad.

A consequence of the new economic policy is that the patchwork of socialist-inspired laws and sub-laws which used to govern economic activities must be replaced with laws and institutions more akin to market principles. Vietnam has made great efforts in this respect, but all cannot be changed overnight and many features of the old order still prevail. The hierarchy between various legal documents is also unclear, and it is not uncommon that administrative provisions are more significant than laws.

A note on terminology is therefore justified. Laws are passed by the National Assembly and are the highest form of legal instruments. Ordinances are passed by the Standing Committee of the National Assembly. Decrees are issued by the Government and provide detailed instructions for the implementation of laws and ordinances. The decrees are often supplemented by even more detailed regulations. Circulars are issued by the line ministries and other state agencies and lay down how a particular law, ordinance or decree will be administrated. There are also guidelines issued by the Prime Minister which indicate the Governments policy in various matters.

A new Civil Code has recently been adopted by the National Assembly and awaits promulgation by the Government. It will be the first comprehensive codification of Vietnamese civil law and contains over 800 detailed articles on issues of ownership, civil obligations, contracts, inheritance, intellectual property, etc. No official translation into the English language is available yet, and the Code is therefore not commented upon in this work.

A distinction is made in the following between general legislation and legislation aiming specifically at foreign investors. Rules on auditing, accounting, taxation, labour, etc. for enterprises operating under the foreign investment legislation are discussed in the section Foreign Investment Law.

II. Laws and Institutions Affecting Business and Commercial Activities

Property Ownership

Laws that provide a clear basis for ownership and transfer of property are   K.02
essential to any market economy. The recent increase in the number of
registered enterprises, the more frequent use of bank accounts, and the great
interest in real estate also indicate that there is an increasing confidence in the
protection of private property in Vietnam.

A legal basis for ownership rights is given in the new 1992 Constitution
which recognizes and protects state, collective and private ownership.[21]
The Constitution also offers legal protection of connected rights, including
inheritance and transfer.[22] Nationalization of private property is prohibited,
while necessary expropriation must be compensated.[23] Land, however, is
still under exclusive ownership of the state and cannot be privately
owned.

The Law on Private Enterprises, the Law on Companies, the Law on
Foreign Investment and the Law on Promotion of Domestic Investment also
contain provisions which protect interests in private ventures.[24]

Rights to Land

Allocation and Protection

State ownership of land is still a cornerstone of the official ideology and the   K.03
1992 Constitution maintains that all land is owned by the People.[25] Domestic
private companies and individuals who wish to use land commercially must
therefore rely on various forms of lesser interests in land, of which the
strongest is a "use right", and pay tax as a form of rent.[26] The allocation of
land is supposed to be based on non-price considerations, but is increasingly
often viewed as a source of revenue. This has lead to local governments
experimenting with different methods of charging for land, such as "infrastructure charges", often amounting to 10 to 15 per cent of the cost of the
proposed project.

The Constitution and the Land Law are not very detailed. The rights of
the land user, the length of tenure and other crucial matters are instead
regulated in various sub-laws or decided on a case-by-case basis and stipulated in the Land Tenure Certificate which is issued to all new land holders.[27]
The length of tenure generally depends on the proposed use of the land. The
largest right is reserved for residential land, which is often allotted for an
unspecified period and can only be recovered upon fairly narrow, specified

conditions. Land for commercial use is often allotted for a shorter term, often between 20 and 50 years for agricultural land and 20 years for industrial use, with no automatic right of renewal.

The *use right* gives the land holder a relatively strong right to the land under their duration. The Constitution states that "land is allocated by the State to organizations and individuals for stable long-term use. . . . They are also entitled by law to transfer the (unexpired) right to use the land allocated by the state."[28] The new 1993 Land Law confirms that "The State shall allocate to economic organizations . . . for use on a stable and long term basis. The State may also allocate to organizations . . . to rent land . . ." and that ". . . households and individuals have the right to exchange, transfer, rent, inherit, or mortgage the land use right".[29]

Expropriation and other forms of reclamation of land are surrounded by a number of constitutional and legal safeguards, but are nevertheless possible in certain situations, for example when national security or strong public interest call for it.[30] The size of the compensation shall be based on current market prices and is determined by the State.[31] Land may also be reclaimed if individual provisions in the land use certificate are violated, if the user has failed to meet the general legal requirements for land use, and under a number of other circumstances as stipulated in the Land Law.[32] The general legal requirements for land use refer to obligations from the side of the state to pay taxes and fees, furnish protection, rational exploitation and economic utilization of land, etc.[33] This duty is most strictly observed in respect of commercial land, which only can be used for its allotted purpose, for example rice production or industrial development.

Transfer and Sublease

K.04   Use rights to land may be transferred to new holders, but only for the purpose for which the land was originally allocated.[34] Certain other restrictions also apply, especially regarding agricultural land.[35] All transfer also require the permission of the competent state authority, usually the People's Committee.[36] It is only the rights that follow from the land use certificate which can be transferred. A transfer can therefore never give the new holder a longer term of tenure or a better right to the land than the original holder had. It is further notable that the parties may not freely determine the price, but that the State stipulates limits for various categories of land within which the price must fall.[37]

Holders of cultivated land who have difficulties effectively utilizing the land, for example because of lack of manpower or a change of profession, may also sublease the land for limited periods of time, usually up to three years.[38] The original holder of the land remains responsible for the land and must ensure that all legal obligations are fulfilled.

Mortgage

Households and individuals may (since the enactment of the 1992 Constitu-   K.05
tion and the 1993 Land Law) mortgage use rights to land.[39] Holders of farm
or forest land may pledge the Land Tenure Certificate as collateral for loans
from the branches of the State Bank and certain other approved credit organizations, while users of residential land may pledge their Certificate with
Vietnamese economic organizations and individuals.[40] It seems, however,
that the right to mortgage land use rights only applies to loans for production
and land improvement, and thus not to loans for the acquisition of additional
use rights.

Dispute Resolution

Disputes over smaller plots of residential or agricultural land have tradition-   K.06
ally been settled through various forms of mediation and conciliation, often
with a focus on achieving a degree of social justice rather than precisely
adjudicating the claims. To the extent disputes were formalized, they were
usually adjudicated by administrative or social bodies such as the People's
Committees or the Association of Farmers. The new Land Law maintains
that conciliation under supervision of social organizations is the favored
form of dispute resolution, but also stipulates that parties with a Land Tenure
Certificate may bring the dispute before the People's Courts if they fail to
reach an agreement. Cases where the users do not have a Certificate, however, still appear to be bound to be resolved administratively by the People's
Committee.[41]

Contract Law

The contract law until recently reflected the principles of a centrally planned   K.07
economy in which contracts served as instruments for the fulfilment of the
state plan rather than as a tool for undertaking voluntary transactions. The
rapid economic development following on the *Doi Moi*, however, made it
clear that mechanisms for contracting which are more akin to market principles had to be created. Vietnam therefore enacted an Ordinance on Economic Contracts in 1989 and an Ordinance on Civil Contracts in 1991.
A Civil Code has also recently been adopted by the National Assembly.
It will be promulgated by the Government in 1996 and will then provide
the first comprehensive set of rules for matters related to contracts in
Vietnam.

Civil Contracts

Vietnam still maintains separate rules depending on the legal status of the   K.08
parties to a contract and the nature of the agreement. Civil contracts are

governed under the 1991 Ordinance on Civil Contracts and are defined as agreements with non-profit purposes concluded between individuals or legal entities without business registration as follows: "[o]n the confirmation, changing or termination of rights and obligations of the parties in relation to: the sale and purchase, renting, borrowing, temporary use and donation of properties; the carrying out of work, services or other agreements under which one or more of the parties aims to satisfy everyday needs and consumption."[42] Civil contracts may also encompass non-profit contracts between a Vietnamese party and one or more party (individual or organization) of foreign nationality, to the extent that Vietnam's international agreements do not stipulate otherwise. The Ordinance provides for a set of general contractual principles, for example rules on offer and acceptance, effectiveness, and remedies for breach.

Economic Contracts

K.09   Most relevant in a business context are economic contracts. The economic contract regime still contains some elements associated with the centrally planned economy, but these provisions are commonly considered obsolete. Economic contracts are governed under the Ordinance on Economic Contracts (1989), the Decree on Economic Contracts (1990) and the Ordinance on Economic Arbitration (1990) and are defined as: "an agreement in writing or an exchange of documents between contracting parties which agreement or documents relate to production, exchange of goods, provision of services, research and application of scientific and technical know-how; or other business agreements which clearly set out the rights and responsibilities of each party, the performance of which rights and responsibilities are required for the objectives of the party to be achieved."[43]

Economic Contracts may only be concluded between registered legal entities or individuals with business registration.[44] A word-by-word interpretation of the Ordinance could thus exclude businessmen without registration (which make up for a substantial part of the Vietnamese economy) from the protection of the Ordinance. However, other provisions in the Ordinance seem to allow contracts between registered legal entities and owners of household businesses, private farmers, fishermen, scientists, technicians and artists.[45] An economic contract which is concluded in contravention to these rules is deemed void and the parties can, at least theoretically, be subject to prosecution.[46]

Economic contracts are also automatically rescinded where they exceed the authorized business objective for the company.[47] There are, however, no reliable means to verify whether a transaction falls within the authorized objective since business licences are not public documents. Third parties who want to ensure that the transaction falls within the business objective must therefore insist on the presentation of a copy of the license before concluding the contract. Without the protection of the license, the individual who entered into the contract on behalf of the company is personally liable and may even be subject to criminal action.

The Ordinance on Economic Contracts provides for a set of general contractual principles such as rules on offer and acceptance, effectiveness, and remedies for breach. The factual constraints to the freedom to determine the essential terms of the agreement are relatively few. The parties may for example stipulate the normal elements of quantity, quality, price, terms of delivery, guarantees and duration.[48] Even matters such as contractual fairness, abuse of market dominance and retail price maintenance may be regulated freely, but changes can here be expected when the Civil Code and new laws on competition and consumer protection are enacted.

Disputes arising from economic contracts are usually resolved through negotiation and conciliation, but may also be referred to the recently established Economic Courts.[49] The courts, however, have little experience of contractual disputes and the means for enforcement are weak. The losing party may have to pay compensatory damages for any property loss resulting from the breach, liquidated damages ranging from 2 per cent to 12 per cent of the value of the contract, and costs for assessment and adjudication caused by the breach.[50]

The absence of experience and commentaries often leads the courts to interpret contracts word by word in order to ensure at least a degree of uniformity and predictability. This means that the provisions in the contracts, at least theoretically, are enforceable according to the letter as long as the formal requirements are fulfilled.

Companies Law

The 1990 Law on Private Enterprises and the 1990 Law on Companies are both inspired by the economic renovation and aim to implement a "multi-sector commodity economy" and encourage investment and business. They provide a similar protection for businesses operating under them: a recognition of their long-term existence and development; equality with other enterprises before the law; lawful generation of profits; freedom to carry out business and make decisions independently, within the scope of the law; and protection of the rights of the owners, *i.e.* to own the means of production and inherit capital and assets.[51] The laws also provide special incentives in order to promote investment in certain areas. Favorable terms for land use, priority in borrowing capital, reduction or exemption of duties, etc., can for example be offered for production of daily necessities, export and import-substitution, and construction of infrastructure.

Four main forms of business are recognized under Vietnamese law:

1. **Private enterprises** are similar to sole proprietorships, and the owner is liable for the activities of the business with all his assets.[52]

K.10

2. **Companies** are enterprises where the members contribute capital and share proportionately the profits and losses, to the extent of their capital contribution.[53] Companies can be in the form of:

3. **Limited liability companies** which do not issue shares. Transfer of ownership to non-members requires approval from members representing at least 75 per cent of the company's charter capital,[54] or

4. **Share holding companies** which issue equal and freely transferable shares. The shares must be distributed among at least seven shareholders.[55]

Legal partnerships are not recognized as legal entities. Note that none of these forms currently permits foreign ownership, which only is permitted under the foreign investment legislation.

Private businesses must possess a decision on establishment (or license) and a business registration.[56] The decision on establishment, which essentially is a permit to lawfully carry out a certain kind of business, is lodged with and granted by the provincial People's Committee.[57] An application should be accompanied by names, addresses and other personal data of the applicants and other founding members, a statement of the objectives and areas of business of the company, chartered capital and the methods for contributing it, an assessment of the environmental impact, a feasibility plan, and medical certification and educational background of the founders. All submitted documents must be certified by a designated authority. There are no detailed provisions for the assessment and approval of applications, but outright rejection is uncommon. The assessment departments may, however, delay or propose modifications to applications which do not correspond to centrally formulated investment policies or local preferences. Excessive charges and fees for infrastructure development, etc., can be imposed if the applicant is unresponsive.

Once the People's Committee has approved an application and granted a license, registration of the company or enterprise must follow in order to give it the status of legal entity and enable it to commence operations.[58] This registration is no longer a mechanical procedure. The authorities are increasingly often re-examining the merits of the application and especially companies within low priority areas may encounter difficulties.

Businesses within certain areas of national interest, among them manufacturing and distribution of explosives, poison and toxic chemicals; mining of precious minerals; production and supply of electricity and water; broadcasting, publication, and telecommunication; international transportation; and international tourism, also require approval from the Government.[59]

Auditing

K.11 Auditing is regulated in Decree No. 07/CP on the Regulating of Independent Auditing in the National Economy and in Circular No. 22/TC-CDKT. The

Circular, which essentially contains provisions for the implementation of the above mentioned Decree, covers, among other things, the functions of independent auditors including inspection and certification of accounting documents and reports of enterprises, specifications for the use of auditors for enterprises in various economic sectors, requirements for registration as professional auditor and rules for the licensing and operation of foreign auditing firms. It also stipulates that auditing services must be carried out in accordance with existing auditing methods and standards approved in Vietnam and international auditing standards recognized by Vietnam. All final auditing reports must address the truthfulness and appropriateness of the data stated in the accounting report, the accounting operation of the establishment and its conformity with accounting regulations, and contain proposals and recommendations of the auditor.

Bankruptcy

Bankruptcy and liquidation matters are mainly regulated in the 1993 Law on Business Bankruptcy. The Law, which is fairly comprehensive, contains concepts commonly found in "western" jurisdictions. It is, however, rather skeletal and more detailed provisions for its implementation are therefore provided for in various sub-laws and instructions. **K.12**

The Law on Business Bankruptcy applies to all forms of businesses which are established and operated under Vietnamese law, including joint-ventures operating under the Foreign Investment Law.[60] Personal bankruptcies appear to fall outside the scope of the law, but article 51 states that the law is applicable in "bankruptcy proceedings involving foreign individuals and organisations", which indicates that foreigners, by the mere fact of being involved in credit arrangements, etc., may risk being dragged into a bankruptcy proceeding.

Bankruptcies are heard and declared by the recently established Provincial Economic Courts organized within the People's Courts.[61] A bankruptcy proceeding can be instituted by a voluntary petition filed by the bankrupt enterprise itself, or by an involuntary petition which is a request for forced bankruptcy submitted by unsecured or undersecured creditors or labour representatives.[62] The filing of a petition does not automatically mean that the matter will be subject for adjudication. The Court will first determine whether the petition is justified and valid for adjudication or should be summarily dismissed.[63]

The law renders illegal all possible fraudulent conveyances and prohibits certain transfers, among them the taking of mortgages and payment of debts after a petition for bankruptcy has been accepted by the court. The personal liability of insiders, for example company directors, in connection with these types of transfers is not explicitly regulated, but the law states that the directors and the members of the board continue to be responsible for the result of the business.[64] The law also stipulates a "halting" of financial obligations, for example to pay interest on debts, when a court has received a petition and decided to proceed with it.

Bankrupt enterprises may be allowed to continue their operations under the supervision of the Court and the Assets Management Committee while the petition for bankruptcy is pending. The treatment of debts which have arisen from continued operations after the petition has been filed and accepted is only summarily regulated. It is stated that: "During a bankruptcy proceeding, new debts which result from the operation of the business and the salary of workers shall be settled under the supervision of the judge."[65]

Bankruptcy proceedings are carried out by the Economic Courts. They are assisted by a Committee of Creditors (or "Meeting of Creditors") and an Assets Management Committee (or "Trustee Committee") formed for the specific bankruptcy. The Committee of Creditors shall review reorganization plans and propose how the remaining assets should be distributed.[66] The Assets Management Committee shall compile a list of the assets, prepare a list of creditors and perform other asset management functions.[67] The list of creditors shall be posted for 10 days, and creditors who have grievances may then appeal to the Assets Management Committee. It may, however, be possible to appeal even after the 10 days have expired.

K.13   The actual proceeding is divided into two phases, the adjudication phase and the assets distribution phase. The adjudication phase begins when the Economic Court has accepted to try a petition for bankruptcy and initiates the proceedings. The court may then either approve a reorganization plan which aims at saving the business from bankruptcy by restructuring debts through contractual agreements and compromises, or give a "declaration of bankruptcy" which formally makes the business bankrupt and adjudicates the assets and liabilities.[68]

The assets distribution phase starts after a declaration of bankruptcy has been given. The case is turned over to the Judgement Enforcement Office (an executive agency organized under the Ministry of Justice). It appoints an Enforcement Officer who is responsible for the implementation and forms a Property Realization Committee which shall recover the enterprises assets, carry out sale or auction of assets, manage the enterprise's bank accounts, etc.[69] It may also petition the Court to issue orders to recover assets that were illegally transferred up to six months before the petition was filed.[70] The registration of the bankrupt enterprise is cancelled when this work is completed.[71]

The Law distinguishes between three classes of creditors, secured, partly secured and unsecured, depending on whether the payment of the debt is "guaranteed" by the assets of the enterprise.[72] It also lays down a priority system between the creditors. Expenses and fees which have arisen after the petition for bankruptcy have the highest priority. Salaries to employees, followed by tax liabilities, come next. Fourth come creditors' claims (as listed with the creditor and presumably covering both secured and unsecured debts). Equity holders have the lowest priority and can expect payment only if all other classes have been satisfied.[73] The treatment of debts within the same class is not regulated in the law. The protection of collateral for the benefit of secured and post-petition creditors is only briefly touched upon. The law states that: "the judge shall order that the pledged or mortgaged property of the business be protected and shall organise the valuation of such property".[74]

The Law on Bankruptcy provides a definition of what constitutes an asset.[75] The owner's private property may also be included if the bankruptcy concerns a "private enterprise", regardless of eventual arrangements to create limited liability at the moment of inception of the enterprise.

Creditors must file a claim in court in order to be considered in the distribution of the assets. They also have the burden of proving their claims with adequate documentation.[76] The claim must be filed within 60 days from the date the court accepts the petition for adjudication. Failure to file a claim within the time limit seems to result in a loss of the right to participate in the Committee of Creditors, but it is unclear whether it also means that the creditor is barred from recovering his claim.[77] Decisions regarding the distribution of the assets are appealed in administrative order, first to the head of the Judgement Enforcement Office and then to the Department of Justice.[78]

The chairman, general director and the members of the board of management of the company are forbidden from serving in similar capacities from one to three years from the date on which the business is declared bankrupt. There are, however, exceptions to this rule, *e.g.* if the bankruptcy is caused by force majeure, if the mentioned persons not are directly responsible for the acts of bankruptcy, or if the chairman or general director voluntarily filed the petition and settled all debts.[79]

Banking and Capital Markets

The 1990 Ordinance on the State Bank and the 1990 Ordinance on Banks,   **K.14**
Credit Cooperatives and Financial Companies (Commercial Bank Ordinance) have provided a framework for financial services and given the financial sector a status more akin to that in a market-oriented society.

The State Bank is no longer exclusively an institution for the direction of credit through the state-owned banks, but also a more "conventional" state bank with competence to regulate monetary, credit and banking activities, act as the "bank of banks", and execute policy control over all financial institutions. The process of licensing, supervising and dissolution of financial institutions under the Commercial Bank Ordinance is also principally handled by the State Bank. It is further entrusted with competence to issue regulations and other legal documents for the implementation of the Ordinance on the State Bank and the Ordinance on Banks, Credit Cooperatives and Financial Companies.

Labor Law

K.15 The 1990 Ordinance on Labour Contracts provides for the formation of voluntary contracts between employers and employees which spell out the legal rights and obligations, specify minimum wages and otherwise regulate the relationship between employer and employees. A model contract is provided by the Ministry of Labour, Invalids and Social Affairs. Three different forms of employment are specified: definite, indefinite and seasonal or specialized jobs. The Ordinance also contains rules for conciliation and arbitration in the case of a dispute. The role and legal status of trade unions are specified in the Law on Trade Unions. Rather extensive changes within the field of labor law can be expected with the enactment of the Labour Code which currently is under preparation.

Environmental Law

K.16 The legal framework for environmental protection and natural resources is still rudimentary, but a Law on Protection of the Environment was enacted in December 1993 and regulations for environmental impact assessment are under drafting. Provisions with an aim at environmental protection can also be found in the Law on Companies, the Law on Private Enterprises, the Ordinance on the Transfer of Technology into Vietnam, the Law on Foreign Investment, the Forestry Law, the Land Law, the Water Law, the Regulations on the Environmental Protection in Marine Petroleum Operations, and several other legal documents. Various local authorities, especially in Hanoi, Ho Chi Minh City and other major cities, also pass regulations to address local environmental problems such as industrial waste, air standards, water quality and noise.[80]

The objective of the Law on the Protection of the Environment is basically in line with prevailing international environmental policies and include protection of a healthy environment, sustainable development of natural resources, etc. All activities which cause decay, pollution and accidental harm to the environment are consequently prohibited, but no specific punishments are stipulated.[81] The rules regarding controlled exploitation lay down that those organizations and individuals who use the environment in productive business may be required to make financial contributions in accordance with regulations to be issued by the Government. The law also stipulates that environmental damages must be compensated or restored in accordance with the provisions of the law.[82]

All entities who propose to carry out projects which may affect the environment must file a report on the environmental impact caused by their proposed activities to the Ministry of Science, Technology and Environment (MOSTE) for an assessment of the environmental impact. Environmental disputes involving foreign parties in Vietnam are to be settled in accordance with Vietnamese law, but also by reference to "international laws and practices".[83]

Foreign Investment Law

Vietnam adopted a Law on Foreign Investment in 1987 in order to attract foreign capital. It was amended in 1990 to allow non-state companies to co-operate and form joint-ventures with foreign companies, a right that previously had been reserved for state-owned companies. The amendment was followed by the enactment of Decree 28/HDBT which provided more detailed regulations for the implementation of the law. A new amendment was made in 1992, followed by Decree No. 18-CP 1993 providing Regulations on Foreign Investment in Vietnam and Decree No. 191-CP 1994 promulgating the Regulations on the Formation, Evaluation and Implementation of Direct Foreign Invested Projects. About 70 other ordinances, instructions and decisions have also been issued by different authorities, among them the Ordinance on Transfer of Technology, the Decree on Labour for Enterprises with Foreign-owned Capital, and the Ordinance on Labour Contracts.

K.17

The new Civil Code will be applicable on all civil relationships, including those involving foreigners, as long as international treaties to which Vietnam is a party do not stipulate otherwise. The parts of the code which regulate matters of legal capacity of foreigners and applicable law in respect to property rights, contracts, civil liability, intellectual property, etc., will therefore be of significance for foreign investors.

Protection and Guarantees

The 1992 Constitution provides explicit protection against expropriation, nationalization and other forms of forced acquisition: "The State encourages foreign organizations and individuals to invest funds and technology in Vietnam in conformity with Vietnamese law and international law and practice; ensures the lawful ownership of capital and assets and other interests of foreign organizations and individuals. Enterprises with foreign investment shall not be nationalized."[84] The Law on Foreign Investment offers a similar protection: "The State of Vietnam guarantees the ownership of the invested capital and other rights of foreign organizations and individuals" ... and "The capital and assets invested by foreign organizations and individuals shall not be expropriated or requisitioned through administrative meas-

K.18

ures. An enterprise with foreign owned capital shall not be nationalized."[85] Additional protection follows from various bilateral investment treaties and international law principles. Decree No. 18-CP also stipulates that treaties on investment incentives and protection signed by the Government of Vietnam with the government of another country shall prevail.[86] The combined protection of these provisions, and Vietnam's urgent need to attract foreign capital, make the risk of nationalization or expropriation low.

Outright expropriation is, however, not the only way a foreign investor can be deprived of his interests. Some areas of Vietnamese society, including the economic area, are subject to immense regulation which can cause cumulative burdensome effects which prevent the investor from operating his venture profitably, and thus force him to dispossess it. The Law on Foreign Investment contains a guarantee against adverse changes in the legislation: "In cases where the benefit of the parties . . . are reduced due to any change in the laws of Vietnam the State shall take appropriate measures to protect the interests of the investor."[87] The "changes" mentioned refer to changes which are detrimental to the terms of the investment as stated in the investment and business licenses. The measures the SCCI can take to guarantee the interests of the investor are essentially alterations of the operational objectives of the project, exemption or reduction of taxes, and to allow the enterprise to continue its operations as stated in the investment license.

A detailed investment license which spells out the conditions on which the investment is made is therefore important. Foreign investors are also wise to negotiate some form of stabilization clause which provides a mechanism to determine whether a new law causes adverse effects and guarantees that favorable provisions will continue to apply. Such clauses also ought to regulate the principles for re-negotiation of the terms of the investment.

Foreign investors are guaranteed a right to transfer abroad: profits from business operations, payments for services and transfer of technology, principal and interest on loans made in the course of business operation, their invested capital, and other sums of money and assets lawfully owned by them.[88] Transfers may, however, only be effected after applicable taxes have been fully paid and the financial year has been concluded. Decree No. 18-CP further restricts these remittances and other currency business expenditures to the enterprise's own foreign currencies earnings from export "and other legal sources".[89] Overseas remittance of profits may also be subject to a special remittance tax varying from 5 per cent to 10 per cent.

Foreign investors may also repatriate or transfer abroad their capital contributions and reinvested capital in terminated and liquidated enterprises after payment of all debts. These repatriations are made in three yearly instalments, but can after permission from the State Bank be made in a shorter period. Transfers of funds are also subject to certain restrictions following on Vietnam's foreign exchange control and other restrictions.

All payments for goods and services within Vietnam must be made in Vietnamese currency and all capital funds and incomes of an enterprise with foreign invested capital must be deposited in an account maintained within one of Vietnam's commercial banks. The commercial banks include the Vietcombank and branches of foreign banks. All payments to foreign countries must be made through bank accounts in Vietnam.

Dispute resolution between foreign investors and the Vietnamese State is not subject to any comprehensive regulation. Decree No. 18-CP stipulates that such disputes "shall be resolved through conciliation" and the dispute may, if the parties fail to reach an agreement, "be brought before a competent governmental authority".[90] An investor may therefore have to accept adjudication by agencies of the same Government with which they are in dispute. Additional methods for dispute resolution can follow from bilateral investment treaties. The treaties with Australia and China currently allow disputes between Vietnam and investors from these countries to be referred to international arbitration. The SCCI is also known to be flexible and also allows international arbitration in situations were the investor's home country and Vietnam have not yet concluded any bilateral treaties. Vietnam, however, has not recognised the Washington Covnention of 1966 concerning conflict resolution between the Government and a foreign party.

Foreign investors are often advised to stress an international arbitration agreement in the investment license and seek risk insurance against inconvertibility of currency, expropriation, war, etc.[91]

Areas and Forms of Investment

All foreign physical and legal persons with legal capacity in their home countries are welcome to invest in Vietnam. The Vietnamese partner to a foreign investment may be a state enterprise, a share holding company, a limited company, or a private enterprise. The Vietnamese partner is always subject to domestic company laws.   **K.19**

Vietnam's officially formulated investment policy, as visualized in the Law on Foreign Investment, especially encourages investment within areas which benefit national development, for example, export-oriented production and import substitution, use of high technology and skilled labour, labour-intensive production using resources available in Vietnam, construction of infrastructure, and currency-earning services such as tourism, ship-repair, ports and airports.[92]

The main forms of investment are contractual business co-operation ventures (business co-operation contracts), joint-ventures, and enterprises with 100 per cent foreign owned capital.[93] Build Operate Transfer Contracts (BOT Contracts) and investment within export processing zones are also open to foreign investors.

Vietnam

Business Cooperation Contracts

K.20 A business cooperation contract is a product sharing or cooperation contract between at least one partner on each side. This investment form does not create a new legal entity. The investment projects where this form is used are mostly investment projects concerning infrastructure.

The provisions on business cooperation contracts in the Law on Foreign Investment are not very detailed. Decree No. 18-CP contains provisions on the application procedure. It is largely left to the parties to stipulate the nature and contents of the cooperation, to spell out their respective rights and obligations, and regulate the mechanisms for interpretation and resolution of disputes, etc.

Joint Ventures

K.21 Most common among the forms of investment are joint ventures, both because they are encouraged by the Government and because they enable the investor to involve local partners with knowledge of Vietnam's economic, political and cultural features.

A joint venture is a legally regulated form of cooperation between a Vietnamese and a foreign partner. It creates a new legal entity under Vietnamese law in which the profits and risks shall be shared by the contracting parties in proportion to their contributed capital.[94]

Joint ventures are established through joint venture contracts agreed upon and signed by all contracting parties.[95] The contract shall contain the nationalities, addresses and representatives of the parties; the name, address and area of business of the enterprise; the prescribed capital and procedure for its contribution; a time plan and a description of the equipment and material for the construction and operation of the enterprise; a description of the products and in what markets they will be sold; the duration of the project; procedures for dispute resolution; etc.[96]

Each party must contribute at least 30 per cent of the totally prescribed capital. The Government determines the minimum allowed proportion of contributed capital in joint-ventures established by more than two parties.[97] The foreign party's capital contribution can be made in foreign currency or in kind (plants, buildings, equipment, machinery, patents, technical know-how, services, etc.), but the licensing authorities seem to prefer cash. The Vietnamese party can contribute with Vietnamese or foreign currency, plants, machinery, patents, etc., but also with natural resources and use rights to land and water.[98] The Vietnamese partners often prefer to contribute with land or other natural resources since currency is generally in scarce supply. The foreign party should then be aware that private ownership of land not is legally recognised and that the regulatory framework for land issues often is fragmented and conflicting. The arrangement may therefore be complicated and hazardous.[99]

A capital contribution schedule which states the time, form and amount of the payments should be agreed upon. The consequences of failure to pay in due time should also be agreed upon. The partners may not reduce the prescribed capital.

The joint venture must also contribute 5 per cent of the annual profits after tax to a reserve fund.[100] All assets of the joint venture enterprise must be insured, either by the Vietnam Insurance Company or another insurance company that the parties have agreed on.[101]

The parties must agree upon a charter for the joint venture. This charter should be made as detailed as possible in order to foreclose potential disputes, but shall as a minimum contain the following information:[102]

- names, addresses and representatives of the parties
- name, address and field of operation of the joint venture
- the size of the invested capital, the prescribed capital and the time and procedure for its contribution
- composition of the board and regulations concerning its powers
- names of the enterprise's general director and its deputies
- representatives of the enterprise in legal matters
- procedures concerning financial matters, accounting, statistics and property insurance
- the proportion on how profits and losses shall be shared between the partners
- the duration of the enterprise and how it will be dissolved
- principles and routines for labour relations
- plans for the training of the management, technicians, other specialists and workers
- procedures for amending the charter.

It is also advisable to define the partners' liability against third parties in the charter or a separate joint venture agreement.

Joint ventures are governed by a Board of Directors. Each party appoints members of the Board in proportion to their contribution to the prescribed capital. Each side shall appoint at least two members, or if the joint venture consists of more than two parties, at least one member. The Managing Director is appointed by and responsible before the Board. The Managing Director or the Director second to him in rank must be a Vietnamese citizen.[103]

Enterprises with 100 Per Cent Foreign Owned Capital

Enterprises with 100 per cent foreign owned capital are similar to limited companies and form legal entities under Vietnamese law.[104] No participation of Vietnamese nationals in the board of managers or the management is required and the enterprise can thus be completely controlled by the foreign investors. Owners of enterprises with 100 per cent foreign capital within certain sectors of the economy which are deemed to have special significance

K.22

must, however, agree to let Vietnamese business entities purchase part of the enterprise and transform it into a joint venture.[105] The licence shall clearly state the form and time for the overtaking,[106] and a common arrangement is to grant local businessmen a pre-emptive right in the case of a sale of the enterprise.

The rights and obligations of the enterprise and the owner are spelled out in the investment licence and the charter.[107] The prescribed capital shall at least amount to 30 per cent of the totally invested capital and may not be reduced during the operation of the enterprise unless approved by the SCCI.[108]

Build Operate Transfer Contracts

K.23 Foreign individuals or organizations and Vietnamese authorities may form Build-Operate-Transfer-Contracts (BOT-contracts) in which the foreign party accepts to build and operate a project, usually within infra-structure, and after an agreed period of time transfer the rights to the project to the Vietnamese Government.[109] BOT-projects must be approved by the Governor of the State Bank of Vietnam and the relevant ministry, for example, projects within infrastructure must be approved of by the Ministry of Construction, projects within transportation by the Ministry of Transportation, etc.

Export Processing Zones

K.24 An Export Processing Zone is a demarcated area under control of the SCCI and Provincial People's Committee were enterprises only produce for ex-port. All the forms of foreign investment accounted for above may be estab-lished within these zones. Vietnamese enterprises may also establish themselves or co-operate with foreigners within the zones.[110]

The same rights and obligations apply to the enterprises operating with export processing zones as to those established in the rest of Vietnam, except that enterprises within these zones do not have to pay import an export duties as long as the products are exported. Goods exchanged between an enterprise within an export processing zone and enterprises in other parts of Vietnam will, however, be considered as imported or exported and conse-quently subject to import-export regulations, customs and duties.[111]

Licensing and Governance

K.25 All ventures operating under the foreign investment legislation need an in-vestment licence. The license gives the venture a status of legal entity, spells out in which economic area it is allowed to operate, how much capital must be contributed, the duration of the investment project, etc.[112] The duration of the investment is decided on a case to case basis, usually longer for projects within infrastructure and production than tourism and hotel development, but seldom longer than 50 years.[113] The investment loses its status of legal entity when the term has expired.

The governmental State Committee for Co-operation and Investment (SCCI) is the principal organ for licensing and supervision of foreign investments.[114] The licensing procedure is supposed to be a "one stop procedure" in which the SCCI guides the foreign investor in the identification of suitable partners, assists in the negotiation and conclusion of contracts, serves as link between the foreign investor and all concerned authorities, and eventually approves the application for investment, determines whether preferential treatment shall be given, considers applications for land lease and supervises the enterprise's operations. The reality, however, is that most applications contain requests or provisions which only can be approved by a specific agency, or that it also is necessary to submit applications to local authorities to determine whether labor, materials, electricity, water and other necessities can be supplied. It is consequently wise to maintain good contacts also with organizations not directly involved in the licensing process. The Vietnamese partner, with his familiarity with details and informal contacts, is crucial in this respect.

The application procedure is basically the same for business co-operation contracts, joint-ventures and enterprises with 100 per cent foreign-owned capital, but investments within certain areas, referred to as "Group A projects", need the approval of the Prime Minister. This group includes infrastructure construction for industrial zones, export processing zones and BOT projects; projects involving investments of more than US$ 40 million in certain specified areas, among them electricity, oil and gas, chemicals, engineering, ports and airports, telecommunications and tourism; projects within culture, press and publication; projects affecting national defence and security; and projects requiring utilisation of more than five hectares of urban land or more than 50 hectares of other types of land.[115] All documents shall be submitted to the SCCI and must be signed by all parties. The application shall be written in both Vietnamese and a widely used foreign language and include the business co-operation or joint-venture contract, the charter of the enterprise if a new legal entity is created, an economic and technical feasibility study of the project.[116] A fee of 0.01 per cent of the invested capital must also be paid upon submission of the application.

The technical and economical feasibility study generally contains a description of: the general policies, aims and basic conditions of the venture, including a market analysis and a description of the products, markets and natural resources; the investment form: advantages, disadvantages and capacity for production; the production strategy: supply of raw materials and plants, etc.; the location and external conditions: environmental, technical, social and economical aspects; the technology: production processes, technology transfers, costs, employees and environmental impact; buildings and installations: architecture, standards, etc.; the organization: management, workers and expenses for employees and operation; the financial situation:

funds and credits; implementation: conclusions and propositions for preferential treatment. The feasibility study is often compiled by the Vietnamese partner in joint venture relationships, but foreign investors can benefit from performing it jointly because it may help to establish own channels in the Vietnamese administration.

The processing of the application is divided into two parts, assessment and approval. The SCCI is supposed to co-ordinate the work between all involved agencies and administer the project evaluation. The reality is that a number of agencies, often with other loyalties and preferences, will have a say in the process. It is also commonly known that the evaluation of new projects can be affected by opportunism and corruption. The regime has enacted special legislation in an attempt to streamline the process and narrow down the room for discretion.[117]

The SCCI shall announce its decision within three months and the parties shall then receive an investment licence if the project is approved.[118] The parties must announce their investment licence in a central or local newspaper within 30 days.[119]

The SCCI and other involved authorities have became more selective as the volumes of foreign investment have increased. Especially smaller enterprises located in Hanoi and Ho Chi Minh City have experienced difficulties in attracting proper attention. Joint ventures are also generally favoured before enterprises with 100 per cent foreign ownership. Preferential treatment, for example in the form of lower taxes and favourable terms for land use, used to be routinely granted but are becoming more difficult to obtain.

Auditing and Accounting

K.26 The Law on Foreign Investment (Art. 18) states that enterprises operating under the foreign investment legislation: "shall keep its books of account in accordance with conventional international principles and standards approved by the Ministry of Finance of the Socialist Republic of Vietnam and shall be subject to audit under the supervision and control of the financial bodies of Vietnam." More detailed rules follow in the form of Decree No. 07/CP on the Regulating of Independent Auditing in the National Economy and Circular No. 22/TC-CDKT and the instructions for their implementation. The Circular covers, among other things, the functions of independent auditors including inspection and certification of accounting documents and reports of enterprises, specifications for the use of auditors for enterprises in various economic sectors, requirements for registration as professional auditor, and rules for the licensing and operation of foreign auditing firms.

The Circular also stipulates that auditing services must be carried out in accordance with existing auditing methods and standards approved in Vietnam and international auditing standards recognized by Vietnam. All final auditing reports must address the truthfulness and appropriateness of the data stated in the accounting report, the accounting operation of the establishment and its conformity with accounting regulations, and contain proposals and recommendations of the auditor. Limited liability companies and share holding companies operating under the foreign investment legislation must implement independent audits annually and the annual accounting report must be submitted to the relevant authority.

Labor Regulations

Special labor regulations for enterprises operating under the foreign investment legislation are provided for in the Law on Foreign Investment, Decree HDBT-233 on Labour for Enterprises with Foreign Owned Capital and in a number of other decrees and ordinances.[120] The Law on Foreign Investment states that Vietnamese citizens shall be given priority in the recruitment of personnel and that foreigners only may be employed if advanced qualifications are required and no Vietnamese with such qualifications are available. The rights and obligations of the Vietnamese employees shall be spelled out in special "labor contracts" which employers and employees are supposed to sign.[121]

K.27

Enterprises with foreign invested capital must deposit funds with the State for social insurance of its staff.[122] The Decree on labour for Enterprises with Foreign Owned Capital stipulates that the enterprise must pay 2 per cent monthly to the local labor office for unemployment benefits and 8 per cent to an enterprise social insurance fund to cover health, maternity and funeral benefits. The employee pays 10 per cent to the local social insurance fund for pension, disability and death benefits.[123]

The Decree also provides rules on work conditions. It allows for employees to work eight hours per day, six days per week. Overtime is limited to 150 hours per year and each employee is entitled to 18 days of paid vacation per year and to have the state holidays off (eight days). Female employees are entitled to 12 weeks of maternity leave.

Dispute Resolution

Disputes between the parties to a business co-operation contract or a joint venture as well as disputes between enterprises with foreign invested capital and Vietnamese organizations shall be subject to negotiation and conciliation. If the parties fail to reach an agreement, they may refer the dispute to a legal fora of their own choice, domestic or international.[124] Most investors tend to prefer arbitration before court adjudication. International arbitration facilities are currently available under the Chamber of Commerce and Industry of Vietnam through the non-governmental Vietnam International Arbitration Centre (VIAC).

K.28

Vietnam has recently signed the 1958 New York convention on enforcement of foreign arbitration awards and enacted an ordinance on recognition and enforcement of foreign arbitration awards for its implementation.

Foreign investors may nevertheless face problems enforcing international arbitral awards since the mechanisms for enforcement as a whole are weak, especially outside the major urban areas.

Tax Laws

K.29 Enterprises with foreign-invested capital and foreign partners to business co-operation ventures have to pay taxes in accordance with Vietnamese law.[125] The applicable rates and terms for eligibility for preferential treatment are not fixed, but decided by the SCCI on a case-by-case basis depending on in which sector of the economy the investment is made, the scale of the capital contribution, the volume of exports, etc.[126]

Turnover Tax

K.30 Enterprises operating under the foreign investment legislation have to pay turnover tax in accordance with the Law on Turnover Tax. The taxable turnover is defined for each kind of business activity, irrespective of whether it has brought income or not. The rate varies between 0 per cent and 40 per cent.

Profit Tax

K.31 The Law on Foreign Investment states that enterprises operating under the foreign investment legislation are liable to pay profit tax. The tax is calculated on the total taxable profits during the year, including financial profits. The rate depends on the nature of the enterprise's business and other factors, but normally ranges between 15 per cent and 25 per cent. Profits derived from exploitation of oil, gas and certain other valuable resources are taxed according to a higher rate, normally over 25 per cent,[127] while enterprises in export processing zones only pay between 10 per cent and 15 per cent profit tax. The applicable tax rate shall always be stated in the business license.

Special tax incentives are available to ventures within incentive categories.[128] Enterprises which satisfy two of the following requirements shall pay 20 per cent profit tax: more than 500 employees; advanced technology is introduced; at least 80 per cent of the production is exported; the prescribed capital is no less than US$ 10 million.

Enterprises which are involved in construction of infrastructure, exploitation of natural resources (except oil, gas, etc.), heavy industry, cultivation of perennial industrial crops, investments in mountainous regions and other regions with unfavorable conditions, projects where the investment is transferred to the Vietnamese partner without compensation when the project term has expired, may be eligible to pay a 15 per cent profit tax.

The lowest tax rate, 10 per cent, is reserved for enterprises involved in building of infrastructure in mountainous regions or regions with unfavorable conditions, reforestation projects and projects of "special importance".

The Law on Foreign Investment also states that joint ventures within priority categories may enjoy a reduction or complete exemption of the profit tax for up to two years from the when venture starts to make a profit, and a reduction of 50 per cent is possible for the two following years. A double tax exemption period (four years) may be granted in special cases. The same terms can be granted to enterprises with 100 per cent foreign owned capital in certain cases where encouragement of investment is needed.[129] Decree 18-CP provides further tax incentives for enterprises within priority categories and states that the profit tax can be exempted for up to four years and reduced to 50 per cent for the successive four years. Reduction of profit tax is, however, not possible for hotel developments, banking, finance, insurance, accounting, auditing and trading services.[130] Losses incurred in one tax year may also generally be turned over to next year and set off against profits in up to five succeeding years. The profit tax is also generally refunded if the profits are reinvested.[131]

Foreign investors who transfer their profits abroad have to pay a transfer tax of between 5 and 10 per cent of the transferred amount. This tax may be exempted in cases where encouragement of investment is needed.[132]

Enterprises which produce cigarettes, liquors and beer for domestic consumption also have to pay special consumption tax as prescribed by the law on Special Consumption Tax. The tax rates are 32 per cent to 70 per cent for cigarettes, 15 per cent to 90 per cent for liquors and 75 per cent to 90 per cent for beer.

Income Tax

The personnel employed in enterprises operating under the foreign investment legislation may have to pay income tax according to the 1990 Ordinance on Income Tax of High Income Earners. The taxable income comprises regular and irregular incomes generated in Vietnam, except some allowances, bonuses and pensions. The tax on regular incomes is partially progressional and ranges between 0 per cent and 60 per cent for Vietnamese citizens and between 0 per cent and 50 per cent for foreigners. The income tax on irregular income varies between 0 per cent and 30 per cent.

K.32

Import and Export Taxes and Duties

All enterprises, including those operating under the foreign investment legislation, have to pay export and import duties according to the Law on Export and Import Duties on Commercial Goods.[133] Some duties amount to over 100 per cent, but many products are not subject to any duties at all, for example raw materials, equipment and spare parts for the operation of the business. A partial or complete exemption from duties may also be granted

K.33

within areas where encouragement of investment is needed. Enterprises within export processing zones are exempted from export and import duties on exported products and imported raw material and equipment.[134]

Rent and Royalties for Lease and Exploitation of land, Water and Sea Surface

K.34 A "rent" is levied from enterprises with foreign owned capital and parties to a business co-operation contracts for the use of land, water and other natural resources.[135] The rate is stipulated by the Ministry of Finance and may be revised every five years. The revised rate may not exceed 15 per cent of the earlier rate. The rents and fees are generally considerably higher in the major urban areas, such as Hanoi and Ho Chi Minh City, than in less exploited areas.

Intellectual Property Law

K.35 Intellectual property rights is a new concept in most south-east Asian societies and the means for enforcement are consequently often weak. Vietnam is no exception. The Government has, however, enacted considerable volumes of new legislation and otherwise attempted to improve the situation.[136]

Vietnam recognizes intellectual property rights in accordance with those international conventions to which it is a party, on the principle of reciprocity. Vietnam has participated in the International Convention on Industrial Property Rights since 1981, is a signatory to the Stockholm Convention on the Establishment of the World Intellectual Property Organization (WIPO), the Paris Convention on Industrial Property Rights and the Madrid Agreement on Registration of Trade Marks.

Registration is a prerequisite for protection. The National Office of Inventions, a governmental body under the State Committee on Science and Technology, is the authority responsible for assessment, approval and supervision of intellectual property. Applications for registration can be filed directly or through an Industrial Property Agent, but foreigners without representation in Vietnam must rely on registered agents to act on their behalf. Such services are offered by the Chamber of Commerce, Investip (a government-affiliated patent and trade mark agent), or one of several independent agencies which have appeared during the last few years.

Owners of intellectual property rights are, once the rights have been registered, entitled to the exclusive use of the protected right and may also transfer it to other persons or organisations. The registration is published in the local gazette. The owner of the right may request the competent authority, usually the Office of Inventions, to stop or prohibit infringement of his rights. He may also bring the matter to the People's Courts.

Patents

Patents are granted for the protection of inventions and are effective for 15 **K.36**
years from the date of application (priority date). Technical solution must
have novelty, inventive creativity, practical applicability and economic and
social usefulness in order to be recognized as an invention. Novelty means
that the solution must not have been disclosed, in Vietnam or abroad, prior
to the filing of the application. It must also be different from previously
registered patents. Creativity means that that the solution must be a result of
a creative effort and not through obvious means. Applicability means that the
solution must be capable of use in Vietnam with present or future technology. Economic and social usefulness means that the solution can contribute
to technological development in Vietnam, for example in the form of increased labor efficiency, improved quality or more efficient utilization of
natural resources.

The patent application shall be written in Vietnamese or another widely
used foreign language. Each application must relate to a single invention and
contain the name, address and nationality of the applicant and inventor; name
of the invention; and international classification of the invention. Special
requests referring to international conventions to which Vietnam is a party
should also be stated. The applicant must also provide a description of the
invention, including the name, technical field and features of the invention
(including drawings in four copies).

The National Office of Inventions examines each application and shall
reach a decision within 18 months. Applications can, however, be rejected
already after a preliminary examination. In that case the applicant may amend
his application or provide additional material. Rejections of applications are
appealed administratively to the same agency, the National Office of Inventions. Appeals can eventually reach the State Committee of Science and
Technology, but appeal to court is not possible at present.

Infringements of patents are usually handled through administrative procedures, but patents and license holders also have the right to institute court
proceedings at the competent Provincial Courts. Cases where foreigners are
involved may be referred to Hanoi or Ho Chi Minh City Provincial (City)
Court.

Trade Marks

Trade marks are protected under the Ordinance on Trade Marks. Decree No. **K.37**
140/HDBT 1990 address issues regarding the handling of counterfeiting
cases.

Protection of marks is available to state bodies, collective or private organisations, and legal and natural persons and is provided through registration.[137] Trade marks may be in the form of words, pictures letters, numbers,
designs, etc. Indistinctive marks, for example simple figures or block letters,
will not be accepted.[138] Marks or symbols which have become part of the

public domain, for example conventional signs, symbols and denominations are also refused registration. Trade marks which are merely descriptive, for example, express place, manufacturing process, type, quantity, purpose, value, etc., and marks which can be misleading or deceptive as to the origin, nature or purpose of the product or are considered similar to a mark of any national or international quality, inspection or warranty organization are not registerable. Marks which consist of state flags, emblems, portraits of national leaders, geographical names, etc., will not be accepted unless specific authorization can be proven. It is also stipulated that any mark or sign deemed to contravene the law, public policy or socialist morality will not be accepted. Socialist morality is not defined, but can be assumed to refer to politically related subjects, pornography and other images which the political establishment considers inappropriate.

Applications for registration are filed with the National Office of Invention (NOI).[139] Foreign applicants without representation in Vietnam must file their application through an authorized Vietnamese industrial property agent, for example the Chamber of Industry and Commerce or Investip. The agent can also carry out a search for identical or similar trade marks already registered.

An application for registration may only regard one trade mark and must be accompanied by a list of the goods that will bear the mark.[140] It is only the use of the mark on designated goods that will be protected. The application should also contain a detailed description of the mark which fully explains the purpose of the mark and the significance of its features. Fifteen specimens of the trade mark in the form of drawings, prints, photos, etc., must also be enclosed. Vietnam adheres to the first-to-file principle, and it is therefore crucial to apply to register before any competing registration is filed.

The application process shall take no longer than six months. The applicant obtains a Certificate of Registration once the mark is registered. The trade mark will also be entered into the National Register of Trademarks and published in the Official Gazette of Inventions and Marks. Rejected applications may be appealed administratively, first to the NOI and then to the State Committee for Science and Technology.

Trade marks are protected for 10 years from the date of application. The term may be renewed for periods of 10 years each. Renewal requires that the owner files a request with the National Office of Invention not later than six months prior to the expiry date.[141] The legal protection of a trade mark can be terminated on the owners request, when the establishment owning the mark ceases to exist by terminating its activities, or when the mark has not been used for five years following the date of application.[142]

The Ordinance allows interested parties to bring cancellation actions at any time, but does not specifically provide for opposition actions. Cancellation actions are filed administratively. This may even be done before a mark is registered if the owner of a mark suspects that a potentially conflicting application has been filed.

The owner of trade mark is entitled to the exclusive use of the mark on designated goods in connection with all productive, commercial and service activities during the term of validity. Any unauthorized use of a registered trade mark or use of a similar which could be confused with the registered mark is considered a violation of the exclusive right of the owner. The owner may also assign the right to use the mark, partially or totally, to others. Contracts of assignment must be registered with the National Office of Invention to have legal effect.[143]

Protection against infringements can be sought administratively or through the People's Courts.[144] Litigation is the only way a trade mark owner can obtain civil damages, but litigation is not a favored way of dispute resolution and the People's Courts have very limited experience of trade mark matters. Administrative action is therefore still the preferred means for enforcement. The National Bureau of Inventions and the Market Management Bureau under the Ministry of Trade and Tourism oversee supervision and enforcement matters. The Bureau may issue orders to stop infringements, seize counterfeit goods, revoke the business licence of the infringer, etc.

It is generally acknowledged that enforcement is a difficult matter. A complaint or a lawsuit may therefore not be enough to make an infringement stop. Trade mark owners can turn to the Chamber of Commerce, Investip or another trademark agency in order to speed up the process and ensure proper action. Representatives for these agencies can help to persuade local agencies to take the matter seriously and to have the infringers cease their operations.

Vietnam is a party to the Madrid Agreement on International Registration of Trade Marks and a member of the Madrid Union, a WIPO-affiliated organization which permits its members to register trade marks in other Union countries.[145] Vietnamese companies can therefore obtain registration in other Union countries on the basis of their trade mark registration in Vietnam, and applicants who have establishments in other Union countries may consequently do the same in Vietnam. It may, however, be doubted whether a trade mark registered in another Union country can actually be enforced.

Copyrights

The 1994 Ordinance on the Protection of Copyrights protects published or **K.38** unpublished works by Vietnamese citizens and organizations, unpublished works by foreign authors which are published for the first time in Vietnam, and works by foreign authors which are published in Vietnam within 30 days of the first publication in another country.[146] Copyrights are defined as the intellectual and material rights of the author and includes written works, acts and plays, films, videos, radio programs, music, architectural works, computer software, scientific works, etc.[147] Documents of State organs, political and social organisations and translations of such documents are not subject to protection.[148]

The Ordinance gives the author the right to ownership of his work. This includes a right to authorize or prohibit others to use, alter or disseminate the work, a right to receive royalties or other forms of remuneration when the work is used or sold, and a right to transfer the copyright, partially or entirely.[149] The right of ownership is protected during the authors lifetime and up to 50 years after his death.[150] Use of protected works by others for non-commercial purposes, for example for commentaries, teaching or preparation of news, is allowed without authorization and obligations to pay royalties as long as the rights of the owner not are violated. The name and origin of the work must, however, be quoted.[151]

Protection under the Ordinance requires registration.[152] The Ministry of Culture and Information is primarily responsible for the registration, management and supervision of copyrights on the national level and the People's Committees are responsible for the implementation on local level.[153] Complaints on the management of copyrights are handled administratively.[154] Infringements can be addressed either through administrative channels or in the People's Courts.[155]

Transfer of Technology and Licensing

K.39 Today Vietnam desperately needs foreign technology to promote economic development and is taking steps to attract foreign investment. At the end of 1988, for example, the government promulgated an ordinance governing the transfer of foreign technology to Vietnam, and has passed other laws and decrees to protect that technology once it is transferred to Vietnam.[156]

Overall, foreign technology transferred to Vietnam has had a positive impact in the country.[157] It has improved production levels, developed broader manufacturing capacities, increased exports, and accelerated development of indigenous technological capability.[158] Nevertheless, technology transfer is hampered by many problems involving the mechanics of transfer, the use of technology, and the environment for foreign technology.[159]

The primary laws governing the transfer of technology in Vietnam are the Ordinance on Transfer of Foreign Technology into Vietnam (hereinafter, the "Technology Transfer Law");[160] the Decree on the Transfer of Foreign Technology into Vietnam, hereinafter the "Implementing Regulations");[161] and the Regulations on Licensing (hereinafter "Licensing Regulations").[162] Under the Licensing Regulations, only certain Vietnamese organizations are authorized to negotiate and enter into technology licensing agreements. Once negotiations are completed and an agreement is finalized, licensing agreements for the transfer of foreign inbound technology in Vietnam must then receive approval from the State Committee on Science and Technology ("SCST"), and also the State Committee Cooperation and Investment ("SCCI"), if the agreement is part of an investment project. In addition, terms which prohibit the free use of technology after a licensing agreement terminates are prohibited.

The Technology Transfer Law deals with the transfer of foreign inbound technology, which includes technical assistance and consultancy services from overseas into Vietnam.[163] The Technology Transfer Law requires that all licensing agreements for the transfer of foreign inbound technology first receive governmental approval. Applications for that approval must be made to the government agency responsible for the particular sector at issue.[164]

Any technology transferred under the Technology Transfer Law is required to enhance technological standards and production efficiency, improve product quality or be capable of developing new products[165] and should make rational use of energy natural resources and manpower.[166] The technology transferred must not be detrimental to the production safety,[167] nor may it adversely affect the environment by causing land, water or air pollution, damage to natural fauna or flora or ecological imbalances.[168] Environmental damage is defined to include "damage to the cultural and social aspects of populated areas".[169]

The SCST is given the power to manage technology transfer contracts.[170] For contracts valued at less than US$1,000,000 (or in the case of contracts financed by the State Treasury less than US$500,000), however, the authority to approve technology transfer contracts is delegated to the relevant ministry, State Committee or Provincial or Town People's Committee depending on the nature of the Vietnamese party, and subject to the right of final approval by the SCST.[171]

All technology transfer contracts are required to be in writing[172] and must contain the following provisions:[173]

1. Names and addresses of the transferor and transferee and the names and addresses of the individual representatives of the parties;[174]
2. Definitions of terms used in the contracts;[175]
3. Details of the technology to be transferred including the name of the technology, a detailed description of its main features, the technical and economic value of each item of technology to be transferred and forecasts of the economic, technical and/or social results to be achieved following the completion of the transfer;[176]
4. In the case of industrial property rights, documentation which describes the rights and other legal documents certifying that the rights are protected;[177]
5. The time and the place of the technology transfer. If the technology transfer contract is part of a joint venture, investment or construction project or other contract, including the sale of equipment, each item of equipment and its delivery schedule must be included and must

    comply with the implementation schedule for the investment or construction project;[178]

6. The price, terms and mode of payment (including the currency to be used and the place of payment). If the contract relates to a number of items of technology the contract must clearly state the terms of payment for each.[179] The price of the technology transferred is required to be fixed on the basis of equality and mutual benefit taking into consideration prices of similar technology on the international markets.[180] Payment may be made either in a lump sum or as a royalty. If royalties are paid, the amount may not exceed 5 per cent of the net selling price of the goods;[181]

7. Undertakings by both parties as to the quality and reliability of the technology; the duration of guarantees; and guarantees of confidentiality and occupational safety;[182]

8. Training details, including provisions setting out which party bears the responsibilities and expenses for training; the form, content and areas of training; the duration and location of training; and the objective of and the level of skills to be achieved by the training;[183]

9. Duration of the contract, including provisions allowing for the extension or shortening of the contract by the parties.[184] Except with approval by the appropriate authority, the contract may not last longer than seven years;[185] and,

10. Dispute resolution, including the laws to be applied, the methods of resolution to be applied and the bodies to be used in the resolution of disputes.[186] This can include arbitration by the Vietnam International Arbitration Committee or by foreign arbitration bodies.

Except in special circumstances relating to the "nature of the technology transferred or the state of the national economy"[187] contracts must not contain the following provisions:[188]

1. Those which require the transferee to purchase raw materials, semi-processed goods, machinery, equipment or vehicles from the transferor, or which require the transferee to use unskilled labor provided by the transferor, except if such purchases are necessary for the implementation of the contracts and these reasons are explained in the contract;[189]

2. Provisions which limit the quantity, prices or terms of sale of goods produced by the transferee, or which specify the appointment of agents or commercial representatives;[190]

3. Provisions which restrict the export of products, except that restrictions may be placed on exports to markets where the transferor is already producing or has granted an exclusive right to another to produce in that market;[191]

4. Provisions which restrict the transferee from research and development or acquisition of similar technology from other sources;[192] or

5. Provisions which prohibit the free use of the technology by the transferee after the contract has expired.[193]

The SCST or other approval bodies are required to approve or reject the **K.40** application within three months after receipt of all the required documents.[194] If the application is approved a technology transfer license will be issued by the SCST.[195] The SCST is charged with keeping a record of all technology transfer contracts.[196] If a contract has been approved by a lower level body, that body is required to forward a copy of the contract to the SCST within two weeks of approval.[197]

The Licensing Regulations apply to the purchase and sale of the right to use inventions, utility solutions, industrial designs, trademarks on goods and technical secrets.[198] The Licensing Regulations allow for the licensing of the right to use inventions, utility solutions, industrial designs and trade marks on goods which have been registered and are legally protected.[199] Technical secrets, defined as know-how, data, documents and secret technical information may also be licensed.[200] Design sketches and models of goods relating to the above forms of intellectual property may also be licensed.[201] The Licensing Regulations have different requirements for contracts made between Vietnamese entities and foreign parties and those made solely between Vietnamese parties.

The Licensing Regulations are effectively divided into two parts. The first part deals with the procedures that need to be followed to license intellectual property. The second part deals with the implementation of licensing agreements, including protection against infringement, dispute resolution and the termination of licensing agreements.[202]

Unlike the Technology Transfer Law only a limited number of Vietnamese organizations are permitted to directly negotiate and sign licensing contracts with foreigners. These are:

(a) Export and import organizations permitted by the State to sign licensing contracts with foreigners;

(b) Organizations permitted by the State to provide services in relation to licensing contracts with foreigners; and,

(c) Units permitted by the State to enter into economic co-operation with foreigners.[203]

All other entities and individuals are required to use the services of one of the above organizations to negotiate and sign licenses.[204] In such cases, the Licensing Regulations provide that the representative of the organization wishing to enter the licensing contract may join in the negotiations with the foreign parties.[205] The Licensing Regulations do not provide in detail the provisions that must be in a licensing contract. Rather, they provide that licensing contracts must be in writing,[206] may not be for a longer period than the monopoly right held by the licensor,[207] and set out the general rights and obligations of the parties.[208] However, as with the technology transfer contracts, there are a number of prohibitions which a licensing contract may not contain such as:[209]

1. Unreasonably limit the licensee in the use, production and marketing (including export) of the product produced under the license;[210]
2. Unreasonably control the market price of the product produced under the license;[211]
3. Prohibit improvements to the subject of the license, or prohibit the licensee from using similar technology of other entities;[212]
4. Prohibit the continued use of the subject of the license after expiry of the license (except for trade marks);[213] or
5. Prohibit the licensee from granting an exclusive sub-license to a third party which is engaged in lawful production and business in Vietnam.[214]

The Licensing Regulations, however, provide that licensing contracts with foreigners which contain one or more of the above provisions may be approved by the SCST, in certain circumstances, when proposed by the relevant administrative agency and "particularly when required by the national economy, defense and security".[215]

The Licensing Regulations encourage the licensing of technology by providing financial incentives, such as reduced tax rates and the payment of bonuses to local inventors working in state-owned enterprises.[216] Foreign individuals and companies are allowed to use the royalties from licensing in Vietnam as if this money had been invested on the basis of the Vietnamese Foreign Investment Law.[217]

Litigation, Arbitration and Other ADR Techniques

K.41 The system for dispute resolution and enforcement is undergoing comprehensive reforms, but some organs only reluctantly accept the new order and other organs are unable of performing their new tasks because of a lack of training and resources.

The judicial system mainly comprises: (a) the organizations for mediation and conciliation; (b) the People's Courts, including the economic courts; and (c) the Military Courts where the judges often are officers with a background in the armed forces.[218] Various organizations for arbitration also fulfil an important function. The recently adopted Law on Amendments to the Law on the Organization of the People's Courts provides for the establishment of Economic Courts (departments) within the present Provincial and Supreme People's Courts. They will be the principal institution for the resolution of disputes related to economic matters, for example contracts, securities, unfair competition and bankruptcies.

Conciliation

The tradition of informal dispute resolution is very long in Vietnam and still   **K.42**
influences the ways disputes are handled. Organized conciliation is currently
undertaken mainly in matters relating to family and civil law and is known to
be rather efficient, achieving voluntary settlement of about one-third of the
disputes.[219] Strong social pressure may, however, be used to make a party give
up lawful rights.

The Civil Courts

Civil and economic disputes are channelled through the system of People's   **K.43**
Courts. The courts have long been under factual influence of the Party and
the Government, but are gradually gaining a more independent status under
law. The Constitution maintains the courts explicit duty to protect socialism,
but also stipulates that the courts are to: ". . . protect the lives, property,
freedom, honor and dignity of citizens".[220] It also stresses that "The verdicts
and decisions of the People's Courts which have already taken legal effect
must be respected by state organs, social and economic organizations, people's armed forces units and all citizens; persons and units concerned must
strictly implement them."[221]

    The first instance in most civil cases is the District People's Courts. The
adoption of the 1993 Law on Amendments to the Law on the Organization
of the People's Courts also meant that the adjudicating of the Economic
Arbitration Organization were transferred to the People's Courts and that
certain judges were designated to settle economic cases. The jurisdiction of
the Districts Courts is, however, limited to 50 million Dong or US\$ 4,500 in
contract disputes.[222]

    Appeal to the provincial People's Court can be made by either party
within 10 days of the courts decision.[223] The Provincial Courts consist of a
Judicial Committee, a criminal court, a civil court, an economic court and a
chancellery. The Provincial Economic Court is the first instance in most
disputes regarding economic contracts, company law, industrial property,
securities, unfair competition, bankruptcies, etc.[224] It is also the first instance
in disputes involving foreigners.

    The final appellate body is the Supreme People's Court. The Supreme
Court is organized in a Council of Judges, a Committee of Judges, a civil
court, a criminal court, a military court, an economic court, and three appeal
courts. The judgments of the Supreme People's Court are not published or
otherwise regularly made available in print.

    Higher courts and representatives for the Procuracy may also request to
review the judgments of lower courts *ex officio*.[225] The grounds for review
are: serious procedural errors, that the judgment is not "appropriate to the
objective facts of the dispute", or there is a serious mistake in the application
of the law.[226] Civil cases, however, especially those settled by higher courts,
are handled with prudence and the use of reviews is decreasing.

Vietnam

The People's Courts on district and provincial level are generally competent with one professional judge and two lay assessors, and in regard to economic cases, with two professional judges and one lay assessor. A significant change since the enactment of the new Constitution is that persons appointed as professional judges are required to have law degree. Judges are appointed by the President for a period of five years and may be re-appointed for another period. The Chief Justice of the Supreme Court is elected by and responsible to the National Assembly.[227] The lay assessors are elected by political assemblies. It is notable that event he Supreme Court contains lay assessors.

Rules for the procedure in the Economic Courts follow from the 1994 Ordinance on Procedure for Settlement of Economic Disputes. The rules are also applicable in cases where one of the parties is a foreign individual or entity, unless otherwise stipulated by an international treaty to which Vietnam is a party.[228]

Individuals and juridical persons are guaranteed a right to initiate legal proceedings to protect their legitimate rights and lawful interests.[229] The petition for the commencement of proceedings must be filed within six months of "the date on which the dispute arises".[230] The defendant must file his defence with the court within ten days from he has been notified.[231] The court may assist the parties in collecting evidence and issuing subpoenas.

The court shall propose an initial conciliatory arrangement prior to the formal hearing.[232] Where the parties fail to conciliate, the court may proceed with a preliminary hearing. Economic disputes are heard in open court unless the dispute involves state secrets or the court otherwise decides to hear the matter in closed court.[233] A party can therefore not legally request that a matter involving trade secrets etc. should be heard in closed court. All proceedings are conducted in the Vietnamese language, but litigants may argue in their own language through an interpreter.[234] The parties are entitled to be represented by a lawyer or another trustworthy person.[235]

The interpretation of laws, regulations and contracts is sometimes difficult because of the lack of preparatory work from the legislator, cases and commentaries. This leads the courts to interpret laws and contracts word by word, a practice which ensures a degree of predictability. The principle of sanctity of promise in commercial relationships is generally upheld and there is hardly any distinction between the meaning of the words and the actual intent or purpose behind a law or contract.

Provisions for the enforcement of judgments are provided for in the 1993 Ordinance on Execution of Civil Judgments. The Enforcement Unit of the Provincial Department of Justice and the Enforcement Group of the District Department of Justice are the organs principally responsible for the enforcement. The Enforcement Officer of the district, with possible assistance from the police, may undertake force measures if a judgment cannot be enforced voluntarily. It is, however, generally recognized that the Enforcement Units lack the necessary authority and material resources to effectively fulfil their tasks.

A consequence of Vietnam's greater involvement in international trade is that enforcement of decisions of foreign courts and tribunals are requested more and more often in Vietnam. Vietnam has signed a number of bilateral agreements on mutual judicial assistance, and the 1989 Ordinance on Execution of Civilian Court Verdicts stipulates that verdicts of foreign tribunals which have been sanctioned by Vietnamese courts shall be executed in Vietnam. Therefore, although Vietnam can in principle give effect to a foreign decision, proceedings to enforce such a decision are virtually unknown.

The Ordinance on the Recognition and Execution of Foreign Tribunal Verdicts and Civilian Decisions within Vietnam attempts to address some of these problems. It empowers Vietnamese courts and tribunals to examine petitions to enforce or reject decisions by foreign courts regarding marriages, labor, property, etc. The Ordinance does not, however, provide for the recognition and enforcement of foreign arbitration awards.

Economic Arbitration

The Economic Arbitration Organization (EAO) was established in 1960 **K.44** with the main purpose to supervise that business was carried out in conformity with the state plan and to solve economic disputes between state enterprises. The EAO also became responsible for the settlement of disputes related foreign trade and investment and continued to be the exclusive alternative to negotiations between the parties in economic disputes until the adoption of the Law on Amendment to Some Articles of the Law on the Organization of the people's Courts in 1993 and the establishment of Economic Courts within the People's Courts.[236]

New and more autonomous institutions for arbitration have also developed. These fora can potentially achieve an important position in the business community, both because of a deeply rooted distrust in formal institutions and a long tradition of avoiding to settle disputes in public. On a lower level, this "arbitration" may take the shape of informal negotiations with the assistance of some trustworthy person, and when the sums and complexity increase, in a more formalized manner with the assistance of skilled jurists.

The Government has also enacted new legislation in an attempt to establish arbitration centers after a uniform model.[237] These centers settle disputes related to economic contracts, the establishment, operation and dissolution of companies, and over securities. The awards are final and binding, and if a party fails to comply with the award, the other party may request the People's Court to resolve the matter in accordance with the procedures for resolution of economic proceedings.[238]

The centers may only try a dispute if the parties have agreed in writing to submit the dispute to this particular center.[239] The parties can unanimously select an arbitrator, or if they fail to reach an agreement, select one each. These arbitrators will then choose a third arbitrator who will act as chairman of the tribunal. The Chairman of the tribunal can also be appointed by the director of the center. The arbitrators must be ethical, honest, impartial, objective, and wise and experienced in the field of law and economics, but a law degree is not required. The parties may attend the proceedings themselves or send a representative. All proceedings are conducted in Vietnamese, but interpretation may be requested.

The Vietnam International Arbitration Center (VIAC), a non-governmental organization under the Vietnam Chamber of Commerce and Industry, was set up in conformity with Decision No. 204/TTg 1993 and replaced the Foreign Trade Arbitration Committee and the Maritime Arbitration Committee as the principal fora for arbitration between foreign parties and Vietnamese entities. It may settle disputes related to international economic relations, for example trade and investment contracts, tourism, international transport, transfer of technology, financial services, etc., where at least one of the parties is a foreign physical or juridical person and there is an agreement to submit the dispute to VIAC. Its awards are final and cannot be appealed before any other court or institution.

VIAC has elaborated special rules for its operation, the Rules of Arbitration of the Vietnam International Arbitration Center at the Chamber of Commerce and Industry of Vietnam. The parties may decide which law that should apply to the substantive issues. The hearing shall take place in Hanoi, but can after permission of the Chairman of VIAC be conducted at some other location in Vietnam. All applicable arbitration fees must be advanced when the request is filed. The parties may attend the hearing themselves or be represented by authorized legal representatives, Vietnamese or foreign. All proceedings are carried out behind closed doors and the vote of the majority decides the case. Agreement between the parties may be recorded and laid down as consent awards.

Vietnam has recently ratified the 1958 New York Convention on Recognition and Enforcement of International Arbitration Awards and enacted a decree for its implementation. Foreign arbitration awards can therefore, at least theoretically, be enforced in Vietnam. It may, however, be doubted whether this is possible in practice, given the weakness of the institutions for enforcement.

The Notary

K.45 There is a governmental public notary organization under the Provincial People's Committee and the Ministry of Justice.[240] Its main areas of activity are essentially the same as in the continental notary system. Most important is its duty to handle various kinds of compulsory registrations and certifications, for example to transfer of use rights to land, legal capital in enterprises, family matters (separate property of spouses, wills, etc.). Negligence to register in accordance with the law can make the legal act or document void. The Notary also offers voluntary registration of economic contracts and control of the legal status of the parties and their authorized representatives.

Notes

[1] Marlita A. Reddy, *Statistical Abstract of the World* 1002 (1994).

[2] *Ibid.* 1004 (1990 estimate).

[3] *Ibid.* (1992 estimate).

[4] *Vietnam Business Yellow Pages* (1994).

[5] *Ibid.*   [6] *Ibid.*

[7] *Ibid.*   [8] *Ibid.*

[9] *Ibid.*   [10] *Ibid.*

[11] "Vietnam's Transition to a Market Economy, II: Growth prospects, Financing Requirements and a Reform Agenda", 16 *East Asian Executive Reports* 8, 26 (January 15, 1994).

[12] *Ibid.*

[13] *The Statesmen's Yearbook* (1994).

[14] "Vietnam's Transition to a Market Economy I: Reform Priorities — Foreign Direct Investment", 15 *East Asian Executive Reports* 9, December 15, 1993.

[15] Vietnam's Transition to a Market Economy III: — Reform Priorities — Foreign Trade, *East Asian Executive Reports*, 8, February 1994.

[16] *Ibid.*

[17] *Ibid.*

[18] *Ibid.*

[19] *Ibid.*

[20] James Taylor, "Vietnam: The Current Legal Environment for U.S. Investors", 25 *Law and Policy in International Business* 469, 472 (Winter 1994).

[21] Constitution 1992, Arts. 15, 19–22.

[22] Art. 58.

[23] Art. 23.

[24] Law on Promotion of Domestic Investment (Arts. 1, 2 and 6) protects investments made by Vietnamese physical and legal persons, overseas Vietnamese and long-term foreign residents and stipulates that investments and profits are protected and guaranteed by the State and that compulsory acquisition must be compensated.

[25] Constitution 1992, Art. 17.

[26] Constitution 1992, Art. 18 and Land Law, Arts. 1 and 20.

[27] Land Law, Art. 2.

[28] Constitution 1992, Art. 18.

[29] Land Law, Arts. 1 and 3.

[30] Constitution 1992, Art. 23; Land Law, Art. 27.

[31] Land Law, Arts. 12 and 27.

[32] The Land Law (Art. 26) mentions a number of situations where land shall revert to the State, among them: if the organization which has been allocated land dissolves, becomes bankrupt, moves, etc., or an individual land user dies and has no successor by will or law; the land user voluntarily gives his use right back to the State; the land, without permission, is left unused for 12 consecutive months; the land user does not fulfil his obligations to the State; the land is used for purposes other than for which it was allocated or the land has been allocated by an agency which did not have competence to do so.

[33] Constitution 1992, Art. 18 and Land Law, Arts. 4 and 79.
[34] Constitution 1992, Art. 18 and Land Law, Arts. 3 and 73.
[35] Use rights to agricultural land can be transferred on certain conditions, for example if the user has to move, change profession or no longer is able to use the land. Land Law, Arts. 74 and 75.
[36] Land Law, Art. 31.
[37] Art. 12.
[38] Art. 78.
[39] Arts. 3 and 77.
[40] Art. 77.
[41] Art. 38.
[42] Ordinance on Civil Contracts, Arts. 1 and 3.
[43] Ordinance on Economic Contracts, Art. 1.
[44] Art. 2.
[45] Art. 42. The State Economic Arbitration, which previously adjudicated disputes arising from economic contracts, also extended the scope of economic contract arbitration to include disputes between registered individual and family traders.
[46] Arts. 8 and 39.
[47] Art. 8.
[48] Quality standards, however, are regulated administratively by the Department of Standards, Weights, Measurement and Quality. Art. 13.
[49] The Ordinance on Economic Contracts (Art. 7) refers to negotiations or economic arbitration before the governmental Economic Arbitration Organization, but this provision has been obsolete since the establishment of the Economic Courts.
[50] Art. 29.
[51] Law on Companies, Arts. 4–5; Law on Private Enterprises, Arts. 3 and 4.
[52] Law on Private Enterprises, Art. 2.
[53] Law on Companies, Art. 2.
[54] Art. 25.
[55] Art. 30. To issue and sell shares to the public does, however, require approval of the People's Committee where the head office is located (Art. 34).
[56] The Vietnamese authorities are currently investigating the possibilities of uniting the decision on establishment and the business registration to only one registration, possibly under the recently established Economic Courts.
[57] Law on Companies, Art. 16 and Law on Private Enterprises, Art. 8.
[58] Law on Companies, Art. 17; Law on Private Enterprises, Art. 11. The laws designate the Economic Arbitration and the People's Committee to take care of registrations of companies and enterprises, but this function is currently subject to discussions and may be transferred to another body, possibly the economic courts.
[59] Law on Companies, Art. 11; Law on Private Enterprises, Art. 5.
[60] Art. 1. Joint ventures, however, can alternatively undergo dissolution, termination or assignment to third parties after approval of the State Committee for Cooperation and Investment.
[61] Art. 4.
[62] Arts. 7, 8 and 9.
[63] The decision may be appealed to and reviewed by the People's Court and can eventually reach the People's Supreme Court (Art. 13).
[64] Art. 18.
[65] Art. 23.
[66] Art. 24.
[67] Arts. 15, 17 and 22.
[68] Arts. 20, 33, 36.

69 Arts. 42, 43 and 44. The Committee consists of a member of the Judgement Enforcement Office, representatives of banks and financial institutions, representatives of creditors and unions, and a representative of the bankrupt enterprise.

70 Art. 45.

71 Art. 48.

72 Art. 3.

73 Article 39. The Assets Management Committee is supposed to prepare a list over the creditors and this list is to be posted for 10 days. Creditors who have grievances may then appeal to the Assets Management Committee. It seems, however, possible to appeal even after the 10 days have expired.

74 Art. 38.

75 Art. 19.

76 Arts. 21 and 22.

77 Art. 22.

78 Art. 47.

79 Art. 50.

80 The Ministry of Science, Technology and Environment (MOSTE), and especially its Department of Environment and Natural Resources, plays the central role in drafting and decision making within the environmental area, but several other agencies also compete for influence.

81 The law states that offenders must implement remedial measures, pay damages and may be punished, administratively or through criminal prosecution, according to the degree and consequences of the violation. The law does not provide any ground for the calculation of compensations, etc. Law on the Protection of the Environment, Arts. 9, 30 and 50.

82 Art. 7.

83 Art. 48.

84 Constitution 1992, Art. 25.

85 Law on Foreign Investment, Arts. 1 and 21.

86 Decree No. 18-CP, Art. 99.

87 Law on Foreign Investment, Art. 21 and Decree No. 18-CP, Art. 99.

88 Law on Foreign Investment, Art. 22.

89 Decree No. 18-CP, Arts. 82 and 83.

90 Art. 102. The provisions regarding disputes between the parties to a joint venture with foreign invested capital, which provide for international arbitration in a fora of the parties' own choice, are therefore hardly applicable.

91 The Multilateral Investment Guarantee Agency (MIGA) considers to extend its policies to Vietnam.

92 Law on Foreign Investment, Art. 3.

93 Art. 4.

94 Law on Foreign Investment, Arts. 6 and 10; Decree No. 18-CP, Art. 19.

95 Decree No. 18-CP, Art. 19.

96 Decree No. 18-CP, Art. 21.

97 Law on Foreign Investment, Art. 8.

98 Art. 7.

99 The Ministry of Finance has attempted to establish price ranges for the evaluation of such land, but land prices are still known to be speculative and fluctuate heavily.

100 Law on Foreign Investment, Art. 30.

101 Art. 9.

102 Decree No. 18-CP, Art. 22.

103 Law on Foreign Investment, Arts. 12 and 13.

104 Law on Foreign Investment, Art. 14; Decree No. 18-CP, Arts. 43 and 44.

105 Law on Foreign Investment, Art. 14.

106 Decree No. 18-CP, Art. 47.
107 The charter shall include essentially the same information as for joint ventures. See Decree No. 18-CP Art. 48.
108 Decree No. 18-CP, Art. 47.
109 Law on Foreign Investment, Art. 19b.
110 Art. 19a.
111 Art. 19a.
112 Joint venture and business co-operation contracts do not have legal effect until the investment licence is granted. Decree No. 18-CP, Arts. 19 and 44.
113 Based on regulations issued by the National Assembly, the Government may authorize projects with a duration up to 70 years. Law on Foreign Investment, Art. 15.
114 Law on Foreign Investment, Art. 36 and Decree No. 18-CP, Art. 6. The SCCI is divided into five sections: Department of Law and Investment Promotion; Department for Project Evaluation; Department for Administration of Export Processing Zone; and Department for Administration and Training of Personnel.
115 Decree No. 191-CP 1994 Providing Regulations on the Formation, Evaluation and Implementation of Direct Foreign Invested Projects, Art. 6.
116 Law on Foreign Investment, Art. 37; Decree No. 18-CP 1993, Arts. 7, 9, 20.
117 Decree No. 191-CP (Art. 5) enumerates the factors which should be considered in the evaluation of new projects. It mentions the legal status and financial capacity of the parties; the relationship between the project and social and economic objectives; the benefits gained from the project for the Vietnamese party and for Vietnam (for example in the form of increased production, new jobs and financial contributions); technology, utilization and protection of natural resources; and taxes and rents for land, water and other natural resources.
118 Law on Foreign Investment, Art. 38.
119 Decree No. 18-CP, Arts. 12, 24, 49.
120 For example Decree 389 on Leases and Labour Hire by Foreigners; Regulations on Leases and Labour Hire by Foreigners; Circular 03 on Leases and Labour Hire by Foreigners; and Circular 03 on Minimum Rent.
121 Law on Foreign Investment, Art. 16.
122 Art. 31.
123 Decree on Labour for Enterprises with Foreign Owned Capital, Arts. 46–47.
124 Law on Foreign Investment, Art. 25.
125 Decree No. 18-CP, Art. 77.
126 Law on Foreign Investment, Art. 27; Decree No. 18-CP, Art. 71.
127 Law on Foreign Investment, Art. 26; Decree No. 18-CP, Art. 66.
128 Law on Foreign Investment, Art. 28; Decree No. 18-CP, Art. 67.
129 Law on Foreign Investment, Arts. 27 and 28.
130 Decree 18-CP, Art. 69.
131 Law on Foreign Investment, Arts. 27 and 32; Decree No. 18-CP, Art. 72.
132 Law on Foreign Investment, Art. 33.
133 Art. 35.
134 Art. 35a.
135 Law on Foreign Investment, Art. 29; Decree No. 18-CP, Art. 79.
136 For example the 1988 Ordinance on Industrial Designs; the 1989 Decree on the Protection of Industrial Property Rights; the 1990 Ordinance on Trademarks; and the 1994 Ordinance on the Protection of Copyrights.
137 Ordinance on Trade Marks, Art. 1.
138 Art. 2. An indistinctive mark may be accepted if it has been widely used for a long period and is recognized in Vietnam as the trade mark of a particular brand or enterprise.

[139] Art. 4.   [140] Art. 4.
[141] Art. 8.   [142] Art. 11.
[143] Art. 9.   [144] Art. 14.
[145] An international registration is obtained by filing a trade mark application in a country in which the applicant has a "real and effective industrial and commercial establishment".
[146] Works of foreign authors which have been published in a foreign country and then are disseminated in Vietnam are protected in accordance with those international conventions on copyright to which Vietnam is a party. Ordinance on the Protection of Copyrights, Art. 3.
[147] Arts. 2 and 4.
[148] Art. 6.
[149] Arts. 10, 22, 24.
[150] Arts. 17, 23.
[151] Art. 16.
[152] Art. 5.
[153] Arts. 39–40.
[154] Art. 41.
[155] Arts.42–45.
[156] Robert L. Wunker "The Laws of Vietnam Affecting Foreign Investment", 28 *International Lawyer* 363, 373, n. 44 (Summer 1994).
[157] "Technology Transfer To Vietnam, an Interim Report": Claes Brundeniux, Tran Hgoc Ca, Vu Vao Dam, Bo Goransson, Hguyen Thanh Ha, Ngu-yen Si Loc, and Luc Gia Thai, Research Policy Institute, Univ. of Lund, Sweden, and Institute for Science Management, Hanoi, Socialist Republic of Vietnam, Discussion Paper No. 181, (1987).
[158] Sesto E. Vecchi, Technology Transfer: Problems and Potential, 13 *East Asian Executive Reports* 8 (January 15, 1991).
[159] *Ibid.*
[160] Dated December 10, 1988.
[161] Decree No. 49/HDBT, dated March 4, 1991.
[162] Dated December 28, 1988.
[163] Stephen Hayward, Technology Transfer and Licensing of Technology in Vietnam, *Patent World*, at 37 (April 1995).
[164] Wunker, above, n. 156, at 373 (Summer 1994).
[165] Technology Transfer Law, Chap. I, Art. 4(1).
[166] *Ibid.*, Chap. I, Art. 4(3).   [167] *Ibid.*, Chap. I, Art. 4(2).
[168] *Ibid.*, Chap. I, Art. 4(4).   [169] *Ibid.*, Chap. I, Art. 4(2)(a).
[170] *Ibid.*, Chap. III, Art. 15.   [171] *Ibid.*, Chap. III, Art. 20(1).
[172] *Ibid.*, Chap. II, Art. 5.   [173] *Ibid.*, Chap. II, Art. 6.
[174] *Ibid.*, Chap. II, Art. 6(1).   [175] *Ibid.*, Chap. II, Art. 6(2).
[176] *Ibid.*, Chap. II, Art. 6(3).   [177] *Ibid.*, Chap. II, Art. 6(4).
[178] *Ibid.*, Chap. II, Art. 6(5).   [179] *Ibid.*, Chap. II, Art. 6(6).
[180] *Ibid.*, Chap. II, Art. 9.   [181] *Ibid.*, Chap. II, Art. 10.
[182] *Ibid.*, Chap. II, Art. 6(7).   [183] *Ibid.*, Chap. II, Art. 6(8).
[184] *Ibid.*, Chap. II, Art. 6(9).   [185] *Ibid.*, Chap. II, Art. 11.
[186] *Ibid.*, Chap. II, Art. 6(10).   [187] *Ibid.*, Chap. II, Art. 8(5).
[188] *Ibid.*, Chap. II, Art. 8.   [189] *Ibid.*, Chap. II, Art. 8(1).
[190] *Ibid.*, Chap. II, Art. 8(2).   [191] *Ibid.*, Chap. II, Art. 8(3).
[192] *Ibid.*, Chap. II, Art. 8(4).   [193] *Ibid.*, Chap. II, Art. 8(5).
[194] *Ibid.*, Chap. III, Art. 17.   [195] *Ibid.*
[196] *Ibid.*, Chap. III, Art. 22.   [197] *Ibid.*, Chap. II, Art. 21.
[198] Regulations on Licensing, Chap. 1, Art. 1.
[199] *Ibid.*, Chap. I, Art. 2(1).   [200] *Ibid.*, Chap. I, Art. 2(2).

201 *Ibid.*

202 Hayward, above n. 313, at 40.

203 *Ibid.*, Chap. III, Art. 10(2).

204 *Ibid.*, Chap. III, Art. 10(3).

205 *Ibid.*, Chap. III, Art. 11.

206 *Ibid.*, Chap. II, Art. 5(1).

207 Hayward, above n. 163, at 41.

208 Regulations on Licensing, Chap. II, Art. 5(2).

209 *Ibid.*, Chap. II, Art. 6.

210 *Ibid.*, Chap. II, Art. 6(1).

211 *Ibid.*, Chap. II, Art. 6(2).

212 *Ibid.*, Chap. II, Art. 6(3).

213 *Ibid.*, Chap. II, Art. 6(4).

214 *Ibid.*, Chap. II, Art. 6(5).

215 *Ibid.*

216 *Ibid.*, Chap. V, Art. 24.

217 *Ibid.*, Chap. V, Art. 25(2).

218 Constitution 1992, Art. 127.

219 The Constitution (Art. 127) states that "Appropriate popular organisations shall be formed at the grass-roots level to deal with minor breaches of law and disputes among the people in accordance with the law".

220 Art. 126.

221 Art. 136.

222 Ordinance on Procedure for Settlement of Economic Disputes, Art. 13.

223 Arts. 59, 61.

224 Arts. 12 and 13.

225 Ordinance on Procedure for Settlement of Economic Disputes, Art. 74.

226 Art. 75.

227 The Chief Justice is elected on recommendation of the President. Law on the Organization of the People's Courts, Arts. 15 and 38. Constitution 1992, Arts. 84 and 103.

228 Ordinance on the Procedure for Settlement of Economic Disputes, Art. 87.

229 Art. 1.

230 Art. 31. The petition can be rejected if the court considers that the claim is not valid, the case has been settled by another court or authorized agency or does not fall within the court's jurisdiction, or the parties have agreed to solve the dispute through arbitration. Art. 32.

231 Art. 34.

232 Art. 36.

233 Constitution 1992, Art. 131; Ordinance on the Procedure for Settlement of Economic Disputes, Art. 7.

234 Ordinance on the Procedure for Settlement of Economic Disputes, Art. 8.

235 Constitution 1992, Art. 132; Ordinance on the Procedure for Settlement of Economic Disputes, Art. 9.

236 The proceedings before the EAO were similar to court proceedings, but paradoxically often more investigative. The arbitrators often took an active role in the settlement of the dispute through extensive questioning and fact-finding investigations, and could often request the parties to present more evidence, ask experts for advice or set up committees with different tasks.

237 Decree No. 116-CP 1994 on the Organization and Operation of Economic Arbitration and Decision No. 204/TTg on the Establishment of the Vietnam International Arbitration Center. The centers are registered with the Ministry of Justice and subject to state supervision.

238 Decree No. 116-CP, Arts. 5 and 31.

239 Art. 3.

240 The organization and function of the notary system follow from Decree No. 45 HDBT of the Council of Ministers and various other regulations.

Index

User's Note: References are to paragraph numbers. The letter prefixes are:

A = Cambodia; B = Hong Kong; C = Indonesia; D = Malaysia; E = People's Republic of China; F = The Philippines; G = Singapore; H = South Korea; I = Taiwan; J = Thailand; K = Vietnam.

Index

Index

Index